TYPES OF ENGLISH *Poetry*

TYPES OF ENGLISH LITERATURE
Hardin Craig, *General Editor*

⚜⚜⚜⚜⚜⚜⚜⚜⚜⚜⚜⚜⚜⚜⚜⚜⚜⚜⚜⚜⚜⚜⚜⚜⚜⚜⚜⚜⚜⚜⚜⚜⚜⚜⚜⚜

TYPES OF ENGLISH *Poetry*
Edited by Rudolf Kirk *and* Clara Marburg Kirk

TYPES OF ENGLISH *Drama*
Edited by John W. Ashton

TYPES OF ENGLISH *Fiction*
Edited by Hardin Craig *and* John W. Dodds

TYPES OF ENGLISH *Prose*
Edited by Virgil B. Heltzel

TYPES OF
ENGLISH *Poetry*

Edited *by* Rudolf Kirk
and Clara Marburg Kirk

RUTGERS UNIVERSITY

New York • 1940

THE MACMILLAN COMPANY

821.08

K

c.1

For Sue and Donald

PREFACE

THIS COLLECTION of English poems is for college students who enjoy reading poetry. It is more especially for those who not only enjoy reading poetry, but who also are pleased by questions as to the nature and quality of their enjoyment. Such questions have to do more or less directly with the meaning of "form" in poetry. Interesting and rewarding as discussions of the religion of Shelley and the pessimism of Hardy may be, they are not so necessary to an understanding of the poetic quality of Shelley and Hardy as is a grasp of the forms in which they wrote.

In order to realize the poetic experience, it is essential to know from the poets themselves what this experience is, by what means the poet is able to bring it about, and how we can share in it. These basic questions, which underlie all discussions of form in poetry, we shall treat in our Introduction —and among other things, we shall discover that, though Sir Philip Sidney's vocabulary is very different from that of Mr. T. S. Eliot, what these poets are saying is not entirely dissimilar. The further question related to form—how poets of different centuries have seen new and fresh possibilities within the unchanging limitations of poetry—is the question which by the arrangement of the poems, we wish to propose. Though the fundamental theory of poetry remains more or less constant, the concrete expression of it in poetry itself is never the same. Between these two points of theory and example lie the answers to all inquiries into poetic form.

The purpose of this anthology, then, is that the student shall emerge with a general historical knowledge of English poetry, and further that he shall learn from a thoughtful reading of a small selection of poems to meditate on the nature of poetry itself. By considering at once the unchanging character of form and the changing styles of different eras and of different poets, he should learn to read poetry more critically and, therefore, more appreciatively. What the poet aims to do—"to please and to instruct"—does not differ very markedly from generation to generation; the basic means at his disposal, rhythm and meter, metaphor and rime, remain fundamentally the same. But for reasons too complex for us entirely to understand, the poet does find himself in a different relation to himself, his reader, and his world, in different periods of history, and these altered relationships are seen in the particular expression he finds for his feelings.

In order to reflect these changing styles within the more or less permanent form, we have arranged our material in three parts, which correspond to three general types of poetry. In each section the work of one or two particular periods of English poetic production will be stressed. Since the earliest poets were moved by little more remote than the desire to tell a story, we shall call the first section of our collection "Narrative Poems." Though lyrics have been written throughout our literary history, the pure and untroubled desire to sing a song seems to have marked particularly the Renaissance, and we shall call the second section of our collection "Lyric Poems." As the influence of science and the reasoning mind discouraged this burst of song, and made the attitude of teaching natural to poets, the later English poetry became more characteristically didactic than that of earlier periods. "Didactic Poems" is, therefore, the title of our third section.

But narrative, lyrical, and didactic poems have, of course, been written in every period, as the examples in each of our three sections will indicate. Students may look at the narratives of Wordsworth and Byron beside those of Chaucer; the lyrics of Browning and Housman beside those of Shakespeare and Herrick; the didactic poems of Hardy beside those of Pope, and speculate as to the effect of the century on the poet's manner of writing. The reader must bear in mind, however, that poetry can not really be classified—a lyric by Donne or a narrative by Browning may also be intended to teach a lesson. In placing the poems in one or another of the three groups, then, we shall try to classify them as nearly as possible according to what seems to us the main purpose of the poet —to tell a story, or to sing a song, or to teach a lesson— realizing that the reader may disagree with our classification. We shall introduce each section with an historical account of narrative, lyrical, and didactic poetry, not because we think that the history of a form explains the form itself, but because we think it makes one's inquiries into poetry some- what more realistic.

One must always remember that there can be no final ex- planation of form. One can, however, come to a closer under- standing of the possible implications of the term, and this is an anthology for those who enjoy speculating about poetry as well as reading it. In our study of the changing and the unchanging elements of poetic form, therefore, the assumption is that the reader will take issue with the editors at every point, and the hope is that he will learn to think independently —with due respect both for theory and example—on the difficult but fascinating question of form in poetry.

Our selection of poetry has been greatly enriched by the suggestions of Charlotte Wing, who for a number of years has been assembling her own private collection of "pure poetry" for the delight of her family and friends. We are indebted to Violet Mignon Couser, who read our introduc- tions and made a number of corrections. Dr. Hardin Craig has made the preparation of this book a pleasure by his tactful criticism and constant encouragement.

A Note on Arrangement

The poems in this collection are arranged both chrono- logically and according to types. The three type divisions themselves—narrative, lyrical, and didactic—reflect in a general way the evolution of poetry, which began as story-telling and developed into sophisticated expressions of philosophical thought. Each division is preceded by an historical sketch which traces this evolution, and indicates that all three tendencies are present in every period, but that one is apt to be more marked than the others. The selections in each of these three divisions make it abundantly clear that the best stories in poetry are told by Chaucer and the ballad singers, that the freest and loveliest lyrics are those written by the Elizabethans, and that the neatest didactic thought comes from such more modern poets as Dryden and Pope. The nineteenth century differs from the preceding centuries in that the poets attempted to excel in all three forms—narrative, lyrical, and philosophical poetry. The narrative power of Arnold, the lyrical reach of Shelley, the ethical penetration of Browning indicate that they were indeed remarkably successful.

Our selection only just reaches into the twentieth century, the assumption being that this anthology is to be used in a basic poetry course, where both the principles and the history of English poetry are to be studied, and that the poetry of our own day will be considered in another course. As an aid to the historical study of poetry the dates of birth and death have been added after the name of each poet in the Index. At the end of each poem a date is given. When this date is placed on the left-hand side, as it is after the poems of Chaucer and a few other writers, it indicates the time of composition. When it is placed on the right hand side, as it usually is, it indicates the year of publication. In a few instances where both dates seem significant, both have been given. The texts of the poems reflect the usage of standard modern editions. The spelling and the capitalization have been modernized except in the cases of Chaucer, the ballad writers, Spenser, and Burns.

An attempt has been made to print all poems in full, but it is obviously impossible to give all of the *Faerie Queene*, for example, or of *Paradise Lost* or of Pope's *Essay on Criticism*. It is assumed that the teacher will enrich the course for which this anthology serves as a basic text by a judicious use of the library. In this book the editors have attempted by the arrangement of material to indicate a method of studying poetry both chronologically and by types.

Undoubtedly readers of this anthology will wish to carry their investigations far beyond the confines of this book. We therefore have appended to each introductory section short bibliographies. For the more general history of English literature students will consult such admirable works as the following: *The Cambridge History of English Literature; A History of English Literature* by Emile Legouis and Louis Cazamian, 1927; *The Voice of England* by Charles G. Osgood, and *A History of English Poetry* by W. J. Courthope. The great source for biographical information is *The Dictionary of National Biography*.

Acknowledgments

The editors and the publishers of *Types of English Poetry* wish to acknowledge with gratitude permission received from holders of copyright of the following works to include them in this volume: to The Macmillan Company for four poems from *Collected Poems* by Thomas Hardy and four poems from *Collected Poems* by William Butler Yeats; to The Clarendon Press, Oxford, for four poems from *The Shorter Poems of Robert Bridges* and for selections from *English Lyrics of the Thirteenth Century* and *Religious Lyrics of the Fourteenth Century*, edited by Professor Carleton Brown; to Henry Holt and Company for five poems from *A Shropshire Lad* by A. E. Housman; and to Charles Scribner's Sons for one poem from the *Poems* of Francis Thompson.

TABLE OF CONTENTS

CONTENTS

TYPES OF ENGLISH *Poetry*

INTRODUCTION

1. The Uses of Poetry

To the true poetry reader the uses of poetry are obvious.

> Bright Star, would I were steadfast as thou art

and many another perfect, imperishable, never quite understood line of poetry, is a possession stored away in the mind and currently used. Who can explain, who wishes to explain, the strange pleasure, made up of joy and sorrow, one feels when one reads aloud,

> Sweet day, so cool, so calm, so bright!
>   The bridal of the earth and sky—
> The dew shall weep thy fall to-night;
>   For thou must die.

or the feeling of despair, redeemed by the dignity of words, with which one pronounces these lines,

> When, in disgrace with fortune and men's eyes,
> I all alone beweep my outcast state,
> And trouble deaf heaven with my bootless cries,
> And look upon myself, and curse my fate.

But in our world of movies, radio, and swing, how many of us can hear the much quieter though more potent sounds of poetry? What defence of its "uses" can poetry make in the face of the economic insecurity and profound moral confusion which accompanies war?

Perhaps I. A. Richards gives us the clearest statement of the case for poetry in our generation. Like Matthew Arnold before him, he observes simply that we dare not overlook the sustaining powers of poetry, especially in "this iron time." The immensely important function of poetry is that it at the same moment brings us to the highest state of consciousness and the most complete state of harmony of which we are capable, and thus puts us more in control of ourselves amid the actual experience of life. This inner state of serene awareness makes possible the life of the spirit in a period when not only our minds but also our physical selves are played upon by the manifold "improvements" presented to a bewildered world by science, unmodified by poetry. In a small volume called *Science and Poetry*, Richards points out to us that we have put our faith in science—or, as Arnold would say, "the fact"—and that it is now clear that science, which does not evaluate, and therefore constructs battleships as readily as model houses, has failed us. For the truth on which science depends is purely quantitative, and is unable even to put the questions which require a qualitative answer. Qualitative truth is the truth of poetry.

But how can this "truth," important as it is, be made available to the ordinary reader? The answer is, it is only available to the lover of poetic experience who allows the poem to become a part of his own rhythmic expression by knowing the poem so thoroughly that it is one with his breathing and walking as he tramps down a country road or along a crowded city street. It is only then that the reader knows what Richards means when he says that poetry gives one at the same instant stimulation and serenity, that it strengthens the spirit thereby, and makes one more able to cope with the actual world. A genuine experience in reading poetry is alike in kind, if not in degree, to that which the poet himself knows when he composes his poem; when he catches a glimpse of truth, and matches it with rhythmic expression which we in turn are able, through the only partially understood power of sound and rhythm, to make a part of our inner selves. Thus we, ordinary people though we be, have the power to share in a kind of eternity, to feel and know truth, to escape from the transitory, the mechanical, and the predatory. After such an association with poetry, the tyranny of the real world can never be absolute, for we have learned to deal with actuality on a level other than that of science, which has no terms with which to think of value or meaning.

The old phrase, that "the purpose of poetry is to please and to instruct," takes on new meaning if we see in it a rather simple effort to say what is so difficult to put into words—that poetry "pleases" by bestowing on us exalted moments of perfect harmony; that it "teaches" by allowing us to live during these moments close to a truth, immaterial and indestructible. It is in some such terms as these that all poet-critics, from Sir Philip Sidney to Matthew Arnold, have philosophised on the "uses of poetry." For poets from the beginning of time have been forced to come to the "defence of sweet poetry" against hard-headed readers who look with mistrust on "poor poets." It is enlightening to enrich our own conception of the uses of poetry by considering the ways in which our five greatest poet-critics—Sidney, Dryden, Wordsworth, Shelley, Arnold—have interpreted the "to please and to instruct" formula according to their temperaments and according to the periods in which they lived. The phrases with which they speak of poetry are quite as beautiful as are the poems they write; to place oneself with such a group as a defender of poetry is to feel indeed that one is on the side of the angels.

Sir Philip Sidney's very noble statement of why "the Planet-like Musick of poetry" will always be important to "earth-creeping" mortals, was called forth by Stephen Gosson's pamphlet, *The School of Abuse* (1579), which attacked poetry on moral grounds. In his *Defence of Poesie* (1583), Sidney says that the poet is not simply the interpreter of the truth, but indeed the only true creator among men—he, by his "inventions," makes a truth truer than truth. The astronomer, geometrician, musician, and physician are always dependent on "what Nature will have set forth," while "onely the Poet, disdayning to be tied to any such subjection, lifted up with the vigor of his owne invention, dooth growe in effect another nature, in making things either better than Nature bringeth

forth, or quite a newe, formes such as never were in Nature."
The poet is not "inclosed within the narrow warrant" of Nature's gifts, but ranges freely "within the Zodiack of his owne
wit." "Nature never set forth the earth in so rich tapestry as
divers Poets have done, neither with pleasant rivers, fruitful
trees, sweet smelling flowers, nor whatsoever els may make the
too much loved earth more lovely. Her world is brasen, the
Poets only deliver a golden." This golden world of the poets
projects for us not what is, but the "perfect picture" of what
should be, for the poet is able to conceive the Idea with a "divine breath"; to bring forth a truer lover, a more constant
friend, a fairer meadow than life itself ever presents.

> Leave me, O Love, which reachest but to dust,
> And thou, my mind, aspire to higher things!
> Grow rich in that which never taketh rust:
> Whatever fades, but fading pleasure brings.
> Draw in thy beams, and humble all thy might
> To that sweet yoke where lasting freedoms be;
> Which breaks the clouds and opens forth the light
> That doth both shine and give us sight to see.
> O take fast hold! let that light be thy guide
> In this small course which birth draws out to death,
> And think how evil becometh him to slide
> Who seeketh Heaven, and comes of heavenly breath.
> Then farewell, world! thy uttermost I see:
> Eternal Love, maintain thy life in me!
>   *Splendidis longum valedico Nugis, 1591*

Thus poetry leads us by "sweetly uttered knowledge" from
the temporary to the eternal; it instructs us by guiding us at
last into a Platonic world of Ideas where we are drawn to "as
high a perfection as our degenerate soules made worse by theyr
clayey lodgings, can be capable of." The end of all knowledge
is "to lift up the mind from the dungeon of the body to the en-
joying his owne divine essence," but poetry is the most perfect
of all knowledges. "The ending of all earthly learning being
vertuous action," the poet is "Prince" over his two rivals, the

philosopher and the historian. Though the moral philosopher "with sullen gravity" attempt to guide us, his "thorny argument" gives only "the bare rule" and "standeth so upon the abstract and generall" that we can scarcely understand him. The historian, on the other hand, is so tied "to the particular truth of things and not to the general reason of things" that we are lost. The "peerelesse Poet" alone gives us both the general concept and the particular example, and is able thus "to take nautiness away, and plant goodnesse even in the secretest cabinet of our soules." The "good felow Poet" becomes "the right Popular Philosopher," and leads us to goodness as if we "tooke a medicine of Cherries." "Ever-praiseworthy Poesie is full of vertue-breeding delightfulness"; he who learns to understand "the sacred misteries of Poesie . . . shall be most fayre, most ritch, most wise, most all." With such beguiling phrases does Sidney in his "not old yeres, and idelest times" take us by the hand and lead us to "this hart-ravishing knowledge" of poetry, and show us how we are "pleased" even while we are "taught."

Dryden, from the eminence of Charles's court listened somewhat patronizingly to the "obsolete language" of Shakespeare and the "ignorant" blank verse of Milton, which the blast from Sidney's golden trumpet helped to usher in. He was, in fact, more concerned with establishing a vigorous and direct prose in England, and with the practical problems of "correct plotting" in plays than with thoughts about poetry itself. To Dryden it seemed that the rhymed couplet had established "learning in verse," which was now "more civilized and better bred" than in the rude days of Sidney; he was pleased that the poets of his generation had at last "taught us to mold our thoughts into easy and significant words, to retrench the superfluities of expression"—and the superfluities of feeling, one suspects.

> I feed a flame within, which so torments me
> That it both pains my heart, and yet contents me:
> 'Tis such a pleasing smart, and I so love it,
> That I had rather die than once remove it.

Though the "reasonableness" of his day made the "divine fury" of an earlier period appear somewhat ill-bred to this supremely intelligent poet of a sophisticated court, Dryden nevertheless in his defense of poetry repeats Sidney's thought. His terse statement, "poesy only instructs as it delights," is after all merely Sidney's more deeply felt belief that "there is no learning so good as that which teacheth and moveth to vertue, and that none can both teach and move thereto so much as Poetry." But whereas Sidney by his sweet phrases ravishes us to an appreciation of the beauties of poetry, Dryden addresses us more sternly in placing the emphasis on the didactic end of our formula, "to please and to instruct." "The moral is the first business of the Poet," says he, taking his position squarely with the rationalists of his day, who believed that man must, above all else, be corrected of his erring ways by "reason," which is securely founded on "nature." Far from finding himself at odds with the members of the Royal Society, who were every day uncovering new laws of nature by which men might direct their moral lives, Dryden felt that the function of the poet was essentially like that of the scientist, since the poet too must discover the general laws under the individual example, and thus teach men how to "defend their inclination by their reason." As Dr. Johnson pointed out a century later, Dryden taught us how to justify our natural love of poetry by showing us that the poets, "by correcting nature from what actually she is in individuals to what she ought to be," presents to us with agreeable ease the rationality of the universe. The imitation of nature is, indeed, the chief concern of the poet, but of the "truth" of the "best nature," of "that which is wrought up to a nobler pitch." The poets give us "images more perfect than the life in any individual; and we have the pleasure to see all the scattered beauties of nature united by a happy chemistry, without its deformities or faults." The poet's highest function, then, was to "instruct" us in as "pleasing" a manner as possible, for only thus can we live in the clear light of reason. Dryden, writing at the dawn of modern science, when it seemed quite possible that men by the sheer act of will might achieve a sensible and rational way of living, in harmony with a divine plan, gives a simple interpretation of our formula, "to please and to instruct." But let us not suppose that his poetry partakes of the blandness of his thoughts on poetry.

> From harmony, from heavenly harmony,
>   This universal frame began,

expresses, in the most resounding poetry, Dryden's vision of the divine plan of the universe whose glory the great poets celebrate.

> As from the power of sacred lays
>   The spheres began to move,
> And sung the great Creator's praise
>   To all the Blest above;
> So when the last and dreadful hour
> This crumbling pageant shall devour,
> The trumpet shall be heard on high,
> The dead shall live, the living die,
> And Music shall untune the sky!
>   *A Song for St. Cecilia's Day, 1687*

Poetry as a means of orchestrating the intricate perfection of the whole, in order to "teach" men to live in closer harmony with each other and with God was indeed the justification of poetry which sustained Pope, Johnson, Gray, and Goldsmith in the eighteenth century.

When Wordsworth, in his Preface to the second edition of the *Lyrical Ballads* (1800), tells us, in terms which sound more familiar to our modern ears, that the "object of poetry is truth, carried alive into the heart by passion . . . to produce excitement with an overbalance of pleasure," he is actually saying again that poetry must "please and instruct," but he is infusing into the old formula a wealth of meaning which makes us feel again the power of poetry. In order to understand what this meaning is, one must first consider Wordsworth's notion of the poet, who does not differ in kind from other men but only in degree. He is a man addressing himself to other men, but "endowed with more lively sensibility, more enthusiasm and tenderness." He consciously enjoys "his own passions and volitions," and "rejoices more than other men in the spirit of life that is in him; delighting to contemplate similar volitions and passions as manifested in the goings-on of the Universe, and habitually impelled to create them where he does not find them." He is capable of thought and feeling, "without immediate external excitement," and is able to express these thoughts and feelings, which are, in fact, "the general passions and thoughts and feelings of men." The poet is the man who, knowing our restlessness in a routine world, can bring us nearer to our natural selves.

> The world is too much with us; late and soon,
> Getting and spending, we lay waste our powers:
> Little we see in Nature that is ours;
> We have given our hearts away, a sordid boon!
> This sea that bares her bosom to the moon;
> The winds that will be howling at all hours,
> And are up-gather'd now like sleeping flowers;
> For this, for everything, we are out of tune;
> It moves us not.—Great God! I'd rather be
> A Pagan suckled in a creed outworn;
> So might I, standing on this pleasant lea,
> Have glimpses that would make me less forlorn;
> Have sight of Proteus rising from the sea;
> Or hear old Triton blow his wreathèd horn.
>
> *The World, 1807*

Wordsworth reminds us of what we all know, that "we lay waste our powers" in getting and spending; he invites us to respond more freely to "the goings on of the Universe," to the sea and the moon and the wind. The poet "pleases and instructs" us because he thinks and feels habitually in the spirit of our deeper human passions and brings us into a truer relationship with "our moral sentiments and animal sensation, and with the causes which excite these; with the operations of the elements and the appearance of the visible universe; with storm and sunshine, with the revolutions of the seasons, with cold and heat, with loss of friends and kindred, with injuries and resentments, gratitude and hope, with fear and sorrow." Poetry is important, then, "in the multiplicity and quality of its moral relations;" it leads to an understanding of "the primary laws of our nature." By a "wise passiveness" we ourselves learn to draw upon the same source of knowledge made use of by the poets, the knowledge of our inner selves, of "emotion recollected in tranquillity," which unites us with the absolute.

The poet must, moreover, produce "immediate pleasure"— nor is this obligation degrading. It is, in fact, "an acknowledgment of the beauty of the universe," a task easy to the poet, "who looks at the world in the spirit of love," and is eager to pay homage "to the native and naked dignity of man, to the grand elementary principle of pleasure, by which he knows and feels and lives and moves." And in paying this homage to the "elementary principle of pleasure," he is obeying the law which governs us all. For "we have no knowledge . . . but what has been built up by pleasure, and exists in us by pleasure alone." The scientist enjoys the truth he discovers in solitude, but the poet, "singing a song in which all human beings join with him, rejoices in the presence of truth as our visible friend and hourly companion." "Poetry is the breath and finer spirit of all knowledge; it is the impassioned expression which is in the countenance of all Science."

Wordsworth gives us a penetrating analysis of how poetry "instructs" us by leading us to the very center of our moral being, and "pleases" us by inviting us to join with the poet in the song which he is perpetually singing to the universe itself. Though Wordsworth, disgusted with the artificial verse of the eighteenth century, wished to speak a "plainer more emphatic language" than had before been used by poets, and though he wished to describe "incidents and situations from common life," yet to him as to Sidney and Dryden, the object of poetry was truth, "not individual and local, but general and operative; not standing upon external testimony, but carried alive into the heart by passion."

Shelley's eloquent *Defence of Poetry* (1821) was called forth, as were all the defences we have been considering, by an unsympathetic attitude toward poetry. Thomas Love Peacock excited Shelley to "a sacred rage" by the scathing irony of *The Four Ages of Poetry* (1820). In phrases which are themselves sheer poetry, Shelley reverts once more to the conception of poetry as universal and eternal truth, not individual and particular. "A poet participates in the eternal, the infinite, and the one." "A poem is the very image of life expressed in its eternal truth"—a truth which lives from age to age, for time "forever develops new and wonderful applications of the eternal truth which it contains."

Like all the poet-defenders of poetry who had gone before him, Shelley felt that the high purpose of poetry was to reveal this everlasting truth by moving and delighting his readers. "Poetry ever communicates all the pleasure which men are capable of receiving." He restates the old phrase, "to please and to instruct," in terms which remind one of his poetry— "A great poem is a fountain forever overflowing with the waters of wisdom and delight"—and then defines his terms with a largeness which makes them as applicable to our day as to his. The "wisdom" of the poet is not the poet's "own conception of right and wrong, which are usually those of his place and time," and therefore necessarily narrow. "All high poetry is infinite." It is the lifting of veil after veil from the "naked and sleeping" beauty of the world which remains forever concealed from ordinary eyes. The familiar world, clothed in the "Elysian light" of poetry, stands forth fresh-made and radiant. All of our senses are washed and renewed by Shelley's rapturous pleasure in the flight of the English skylark starting up from any English meadow.

In the golden light'ning
Of the sunken sun,
O'er which clouds are bright'ning,
Thou dost float and run,
Like an unbodied joy whose race is just begun.

The pale purple even
Melts around thy flight;
Like a star of heaven,
In the broad daylight
Thou art unseen, but yet I hear thy shrill delight.

To a Skylark, 1820

Like Shelley listening to the skylark, those who respond to poetry are "as men entranced by the melody of an unseen musician, who feel that they are moved and softened, yet know not whence or why."

The wisdom to be found in poetry, then, is that which one feels when "the veil of the familiar" is removed, when the mind is awakened and enlarged so that it becomes "the receptacle of a thousand unapprehended combinations" of thought and feelings which make "the pains and pleasures of his species become his own." Men, thus moved by poetry, are no longer victims of "the selfish and calculating principle" which burdens society with "the accumulation of the materials of external life," and exceeds "the power of assimilating them to the internal laws of human nature." By gazing at the very center of beauty which lies about us, we learn that "the great secret of morals is love; or a going out of our own nature, and an identification of ourselves with the beautiful which exists in thought, action or person, not our own." An understanding of love grows from an insight into the beauty of the universe. The function of the poet, "to please and to instruct," becomes in Shelley's mind a most important one. For the poets, by making us feel the wisdom of universal love, are our "most unfailing heralds;" they are "the mirrors of the gigantic shadows which futurity casts upon the present," "the trumpets which sing to battle and feel not what they inspire." "Poets are the unacknowledged legislators of the world."

The power of poetry, according to Shelley, is the power to move men to sympathetic understanding of the divinity of all things, by means of which man is able to throw off the slavery of custom and wealth and to conceive of a new society. But more important still, poetry is that which "makes immortal all that is best and most beautiful in the world; it arrests the vanishing apparitions which haunt the interlunations of life," and "redeems from decay the visitations of the divinity in man." "It is the perfect and consummate surface and bloom of all things," more sensitively felt and more exquisitely described by those among us who make of poetry "the record of the best and happiest moments of the happiest and best minds."

Like Shelley, Matthew Arnold gives a distinctly social meaning to the phrase "to please and to instruct." But he, observing a later phase of the social injustices which accompanied the introduction of machinery into the industrial world, speaks of the hope of poetry in a quieter, less enthusiastic language than that which Shelley uses. In *The Art of Poetry* (1880), he says simply that poetry is an "ever surer and surer stay" in a world where "there is not a creed which is not shaken, not an accredited dogma which is not shown to be questionable, not a received tradition which does not threaten to dissolve." In a growing empire of vast material wealth, Matthew Arnold called into question the final worth of "the fact" discovered by science. "Our religion has materialised itself in the fact . . . and now the fact is failing it. But for poetry the idea is everything; the rest is a world of illusion, of divine illusion. Poetry attaches its emotion to the idea; the idea *is* the fact." And "the fact" of poetry never changes from age to age. Apollo is still leading the Muses over misty mountains.

> They are lost in the hollows.
> They stream up again.
> What seeks on this mountain
> The glorified train?—

They bathe on this mountain,
In the spring by their road.
Then on to Olympus,
Their endless abode.

—Whose praise do they mention:
Of what is it told?—
What will be for ever.
What was from of old.

First hymn they the Father
Of all things: and then,
The rest of Immortals,
The action of men.

The Day in his hotness,
The strife with the palm;
The Night in her silence,
The Stars in their calm.

The Song of Callicles, 1852

Here again is Sidney's "golden world" which only poets create, the world of the spirit, built within and above the "brazen world" of daily routine. This is Dryden's "truth," which was for him one with the very laws of nature, and this is the shadow of eternity traced by Wordsworth and Shelley. The immeasurable power of the spirit, fortified by beauty, moves Arnold to announce that "the future of poetry is immense," and to declare that though poetry at times might lose currency in the Philistine world, it will never lose supremacy, which is finally insured to poetry, "not indeed by the world's deliberate and conscious choice, but by something far deeper,—by the instinct of self-preservation in humanity." We live by the spirit, or else we sink again into barbarism; these surely are words peculiarly applicable to our generation, which is experiencing the reversion Arnold predicted.

To lend ourselves to the enchantment of the "best poetry" is to discover that it has a power of forming, sustaining, and delighting us as nothing else can—that it is as able "to delight and to instruct" now as it was when Sidney and Shakespeare awakened all England with their songs. But we must conceive of poetry, Arnold warns us, worthily and accept only the best, "since poetry, to be capable of fulfilling such high destinies, must be poetry of a high order of excellence," able to interpret life for us, to console us, and to sustain us. The strength and joy drawn from "the classics"—a term used by Arnold to describe "the best"—is open to all who are willing to familiarize themselves with poetry itself for its own sake alone. Only through years of reading the very best can we come to an intuitively felt "real" estimate of poetic values, which provides us with a "touchstone" for judging all poetry. The great thing is "to feel and enjoy the best" as deeply as we can, and to appreciate the wide difference between it and all poetry which has not the same high character. It is misleading to accept uncritically the "historical" estimate of poetry; it is superficial to judge by a too "personal" standard. Only long and patient attention to "the great masters" can so infuse us with their very lines and expressions that we are impatient of poetry which lacks a certain "high poetic quality." What this "high poetic quality" is Arnold himself nowhere says precisely, for to attempt an exact definition of the "beauty, worth and power" of poetry would be not to clarify but to darken our understanding. There must be a "thorough truth of substance," he says, and "an answering truth of style" in all poetry which is "sound to the core"; it must possess "in an eminent degree, truth and seriousness," the seriousness "which comes from absolute sincerity." More than this we would not wish Arnold to say, for the discovery of poetry, like all other discoveries of the spirit, is one which each reader must make alone. Having trained our ear and eye and mind and feeling to the point where we are able to share in the "very best," we know that Arnold is right in saying that poetry is our stay in a materialistic world. Depending on the "idea" rather than on the "fact," it provides an abiding place for man's harried spirit, and is thus able truly "to please and to instruct"—as it has always done. It is especially important to us now, when

> . . . this strange disease of modern life
> With its sick hurry, its divided aims,
> Its heads o'ertaxed, its palsied hearts

is testing us severely.

Each of our critics uses the language of his time to remind an inattentive world of the uses of poetry, from Sir Philip Sidney, who speaks in terms of Renascence Neo-Platonism, to I. A. Richards, who uses the language of psycho-analysis; each is saying essentially the same thing, "A great poem is a fountain forever overflowing with the waters of wisdom and delight."

II. The Methods of Poetry

We have said that the poet "teaches" and "delights," by stirring the reader to an unusual pitch of excitement and by making all the discordant elements of his mind and body move together in perfect harmony. But what is the poet's secret, that he, with only the materials of the daily round of existence which we all share, can render back to us a heightened sense of the significance of our own lives together with a more serene detachment? The answer is—we do not know. We know simply that the poet probably does respond to what is going on about him more finely, more deeply, and with more variety than most of us do; we know further, that together with a delicate emotional nature the poet has a power to organize and arrange his thoughts and to fit them into ordered words; we suspect that this instinct for form not only helps the poet relieve his inner tension, but also actually enhances his original experience. Which moment was more precious to Wordsworth—when the host of golden daffodils burst upon him as he walked beside the lake, or when, long afterwards, the vision became material for poetry, and flashed "upon the inward eye, which is the bliss of solitude"?

> And then my heart with pleasure fills
> And dances with the daffodils.

The daffodils in the poem are singled out; irrelevancies have disappeared. The meaning of the experience is felt and has achieved permanency through form, not only in the mind of Wordsworth, but in the minds of all who read the poem. The freshness, the surprise of daffodils in early spring is caught forever, while the memory of the actual walk died when Wordsworth died. "The emotion of art is impersonal," says T. S. Eliot. It has its life in the poem itself, not in the personal biography of the poet. The only word we have to explain this transformation of personal feeling into the complete and perfect poem is "form."

What we mean by the word can best be discovered by a further consideration of the elements of form—rhythm and meter, rime, and images. But we must always remember that there are no definite and fixed laws to help us. "In English, by the grace of God and the Muses, the poetry makes the rules, not the rules the poetry," says Saintsbury. Repeated and sympathetic reading of a poem leads one to tentative observations as to how it is organized, and curiously enough these observations as to the form of a poem usually bring one to a deeper and more satisfying understanding of its meaning. For form and meaning are inextricably bound together; in a sense, the one *is* the other.

Let us select Milton's poem *On Time* for such a reading, and let us approach it pencil in hand, prepared to mark and underline it in any way we please. But first let us read and re-read it, until a general sense of its meaning has been borne in upon us, and we feel fairly satisfied with our way of rendering it aloud.

> Fly, envious Time, till thou run out thy race,
> Call on the lazy leaden-stepping hours,
> Whose speed is but the heavy Plummets pace;
> And glut thy self with what thy womb devours,
> Which is no more then what is false and vain,
> And meerly mortal dross;
> So little is our loss,

So little is thy gain.
For when as each thing bad thou hast entomb'd,
And last of all, thy greedy self consum'd,
Then long Eternity shall greet our bliss
With an individual kiss;
And Joy shall overtake us as a flood,
When every thing that is sincerely good
And perfectly divine,
With Truth, and Peace, and Love shall ever shine
About the supreme Throne
Of him, t'whose happy-making sight alone,
When once our heav'nly-guided soul shall clime,
Then all this Earthy grosnes quit,
Attir'd with Stars, we shall for ever sit,
    Triumphing over Death, and Chance, and thee, O Time.

After one has enjoyed to the full saying aloud these resounding lines, while they are still echoing in one's mind, one begins
to realize that Milton is dealing with a problem which has always fascinated poets and scientists alike, the problem of time.
He is, in this poem, placing Time in its relation to Eternity
and doing it so effectively that, though the lines are for the
most part of a regular alternating heavy and light stress
throughout, the pitch and intensity with which one reads them
change from a nervous, almost irritable impatience while one is
still concerned with Time, to a serene calm when one mounts
with the poet to Eternity itself, there at last to triumph over
Death and Chance and Time. The metrical scheme of the lines
is stretched and enlarged by the rhythmic urge which animates
the whole.

Notice that though the two lines,

        Fly envious Time, till thou run out thy race

and

        Attir'd with Stars, we shall for ever sit

have each ten syllables and five stresses, we read them with a
more solemn tone and a more deliberate emphasis because of

our sense of the slowly emerging meaning of the poem. The
meter is fairly regular, except for the three-stress lines which
do not really break the meter, for one fills out these lines with
pauses. The rhythm, however, is varied and shifted by the
sense of the poem, which every reader will respond to with
slightly different stress, for the thought itself may be said to
have a sort of rhythmic urge, quite apart from the metrical
scheme of the lines. It is, in fact, this never-ending conflict between the meter of the line and the rhythm of the whole which
gives to this poem, and to all poems, poetic intensity.

But there are other ways in which Milton "organizes" the
poem, besides his use of meter and rhythm. Let us read the
poem again. Beginning with impatience earth-bound, confused, we finally are wafted into remote and shining regions
where everything

is sincerely good
And perfectly divine

Dividing the poem directly in two parts of ten lines each comes
the "individual kiss" of long Eternity, which frees us from
our bonds. Notice that the rime scheme which Milton uses
varies as the emotion mounts. Though the poem sweeps us
along in one unbroken sentence with no complete stop until
Time is finally vanquished, we might, if we like, consider the
first two sets of four lines as two units each marked by its own
rime scheme. Milton's riming in this poem follows no established rules at all; its effectiveness makes us realize his power to
create form for his own purposes. The second four-line unit
gains a kind of high and proud defiance by urging the reader
through the two short intervening lines in order to bear down
on the word *gain*, answering with such firmness to *vain*. These
two units are then followed by five sets of riming couplets
which whirl us up to the "supreme Throne," and there with
the support of our final unit of four lines, linked as our second
unit was linked, we find ourselves in a freer, milder atmosphere
where Time cannot endure. Again the form fills out the mean-

ing and the meaning gives the form significance, and that is the purpose of rime—to make more secure, more firm, more concentrated, the intricately bound thought, which is always attempting to free itself.

Besides Milton's subtle use of rhythm, meter, rime, he makes a demand upon our power of seeing, which is another demand of form. One cannot see Time, Eternity, Joy, Truth, Peace, Love, Death and Chance, and yet in this soaring poem, as in the music of Bach, as in the paintings of El Greco, something visual accompanies our enjoyment of the mounting thought. Perhaps the fact that Time is addressed directly—"run out thy race," "glut thy self with what thy womb devours"—gives us a sense of large and shrouded figures of an allegorical sort on a canvass varying from stormy dark to shining light. Visualize one must; it is probable that our images are never more than approximately akin to those in the mind of the poet. The important thing is that by calling upon our power to summon up the actual color and shape of the figures involved we thereby are made to feel more completely the final serenity, when "our heavenly-guided soul" shall sit "attir'd with Stars," triumphant over Death and Chance and Time. Though the images are intentionally shrouded in this poem, the words themselves have a clarity and precision which cancel the vagueness of the images. One loves to pronounce the words, especially the vowels, as distinctly as possible, each one presenting itself as peculiarly perfect. We do not merely imagine that the very sounds of the words fit themselves to the nervous impatience of "Fly envious Time, till thou run out thy race," with its array of sharp vowels, and that the *l*'s of the next line are actually heavy. There is a fullness and roundness to the line, "And Joy shall overtake us as a flood"; there is a special pleasure in hearing the last phrase of the poem, "and thee O Time," chime with the first. The poet's power to fit the very sounds of words to the mood of the poem is an aspect of the poet's sense of organic form, which can never be precisely defined because it varies in every poem.

It is form which gives a poem "life," quite apart from the actual daily life of the poet. Who knows—and indeed does it matter?—what personal reasons moved Milton with such truly divine words to express for us our mortal defeat in terms of Time, our immortal triumph in terms of Eternity? The poem is "impersonal"; it has what is called form. And now let us examine in more detail each of the four aspects of form touched on here—rhythm and meter, rime and images—remembering that it is not a mechanical sort of form, dependent on rules, which interests us, but form which grows out of the thought itself, or, as Coleridge would say, "organic form."

Rhythm

John Livingston Lowes, in an interesting lecture on Shelley's poetic methods, based on a series of Shelley's revisions of a single poem, pointed out that the poet in his first sketch for his poem marked out the time with dashes, and only filled in with an occasional word. More words took their place among the dashes as the rhythm became established in his mind and he felt his way towards an articulate expression:

> O world! O life! O time!
> On whose last steps I climb,
> Trembling at that where I had stood before;
> When will return the glory of your prime?
> No more—Oh, never more!

Notice the heavy drag of the first two lines; the balance and poise of the third, which in the next line is gathered together in one despairing question—"When will return the glory of your prime?"—to sink away at last into utter dejection. The strong rhythmic feeling of Shelley's mood came to him before words were found to give it expression. It is to rhythmic feeling, then, that we must ourselves first respond; the poem will yield its meaning gradually as we surrender ourselves to its emotion.

The physiological fact that we are ourselves creatures of rhythm is the reason we are able to share in the rhythmic expression, and thence in the thought and feeling, of the poets of all ages. Our breathing, our walking, the tempo with which we type a letter, is rhythmic, slow or rapid, regular or disjointed, according to the mood which we are thus unconsciously expressing in every gesture. Rhythm, then, underlies all life; it is not confined to art alone, and it may be defined as that in us which responds to recurrent time intervals. As in music and dancing, so in poetry, time is the chief factor. It was in terms of time that Shelley found expression for his melancholy mood, and it is in terms of time that we come to share his mood.

Not only is there a definite rhythm to each line to which one responds as completely as one can; there is also a rhythm to the whole, and this is indicated by the stanzas, by refrains, by words repeated, by the thought enlarged and finally brought to a close. The second stanza—and there are but two—of this poem reflects back upon the first stanza when we reread the whole and subtly influences our way of modulating our voices. And for this reason one must read the poem again and again, that the whole may play upon each part, backwards and forwards.

> Out of the day and night
> A joy has taken flight;
>   Fresh spring, and summer, and winter hoar,
> Move my faint heart with grief, but with delight
>   No more—Oh, never more!

The resignation, the exhaustion, of the second stanza, make the line, "No more—Oh, never more!" sound on our ears more sadly than the same line at the end of the first stanza. One reads it the first time with less finality, with something of an upward urge; one reads it the second time with the quiet, even tone of despair.

To D. H. Lawrence "the hidden emotional pattern" of poetry, the rhythm shaped by the feeling of the poet, was more important than meter:

I think more of a bird with broad wings flying and lapsing through the air, than anything, when I think of meter . . . It all depends on the *pause*—the natural pause, the natural lingering of the voice according to the feeling—it is the hidden emotional pattern that makes poetry, not the obvious form.

and this "hidden emotional pattern" is the pattern of rhythm.

Meter

Metrical pattern, however, seems to be essential to transport us to the level of consciousness experienced by the poet himself, to enable us to share the thoughts and emotions which are beyond our ordinary range. Rhythm marks prose as well as poetry; meter, or regularity of time parts within a line, is the distinguishing sign of poetry. One has only to repeat with exaggerated emphasis Lawrence's sentence above to observe that it has very beautiful rhythm. But it is equally clear that it has no regular pattern of sound. For the sake of the contrast, repeat Shelley's stanzas. The time-pattern is very regular; each stanza is made up of two three-stress lines, followed by two five-stress lines, and ending with a three-stress line. Perhaps irregular rhythmic patterns, such as those used by D. H. Lawrence himself, and many other writers of free verse, will finally displace the more regular metrical organization of traditional verse. But it is not probable, since the physiological fact remains that in moments of excitement our speech, gestures and steps fall into a more definitely marked rhythm, and poetry is the language of strong feeling. Though we enjoy free verse very much, our enjoyment is essentially that of our pleasure in rhythmic prose.

But to say that meter is essential to poetry is not to say that the poet is bound by an unalterable metric pattern. Though the beat of Shelley's poem is strong and firm, it only approximates an exact rhythm which we feel subconsciously should be there; though the meter seems clearly defined for a line or two, it is swiftly shifted only to regain again its original pattern. For the principle behind all art, which is always a struggle between inner spontaneity and outer control, is that the rigidity of the scheme be constantly modified by the life which flows through it. After two lines of alternating unstressed and stressed syllables, Shelley, for instance, reverses his pattern and writes,

> Trembling at that where I had stood before
> When will return the glory of your prime
> No more—Oh, never more.

The first foot in each of these lines begins with a stressed syllable, perhaps to make us feel the physical strain of the weary climb. In spite of this irregularity of meter, we stay close enough to the established pattern to feel the variation only as a deeply satisfying conflict between the urge of the emotion and the control of the form. And it is in this conflict, shifting and changing with every line, that the pleasure of reading poetry aloud is found. Should one read "O world! O life! O time!" with a mounting emphasis, or should one almost ignore the stress on "whose" in the next line, and place a borrowed emphasis on "last," which actually does not carry the stress? How long should one pause at the end of lines 1 and 2, and at the beginning of line 5? For a whole beat, silently felt? The answer depends on the reader's age, his temperament, his mood at the moment, for he, with the poet, is the "creator," by means of his rhythmic expressiveness, of the poem which emerges.

It is clear, then, that though we mark all the stresses of a line in the same way, no two stresses are precisely alike. We shall, however, use the word "foot" in our discussion of various familiar meters to indicate a certain number of syllables in a unit, for one's perception of the basic rhythm of the poem is enlarged by training one's ear to hear more accurately the different patterns used by English poets. They are:

Iambus: One unstressed and one stressed syllable

> Impé | rious Cae | sar dead | and turned | to clay.

Trochee: One stressed and one unstressed syllable

> Creép in | tó thy | nárrow | bed.

Spondee: Two stressed syllables

> The gray seá | and the long | black land.

Anapest: Two unstressed and one stressed syllable

> I am lórd | of the fówl | and the brúte.

Dactyl: One stressed and two unstressed syllables

> Swíftly walk | óver the | Wéstern wave.

The first three kinds of feet are sometimes called "duple" rhythm, each beat representing two counts. This is the rhythm of walking. The last two kinds of feet are often called "triple" rhythm, and may be compared to waltzing. Very little experience in reading poetry teaches one that poetry is not a matter of syllable counting. But a certain amount of syllable counting actually seems to make one's ear more sensitive to the organic rhythm underlying the whole.

English verse was strongly marked by meter long before rime was considered a necessary adornment of poetry. Though there has not been a revival of the alliterative verse of Anglo-Saxon and Middle English poetry since the fourteenth century, blank verse which came into vogue with the great Elizabethan dramas, is still the favorite meter for full-bodied, dignified poetry. Perhaps the essential reason for the hold of this five-stress iambic line is simply that it does not fall apart into two equal halves, as the four- and the six-stress lines are always in danger of doing. For instance, observe the four-stress line:

> Bínd up, bínd up, your yéllow háir
> And tíe it ón your néck;
> And seé you loók as máiden-líke
> As the dáy that wé first mét

And now consider the six-stress line:

Then labour in the deep mid-ocean, wind and wave and oar;
O rest ye, brother Mariners, we will not wander more

Nor has the five-stress iambic line the song-like quality of the three-stress line,

Hail to thee, blithe spirit!
Bird thou never wert—
That from heaven or near it
Pourest thy full heart.

But probably the real glory of blank verse is that, though the iambic beat of the ten-syllable line is maintained, the pressure of the thought is felt filling out the lines with its own strength, disregarding rime, letting the pauses fall where they will, often, indeed, shifting the meter from iambic to trochee or to spondee. Othello's greeting to Desdemona when she joins him in Cyprus illustrates the variety, the plasticity, the strength of blank verse.

OTHELLO:

It gives me wonder great as my content
To see you here before me. O my soul's joy!
If after every tempest come such calms,
May the winds blow till they have waken'd death!
And let the labouring bark climb hills of seas
Olympus-high, and duck again as low
As hell's from heaven! If it were now to die,
'T were now to be most happy; for, I fear,
My soul hath her content so absolute
That not another comfort like to this
Succeeds in unknown fate.

DESDEMONA:

The heávens forbid. . . .

One observes, in the first place, that one pauses only for the
fraction of a second at the end of the first line, that the real
pause comes in the middle of the second. But notice, too, that
Shakespeare does not let us stray too far from the rhythmic
effect of the pause at the end of a line. For the next three lines
the pause and the line end together and then we mount again,
and with

> . . . the labouring bark climb hills of seas
> Olympus-high, and duck again as low
> As hell's from heaven!

Then a long pause, the longest in the speech, for here the
whole mood shifts, and Othello begins again in quite a different
key, as though he were conversing with himself:

> If it were now to die,
> 'T were now to be most happy; for, I fear,
> My soul hath her content so absolute
> That not another comfort like to this
> Succeeds in unknown fate.

And Desdemona quickly takes him up, filling out the line with,

> The heavens forbid.

One observes, in the second place, that Shakespeare does not
maintain the regularity of his stressed and unstressed syllables
for long, but gives us a sense of the variety of rhythmic con-
versation by a quick change of pattern:

> It gíves me wónder gréat as mý content
> To sée you hére befóre me. Ó my sóul's jóy!

By disregarding the stress entirely at times, or else by letting it
fall lightly, the poet keeps us from feeling the artificiality of
meter:

May the winds blow till they have waken'd death.

Neither *the* nor *they* are strong enough to bear the stress nor are they required to do so, for the essential time beat is maintained by the rhythm of the whole passage.

The language of Shakespeare, Marlowe, Milton, and many others found scope in the freest and yet the most sustained of English meters. The greatness of the Elizabethan drama rests in part on the fact that the dramatists discovered the strength and range of blank verse by matching impassioned language to the meter of poetry, and by lending to poetry the naturalness of prose.

Rime

The greater part of English verse since the time of Chaucer has been rimed—that is to say, the stressed vowels and the following consonants are alike at the end of two or more lines of verse. Rimes are frequently arranged in pairs or couplets (aa, bb, cc, dd, and so forth), or else alternately (abab). There may be variations and combinations of these two principles. Such as, ababab; ababcc; aabcbc; abababcc; and so forth. In quatrains, alternate lines are sometimes left unrimed, thus: xaya. Let us now consider why it is that one's ears are pleased by rime, which is, after all, not essential to poetry, as rhythm and meter are.

In the seventeenth and eighteenth centuries, the iambic pentameter line of blank verse was written in rhythmical couplets and was called "heroic" verse, though it sounds much less heroic to our ears than blank verse. Sir John Denham, standing on Cooper's Hill in 1642, looked down on the swiftly-flowing, but self-contained Thames and thought of the river as a perfect example of how noble verse might be made to flow:

> O could I flow like thee, and make thy stream
> My great example, as it is my theme!
> Though deep, yet clear, though gentle yet not dull,
> Strong without rage, without o'er-flowing full.

One notices at once that the pauses coincide with the ends of the line, though in each line there is also a definitely marked pause in the middle; one observes that the stresses fall on the important words and that there is only a slight disparity between the rhythmic emphasis which the reader is moved to place upon the lines and the metrical stresses of the lines. And this is one of the chief reasons for rime, that it marks clearly the metric pattern. The conflict between rhythm and meter is almost resolved in the heroic couplet; the result is that one does not feel any very strong emotion and is quite willing to agree that now "sense" and "reason" are in control. Rimed couplets are easier to write than blank verse, for the rimes themselves are pleasantly distracting and the reader demands less of real excellence. Dryden, at the end of the seventeenth century, and many others after him, did indeed add a fresh intellectual quality and a sharp satiric turn, which, as Dryden said, "tickles even while it hurts." Of George Villiers, Second Duke of Buckingham, he wrote:

> Stiff in opinions, always in the wrong
> Was everything by starts and nothing long.

Moreover, Dryden was able to use the same meter to express his mood of lonely doubt, as well as his bursts of personal venom:

> Dim as the borrowed beams of moon and stars
> To lonely weary wandring travellers
> Is Reason to the soul. . . .

Though heroic verse stays more serenely within the limits of the line, the conflict between meter and rhythm remains, as it does in all poetry. But in this verse, in contrast to blank verse, the line structure is reinforced by the rime, and the effect is that the grip of the pattern is tightened.

Rime is not only used to make blank verse walk in more orderly heroic couplets, but it is also used to organize groups of lines into stanzas, from the simplest ballad form, really intended to be sung,

> In somer when the shawes be sheyne,
>   And leves be large and long,
> Hit is full merry in feyre foreste
>   To here the foulys song,

to the complicated rime royal, Spenserian stanza, ode, sonnet
and other patterns. All of these verse forms are different
devices to achieve the same end—to reinforce the rhythm of
the verse and hence to make more inevitable our understanding
of the poem. Though various patterns have names, the truth is
that each poet does what he pleases with the inherited form.
Since each poet responds to experience in his own way, the
conflict he makes us feel between rhythm and meter is in every
case essentially unique. Rime is simply another way of tighten-
ing the organization of the poem against which the larger
rhythm struggles. Listen to the use Wordsworth makes of
rime, for instance, in his *Intimations of Immortality:*

> There was a time when meadow, grove, and stream,
>   The earth, and every common sight,
>   To me did seem
>   Apparell'd in celestial light,
> The glory and the freshness of a dream.

How one holds to the rime in this free and drifting rhythm,
and how skillfully and quickly Wordsworth shifts his rime
schemes:

> The rainbow comes and goes
> And lovely is the rose;
> The moon doth with delight
> Look round her when the heavens are bare;
>   Waters on a starry night
>   Are beautiful and fair . . .

The conflict between the larger rhythm and the meter is felt
more strongly in rimed stanzas than in heroic couplets because
the thought in rimed stanzas tends to be more discursive. But
this is only a tendency; the real poet, by the very strength of
his feeling, bends any form to his use and makes the reader feel,

in the very midst of the conflict between spontaneity and control, the power of poetry.

Images and Words

We have said that organic form is the essence of poetry; that because of our common human response to rhythm, made stronger by meter and rime, the poet and the reader of poetry are able to share experience. What we wish to seize from this sharing of experience is a kind of truth, the poet's truth, and this, after all, is said to us in words, not in rhythm.

Because of the heightened emotional state of the poet, his words are never entirely abstract; because of our heightened emotional state when we read the poem, we are able—we hardly know how—to understand the abstract truth behind the concrete pictures the poet gives us. For the poet's language is the language of imagery, and his images, perfect and satisfying as they are, always represent a truth, no matter how simple, no matter how difficult to translate again into abstract words. It is for the sake of this truth, which Keats says is the same as beauty, that we are eager to enter completely into the thought of a poem.

Though the language of poetry is images, the vocabulary of poetry is the vocabulary we hear around us. Wordsworth settled the question nearly a hundred and fifty years ago when he issued a blast against "poetic" words in his famous *Preface,* and declared that he was going to use "a selection of language really used by men." At the same time Wordsworth hoped to cast over his words "a certain colouring of imagination whereby ordinary things should be presented to the mind in an unusual way." By the strength of the feeling of the poet ordinary words are made to sing themselves into our hearts and to speak their meaning. Masefield, in *Cargoes,* gives us two stanzas of "poetic" language, and then, in the third, makes use of "the language really used by men," over which "a certain colouring of imagination" has been cast.

Quinquireme of Nineveh from distant Ophir,
Rowing home to haven in sunny Palestine,
With a cargo of ivory,
And apes and peacocks,
Sandalwood, cedarwood, and sweet white wine.

Stately Spanish galleon coming from the Isthmus,
Dipping through the Tropics by the palm-green shores,
With a cargo of diamonds,
Emeralds, amethysts,
Topazes, and cinnamon, and gold moidores.

Dirty British coaster with a salt-caked smoke-stack,
Butting through the Channel in the mad March days,
With a cargo of Tyne coal,
Road-rails, pig-lead,
Firewood, iron-ware, and cheap tin trays.

Though the vocabulary of the third stanza may be said to be less "poetic" than that of the first two, the sounds of the last stanza are actually just as beautiful. By the sharp contrast of the images, Masefield makes us understand the romantic feeling with which he observes British ships in the Channel on a windy March day.

Presenting to us familiar images in our own daily language, the poet is able by the way in which he groups and associates his words and images to cast "a certain colouring of the imagination" over ordinary things and thus to express truth for us. For we emerge finally with a sense of having understood what before we missed, of having extended the realms of our awareness. As John Livingston Lowes puts it, "Poetry starts from the actual and ends in the true."

Keats tells us in one of his letters, that he spent a morning in a somewhat moody state of mind, listening to the song of a nightingale in a nearby tree. A simple prose statement of how he sat in the garden listening to the bird does not tell us what really happened in this transition from "the actual" to "the true." It can be said only in poetry; it can be said only by images:

> My heartaches, and a drowsy numbness pains
> My sense, as though of hemlock I had drunk,
> Or emptied some dull opiate to the drains
> One minute past, and Lethe-wards had sunk.

And we, with Keats, sink Lethe-wards, release our hold on the world about us, and let the song of a bird lead us to a comprehension of—what? Let us listen first, and let each image form itself in our minds:

> Tis not through envy of thy happy lot,
> But being too happy in thy happiness,
> That thou, light-wingèd Dryad of the trees,
> In some melodious plot
> Of beechen green, and shadows numberless,
> Singest of summer in full-throated ease.

The bird, invisible, is a "light-wingèd Dryad of the trees." The very metaphor, together with the reference to hemlock and to Lethe, reminds us that birds were singing as freshly many centuries ago as they are now. Their unchanging music helps us to leave the present world unseen, and to "fade away into the forest dim,"

> Fade far away, dissolve, and quite forget
> What thou among the leaves hast never known,
> The weariness, the fever, and the fret
> Here, where men sit and hear each other groan.

"Though the dull brain perplexes and retards," the song of the invisible bird is enough to release Keats, to release us, to let him "fly to thee" "on the viewless wings of poesy." For now the garden in which Keats is seated has become remote:

> I cannot see what flowers are at my feet,
> Nor what soft incense hangs upon the boughs.

But in "embalmèd darkness," a darkness made sweet by "the grass, the thicket and the fruit-tree wild," does Keats, in his mood of restlessness, let the sound of the bird's song lead him

further and further away from the "actual," nearer and nearer
to the "true," the true, which, in this poem, is an apprehension
of the meaning of the death of the individual:

> Darkling I listen; and for many a time
> I have been half in love with easeful Death . . .

> Now more than ever seems it rich to die
> To cease upon the midnight with no pain,

And the immortality of beauty itself:

> Thou wast not born for death, immortal Bird!
> No hungry generations tread thee down;
> The voice I hear this passing night was heard
> In ancient days by emperor and clown:
> Perhaps the self-same song that found a path
> Through the sad heart of Ruth, when, sick for home,
> She stood in tears amid the alien corn;
> The same that ofttimes hath
> Charm'd magic casements, opening on the foam
> Of perilous seas, in faery lands forlorn.

The song of the bird, and all the associations which cluster
around the song in Keats's mind, have led him in terms of
imagery to a comprehension of the relation between our transitory selves and all the imperishable beauty of the world, a comprehension which we share as we ourselves, led by Keats as
he was led by the bird, enter the "forest dim" of our own
minds and emerge again into the actual world, deepened and
harmonized:

> Fled is that music:—do I wake or sleep?

Just as we can never hope to recapture the exact rhythmic
stress with which Keats read over his poem, so we can never
see the same images. Our images of the flowers in the garden,
"fast fading violets cover'd up in leaves," and of Ruth

> . . . when, sick for home,
> She stood in tears amid the alien corn

are different from the images in Keats's mind. No matter. The point is that we too create the images as vividly, as wholly, as we can, with as rich association as we are able to evoke—and that the images do give up their meanings to us. For images are the language with which the poet expresses the truths of his heart; all that the poet has enjoyed and suffered, all that he has observed, will be fused and distilled again by this "image-making faculty," which Sir Philip Sidney says is the very mark of the poet.

Why this should be so we do not know. We do know, however, that after moments of excitement, when our minds and emotions seem to be deeply involved, we are apt to call up again isolated images stored in our imaginations—the gesture of a hand, the quality of a voice—which forever symbolize for us the whole experience. The poet, finer in his responses, richer in his power of association, must be able by means of these symbols to fuse the experience for us into one perfect unity, making us feel the abstract in the concrete, and the concrete in the abstract, and thus to give meaning to our otherwise not quite realized lives. Coleridge's description of "the streamy nature of association which thinking curbs and rudders," helps us to understand the mental process of the poet searching for expression, in which images are integral parts, not superimposed ornaments with which the poet adorns his poem. How better, except by associating the song of an invisible bird to undying music, could Keats have told us that, though we die, beauty is never vanquished? Evoking images of familiar sights and sounds, the poet makes us feel their import by suggesting the shadowed truth which they express. Using words that are thoroughly familiar to us, he so orders them that they reverberate in our minds and suggest more than words can ever say explicitly.

Poetry, then, does not make us experience directly the feeling of love, or hate, or hunger, or humiliation, or relief; by a process only partially understood the poet takes these emotions known to us all, and bodies them forth in ordered words.

By responding as fully as we can to the demands made upon us by poetry to hear it, and see it, and share in its mood, we ourselves learn indirectly the meaning of these basic emotions. Like the poet, we feel a new inner harmony which makes us at once more detached from the world about us and more completely a part of it. The terms of poetry which we have been discussing here—rhythm, meter, rime, and images—are only words which we use to describe an experience of concentrated intensity, the exact nature of which we do not understand. True form is a part of the very life of the poem itself. As Coleridge wrote in his essay on "Shakespeare, a Poet Generally":

The form is mechanic, when on any given material we impress a pre-determined form, not necessarily arising out of the properties of the material;—as when to a mass of wet clay we give whatever shape we wish it to retain when hardened. The organic form, on the other hand, is innate; it shapes, as it develops, itself from within, and the fulness of its development is one and the same with the perfection of its outward form. Such as the life is, such is the form. Nature, the prime genial artist, inexhaustible in diverse powers, is equally inexhaustible in forms;—each exterior is the physiognomy of the being within—its true image reflected and thrown out from the concave mirror.

FURTHER READING

Lascelles Abercrombie, *Poetry, Its Music and Meaning*, 1932.
Clarence E. Andrews, *The Writing and Reading of Verse*, 1932.
Elizabeth Drew, *Discovering Poetry*, 1933.
Max Eastman, *The Enjoyment of Poetry*, 1916.
Thomas S. Eliot, *The Sacred Wood*, 1920.
Alfred E. Housman, *The Name and Nature of Poetry*, 1933.
Reginald B. Johnson, *Poetry and the Poets*, 1926.
W. P. Ker, *Form and Style in Poetry*, 1929.
John Livingston Lowes, *Convention and Revolt in Poetry*, 1931.
I. A. Richards, *Science and Poetry*, 1926.
George Saintsbury, *History of English Prosody*, 1923.

NARRATIVE POETRY

FROM THE EARLIEST TIMES the character of a story has been to a large extent determined by the audiences for which it has been composed. The book of *Esther* was written for Jews who, after the tortures of the Captivity, were eager to rejoice in a glorious tale of their release. The *Iliad* was made to be recited by a bard before royal warriors. Modern stories in verse such as John Masefield's *Reynard the Fox* are produced for readers whose interest must be held while they wait for trains on railroad platforms. In reading English narrative poetry from the Middle Ages to the present, therefore, one must keep in mind the audiences for whom the poems were written and the conditions under which they were read.

Narrative Poetry of the Middle Ages

The earliest period of English poetry with which we are concerned is that of the fourteenth century, the time when English literature came into its first glory. The French literary culture which had come to dominate England after the Conquest in 1066 had by this time been thoroughly assimilated by the native Anglo-Saxon culture, which had itself been altered in its contact with foreign forms and techniques. From this combination of the two, a new English language, ready to be cast into some of the most beautiful literary forms of the Middle Ages, had grown up, and a new English literature had appeared. The English people, moreover, were growing in wealth and power, and both high and low could afford the luxury of supporting writers of good stories.

The medieval English audience may, in general, be divided into two groups: the one was noble and cultured; the other was made up of the common people, somewhat rough, but sturdy, hearty, and vigorous. The upper-class audience, which was ruled over in artistic matters by ladies, loved to hear romances of courtly love and tales of high adventure; the middle and lower classes, knowing little of the rules of chivalry, were more apt to listen to accounts of deeds in which they themselves might have played a part. But, of course, each group also enjoyed the poetry of the other.

Appealing to both groups but springing more particularly from the second was the popular ballad, the earliest form of narrative verse with which we shall deal. Who first sang the ballads is unknown. Some students have thought they were made up by groups of men and women singing and dancing together—first one line contributed by one person and then another by a second, and the group joining in the refrain. Other students have maintained that they were composed by individual poets whose names died with them but whose poems were preserved in the memory of the community. Still others believe that the ballads were the result of both methods of composition. However they were made, they were recited from memory and were only written down by antiquaries many centuries later. Indeed, it was not until Dr. Thomas Percy in the eighteenth century gathered together a large number of old ballads and published them as *Reliques of Ancient English Poetry* (1765) that poets and scholars came to know the medieval ballads at first hand. In the early nineteenth century Sir Walter Scott collected many more from the mouths of persons who were still in his day carrying on the tradition; and at the end of the nineteenth century Professor F. J. Child compiled a great anthology of over three hundred extant early English ballads. It is interesting to learn that some of these very ballads came to this country with the immigrants from England and Scotland and are still to be heard from the lips of fishermen in Maine and mountaineers in Kentucky and Tennessee. Ballads thus began with the people and still live with them.

Ballads were concerned with all sorts of subjects, but the feeling evoked was always very dear to people's hearts. We find stark tragedy in *Edward* and *Barbara Allen,* and comedy in *Get up and Bar the Door. Sweet William's Ghost* and *Thomas Rymer* show the taste of the people for the supernatural. Probably the most popular of all the ballads tell of the adventures and death of Robin Hood. In these accounts the common people could enjoy, at least imaginatively, the triumphs of their hero over their rich and powerful oppressors. The popular ballads give an insight into the lives, both imaginative and actual, of the poor people. They do not, however, portray individual characters. On the contrary, the story is the whole interest, and the persons who participate in the actions are almost counters. It is true that in such ballads as those of Robin Hood one does receive impressions of strong or weak, brave or cowardly men. But personality is subordinated.

Geoffrey Chaucer, the first great individual poet, knew how to touch this same audience. Although he wrote for the courtly circles, he knew the common people as well, and in *The Canterbury Tales* we find all kinds of stories. The *Tales* are presented in a "frame," a familiar device of medieval story tellers. Chaucer arranges his stories as if they were being told by a group of pilgrims making a trip to the shrine of St. Thomas à Becket at Canterbury. In the General Prologue, he outlined his plan and described each one of the pilgrims. The worthy Knight, the epicurean Franklin, the hearty Wife of Bath, the shrewd Reeve, the devoted Parson, all are miniatures taken from the life of the fourteenth century. Then as the procession starts its journey, the various members under the leadership of Harry Bailey, the Host of the Tabard Inn in Southwark, begin their stories. From the Knight, as was fitting, we have a romance of courtly love. The high tone of such a good beginning could not be maintained long, however, for at once after the story ended, the Miller and the Reeve had to rush in to tell vulgar tales of their lowly lives. Other stories succeeded one another, some sad, some humorous, interspersed

with prologues and epilogues which throw light on the characters of the pilgrims and relate incidents which took place on
the journey. The Summoner and the Friar almost have a fight
but are prevented by the stout leader of the party. The
Prioress tells a tale of a little Christian boy who was persecuted
by the Jews, and the whole group of pilgrims are moved to
tears. The Nun's Priest later delights everyone by the tale of a
cock and a hen. Finally, the pilgrimage ends with a long
sermon by the Parson. Chaucer has employed nearly all the
narrative devices known to the medieval English poet.

We have seen that in the ballad poetry of this period, individual character is absent. When we come to Chaucer,
however, we see actual persons who live and move before our
eyes as definite personalities. The pictures of the pilgrims as
they are drawn in the sketches of the *Prologue* are so clearly
taken from life that scholars have been able to identify with
some degree of likelihood the persons of the fourteenth century whom Chaucer was depicting. Within the *Tales*, too, one
seems to see individuals move before one's eyes. Though the
"povre Widwe" of *The Nonne Preestes Tale* may not be
distinguishable from other widows of the age; nevertheless, the
account of her and her daughters and their dwelling is memorable and is a definite picture of life among the poor of the
fourteenth century. In *The Miller's Tale* the poet has given a
description of Absolon so accurately that one is sure he had a
definite small town "slicker" in mind:

> Crul was his heer, and as the gold it shoon,
> And strouted as a fanne large and brode;
> Ful streight and evene lay his joly shode.
> His rode was reed, his eyen greye as goos.
> With Powles wyndow corven on his shoos,
> In hoses rede he wente fetisly.
> Y-clad he was ful smal and properly,
> Al in a kirtel of lyght waget,
> Ful faire and thikke been the poyntes set.
> And therupon he hadde a gay surplys,

As whit as is the blosme upon the rys.
A myrie child he was, so God me save.
Wel koude he laten blood and clippe and shave,
And maken a chartre of lond or acquitaunce.
In twenty manere koude he trippe and daunce
(After the scole of Oxenforde tho)
And with his legges casten to and fro,
And pleyen songes on a smal rubible:
Therto he song somtyme a loud quynyble;
And as wel koude he pleye on his giterne.
In al the toun nas brewhous ne taverne
That he ne visited with his solas,
Ther any gaylard tappestere was.

With Chaucer the art of character development in English
poetry began, and, one must add, it has never reached greater
perfection.

Narrative Poetry of the Sixteenth and Seventeenth Centuries

Beginning in the fourteenth century and extending to the
late sixteenth a change which we call the Renascence took
place in the culture of Europe. Men travelled more widely
than before, and commerce increased between nations. In the
field of literature the reading of the Greek and Latin classics
was revived, new colleges were founded at Oxford and
Cambridge, and many long forgotten texts were again put in
circulation. The introduction of the printing press to Western
Europe about the middle of the fifteenth century came just at
the right moment to make these books more easily available to
thousands of readers. To meet the demands of this new audience, the forms of narrative poetry gradually changed, for
now, for the first time, there was a reading, rather than a listening, public.

The old ballads for the time being seemed to drop out of
sight entirely, though country people still sang them on the
village greens where they had originated. But though they

were not printed for hundreds of years and seemed forgotten, they did exert an influence on the new poetry which was being written. Their attractive meter was frequently used, as we shall see in the introduction to the second section of this book, by the lyric poets, and the writers of broadsides commonly employed it. In a somewhat adapted form we find the popular ballad meter in such a poem as Drayton's *Ballad of Agincourt*. Here also, though one realizes that the poet is now the conscious artist writing for a literary audience, we get much of the spirit of the old ballads. The day of the ballad was coming to an end, however, and that of its literary imitations was still two centuries in the future.

The verse romance and the tale, which formerly had been read aloud to groups in the great halls and in the chambers of the ladies, began also to disappear when men and women tended more and more to read for themselves. Possibly this change came about because prose seemed more realistic than poetry—and consequently closer to the imaginative range of the middle-class reader—or possibly it came because of the example of Malory, who told in prose his stories of King Arthur and his knights. Whatever the cause, the sixteenth- and seventeenth-century romance writers, responding to a shift in public taste, abandoned verse almost entirely. To this change of taste may be attributed the great popularity attained at the end of the sixteenth century and during the first half of the seventeenth by the prose romances. Of these Lyly's *Euphues* and Sydney's *Arcadia* went through many editions during this period.

But though the medieval versified romance dropped out of favor, many readers found in poetry something more ennobling than in prose. As if in response to the need created by the disappearance of the metrical romance, Edmund Spenser, in 1590 and 1596, published *The Færie Queene*. This poem, dedicated to Queen Elizabeth, seems in many respects to be a medieval work. The allegory is characteristic of the older tradition. The deeds of armored knights fighting for their ladies carry one back to the medieval legends told by Malory and the earlier romancers. The delineation of character is neglected in the allegorical maze. But the spirit of the Renascence pervades the poem. The stanza form is original. The constant appeals to the senses of sight, taste, smell, feeling, and hearing thrill us, and must have thrilled Spenser's sixteenth-century readers too, for Spenser's influence is reflected in the new poetry which was written in such abundance in the next two generations. The classical reading of Spenser, a typical scholar-poet of the sixteenth century, appears in almost every stanza. The virtues of Aristotle, the thoughts on love and beauty of Plato, and the countless allusions to Greek and Roman mythology mark *The Faerie Queene* as a poem of the new age.

Another of the classical influences on Spenser, and one which became of increasing importance in the narrative poetry of the sixteenth and seventeenth centuries, reaching its height in the work of Milton, was that of the ancient epic poets. Homer and Virgil had become the models for all those whose ambition it was to compose the great English poem. Though *The Faerie Queene* was not constructed as an epic, in its use of classical story material and of simile and epithet, it shows throughout the influence of the ancient heroic poets.

The greatest narrative poem of the seventeenth century was, of course, John Milton's *Paradise Lost*, where the classical epic was very nearly naturalized in English literature. Structurally this poem is modeled on the epics of antiquity. Its theme is heroic; it contains twelve books, the number of Virgil's *Aeneid*; it plunges *in medias res*. Milton first invokes the Muse, as do Homer and Virgil, but in his case it is the Christian Muse, the Holy Spirit, from whom he implores inspiration and strength. In the manner of the ancients he has filled his epic with similes, epithets, and hundreds of allusions to the legends of antiquity. The poem is thoroughly original, however, for as a Christian and an Englishman, the author poured into his writing all the fervor which these two words implied in his day, and he seasoned all with genius. The character sketches of many of the figures, however, do not reveal living persons so much as types. One feels Beelzebub, Moloch, and Belial more as abstractions than as persons of flesh and blood. But Adam and Eve and Satan are creations of genius who live as individuals.

Narrative Poetry of the Eighteenth Century

But even before *Paradise Lost* was published in 1667, the literary atmosphere had changed. Beginning about the time of the Restoration and continuing until the latter eighteenth century came the period which we rather vaguely call "The Age of Reason." It was a time when men were preoccupied with science and with the precise expression of scientific ideas in prose. The two went together because the accurate observation of scientific data required exactitude in writing in order to describe them. The use of the reason in science, moreover, caused all writers and thinkers to scrutinize more carefully than formerly every sort of intellectual process. In literature the first result of this attitude of mind was to make men seek scientific verification for all they wrote. This in turn caused them to attempt to write "reasonable" poetry. Though the people of the time admired *The Faerie Queene* and *Paradise Lost,* they deplored the improbabilities which appear throughout them. Who, they thought, could now write seriously of the Red Cross Knight or of conversations in Heaven for which the Bible gives no authority?

One use, however, the Restoration and eighteenth century could find for narrative poetry. It proved to be a magnificent instrument of satire. John Dryden tells a story of the Duke of Monmouth and the Earl of Shaftesbury under the biblical names of Absalom and Achitophel. His aim was to attack Shaftesbury who was at the time imprisoned in the Tower for political reasons. A few lines from the sketch of the Earl's character may be quoted here to illustrate the power and discernment of Dryden's satire:

> Of these the false Achitophel was first,
> A name to all succeeding ages curst:
> For close designs and crooked counsels fit;
> Sagacious, bold, and turbulent of wit;
> Restless, unfix'd in principles and place;
> In pow'r unpleas'd, impatient of disgrace.
> A fiery soul, which, working out its way,
> Fretted the pigmy body to decay,
> And o'er inform'd the tenement of clay.
> A daring pilot in extremity;
> Pleas'd with the danger, when the waves went high,
> He sought the storms; but, for a calm unfit,
> Would steer too nigh the sands, to boast his wit.
> Great wits are sure to madness near allied,
> And thin partitions do their bounds divide;
> Else why should he, with wealth and honor blest,
> Refuse his age the needful hours of rest?
> Punish a body which he could not please;
> Bankrupt of life, yet prodigal of ease?
> And all to leave what with his toil he won,
> To that unfeather'd two-legg'd thing, a son;
> Got, while his soul did huddled notions try;
> And born a shapeless lump, like anarchy.

The character continues for many lines more, marked by the clear recitation of facts, such as those alluding to Shaftesbury's weak and hunch-backed body. Dryden, like the true satirist, did not make up his facts; he merely distorted what nature supplied.

Writing in the next generation after Dryden, Pope's satirical narratives are even more personally biting, but they are sometimes marked by greater humor. Thus, when addressing a clever social public that enjoyed good company, balls, and wit, he seized on the method of the classical epic, which had inspired Spenser and Milton to their most sublime thoughts, to ridicule the parties to a social squabble. *The Rape of the Lock* begins with an invocation to the epic muse, which sets the tone of the whole poem:

> What dire offense from amorous causes springs,
> What mighty contests rise from trivial things,
> I sing—

From this point on one learns in mock heroic terms of the affairs of beaus and beauties, instead of the deeds of warlike heroes. One is told of a naughty young gentleman who had the temerity to cut a lock of hair from the head of a lovely young lady and of the dreadful consequences which ensued. Pope liked the mock-epic technique and employed it again in *The Dunciad*, which begins,

> Books and the Man I sing, the first who brings
> The Smithfield Muses to the Ear of Kings,

in imitation of Virgil. Throughout the satire Pope strews character sketches of his victims, the poets, publishers, and wits against whom he had a grudge.

In the realm of the romance and tale told in verse, the eighteenth century did little. But we must not forget to mention *Eloisa to Abelard,* in which Pope adapted the rimed couplet to the medieval, romantic subject matter, nor, at the other end of the century, Robert Burns' *Tam O'Shanter,* an amusing tale in the Scottish dialect. The tradition of the poetic narrative was at least kept alive by two of the great poets of the age.

Narrative Poetry of the Late Eighteenth and Nineteenth Centuries

Toward the middle of the eighteenth century a revival of medieval art, literature, and legend occurred which has continued to this day. Gothic architecture became fashionable and "Gothic" novels were the fad. As time went on, medieval legends caught the imaginations of the poets who revived them in the late eighteenth- and in nineteenth-century poetry. One of the earliest narrative forms to feel this new impulse, and one which has continued until the present was the ballad. We have already noticed that Dr. Thomas Percy collected and published the old English ballads, which had been neglected for centuries. Immediately the poets saw in these poems materials for their purposes and started to imitate both the form and subjects of the ballads. Thomas Chatterton, a boy of seventeen, wrote the pseudo-medieval *Bristowe Tragedie,* and many other poets delighted their eighteenth century public by their adaptations of this old form. So well established was the ballad revival by 1782 that Cowper could use it with tremendous success in *The Diverting History of John Gilpin.* Then, at the end of the century, came the group of poets whom we call the "Romantics," nearly all of whom wrote in the neo-ballad manner.

The best known of all the imitative ballads is *The Rime of the Ancient Mariner.* The stanza form is that of the old ballads, and the story might well have been told by one of the early rustic singers. But as it so well illustrates the naturalization of the medieval ballad meter and theme, it also exemplifies attitudes of mind in the poet which were foreign to the old ballad makers of the Middle Ages. In the fourteenth and fifteenth centuries one would not expect to hear the self-conscious praise of the "sweet voice" of the Hermit who "loves to talk with mariners." Nor would the medieval balladers have moralized as does Coleridge in such stanzas as, "He loveth well who prayeth well." From the old materials the poet has made a work wonderfully true to himself and to his time.

The ballad continued to be popular with poets through the entire nineteenth century. The neo-medievalism, so dearly loved by the romantics, comes out in *La Belle Dame sans Merci* by Keats, where in a slightly modified stanza the author told a story of a knight and a lady. Scott's *Hunting Song* catches the spirit of the medieval ballads both in theme and rhythm. The Victorians too enjoyed the beauties of the old ballad. To mention only a few examples out of many, Tennyson employed the ballad technique in *The Revenge*, Browning used it in *How They Brought the Good News from Ghent to Aix*, Rossetti adapted it in *Sister Helen*, and, at the end of the century, Kipling found in it a ringing medium for the *Ballad of East and West*. Just as the ballad was useful to humorous poets in the eighteenth century, for example, Cowper, so also in the late nineteenth it proved very success-ful in W. S. Gilbert's *Rime of the Nancy Bell*, a mock-serious ballad modeled on *The Rime of the Ancient Mariner*.

But though the old meter, sometimes slightly altered and sometimes exactly followed, had proved so valuable to modern writers, the subject matters in which these later poets dealt had gone far from those of the medieval singers. Scott, per-haps, kept most closely to the original spirit of the ballad; Rossetti went far afield.

The nineteenth century, which adapted all the earlier liter-ary forms to its purposes, also fostered the tale and the ro-mance, forms which have flourished from the late eighteenth century straight down to the present. In *Michael, A Pastoral Poem*, Wordsworth has given us a kind of tale, but one which is a combination of the reflective poem and the character sketch. One of the early examples of the neo-medieval ro-mance is Coleridge's incomplete *Christobel*, which reflects a nostalgic longing for Gothic castles and the adventures that ideally might take place in them. Its mood is declared in the opening lines, where owls and the crowing cock cast their artificial "Gothic" spell. But whether he will or no, the reader's imagination is enthralled by the lovely poetry. With more power, perhaps because of the poet's greater mastery of narrative technique, Keats' *Eve of St. Agnes* succeeds in carry-ing one back into the Middle Ages. The Spenserian stanza supports the story, lending it dignity and strength, and the simplicity of the plot allows one to dwell on the sensuous descriptions.

We cannot mention the tales and romances of the Romantic poets without naming Byron and Scott, whose verse romances so delighted their contemporaries and their descendants almost to the end of the century. Byron's curious stories have little in common either with a Wordsworthian tale or with a neo-medieval romance. He seems always to have been striving for the exotic and for stories of personal adventure and heroism. One witnesses physical courage, physical suffering, and physical hatred in *The Corsair*, a poem with an Eastern setting, and in *The Prisoner of Chillon*, one with a medieval setting. He strives for the "Gothic," but only achieves the pseudo-"Gothic." The ability, moreover, to portray character truly in verse was denied to Byron as it was to most of the other poets who attempted to write romances. The long poems of Scott were less exotic than those of Byron, for the author of

> Breathes there a man with soul so dead
> Who never to himself hath said
> This is my own my native land,

was not likely to go far afield for the subjects of his romances. He loved the Middle Ages and the period of the Renascence, and in *Marmion* and *The Lady of the Lake* he thrilled all his readers of the British tradition by portraying highly romanticized pictures of stirring events in the long border struggle of England and Scotland. He achieved a high patriotic note, so dear to the nineteenth century imperialists, but his characters tend to be all hero or all knave. The most memorable parts of his long poems are the fine warlike or sentimental lyrics interspersed through the narratives.

Among the Victorians the story based on romantic materials continued in popularity. Tennyson's *The Lady of Shalott*, a narrative meditation on a legend from Malory, suggests the dangers and the folly of watching life in a mirror instead of directly participating in the struggle. Because of his less obviously moral intent in the *Idylls of the King*, Tennyson was more successful in developing character, which be portrayed for the sake of setting examples of conduct before the youth of his generation. Indeed, in telling his tales he was nearly always preoccupied by pointing a moral, a habit which should place many of his narrative poems in the didactic section of the present volume. William Morris in *The Haystack in the Floods* probably comes nearest to telling a story simply for the effect of the tale. One might continue citing examples of romantic narratives, and include the dramas of Synge and Yeats, which are directly in the tradition with which we are dealing, but enough has been said to indicate the uses made of this literary type. The poets of the nineteenth century had turned to the romances of the Middle Ages for story material, but their treatment of them was far more philosophical than that of the medieval writers. The modern poets sometimes longed for the old days, sometimes pointed a moral, and sometimes were humorous; very seldom were they pleased with the legend merely for the sake of the story.

In this nineteenth century, which chewed and digested nearly all verse forms, we also find at least one interesting example of the modern epic. In *Sohrab and Rustum*, Matthew Arnold created in miniature a Victorian epic which derived from the classical epic as much as might be crammed within so narrow a compass. Its subject-matter might appropriately have been used as romance material, but the poet evidently felt that the theme was heroic and so cast it in a small epic mould. The expression is so dignified and restrained that the Victorian sentimentality is kept within bounds. It may fairly be regarded as an epic closely allied to the imitative romances of the period.

One last narrative form of the nineteenth century must be mentioned before we end this review of English story-telling in verse. The dramatic monologue of Robert Browning is at once a poetic soliloquy and a dramatic narrative for meditative reading rather than for the stage. In *My Last Duchess*, Browning has the speaker reveal his character by the quiet recital of facts; the result is a subtle character study. *Fra Lippo Lippi* is an autobiography of an artist. Here, however, the facts are not always so objective as in *My Last Duchess*. Browning had the gifts of a playwright in an age when the atmosphere was unfavorable to the theater. In the dramatic monologue he was able to rescue his gifts both as a story-teller and as a dramatist.

With the coming of the twentieth century we find the poets continuing the narrative forms with which their predecessors worked. Old devices in new settings are also still being tried. In *Renard the Fox*, for instance, John Masefield has adapted Chaucer's method of character delineation as an introduction to the participants in a long tale. Both the old poet and the new are attempting to portray human beings as they live and act, and the devices of the one are suggestive for the other. Like all successful narrative poets, both derive their vitality from their ability to tell a good story and to portray characters of flesh and blood.

The audience for whom twentieth-century narrative poets write is, on the whole, one which reads rather than one which listens, for the listening audience is entirely preoccupied with the radio and the movies. It is an intellectual rather than a popular audience, highly trained in the traditions of English poetry from Chaucer to the present. In these ways it differs greatly from the audience for whom the fourteenth- and sixteenth-century poets made their verses. With them the story was of first importance, for it gave a thread to which the listeners could cling. When Chaucer portrayed character skillfully, the people were delighted, but had he neglected his story for too extended psychological disquisitions, they probably would have yawned. Countless readers of Spenser and Milton have delighted in the stories related long before they have attended to the allegory and the morals. As we shall see in the introduction to didactic poetry, the eighteenth century was on the whole more devoted to the moral and satirical aspects of its narrative poems than to the tales themselves. With the greatly enlarged audience which read its poetry to itself and seldom listened to it aloud, the poets of the nineteenth century were able to center their attentions more on subtleties of character and psychological processes than could their predecessors.

FURTHER READING

William Mac Neile Dixon, *English Epic and Heroic Poetry*, 1912.
Francis B. Gummere, *The Popular Ballad*, 1907.
W. P. Ker, *Epic and Romance*, 1897.
William W. Lawrence, *Medieval Story*, 1926.

GEOFFREY CHAUCER

THE CANTERBURY TALES

The Prologue

Whan that Aprille with his shoures sote
The droghte of Marche hath perced to the rote,
And bathed every veyne in swich licour,
Of which vertu engendred is the flour;
Whan Zephirus eek with his swete breeth
Inspired hath in every holt and heeth
The tendre croppes, and the yonge sonne
Hath in the Ram his halfe cours y-ronne,
And smale fowles maken melodye,
That slepen al the night with open yë,   10
(So priketh hem nature in hir corages):
Than longen folk to goon on pilgrimages
(And palmers for to seken straunge strondes)
To ferne halwes, couthe in sondry londes;
And specially, from every shires ende
Of Engelond, to Caunterbury they wende,
The holy blisful martir for to seke,
That hem hath holpen, whan that they were seke.
      Bifel that, in that seson on a day,
In Southwerk at the Tabard as I lay   20

1. *shoures sote*, showers sweet.   3. *swich*, such.   4. *vertu*, power.
5. *Zephirus*, the west wind.   6. *inspired*, breathed into.
7. *croppes*, shoots.
8. *Hath . . . y-ronne*. The new spring sun had completed running through half of the sign of the Ram, one of the signs of the zodiac, on April 11.
9. *fowles*, birds.
11. *So . . . corages*, So nature stirs them in their hearts.
13. *straunge strondes*, foreign strands.   14. *ferne*, far; *couthe*, known.
17. St. Thomas à Becket, Archbishop of Canterbury, who was assassinated in 1170 and canonized in 1173.
20. *Tabard*, the name of an actual inn in Southwark, just across the Thames river from London. The name was taken from the painted sign in front of the inn, a sleeveless shirt.

Redy to wenden on my pilgrimage
To Caunterbury with ful devout corage,
At night was come in-to that hostelrye
Wel nyne and twenty in a companye,
Of sondry folk, by aventure y-falle
In felawshipe, and pilgrims were they alle,
That toward Caunterbury wolden ryde;
The chambres and the stables weren wyde,
And wel we weren esed atte beste.
And shortly, whan the sonne was to reste,   30
So hadde I spoken with hem everichon,
That I was of hir felawshipe anon,
And made forward erly for to ryse,
To take our wey, ther as I yow devyse.
     But natheles, whyl I have tyme and space,
Er that I ferther in this tale pace,
Me thinketh it acordaunt to resoun,
To telle yow al the condicioun
Of ech of hem, so as it semed me,
And whiche they weren, and of what degree;   40
And eek in what array that they were inne:
And at a knight than wol I first biginne.
     A KNIGHT ther was, and that a worthy man,
That fro the tyme that he first bigan
To ryden out, he loved chivalrye,
Trouthe and honour, fredom and curteisye.
Ful worthy was he in his lordes werre,
And therto hadde he riden (no man ferre)
As wel in Cristendom as hethenesse,
And ever honoured for his worthinesse.   50
     At Alisaundre he was, whan it was wonne;
Ful ofte tyme he hadde the bord bigonne

22. *corage*, heart.   25. *aventure*, chance.
29. *esed atte beste*, served with the best.   31. *everichon*, every one.
33. *forward*, agreement.   34. *devyse*, describe.   36. *pace*, pass.
37. *accordaunt to resoun*, reasonable.   43. *worthy*, honorable.
46. *fredom*, generosity.   47. *werre*, war.   49. *hethenesse*, heathen lands.
51. *Alisaundre*, Alexandria, which was captured from the "Heathens" in 1365.
52. *the bord bigonne*, sat at the head of the table.

Aboven alle naciouns in Pruce.
In Lettow hadde he reysed and in Ruce,
No Cristen man so ofte of his degree.
In Gernade at the sege eek hadde he be
Of Algezir, and riden in Belmarye.
At Lyeys was he, and at Satalye,
Whan they were wonne; and in the Grete See
At many a noble aryve hadde he be.   60
At mortal batailles hadde he been fiftene,
And foughten for our feith at Tramissene
In listes thryes, and ay slayn his fo.
This ilke worthy knight had been also
Somtyme with the lord of Palatye,
Ageyn another hethen in Turkye:
And evermore he hadde a sovereyn prys.
And though that he were worthy, he was wys,
And of his port as meke as is a mayde.
He never yet no vileinye ne sayde   70
In al his lyf, un-to no maner wight.
He was a verray parfit gentil knight.
But for to tellen yow of his array,
His hors were gode, but he was nat gay.
Of fustian he wered a gipoun
Al bismotered with his habergeoun;
For he was late y-come from his viage,
And wente for to doon his pilgrimage.
    With him ther was his sone, a yong SQUYER,
A lovyere, and a lusty bacheler,   80

53–58. *Pruce*, Prussia; *Lettow*, Lithuania; *reysed*, gone on a military expedition; *Ruce*, Russia; *Gernade*, Granada; *Algezir*, Algeciras; *Belmarye*, a
Moorish city in Africa; *Lyeys*, in Armenia; *Satalye*, Attalia. Crusading
knights from England fought at all of these places in the 1360s.
    59. *Grete See*, Mediterranean Sea.   60. *aryve*, military disembarcation.
    62. *Tramissene*, a Moorish kingdom.
    63. *In listes thryes*, in three tournaments.   64. *ilke*, same.
    65. *Palatye*, Christian lordship in Asia Minor.
    67. *sovereyn prys*, high reputation.   69. *port*, bearing.
    71. *no maner wight*, any sort of person.   75. *gipoun*, a short coat.
    76. *habergeoun*, coat of mail.   77. *viage*, expedition.
    80. *bachelor*, candidate for knighthood.

With lokkes crulle, as they were leyd in presse.
Of twenty yeer of age he was, I gesse.
Of his stature he was of evene lengthe,
And wonderly deliver, and greet of strengthe.
And he had been somtyme in chivachye,
In Flaundres, in Artoys, and Picardye,
And born him wel, as of so litel space,
In hope to stonden in his lady grace.
Embrouded was he, as it were a mede
Al ful of fresshe floures, whyte and rede.   90
Singinge he was, or floytinge, al the day;
He was as fresh as is the month of May.
Short was his goune, with sleves longe and wyde.
Wel coude he sitte on hors, and faire ryde.
He coude songes make and wel endyte,
Juste and eek daunce, and wel purtreye and wryte.
So hote he lovede, that by nightertale
He sleep namore than dooth a nightingale.
Curteys he was, lowly, and servisable,
And carf biforn his fader at the table.   100

  Ther was also a Nonne, a PRIORESSE,
That of hir smyling was ful simple and coy;
Hir gretteste ooth was but by sëynt Loy;
And she was cleped madame Eglentyne.
Ful wel she song the service divyne,
Entuned in hir nose ful semely;
And Frensh she spak ful faire and fetisly,
After the scole of Stratford atte Bowe,
For Frensh of Paris was to hir unknowe.
At mete wel y-taught was she with-alle;   110

81. *crulle,* curled.   83. *evene lengthe,* good proportions.
84. *deliver,* active.   85. *chivachye,* military expedition.   87. *space,* age.
88. *lady,* the genitive singular.   91. *floytinge,* playing on the flute.
95. *endyte,* compose.   96. *purtrye,* draw.   97. *nightertale,* nighttime.
102. *coy,* quiet.   103. *seynt Loy,* St. Eligius, famed for courtesy.
104. *cleped,* called.   107. *fetisly,* gracefully.
108–109. *After . . . unknowe,* The nuns of the Benedictine nunnery of St.
Leonard's in Middlesex, adjoining Stratford-Bow, learned French, but it was
not very good French such as one learned in Paris.

She leet no morsel from hir lippes falle,
Ne wette hir fingres in hir sauce depe.
Wel coude she carie a morsel, and wel kepe,
That no drope ne fille up-on hir brest.
In curteisye was set ful muchel hir lest.
Hir over lippe wyped she so clene,
That in hir coppe was no ferthing sene
Of grece, whan she dronken hadde hir draughte.
Ful semely after hir mete she raughte,
And sikerly she was of greet disport,   120
And ful plesaunt, and amiable of port,
And peyned hir to countrefete chere
Of court, and been estatlich of manere,
And to ben holden digne of reverence.
But, for to speken of hir conscience,
She was so charitable and so pitous,
She wolde wepe, if that she sawe a mous
Caught in a trappe, if it were deed or bledde.
Of smale houndes had she, that she fedde
With rosted flesh, or milk and wastel-breed.   130
But sore weep she if oon of hem were deed,
Or if men smoot it with a yerde smerte:
And al was conscience and tendre herte.
Ful semely hir wimpel pinched was;
Hir nose tretys; hir eyen greye as glas;
Hir mouth ful smal, and ther-to softe and reed;
But sikerly she hadde a fair forheed;
It was almost a spanne brood, I trowe;
For, hardily, she was nat undergrowe.
Ful fetis was hir cloke, as I was war.   140
Of smal coral aboute hir arm she bar

---

115. *lest*, pleasure.   117. *ferthing*, fourth part, small bit.
119. *raughte*, reached.   120. *sikerly*, surely; *disport*, good humor.
122–123. "She took pains to imitate the behavior of court, and to be stately
of manner."
124. *digne*, worthy. 130. *wastel-breed*, bread made from fine white flour.
132. *yerde*, stick; *smerte*, sharply.   134. *pinched*, pleated.
135. *tretys*, streight and well shaped.   139. *hardily*, certainly.
140. *fetis*, neat.

A peire of bedes, gauded al with grene;
And ther-on heng a broche of gold ful shene,
On which there was first write a crowned A,
And after, *Amor vincit omnia.*
Another NONNE with hir hadde she,
That was hir chapeleyne, and PREESTES THREE.
A MONK ther was, a fair for the maistrye,
An out-rydere, that lovede venerye;
A manly man, to been an abbot able.   150
Ful many a deyntee hors hadde he in stable:
And, whan he rood, men mighte his brydel here
Ginglen in a whistling wind as clere,
And eek as loude as dooth the chapel-belle
Ther as this lord was keper of the celle.
The reule of seint Maure or of seint Beneit,
By-cause that it was old and som-del streit,
This ilke monk leet olde thinges pace,
And held after the newe world the space.
He yaf nat of that text a pulled hen,   160
That seith, that hunters been nat holy men;
Ne that a monk, whan he is cloisterlees,
Is lykned til a fish that is waterlees;
This is to seyn, a monk out of his cloistre.
But thilke text held he nat worth an oistre;
And I seyde, his opinioun was good.
What sholde he studie, and make him-selven wood,
Upon a book in cloistre alwey to poure,
Or swinken with his handes, and laboure,
As Austin bit? How shal the world be served?   170

142. *peire of bedes*, rosary; *gauded*, having large green beads for the Lord's
Prayer.
143. *shene*, bright.   145. *Armor vincit omnia*, Love conquers all.
148. *for the maistrye*, superior to all others.
149. *out-rydere*, a monk who visited various properties owned by a monastery; *venerye*, hunting.
151. *deyntee*, fine.
155. *celle*, a small monastery subordinate to a larger one.
156. *seint Maure*, a disciple of St. Benedict; *seint Beneit*, St. Benedict.
157. *som-del streit*, somewhat strict.   159. *space*, course.
160. *yaf*, gave; *pulled*, plucked.   167. *wood*, mad.   169. *swinken*, work.
170. *Austin*, St. Augustine, who taught that monks should both work with
their hands and study with their heads; *bit*, biddeth.

Lat Austin have his swink to him reserved.
Therfore he was a pricasour aright;
Grehoundes he hadde, as swifte as fowel in flight;
Of priking and of hunting for the hare
Was al his lust, for no cost wolde he spare.
I seigh his sleves purfiled at the hond
With grys, and that the fyneste of a lond;
And, for to festne his hood under his chin,
He hadde of gold y-wroght a curious pin:
A love-knotte in the gretter ende ther was.   180
His heed was balled, that shoon as any glas,
And eek his face, as he had been anoint.
He was a lord ful fat and in good point;
His eyen stepe, and rollinge in his heed,
That stemed as a forneys of a leed;
His botes souple, his hors in greet estat.
Now certeinly he was a fair prelat;
He was nat pale as a for-pyned goost.
A fat swan loved he best of any roost.
His palfrey was as broun as is a berye.   190

A CLERK ther was of Oxenford also,
That un-to logik hadde longe y-go.
As lene was his hors as is a rake,
And he nas nat right fat, I undertake;
But loked holwe, and ther-to soberly.
Ful thredbar was his overest courtepy;
For he had geten him yet no benefyce,
Ne was so worldly for to have offyce.
For him was lever have at his beddes heed
Twenty bokes, clad in blak or reed,   200
Of Aristotle and his philosophye,

172. *pricasour*, hard rider.   174. *priking*, hunting a hare.
176. *seigh*, saw; *purfiled*, fringed.   177. *grys*, gray fur.
183. *in good point*, in good condition.   185. *stepe*, large.
186. *stemed*, shone; *of a leed*, under a cauldron.
188. *for-pyned goost*, emaciated ghost.   192. *y-go*, gone.
194. *nas nat*, ne was not, was not.
196. *overest courtepy*, outer short coat.   197. *benefyce*, a church living.
198. *offyce*, secular employment.

Than robes riche, or fithele, or gay sautrye.
But al be that he was a philosophre,
Yet hadde he but litel gold in cofre;
But al that he mighte of his freendes hente,
On bokes and on lerninge he it spente,
And bisily gan for the soules preye
Of hem that yaf him wher-with to scoleye.
Of studie took he most cure and most hede.
Noght o word spak he more than was nede,   210
And that was seyd in forme and reverence,
And short and quik, and ful of hy sentence.
Souninge in moral vertu was his speche,
And gladly wolde he lerne, and gladly teche.

A good WYF was ther of bisyde BATHE,
But she was som-del deef, and that was scathe.
Of clooth-making she hadde swiche an haunt,
She passed hem of Ypres and of Gaunt.
In all the parisshe wyf ne was ther noon
That to th'offring bifore hir sholde goon;   220
And if ther dide, certeyn, so wrooth was she,
That she was out of alle charitee.
Hir coverchiefs ful fyne were of ground;
I dorste swere they weyeden ten pound
That on a Sonday were upon hir heed.
Hir hosen weren of fyn scarlet reed,
Ful streite y-teyd, and shoos ful moiste and newe.
Bold was hir face, and fair, and reed of hewe.
She was a worthy womman al hir lyve,
Housbondes at chirche-dore she hadde fyve,   230

202. *fithele*, fiddle; *sautrye*, psaltery, a stringed musical instrument.
205. *hente*, seize.   208. *scoleye*, go to school.   209. *cure*, care.
211. *in forme and reverence*, in proper form and with respect.
213. *Souninge*, sounding.   216. *scathe*, unfortunate.   217. *haunt*, skill.
218. *Ypres . . . Gaunt*, cities of Flanders which had a reputation for cloth-making.
223. *coverchiefs*, covering for the head; *ground*, texture.
230. *at chirche-dore*, weddings took place by the church door until the sixteenth century. After the wedding proper, the couple would go to the front of the church for the celebration of the Mass.

Withouten other companye in youthe;
But therof nedeth nat to speke as nouthe.
And thryes hadde she been at Jerusalem;
She hadde passed many a straunge streem;
At Rome she hadde been, and at Boloigne,
In Galice at seint Jame, and at Coloigne.
She coude muche of wandring by the weye:
Gat-tothed was she, soothly for to seye.
Up-on an amblere esily she sat,
Y-wimpled wel, and on hir heed an hat   240
As brood as is a bokeler or a targe;
A foot-mantel aboute hir hipes large,
And on hir feet a paire of spores sharpe.
In felawschip wel coude she laughe and carpe.
Of remedyes of love she knew per-chaunce,
For she coude of that art the olde daunce.
About 1387

The Nonne Preestes Tale

A povre widwe, somdel stape in age,
Was whylom dwelling in a narwe cotage,
Bisyde a grove, stonding in a dale.
This widwe, of which I telle yow my tale,
Sin thilke day that she was last a wyf,
In pacience ladde a ful simple lyf,
For litel was hir catel and hir rente;
By housbondrye, of such as God hir sente,
She fond hir-self, and eek hir doghtren two.

231. *Withouten other companye in youthe,* not to mention other love affairs in youth.
232. *as nouthe,* for the present.
236. *In Galice,* the shrine of St. James at Compostella, Spain.
238. *Gat-tothed,* widespaced between the teeth, a sign of a lascivious nature.
239. *amblere,* a horse with an ambling gait.   241. *targe,* shield.
242. *foot-mantel,* outer skirt.   243. *spores,* spurs.   244. *carpe,* prate.
246. *the olde daunce,* the old game.
1. *stape,* advanced.   2. *whylom,* once upon a time.
7. *catel,* property; *rente,* income.

Three large sowes hadde she, and namo,   10
Three kyn, and eek a sheep that highte Malle.
Ful sooty was hir bour, and eek hir halle,
In which she eet ful many a sclendre meel.
Of poynaunt sauce hir neded never a deel.
No deyntee morsel passed thurgh hir throte;
Hir dyete was accordant to hir cote.
Repleccioun ne made hir never syk;
Attempree dyete was al hir phisyk,
And exercyse, and hertes suffisaunce.
The goute lette hir no-thing for to daunce,   20
N'apoplexye shente nat hir heed;
No wyn ne drank she, neither whyt ne reed;
Hir bord was served most with whyt and blak,
Milk and broun breed, in which she fond no lak,
Seynd bacoun, and somtyme an ey or tweye,
For she was as it were a maner deye.
   A yerd she hadde, enclosed al aboute
With stikkes, and a drye dich with-oute,
In which she hadde a cok, hight Chauntecleer,
In al the land of crowing nas his peer.   30
His vois was merier than the mery orgon
On messe-dayes that in the chirche gon;
Wel sikerer was his crowing in his logge,
Than is a clokke, or an abbey orlogge.
By nature knew he ech ascencioun
Of equinoxial in thilke toun;
For whan degrees fiftene were ascended,
Thanne crew he, that it mighte nat been amended.
His comb was redder than the fyn coral,
And batailed, as it were a castel-wal.   40

11. *highte*, named.   12. *bour*, inner room.
13. *sclendre meel*, slender meal.   14. *deel*, bit.   16. *cote*, cottage.
19. *suffisaunce*, satisfaction.   20. *lette*, hindered.   21. *shente*, injured.
25. *Seynd*, singed; *ey*, egg.   26. *a maner deye*, a sort of dairy woman.
30. *nas*, was not.   32. *messe-dayes*, mass-days.
33. *sikerer*, surer; *logge*, lodging place.   34. *orlogge*, clock.
35–38. Chanticleer crowed regularly every hour, that is, every fifteen degrees of the sun's progress.
40. *batailed*, serrated like a castle wall.

His bile was blak, and as the jeet it shoon;
Lyk asur were his legges, and his toon;
His nayles whytter than the lilie flour,
And lyk the burned gold was his colour.
This gentil cok hadde in his governaunce
Sevene hennes, for to doon al his plesaunce,
Whiche were his sustres and his paramours,
And wonder lyk to him, as of colours.
Of whiche the faireste hewed on hir throte
Was cleped faire damoysele Pertelote.   50
Curteys she was, discreet, and debonaire,
And compaignable, and bar hir-self so faire,
Sin thilke day that she was seven night old,
That trewely she hath the herte in hold
Of Chauntecleer loken in every lith;
He loved hir so, that wel was him therwith.
But such a joye was it to here hem singe,
Whan that the brighte sonne gan to springe,
In swete accord, "my lief is faren in londe."
For thilke tyme, as I have understonde,   60
Bestes and briddes coude speke and singe.
    And so bifel, that in a daweninge,
As Chauntecleer among his wyves alle
Sat on his perche, that was in the halle,
And next him sat this faire Pertelote,
This Chauntecleer gan gronen in his throte,
As man that in his dreem is drecched sore.
And whan that Pertelote thus herde him rore,
She was agast, and seyde, "O herte dere,
What eyleth yow, to grone in this manere?   70
Ye been a verray sleper, fy for shame!"
And he answerde and seyde thus, "madame,
I pray yow, that ye take it nat a-grief:
By god, me mette I was in swich meschief

41. *bile*, bill; *jeet*, jet.   42. *toon*, toes.   50. *cleped*, named.
51. *debonaire*, gracious.   52. *compaignable*, companionable.
54. *in hold*, in possession.   55. *loken in every lith*, locked in every limb.
59. *lief*, beloved. The quotation is from a contemporary song.
67. *drecched*, troubled.   70. *eyleth*, ails.   74. *me mette*, I dreamed.

Right now, that yet myn herte is sore afright.
Now god," quod he, "my swevene recche aright,
And keep my body out of foul prisoun!
Me mette, how that I romed up and doun
Withinne our yerde, wher-as I saugh a beste,
Was lyk an hound, and wolde han maad areste   80
Upon my body, and wolde han had me deed.
His colour was bitwixe yelwe and reed;
And tipped was his tail, and bothe his eres,
With blak, unlyk the remenant of his heres;
His snowte smal, with glowinge eyen tweye.
Yet of his look for fere almost I deye;
This caused me my groning, doutelees."
     "Avoy!" quod she, "fy on yow, hertelees!
Allas!" quod she, "for, by that god above,
Now han ye lost myn herte and al my love;   90
I can nat love a coward, by my feith.
For certes, what so any womman seith,
We alle desyren, if it mighte be,
To han housbondes hardy, wyse, and free,
And secree, and no nigard, ne no fool,
Ne him that is agast of every tool,
Ne noon avauntour, by that god above!
How dorste ye seyn for shame unto your love,
That any thing mighte make yow aferd?
Have ye no mannes herte, and han a berd?   100
Allas! and conne ye been agast of swevenis?
No-thing, god wot, but vanitee, in sweven is.
Swevenes engendren of replecciouns,
And ofte of fume, and of complecciouns,
Whan humours been to habundant in a wight.
Certes this dreem, which ye han met to-night,
Cometh of the grete superfluitee

76. *swevene*, dream; *recche*, interpret.   79. *saugh*, saw.   80. *han*, have.
85. *tweye*, two.   88. *Avoy*, fie; *hertelees*, coward.   94. *free*, generous.
95. *secree*, secret.   97. *tool*, weapon.   98. *avaunter*, boaster.
103. *replecciouns*, gluttony.
104. *fume*, vapor from indigestion; *complecciouns*, temperament caused by
the mingling of the four humors of the body—blood, phlegm, bile, and black
bile.

Of youre rede *colera*, pardee,
Which causeth folk to dreden in here dremes
Of arwes, and of fyr with rede lemes,   110
Of grete bestes, that they wol hem byte,
Of contek, and of whelpes grete and lyte;
Right as the humour of malencolye
Causeth ful many a man, in sleep, to crye,
For fere of blake beres, or boles blake,
Or elles, blake develes wole hem take.
Of othere humours coude I telle also,
That werken many a man in sleep ful wo;
But I wol passe as lightly as I can.
    Lo Catoun, which that was so wys a man,   120
Seyde he nat thus, ne do no fors of dremes?
Now, sire," quod she, "whan we flee fro the bemes,
For Goddes love, as tak som laxatyf;
Up peril of my soule, and of my lyf,
I counseille yow the beste, I wol nat lye,
That bothe of colere and of malencolye
Ye purge yow; and for ye shul nat tarie,
Though in this toun is noon apotecarie,
I shal my-self to herbes techen yow,
That shul ben for your hele, and for your prow;   130
And in our yerd tho herbes shal I finde,
The whiche han of hir propretee, by kinde,
To purgen yow binethe, and eek above.
Forget not this, for goddes owene love!
Ye been ful colerik of compleccioun.
Ware the sonne in his ascencioun
Ne fynde yow nat repleet of humours hote;
And if it do, I dar wel leye a grote,
That ye shul have a fevere terciane,

108. *colera*, red bile.   110. *lemes*, flames.   112. *contek*, strife.
113. *malencolye*, black bile.   115. *boles*, bulls.
120. *Catoun*, Dionisius Cato, a medieval writer.
121. *ne do no fors*, pay no attention to.   122. *flee*, fly.
124. *Up*, upon.   130. *hele*, health; *prow*, profit.   131. *tho*, those.
132. *kinde*, nature.   136. *Ware*, beware.   138. *grote*, groat.
139. *fevere terciane*, tertian fever.

Or an agu, that may be youre bane.   140
A day or two ye shul have digestyves
Of wormes, er ye take your laxatyves,
Of lauriol, centaure, and fumetere,
Or elles of ellebor, that groweth there,
Of catapuce, or of gaytres beryis,
Of erbe yve, growing in our yerd, that mery is;
Pekke hem up right as they growe, and ete hem in.
Be mery, housbond, for your fader kin!
Dredeth no dreem; I can say yow namore."
    "Madame," quod he, "*graunt mercy* of your lore. 150
But nathelees, as touching daun Catoun,
That hath of wisdom such a greet renoun,
Though that he bad no dremes for to drede,
By god, men may in olde bokes rede
Of many a man, more of auctoritee
Than ever Catoun was, so mote I thee,
That al the revers seyn of his sentence,
And han wel founden by experience,
That dremes ben significaciouns,
As wel of joye as tribulaciouns   160
That folk enduren in this lyf present.
Ther nedeth make of this noon argument;
The verray preve sheweth it in dede.
    Oon of the gretteste auctours that men rede
Seith, thus, that whylom two felawes wente
On pilgrimage, in a ful good entente;
And happed so, thay come into a toun,
Wher-as ther was swich congregacioun
Of peple, and eek so streit of herbergage,
That they ne founde as muche as o cotage   170
In which they bothe mighte y-logged be.
Wherfor thay mosten, of necessitee,

143–146. *lauriol*, laurel; *centaure*, centaury; *fumetere*, fumitory; *ellebor*,
hellebore; *catapuce*, spurge; *gaytres beryis*, dogwood burries; *yve*, ivy. All
herbs which were used as medicines.
    150. *graunt mercy*, great thanks.   156. *so mote I thee*, as I may thrive.
157. *sentence*, sense.
169. *so streit of herbergage*, so cramped for accommodations.
170. *o*, one.

As for that night, departen compaignye;
And ech of hem goth to his hostelrye,
And took his logging as it wolde falle.
That oon of hem was logged in a stalle,
Fer in a yerd, with oxen of the plough;
That other man was logged wel y-nough,
As was his aventure, or his fortune,
That us governeth alle as in commune.   180
    And so bifel, that, longe er it were day,
This man mette in his bed, ther-as he lay,
How that his felawe gan up-on him calle,
And seyde, 'allas! for in an oxes stalle
This night I shal be mordred ther I lye.
Now help me, dere brother, er I dye;
In alle haste com to me,' he sayde.
This man out of his sleep for fere abrayde;
But whan that he was wakned of his sleep,
He turned him, and took of this no keep;   190
Him thoughte his dreem nas but a vanitee.
Thus twyës in his sleping dremed he.
And atte thridde tyme yet his felawe
Cam, as him thoughte, and seide, 'I am now slawe;
Bihold my blody woundes, depe and wyde!
Arys up erly in the morwe-tyde,
And at the west gate of the toun,' quod he,
'A carte ful of dong ther shaltow see,
In which my body is hid ful prively;
Do thilke carte aresten boldely.   200
My gold caused my mordre, sooth to sayn';
And tolde him every poynt how he was slayn,
With a ful pitous face, pale of hewe.
And truste wel, his dreem he fond ful trewe;
For on the morwe, as sone as it was day,
To his felawes in he took the way;
And whan that he cam to this oxes stalle,
After his felawe he bigan to calle.
    The hostiler answered him anon,

177. *fer*, far.   179. *aventure*, chance.   188. *abrayde*, started up.
190. *took . . . no keep*, paid no attention.   194. *slawe*, slain.

And seyde, 'sire, your felawe is agon,   210
As sone as day he wente out of the toun.'
This man gan fallen in suspecioun,
Remembring on his dremes that he mette,
And forth he goth, no lenger wolde he lette,
Unto the west gate of the toun, and fond
A dong-carte, as it were to donge lond,
That was arrayed in the same wyse
As ye han herd the dede man devyse;
And with an hardy herte he gan to crye
Vengeaunce and justice of this felonye:—   220
'My felawe mordred is this same night,
And in this carte he lyth gapinge upright.
I crye out on the ministres,' quod he,
'That sholden kepe and reulen this citee;
Harrow! allas! her lyth my felawe slayn!'
What sholde I more un-to this tale sayn?
The peple out-sterte, and caste the cart to grounde,
And in the middel of the dong they founde
The dede man, that mordred was al newe.
    O blisful god, that art so just and trewe!   230
Lo, how that thou biwreyest mordre alway!
Mordre wol out, that see we day by day.
Mordre is so wlatsom and abhominable
To God, that is so just and resonable,
That he ne wol nat suffre it heled be;
Though it abyde a yeer, or two, or three,
Mordre wol out, this my conclusioun.
And right anoon, ministres of that toun
Han hent the carter, and so sore him pyned,
And eek the hostiler so sore engyned,   240
That they biknewe hir wikkednesse anoon,
And were an-hanged by the nekke-boon.
    Here may men seen that dremes been to drede,
And certes, in the same book I rede,

214. *lette*, delay.   222. *upright*, flat on his back.
231. *biwreyest*, makest known.   233. *wlatsom*, dreadful.
235. *heled*, concealed.   239. *pyned*, punished.   240. *engyned*, tortured.
241. *biknewe*, confessed.

Right in the nexte chapitre after this
(I gabbe nat, so have I joye or blis),
Two men that wolde han passed over see,
For certeyn cause, in-to a fer contree,
If that the wind ne hadde been contrarie,
That made hem in a citee for to tarie,   250
That stood ful mery upon an haven-syde.
But on a day, agayn the even-tyde,
The wind gan chaunge, and blew right as hem leste.
Jolif and glad they wente un-to hir reste,
And casten hem ful erly for to saille;
But to that oo man fil a greet mervaille.
That oon of hem, in sleping as he lay,
Him mette a wonder dreem, agayn the day;
Him thoughte a man stood by his beddes syde,
And him comaunded, that he sholde abyde,   260
And seyde him thus, 'if thou to-morwe wende,
Thou shalt be dreynt; my tale is at an ende.'
He wook, and tolde his felawe what he mette,
And preyde him his viage for to lette;
As for that day, he preyde him to abyde.
His felawe, that lay by his beddes syde,
Gan for to laughe, and scorned him ful faste.
'No dreem,' quod he, 'may so myn herte agaste,
That I wol lette for to do my thinges.
I sette not a straw by thy dreminges,   270
For swevenes been but vanitees and japes.
Men dreme al-day of owles or of apes,
And eke of many a mase therwithal;
Men dreme of thing that never was ne shal.
But sith I see that thou wolt heer abyde,
And thus for-sleuthen wilfully thy tyde,
God wot it reweth me; and have good day.'
And thus he took his leve, and wente his way.

246. *gabbe*, lie.   252. *agayn*, toward.   253. *as hem leste*, as they desired.
254. *Jolif*, cheerful; *hir*, their.   256. *oo*, one.   262. *dreynt*, drowned.
271. *japes*, deceptions.   273. *mase*, maze.   275. *sith*, since.
276. *for-sleuthen*, lose through sloth; *tyde*, time.
277. *it reweth me*, it causes me sorrow.

But er that he hadde halfe his cours y-seyled,
Noot I nat why, ne what mischaunce it eyled,   280
But casuelly the shippes botme rente,
And ship and man under the water wente
In sighte of othere shippes it byside,
That with hem seyled at the same tyde.
And therfor, faire Pertelote so dere,
By swiche ensamples olde maistow lere,
That no man sholde been to recchelees
Of dremes, for I sey thee, doutelees,
That many a dreem ful sore is for to drede.
    Lo, in the lyf of seint Kenelm, I rede,   290
That was Kenulphus sone, the noble king
Of Mercenrike, how Kenelm mette a thing;
A lyte er he was mordred, on a day,
His mordre in his avisioun he say.
His norice him expouned every del
His sweven, and bad him for to kepe him wel
For traisoun; but he nas but seven yeer old,
And therfore litel tale hath he told
Of any dreem, so holy was his herte.
By god, I hadde lever than my sherte   300
That ye had rad his legende, as have I.
Dame Pertelote, I sey yow trewely,
Macrobeus, that writ th'avisioun
In Affrike of the worthy Cipioun,
Affermeth dremes, and seith that they been
Warning of thinges that men after seen.
    And forther-more, I pray yow loketh wel
In th'olde testament, of Daniel,
If he held dremes any vanitee.

281. *casuelly,* accidentally.   286. *maistow lere,* mayest thou learn.
287. *recchelees,* reckless.
  290. *seint Kenelm,* became king of Mercia in 821, later was murdered by order of his aunt, and afterwards was canonized.
  292. *Mercenrike,* Mercia.   293. *A lyte er,* a short time before.
  294. *avisioun,* vision; *say,* saw.   295. *norice,* nurse; *del,* bit.
  300. *lever,* rather.
  303. *Macrobeus,* wrote a commentary on the *Dream of Scipio,* by Cicero.
  304. *Cipioun,* Scipio Africanus.   308. *Daniel,* See the Book of Daniel 7.

Reed eek of Joseph, and ther shul ye see 310
Wher dremes ben somtyme (I sey nat alle)
Warning of thinges that shul after falle.
Loke of Egipt the king, daun Pharao,
His bakere and his boteler also,
Wher they ne felte noon effect in dremes.
Who-so wol seken actes of sondry remes,
May rede of dremes many a wonder thing.
    Lo Cresus, which that was of Lyde king,
Mette he nat that he sat upon a tree,
Which signified he sholde anhanged be? 320
Lo heer Andromacha, Ectores wyf,
That day that Ector sholde lese his lyf,
She dremed on the same night biforn,
How that the lyf of Ector sholde be lorn,
If thilke day he wente in-to bataille;
She warned him, but it mighte nat availle;
He wente for to fighte nathelees,
But he was slayn anoon of Achilles.
But thilke tale is al to long to telle,
And eek it is ny day, I may nat dwelle. 330
Shortly I seye, as for conclusioun,
That I shal han of this avisioun
Adversitee; and I seye forther-more,
That I ne telle of laxatyves no store,
For they ben venimous, I woot it wel;
I hem defye, I love hem never a del.
    Now let us speke of mirthe, and stinte al this;
Madame Pertelote, so have I blis,
Of o thing god hath sent me large grace;
For whan I see the beautee of your face, 340
Ye ben so scarlet-reed about your yën,
It maketh al my drede for to dyen;

310. *Joseph*, See Genesis 39–41.   316. *actes*, history; *remes*, realms.
318. *Cresus*, the fabulously wealthy king Croesus.
    321. *Andromacha*, the wife of Hector. The story of her dream is not told
by Homer but by Dares Phrygius.
324. *lorn*, lost.   327. *nathelees*, nevertheless.   330. *ny*, nigh.
334. *I ne telle of laxatyves no store*, I put no faith in laxatives.
335. *woot*, know.

For, also siker as *In principio,*
Mulier est hominis confusio;
Madame, the sentence of this Latin is—
Womman is mannes joye and al his blis.
For whan I fele a-night your softe syde,
Al-be-it that I may nat on you ryde,
For that our perche is maad so narwe, alas!
I am so ful of joye and of solas   350
That I defye bothe sweven and dreem."
And with that word he fley doun fro the beem,
For it was day, and eek his hennes alle;
And with a chuk he gan hem for to calle,
For he had founde a corn, lay in the yerd.
Royal he was, he was namore aferd;
He fethered Pertelote twenty tyme,
And trad as ofte, er that it was pryme.
He loketh as it were a grim leoun;
And on his toos he rometh up and doun,   360
Him deyned not to sette his foot to grounde.
He chukketh, whan he hath a corn y-founde,
And to him rennen thanne his wyves alle.
Thus royal, as a prince is in his halle,
Leve I this Chauntecleer in his pasture;
And after wol I telle his aventure.

    Whan that the month in which the world bigan,
That highte March, whan god first maked man,
Was complet, and [y]-passed were also,
Sin March bigan, thritty dayes and two,   370
Bifel that Chauntecleer, in all his pryde,
His seven wyves walking by his syde,
Caste up his eyen to the brighte sonne,
That in the signe of Taurus hadde y-ronne
Twenty degrees and oon, and somwhat more;

343–344. "In the beginning, woman is the confusion of man."
345. *sentence,* meaning.   359. *leoun,* lion.
367. *month . . . began* The old calendar began with the vernal equinox,
which was supposed to be the time of the year when the world was created.
370. That is, May 3.   374. *Taurus,* the Bull, a sign of the zodiac.

And knew by kynde, and by noon other lore,
That it was pryme, and crew with blisful stevene.
"The sonne," he sayde, "is clomben up on hevene
Fourty degrees and oon, and more, y-wis.
Madame Pertelote, my worldes blis,   380
Herkneth thise blisful briddes how they singe,
And see the fresshe floures how they springe;
Ful is myn herte of revel and solas."
But sodeinly him fil a sorweful cas;
For ever the latter ende of joye is wo.
God woot that worldly joye is sone ago;
And if a rethor coude faire endyte,
He in a cronique saufly mighte it wryte,
As for a sovereyn notabilitee.
Now every wys man, lat him herkne me;   390
This storie is al-so trewe, I undertake,
As is the book of Launcelot de Lake,
That wommen holde in ful gret reverence.
Now wol I torne agayn to my sentence.
    A col-fox, ful of sly iniquitee,
That in the grove hadde woned yeres three,
By heigh imaginacioun forn-cast,
The same night thurgh-out the hegges brast
Into the yerd, ther Chauntecleer the faire
Was wont, and eek his wyves, to repaire;   400
And in a bed of wortes stille he lay,
Til it was passed undern of the day,
Wayting his tyme on Chauntecleer to falle,
As gladly doon thise homicydes alle,
That in awayt liggen to mordre men.

376. *kynde,* nature.   377. *pryme,* nine o'clock; *stevene,* voice.
383. *solas,* mirth.   384. *him fil,* there befell him; *cas,* occurrence.
387. *rethor,* rhetorician; *endyte,* relate.
388. *cronique,* chronicle; *saufly,* safely.
389. *sovereyn notabilitee,* a very notable saying.   391. *undertake,* affirm.
392. *book of Launcelot de Lake,* a famous romance of the Middle Ages.
395. *col-fox,* coal, or black tipped, fox.   396. *woned,* dwelt.
397. *heigh imaginacioun forn-cast,* divine foreknowledge.
398. *hegges,* hedges.   401. *wortes,* herbs.
402. *undern,* the latter forenoon.   405. *liggen,* lie.

O false mordrer, lurking in thy den!
O newe Scariot, newe Genilon!
False dissimilour, O Greek Sinon,
That broghtest Troye al outrely to sorwe!
O Chauntecleer, acursed be that morwe,   410
That thou into that yerd flough fro the bemes!
Thou were ful wel y-warned by thy dremes,
That thilke day was perilous to thee.
But what that god forwoot mot nedes be,
After the opinioun of certeyn clerkis.
Witnesse on him, that any perfit clerk is,
That in scole is gret altercacioun
In this matere, and greet disputisoun,
And hath ben of an hundred thousand men.
But I ne can not bulte it to the bren,   420
As can the holy doctour Augustyn,
Or Boëce, or the bishop Bradwardyn,
Whether that goddes worthy forwiting
Streyneth me nedely for to doon a thing,
(Nedely clepe I simple necessitee);
Or elles, if free choys be graunted me
To do that same thing, or do it noght,
Though god forwoot it, er that it was wroght;
Or if his witing streyneth nevere a del
But by necessitee condicionel.   430
I wol not han to do of swich matere;
My tale is of a cok, as ye may here,
That took his counseil of his wyf, with sorwe,
To walken in the yerd upon that morwe

407. *Scariot,* Judas Iscariot; *Genilon,* Ganelon who betrayed Roland.
408. *dissimilour,* deceiver; *Sinon,* the Greek spy who urged the Trojans to admit the wooden horse into Troy.
411. *flough,* flew.   414. *forwoot,* foreknew.   420. *bolt,* sift; *bren,* bran.
421. *Augustyn,* St. Augustine of Hippo, a famous theologian.
422. *Bradwardyn,* Thomas Bradwardine, an English theologian of the fourteenth century, who wrote on the subject of free will and predestination.
423. *forwiting,* foreknowledge.   424. *Streyneth,* constraineth.
425. *Nedely,* necessarily; *clepe,* call or name.
430. *necessitee condicionel,* mere foreknowledge on the part of God without divine compulsion.

That he had met the dreem, that I yow tolde.
Wommennes counseils been ful ofte colde;
Wommannes counseil broghte us first to wo,
And made Adam fro paradys to go,
Wher-as he was ful mery, and wel at ese.—
But for I noot, to whom it mighte displese,   440
If I counseil of wommen wolde blame,
Passe over, for I seyde it in my game.
Rede auctours, wher they trete of swich matere,
And what thay seyn of wommen ye may here.
Thise been the cokkes wordes, and nat myne;
I can noon harm of no womman divyne.—
     Faire in the sond, to bathe hir merily,
Lyth Pertelote, and alle hir sustres by,
Agayn the sonne; and Chauntecleer so free
Song merier than the mermayde in the see;   450
For Phisiologus seith sikerly,
How that they singen wel and merily.
And so bifel that, as he caste his yë,
Among the wortes, on a boterflye,
He was war of this fox that lay ful lowe.
No-thing ne liste him thanne for to crowe,
But cryde anon, "cok, cok," and up he sterte,
As man that was affrayed in his herte.
For naturelly a beest desyreth flee
Fro his contrarie, if he may it see,   460
Though he never erst had seyn it with his yë.
     This Chauntecleer, whan he gan him espye,
He wolde han fled, but that the fox anon
Seyde, "Gentil sire, allas! wher wol ye gon?
Be ye affrayed of me that am your freend?
Now certes, I were worse than a feend,
If I to yow wolde harm or vileinye.
I am nat come your counseil for t'espye;
But trewely, the cause of my cominge

---

440. *noot*, know not.   447. *sond*, sand.   448. *sustres*, sisters.
     451. *Phisiologus*, a medieval Latin bestiary which gave wonderful accounts
of animals.
     456. "Then nothing made him wish to crow."

Was only for to herkne how that ye singe.   470
For trewely ye have as mery a stevene
As eny aungel hath, that is in hevene;
Therwith ye han in musik more felinge
Than hadde Boëce, or any that can singe.
My lord your fader (god his soule blesse!)
And eek your moder, of hir gentilesse,
Han in myn hous y-been, to my gret ese;
And certes, sire, ful fayn wolde I yow plese.
But for men speke of singing, I wol saye,
So mote I brouke wel myn eyen tweye,   480
Save yow, I herde never man so singe,
As dide your fader in the morweninge;
Certes, it was of herte, al that he song.
And for to make his voys the more strong,
He wolde so peyne him, that with bothe his yën
He moste winke, so loude he wolde cryen,
And stonden on his tiptoon ther-with-al,
And strecche forth his nekke long and smal.
And eek he was of swich discrecioun,
That ther nas no man in no regioun   490
That him in song or wisdom mighte passe.
I have wel rad in daun Burnel the Asse,
Among his vers, how that ther was a cok,
For that a preestes sone yaf him a knok
Upon his leg, whyl he was yong and nyce,
He made him for to lese his benefyce.
But certeyn, ther nis no comparisoun
Bitwix the wisdom and discrecioun
Of youre fader, and of his subtiltee.
Now singeth, sire, for seinte Charitee,   500
Let see, conne ye your fader countrefete?"
This Chauntecleer his winges gan to bete,
As man that coude his tresoun nat espye,

471. *stevene*, voice.   472. *eny*, any.
474. *Boece*, Boethius, a famous medieval philosopher.
480. *brouke*, keep.   485. *peyne*, take pains.   486. *wynke*, shut both eyes.
492. *Brunel the Asse*, a satirical medieval Latin poem.   496. *lese*, lose.
500. *seinte*, holy.   501. *conne*, can.

So was he ravisshed with his flaterye.
    Allas! ye lordes, many a fals flatour
Is in your courtes, and many a losengeour,
That plesen yow wel more, by my feith,
Than he that soothfastnesse unto yow seith.
Redeth Ecclesiaste of flaterye;
Beth war, ye lordes, of hir trecherye.   510
    This Chauntecleer stood hye up-on his toos,
Strecching his nekke, and heeld his eyen cloos,
And gan to crowe loude for the nones;
And daun Russel the fox sterte up at ones,
And by the gargat hente Chauntecleer,
And on his bak toward the wode him beer,
For yet ne was ther no man that him sewed.
O destinee, that mayst nat been eschewed!
Allas, that Chauntecleer fleigh fro the bemes!
Allas, his wyf ne roghte nat of dremes!   520
And on a Friday fil al this meschaunce.
O Venus, that art goddesse of plesaunce,
Sin that thy servant was this Chauntecleer,
And in thy service dide al his poweer,
More for delyt, than world to multiplye,
Why woldestow suffre him on thy day of dye?
O Gaufred, dere mayster soverayn,
That, whan thy worthy king Richard was slayn
With shot, compleynedest his deth so sore,
Why ne hadde I now thy sentence and thy lore,   530
The Friday for to chyde, as diden ye?
(For on a Friday soothly slayn was he.)
Than wolde I shewe yow how that I coude pleyne
For Chauntecleres drede, and for his peyne.
    Certes, swich cry ne lamentacioun
Was never of ladies maad, whan Ilioun

506. *losengeour,* liar.   509. *Ecclesiaste,* Ecclesiasticus.
513. *for the nones,* for the occasion.   515. *gargat,* throat.
518. *eschewed,* avoided.   520. *ne roghte nat of,* believed not in.
522. Friday was the day of Venus and was also an unlucky day; *plesaunce,*
pleasure.
527. *Gaufred,* Geoffrey de Vinsauf, who wrote *Nova Poetica,* which contains an account of the death of Richard I.

Was wonne, and Pirrus with his streite swerd,
Whan he hadde hent king Priam by the berd,
And slayn him (as saith us *Eneydos*),
As maden alle the hennes in the clos,   540
Whan they had seyn of Chauntecleer the sighte.
But sovereynly dame Pertelote shrighte,
Ful louder than dide Hasdrubales wyf,
Whan that hir housbond hadde lost his lyf,
And that the Romayns hadde brend Cartage;
She was so ful of torment and of rage,
That wilfully into the fyr she sterte,
And brende hir-selven with a stedfast herte.
O woful hennes, right so cryden ye,
As, whan that Nero brende the citee   550
Of Rome, cryden senatoures wyves,
For that hir housbondes losten alle hir lyves;
Withouten gilt this Nero hath hem slayn.
Now wol I torne to my tale agayn:—
      This sely widwe, and eek hir doghtres two,
Herden thise hennes crye and maken wo,
And out at dores sterten they anoon,
And syen the fox toward the grove goon,
And bar upon his bak the cok away;
And cryden, "Out! harrow! and weylaway!   560
Ha, ha, the fox!" and after him they ran,
And eek with staves many another man;
Ran Colle our dogge, and Talbot, and Gerland,
And Malkin, with a distaf in hir hand;
Ran cow and calf, and eek the verray hogges
So were they fered for berking of the dogges
And shouting of the men and wimmen eke,
They ronne so, hem thoughte hir herte breke,
They yelleden as feendes doon in helle;
The dokes cryden as men wolde hem quelle;   570
The gees for fere flowen over the trees;

537. *Pirrus*, Pyrrhus; *streite swerd*, drawn sword.
539. *Eneydos*, the *Aeneid* of Virgil.
543. *Hasbrubales*, Hasdrubal was king of Carthage.   547. *sterte*, rushed.
555. *sely*, simple.   570. *quelle*, kill.

Out of the hyve cam the swarm of bees;
So hidous was the noyse, a! *benedicite!*
Certes, he Jakke Straw, and his meynee,
Ne made never shoutes half so shrille,
Whan that they wolden any Fleming kille,
As thilke day was maad upon the fox.
Of bras thay broghten bemes, and of box,
Of horn, of boon, in whiche they blewe and pouped,
And therwithal thay shryked and they houped;   580
It semed as that heven sholde falle.
Now, gode men, I pray yow herkneth alle!
   Lo, how fortune turneth sodeinly
The hope and pryde eek of hir enemy!
This cok, that lay upon the foxes bak,
In al his drede, un-to the fox he spak,
And seyde, "sire, if that I were as ye,
Yet sholde I seyn (as wis god helpe me),
Turneth agayn, ye proude cherles alle!
A verray pestilence up-on yow falle!   590
Now am I come un-to this wodes syde,
Maugree your heed, the cok shal heer abyde
I wol him ete in feith, and that anon."—
The fox answerde, "in feith, it shal be don,"—
And as he spak that word, al sodeinly
This cok brak from his mouth deliverly,
And heighe up-on a tree he fleigh anon.
And whan the fox saugh that he was y-gon,
"Allas!" quod he, "O Chauntecleer, allas!
I have to yow," quod he, "y-doon trespas,   600
In-as-muche as I maked yow aferd,
Whan I yow hente, and broghte out of the yerd;
But, sire, I dide it in no wikke entente;
Com doun, and I shal telle yow what I mente.
I shal seye sooth to yow, god help me so."
"Nay than," quod he, "I shrewe us bothe two,

---

574. *Jakke Straw*, leader of the Peasants' Revolt in 1381; *meynee*, crowd.
576. *any Fleming kille*, English workers were jealous of foreign labor.
578. *bemes*, horns; *box*, boxwood.   579. *pouped*, puffed, blew.
592. *Maugree*, in spite of.   596. *deliverly*, suddenly.   606. *shrewe*, curse.

And first I shrewe my-self, bothe blood and bones,
If thou bigyle me ofter than ones.
Thou shalt na-more, thurgh thy flaterye,
Do me to singe and winke with myn yë.   610
For he that winketh, whan he sholde see,
Al wilfully, god lat him never thee!"
"Nay," quod the fox, "but god yeve him meschaunce,
That is so undiscreet of governaunce,
That jangleth whan he sholde holde his pees."
    Lo, swich it is for to be recchelees,
And necligent, and truste on flaterye.
But ye that holden this tale a folye,
As of a fox, or of a cok and hen,
Taketh the moralitee, good men.   620
For seint Paul seith, that al that writen is,
To our doctryne it is y-write, y-wis.
Taketh the fruyt, and lat the chaf be stille.
    Now, gode god, if that it be thy wille,
As seith my lord, so make us alle good men;
And bringe us to his heighe blisse. Amen.
About 1398

BALLADS

Barbara Allan

It was in and about the Martinmas time,
    When the green leaves were a falling,
That Sir John Graeme, in the West Country,
    Fell in love with Barbara Allan.

He sent his man down through the town,
    To the place where she was dwelling:
"O haste and come to my master dear,
    Gin ye be Barbara Allan."

612. *thee*, thrive.   614. *governaunce*, conduct.   615. *jangleth*, chatters.
616. *recchlees*, reckless.   621. See II Timothy 3.   622. *y-wis*, certainly.
625. *my lord*, the Archbishop of Canterbury, William Courtenay.

O hooly, hooly rose she up,
   To the place where he was lying,   10
And when she drew the curtain by,
   "Young man, I think you're dying."

"O it's I'm sick, and very, very sick,
   And 'tis a' for Barbara Allan;"
"O the better for me ye's never be,
   Tho your heart's blood were a spilling.

"O dinna ye mind, young man," said she,
   "When ye was in the tavern a drinking,
That ye made the healths gae round and round,
   And slighted Barbara Allan?"   20

He turnd his face unto the wall,
   And death was with him dealing:
"Adieu, adieu, my dear friends all,
   And be kind to Barbara Allan."

And slowly, slowly raised she up,
   And slowly, slowly left him,
And sighing said, she could not stay,
   Since death of life had reft him.

She had not gane a mile but twa,
   When she heard the dead-bell ringing,   30
And every jow that the dead-bell geid,
   It cry'd "Woe to Barbara Allan!"

"O mother, mother, make my bed!
   O make it soft and narrow!
My love has died for me today,
   I'll die for him tomorrow."

Thomas Rymer

True Thomas lay oer yond grassy bank,
   And he beheld a ladie gay,
A ladie that was brisk and bold,
   Come riding oer the fernie brae.

9. *hooly*, slowly.   15. *ye's never be*, you had never been.
31. *jow*, stroke; *geid*, gave.   4. *brae*, slope.

Her skirt was of the grass-green silk,
   Her mantel of the velvet fine,
At ilka tett of her horse's mane
   Hung fifty silver bells and nine.

True Thomas he took off his hat,
   And bowed him low down till his knee: 10
"All hail, thou mighty Queen of Heaven!
   For your peer on earth I never did see."

"O no, O no, True Thomas," she says,
   "That name does not belong to me;
I am but the queen of fair Elfland,
   And I'm come here for to visit thee.

"But ye maun go wi me now, Thomas,
   True Thomas, ye maun go wi me,
For ye maun serve me seven years,
   Thro weel or wae as may chance to be."   20

She turned about her milk-white steed,
   And took True Thomas up behind,
And aye wheneer her bridle rang,
   The steed flew swifter than the wind.

For forty days and forty nights
   He wade thro red blude to the knee,
And he saw neither sun nor moon,
   But heard the roaring of the sea.

O they rade on, and further on,
   Until they came to a garden green: 30
"Light down, light down, ye ladie free,
   Some of that fruit let me pull to thee."

"O no, O no, True Thomas," she says,
   "That fruit maun not be touched by thee,
For a' the plagues that are in hell
   Light on the fruit of this countrie.

7. *tett*, lock.

"But I have a loaf here in my lap,
   Likewise a bottle of claret wine,
And now ere we go farther on,
   We'll rest a while, and ye may dine."   40

When he had eaten and drunk his fill,
   "Lay down your head upon my knee,"
The lady sayd, "ere we climb yon hill,
   And I will show you fairlies three.

"O see not ye yon narrow road,
   So thick beset wi thorns and briers?
That is the path of righteousness,
   Tho after it but few enquires.

"And see not ye that braid braid road,
   That lies across yon lillie leven?   50
That is the path of wickedness,
   Tho some call it the road to heaven.

"And see not ye that bonny road,
   Which winds about the fernie brae?
That is the road to fair Elfland,
   Whe[re] you and I this night maun gae.

"But Thomas, ye maun hold your tongue,
   Whatever you may hear or see,
For gin ae word you should chance to speak,
   You will neer get back to your ain countrie."   60

He has gotten a coat of the even cloth,
   And a pair of shoes of velvet green,
And till seven years were past and gone
   True Thomas on earth was never seen.

Robin Hood and Allen-a-Dale

Come listen to me, you gallants so free,
   All you that loves mirth for to hear,
And I will you tell of a bold outlaw,
   That lived in Nottinghamshire.

44. *fairlies*, marvels.   50. *leven*, lawn.

As Robin Hood in the forest stood,
  All under the greenwood tree,
There was he ware of a brave young man
  As fine as fine might be.

The youngster was clothed in scarlet red,
  In scarlet fine and gay,   10
And he did frisk it over the plain,
  And chanted a roundelay.

As Robin Hood next morning stood,
  Amongst the leaves so gay,
There did he espy the same young man
  Come drooping along the way.

The scarlet he wore the day before,
  It was clean cast away;
And every step he fetcht a sigh,
  "Alack and a well a day!"   20

Then stepped forth brave Little John,
  And Nick the miller's son,
Which made the young man bend his bow,
  When as he see them come.

"Stand off, stand off," the young man said,
  "What is your will with me?"
"You must come before our master straight,
  Under yon greenwood tree."

And when he came bold Robin before,
  Robin asked him courteously,   30
"O hast thou any money to spare
  For my merry men and me?"

"I have no money," the young man said,
  "But five shillings and a ring;
And that I have kept this seven long years,
  To have it at my wedding.

"Yesterday I should have married a maid,
   But now she is from me tane,
And chosen to be an old knight's delight,
   Whereby my poor heart is slain."   40

"What is thy name?" then said Robin Hood,
   "Come tell me, without any fail."
"By the faith of my body," then said the young man,
   "My name it is Allen-a-Dale."

"What wilt thou give me," said Robin Hood,
   "In ready gold or fee,
To help thee to thy true-love again,
   And deliver her unto thee?"

"I have no money," then quoth the young man,
   "No ready gold nor fee.   50
But I will swear upon a book
   Thy true servant for to be."

"How many miles is it to thy true-love?
   Come tell me without any guile."
"By the faith of my body," then said the young man,
   "It is but five little mile."

Then Robin he hasted over the plain,
   He did neither stint nor lin,
Until he came unto the church
   Where Allin should keep his wedding.   60

"What dost thou do here?" the bishop he said,
   "I prethee now tell to me."
"I am a bold harper," quoth Robin Hood,
   "And the best in the north countrey."

"O welcome, O welcome," the bishop he said,
   "That music best pleaseth me."
"You shall have no music," quoth Robin Hood,
   "Till the bride and the bridegroom I see."

58. *stint nor lin*, stop nor pause.

With that came in a wealthy knight,
　　Which was both grave and old,   70
And after him a finikin lass,
　　Did shine like glistering gold.

"This is no fit match," quoth bold Robin Hood,
　　"That you do seem to make here;
For since we are come into the church,
　　The bride she shall choose her own dear."

Then Robin Hood put his horn to his mouth,
　　And blew blasts two or three;
When four and twenty bowmen bold
　　Came leaping over the lea.   80

And when they came into the churchyard,
　　Marching all on a row,
The first man was Allin-a-Dale,
　　To give bold Robin his bow.

"This is thy true-love," Robin he said,
　　"Young Allin, as I hear say;
And you shall be married at this same time,
　　Before we depart away."

"That shall not be," the bishop he said,
　　"For thy word shall not stand;   90
They shall be three times askt in the church,
　　As the law is of our land."

Robin Hood pulled off the bishop's coat,
　　And put it upon Little John;
"By the faith of my body," then Robin said,
　　"This cloath doth make thee a man."

When Little John went into the quire,
　　The people began for to laugh;
He askt them seven times in the church,
　　Lest three times should not be enough.   100

71. *finikin*, well-dressed.

"Who gives me this maid?" then said Little John;
   Quoth Robin, "That do I,
And he that doth take her from Allin-a-Dale
   Full dearly he shall her buy."

And thus having ended this merry wedding,
   The bride lookt as fresh as a queen,
And so they returned to the merry greenwood,
   Amongst the leaves so green.

Get Up and Bar the Door

It fell about the Martinmas time,
   And a gay time it was then,
When our goodwife got puddings to make,
   And she's boild them in the pan.

The wind sae cauld blew south and north,
   And blew into the floor;
Quoth our goodman to our goodwife,
   "Gae out and bar the door."

"My hand is in my hussyfskap,
   Goodman, as ye may see;   10
An it should nae be barrd this hundred year,
   It's no be barrd for me."

They made a paction tween them twa,
   They made it firm and sure,
That the first word whaeer shoud speak,
   Shoud rise and bar the door.

Then by there came two gentlemen,
   At twelve o clock at night,
And they could neither see house nor hall,
   Nor coal nor candle-light.   20

"Now whether is this a rich man's house,
   Or whether is it a poor?"
But neer a word wad ane o them speak,
   For barring of the door.

9. *hussyfskap*, household affairs.

And first they ate the white puddings,
    And then they ate the black;
Tho muckle thought the goodwife to hersel,
    Yet neer a word she spake.

Then said the one unto the other,
    "Here, man, tak ye my knife;   30
Do ye tak aff the auld man's beard,
    And I'll kiss the goodwife."

"But there's nae water in the house,
    And what shall we do than?"
"What ails ye at the pudding-broo,
    That boils into the pan?"

O up then started our goodman,
    An angry man was he:
"Will ye kiss my wife before my een,
    And scad me wi pudding-bree?"   40

Then up and started our goodwife,
    Gied three skips on the floor:
"Goodman, you've spoken the foremost word,
    Get up and bar the door."

EDMUND SPENSER

The Faerie Queene

BOOK I, CANTO I

The Patron of true Holinesse,
Foule Errour doth defeate:
Hypocrisie him to entrappe,
Doth to his home entreate.

I

A Gentle Knight was pricking on the plaine,
    Ycladd in mightie armes and siluer shielde,
Wherein old dints of deepe wounds did remaine,
    The cruell markes of many' a bloudy fielde;
    Yet armes till that time did he neuer wield:

1. *pricking,* riding.

His angry steede did chide his foming bitt,
As much disdayning to the curbe to yield:
Full iolly knight he seemd, and faire did sitt,
As one for knightly giusts and fierce encounters fitt.

2

But on his brest a bloudie Crosse he bore,   10
    The deare remembrance of his dying Lord,
    For whose sweete sake that glorious badge he wore,
    And dead as liuing euer him ador'd:
    Vpon his shield the like was also scor'd,
    For soueraine hope, which in his helpe he had:
    Right faithfull true he was in deede and word,
    But of his cheere did seeme too solemne sad;
Yet nothing did he dread, but euer was ydrad.

3

Vpon a great aduenture he was bond,
    That greatest *Gloriana* to him gaue,   20
    That greatest Glorious Queene of *Faerie* lond,
    To winne him worship, and her grace to haue,
    Which of all earthly things he most did craue;
    And euer as he rode, his hart did earne
    To proue his puissance in battell braue
    Vpon his foe, and his new force to learne;
Vpon his foe, a Dragon horrible and stearne.

4

A louely Ladie rode him faire beside,
    Vpon a lowly Asse more white then snow,
    Yet she much whiter, but the same did hide   30
    Vnder a vele, that wimpled was full low,
    And ouer all a blacke stole she did throw,
    As one that inly mournd: so was she sad,
    And heauie sat vpon her palfrey slow:
    Seemed in heart some hidden care she had,
And by her in a line a milke white lambe she lad.

20. *Gloriana*, Queen Elizabeth.   24. *earne*, yearn.
31. *wimpled*, pleated.

5

So pure an innocent, as that same lambe,
  She was in life and euery vertuous lore,
  And by descent from Royall lynage came
  Of ancient Kings and Queenes, that had of yore   40
  Their scepters stretcht from East to Western shore,
  And all the world in their subiection held;
  Till that infernall feend with foule vprore
  Forwasted all their land, and them expeld:
Whom to auenge, she had this Knight from far compeld.

6

Behind her farre away a Dwarfe did lag,
  That lasie seemd in being euer last,
  Or wearied with bearing of her bag
  Of needments at his backe. Thus as they past,
  The day with cloudes was suddeine ouercast,   50
  And angry *Ioue* an hideous storme of raine
  Did poure into his Lemans lap so fast,
  That euery wight to shrowd it did constrain,
And this faire couple eke to shroud themselues were fain.

7

Enforst to seeke some couert nigh at hand,
  A shadie groue not far away they spide,
  That promist ayde the tempest to withstand:
  Whose loftie trees yclad with sommers pride,
  Did spred so broad, that heauens light did hide,
  Not perceable with power of any starre: 60
  And all within were pathes and alleies wide,
  With footing worne, and leading inward farre:
Faire harbour that them seems; so in they entred arre.

8

And foorth they passe, with pleasure forward led,
  Ioying to heare the birdes sweete harmony,
  Which therein shrouded from the tempest dred,

52. *lemans,* sweetheart's.

Seemd in their song to scorne the cruell sky.
Much can they prayse the trees so straight and hy,
The sayling Pine, the Cedar proud and tall,
The vine-prop Elme, the Poplar neuer dry,   70
The builder Oake, sole king of forrests all,
The Aspine good for staues, the Cypresse funerall.

9

The Laurell, meed of mightie Conquerours
And Poets sage, the Firre that weepeth still,
The Willow worne of forlorne Paramours,
The Eugh obedient to the benders will,
The Birch for shaftes, the Sallow for the mill,
The Mirrhe sweete bleeding in the bitter wound,
The warlike Beech, the Ash for nothing ill,
The fruitfull Oliue, and the Platane round,   80
The caruer Holme, the Maple seeldom inward sound.

10

Led with delight, they thus beguile the way,
Vntill the blustring storme is ouerblowne;
When weening to returne, whence they did stray,
They cannot finde that path, which first was showne,
But wander too and fro in wayes vnknowne,
Furthest from end then, when they neerest weene,
That makes them doubt, their wits be not their owne:
So many pathes, so many turnings seene,
That which of them to take, in diuerse doubt they been. 90

11

At last resoluing forward still to fare,
Till that some end they finde or in or out,
That path they take, that beaten seemd most bare,
And like to lead the labyrinth about;
Which when by tract they hunted had throughout,
At length it brought them to a hollow caue,
Amid the thickest woods. The Champion stout
Eftsoones dismounted from his courser braue,
And to the Dwarfe a while his needlesse spere he gaue.

98. *eftsoones*, at once.

12

Be well aware, quoth then that Ladie milde,   100
   Least suddaine mischiefe ye too rash prouoke:
   The danger hid, the place vnknowne and wilde,
   Breedes dreadfull doubts: Oft fire is without smoke,
   And perill, without show: therefore your stroke
   Sir knight with-hold, till further triall made.
   Ah Ladie (said he) shame were to reuoke
   The forward footing for an hidden shade:
Vertue giues her selfe light, through darkenesse for to wade.

13

Yea but (quoth she) the perill of this place
   I better wot then you, though now too-late   110
   To wish you backe returne with foule disgrace,
   Yet wisedome warnes, whilest foot is in the gate,
   To stay the steppe, ere forced to retrate.
   This is the wandring wood, this *Errours den*,
   A monster vile, whom God and man does hate:
   Therefore I read beware. Fly fly (quoth then
The fearefull Dwarfe:) this is no place for liuing men.

14

But full of fire and greedy hardiment,
   The youthful knight could not for ought be staide,
   But forth vnto the darksome hole he went,   120
   And looked in: his glistring armor made
   A litle glooming light, much like a shade,
   By which he saw the vgly monster plaine,
   Halfe like a serpent horribly displaide,
   But th'other halfe did womans shape retaine,
Most lothsom, filthie, foule, and full of vile disdaine.

15

And as she lay vpon the durtie ground,
   Her huge long taile her den all ouerspred,
   Yet was in knots and many boughtes vpwound,

116. *read*, counsel.   129. *boughtes*, coils.

Pointed with mortall sting. Of her there bred   130
  A thousand yong ones, which she dayly fed,
  Sucking vpon her poisonous dugs, each-one
  Of sundry shapes, yet all ill fauored:
  Soone as that vncouth light vpon them shone,
Into her mouth they crept, and suddain all were gone.

16

Their dam vpstart, out of her den effraide,
  And rushed forth, hurling her hideous taile
  About her cursed head, whose folds displaid
  Were stretcht now forth at length without entraile.
  She lookt about, and seeing one in mayle   140
  Armed to point, sought backe to turne againe:
  For light she hated as the deadly bale,
  Ay wont in desert darknesse to remaine,
Where plaine none might her see, nor she see any plaine.

17

Which when the valiant Elfe perceiu'd, he lept
  As Lyon fierce vpon the flying pray,
  And with his trenchand blade her boldly kept
  From turning backe, and forced her to stay:
  Therewith enrag'd she loudly gan to bray,
  And turning fierce, her speckled taile aduaunst,   150
  Threatning her angry sting, him to dismay:
  Who nought aghast, his mightie hand enhaunst:
The stroke down from her head vnto her shoulder glaunst.

18

Much daunted with that dint, her sence was dazd,
  Yet kindling rage, her selfe she gathered round,
  And all attonce her beastly body raizd
  With double forces high aboue the ground:
  Tho wrapping vp her wrethed sterne arownd,
  Lept fierce vpon his shield, and her huge traine
  All suddenly about his body wound,   160
  That hand or foot to stirre he stroue in vaine:
God helpe the man so wrapt in *Errours* endless traine.

139. *without entraile,* uncoiled.

19

His Lady sad to see his sore constraint,
    Cride out, Now now Sir knight, shew what ye bee,
    Add faith vnto your force, and be not faint:
    Strangle her, else she sure will strangle thee.
    That when he heard, in great perplexitie,
    His gall did grate for griefe and high disdaine,
    And knitting all his force got one hand free,
    Wherewith he grypt her gorge with so great paine,   170
That soone to loose her wicked bands did her constraine.

20

Therewith she spewd out of her filthy maw
    A floud of poyson horrible and blacke,
    Full of great lumpes of flesh and gobbets raw,
    Which stunck so vildly, that it forst him slacke
    His grasping hold, and from her turne him backe:
    Her vomit full of bookes and papers was,
    With loathly frogs and toades, which eyes did lacke,
    And creeping sought way in the weedy gras:
Her filthy parbreake all the place defiled has.   180

21

As when old father *Nilus* gins to swell
    With timely pride aboue the *Aegyptian* vale,
    His fattie waues do fertile slime outwell,
    And ouerflow each plaine and lowly dale:
    But when his later spring gins to avale,
    Huge heapes of mudd he leaues, wherein there breed
    Ten thousand kindes of creatures, partly male
    And partly female of his fruitfull seed;
Such vgly monstrous shapes elswhere may no man reed.

22

The same so sore annoyed has the knight,   190
    That welnigh choked with the deadly stinke,
    His forces faile, ne can no longer fight.

189. *reed*, see.

Whose corage when the feend perceiu'd to shrinke,
She poured forth out of her hellish sinke
Her fruitfull cursed spawne of serpents small,
Deformed monsters, fowle, and blacke as inke,
Which swarming all about his legs did crall,
And him encombred sore, but could not hurt at all.

23

As gentle Shepheard in sweete euen-tide,
    When ruddy *Phœbus* gins to welke in west,   200
    High on an hill, his flocke to vewen wide,
    Markes which do byte their hasty supper best;
    A cloud of combrous gnattes do him molest,
    All striuing to infixe their feeble stings,
    That from their noyance he no where can rest,
    But with his clownish hands their tender wings
He brusheth oft, and oft doth mar their murmurings.

24

Thus ill bestedd, and fearefull more of shame,
    Then of the certaine perill he stood in,
    Halfe furious vnto his foe he came,   210
    Resolv'd in minde all suddenly to win,
    Or soone to lose, before he once would lin;
    And strooke at her with more then manly force,
    That from her body full of filthie sin
    He raft her hatefull head without remorse;
A streame of cole black bloud forth gushed from her corse.

25

Her scattred brood, soone as their Parent deare
    They saw so rudely falling to the ground,
    Groning full deadly, all with troublous feare,
    Gathred themselues about her body round,   220
    Weening their wonted entrance to haue found
    At her wide mouth: but being there withstood
    They flocked all about her bleeding wound,

200. *welke*, fade.   212. *lin*, cease.

And sucked vp their dying mothers blood,
Making her death their life, and eke her hurt their good.

26

That detestable sight him much amazde,
   To see th'vnkindly Impes of heauen accurst,
   Deuoure their dam; on whom while so he gazd,
   Hauing all satisfide their bloudy thurst,
   Their bellies swolne he saw with fulnesse burst,   230
   And bowels gushing forth: well worthy end
   Of such as drunke her life, the which them nurst;
   Now needeth him no lenger labour spend,
His foes haue slaine themselues, with whom he should
   contend.

27

His Ladie seeing all, that chaunst, from farre
   Approcht in hast to greet his victorie,
   And said, Faire knight, borne vnder happy starre,
   Who see your vanquisht foes before you lye;
   Well worthy be you of that Armorie,
   Wherein ye haue great glory wonne this day,   240
   And proou'd your strength on a strong enimie,
   Your first aduenture: many such I pray,
And henceforth euer wish, that like succeed it may.

28

Then mounted he vpon his Steed againe,
   And with the Lady backward sought to wend;
   That path he kept, which beaten was most plaine,
   Ne euer would to any by-way bend,
   But still did follow one vnto the end,
   The which at last out of the wood them brought.
   So forward on his way (with God to frend)   250
   He passed forth, and new aduenture sought;
Long way he trauelled, before he heard of ought.

29

At length they chaunst to meet vpon the way
   An aged Sire, in long blacke weedes yclad,

His feete all bare, his beard all hoarie gray,
And by his belt his booke he hanging had;
Sober he seemde, and very sagely sad,
And to the ground his eyes were lowly bent,
Simple in shew, and voyde of malice bad,
And all the way he prayed, as he went,   260
And often knockt his brest, as one that did repent.

30

He faire the knight saluted, louting low,
Who faire him quited, as that courteous was:
And after asked him, if he did know
Of straunge aduentures, which abroad did pas.
Ah my deare Sonne (quoth he) how should, alas,
Silly old man, that liues in hidden cell,
Bidding his beades all day for his trespas,
Tydings of warre and worldly trouble tell?
With holy father sits not with such things to mell.   270

31

But if of daunger which hereby doth dwell,
And homebred euill ye desire to heare,
Of a straunge man I can you tidings tell,
That wasteth all his countrey farre and neare.
Of such (said he) I chiefly do inquere,
And shall you well reward to shew the place,
In which that wicked wight his dayes doth weare:
For to all knighthood it is foule disgrace,
That such a cursed creature liues so long a space.

32

For hence (quoth he) in wastfull wildernesse   280
His dwelling is, by which no liuing wight
May euer passe, but thorough great distresse.
Now (sayd the Lady) draweth toward night,
And well I wote, that of your later fight
Ye all forwearied be: for what so strong,

262. *louting*, bowing.   267. *Silly*, simple.   270. *mell*, meddle.

But wanting rest will also want of might?
The Sunne that measures heauen all day long,
At night doth baite his steedes the *Ocean* waues emong.

33

Then with the Sunne take Sir, your timely rest,
And with new day new worke at once begin: 290
Vntroubled night they say giues counsell best.
Right well Sir knight ye haue aduised bin,
(Quoth then that aged man;) the way to win
Is wisely to aduise: now day is spent;
Therefore with me ye may take vp your In
For this same night. The knight was well content:
So with that godly father to his home they went.

34

A little lowly Hermitage it was,
Downe in a dale, hard by a forests side,
Far from resort of people, that did pas   300
In trauell to and froe: a little wyde
There was an holy Chappell edifyde,
Wherein the Hermite dewly wont to say
His holy things each morne and euentyde:
Thereby a Christall streame did gently play,
Which from a sacred fountaine welled forth alway.

35

Arriued there, the little house they fill,
Ne looke for entertainement, where none was:
Rest is their feast, and all things at their will;
The noblest mind the best contentment has.   310
With faire discourse the euening so they pas:
For that old man of pleasing wordes had store,
And well could file his tongue as smooth as glas;
He told of Saintes and Popes, and euermore
He strowd an *Aue-Mary* after and before.

36

The drouping Night thus creepeth on them fast,
And the sad humour loading their eye liddes,

As messenger of *Morpheus* on them cast
Sweet slombring deaw, the which to sleepe them biddes.
Vnto their lodgings then his guestes he riddes: 320
Where when all drownd in deadly sleepe he findes,
He to his study goes, and there amiddes
His Magick bookes and artes of sundry kindes,
He seekes out mighty charmes, to trouble sleepy mindes.

37

Then choosing out few wordes most horrible,
   (Let none them read) thereof did verses frame,
With which and other spelles like terrible,
He bad awake blacke *Plutoes* griesly Dame,
And cursed heauen, and spake reprochfull shame
Of highest God, the Lord of life and light;   330
A bold bad man, that dar'd to call by name
Great *Gorgon*, Prince of darknesse and dead night,
At which *Cocytus* quakes, and *Styx* is put to flight.

38

And forth he cald out of deepe darknesse dred
   Legions of Sprights, the which like little flyes
Fluttring about his euer damned hed,
A-waite whereto their seruice he applyes,
To aide his friends, or fray his enimies:
Of those he chose out two, the falsest twoo,
And fittest for to forge true-seeming lyes;   340
The one of them he gaue a message too,
The other by him selfe staide other worke to doo.

39

He making speedy way through spersed ayre,
   And through the world of waters wide and deepe,
To *Morpheus* house doth hastily repaire.
Amid the bowels of the earth full steepe,
And low, where dawning day doth neuer peepe,
His dwelling is; there *Tethys* his wet bed
Doth euer wash, and *Cynthia* still doth steepe

328. *Plutoes griesly dame*, Proserpine, the hideous wife of Pluto.

In siluer deaw his euer-drouping hed,   350
Whiles sad Night ouer him her mantle black doth spred.

                    40

Whose double gates he findeth locked fast,
    The one faire fram'd of burnisht Yuory,
    The other all with siluer ouercast;
    And wakefull dogges before them farre do lye,
    Watching to banish Care their enimy,
    Who oft is wont to trouble gentle Sleepe.
    By them the Sprite doth passe in quietly,
    And vnto *Morpheus* comes, whom drowned deepe
In drowsie fit he findes: of nothing he takes keepe.   360

                    41

And more, to lulle him in his slumber soft,
    A trickling streame from high rocke tumbling downe
    And euer-drizling raine vpon the loft,
    Mixt with a murmuring winde, much like the sowne
    Of swarming Bees, did cast him in a swowne:
    No other noyse, nor peoples troublous cryes,
    As still are wont t'annoy the walled towne,
    Might there be heard: but carelesse Quiet lyes,
Wrapt in eternall silence farre from enemyes.

                    42

The messenger approching to him spake,   370
    But his wast wordes returned to him in vaine:
    So sound he slept, that nought mought him awake.
    Then rudely he him thrust, and pusht with paine,
    Whereat he gan to stretch: but he againe
    Shooke him so hard, that forced him to speake.
    As one then in a dreame, whose dryer braine
    Is tost with troubled sights and fancies weake,
He mumbled soft, but would not all his silence breake.

                    43

The Sprite then gan more boldly him to wake,
    And threatned vnto him the dreaded name   380

Of *Hecate:* whereat he gan to quake,
And lifting vp his lumpish head, with blame
Halfe angry asked him, for what he came.
Hither (quoth he) me *Archimago* sent,
He that the stubborne Sprites can wisely tame,
He bids thee to him send for his intent
A fit false dreame, that can delude the sleepers sent.

44

The God obayde, and calling forth straight way
  A diuerse dreame out of his prison darke,
  Deliuered it to him, and downe did lay   390
  His heauie head, deuoide of carefull carke
  Whose sences all were straight benumbd and starke.
  He backe returning by the Yuorie dore,
  Remounted vp as light as chearefull Larke,
  And on his litle winges the dreame he bore
In hast vnto his Lord, where he him left afore.

45

Who all this while with charmes and hidden artes,
  Had made a Lady of that other Spright,
  And fram'd of liquid ayre her tender partes
  So liuely, and so like in all mens sight,   400
  That weaker sence it could haue rauisht quight:
  The maker selfe for all his wondrous witt,
  Was nigh beguiled with so goodly sight:
  Her all in white he clad, and ouer it
Cast a blacke stole, most like to seeme for *Vna* fit.

46

Now when that ydle dreame was to him brought,
  Vnto that Elfin knight he bad him fly,
  Where he slept soundly void of euill thought,
  And with false shewes abuse his fantasy,
  In sort as he him schooled priuily: 410
  And that new creature borne without her dew,
  Full of the makers guile, with vsage sly

387. *sent,* sense.   389. *diverse,* distracting.

He taught to imitate that Lady trew,
Whose semblance she did carrie vnder feigned hew.

47

Thus well instructed, to their worke they hast,
    And comming where the knight in slomber lay,
    The one vpon his hardy head him plast,
    And made him dreame of loues and lustfull play,
    That nigh his manly hart did melt away,
    Bathed in wanton blis and wicked ioy: 420
    Then seemed him his Lady by him lay,
    And to him playnd, how that false winged boy
Her chast hart had subdewd, to learne Dame pleasures toy.

48

And she her selfe of beautie soueraigne Queene,
    Faire *Venus* seemde vnto his bed to bring
    Her, whom he waking euermore did weene
    To be the chastest flowre, that ay did spring
    On earthly braunch, the daughter of a king,
    Now a loose Leman to vile seruice bound:
    And eke the *Graces* seemed all to sing,   430
    Hymen io Hymen, dauncing all around,
Whilst freshest *Flora* her with Yuie girlond crownd.

49

In this great passion of vnwonted lust,
    Or wonted feare of doing ought amis,
    He started vp, as seeming to mistrust
    Some secret ill, or hidden foe of his:
    Lo there before his face his Lady is,
    Vnder blake stole hyding her bayted hooke,
    And as halfe blushing offred him to kis,
    With gentle blandishment and louely looke,   440
Most like that virgin true, which for her knight him took.

50

All cleane dismayd to see so vncouth sight,
    And halfe enraged at her shamelesse guise,

He thought haue slaine her in his fierce despight:
But hasty heat tempring with sufferance wise,
He stayde his hand, and gan himselfe aduise
To proue his sense, and tempt her faigned truth.
Wringing her hands in wemens pitteous wise,
Tho can she weepe, to stirre vp gentle ruth,
Both for her noble bloud, and for her tender youth.   450

51

And said, Ah Sir, my liege Lord and my loue,
Shall I accuse the hidden cruell fate,
And mightie causes wrought in heauen aboue,
Or the blind God, that doth me thus amate,
For hoped loue to winne me certaine hate?
Yet thus perforce he bids me do, or die.
Die is my dew: yet rew my wretched state
You, whom my hard auenging destinie
Hath made iudge of my life or death indifferently.

52

Your owne deare sake forst me at first to leaue   460
My Fathers kingdome, There she stopt with teares;
Her swollen hart her speach seemd to bereaue,
And then againe begun, My weaker yeares
Captiu'd to fortune and frayle worldly feares,
Fly to your faith for succour and sure ayde:
Let me not dye in languor and long teares.
Why Dame (quoth he) what hath ye thus dismayd?
What frayes ye, that were wont to comfort me affrayd?

53

Loue of your selfe, she said, and deare constraint
Lets me not sleepe, but wast the wearie night   470
In secret anguish and vnpittied plaint,
Whiles you in carelesse sleepe are drowned quight.
Her doubtfull words made that redoubted knight
Suspect her truth: yet since no'vntruth he knew,

454. *amate*, dismay.

Her fawning loue with foule disdainefull spight
He would not shend, but said, Deare dame I rew,
That for my sake vnknowne such griefe vnto you grew.

54

Assure your selfe, it fell not all to ground;
   For all so deare as life is to my hart,
   I deeme your loue, and hold me to you bound;   480
   Ne let vaine feares procure your needlesse smart,
   Where cause is none, but to your rest depart.
   Not all content, yet seemd she to appease
   Her mournefull plaintes, beguiled of her art,
   And fed with words, that could not chuse but please,
So slyding softly forth, she turnd as to her case.

55

Long after lay he musing at her mood,
   Much grieu'd to thinke that gentle Dame so light,
   For whose defence he was to shed his blood.
   At last dull wearinesse of former fight   490
   Hauing yrockt a sleepe his irkesome spright,
   That troublous dreame gan freshly tosse his braine,
   With bowres, and beds, and Ladies deare delight:
   But when he saw his labour all was vaine,
With that misformed spright he backe returnd againe.

1590

MICHAEL DRAYTON

To the Cambro-Britons and Their Harp, His Ballad of Agincourt [1]

Fair stood the wind for France,
   When we are sails advance,
   Nor now to prove our chance,
      Longer will tarry;
   But putting to the main

476. *shend*, repel.
[1] In the Battle of Agincourt Henry V of England defeated the French, 1415.

At Caux, the mouth of Seine,
With all his martial train,
Landed King Harry.

And taking many a fort,
Furnished in warlike sort,   10
Marcheth towards Agincourt,
   In happy hour;
Skirmishing day by day
With those that stopped his way,
Where the French gen'ral lay
   With all his power.

Which in his height of pride,
King Henry to deride,
His ransom to provide
   To the King sending;   20
Which he neglects the while
As from a nation vile,
Yet with an angry smile
   Their fall portending.

And turning to his men,
Quoth our brave Henry then:
Though they to one be ten,
   Be not amazéd.
Yet have we well begun,
Battles so bravely won   30
Have ever to the sun
   By fame been raiséd.

And for myself, quoth he,
This my full rest shall be,
England ne'er mourn for me,
   Nor more esteem me;
Victor I will remain,
Or on this earth lie slain,
Never shall she sustain
   Loss to redeem me.   40

Poitiers and Crécy tell,
When most their pride did swell,
Under our swords they fell;
    No less our skill is
Than when our grandsire great,
Claiming the regal seat
By many a warlike feat,
    Lopped the French lilies.

The Duke of York so dread
The eager vaward led;   50
With the main Henry sped
    Amongst his henchmen.
Excester had the rear,
A braver man not there,
O Lord, how hot they were
    On the false Frenchmen!

They now to fight are gone,
Armor on armor shone,
Drum now to drum did groan,
    To hear was wonder,   60
That with the cries they make
The very earth did shake,
Trumpet to trumpet spake,
    Thunder to thunder.

Well it thine age became,
O noble Erpingham,
Which didst the signal aim
    To our hid forces;
When from a meadow by,
Like a storm suddenly,   70
The English archery
    Stuck the French horses.

With Spanish yew so strong,
Arrows a cloth-yard long,
That like to serpents stung,
    Piercing the weather;

45. Edward III, great grandfather of Henry.   50. *vaward*, vanguard.

None from his fellow starts,
But playing manly parts,
And like true English hearts,
    Stuck close together.   80

When down their bows they threw,
And forth their bilboes drew,
And on the French they flew,
    Not one was tardy;
Arms were from shoulders sent,
Scalps to the teeth were rent,
Down the French peasants went;
    Our men were hardy.

This while our noble King,
His broad sword brandishing,   90
Down the French host did ding,
    As to o'erwhelm it;
And many a deep wound lent,
His arms with blood besprent,
And many a cruel dent
    Bruiséd his helmet.

Gloster, that Duke so good,
Next of the royal blood,
For famous England stood
    With his brave brother;   100
Clarence, in steel so bright,
Though but a maiden knight,
Yet in that furious fight,
    Scarce such another.

Warwick in blood did wade,
Oxford the foe invade,
And cruel slaughter made,
    Still as they ran up;
Suffolk his axe did ply,
Beaumont and Willoughby   110
Bare them right doughtily,
    Ferrers and Fanhope.

Upon Saint Crispin's day
Fought was this noble fray,
Which fame did not delay
To England to carry;
Oh, when shall English men
With such acts fill a pen,
Or England breed again
Such a King Harry?   120

1619

JOHN MILTON

Paradise Lost

BOOK I

Of man's first disobedience, and the fruit
Of that forbidden tree whose mortal taste
Brought death into the World, and all our woe,
With loss of Eden, till one greater Man
Restore us, and regain the blissful seat,
Sing, Heavenly Muse, that, on the secret top
Of Oreb, or of Sinai, didst inspire
That shepherd who first taught the chosen seed
In the beginning how the heavens and earth
Rose out of Chaos: or, if Sion hill   10
Delight thee more, and Siloa's brook that flowed
Fast by the oracle of God, I thence
Invoke thy aid to my adventrous song,
That with no middle flight intends to soar
Above the Aonian mount, while it pursues
Things unattempted yet in prose or rime.
And chiefly thou, O Spirit, that does prefer
Before all temples the upright heart and pure,

6. *Heavenly Muse,* Milton does not address the muse of poetry whom Homer and Virgil invoked but the Holy Spirit of the Christian.
7. *Oreb . . . Sinai,* Horeb is a mountain range of which Sinai is one peak.
11. *Siloa's brook,* a pool at the foot of the hill of Sion in Jerusalem on which the Temple stood.
15. *Aonian mount,* Helicon, the home of the muses of ancient Greece.

Instruct me, for thou know'st; thou from the first
Wast present, and, with mighty wings outspread, 20
Dove-like sat'st brooding on the vast Abyss,
And mad'st it pregnant: what in me is dark
Illumine, what is low raise and support;
That, to the highth of this great argument,
I may assert Eternal Providence,
And justify the ways of God to men.
　　Say first—for Heaven hides nothing from thy view,
Nor the deep tract of Hell—say first what cause
Moved our grand Parents, in that happy state,
Favored of Heaven so highly, to fall off 30
From their Creator, and transgress his will
For one restraint, lords of the World besides.
Who first seduced them to that foul revolt?
　　The infernal Serpent; he it was whose guile,
Stirred up with envy and revenge, deceived
The mother of mankind, what time his pride
Had cast him out from Heaven, with all his host
Of rebel Angels, by whose aid, aspiring
To set himself in glory above his peers,
He trusted to have equaled the Most High, 40
If he opposed, and, with ambitious aim
Against the throne and monarchy of God,
Raised impious war in Heaven and battle proud,
With vain attempt. Him the Almighty Power
Hurled headlong flaming from the ethereal sky,
With hideous ruin and combustion, down
To bottomless perdition, there to dwell
In adamantine chains and penal fire,
Who durst defy the Omnipotent to arms.
　　Nine times the space that measure day and night 50
To mortal men, he, with his horrid crew,
Lay vanquished, rolling in the fiery gulf,
Confounded, though immortal. But his doom
Reserved him to more wrath; for now the thought
Both of lost happiness and lasting pain
Torments him: round he throws his baleful eyes,

25. *assert*, vindicate.

That witnessed huge affliction and dismay,
Mixed with obdurate pride and steadfast hate.
At once, as far as Angels ken, he views
The dismal situation waste and wild.   60
A dungeon horrible, on all sides round,
As one great furnace flamed; yet from those flames
No light; but rather darkness visible
Served only to discover sights of woe,
Regions of sorrow, doleful shades, where peace
And rest can never dwell, hope never comes
That comes to all, but torture without end
Still urges, and a fiery deluge, fed
With ever-burning sulphur unconsumed.
Such place Eternal Justice had prepared   70
For those rebellious; here their prison ordained
In utter darkness, and their portion set,
As far removed from God and light of Heaven
As from the center thrice to the utmost pole.
Oh how unlike the place from whence they fell!
There the companions of his fall, o'erwhelmed
With floods and whirlwinds of tempestuous fire,
He soon discerns; and, weltering by his side,
One next himself in power, and next in crime,
Long after known in Palestine, and named   80
BEËLZEBUB. To whom the Arch-Enemy,
And thence in Heaven called SATAN, with bold words
Breaking the horrid silence, thus began:—
     "If thou beest he—but Oh how fallen! how changed
From him!—who, in the happy realms of light,
Clothed with transcendent brightness, didst outshine
Myriads, though bright—if he whom mutual league,
United thoughts and counsels, equal hope
And hazard in the glorious enterprise,
Joined with me once, now misery hath joined   90
In equal ruin; into what pit thou seest
From what highth fallen: so much the stronger proved
He with his thunder: and till then who knew
The force of those dire arms? Yet not for those,

72. *utter,* outer.

Nor what the potent Victor in his rage
Can else inflict, do I repent, or change,
Though changed in outward luster, that fixed mind,
And high disdain from sense of injured merit,
That with the Mightiest raised me to contend,
And to the fierce contention brought along   100
Innumerable force of Spirits armed,
That durst dislike his reign, and, me preferring,
His utmost power with adverse power opposed
In dubious battle on the plains of Heaven,
And shook his throne. What though the field be lost?
All is not lost—the unconquerable will,
And study of revenge, immortal hate,
And courage never to submit or yield;
And what is else not to be overcome?
That glory never shall his wrath or might   110
Extort from me. To bow and sue for grace.
With suppliant knee, and deify his power
Who, from the terror of this arm, so late
Doubted his empire—that were low indeed;
That were an ignominy and shame beneath
This downfall; since, by fate, the strength of Gods,
And this empyreal substance, cannot fail;
Since, through experience of this great event,
In arms not worse, in foresight much advanced,
We may with more successful hope resolve   120
To wage by force or guile eternal war,
Irreconcilable to our grand Foe,
Who now triumphs, and in the excess of joy
Sole reigning holds the tyranny of Heaven."
    So spake the apostate Angel, though in pain,
Vaunting aloud, but racked with deep despair;
And him thus answered soon his bold compeer:—
    "O Prince, O Chief of many thronéd Powers
That led the embattled Seraphim to war
Under thy conduct, and, in dreadful deeds   130
Fearless, endangered Heaven's perpetual King,
And put to proof his high supremacy,
Whether upheld by strength, or chance, or fate,

Too well I see and rue the dire event
That, with sad overthrow and foul defeat,
Hath lost us Heaven, and all this mighty host
In horrible destruction laid thus low,
As far as Gods and Heavenly Essences
Can perish: for the mind and spirit remains
Invincible, and vigor soon returns,   140
Though all our glory extinct, and happy state
Here swallowed up in endless misery.
But what if he our Conqueror (whom I now
Of force believe almighty, since no less
Than such could have o'erpowered such force as ours)
Have left us this our spirit and strength entire,
Strongly to suffer and support our pains,
That we may so suffice his vengeful ire,
Or do him mightier service as his thralls
By right of war, whate'er his busines be,   150
Here in the heart of Hell to work in fire,
Or do his errands in the gloomy Deep?
What can it then avail though yet we feel
Strength undiminished, or eternal being
To undergo eternal punishment?"
    Whereto with speedy words the Arch-Fiend re-
      plied:—
"Fallen Cherub, to be weak is miserable,
Doing or suffering: but of this be sure—
To do ought good never will be our task,
But ever to do ill our sole delight,   160
As being the contrary to his high will
Whom we resist. If then his providence
Out of our evil seek to bring forth good,
Our labor must be to pervert that end,
And out of good still to find means of evil;
Which ofttimes may succeed so as perhaps
Shall grieve him, if I fail not, and disturb
His inmost counsels from their destined aim.
But see! the angry Victor hath recalled
His ministers of vengeance and pursuit   170

167. *fail*, mistake.

Back to the gates of Heaven: the sulphurous hail,
Shot after us in storm, o'erblown hath laid
The fiery surge that from the precipice
Of Heaven received us falling; and the thunder,
Winged with red lightning and impetuous rage,
Perhaps hath spent his shafts, and ceases now
To bellow through the vast and boundless Deep.
Let us not slip the occasion, whether scorn
Or satiate fury yield it from our Foe.
Seest thou yon dreary plain, forlorn and wild,   180
The seat of desolation, void of light,
Save what the glimmering of these livid flames
Casts pale and dreadful? Thither let us tend
From off the tossing of these fiery waves;
There rest, if any rest can harbor there;
And, re-assembling our afflicted powers,
Consult how we may henceforth most offend
Our enemy, our own loss how repair,
How overcome this dire calamity,
What reinforcement we may gain from hope,   190
If not, what resolution from despair."
    Thus Satan, talking to his nearest mate,
With head uplift above the wave, and eyes
That sparkling blazed; his other parts besides
Prone on the flood, extended long and large,
Lay floating many a rood, in bulk as huge
As whom the fables name of monstrous size,
Titanian or Earth-born, that warred on Jove,
Briareos or Typhon, whom the den
By ancient Tarsus held, or that sea-beast   200
Leviathan, which God of all his works
Created hugest that swim the ocean-stream.
Him, haply slumbering on the Norway foam,
The pilot of some small night-foundered skiff,
Deeming some island, oft, as seamen tell,
With fixéd anchor in his scaly rind,
Moors by his side under the lee, while night
Invests the sea, and wishéd morn delays.
So stretched out huge in length the Arch-Fiend lay,

Chained on the burning lake; nor ever thence   210
Had risen, or heaved his head, but that the will
And high permission of all-ruling Heaven
Left him at large to his own dark designs,
That with reiterated crimes he might
Heap on himself damnation, while he sought
Evil to others, and enraged might see
How all his malice served but to bring forth
Infinite goodness, grace, and mercy, shown
On Man by him seduced, but on himself
Treble confusion, wrath, and vengeance poured.   220
   Forthwith upright he rears from off the pool
His mighty stature; on each hand the flames
Driven backward slope their pointing spires, and, rolled
In billows, leave i'the midst a horrid vale.
Then with expanded wings he steers his flight
Aloft, incumbent on the dusky air,
That felt unusual weight; till on dry land
He lights—if it were land that ever burned
With solid, as the lake with liquid fire,
And such appeared in hue as when the force   230
Of subterranean wind transports a hill
Torn from Pelorus, or the shattered side
Of thundering Ætna, whose combustible
And fueled entrails, thence conceiving fire,
Sublimed with mineral fury, aid the winds,
And leave a singéd bottom all involved
With stench and smoke. Such resting found the sole
Of unblest feet. Him followed his next mate;
Both glorying to have scaped the Stygian flood
As gods, and by their own recovered strength,   240
Not by the sufferance of supernal power.
   "Is this the region, this the soil, the clime,"
Said then the lost Archangel, "this the seat
That we must change for Heaven?—this mournful
   gloom
For that celestial light? Be it so, since he
Who now is sovran can dispose and bid
What shall be right: farthest from him is best,

Whom reason hath equaled, force hath made supreme
Above his equals. Farewell, happy fields,
Where joy for ever dwells! Hail, horrors! hail,   250
Infernal World! and thou, profoundest Hell,
Receive thy new possessor—one who brings
A mind not to be changed by place or time.
The mind is its own place, and in itself
Can make a Heaven of Hell, a Hell of Heaven.
What matter where, if I be still the same,
And what I should be, all but less than he
Whom thunder hath made greater? Here at least
We shall be free; the Almighty hath not built
Here for his envy, will not drive us hence: 260
Here we may reign secure; and, in my choice,
To reign is worth ambition, though in Hell:
Better to reign in Hell than serve in Heaven.
But wherefore let we then our faithful friends,
The associates and co-partners of our loss,
Lie thus astonished on the oblivious pool,
And call them not to share with us their part
In this unhappy mansion, or once more
With rallied arms to try what may be yet
Regained in Heaven, or what more lost in Hell?"   270
    So Satan spake; and him Beëlzebub
Thus answered:—"Leader of those armies bright
Which, but the Omnipotent, none could have foiled!
If once they hear that voice, their liveliest pledge
Of hope in fears and dangers—heard so oft
In worst extremes, and on the perilous edge
Of battle, when it raged, in all assaults
Their surest signal—they will soon resume
New courage and revive, though now they lie
Groveling and prostrate on yon lake of fire,   280
As we erewhile, astounded and amazed;
No wonder, fallen such a pernicious highth!"
    He scarce had ceased when the superior Fiend
Was moving toward the shore; his ponderous shield,
Ethereal temper, massy, large, and round,

266. *oblivious pool,* pool of oblivion.

Behind him cast. The broad circumference
Hung on his shoulders like the moon, whose orb
Through optic glass the Tuscan artist views
At evening, from the top of Fesolè,
Or in Valdarno, to descry new lands,   290
Rivers, or mountains, in her spotty globe.
His spear—to equal which the tallest pine
Hewn on Norwegian hills, to be the mast
Of some great Ammiral, were but a wand—
He walked with, to support uneasy steps
Over the burning marl, not like those steps
On Heaven's azure; and the torrid clime
Smote on him sore besides, vaulted with fire.
Nathless he so endured, till on the beach
Of that inflamèd sea he stood, and called   300
His legions—Angel Forms, who lay entranced
Thick as autumnal leaves that strow the brooks
In Vallombrosa, where the Etrurian shades
High over-arched embower; or scattered sedge
Afloat, when with fierce winds Orion armed
Hath vexed the Red-Sea coast, whose waves o'erthrew
Busiris and his Memphian chivalry,
While with perfidious hatred they pursued
The sojourners of Goshen, who beheld
From the safe shore their floating carcases   310
And broken chariot-wheels. So thick bestrown,
Abject and lost, lay these, covering the flood,
Under amazement of their hideous change.
He called so loud that all the hollow deep
Of Hell resounded:—"Princes, Potentates,
Warriors, the Flower of Heaven—once yours; now lost,
If such astonishment as this can seize
Eternal Spirits! Or have ye chosen this place
After the toil of battle to repose
Your wearied virtue, for the ease you find   320

288. *Tuscan artist,* Galileo, inventor of the telescope.
289. *Fesole,* Fiesole, a hill outside of Florence.
290. *Valdarno,* the valley of the Arno on which Florence is situated.
303. *Vallombrosa,* a valley not far from Florence.

To slumber here, as in the vales of Heaven?
Or in this abject posture have ye sworn
To adore the Conqueror, who now beholds
Cherub and Seraph rolling in the flood
With scattered arms and ensigns, till anon
His swift pursuers from Heaven-gates discern
The advantage, and, descending, tread us down
Thus drooping, or with linkéd thunderbolts
Transfix us to the bottom of this gulf?—
Awake, arise, or be for ever fallen!"   330
    They heard, and were abashed, and up they sprung
Upon the wing, as when men wont to watch,
On duty sleeping found by whom they dread,
Rouse and bestir themselves ere well awake.
Nor did they not perceive the evil plight
In which they were, or the fierce pains not feel;
Yet to their General's voice they soon obeyed
Innumerable. As when the potent rod
Of Amram's son, in Egypt's evil day,
Waved round the coast, up-called a pitchy cloud   340
Of locusts, warping on the eastern wind,
That o'er the realm of impious Pharaoh hung
Like Night, and darkened all the land of Nile;
So numberless were those bad Angels seen
Hovering on wing under the cope of Hell,
'Twixt upper, nether, and surrounding fires;
Till, as a signal given, the uplifted spear
Of their great Sultan waving to direct
Their course, in even balance down they light
On the firm brimstone, and fill all the plain: 350
A multitude like which the populous North
Poured never from her frozen loins to pass
Rhene or the Danaw, when her barbarous sons
Came like a deluge on the South, and spread
Beneath Gibraltar to the Libyan sands.
Forthwith, from every squadron and each band,
The heads and leaders thither haste where stood
Their great Commander—godlike Shapes, and Forms

339. *Amram's son*, Moses.   353. *Danaw*, Danube.

Excelling human; princely Dignities;
And Powers that erst in Heaven sat on thrones,   360
Though of their names in Heavenly records now
Be no memorial, blotted out and razed
By their rebellion from the Books of Life.
Nor had they yet among the sons of Eve
Got them new names, till, wandering o'er the earth,
Through God's high sufferance for the trial of man,
By falsities and lies the greatest part
Of mankind they corrupted to forsake
God their Creator, and the invisible
Glory of him that made them, to transform   370
Oft to the image of a brute, adorned
With gay religions full of pomp and gold,
And devils to adore for deities:
Then were they known to men by various names,
And various idols through the Heathen World.
    Say, Muse, their names then known, who first, who
        last,
Roused from the slumber on that fiery couch,
At their great Emperor's call, as next in worth
Came singly where he stood on the bare strand,
While the promiscuous crowd stood yet aloof.   380
    The chief were those who, from the pit of Hell
Roaming to seek their prey on Earth, durst fix
Their seats, long after, next the seat of God,
Their altars by his altar, gods adored
Among the nations round, and durst abide
Jehovah thundering out of Sion, throned
Between the Cherubim; yea, often placed
Within his sanctuary itself their shrines,
Abominations; and with cursèd things
His holy rites and solemn feasts profaned,   390
And with their darkness durst affront his light.
First, *Moloch*, horrid king, besmeared with blood
Of human sacrifice, and parents' tears;
Though, for the noise of drums and timbrels loud,
Their children's cries unheard that passed through fire
To his grim idol. Him the Ammonite

Worshiped in Rabba and her watery plain,
In Argob and in Basan, to the stream
Of utmost Arnon. Nor content with such
Audacious neighborhood, the wisest heart   400
Of Solomon he led by fraud to build
His temple right against the temple of God
On that opprobrious hill, and made his grove
The pleasant valley of Hinnom, Tophet thence
And black Gehenna called, the type of Hell.
Next *Chemos*, the obscene dread of Moab's sons,
From Aroar to Nebo and the wild
Of southmost Abarim; in Hesebon
And Horonaim, Seon's realm, beyond
The flowery dale of Sibma clad with vines,   410
And Elealé to the Asphaltic Pool:
Peor his other name, when he enticed
Israel in Sittim on their march from Nile,
To do him wanton rites, which cost them woe.
Yet thence his lustful orgies he enlarged
Even to that hill of scandal, by the grove
Of Moloch homicide, lust hard by hate,
Till good Josiah drove them thence to Hell.
With these came they who, from the bordering flood
Of old Euphrates to the brook that parts   420
Egypt from Syrian ground, had general names
Of *Baälim* and *Ashtaroth*—those male,
These feminine. For spirits, when they please,
Can either sex assume, or both; so soft
And uncompounded is their essence pure,
Not tied or manacled with joint or limb,
Nor founded on the brittle strength of bones,
Like cumbrous flesh; but, in what shape they choose,
Dilated or condensed, bright or obscure,
Can execute their aery purposes,   430
And works of love or enmity fulfill.
For those the race of Israel oft forsook
Their Living Strength, and unfrequented left

403. *that opprobrious hill*, the Mount of Olives.
411. *Asphaltic Pool*, the Dead Sea.

His righteous altar, bowing lowly down
To bestial gods; for which their heads, as low
Bowed down in battle, sunk before the spear
Of despicable foes. With these in troop
Came *Astoreth*, whom the Phœnicians called
Astarté, queen of heaven, with crescent horns;
To whose bright image nightly by the moon   440
Sidonian virgins paid their vows and songs;
In Sion also not unsung, where stood
Her temple on the offensive mountain, built
By that uxorious king whose heart, though large,
Beguiled by fair idolatresses, fell
To idols foul. *Thammuz* came next behind,
Whose annual wound in Lebanon allured
The Syrian damsels to lament his fate
In amorous ditties all a summer's day,
While smooth Adonis from his native rock   450
Ran purple to the sea, supposed with blood,
Of Thammuz yearly wounded: the love-tale
Infected Sion's daughters with like heat,
Whose wanton passions in the sacred porch
Ezekiel saw, when, by the vision led,
His eyes surveyed the dark idolatries
Of alienated Judah. Next came one
Who mourned in earnest, when the captive ark
Maimed his brute image, head and hands lopped off,
In his own temple, on the grunsel edge,   460
Where he fell flat and shamed his worshipers:
Dagon his name, sea-monster, upward man
And downward fish; yet had his temple high
Reared in Azotus, dreaded through the coast
Of Palestine, in Gath and Ascalon,
And Accaron and Gaza's frontier bounds.
Him followed *Rimmon*, whose delightful seat
Was fair Damascus, on the fertile banks
Of Abbana and Pharphar, lucid streams.
He also against the house of God was bold: 470
A leper once he lost, and gained a king—

444. *that uxorious king,* Solomon.

Ahaz, his sottish conqueror, whom he drew
God's altar to disparage and displace
For one of Syrian mode, whereon to burn
His odious offerings, and adore the gods
Whom he had vanquished. After these appeared
A crew who, under names of old renown—
Osiris, Isis, Orus, and their train—
With monstrous shapes and sorceries abused
Fanatic Egypt and her priests to seek   480
Their wandering gods disguised in brutish forms
Rather than human. Nor did Israel scape
The infection, when their borrowed gold composed
The calf in Oreb; and the rebel king
Doubled that sin in Bethel and in Dan,
Likening his Maker to the grazéd ox—
Jehovah, who, in one night, when he passed
From Egypt marching, equaled with one stroke
Both her first-born and all her bleating gods.
Belial came last; than whom a Spirit more lewd   490
Fell not from Heaven, or more gross to love
Vice for itself. To him no temple stood
Or altar smoked; yet who more oft than he
In temples and at altars, when the priest
Turns atheist, as did Eli's sons, who filled
With lust and violence the house of God?
In courts and palaces he also reigns,
And in luxurious cities, where the noise
Of riot ascends above their loftiest towers,
And injury and outrage; and, when night   500
Darkens the streets, then wander forth the sons
Of Belial, flown with insolence and wine.
Witness the streets of Sodom, and that night
In Gibeah, when the hospitable door
Exposed a matron, to avoid worse rape.
    These were the prime in order and in might:
The rest were long to tell; though far renowned
The Ionian gods—of Javan's issue held
Gods, yet confessed later than Heaven and Earth,

508. *Ionian gods,* Greek gods.

Their boasted parents;—*Titan*, Heaven's first-born,   510
With his enormous brood, and birthright seized
By younger *Saturn:* he from mightier Jove,
His own and Rhea's son, like measure found;
So *Jove* usurping reigned. These, first in Crete
And Ida known, thence on the snowy top
Of cold Olympus ruled the middle air,
Their highest heaven; or on the Delphian cliff,
Or in Dodona, and through all the bounds
Of Doric land; or who with Saturn old
Fled over Adria to the Hesperian fields,   520
And o'er the Celtic roamed the utmost Isles.
    All these and more came flocking; but with looks
Downcast and damp; yet such wherein appeared
Obscure some glimpse of joy to have found their Chief
Not in despair, to have found themselves not lost
In loss itself; which on his countenance cast
Like doubtful hue. But he, his wonted pride
Soon recollecting, with high words, that bore
Semblance of worth, not substance, gently raised
Their fainting courage, and dispelled their fears: 530
Then straight commands that, at the warlike sound
Of trumpets loud and clarions, be upreared
His mighty standard. That proud honor claimed
Azazel as his right, a Cherub tall:
Who forthwith from the glittering staff unfurled
The imperial ensign; which, full high advanced,
Shone like a meteor streaming to the wind,
With gems and golden luster rich emblazed;
Seraphic arms and trophies; all the while
Sonorous metal blowing martial sounds: 540
At which the universal host up-sent
A shout that tore Hell's concave, and beyond
Frighted the reign of Chaos and old Night.
All in a moment through the gloom were seen
Ten thousand banners rise into the air,
With orient colors waving: with them rose
A forest huge of spears; and thronging helms
Appeared, and serried shields in thick array

Of depth immeasurable. Anon they move
In perfect phalanx to the Dorian mood   550
Of flutes and soft recorders—such as raised
To highth of noblest temper heroes old
Arming to battle, and instead of rage
Deliberate valor breathed, firm, and unmoved
With dread of death to flight or foul retreat;
Nor wanting power to mitigate and swage
With solemn touches troubled thoughts, and chase
Anguish and doubt and fear and sorrow and pain
From mortal or immortal minds. Thus they,
Breathing united force with fixéd thought,   560
Moved on in silence to soft pipes that charmed
Their painful steps o'er the burnt soil. And now
Advanced in view they stand—a horrid front
Of dreadful length and dazzling arms, in guise
Of warriors old, with ordered spear and shield,
Awaiting what command their mighty Chief
Had to impose. He through the arméd files
Darts his experienced eye, and soon traverse
The whole battalion views—their order due,
Their visages and stature as of gods;   570
Their number last he sums. And now his heart
Distends with pride, and, hardening in his strength,
Glories: for never, since created Man,
Met such embodied force as, named with these,
Could merit more than that small infantry
Warred on by cranes—though all the giant brood
Of Phlegra with the heroic race were joined
That fought at Thebes and Ilium, on each side
Mixed with auxiliar gods; and what resounds
In fable or romance of Uther's son   580
Begirt with British and Armoric knights;
And all who since, baptized or infidel,
Jousted in Aspramont, or Montalban,

550. *Dorian mood*, the musical scale in which martial tunes were composed.
551. *recorders*, musical instruments.
580. *Uther's son*, King Arthur.

Damasco, or Marocco, or Trebisond,
Or whom Biserta sent from Afric shore
When Charlemagne with all his peerage fell
By Fontarabbia. Thus far these beyond
Compare of mortal prowess, yet observed
Their dread Commander. He, above the rest
In shape and gesture proudly eminent,   590
Stood like a tower. His form had yet not lost
All her original brightness, nor appeared
Less than Archangel ruined, and the excess
Of glory obscured: as when the sun new-risen
Looks through the horizontal misty air
Shorn of his beams, or from behind the moon,
In dim eclipse, disastrous twilight sheds
On half the nations, and with fear of change
Perplexes monarchs. Darkened so, yet shone
Above them all the Archangel: but his face   600
Deep scars of thunder had intrenched, and care
Sat on his faded cheek, but under brows
Of dauntless courage, and considerate pride
Waiting revenge. Cruel his eye, but cast
Signs of remorse and passion, to behold
The fellows of his crime, the followers rather
(Far other once beheld in bliss), condemned
For ever now to have their lot in pain—
Millions of Spirits for his fault amerced
Of Heaven, and from eternal splendors flung   610
For his revolt—yet faithful how they stood,
Their glory withered; as, when heaven's fire
Hath scathed the forest oaks or mountain pines,
With singéd top their stately growth, though bare,
Stands on the blasted heath. He now prepared
To speak; whereat their doubled ranks they bend
From wing to wing, and half enclose him round
With all his peers: Attention held them mute.
Thrice he assayed, and thrice, in spite of scorn,
Tears, such as angels weep, burst forth: at last   620
Words interwove with sighs found out their way:—

603. *considerate*, carefully considered.

"O myriads of immortal Spirits! O Powers
Matchless, but with the Almighty!—and that strife
Was not inglorious, though the event was dire,
As this place testifies, and this dire change,
Hateful to utter. But what power of mind,
Foreseeing or presaging, from the depth
Of knowledge past or present, could have feared
How such united force of gods, how such
As stood like these, could ever know repulse?   630
For who can yet believe, though after loss,
That all these puissant legions, whose exile
Hath emptied Heaven, shall fail to re-ascend,
Self-raised, and re-possess their native seat?
For me, be witness all the host of Heaven,
If counsels different, or danger shunned
By me, have lost our hopes. But he who reigns
Monarch in Heaven till then as one secure
Sat on his throne, upheld by old repute,
Consent or custom, and his regal state   640
Put forth at full, but still his strength concealed—
Which tempted our attempt, and wrought our fall.
Henceforth his might we know, and know our own,
So as not either to provoke, or dread
New war provoked: our better part remains
To work in close design, by fraud or guile,
What force effected not; that he no less
At length from us may find, who overcomes
By force hath overcome but half his foe.
Space may produce new Worlds; whereof so rife   650
There went a fame in Heaven that he ere long
Intended to create, and therein plant
A generation whom his choice regard
Should favor equal to the Sons of Heaven.
Thither, if but to pry, shall be perhaps
Our first eruption—thither, or elsewhere;
For this infernal pit shall never hold
Celestial Spirits in bondage, nor the Abyss
Long under darkness cover. But these thoughts
Full counsel must mature. Peace is despaired;   660

For who can think submission? War, then, war
Open or understood, must be resolved."
   He spake; and, to confirm his words, outflew
Millions of flaming swords, drawn from the thighs
Of mighty Cherubim; the sudden blaze
Far round illumined Hell. Highly they raged
Against the Highest, and fierce with graspéd arms
Clashed on their sounding shields the din of war,
Hurling defiance toward the vault of Heaven.
   There stood a hill not far, whose grisly top   670
Belched fire and rolling smoke; the rest entire
Shone with a glossy scurf—undoubted sign
That in his womb was hid metallic ore,
The work of sulphur. Thither, winged with speed,
A numerous brigad hastened: as when bands
Of pioneers, with spade and pickax armed,
Forerun the royal camp, to trench a field,
Or cast a rampart. Mammon led them on—
Mammon, the least erected Spirit that fell
From Heaven; for even in Heaven his looks and
     thoughts   680
Were always downward bent, admiring more
The riches of Heaven's pavement, trodden gold,
Than aught divine or holy else enjoyed
In vision beatific. By him first
Men also, and by his suggestion taught,
Ransacked the center, and with impious hands
Rifled the bowels of their mother earth
For treasures better hid. Soon had his crew
Opened into the hill a spacious wound,
And digged out ribs of gold. Let none admire   690
That riches grow in Hell; that soil may best
Deserve the precious bane. And here let those
Who boast in mortal things, and wondering tell
Of Babel, and the works of Memphian kings,
Learn how their greatest monuments of fame
And strength, and art, are easily outdone

694. *works of Memphian kings*, the Pyramids.

By Spirits reprobate, and in an hour
What in an age they, with incessant toil
And hands innumerable, scarce perform.
Nigh on the plain, in many cells prepared,   700
That underneath had veins of liquid fire
Sluiced from the lake, a second multitude
With wondrous art founded the massy ore,
Severing each kind, and scummed the bullion-dross.
A third as soon had formed within the ground
A various mold, and from the boiling cells
By strange conveyance filled each hollow nook;
As in an organ, from one blast of wind,
To many a row of pipes the sound-board breathes.
Anon out of the earth a fabric huge   710
Rose like an exhalation, with the sound
Of dulcet symphonies and voices sweet—
Built like a temple, where pilasters round
Were set, and Doric pillars overlaid
With golden architrave; nor did there want
Cornice or frieze, with bossy sculptures graven;
The roof was fretted gold. Not Babylon
Nor great Alcairo such magnificence
Equaled in all their glories, to enshrine
Belus or Serapis their gods, or seat   720
Their kings, when Egypt with Assyria strove
In wealth and luxury. The ascending pile
Stood fixed her stately highth; and straight the doors,
Opening their brazen folds, discover, wide
Within, her ample spaces o'er the smooth
And level pavement: from the archéd roof,
Pendent by subtle magic, many a row
Of starry lamps and blazing cressets, fed
With naphtha and asphaltus, yielded light
As from a sky. The hasty multitude   730
Admiring entered; and the work some praise,
And some the architect. His hand was known
In Heaven by many a towered structure high,
Where sceptered Angels held their residence,
And sat as Princes, whom the supreme King

Exalted to such power, and gave to rule,
Each in his hierarchy, the Orders bright.
Nor was his name unheard or unadored
In ancient Greece; and in Ausonian land
Men called him Mulciber; and how he fell   740
From Heaven they fabled, thrown by angry Jove
Sheer o'er the crystal battlements: from morn
To noon he fell, from noon to dewy eve,
A summer's day, and with the setting sun
Dropped from the zenith, like a falling star,
On Lemnos, the Ægæan isle. Thus they relate,
Erring; for he with this rebellious rout
Fell long before; nor aught availed him now
To have built in Heaven high towers; nor did he scape
By all his engines, but was headlong sent,   750
With his industrious crew, to build in Hell.
    Meanwhile the wingéd heralds, by command
Of sovran power, with awful ceremony
And trumpet's sound, throughout the host proclaim
A solemn council forthwith to be held
At Pandemonium, the high capital
Of Satan and his peers. Their summons called
From every band and squaréd regiment
By place or choice the worthiest: they anon
With hundreds and with thousands trooping came   760
Attended. All access was thronged; the gates
And porches wide, but chief the spacious hall
(Though like a covered field, where champions bold
Wont ride in armed, and at the soldan's chair
Defied the best of paynim chivalry
To mortal combat, or career with lance),
Thick swarmed, both on the ground and in the air,
Brushed with the hiss of rustling wings. As bees
In spring-time, when the Sun with Taurus rides,
Pour forth their populous youth about the hive   770

737. Celestial beings were graded into nine orders: Seraphim, Cherubim, Thrones, Virtues, Dominations, Powers, Principalities, Archangels, and Angels.
739. *Ausonian*, Italian.

In clusters; they among fresh dews and flowers
Fly to and fro, or on the smoothéd plank,
The suburb of their straw-built citadel,
New rubbed with balm, expatiate, and confer
Their state-affairs: so thick the aery crowd
Swarmed and were straitened; till, the signal given,
Behold a wonder! They but now who seemed
In bigness to surpass earth's giant sons,
Now less than smallest dwarfs, in narrow room
Throng numberless—like that pygmean race   780
Beyond the Indian mount; or faery elves,
Whose midnight revels, by a forest-side
Or fountain, some belated peasant sees,
Or dreams he sees, while overhead the Moon
Sits arbitress, and nearer to the earth
Wheels her pale course: they, on their mirth and dance
Intent, with jocund music charm his ear;
At once with joy and fear his heart rebounds.
Thus incorporeal Spirits to smallest forms
Reduced their shapes immense, and were at large,   790
Though without number still, amidst the hall
Of that infernal court. But far within,
And in their own dimensions like themselves,
The great Seraphic Lords and Cherubim
In close recess and secret conclave sat,
A thousand demi-gods on golden seats,
Frequent and full. After short silence then,
And summons read, the great consult began.
                                            1667

774. *expatiate*, walk about.

ALEXANDER POPE

The Rape of the Lock

CANTO I

What dire offense from amorous causes springs,
What mighty contests rise from trivial things,
I sing—This verse to Caryl, Muse! is due:
This, even Belinda may vouchsafe to view:
Slight is the subject, but not so the praise,
If she inspire, and he approve my lays.

Say what strange motive, goddess! could compel
A well-bred lord to assault a gentle belle?
Oh, say what stranger cause, yet unexplored,
Could make a gentle belle reject a lord?   10
In tasks so bold, can little men engage,
And in soft bosoms dwells such mighty rage?

Sol through white curtains shot a timorous ray,
And oped those eyes that must eclipse the day;
Now lap-dogs give themselves the rousing shake,
And sleepless lovers, just at twelve, awake;
Thrice rung the bell, the slipper knocked the ground,
And the pressed watch returned a silver sound.
Belinda still her downy pillow pressed,
Her guardian sylph prolonged the balmy rest: 20
'Twas he had summoned to her silent bed
The morning dream that hovered o'er her head;
A youth more glittering than a birth-night beau
(That e'en in slumber caused her cheek to glow)
Seemed to her ear his winning lips to lay,
And thus in whispers said, or seemed to say:
"Fairest of mortals, thou distinguished care
Of thousand bright inhabitants of air!

3. *Caryl*, John Caryll, who suggested to Pope that he write the poem.
4. *Belinda*, Miss Arabella Fermor, a well-known beauty of the period.
8. *well-bred lord*, Lord Petre, who actually cut off Miss Fermor's lock.
   23. *birth-night beau*, one dressed to attend court on the night of the birthday of a member of the royal family.

If e'er one vision touched thy infant thought,
Of all the nurse and all the priest have taught   30
Of airy elves by moonlight shadows seen,
The silver token, and the circled green,
Or virgins visited by angel powers,
With golden crowns and wreaths of heavenly flowers;
Hear and believe! thy own importance know,
Nor bound thy narrow views to things below.
Some secret truths, from learned pride concealed,
To maids alone and children are revealed;
What though no credit doubting wits may give?
The fair and innocent shall still believe.   40
Know, then, unnumbered spirits round thee fly,
The light militia of the lower sky:
These, though unseen, are ever on the wing,
Hang o'er the box, and hover round the Ring,
Think what an equipage thou hast in air,
And view with scorn two pages and a chair.
As now your own, our beings were of old,
And once enclosed in woman's beauteous mold;
Thence, by a soft transition, we repair
From earthly vehicles to these of air.   50
Think not, when woman's transient breath is fled,
That all her vanities at once are dead;
Succeeding vanities she still regards,
And though she plays no more, o'erlooking cards.
Her joy in gilded chariots, when alive,
And love of ombre, after death survive.
For when the fair in all their pride expire,
To their first elements their souls retire:
The sprites of fiery termagants in flame
Mount up, and take a salamander's name.   60
Soft yielding minds to water glide away,
And sip, with nymphs, their elemental tea.
The graver prude sinks downward to a gnome,
In search of mischief still on earth to roam.

44. *box*, a box in the theater; *Ring*, the road in Hyde Park where people
of fashion drove.
56. *ombre*, a game of cards.

The light coquettes in sylphs aloft repair,
And sport and flutter in the fields of air.

"Know further yet; whoever fair and chaste
Rejects mankind, is by some sylph embraced;
For spirits, freed from mortal laws, with ease
Assume what sexes and what shapes they please.   70
What guards the purity of melting maids,
In courtly balls, and midnight masquerades,
Safe from the treacherous friend, the daring spark,
The glance by day, the whisper in the dark,
When kind occasion prompts their warm desires,
When music softens, and when dancing fires?
'Tis but their sylph, the wise celestials know,
Though honor is the word with men below.
Some nymphs there are, too conscious of their face,
For life predestined to the gnomes' embrace.   80
These swell their prospects and exalt their pride,
When offers are disdained, and love denied:
Then gay ideas crowd the vacant brain,
While peers, and dukes, and all their sweeping train,
And garters, stars, and coronets appear,
And in soft sounds 'Your Grace' salutes their ear.
'Tis these that early taint the female soul,
Instruct the eyes of young coquettes to roll,
Teach infant cheeks a bidden blush to know,
And little hearts to flutter at a beau.   90

"Oft, when the world imagine women stray,
The sylphs through mystic mazes guide their way,
Through all the giddy circle they pursue,
And old impertinence expel by new.
What tender maid but must a victim fall
To one man's treat, but for another's ball?
When Florio speaks, what virgin could withstand,
If gentle Damon did not squeeze her hand?
With varying vanities, from every part,
They shift the moving toyshop of their heart;   100
Where wigs with wigs, with sword-knots sword-knots
    strive,

Beaux banish beaux, and coaches coaches drive.
This erring mortals levity may call;
Oh, blind to truth! the sylphs contrive it all.

"Of these am I, who thy protection claim,
A watchful sprite, and Ariel is my name.
Late, as I ranged the crystal wilds of air,
In the clear mirror of thy ruling star
I saw, alas! some dread event impend,
Ere to the main this morning sun descend,   110
But Heaven reveals not what, or how, or where:
Warned by the sylph, O pious maid, beware!
This to disclose is all thy guardian can:
Beware of all, but most beware of man!"

He said; when Shock, who thought she slept too long,
Leaped up, and waked his mistress with his tongue.
'Twas then, Belinda, if report say true,
Thy eyes first opened on a billet-doux;
Wounds, charms, and ardors were no sooner read,
But all the vision vanished from thy head.   120

And now, unveiled, the toilet stands displayed,
Each silver vase in mystic order laid.
First, robed in white, the nymph intent adores,
With head uncovered, the cosmetic powers.
A heavenly image in the glass appears.
To that she bends, to that her eyes she rears;
The inferior priestess, at her altar's side,
Trembling begins the sacred rites of pride.
Unnumbered treasures ope at once, and here
The various offerings of the world appear;   130
From each she nicely culls with curious toil,
And decks the goddess with the glittering spoil.
This casket India's glowing gems unlocks,
And all Arabia breathes from yonder box.
The tortoise here and elephant unite,
Transformed to combs, the speckled, and the white.
Here files of pins extend their shining rows,
Puffs, powders, patches, bibles, billets-doux.

Now awful beauty puts on all its arms;
The fair each moment rises in her charms,   140
Repairs her smiles, awakens every grace,
And calls forth all the wonders of her face;
Sees by degrees a purer blush arise,
And keener lightnings quicken in her eyes.
The busy sylphs surround their darling care,
These set the head, and those divide the hair,
Some fold the sleeve, whilst others plait the gown;
And Betty's praised for labors not her own.

CANTO II

Not with more glories, in the ethereal plain,
The sun first rises o'er the purpled main,
Than, issuing forth, the rival of his beams
Launched on the bosom of the silver Thames.
Fair nymphs, and well-dressed youths around her shone,
But every eye was fixed on her alone.
On her white breast a sparkling cross she wore,
Which Jews might kiss, and infidels adore.
Her lively looks a sprightly mind disclose,
Quick as her eyes, and as unfixed as those;   10
Favors to none, to all she smiles extends;
Oft she rejects, but never once offends.
Bright as the sun, her eyes the gazers strike,
And, like the sun, they shine on all alike.
Yet graceful ease, and sweetness void of pride,
Might hide her faults, if belles had faults to hide;
If to her share some female errors fall,
Look on her face, and you'll forget 'em all.

This nymph, to the destruction of mankind,
Nourished two locks, which graceful hung behind   20
In equal curls, and well conspired to deck
With shining ringlets the smooth ivory neck.
Love in these labyrinths his slaves detains,
And mighty hearts are held in slender chains.
With hairy springes, we the birds betray,

Slight lines of hair surprise the finny prey,
Fair tresses man's imperial race ensnare,
And beauty draws us with a single hair.

The adventurous baron the bright locks admired;
He saw, he wished, and to the prize aspired.   30
Resolved to win, he meditates the way,
By force to ravish, or by fraud betray;
For when success a lover's toil attends,
Few ask, if fraud or force attained his ends.

For this, ere Phoebus rose, he had implored
Propitious Heaven, and every power adored,
But chiefly Love—to Love an altar built,
Of twelve vast French romances, neatly gilt.
There lay three garters, half a pair of gloves;
And all the trophies of his former loves;   40
With tender billets-doux he lights the pyre,
And breathes three amorous sighs to raise the fire.
Then prostrate falls, and begs with ardent eyes
Soon to obtain, and long possess the prize;
The powers gave ear, and granted half his prayer,
The rest, the winds dispersed in empty air.

But now secure the painted vessel glides,
The sunbeams trembling on the floating tides:
While melting music steals upon the sky,
And softened sounds along the waters die;   50
Smooth flow the waves, the zephyrs gently play,
Belinda smiled, and all the world was gay.
All but the sylph—with careful thoughts oppressed,
The impending woe sat heavy on his breast.
He summons straight his denizens of air;
The lucid squadrons round the sails repair:
Soft o'er the shrouds aërial whispers breathe,
That seemed but zephyrs to the train beneath.
Some to the sun their insect wings unfold,
Waft on the breeze, or sink in clouds of gold;   60
Transparent forms, too fine for mortal sight,
Their fluid bodies half dissolved in light.

Loose to the wind their airy garments flew,
Thin glittering textures of the filmy dew,
Dipped in the richest tincture of the skies,
Where light disports in ever-mingling dyes,
While every beam new transient colors flings,
Colors that change whene'er they wave their wings.
Amid the circle, on the gilded mast,
Superior by the head, was Ariel placed;   70
His purple pinions opening to the sun,
He raised his azure wand, and thus begun.

    "Ye sylphs and sylphids, to your chief give ear!
Fays, fairies, genii, elves, and demons, hear!
Ye know the spheres, and various tasks assigned
By laws eternal to the aërial kind.
Some in the fields of purest ether play,
And bask and whiten in the blaze of day.
Some guide the course of wandering orbs on high,
Or roll the planets through the boundless sky.   80
Some less refined, beneath the moon's pale light
Pursue the stars that shoot athwart the night,
Or suck the mists in grosser air below,
Or dip their pinions in the painted bow,
Or brew fierce tempests on the wintry main,
Or o'er the glebe distil the kindly rain.
Others on earth o'er human race preside,
Watch all their ways, and all their actions guide:
Of these the chief, the care of nations own,
And guard with arms divine the British throne.   90

    "Our humbler province is to tend the fair.
Not a less pleasing, though less glorious care;
To save the powder from too rude a gale,
Nor let the imprisoned essences exhale;
To draw fresh colors from the vernal flowers;
To steal from rainbows ere they drop in showers,
A brighter wash; to curl their waving hairs,
Assist their blushes, and inspire their airs;
Nay, oft in dreams, invention we bestow,
To change a flounce, or add a furbelow.   100

"This day, black omens threat the brightest fair
That e'er deserved a watchful spirit's care;
Some dire disaster, or by force, or slight;
But what, or where, the fates have wrapped in night.
Whether the nymph shall break Diana's law,
Or some frail china jar receive a flaw;
Or stain her honor, or her new brocade;
Forget her prayers, or miss a masquerade;
Or lose her heart, or necklace, at a ball;
Or whether Heaven has doomed that Shock must fall. 110
Haste, then, ye spirits! to your charge repair;
The fluttering fan be Zephyretta's care;
The drops to thee, Brillante, we consign;
And, Momentilla, let the watch be thine;
Do thou, Crispissa, tend her favorite lock;
Ariel himself shall be the guard of Shock.

"To fifty chosen sylphs, of special note,
We trust the important charge, the petticoat:
Oft have we known that seven-fold fence to fail,
Though stiff with hoops, and armed with ribs of
        whale;   120
Form a strong line about the silver bound,
And guard the wide circumference around.

"Whatever spirit, careless of his charge,
His post neglects, or leaves the fair at large,
Shall feel sharp vengeance soon o'ertake his sins,
Be stopped in vials, or transfixed with pins;
Or plunged in lakes of bitter washes lie,
Or wedged whole ages in a bodkin's eye:
Gums and pomatums shall his flight restrain,
While clogged he beats his silken wings in vain;   130
Or alum styptics with contracting power
Shrink his thin essence like a rivelled flower:
Or, as Ixion fixed, the wretch shall feel
The giddy motion of the whirling mill,
In fumes of burning chocolate shall glow,
And tremble at the sea that froths below!"

134. *whirling mill,* mill for preparing chocolate.

He spoke; the spirits from the sails descend;
Some, orb in orb, around the nymph extend;
Some thrid the mazy ringlets of her hair;
Some hang upon the pendants of her ear;   140
With beating hearts the dire event they wait,
Anxious, and trembling for the birth of fate.

CANTO III

Close by those meads, forever crowned with flowers,
Where Thames with pride surveys his rising towers,
There stands a structure of majestic frame,
Which from the neighboring Hampton takes its name.
Here Britain's statesmen oft the fall foredoom
Of foreign tyrants and of nymphs at home;
Here thou, great Anna! whom three realms obey,
Dost sometimes counsel take—and sometimes tea.

Hither the heroes and the nymphs resort,
To taste awhile the pleasures of a court;   10
In various talk the instructive hours they passed,
Who gave the ball, or paid the visit last;
One speaks the glory of the British queen,
And one describes a charming Indian screen;
A third interprets motions, looks, and eyes;
At every word a reputation dies.
Snuff, or the fan, supply each pause of chat,
With singing, laughing, ogling, and all that.

Meanwhile, declining from the noon of day,
The sun obliquely shoots his burning ray;   20
The hungry judges soon the sentence sign,
And wretches hang that jurymen may dine;
The merchant from the Exchange returns in peace,
And the long labors of the toilet cease.
Belinda now, whom thirst of fame invites,
Burns to encounter two adventurous knights,

3-4. The royal palace of Hampton Court.
   7. *Anna*, Queen Ann (1702-1714).

At ombre singly to decide their doom;
And swells her breast with conquests yet to come.
Straight the three bands prepare in arms to join,
Each band the number of the sacred nine.   30
Soon as she spreads her hand, the aërial guard
Descend, and sit on each important card:
First, Ariel perched upon a Matadore,
Then each, according to the rank they bore;
For sylphs, yet mindful of their ancient race,
Are, as when women, wondrous fond of place.

Behold, four kings in majesty revered,
With hoary whiskers and a forky beard;
And four fair queens whose hands sustain a flower,
The expressive emblem of their softer power;   40
Four knaves in garbs succinct, a trusty band,
Caps on their heads, and halberts in their hand;
And parti-colored troops, a shining train,
Draw forth to combat on the velvet plain.

The skillful nymph reviews her force with care:
Let spades be trumps! she said, and trumps they were.

Now moved to war her sable Matadores,
In show like leaders of the swarthy Moors.
Spadillio first, unconquerable lord!
Led off two captive trumps, and swept the board.   50
As many more Manillio forced to yield,
And marched a victor from the verdant field.
Him Basto followed, but his fate more hard
Gained but one trump and one plebeian card.
With his broad saber next, a chief in years,
The hoary majesty of spades appears,
Puts forth one manly leg, to sight revealed,
The rest, his many-colored robe concealed.

33. *Matadore*, in the game ombre the three best cards were called matadores.
49. *Spadillio*, the ace of spades.   51. *Manillio*, the two of trumps.
53. *Basto*, the ace of clubs.

The rebel knave, who dares his prince engage,
Proves the just victim of his royal rage.   60
Even mighty Pam, that kings and queens o'erthrew,
And mowed down armies in the fights of Loo,
Sad chance of war! now destitute of aid,
Falls undistinguished by the victor spade!

Thus far both armies to Belinda yield;
Now to the baron fate inclines the field.
His warlike Amazon her host invades,
The imperial consort of the crown of spades,
The club's black tyrant first her victim died,
Spite of his haughty mien, and barbarous pride: 70
What boots the regal circle on his head,
His giant limbs, in state unwieldy spread;
That long behind he trails his pompous robe,
And of all monarchs only grasps the globe?

The baron now his diamonds pours apace;
The embroidered king who shows but half his face,
And his refulgent queen, with powers combined,
Of broken troops an easy conquest find.
Clubs, diamonds, hearts, in wild disorder seen,
With throngs promiscuous strew the level green.   80
Thus when dispersed a routed army runs,
Of Asia's troops, and Afric's sable sons,
With like confusion different nations fly,
Of various habit, and of various dye,
The pierced battalions disunited fall,
In heaps on heaps; one fate o'erwhelms them all.

The knave of diamonds tries his wily arts,
And wins (oh, shameful chance!) the queen of hearts.
At this the blood the virgin's cheek forsook,
A livid paleness spreads o'er all her look;   90
She sees, and trembles at the approaching ill,
Just in the jaws of ruin, and codille.
And now (as oft in some distempered state)

61. *Pam*, the jack of clubs.   62. *Loo*, a game of cards.
92. *codille*, failure to get a majority of tricks.

On one nice trick depends the general fate,
An ace of hearts steps forth; the king unseen
Lurked in her hand, and mourned his captive queen:
He springs to vengeance with an eager pace,
And falls like thunder on the prostrate ace.
The nymph exulting fills with shouts the sky;
The walls, the wood, and long canals reply.   100

Oh, thoughtless mortals! ever blind to fate,
Too soon dejected, and too soon elate.
Sudden, these honors shall be snatched away,
And cursed forever this victorious day.

For lo! the board with cups and spoons is crowned,
The berries crackle, and the mill turns round;
On shining altars of Japan they raise
The silver lamp; the fiery spirits blaze:
From silver spouts the grateful liquors glide,
While China's earth receives the smoking tide: 110
At once they gratify their scent and taste,
And frequent cups prolong the rich repast.
Straight hover round the fair her airy band;
Some, as she sipped, the fuming liquor fanned,
Some o'er her lap their careful plumes displayed,
Trembling, and conscious of the rich brocade.
Coffee (which makes the politician wise,
And see through all things with his half-shut eyes)
Sent up in vapors to the baron's brain
New stratagems the radiant lock to gain.   120
Ah, cease, rash youth! desist ere 'tis too late,
Fear the just gods, and think of Scylla's fate!
Changed to a bird, and sent to flit in air,
She dearly pays for Nisus' injured hair!

But when to mischief mortals bend their will,
How soon they find fit instruments of ill!
Just then Clarissa drew with tempting grace
A two-edged weapon from her shining case;

106. *berries crackle*, coffee berries being prepared for grinding in the *mill*.
107. *altars of Japan*, japanese tables.

So ladies in romance assist their knight,
Present the spear, and arm him for the fight.   130
He takes the gift with reverence, and extends
The little engine on his fingers' ends;
This just behind Belinda's neck he spread,
As o'er the fragrant steams she bends her head.
Swift to the lock a thousand sprites repair,
A thousand wings, by turns, blow back her hair;
And thrice they twitched the diamond in her ear;
Thrice she looked back, and thrice the foe drew near.
Just in that instant, anxious Ariel sought
The close recesses of the virgin's thought;   140
As on the nosegay in her breast reclined,
He watched the ideas rising in her mind,
Sudden he viewed, in spite of all her art,
An earthly lover lurking at her heart.
Amazed, confused, he found his power expired,
Resigned to fate, and with a sigh retired.

    The peer now spreads the glittering forfex wide,
To inclose the lock; now joins it, to divide.
Even then, before the fatal engine closed,
A wretched sylph too fondly interposed;   150
Fate urged the shears, and cut the sylph in twain,
(But airy substance soon unites again)
The meeting points the sacred hair dissever
From the fair head, forever, and forever!

    Then flashed the living lightning from her eyes,
And screams of horror rend the affrighted skies.
Not louder shrieks to pitying Heaven are cast,
When husbands or when lap-dogs breathe their last;
Or when rich China vessels, fallen from high,
In glittering dust and painted fragments lie!   160

    "Let wreaths of triumph now my temples twine,"
(The victor cried); "the glorious prize is mine!
While fish in streams, or birds delight in air,
Or in a coach and six the British fair,

As long as Atalantis shall be read,
Or the small pillow grace a lady's bed,
While visits shall be paid on solemn days,
When numerous wax-lights in bright order blaze,
While nymphs take treats, or assignations give,
So long my honor, name, and praise shall live!   170
What Time would spare, from steel receives its date,
And monuments, like men, submit to fate!
Steel could the labor of the gods destroy,
And strike to dust the imperial towers of Troy;
Steel could the works of mortal pride confound,
And hew triumphal arches to the ground.
What wonder then, fair nymph! thy hairs should feel
The conquering force of unresisted steel?"

CANTO IV

But anxious cares the pensive nymph oppressed,
And secret passions labored in her breast.
Not youthful kings in battle seized alive,
Not scornful virgins who their charms survive,
Not ardent lovers robbed of all their bliss,
Not ancient ladies when refused a kiss,
Not tyrants fierce that unrepenting die,
Not Cynthia when her manteau's pinned awry,
E'er felt such rage, resentment, and despair,
As thou, sad virgin, for thy ravished hair.   10
For, that sad moment, when the sylphs withdrew
And Ariel weeping from Belinda flew,
Umbriel, a dusky, melancholy sprite,
As ever sullied the fair face of light,
Down to the central earth, his proper scene,
Repaired to search the gloomy cave of Spleen.

Swift on his sooty pinions flits the gnome,
And in a vapor reached the dismal dome.
No cheerful breeze this sullen region knows,
The dreaded east is all the wind that blows.   20

165. *Atalantis*, a book by Mrs. Manley.

Here in a grotto, sheltered close from air,
And screened in shades from day's detested glare,
She sighs forever on her pensive bed,
Pain at her side, and Megrim at her head.
Two handmaids wait the throne, alike in place,
But differing far in figure and in face.
Here stood Ill-nature like an ancient maid,
Her wrinkled form in black and white arrayed;
With store of prayers, for mornings, nights, and noons,
Her hand is filled; her bosom with lampoons.   30

There Affectation, with a sickly mien,
Shows in her cheek the roses of eighteen,
Practiced to lisp, and hang the head aside,
Faints into airs, and languishes with pride,
On the rich quilt sinks with becoming woe,
Wrapped in a gown, for sickness, and for show.
The fair ones feel such maladies as these,
When each new night-dress gives a new disease.

A constant vapor o'er the palace flies;
Strange phantoms rising as the mists arise;   40
Dreadful, as hermit's dreams in haunted shades,
Or bright, as visions of expiring maids.
Now glaring fiends, and snakes on rolling spires,
Pale specters, gaping tombs, and purple fires:
Now lakes of liquid gold, Elysian scenes,
And crystal domes, and angels in machines.

Unnumbered throngs on every side are seen,
Of bodies changed to various forms by Spleen.
Here living tea-pots stand, one arm held out,
One bent; the handle this, and that the spout: 50
A pipkin there, like Homer's tripod, walks;
Here sighs a jar, and there a goose-pie talks;
Men prove with child, as powerful fancy works,
And maids, turned bottles, call aloud for corks.

51. *Homer's tripod*, a self-moving tripod.

Safe passed the gnome through this fantastic band,
A branch of healing spleenwort in his hand.
Then thus addressed the power: "Hail, wayward queen!
Who rule the sex, to fifty from fifteen;
Parent of vapors and of female wit,
Who give the hysteric, or poetic fit,   60
On various tempers act by various ways,
Make some take physic, others scribble plays;
Who cause the proud their visits to delay,
And send the godly in a pet to pray.
A nymph there is, that all thy power disdains,
And thousands more in equal mirth maintains.
But oh! if e'er thy gnome could spoil a grace,
Or raise a pimple on a beauteous face,
Like citron-waters matrons' cheeks inflame,
Or change complexions at a losing game;   70
If e'er with airy horns I planted heads,
Or rumpled petticoats, or tumbled beds,
Or caused suspicion when no soul was rude,
Or discomposed the head-dress of a prude,
Or e'er to costive lap-dog gave disease,
Which not the tears of brightest eyes could ease;
Hear me, and touch Belinda with chagrin,
That single act gives half the world the spleen."

The goddess with a discontented air
Seems to reject him, though she grants his prayer.   80
A wondrous bag with both her hands she binds,
Like that where once Ulysses held the winds;
There she collects the force of female lungs,·
Sighs, sobs, and passions, and the war of tongues.
A vial next she fills with fainting fears,
Soft sorrows, melting griefs, and flowing tears.
The gnome rejoicing bears her gifts away,
Spreads his black wings, and slowly mounts to day.

82. Homer tells in the *Odyssey* how Aeolus gave Ulysses all the winds in a
bag.

Sunk in Thalestris' arms the nymph he found,
Her eyes dejected and her hair unbound.   90
Full o'er their heads, the swelling bag he rent,
And all the furies issued at the vent.
Belinda burns with more than mortal ire,
And fierce Thalestris fans the rising fire.
"O wretched maid!" she spread her hands, and cried,
(While Hampton's echoes, "Wretched maid!" replied)
"Was it for this you took such constant care
The bodkin, comb, and essence to prepare?
For this your locks in paper durance bound,
For this with torturing irons wreathed around?   100
For this with fillets strained your tender head,
And bravely bore the double loads of lead?
Gods! shall the ravisher display your hair,
While the fops envy, and the ladies stare!
Honor forbid! at whose unrivalled shrine
Ease, pleasure, virtue, all our sex resign.
Methinks already I your tears survey,
Already hear the horrid things they say,
Already see you a degraded toast,
And all your honor in a whisper lost!   110
How shall I, then, your helpless fame defend?
'Twill then be infamy to seem your friend!
And shall this prize, the inestimable prize,
Exposed through crystal to the gazing eyes,
And heightened by the diamond's circling rays,
On that rapacious hand forever blaze?
Sooner shall grass in Hyde Park Circus grow,
And wits take lodgings in the sound of Bow;
Sooner let earth, air, sea, to chaos fall,
Men, monkeys, lap-dogs, parrots, perish all!"   120

She said; then raging to Sir Plume repairs,
And bids her beau demand the precious hairs.

89. *Thalestris*, Mrs. Morley, a friend of the Fermors'.
118. *in the sound of Bow*, within ear-shot of Bow bells, the unfashionable
part of London.
121. *Sir Plume*, Sir George Brown, the brother of Mrs. Morley and another friend of the Fermors.

(Sir Plume, of amber snuff-box justly vain,
And the nice conduct of a clouded cane)
With earnest eyes, and round unthinking face,
He first the snuff-box opened, then the case,
And thus broke out—"My lord, why, what the devil?
Z——ds! damn the lock! 'fore Gad, you must be civil!
Plague on't! 'tis past a jest—nay prithee, pox!
Give her the hair," he spoke, and rapped his box.   130
"It grieves me much," replied the peer again,
"Who speaks so well should ever speak in vain.
But by this lock, this sacred lock, I swear,
(Which never more shall join its parted hair;
Which never more its honors shall renew,
Clipped from the lovely head where late it grew)
That while my nostrils draw the vital air,
This hand, which won it, shall forever wear."
He spoke, and speaking, in proud triumph spread
The long-contended honors of her head.   140

But Umbriel, hateful gnome! forbears not so;
He breaks the vial whence the sorrows flow.
Then see! the nymph in beauteous grief appears,
Her eyes half languishing, half drowned in tears;
On her heaved bosom hung her drooping head,
Which, with a sigh, she raised; and thus she said:

"Forever cursed be this detested day,
Which snatched my best, my favorite curl away!
Happy! ah, ten times happy had I been,
If Hampton Court these eyes had never seen!   150
Yet am not I the first mistaken maid,
By love of courts to numerous ills betrayed.
Oh, had I rather unadmired remained
In some lone isle or distant northern land;
Where the gilt chariot never marks the way,
Where none learn ombre, none e'er taste bohea!
There kept my charms concealed from mortal eye,
Like roses, that in deserts bloom and die.
What moved my mind with youthful lords to roam?

156. *bohea*, a kind of black tea.

Oh, had I stayed, and said my prayers at home!   160
'Twas this, the morning omens seemed to tell,
Thrice from my trembling hand the patch-box fell;
The tottering china shook without a wind.
Nay, Poll sat mute, and Shock was most unkind!
A sylph, too, warned me of the threats of fate,
In mystic visions, now believed too late!
See the poor remnants of these slighted hairs!
My hands shall rend what e'en thy rapine spares;
These in two sable ringlets taught to break,
Once gave new beauties to the snowy neck;   170
The sister lock now sits uncouth, alone,
And in its fellow's fate forsees its own;
Uncurled it hangs, the fatal shears demands,
And tempts once more, thy sacrilegious hands.
Oh, hadst thou, cruel! been content to seize
Hairs less in sight, or any hairs but these!"

CANTO V

She said; the pitying audience melt in tears.
But Fate and Jove had stopped the baron's ears.
In vain Thalestris with reproach assails,
For who can move when fair Belinda fails?
Not half so fixed the Trojan could remain,
While Anna begged and Dido raged in vain.
Then grave Clarissa graceful waved her fan;
Silence ensued, and thus the nymph began:

"Say, why are beauties praised and honored most,
The wise man's passion, and the vain man's toast?   10
Why decked with all that land and sea afford,
Why angels called, and angel-like adored?
Why 'round our coaches crowd the white-gloved beaux,
Why bows the side-box from its inmost rows?
How vain are all these glories, all our pains,

5. the Trojan, Aneas, parted with Dido in the presence of Dido's sister,
Anna.

Unless good sense preserve what beauty gains:
That men may say, when we the front-box grace:
'Behold the first in virtue as in face!'
Oh! if to dance all night, and dress all day,
Charmed the smallpox, or chased old age away;   20
Who would not scorn what housewife's cares produce,
Or who would learn one earthly thing of use?
To patch, nay ogle, might become a saint,
Nor could it sure be such a sin to paint.
But since, alas! frail beauty must decay,
Curled or uncurled, since locks will turn to gray;
Since painted, or not painted, all shall fade,
And she who scorns a man must die a maid;
What then remains but well our power to use,
And keep good humor still whate'er we lose?   30
And trust me, dear! good humor can prevail,
When airs, and flights, and screams, and scolding fail.
Beauties in vain their pretty eyes may roll;
Charms strike the sight, but merit wins the soul."

   So spoke the dame, but no applause ensued;
Belinda frowned, Thalestris called her prude.
"To arms, to arms!" the fierce virago cries,
And swift as lightning to the combat flies.
All side in parties, and begin th' attack;
Fans clap, silks rustle, and tough whale-bones crack;   40
Heroes' and heroines' shouts confusedly rise,
And bass and treble voices strike the skies.
No common weapons in their hands are found,
Like gods they fight, nor dread a mortal wound.

   So when bold Homer makes the gods engage,
And heavenly breasts with human passions rage;
'Gainst Pallas, Mars; Latona, Hermes arms;
And all Olympus rings with loud alarms:
Jove's thunder roars, Heaven trembles all around,
Blue Neptune storms, the bellowing deeps resound: 50
Earth shakes her nodding towers, the ground gives way,
And the pale ghosts start at the flash of day!

Triumphant Umbriel on a sconce's height
Clapped his glad wings, and sat to view the fight:
Propped on their bodkin spears, the sprites survey
The growing combat, or assist the fray.

While through the press enraged Thalestris flies,
And scatters death around from both her eyes,
A beau and witling perished in the throng,
One died in metaphor, and one in song.   60
"O cruel nymph! a living death I bear,"
Cried Dapperwit, and sunk beside his chair.
A mournful glance Sir Fopling upwards cast,
"Those eyes are made so killing"—was his last.
Thus on Meander's flowery margin lies
The expiring swan, and as he sings he dies.

When bold Sir Plume had drawn Clarissa down,
Chloe stepped in and killed him with a frown;
She smiled to see the doughty hero slain,
But, at her smile, the beau revived again.   70
Now Jove suspends his golden scales in air,
Weighs the men's wits against the lady's hair;
The doubtful beam long nods from side to side;
At length the wits mount up, the hairs subside.

See, fierce Belinda on the baron flies,
With more than usual lightning in her eyes;
Nor feared the chief the unequal fight to try,
Who sought no more than on his foe to die.
But this bold lord with manly strength endued,
She with one finger and a thumb subdued;   80
Just where the breath of life his nostrils drew,
A charge of snuff the wily virgin threw;
The gnomes direct, to every atom just,
The pungent grains of titillating dust.
Sudden, with starting tears each eye o'erflows,
And the high dome re-echoes to his nose.

"Now meet thy fate," incensed Belinda cried,
And drew a deadly bodkin from her side.
(The same, his ancient personage to deck,

Her great great grandsire wore about his neck,   90
In three seal-rings; which after, melted down,
Formed a vast buckle for his widow's gown;
Her infant grandame's whistle next it grew,
The bells she jingled, and the whistle blew;
Then in a bodkin graced her mother's hairs,
Which long she wore, and now Belinda wears.)

"Boast not my fall," he cried, "insulting foe!
Thou by some other shalt be laid as low,
Nor think to die dejects my lofty mind;
All that I dread is leaving you behind!   100
Rather than so, ah, let me still survive,
And burn in Cupid's flames—but burn alive."

"Restore the lock!" she cries; and all around
"Restore the lock!" the vaulted roofs rebound.
Not fierce Othello in so loud a strain
Roared for the handkerchief that caused his pain.
But see how oft ambitious aims are crossed,
And chiefs contend till all the prize is lost!
The lock, obtained with guilt, and kept with pain,
In every place is sought, but sought in vain: 110
With such a prize no mortal must be blessed,
So Heaven decrees! with Heaven who can contest?

Some thought it mounted to the lunar sphere,
Since all things lost on earth are treasured there.
There heroes' wits are kept in ponderous vases,
And beaux' in snuff-boxes and tweezer cases.
There broken vows and death-bed alms are found,
And lovers' hearts with ends of riband bound,
The courtier's promises, and sick man's prayers,
The smiles of harlots, and the tears of heirs,   120
Cages for gnats, and chains to yoke a flea,
Dried butterflies, and tomes of casuistry.

But trust the Muse—she saw it upward rise,
Though marked by none but quick, poetic eyes:
(So Rome's great founder to the heavens withdrew,

125. *Rome's great founder*, Romulus.

Assist their blushes, and inspire their airs;
To Proculus alone confessed in view)
A sudden star, it shot through liquid air,
And drew behind a radiant trail of hair.
Not Berenice's locks first rose so bright,
The heavens bespangling with disheveled light.   130
The sylphs behold it kindling as it flies,
And pleased pursue its progress through the skies.

    This the beau monde shall from the Mall survey,
And hail with music its propitious ray.
This the blest lover shall for Venus take,
And send up vows from Rosamonda's lake.
This Partridge soon shall view in cloudless skies.
When next he looks through Galileo's eyes;
And hence the egregious wizard shall foredoom
The fate of Louis and the fall of Rome.   140

    Then cease, bright nymph! to mourn thy ravished hair,
Which adds new glory to the shining sphere!
Not all the tresses that fair head can boast,
Shall draw such envy as the lock you lost.
For, after all the murders of your eye,
When, after millions slain, yourself shall die:
When those fair suns shall set, as set they must,
And all those tresses shall be laid in dust,
This lock, the Muse shall consecrate to fame,
And 'midst the stars inscribe Belinda's name.   150

1712, 1714

126. *Proculus,* a Roman senator who told the people that Romulus had become a god.
129. *Berenice's locks,* a constellation.
136. *Rosamonda's lake,* a lake in St. James's Park.
137. *Partridge,* an astrologer of the time.
138. *Galileo's eyes,* the telescope.
140. *Louis,* Louis XIV of France; *Rome,* the Roman Catholic Church.

ROBERT BURNS

Tam O' Shanter

A TALE

When chapman billies leave the street,
And drouthy neibors neibors meet,
As market-days are wearing late,
An' folk begin to tak the gate;
While we sit bousing at the nappy,
An' getting fou and unco happy,
We think na on the lang Scots miles,
The mosses, waters, slaps, and styles,
That lie between us and our hame,
Where sits our sulky sullen dame,   10
Gathering her brows like gathering storm,
Nursing her wrath to keep it warm.
    This truth fand honest Tam o' Shanter,
As he frae Ayr ae night did canter—
(Auld Ayr, wham ne'er a town surpasses
For honest men and bonnie lasses).
    O Tam! hadst thou but been sae wise
As ta'en thy ain wife Kate's advice!
She tauld thee weel thou was a skellum,
A bletherin', blusterin', drunken blellum;   20
That frae November till October,
Ae market-day thou was na sober;
That ilka melder wi' the miller
Thou sat as lang as thou had siller;
That every naig was ca'd a shoe on,
The smith and thee gat roarin' fou on;
That at the Lord's house, even on Sunday,
Thou drank wi' Kirkton Jean till Monday.
She prophesied that, late or soon,
Thou would be found deep drowned in Doon;   30

1. *billies*, peddlers.   2. *drouthy*, thirsty.   5. *nappy*, ale house.
8. *slaps*, gaps in fences.   19. *skellum*, scamp.   20. *bletherin'*, chattering.
20. *blellum*, idle talker.   23. *melder*, meal-grinding.   25. *ca'd*, driven.

Or catched wi' warlocks in the mirk
By Alloway's auld haunted kirk.
    Ah, gentle dames! it gars me greet
To think how mony counsels sweet,
How mony lengthened sage advices,
The husband frae the wife despises!
    But to our tale: Ae market night,
Tam had got planted unco right,
Fast by an ingle, bleezing finely,
Wi' reaming swats, that drank divinely;   40
And at his elbow, Souter Johnny,
His ancient, trusty, drouthy crony;
Tam lo'ed him like a very brither;
They had been fou for weeks thegither.
The night drave on wi' sangs and clatter,
And aye the ale was growing better:
The landlady and Tam grew gracious,
Wi' favors secret, sweet, and precious;
The souter tauld his queerest stories;
The landlord's laugh was ready chorus: 50
The storm without might rair and rustle,
Tam did na mind the storm a whistle.
    Care, mad to see a man sae happy,
E'en drowned himself amang the nappy.
As bees flee hame wi' lades o' treasure,
The minutes winged their way wi' pleasure;
Kings may be bless'd, but Tam was glorious,
O'er a' the ills o' life victorious!
    But pleasures are like poppies spread—
You seize the flow'r, its bloom is shed;   60
Or like the snow falls in the river—
A moment white, then melts for ever;
Or like the borealis race,
That flit ere you can point their place;
Or like the rainbow's lovely form
Evanishing amid the storm.
Nae man can tether time nor tide;

33. *gars me greet*, makes me cry.   40. *swats*, foaming ale.
41. *Souter*, shoemaker.

The hour approaches Tam maun ride;
That hour, o' night's black arch the keystane,
That dreary hour, he mounts his beast in;   70
And sic a night he taks the road in,
As ne'er poor sinner was abroad in.
　　The wind blew as 'twad blawn its last;
The rattling show'rs rose on the blast;
The speedy gleams the darkness swallowed;
Loud, deep, and lang, the thunder bellowed:
That night, a child might understand,
The Deil had business on his hand.
　　Weel mounted on his gray mare, Meg,
A better never lifted leg,   80
Tam skelpit on thro' dub and mire,
Despising wind, and rain, and fire;
Whiles holding fast his gude blue bonnet;
Whiles crooning o'er some auld Scots sonnet;
Whiles glow'ring round wi' prudent cares,
Lest bogles catch him unawares.
Kirk-Alloway was drawing nigh,
Whare ghaists and houlets nightly cry.
　　By this time he was cross the ford,
Where in the snaw the chapman smoor'd;   90
And past the birks and meikle stane,
Where drunken Charlie brak's neck-bane;
And thro' the whins, and by the cairn,
Where hunters fand the murdered bairn;
And near the thorn, aboon the well,
Where Mungo's mither hanged hersel.
Before him Doon pours all his floods;
The doubling storm roars thro' the woods;
The lightnings flash from pole to pole;
Near and more near the thunders roll: 100
When, glimmering thro' the groaning trees,
Kirk-Alloway seem'd in a bleeze;
Thro' ilka bore the beams were glancing;

86. *bogles*, bogies.　90. *smoor'd*, smothered.　91. *meikle stane*, big stone.
93. *whins*, furze.　　　93. *cairn*, pile of stone.　　94. *bairn*, child.
103. *bore*, chink.

And loud resounded mirth and dancing.
   Inspiring bold John Barleycorn!
What dangers thou canst make us scorn!
Wi' tippenny, we fear nae evil;
Wi' usquebae, we'll face the devil!
The swats sae reamed in Tammie's noddle,
Fair play, he cared na deils a boddle!   110
But Maggie stood right sair astonished,
Till, by the heel and hand admonished,
She ventured forward on the light;
And, vow! Tam saw an unco sight!
   Warlocks and witches in a dance!
Nae cotillon brent new frae France,
But hornpipes, jigs, strathspeys, and reels,
Put life and mettle in their heels.
A winnock-bunker in the east,
There sat auld Nick, in shape o' beast—   120
A touzie tyke, black, grim, and large!
To gie them music was his charge:
He screwed the pipes and gart them skirl,
Till roof and rafters a' did dirl.
Coffins stood round like open presses,
That shawed the dead in their last dresses;
And by some devilish cantraip sleight
Each in its cauld hand held a light,
By which heroic Tam was able
To note upon the haly table   130
A murderer's banes in gibbet-airns;
Twa span-lang, wee, unchristened bairns;
A thief new-cutted frae the rape,
Wi' his last gasp his gab did gape;
Five tomahawks, wi' blude red rusted;
Five scymitars, wi' murder crusted;
A garter, which a babe had strangled;
A knife, a father's throat had mangled,

107. *tippenny*, ale.   108. *usquebae*, whiskey.   110. *boddle*, penny.
116. *brent*, brand.   119. *winnock-bunker*, window-seat.
121. *touzie tyke*, shaggy dog.   123. *skirl*, squeal.   124. *dirl*, ring.
134. *gab*, mouth.

Whom his ain son o' life bereft—
The gray hairs yet stack to the heft;   140
Wi' mair of horrible and awfu',
Which even to name wad be unlawfu'.
  As Tammie glowred, amazed, and curious,
The mirth and fun grew fast and furious:
The piper loud and louder blew;
The dancers quick and quicker flew;
They reeled, they set, they crossed, they cleekit,
Till ilka carlin swat and reekit,
And coost her duddies to the wark,
And linkit at it in her sark!   150
  Now Tam, O Tam! had thae been queans,
A' plump and strapping in their teens;
Their sarks, instead o' creeshie flannen,
Been snaw-white seventeen hunder linen!
Thir breeks o' mine, my only pair,
That ance were plush, o' gude blue hair,
I wad hae gi'en them off my hurdies,
For ae blink o' the bonnie burdies!
  But withered beldams, auld and droll,
Rigwoodie hags wad spean a foal,   160
Louping and flinging on a crummock,
I wonder didna turn thy stomach.
  But Tam kent what was what fu' brawlie:
There was ae winsome wench and walie
That night enlisted in the core,
Lang after kent on Carrick shore!
(For mony a beast to dead she shot,
And perished mony a bonnie boat,
And shook baith meikle corn and bear,
And kept the country-side in fear.)   170
Her cutty sark, o' Paisley harn,

147. *cleekit*, linked arms. 148. *carlin*, old woman. 149. *coost*, threw off.
149. *duddies*, clothes.   149. *wark*, work.   150. *sark*, shirt.
151. *queans*, young women. 153. *creeshie*, greasy. 155. *breeks*, breaches.
157. *hurdies*, hips.   160. *spean*, wean.   161. *louping*, leaping.
161. *flinging*, kicking.   161. *crummock*, staff.   163. *brawlie*, well.
164. *walie*, goodly.   171. *cutty*, short.   171. *harn*, linen.

That while a lassie she had worn,
In longitude tho' sorely scanty,
It was her best, and she was vauntie.
Ah! little kent thy reverend grannie
That sark she coft for her wee Nannie
Wi' twa pund Scots ('twas a' her riches)
Wad ever graced a dance of witches!
    But here my muse her wing maun cour;
Sic flights are far beyond her pow'r—   180
To sing how Nannie lap and flang
(A souple jade she was, and strang);
And how Tam stood, like ane bewitched,
And thought his very e'en enriched;
Even Satan glowred, and fidget fu' fain,
And hotched and blew wi' might and main:
Till first ae caper, syne anither,
Tam tint his reason a' thegither,
And roars out, "Weel done, Cutty-sark!"
And in an instant all was dark!   190
And scarcely had he Maggie rallied,
When out the hellish legion sallied.
    As bees bizz out wi' angry fyke
When plundering herds assail their byke,
As open pussie's mortal foes
When, pop! she starts before their nose,
As eager runs the market-crowd,
When "Catch the thief!" resounds aloud,
So Maggie runs; the witches follow,
Wi' mony an eldritch skriech and hollow.   200
    Ah, Tam! ah, Tam! thou'll get thy fairin'!
In hell they'll roast thee like a herrin'!
In vain thy Kate awaits thy comin'!
Kate soon will be a woefu' woman!
Now do thy speedy utmost, Meg,
And win the key-stane o' the brig:

176. *coft*, bought.   186. *hotched*, jerked.   188. *tint*, lost.
193. *fyke*, buzz.   194. *byke*, hive.   195. *pussie's*, hare's.
200. *eldritch*, unearthly.   201. *fairin'*, reward, i.e., beating.
206. *brig*, bridge.

There at them thou thy tail may toss,
A running stream they darena cross.
But ere the key-stane she could make,
The fient a tail she had to shake!   210
For Nannie, far before the rest,
Hard upon noble Maggie pressed,
And flew at Tam wi' furious ettle;
But little wist she Maggie's mettle!
Ae spring brought off her master hale,
But left behind her ain gray tail:
The carlin claught her by the rump,
And left poor Maggie scarce a stump.
    Now, wha this tale o' truth shall read,
Each man and mother's son, take heed;   220
Whene'er to drink you are inclined,
Or cutty-sarks run in your mind,
Think! ye may buy the joys o'er dear;
Remember Tam o' Shanter's mare.

1791

WILLIAM WORDSWORTH

Michael

A PASTORAL POEM

If from the public way you turn your steps
Up the tumultuous brook of Greenhead Ghyll,
You will suppose that with an upright path
Your feet must struggle; in such bold ascent
The pastoral mountains front you, face to face.
But, courage! for around that boisterous brook
The mountains have all opened out themselves,
And made a hidden valley of their own.
No habitation can be seen; but they
Who journey thither find themselves alone   10
With a few sheep, with rocks and stones, and kites
That overhead are sailing in the sky.

210. *fient*, devil.   213. *ettle*, aim.   217. *claught*, seized

It is in truth an utter solitude;
Nor should I have made mention of this Dell
But for one object which you might pass by,
Might see and notice not. Beside the brook
Appears a straggling heap of unhewn stones!
And to that simple object appertains
A story—unenriched with strange events,
Yet not unfit, I deem, for the fireside,   20
Or for the summer shade. It was the first
Of those domestic tales that spake to me
Of shepherds, dwellers in the valleys, men
Whom I already loved; not verily
For their own sakes, but for the fields and hills
Where was their occupation and abode.
And hence this Tale, while I was yet a Boy
Careless of books, yet having felt the power
Of Nature, by the gentle agency
Of natural objects, led me on to feel   30
For passions that were not my own, and think
(At random and imperfectly indeed)
On man, the heart of man, and human life.
Therefore, although it be a history
Homely and rude, I will relate the same
For the delight of a few natural hearts;
And, with yet fonder feeling, for the sake
Of youthful Poets, who among these hills
Will be my second self when I am gone.

    Upon the forest-side in Grasmere Vale   40
There dwelt a Shepherd, Michael was his name;
An old man, stout of heart, and strong of limb.
His bodily frame had been from youth to age
Of an unusual strength: his mind was keen,
Intense, and frugal, apt for all affairs,
And in his shepherd's calling he was prompt
And watchful more than ordinary men.
Hence had he learned the meaning of all winds,
Of blasts of every tone; and oftentimes,
When others heeded not, He heard the South   50

Make subterraneous music, like the noise
Of bagpipers on distant Highland hills.
The Shepherd, at such warning, of his flock
Bethought him, and he to himself would say,
"The winds are now devising work for me!"
And, truly, at all times, the storm, that drives
The traveler to a shelter, summoned him
Up to the mountains: he had been alone
Amid the heart of many thousand mists,
That came to him, and left him, on the heights.   60
So lived he till his eightieth year was past.
And grossly that man errs, who should suppose
That the green valleys, and the streams and rocks,
Were things indifferent to the Shepherd's thoughts.
Fields, where with cheerful spirits he had breathed
The common air; hills, which with vigorous step
He had so often climbed; which had impressed
So many incidents upon his mind
Of hardship, skill or courage, joy or fear;
Which, like a book, preserved the memory   70
Of the dumb animals, whom he had saved,
Had fed or sheltered, linking to such acts
The certainty of honorable gain;
Those fields, those hills—what could they less? had laid
Strong hold on his affections, were to him
A pleasurable feeling of blind love,
The pleasure which there is in life itself.
    His days had not been passed in singleness.
His Helpmate was a comely matron, old—
Though younger than himself full twenty years.   80
She was a woman of a stirring life,
Whose heart was in her house: two wheels she had
Of antique form; this large, for spinning wool;
That small, for flax; and if one wheel had rest
It was because the other was at work.
The Pair had but one inmate in their house,
An only Child, who had been born to them
When Michael, telling o'er his years, began
To deem that he was old,—in shepherd's phrase,

With one foot in the grave. This only Son,   90
With two brave sheep-dogs tried in many a storm,
The one of an inestimable worth,
Made all their household. I may truly say,
That they were as a proverb in the vale
For endless industry. When day was gone,
And from their occupations out of doors
The Son and Father were come home, even then,
Their labor did not cease; unless when all
Turned to the cleanly supper-board, and there,
Each with a mess of pottage and skimmed milk,   100
Sat round the basket piled with oaten cakes,
And their plain home-made cheese. Yet when the meal
Was ended, Luke (for so the Son was named)
And his old Father both betook themselves
To such convenient work as might employ
Their hands by the fireside; perhaps to card
Wool for the Housewife's spindle, or repair
Some injury done to sickle, flail, or scythe,
Or other implement of house or field.
     Down from the ceiling, by the chimney's edge,   110
That in our ancient uncouth country style
With huge and black projection overbrowed
Large space beneath, as duly as the light
Of day grew dim the Housewife hung a lamp;
An agéd utensil, which had performed
Service beyond all others of its kind.
Early at evening did it burn—and late,
Surviving comrade of uncounted hours,
Which, going by from year to year, had found,
And left, the couple neither gay perhaps   120
Nor cheerful, yet with objects and with hopes,
Living a life of eager industry.
And now, when Luke had reached his eighteenth year,
There by the light of this old lamp they sat,
Father and Son, while far into the night
The Housewife plied her own peculiar work,
Making the cottage through the silent hours
Murmur as with the sound of summer flies.

This light was famous in its neighborhood,
And was a public symbol of the life   130
That thrifty Pair had lived. For, as it chanced,
Their cottage on a plot of rising ground
Stood single, with large prospect, north and south,
High into Easdale, up to Dunmail-Raise,
And westward to the village near the lake;
And from this constant light, so regular
And so far seen, the House itself, by all
Who dwelt within the limits of the vale,
Both old and young, was named the *Evening Star.*
    Thus living on through such a length of years,   140
The Shepherd, if he loved himself, must needs
Have loved his Helpmate; but to Michael's heart
This son of his old age was yet more dear—
Less from instinctive tenderness, the same
Fond spirit that blindly works in the blood of all—
Than that a child, more than all other gifts
That earth can offer to declining man,
Brings hope with it, and forward-looking thoughts,
And stirrings of inquietude, when they
By tendency of nature needs must fail.   150
Exceeding was the love he bare to him,
His heart and his heart's joy! For oftentimes
Old Michael, while he was a babe in arms,
Had done him female service, not alone
For pastime and delight, as is the use
Of fathers, but with patient mind enforced
To acts of tenderness; and he had rocked
His cradle, as with a woman's gentle hand.
    And, in a later time, ere yet the Boy
Had put on boy's attire, did Michael love,   160
Albeit of a stern unbending mind,
To have the Young-one in his sight, when he
Wrought in the field, or on his shepherd's stool
Sat with a fettered sheep before him stretched
Under the large old oak, that near his door
Stood single, and, from matchless depth of shade,
Chosen for the Shearer's covert from the sun,

Thence in our rustic dialect was called
The *Clipping Tree*, a name which yet it bears.
There, while they two were sitting in the shade,   170
With others round them, earnest all and blithe,
Would Michael exercise his heart with looks
Of fond correction and reproof bestowed
Upon the Child, if he disturbed the sheep
By catching at their legs, or with his shouts
Scared them, while they lay still beneath the shears.
    And when by Heaven's good grace the boy grew up
A healthy Lad, and carried in his cheek
Two steady roses that were five years old;
Then Michael from a winter coppice cut   180
With his own hand a sapling, which he hooped
With iron, making it throughout in all
Due requisites a perfect shepherd's staff,
And gave it to the Boy; wherewith equipped
He as a watchman oftentimes was placed
At gate or gap, to stem or turn the flock;
And, to his office prematurely called,
There stood the urchin, as you will divine,
Something between a hindrance and a help;
And for this cause not always, I believe,   190
Receiving from his Father hire of praise;
Though nought was left undone which staff, or voice,
Or looks, or threatening gestures, could perform.
    But soon as Luke, full ten years old, could stand
Against the mountain blasts; and to the heights,
Not fearing toil, nor length of weary ways,
He with his Father daily went, and they
Were as companions, why should I relate
That objects which the Shepherd loved before
Were dearer now? that from the Boy there came   200
Feelings and emanations—things which were
Light to the sun and music to the wind;
And that the old Man's heart seemed born again?
    Thus in his Father's sight the Boy grew up:
And now, when he had reached his eighteenth year,
He was his comfort and his daily hope.

  While in this sort the simple household lived
From day to day, to Michael's ear there came
Distressful tidings. Long before the time
Of which I speak, the Shepherd had been bound   210
In surety for his brother's son, a man
Of an industrious life, and ample means;
But unforeseen misfortunes suddenly
Had pressed upon him; and old Michael now
Was summoned to discharge the forfeiture,
A grievous penalty, but little less
Than half his substance. This unlooked-for claim,
At the first hearing, for a moment took
More hope out of his life than he supposed
That any old man ever could have lost.   220
As soon as he had armed himself with strength
To look his trouble in the face, it seemed
The Shepherd's sole resource to sell at once
A portion of his patrimonial fields.
Such was his first resolve; he thought again,
And his heart failed him. "Isabel," said he,
Two evenings after he had heard the news,
"I have been toiling more than seventy years,
And in the open sunshine of God's love
Have we all lived; yet if these fields of ours   230
Should pass into a stranger's hand, I think
That I could not lie quiet in my grave.
Our lot is a hard lot; the sun himself
Has scarcely been more diligent than I;
And I have lived to be a fool at last
To my own family. An evil man
That was, and made an evil choice, if he
Were false to us; and if he were not false,
There are ten thousand to whom loss like this
Had been no sorrow. I forgive him;—but   240
'Twere better to be dumb than to talk thus.
  "When I began, my purpose was to speak
Of remedies and of a cheerful hope.
Our Luke shall leave us, Isabel; the land
Shall not go from us, and it shall be free;

He shall possess it, free as is the wind
That passes over it. We have, thou know'st,
Another kinsman—he will be our friend
In this distress. He is a prosperous man,
Thriving in trade—and Luke to him shall go,   250
And with his kinsman's help and his own thrift
He quickly will repair this loss, and then
He may return to us. If here he stay,
What can be done? Where every one is poor,
What can be gained?"
              At this the old Man paused,
And Isabel sat silent, for her mind
Was busy, looking back into past times.
There's Richard Bateman, thought she to herself,
He was a parish-boy—at the church-door
They made a gathering for him, shillings, pence,   260
And halfpennies, wherewith the neighbors bought
A basket, which they filled with peddler's wares;
And, with this basket on his arm, the lad
Went up to London, found a master there,
Who, out of many, chose the trusty boy
To go and overlook his merchandise
Beyond the seas; where he grew wondrous rich,
And left estates and monies to the poor.
And, at his birthplace, built a chapel, floored
With marble which he sent from foreign lands.   270
These thoughts, and many others of like sort,
Passed quickly through the mind of Isabel,
And her face brightened. The old Man was glad,
And thus resumed:—"Well, Isabel! this scheme
These two days has been meat and drink to me.
Far more than we have lost is left us yet.
—We have enough—I wish indeed that I
Were younger;—but this hope is a good hope.
—Make ready Luke's best garments, of the best
Buy for him more, and let us send him forth   280
To-morrow, or the next day, or to-night:
—If he *could* go, the Boy should go to-night."
    Here Michael ceased, and to the fields went forth

With a light heart. The Housewife for five days
Was restless morn and night, and all day long
Wrought òn with her best fingers to prepare
Things needful for the journey of her son.
But Isabel was glad when Sunday came
To stop her in her work: for, when she lay
By Michael's side, she through the last two nights 290
Heard him, how he was troubled in his sleep:
And when they rose at morning she could see
That all his hopes were gone. That day at noon,
She said to Luke, while they two by themselves
Were sitting at the door, "Thou must not go:
We have no other Child but thee to lose—
None to remember—do not go away,
For if thou leave thy Father he will die."
The Youth made answer with a jocund voice;
And Isabel, when she had told her fears, 300
Recovered heart. That evening her best fare
Did she bring forth, and all together sat
Like happy people round a Christmas fire.
    With daylight Isabel resumed her work;
And all the ensuing week the house appeared
As cheerful as a grove in Spring: at length
The expected letter from their kinsman came.
With kind assurances that he would do
His utmost for the welfare of the Boy;
To which, requests were added, that forthwith 310
He might be sent to him. Ten times or more
The letter was read over; Isabel
Went forth to show it to the neighbors round;
Nor was there at that time on English land
A prouder heart than Luke's. When Isabel
Had to her house returned, the old Man said,
"He shall depart to-morrow." To this word
The Housewife answered, talking much of things
Which, if at such short notice he should go,
Would surely be forgotten. But at length 320
She gave consent, and Michael was at ease.
    Near the tumultuous brook of Greenhead Ghyll,

In that deep valley, Michael had designed
To build a Sheepfold; and, before he heard
The tidings of his melancholy loss,
For this same purpose he had gathered up
A heap of stones, which by the streamlet's edge
Lay thrown together, ready for the work.
With Luke that evening thitherward he walked:
And soon as they had reached the place he stopped, 330
And thus the old Man spake to him:—"My Son,
To-morrow thou wilt leave me: with full heart
I look upon thee, for thou art the same
That wert a promise to me ere thy birth,
And all thy life hast been my daily joy.
I will relate to thee some little part
Of our two histories; 'twill do thee good
When thou art from me, even if I should touch
On things thou canst not know of.—After thou
First cam'st into the world—as oft befalls   340
To new-born infants—thou didst sleep away
Two days, and blessings from thy Father's tongue
Then fell upon thee. Day by day passed on,
And still I loved thee with increasing love.
Never to living ear came sweeter sounds
Than when I heard thee by our own fireside
First uttering, without words, a natural tune;
While thou, a feeding babe, didst in thy joy
Sing at thy Mother's breast. Month followed month,
And in the open fields my life was passed   350
And on the mountains; else I think that thou
Hadst been brought up upon thy Father's knees.
But we were playmates, Luke: among these hills,
As well thou knowest, in us the old and young
Have played together, nor with me didst thou
Lack any pleasure which a boy can know."
Luke had a manly heart; but at these words
He sobbed aloud. The old Man grasped his hand,
And said, "Nay, do not take it so—I see
That these are things of which I need not speak. 360
—Even to the utmost I have been to thee

A kind and a good Father: and herein
I but repay a gift which I myself
Received at others' hands; for, though now old
Beyond the common life of man, I still
Remember them who loved me in my youth.
Both of them sleep together: here they lived,
As all their Forefathers had done; and when
At length their time was come, they were not loath
To give their bodies to the family mold.   370
I wished that thou should'st live the life they lived:
But, 'tis a long time to look back, my Son,
And see so little gain from threescore years.
These fields were burthened when they came to me;
Till I was forty years of age, not more
Than half of my inheritance was mine.
I toiled and toiled; God blessed me in my work,
And till these three weeks past the land was free.
—It looks as if it never could endure
Another Master. Heaven forgive me, Luke,   380
If I judge ill for thee, but it seems good
That thou should'st go."
                    At this the old Man paused;
Then, pointing to the stones near which they stood,
Thus, after a short silence, he resumed:
"This was a work for us; and now, my Son,
It is a work for me. But, lay one stone—
Here, lay it for me, Luke, with thine own hands.
Nay, Boy, be of good hope;—we both may live
To see a better day. At eighty-four
I still am strong and hale;—do thou thy part;   390
I will do mine.—I will begin again
With many tasks that were resigned to thee:
Up to the heights, and in among the storms,
Will I without thee go again, and do
All works which I was wont to do alone,
Before I knew thy face.—Heaven bless thee, Boy!
Thy heart these two weeks has been beating fast
With many hopes; it should be so—yes—yes—
I knew that thou could'st never have a wish

To leave me, Luke: thou hast been bound to me   400
Only by links of love: when thou art gone,
What will be left to us!—But, I forget
My purposes. Lay now the corner-stone,
As I requested; and hereafter, Luke,
When thou art gone away, should evil men
Be thy companions, think of me, my Son,
And of this moment; hither turn thy thoughts,
And God will strengthen thee: amid all fear
And all temptation, Luke, I pray that thou
May'st bear in mind the life thy Fathers lived,   410
Who, being innocent, did for that cause
Bestir them in good deeds. Now, fare thee well—
When thou return'st, thou in this place wilt see
A work which is not here: a covenant
'Twill be between us; but, whatever fate
Befall thee, I shall love thee to the last,
And bear thy memory with me to the grave."
　　The Shepherd ended here; and Luke stooped down,
And, as his Father had requested, laid
The first stone of the Sheepfold. At the sight   420
The old Man's grief broke from him; to his heart
He pressed his Son, he kisséd him and wept:
And to the house together they returned.
—Hushed was that House in peace, or seeming peace,
Ere the night fell:—with morrow's dawn the Boy
Began his journey, and when he had reached
The public way, he put on a bold face;
And all the neighbors, as he passed their doors,
Came forth with wishes and with farewell prayers,
That followed him till he was out of sight.   430
　　A good report did from their Kinsman come,
Of Luke and his well-doing: and the Boy
Wrote loving letters, full of wondrous news,
Which, as the Housewife phrased it, were throughout
"The prettiest letters that were ever seen."
Both parents read them with rejoicing hearts.
So, many months passed on: and once again
The Shepherd went about his daily work

With confident and cheerful thoughts; and now
Sometimes when he could find a leisure hour   440
He to that valley took his way, and there
Wrought at the Sheepfold. Meantime Luke began
To slacken in his duty; and, at length,
He in the dissolute city gave himself
To evil courses: ignominy and shame
Fell on him, so that he was driven at last
To seek a hiding-place beyond the seas.
   There is a comfort in the strength of love;
'Twill make a thing endurable, which else
Would overset the brain, or break the heart: 450
I have conversed with more than one who well
Remember the old Man, and what he was
Years after he had heard this heavy news.
His bodily frame had been from youth to age
Of an unusual strength. Among the rocks
He went, and still looked up to sun and cloud,
And listened to the wind; and, as before,
Performed all kinds of labor for his sheep,
And for the land, his small inheritance.
And to that hollow dell from time to time   460
Did he repair, to build the Fold, of which
His flock had need. 'Tis not forgotten yet
The pity which was then in every heart
For the old Man—and 'tis believed by all
That many and many a day he thither went,
And never lifted up a single stone.
   There, by the Sheepfold, sometimes was he seen
Sitting alone, or with his faithful Dog,
Then old, beside him, lying at his feet.
The length of full seven years, from time to time,   470
He at the building of this Sheepfold wrought,
And left the work unfinished when he died.
Three years, or little more, did Isabel
Survive her Husband: at her death the estate
Was sold, and went into a stranger's hand.
The Cottage which was named the *Evening Star*
Is gone—the plowshare has been through the ground

On which it stood; great changes have been wrought
In all the neighborhood:—yet the oak is left
That grew beside their door; and the remains   480
Of the unfinished Sheepfold may be seen
Beside the boisterous brook of Greenhead Ghyll.

                                        1800

SAMUEL TAYLOR COLERIDGE

The Rime of the Ancient Mariner

IN SEVEN PARTS

ARGUMENT

*How a Ship having passed the Line was driven by storms to the
cold Country towards the South Pole; and how from thence she
made her course to the tropical Latitude of the Great Pacific
Ocean; and of the strange things that befell; and in what manner
the Ancyent Marinere came back to his own Country.*

PART I

It is an ancient Mariner,
And he stoppeth one of three.
"By thy long gray beard and glittering eye,
Now wherefore stopp'st thou me?

An ancient Mariner meeteth three Gallants bidden to a wedding-feast, and detaineth one.

"The Bridegroom's doors are opened wide,
And I am next of kin;
The guests are met, the feast is set:
May'st hear the merry din."

He holds him with his skinny hand,
"There was a ship," quoth he.   10
"Hold off! unhand me, gray-beard loon!"
Eftsoons his hand dropped he.

He holds him with his glittering eye—
The Wedding-Guest stood still,
And listens like a three years' child:
The Mariner hath his will.

The Wedding-Guest is spell-bound by the eye of the old seafaring man, and constrained to hear his tale.

The Wedding-Guest sat on a stone:
He cannot choose but hear;
And thus spake on that ancient man,
The bright-eyed Mariner.   20

"The ship was cheered, the harbor cleared,
Merely did we drop
Below the kirk, below the hill,
Below the lighthouse top.

"The sun came up upon the left,
Out of the sea came he!
And he shone bright, and on the right
Went down into the sea.

The Mariner tells how the ship sailed southward with a good wind and fair weather, till it reached the Line.

"Higher and higher every day,
Till over the mast at noon—"   30
The Wedding-Guest here beat his breast,
For he heard the loud bassoon.

The bride hath paced into the hall,
Red as a rose is she;
Nodding their heads before her goes
The merry minstrelsy.

The Wedding-Guest heareth the bridal music; but the Mariner continueth his tale.

The Wedding-Guest he beat his breast,
Yet he cannot choose but hear;
And thus spake on that ancient man,
The bright-eyed Mariner.   40

"And now the Storm-blast came, and he
Was tyrannous and strong:
He struck with his o'ertaking wings,
And chased us south along.

The ship driven by a storm toward the south pole.

"With sloping masts and dipping prow,
As who pursued with yell and blow
Still treads the shadow of his foe,
And forward bends his head,
The ship drove fast, loud roared the blast,
And southward aye we fled.   50

"And now there came both mist and snow,
And it grew wondrous cold:
And ice, mast-high, came floating by,
As green as emerald.

"And through the drifts the snowy clifts
Did send a dismal sheen:
Nor shapes of men nor beasts we ken—
The ice was all between.

The land of ice, and of fearful sounds where no living thing was to be seen.

"The ice was here, the ice was there,
The ice was all around: 60
It cracked and growled, and roared and howled,
Like noises in a swound!

"At length did cross an Albatross,
Thorough the fog it came;
As if it had been a Christian soul,
We hailed it in God's name.

Till a great sea-bird, called the Albatross, came through the snow-fog, and was received with great joy and hospitality.

"It ate the food it ne'er had eat,
And round and round it flew.
The ice did split with a thunder-fit;
The helmsman steered us through!   70

"And a good south wind sprung up behind;
The Albatross did follow,
And every day, for food or play,
Came to the mariner's hollo!

And lo! the Albatross proveth a bird of good omen, and followeth the ship as it returned northward through fog and floating ice.

"In mist or cloud, on mast or shroud,
It perched for vespers nine;
Whiles all the night, through fog-smoke white,
Glimmered the white moon-shine."

"God save thee, ancient Mariner!
From the fiends, that plague thee thus!—   80
Why look'st thou so?"—"With my cross-bow
I shot the Albatross!"

The ancient Mariner inhospitably killeth the pious bird of good omen.

PART II

"The Sun now rose upon the right:
Out of the sea came he,
Still hid in mist, and on the left
Went down into the sea.

"And the good south wind still blew behind,
But no sweet bird did follow,
Nor any day for food or play
Came to the mariner's hollo!   90

"And I had done a hellish thing,
And it would work 'em woe:
For all averred, I had killed the bird
That made the breeze to blow.
Ah wretch! said they, the bird to slay,
That made the breeze to blow!

His shipmates cry
out against the
ancient Mariner,
for killing the bird
of good luck.

"Nor dim nor red, like God's own head,
The glorious Sun uprist:
Then all averred, I had killed the bird
That brought the fog and mist.   100
'Twas right, said they, such birds to slay,
That bring the fog and mist.

But when the fog
cleared off they
justify the same,
and thus make
themselves accom-
plices in the crime.

"The fair breeze blew, the white foam flew,
The furrow followed free;
We were the first that ever burst
Into that silent sea.

The fair breeze
continues; the ship
enters the Pacific
Ocean, and sails
northward, even
till it reaches the
Line.

"Down dropped the breeze, the sails dropped
    down,
'Twas sad as sad could be;
And we did speak only to break
The silence of the sea!   110

The ship hath been
suddenly becalmed.

"All in a hot and copper sky,
The bloody Sun, at noon,
Right up above the mast did stand,
No bigger than the Moon.

"Day after day, day after day,
We stuck, nor breath nor motion;
As idle as a painted ship
Upon a painted ocean.

"Water, water, everywhere,
And all the boards did shrink,   120
Water, water, everywhere,
Nor any drop to drink.

And the Albatross
begins to be
avenged.

"The very deep did rot: O Christ!
That ever this should be!
Yea, slimy things did crawl with legs
Upon the slimy sea.

"About, about, in reel and rout
The death-fires danced at night;
The water, like a witch's oils,
Burned green, and blue and white.   130

"And some in dreams assured were
Of the Spirit that plagued us so;
Nine fathom deep he had followed us
From the land of mist and snow.

A Spirit had fol-
lowed them; one
of the invisible in-
habitants of this
planet, neither de-
parted souls nor
angels; concerning
whom the learned
Jew, Josephus,
and the Platonic
Constantinopolitan,
Michael Psellus,
may be consulted.
They are very
numerous, and
there is no climate
or element without
one or more.

"And every tongue, through utter drought,
Was withered at the root;
We could not speak, no more than if
We had been choked with soot.

"Ah! well-a-day! what evil looks
Had I from old and young!   140
Instead of the cross, the Albatross
About my neck was hung.

The shipmates, in
their sore distress,
would fain throw
the whole guilt on
the ancient Mari-
ner: in sign
whereof they hang
the dead sea-bird
round his neck.

PART III

"There passed a weary time. Each throat
Was parched, and glazed each eye.
A weary time! a weary time!

How glazed each weary eye,
When looking westward, I beheld
A something in the sky.

The ancient Mariner beholdeth a sign in the element afar off.

"At first it seemed a little speck,
And then it seemed a mist;   150
It moved and moved, and took at last
A certain shape, I wist.

"A speck, a mist, a shape, I wist!
And still it neared and neared:
As if it dodged a water-sprite,
It plunged and tacked and veered.

"With throats unslaked, with black lips baked,
We could nor laugh nor wail;
Through utter drought all dumb we stood!
I bit my arm, I sucked the blood,   160
And cried, A sail! a sail!

At its nearer approach, it seemeth him to be a ship; and at a dear ransom he freeth his speech from the bonds of thirst.

"With throats unslaked, with black lips baked,
Agape they heard me call:
Gramercy! they for joy did grin,
And all at once their breath drew in,
As they were drinking all.

A flash of joy;

"See! see! (I cried) she tacks no more!
Hither to work us weal;
Without a breeze, without a tide,
She steadies with upright keel!   170

And horror follows. For can it be a ship that comes onward without wind or tide?

"The western wave was all aflame,
The day was well nigh done!
Almost upon the western wave
Rested the broad bright Sun;
When that strange shape drove suddenly
Betwixt us and the Sun.

"And straight the Sun was flecked with bars,
(Heaven's Mother send us grace!)
As if through a dungeon-grate he peered
With broad and burning face.   180

It seemeth him but the skeleton of a ship.

"Alas! (thought I, and my heart beat loud)
How fast she nears and nears!

And its ribs are
seen as bars on the
face of the setting
Sun.

Are those *her* sails that glance in the Sun,
Like restless gossameres?

"Are those *her* ribs through which the Sun
Did peer, as through a grate?
And is that Woman all her crew?

The Specter-
Woman and her
Deathmate, and no
other on board the
skeleton-ship.

Is that a Death? and are there two?
Is death that woman's mate?

"*Her* lips were red, *her* looks were free,   190
Her locks were yellow as gold:

Like vessel,
like crew!

Her skin was as white as leprosy,
The Nightmare Life-in-Death was she,
Who thicks man's blood with cold.

"The naked hulk alongside came,
And the twain were casting dice;

Death and
Life-in-Death have
diced for the
ship's crew, and
she (the latter)
winneth the
ancient Mariner.

'The game is done! I've won, I've won!'
Quoth she, and whistles thrice.

"The Sun's rim dips; the stars rush out:

No twilight within
the courts of the
Sun.

At one stride comes the dark;   200
With far-heard whisper, o'er the sea,
Off shot the specter-bark.

"We listened and looked sideways up!

At the rising of
the Moon,

Fear at my heart, as at a cup,
My life-blood seemed to sip!
The stars were dim, and thick the night,
The steersman's face by his lamp gleamed white;
From the sails the dew did drip—
Till clomb above the eastern bar
The hornèd Moon with one bright star   210
Within the nether tip.

"One after one, by the star-dogged Moon,

One after another,

Too quick for groan or sigh,
Each turned his face with a ghastly pang,
And cursed me with his eye.

"Four times fifty living men
(And I heard nor sigh nor groan),
With heavy thump, a lifeless lump,
They dropped down one by one.

His shipmates drop down dead.

"The souls did from their bodies fly—
They fled to bliss or woe!
And every soul, it passed me by,
Like the whizz of my cross-bow!"

220   *But Life-in-Death begins her work on the ancient Mariner.*

PART IV

"I fear thee, ancient Mariner!
I fear thy skinny hand!
And thou art long, and lank, and brown,
As is the ribbed sea-sand.

The Wedding-Guest feareth that a Spirit is talking to him.

"I fear thee and thy glittering eye,
And thy skinny hand, so brown."—
"Fear not, fear not, thou Wedding-Guest!
This body dropped not down.

230   *But the ancient Mariner assureth him of his bodily life, and proceedeth to relate his horrible penance.*

"Alone, alone, all, all alone,
Alone on a wide wide sea!
And never a saint took pity on
My soul in agony.

"The many men, so beautiful!
And they all dead did lie:
And a thousand thousand slimy things
Lived on; and so did I.

He despiseth the creatures of the calm

"I looked upon the rotting sea,
And drew my eyes away;
I looked upon the rotting deck,
And there the dead men lay.

240   *And envieth that they should live, and so many lie dead.*

"I looked to heaven, and tried to pray;
But or ever a prayer had gushed,
A wicked whisper came, and made
My heart as dry as dust.

"I closed my lids, and kept them close,
And the balls like pulses beat;
For the sky and the sea, and the sea and the
    sky,   250
Lay like a load on my weary eye,
And the dead were at my feet.

"The cold sweat melted from their limbs,   But the curse
Nor rot nor reek did they: liveth for him in
                                                 the eye of the
The look with which they looked on me   dead men.
Had never passed away.

"An orphan's curse would drag to hell
A spirit from on high;
But oh! more horrible than that
Is the curse in a dead man's eye!   260
Seven days, seven nights, I saw that curse,
And yet I could not die.

"The moving Moon went up the sky,   In his loneliness
And nowhere did abide: and fixedness he
                                                 yearneth   towards
Softly she was going up,   the journeying
And a star or two beside—   Moon, and the
                                                 stars that still so-
                                                 journ, yet still
"Her beams bemocked the sultry main,   move onward; and
                                                 everywhere the
Like April hoar-frost spread;   blue sky belongs
But where the ship's huge shadow lay,   to them, and is
The charmèd water burned alway   270   their appointed
                                                 rest, and their na-
A still and awful red.   tive country and
                                                 their own natural
                                                 homes, which they
"Beyond the shadow of the ship,   enter unan-
I watched the water-snakes: nounced, as lords
                                                 that are certainly
They moved in tracks of shining white,   expected, and yet
And when they reared, the elfish light   there is a silent
                                                 joy at their
Fell off in hoary flakes.   arrival.

"Within the shadow of the ship   By the light of
                                                 the Moon he be-
I watched their rich attire: holdeth God's
Blue, glossy green, and velvet black,   creatures of the
They coiled and swam; and every track   280   great calm.
Was a flash of golden fire.

"O happy living things! no tongue
Their beauty might declare:
A spring of love gushed from my heart,
And I blessed them unaware;
Sure my kind saint took pity on me,
And I blessed them unaware.

Their beauty and their happiness.

He blesseth them in his heart.

The spell begins to break.

"The selfsame moment I could pray;
And from my neck so free
The Albatross fell off, and sank   290
Like lead into the sea."

PART V

"Oh sleep! it is a gentle thing,
Beloved from pole to pole!
To Mary Queen the praise be given!
She sent the gentle sleep from Heaven,
That slid into my soul.

"The silly buckets on the deck,
That had so long remained,
I dreamt that they were filled with dew;
And when I awoke, it rained.   300

By grace of the holy Mother, the ancient Mariner is refreshed with rain.

"My lips were wet, my throat was cold,
My garments all were dank;
Sure I had drunken in my dreams,
And still my body drank.

"I moved, and could not feel my limbs:
I was so light—almost
I thought that I had died in sleep,
And was a blessed ghost.

"And soon I heard a roaring wind:
It did not come anear;   310
But with its sound it shook the sails,
That were so thin and sere.

He heareth sounds and seeth strange sights and commotions in the sky and the element.

"The upper air burst into life!
And a hundred fire-flags sheen,
To and fro they were hurried about!
And to and fro, and in and out,
The wan stars danced between.

"And the coming wind did roar more loud,
And the sails did sigh like sedge;
And the rain poured down from one black
        cloud;   320
The Moon was at its edge.

"The thick black cloud was cleft, and still
The Moon was at its side:
Like waters shot from some high crag,
The lightning fell with never a jag,
A river steep and wide.

"The loud wind never reached the ship,
Yet now the ship moved on!
Beneath the lightning and the Moon
The dead men gave a groan.   330

The bodies of the ship's crew are inspired, and the ship moves on;

"They groaned, they stirred, they all uprose,
Nor spake, nor moved their eyes;
It had been strange, even in a dream,
To have seen those dead men rise.

"The helmsman steered, the ship moved on;
Yet never a breeze up blew;
The mariners all 'gan work the ropes,
Where they were wont to do;
They raised their limbs like lifeless tools—
We were a ghastly crew.   340

"The body of my brother's son
Stood by me, knee to knee:
The body and I pulled at one rope,
But he said nought to me."

"I fear thee, ancient Mariner!"
"Be calm, thou Wedding-Guest!
'Twas not those souls that fled in pain,
Which to their corses came again,
But a troop of spirits blest:

But not by the
souls of the men,
nor by demons of
earth or middle
air, but by a
blessed troop of
angelic spirits,
sent down by the
invocation of the
guardian saint.

"For when it dawned—they dropped their
    arms,   350
And clustered round the mast;
Sweet sounds rose slowly through their mouths,
And from their bodies passed.

"Around, around, flew each sweet sound,
Then darted to the Sun;
Slowly the sounds come back again,
Now mixed, now one by one.

"Sometimes a-dropping from the sky
I heard the sky-lark sing;
Sometimes all little birds that are,   360
How they seemed to fill the sea and air
With their sweet jargoning!

"And now 'twas like all instruments,
Now like a lonely flute;
And now it is an angel's song,
That makes the heavens be mute.

"It ceased; yet still the sails made on
A pleasant noise till noon,
A noise like of a hidden brook
In the leafy month of June,   370
That to the sleeping woods all night
Singeth a quiet tune.

"Till noon we quietly sailed on,
Yet never a breeze did breathe:
Slowly and smoothly went the ship,
Moved onward from beneath.

"Under the keel nine fathom deep,
From the land of mist and snow,
The spirit slid; and it was he
That made the ship to go.   380
The sails at noon left off their tune,
And the ship stood still also.

The lonesome Spirit from the south-pole carries on the ship as far as the Line, in obedience to the angelic troop, but still requireth vengeance.

"The Sun, right up above the mast,
Had fixed her to the ocean;
But in a minute she 'gan stir,
With a short uneasy motion—
Backwards and forwards half her length,
With a short uneasy motion.

"Then like a pawing horse let go,
She made a sudden bound: 390
It flung the blood into my head,
And I fell down in a swound.

"How long in that same fit I lay,
I have not to declare;
But ere my living life returned,
I heard, and in my soul discerned
Two voices in the air.

The Polar Spirit's fellow-demons, the invisible inhabit-ants of the ele-ment, take part in his wrong; and two of them relate one to the other, that penance long and heavy for the ancient Mariner hath been accorded to the Polar Spirit, who returneth southward.

" 'Is it he?' quoth one, 'is this the man?
By Him who died on cross,
With his cruel bow he laid full low   400
The harmless Albatross.

" 'The spirit who bideth by himself
In the land of mist and snow,
He loved the bird that loved the man
Who shot him with his bow.'

"The other was a softer voice,
As soft as honey-dew:
Quoth he, 'The man hath penance done,
And penance more will do.'

PART VI

FIRST VOICE

" 'But tell me, tell me! speak again   410
Thy soft response renewing—
What makes that ship drive on so fast?
What is the ocean doing?'

SECOND VOICE

" 'Still as a slave before his lord,
The ocean hath no blast;
His great bright eye most silently
Up to the Moon is cast—

" 'If he may know which way to go;
For she guides him, smooth or grim.
See, brother, see! how graciously   420
She looketh down on him.'

FIRST VOICE

" 'But why drives on that ship so fast,
Without or wave or wind?'

The Mariner hath been cast into a trance; for the angelic power causeth the vessel to drive northward faster than human life could endure.

SECOND VOICE

" 'The air is cut away before,
And closes from behind.'

" 'Fly, brother, fly! more high, more high!
Or we shall be belated:
For slow and slow that ship will go,
When the Mariner's trance is abated.'

"I woke, and we were sailing on   430
As in a gentle weather:
'Twas night, calm night, the moon was high;
The dead men stood together.

The supernatural motion is retarded; the Mariner awakes, and his penance begins anew.

"All stood together on the deck,
For a charnel-dungeon fitter:
All fixed on me their stony eyes,
That in the Moon did glitter.

"The pang, the curse, with which they died,
Had never passed away:
I could not draw my eyes from theirs,   440
Nor turn them up to pray.

"And now this spell was snapped: once more
I viewed the ocean green,
And looked far forth, yet little saw
Of what had else been seen—

The curse is
finally expiated.

"Like one, that on a lonesome road
Doth walk in fear and dread,
And having once turned round, walks on,
And turns no more his head;
Because he knows, a frightful fiend   450
Doth close behind him tread.

"But soon there breathed a wind on me,
Nor sound nor motion made:
Its path was not upon the sea,
In ripple or in shade.

"It raised my hair, it fanned my cheek
Like a meadow-gale of spring—
It mingled strangely with my fears,
Yet it felt like a welcoming.

"Swiftly, swiftly flew the ship,   460
Yet she sailed softly too:
Sweetly, sweetly blew the breeze—
On me alone it blew.

"Oh! dream of joy! is this indeed
The light-house top I see?
Is this the hill? is this the kirk?
Is this mine own countree?

And the ancient
Mariner beholdeth
his native country.

"We drifted o'er the harbor-bar,
And I with sobs did pray—
O let me be awake, my God!   470
Or let me sleep alway.

"The harbor-bay was clear as glass,
So smoothly it was strewn!
And on the bay the moonlight lay,
And the shadow of the Moon.

"The rock shone bright, the kirk no less,
That stands above the rock:
The moonlight steeped in silentness
The steady weathercock.

"And the bay was white with silent light,   480
Till, rising from the same,
Full many shapes, that shadows were,   The angelic spirits leave the dead bodies,
In crimson colors came.

"A little distance from the prow   And appear in their own forms of light.
Those crimson shadows were:
I turned my eyes upon the deck—
Oh, Christ! what saw I there!

"Each corse lay flat, lifeless and flat,
And, by the holy rood!
A man all light, a seraph-man,   490
On every corse there stood.

"This seraph-band, each waved his hand:
It was a heavenly sight!
They stood as signals to the land,
Each one a lovely light;

"This seraph-band, each waved his hand,
No voice did they impart—
No voice; but oh! the silence sank
Like music on my heart.

"But soon I heard the dash of oars,   500
I heard the Pilot's cheer;
My head was turned perforce away,
And I saw a boat appear.

"The Pilot and the Pilot's boy,
I heard them coming fast:
Dear Lord in Heaven! it was a joy
The dead men could not blast.

"I saw a third—I heard his voice:
It is the Hermit good!
He singeth loud his godly hymns   510
That he makes in the wood.
He'll shrieve my soul, he'll wash away
The Albatross's blood.

PART VII

"This Hermit good lives in that wood   The Hermit of
Which slopes down to the sea.   the Wood,
How loudly his sweet voice he rears!
He loves to talk with marineres
That come from a far countree.

"He kneels at morn, and noon, and eve—
He hath a cushion plump: 520
It is the moss that wholly hides
The rotted old oak-stump.

"The skiff-boat neared: I heard them talk,
'Why, this is strange, I trow!
Where are those lights so many and fair,
That signal made but now?'

" 'Strange, by my faith!' the Hermit said— Approacheth
'And they answered not our cheer!   the ship
The planks look warped! and see those sails, with wonder.
How thin they are and sere!   530
I never saw aught like to them,
Unless perchance it were

" 'Brown skeletons of leaves that lag
My forest-brook along;
When the ivy-tod is heavy with snow,
And the owlet whoops to the wolf below,
That eats the she-wolf's young.'

" 'Dear Lord! it hath a fiendish look—
(The pilot made reply)
I am a-feared'—'Push on, push on!'   540
Said the Hermit cheerily.

"The boat came closer to the ship,
But I nor spake nor stirred;
The boat came close beneath the ship,
And straight a sound was heard.

"Under the water it rumbled on,   The ship suddenly
Still louder and more dread: sinketh.
It reached the ship, it split the bay;
The ship went down like lead.

"Stunned by that loud and dreadful sound,   550   The ancient Mari-
Which sky and ocean smote,   ner is saved in the
                                                    Pilot's boat.
Like one that hath been seven days drowned,
My body lay afloat;
But swift as dreams, myself I found
Within the Pilot's boat.

"Upon the whirl, where sank the ship,
The boat spun round and round;
And all was still, save that the hill
Was telling of the sound.

"I moved my lips—the Pilot shrieked,   560
And fell down in a fit;
The holy Hermit raised his eyes,
And prayed where he did sit.

"I took the oars: the Pilot's boy,
Who now doth crazy go,
Laughed loud and long, and all the while
His eyes went to and fro.
'Ha! ha!' quoth he, 'full plain I see,
The Devil knows how to row.'

"And now, all in my own countree,   570
I stood on the firm land!
The Hermit stepped forth from the boat,
And scarcely he could stand.

" 'O shrieve me, shrieve me, holy man!'
The Hermit crossed his brow.
'Say quick,' quoth he, 'I bid thee say—
What manner of man art thou?'

The ancient Mari-
ner earnestly en-
treateth the
Hermit to shrieve
him; and the
penance of life
falls on him.

"Forthwith this frame of mine was wrenched
With a woeful agony,
Which forced me to begin my tale;   580
And then it left me free.

"Since then at an uncertain hour,
That agony returns;
And till my ghastly tale is told,
This heart within me burns.

And ever and
anon throughout
his future life an
agony constraineth
him to travel
from land to
land,

"I pass, like night, from land to land;
I have strange power of speech;
That moment that his face I see,
I know the man that must hear me:
To him my tale I teach.   590

"What loud uproar bursts from that door!
The wedding-guests are there;
But in the garden-bower the bride
And bride-maids singing are;
And hark the little vesper bell,
Which biddeth me to prayer!

"O Wedding-Guest! this soul hath been
Alone on a wide, wide sea:
So lonely 'twas, that God himself
Scarce seemèd there to be.   600

"O sweeter than the marriage-feast,
'Tis sweeter far to me,
To walk together to the kirk
With a goodly company!—

"To walk together to the kirk,
And all together pray,
While each to his great Father bends,
Old men, and babes, and loving friends,
And youths and maidens gay!

"Farewell, farewell! but this I tell   610   And to teach by
To thee, thou Wedding-Guest!   his own example
                                                    love and reverence
He prayeth well, who loveth well   to all things that
                                                    God made and
Both man and bird and beast.   loveth.

"He prayeth best, who loveth best
All things both great and small;
For the dear God who loveth us,
He made and loveth all."

The Mariner, whose eye is bright,
Whose beard with age is hoar,
Is gone: and now the Wedding-Guest   620
Turned from the bridegroom's door.

He went like one that hath been stunned,
And is of sense forlorn:
A sadder and a wiser man,
He rose the morrow morn.

                    1798

SIR WALTER SCOTT

Brignal Banks

O, Brignal banks are wild and fair,
    And Greta woods are green,
And you may gather garlands there
    Would grace a summer queen.
And as I rode by Dalton-hall,
    Beneath the turrets high,
A maiden on the castle wall
    Was singing merrily,—
'O, Brignal banks are fresh and fair,
    And Greta woods are green;   10

I'd rather rove with Edmund there,
　　Than reign our English queen.'

'If, maiden, thou wouldst wend with me,
　　To leave both tower and town,
Thou first must guess what life lead we,
　　That dwell by dale and down.
And if thou canst that riddle read,
　　As read full well you may,
Then to the greenwood shalt thou speed,
　　As blithe as Queen of May.'   20
Yet sung she, 'Brignal banks are fair,
　　And Greta woods are green;
I'd rather rove with Edmund there,
　　Than reign our English queen.

'I read you, by your bugle-horn,
　　And by your palfrey good,
I read you for a ranger sworn,
　　To keep the king's greenwood.'
'A ranger, lady, winds his horn,
　　And 'tis at peep of light;
His blast is heard at merry morn,
　　And mine at dead of night.'
Yet sung she, 'Brignal banks are fair,
　　And Greta woods are gay;   10
I would I were with Edmund there,
　　To reign his Queen of May!

'With burnish'd brand and musketoon,
　　So gallantly you come,
I read you for a bold dragoon,
　　That lists the tuck of drum.'
'I list no more the tuck of drum,
　　No more the trumpet hear;
But when the beetle sounds his hum,
　　My comrades take the spear.   20
And O! though Brignal banks be fair,
　　And Greta woods be gay,

Yet mickle must the maiden dare,
   Would reign my Queen of May!

'Maiden! a nameless life I lead,
   A nameless death I'll die;
The fiend, whose lantern lights the mead,
   Were better mate than I!
And when I'm with my comrades met
   Beneath the greenwood bough,   30
What once we were we all forget,
   Nor think what we are now.
Yet Brignal banks are fresh and fair,
   And Greta woods are green,
And you may gather garlands there
   Would grace a summer queen.'

1812

GEORGE GORDON, LORD BYRON

The Prisoner of Chillon [1]

My hair is gray, but not with years;
   Nor grew it white
   In a single night,
As men's have grown from sudden fears:
My limbs are bowed, though not with toil,
   But rusted with a vile repose,
For they have been a dungeon's spoil,
   And mine has been the fate of those
To whom the goodly earth and air
Are banned, and barred—forbidden fare;   10
But this was for my father's faith
I suffered chains and courted death:
That father perished at the stake
For tenets he would not forsake;
And for the same his lineal race
In darkness found a dwelling-place.

[1] Chillon is a castle in Switzerland where the Swiss patriot Bonnivard was imprisoned in the sixteenth century.

We were seven—who now are one;
    Six in youth, and one in age,
Finished as they had begun,
    Proud of Persecution's rage;   20
One in fire, and two in field,
Their belief with blood have sealed
Dying as their father died,
For the God their foes denied;—
Three were in a dungeon cast,
Of whom this wreck is left the last.
There are seven pillars of Gothic mould,
In Chillon's dungeons deep and old;
There are seven columns, massy and gray,
Dim with a dull imprisoned ray,   30
A sunbeam which hath lost its way,
And through the crevice and the cleft
Of the thick wall is fallen and left:
Creeping o'er the floor so damp,
Like a marsh's meteor lamp:
And in each pillar there is a ring,
    And in each ring there is a chain;
That iron is a cankering thing,
    For in these limbs its teeth remain,
With marks that will not wear away,   40
Till I have done with this new day,
Which now is painful to these eyes,
Which have not seen the sun so rise
For years—I cannot count them o'er;
I lost their long and heavy score
When my last brother drooped and died,
And I lay living by his side.

They chained us each to a column stone,
And we were three—yet each alone;
We could not move a single pace,   50
We could not see each other's face,
But with that pale and livid light
That made us strangers in our sight:
And thus together—yet apart,

Fettered in hand, but joined in heart,
'Twas still some solace in the dearth
Of the pure elements of earth,
To hearken to each other's speech,
And each turn comforter to each,
With some new hope, or legend old,   60
Or song heroically bold;
But even these at length grew cold.
Our voices took a dreary tone,
An echo of the dungeon-stone,
    A grating sound—not full and free
    As they of yore were wont to be:
    It might be fancy—but to me
They never sounded like our own.

I was the eldest of the three;
    And to uphold and cheer the rest   70
    I ought to do—and did—my best,
And each did well in his degree.
    The youngest, whom my father loved,
Because our mother's brow was given
To him—with eyes as blue as heaven,—
    For him my soul was sorely moved.
And truly might it be distressed
To see such bird in such a nest;
For he was beautiful as day—
    (When day was beautiful to me   80
    As to young eagles, being free)—
    A polar day, which will not see
A sunset till its summer's gone,
    Its sleepless summer of long light,
The snow-clad offspring of the sun:
    And thus he was as pure and bright,
And in his natural spirit gay,
With tears for naught but others' ills,
And then they flowed like mountain rills,
Unless he could assuage the woe   90
Which he abhorred to view below.

The other was as pure of mind,
But formed to combat with his kind;
Strong in his frame, and of a mood
Which 'gainst the world in war had stood,
And perished in the foremost rank
   With joy—but not in chains to pine:
His spirit withered with their clank,
   I saw it silently decline—
   And so perchance in sooth did mine;   100
But yet I forced it on to cheer
Those relics of a home so dear.
He was a hunter of the hills,
   Had followed there the deer and wolf;
   To him this dungeon was a gulf,
And fettered feet the worst of ills.

   Lake Leman lies by Chillon's walls:
A thousand feet in depth below
Its massy waters meet and flow;
Thus much the fathom line was sent   110
From Chillon's snow-white battlement,
   Which round about the wave enthralls:
A double dungeon wall and wave
Have made—and like a living grave.
Below the surface of the lake
The dark vault lies wherein we lay;
We heard it ripple night and day;
   Sounding o'er our heads it knocked;
And I have felt the winter's spray
Wash through the bars when winds were high   120
And wanton in the happy sky;
   And then the very rock hath rocked,
   And I have felt it shake, unshocked,
Because I could have smiled to see
The death that would have set me free.

I said my nearer brother pined,
I said his mighty heart declined,
He loathed and put away his food:
It was not that 'twas coarse and rude

For we were used to hunter's fare,   130
And for the like had little care:
The milk drawn from the mountain goat
Was changed for water from the moat,
Our bread was such as captive's tears
Have moistened many a thousand years,
Since man first pent his fellow men
Like brutes within an iron den;
But what were these to us or him?
These wasted not his heart or limb;
My brother's soul was of that mould   140
Which in a palace had grown cold,
Had his free breathing been denied
The range of the steep mountain's side;
But why delay the truth?—he died.

I saw, and could not hold his head,
Nor reach his dying hand—nor dead,—
Though hard I strove, but strove in vain,
To rend and gnash my bonds in twain.
He died—and they unlocked his chain,
And scooped for him a shallow grave   150
Even from the cold earth of our cave.
I begged them, as a boon, to lay
His corse in dust whereon the day
Might shine—it was a foolish thought,
But then within my brain it wrought,
That even in death his freeborn breast
In such a dungeon could not rest.
I might have spared my idle prayer—
They coldly laughed—and laid him there:
The flat and turfless earth above   160
The being we so much did love;
His empty chain above it leant,
Such murder's fitting monument!
But he, the favorite and the flower,
Most cherished since his natal hour,
His mother's image in fair face,
The infant love of all his race,

His martyred father's dearest thought,
My latest care, for whom I sought
To hoard my life, that his might be   170
Less wretched now, and one day free;
He, too, who yet had held untired
A spirit natural or inspired—
He, too, was struck, and day by day
Was withered on the stalk away.
Oh, God! it is a fearful thing
To see the human soul take wing
In any shape, in any mood:—
I've seen it rushing forth in blood,
I've seen it on the breaking ocean   180
Strive with a swoln convulsive motion,
I've seen the sick and ghastly bed
Of Sin delirious with its dread:
But these were horrors—this was woe
Unmixed with such—but sure and slow:
He faded, and so calm and meek,
So softly worn, so sweetly weak,
So tearless, yet so tender—kind,
And grieved for those he left behind;
With all the while a cheek whose bloom   190
Was as a mockery of the tomb,
Whose tints as gently sunk away
As a departing rainbow's ray;
An eye of most transparent light,
That almost made the dungeon bright;
And not a word of murmur, not
A groan o'er his untimely lot,—
A little talk of better days,
A little hope my own to raise,
For I was sunk in silence—lost   200
In this last loss, of all the most;
And then the sighs he would suppress
Of fainting nature's feebleness,
More slowly drawn, grew less and less:
I listened, but I could not hear;
I called, for I was wild with fear;

I knew 'twas hopeless, but my dread
Would not be thus admonishèd;
I called, and thought I heard a sound—
I burst my chain with one strong bound,   210
And rushed to him:—I found him not,
I only stirred in this black spot,
I only lived, *I* only drew
The accursed breath of dungeon-dew;
The last, the sole, the dearest link
Between me and the eternal brink,
Which bound me to my failing race,
Was broken in this fatal place.
One on the earth, and one beneath—
My brothers—both had ceased to breathe: 220
I took that hand which lay so still,
Alas! my own was full as chill;
I had not strength to stir, or strive,
But felt that I was still alive—
A frantic feeling, when we know
That what we love shall ne'er be so.
     I know not why
     I could not die,
I had no earthly hope but faith,
And that forbade a selfish death.   230

What next befell me then and there
   I know not well—I never knew—
First came the loss of light, and air,
   And then of darkness too:
I had no thought, no feeling—none—
Among the stones I stood a stone,
And was, scarce conscious what I wist,
As shrubless crags within the mist;
For all was blank, and bleak, and gray,
It was not night—it was not day;   240
It was not even the dungeon-light,
So hateful to my heavy sight,
But vacancy absorbing space,
And fixedness, without a place:

There were no stars,—no earth,—no time,—
No check,—no change,—no good,—no crime,—
But silence, and a stirless breath
Which neither was of life nor death;
A sea of stagnant idleness,
Blind, boundless, mute, and motionless!   250

A light broke in upon my brain—
   It was the carol of a bird;
It ceased, and then it came again.
   The sweetest song ear ever heard;
And mine was thankful, till my eyes
Ran over with the glad surprise.
And they that moment could not see
I was the mate of misery;
But then by dull degrees came back
My senses to their wonted track,   260
I saw the dungeon walls and floor
Close slowly round me as before,
I saw the glimmer of the sun
Creeping as it before had done,
But through the crevice where it came
That bird was perched, as fond and tame,
   And tamer than upon the tree;
A lovely bird, with azure wings,
And song that said a thousand things,
   And seemed to say them all for me!   270

I never saw its like before.
I ne'er shall see its likeness more!
It seemed, like me, to want a mate,
But was not half so desolate,
And it was come to love me when
None lived to love me so again,
And cheering from my dungeon's brink,
Had brought me back to feel and think.
I know not if it late were free,
   Or broke its cage to perch on mine,   280
But knowing well captivity,
   Sweet bird, I could not wish for thine!

Or if it were, in wingèd guise,
A visitant from Paradise;
For—Heaven forgive that thought! the while
Which made me both to weep and smile;
I sometimes deemed that it might be
My brother's soul come down to me;
But then at last away it flew,
And then 'twas mortal—well I knew,   290
For he would never thus have flown,
And left me twice so doubly lone—
Lone,—as the corse within its shroud;
Lone,—as a solitary cloud,
    A single cloud on a sunny day,
While all the rest of heaven is clear,
A frown upon the atmosphere,
That hath no business to appear
    When skies are blue and earth is gay.

A kind of change came in my fate,   300
My keepers grew compassionate:
I know not what had made them so,
They were inured to sights of woe;
But so it was—my broken chain
With links unfastened did remain,
And it was liberty to stride
Along my cell from side to side,
And up and down, and then athwart,
And tread it over every part;
And round the pillars one by one,   310
Returning where my walk begun,
Avoiding only, as I trod,
My brothers' graves without a sod;
For if I thought with heedless tread
My step profaned their lowly bed,
My breath came gaspingly and thick,
And my crushed heart fell blind and sick.

I made a footing in the wall,
    It was not therefrom to escape,
For I had buried one and all   320

Who loved me in a human shape;
And the whole earth would henceforth be
A wider prison unto me:
No child—no sire—no kin had I,
No partner in my misery;
I thought of this, and I was glad,
For thought of them had made me mad;
But I was curious to ascend
To my barred windows, and to bend
Once more, upon the mountains high,   330
The quiet of a loving eye.
I saw them—and they were the same,
They were not changed like me in frame;
I saw their thousand years of snow
On high—their wide long lake below,
And the blue Rhone in fullest flow;
I heard the torrents leap and gush
O'er channeled rock and broken bush;
I saw the white-walled distant town,
And whiter sails go skimming down;   340
And then there was a little isle,
Which in my very face did smile,
     The only one in view:
A small green isle, it seemed no more,
Scarce broader than my dungeon floor;
But in it there were three tall trees,
And o'er it blew the mountain breeze,
And by it there were waters flowing,
And on it there were young flowers growing,
     Of gentle breath and hue.   350
The fish swam by the castle wall,
And they seemed joyous, each and all;
The eagle rode the rising blast,
Methought he never flew so fast
As then to me he seemed to fly,
And then new tears came in my eye,
And I felt troubled—and would fain
I had not left my recent chain;
And when I did descend again,

The darkness of my dim abode   360
Fell on me as a heavy load;
It was as is a new-dug grave,
Closing o'er one we sought to save.
And yet my glance, too much oppressed,
Had almost need of such a rest.

It might be months, or years, or days,
    I kept no count—I took no note,
I had no hope my eyes to raise,
    And clear them of their dreary mote;
At last men came to set me free,   370
    I asked not why, and recked not where;
It was at length the same to me,
Fettered or fetterless to be,
    I learned to love despair.
And thus, when they appeared at last,
And all my bonds aside were cast,
These heavy walls to me had grown
A hermitage—and all my own!
And half I felt as they were come
To tear me from a second home: 380
With spiders I had friendship made,
And watched them in their sullen trade,
Had seen the mice by moonlight play,
And why should I feel less than they?
We were all inmates of one place,
And I, the monarch of each race,
Had power to kill—yet, strange to tell!
In quiet we had learned to dwell—
My very chains and I grew friends.
So much a long communion tends   390
To make us what we are:—even I
Regained my freedom with a sigh.

                                    1816

JOHN KEATS

The Eve of St. Agnes [1]

St. Agnes' Eve—ah, bitter chill it was!
The owl, for all his feathers, was a-cold;
The hare limped trembling through the frozen grass,
And silent was the flock in woolly fold;
Numb were the Beadsman's fingers while he told
His rosary, and while his frosted breath,
Like pious incense from a censer old,
Seemed taking flight for heaven without a death,
Past the sweet Virgin's picture, while his prayer he saith.

His prayer he saith, this patient, holy man;   10
Then takes his lamp, and riseth from his knees,
And back returneth, meager, barefoot, wan,
Along the chapel aisle by slow degrees:
The sculptured dead, on each side, seem to freeze,
Emprisoned in black, purgatorial rails:
Knights, ladies, praying in dumb orat'ries,
He passeth by; and his weak spirit fails
To think how they may ache in icy hoods and mails.

Northward he turneth through a little door,
And scarce three steps, ere Music's golden tongue   20
Flattered to tears this agéd man and poor.
But no—already had his death-bell rung;
The joys of all his life were said and sung;
His was harsh penance on St. Agnes' Eve:
Another way he went, and soon among
Rough ashes sat he for his soul's reprieve,
And all night kept awake, for sinners' sake to grieve.

That ancient Beadsman heard the prelude soft;
And so it chanced, for many a door was wide,
From hurry to and fro. Soon, up aloft,   30
The silver, snarling trumpets 'gan to chide:

[1] The Eve of St. Agnes falls on January 20. On this night maidens may, by fasting, see their future husbands in a glass.

The level chambers, ready with their pride,
Were glowing to receive a thousand guests:
The carvéd angels, ever eager-eyed,
Stared, where upon their heads the cornice rests,
With hair blown back, and wings put cross wise on their
    breasts.

At length burst in the argent revelry,
With plume, tiara, and all rich array,
Numerous as shadows haunting fairily
The brain, new-stuffed, in youth, with triumphs gay   40
Of old romance. These let us wish away.
And turn, sole-thoughted, to one Lady there,
Whose heart had brooded, all that wintry day,
On love, and winged St. Agnes' saintly care,
As she had heard old dames full many times declare.

They told her how, upon St. Agnes' Eve,
Young virgins might have visions of delight,
And soft adorings from their loves receive
Upon the honeyed middle of the night,
If ceremonies due they did aright;   50
As, supperless to bed they must retire,
And couch supine their beauties, lily white;
Nor look behind, nor sideways, but require
Of Heaven with upward eyes for all that they desire.

Full of this whim was thoughtful Madeline:
The music, yearning like a God in pain,
She scarcely heard: her maiden eyes divine,
Fixed on the floor, saw many a sweeping train
Pass by—she heeded not at all: in vain
Came many a tiptoe, amorous cavalier,   60
And back retired; not cooled by high disdain,
But she saw not: her heart was otherwhere;
She sighed for Agnes' dreams, the sweetest of the year.

She danced along with vague, regardless eyes,
Anxious her lips, her breathing quick and short:
The hallowed hour was near at hand: she sighs
Amid the timbrels, and the thronged resort

Of whisperers in anger or in sport;
'Mid looks of love, defiance, hate, and scorn,
Hoodwinked with fairy fancy; all amort,   70
Save to St. Agnes and her lambs unshorn,
And all the bliss to be before to-morrow morn.

So, purposing each moment to retire,
She lingered still. Meantime, across the moors,
Had come young Porphyro, with heart on fire
For Madeline. Beside the portal doors,
Buttressed from moonlight, stands he, and implores
All saints to give him sight of Madeline,
But for one moment in the tedious hours,
That he might gaze and worship all unseen;   80
Perchance speak, kneel, touch, kiss—in sooth such things have
    been.

He ventures in: let no buzzed whisper tell;
All eyes be muffled, or a hundred swords
Will storm his heart, Love's fev'rous citadel:
For him, those chambers held barbarian hordes,
Hyena foemen, and hot-blooded lords,
Whose very dogs would execrations howl
Against his lineage; not one breast affords
Him any mercy in that mansion foul,
Save one old beldame, weak in body and in soul.   90

Ah, happy chance! the agéd creature came
Shuffling along with ivory-headed wand,
To where he stood, hid from the torch's flame,
Behind a broad hall-pillar, far beyond
The sound of merriment and chorus bland.
He startled her; but soon she knew his face,
And grasped his fingers in her palsied hand,
Saying, "Mercy, Porphyro! hie thee from this place;
They are all here to-night, the whole blood-thirsty race!

"Get hence! get hence! there's dwarfish Hildebrand;   100
He had a fever late, and in the fit

71. St. Agnes always appears with lambs.

He curséd thee and thine, both house and land:
Then there's that old Lord Maurice, not a whit
More tame for his gray hairs—Alas me! flit!
Flit like a ghost away."—"Ah, Gossip dear,
We're safe enough; here in this arm-chair sit,
And tell me how"—"Good saints! not here, not here;
Follow me, child, or else these stones will be thy bier."

He followed through a lowly archéd way,
Brushing the cobwebs with his lofty plume,   110
And as she muttered "Well-a—well-a-day!"
He found him in a little moonlight room,
Pale, latticed, chill, and silent as a tomb.
"Now tell me where is Madeline," said he,
"O tell me, Angela, by the holy loom
Which none but secret sisterhood may see,
When they St. Agnes' wool are weaving piously."

"St. Agnes! Ah! it is St. Agnes' Eve—
Yet men will murder upon holy days:
Thou must hold water in a witch's sieve,   120
And be liege-lord of all the Elves and Fays
To venture so: it fills me with amaze
To see thee, Porphyro!—St. Agnes' Eve!
God's help! my lady fair the conjurer plays
This very night: good angels her deceive!
But let me laugh awhile,—I've mickle time to grieve."

Feebly she laugheth in the languid moon,
While Porphyro upon her face doth look,
Like puzzled urchin on an agéd crone
Who keepeth closed a wondrous riddle-book,   130
As spectacled she sits in chimney nook.
But soon his eyes grew brilliant, when she told
His lady's purpose; and he scarce could brook
Tears, at the thought of those enchantments cold,
And Madeline asleep in lap of legends old.

Sudden a thought came like a full-blown rose,
Flushing his brow, and in his painéd heart

Made purple riot: then doth he propose
A stratagem, that makes the beldame start:
"A cruel man and impious thou art: 140
Sweet lady! let her pray, and sleep, and dream
Alone with her good angels, far apart
From wicked men like thee. Go, go! I deem
Thou canst not surely be the same that thou didst seem."

"I will not harm her, by all saints I swear,"
Quoth Porphyro: "O may I ne'er find grace
When my weak voice shall whisper its last prayer,
If one of her soft ringlets I displace,
Or look with ruffian passion in her face.
Good Angela, believe me, by these tears,   150
Or I will, even in a moment's space,
Awake, with horrid shout, my foemen's ears,
And beard them, though they be more fanged than wolves
    and bears."

"Ah! why wilt thou affright a feeble soul?
A poor, weak, palsy-stricken, churchyard thing,
Whose passing-bell may ere the midnight toll;
Whose prayers for thee, each morn and evening,
Were never missed." Thus plaining, doth she bring
A gentler speech from burning Porphyro;
So woeful, and of such deep sorrowing,   160
That Angela gives promise she will do
Whatever he shall wish, betide her weal or woe.

Which was, to lead him, in close secrecy,
Even to Madeline's chamber, and there hide
Him in a closet, of such privacy
That he might see her beauty unespied,
And win perhaps that night a peerless bride,
While legioned fairies paced the coverlet,
And pale enchantment held her sleepy-eyed.
Never on such a night have lovers met,   170
Since Merlin paid his Demon all the monstrous debt.

"It shall be as thou wishest," said the Dame:
"All cates and dainties shall be stored there

Quickly on this feast-night: by the tambour-frame
Her own lute thou wilt see: no time to spare,
For I am slow and feeble, and scarce dare
On such a catering trust my dizzy head.
Wait here, my child, with patience; kneel in prayer
The while. Ah! thou must needs the lady wed,
Or may I never leave my grave among the dead." 180

So saying, she hobbled off with busy fear.
The lover's endless minutes slowly passed;
The dame returned, and whispered in his ear
To follow her; with agéd eyes aghast
From fright of dim espial. Safe at last,
Through many a dusky gallery, they gain
The maiden's chamber, silken, hushed, and chaste;
Where Porphyro took covert, pleased amain.
His poor guide hurried back with agues in her brain.

Her faltering hand upon the balustrade, 190
Old Angela was feeling for the stair,
When Madeline, St. Agnes' charméd-maid,
Rose, like a missioned spirit, unaware:
With silver taper's light, and pious care,
She turned, and down the agéd gossip led
To a safe level matting. Now prepare,
Young Porphyro, for gazing on that bed;
She comes, she comes again, like ring-dove frayed and fled.

Out went the taper as she hurried in;
Its little smoke, in pallid moonshine, died: 200
She closed the door, she panted, all akin
To spirits of the air, and visions wide:
No uttered syllable, or, woe betide!
But to her heart, her heart was voluble,
Paining with eloquence her balmy side;
As though a tongueless nightingale should swell
Her throat in vain, and die, heart-stifled, in her dell.

A casement high and triple-arched there was,
All garlanded with carven imag'ries,
Of fruits and flowers, and bunches of knot-grass, 210

And diamonded with panes of quaint device,
Innumerable of stains and splendid dyes,
As are the tiger-moth's deep-damasked wings;
And in the midst, 'mong thousand heraldries,
And twilight saints, and dim emblazonings,
A shielded scutcheon blushed with blood of queens and kings.

Full on this casement shone the wintry moon,
And threw warm gules on Madeline's fair breast,
As down she knelt for Heaven's grace and boon;
Rose-bloom fell on her hands, together pressed,   220
And on her silver cross soft amethyst,
And on her hair a glory, like a saint:
She seemed a splendid angel, newly dressed,
Save wings, for heaven:—Porphyro grew faint:
She knelt, so pure a thing, so free from mortal taint.

Anon his heart revives: her vespers done,
Of all its wreathéd pearls her hair she frees;
Unclasps her warméd jewels one by one;
Loosens her fragrant bodice; by degrees
Her rich attire creeps rustling to her knees: 230
Half-hidden, like a mermaid in sea-weed,
Pensive awhile she dreams awake, and sees,
In fancy, fair St. Agnes in her bed,
But dares not look behind, or all the charm is fled.

Soon, trembling in her soft and chilly nest,
In sort of wakeful swoon, perplexed she lay,
Until the poppied warmth of sleep oppressed
Her soothéd limbs, and soul fatigued away;
Flown, like a thought, until the morrow-day;
Blissfully havened both from joy and pain;   240
Clasped like a missal where swart Paynims pray;
Blinded alike from sunshine and from rain,
As though a rose should shut, and be a bud again.

Stol'n to this paradise, and so entranced,
Porphyro gazed upon her empty dress,
And listened to her breathing, if it chanced
To wake into a slumberous tenderness;

Which when he heard, that minute did he bless,
And breathed himself: then from the closet crept,
Noiseless as fear in a wide wilderness, 250
And over the hushed carpet, silent, stepped,
And 'tween the curtains peeped, where, lo!—how fast she
    slept.

Then by the bedside, where the faded moon
Made a dim, silver twilight, soft he set
A table, and, half anguished, threw thereon
A cloth of woven crimson, gold, and jet:—
O for some drowsy Morphean amulet!
The boisterous, midnight, festive clarion,
The kettle-drum, and far-heard clarinet,
Affray his ears, though but in dying tone:— 260
The hall-door shuts again, and all the noise is gone.

And still she slept an azure-lidded sleep,
In blanchéd linen, smooth, and lavendered,
While he from forth the closet brought a heap
Of candied apple, quince, and plum, and gourd;
With jellies soother than the creamy curd,
And lucent syrops, tinct with cinnamon;
Manna and dates, in argosy transferred
From Fez; and spicéd dainties, every one,
From silken Samarcand to cedared Lebanon. 270

These delicates he heaped with glowing hand
On golden dishes and in baskets bright
Of wreathéd silver: sumptuous they stand
In the retiréd quiet of the night,
Filling the chilly room with perfume light.—
"And now, my love, my seraph fair, awake!
Thou art my heaven, and I thine eremite:
Open thine eyes, for meek St. Agnes' sake,
Or I shall drowse beside thee, so my soul doth ache."

Thus whispering, his warm, unnervéd arm 280
Sank in her pillow. Shaded was her dream
By the dusk curtains:—'twas a midnight charm
Impossible to melt as icéd stream:

The lustrous salvers in the moonlight gleam;
Broad golden fringe upon the carpet lies:
It seemed he never, never could redeem
From such a steadfast spell his lady's eyes;
So mused awhile, entoiled in wooféd phantasies.

Awakening up, he took her hollow lute,—
Tumultuous,—and, in chords that tenderest be,   290
He played an ancient ditty, long since mute,
In Provence called "La belle dame sans mercy":
Close to her ear touching the melody;—
Wherewith disturbed, she uttered a soft moan:
He ceased—she panted quick—and suddenly
Her blue affrayéd eyes wide open shone:
Upon his knees he sank, pale as smooth-sculptured stone.

Her eyes were open, but she still beheld,
Now wide awake, the vision of her sleep:
There was a painful change, that nigh expelled   300
The blisses of her dream so pure and deep,
At which fair Madeline began to weep,
And moan forth witless words with many a sigh,
While still her gaze on Porphyro would keep;
Who knelt, with joinéd hands and piteous eye,
Fearing to move or speak, she looked so dreamingly.

"Ah, Porphyro!" said she, "but even now
Thy voice was at sweet tremble in mine ear,
Made tunable with every sweetest vow;
And those sad eyes were spiritual and clear: 310
How changed thou art! how pallid, chill, and drear!
Give me that voice again, my Porphyro,
Those looks immortal, those complainings dear!
Oh leave me not in this eternal woe,
For if thou diest, my Love, I know not where to go."

Beyond a mortal man impassioned far
At these voluptuous accents, he arose,
Ethereal, flushed, and like a throbbing star
Seen 'mid the sapphire heaven's deep repose;
Into her dream he melted, as the rose   320

Blendeth its odor with the violet,—
Solution sweet: meantime the frost-wind blows
Like Love's alarum, pattering the sharp sleet
Against the window-panes; St. Agnes' moon hath set.

'Tis dark: quick pattereth the flaw-blown sleet:
"This is no dream, my bride, my Madeline!"
'Tis dark: the icéd gusts still rave and beat:
"No dream, alas! alas! and woe is mine!
Porphyro will leave me here to fade and pine.
Cruel! what traitor could thee hither bring?   330
I curse not, for my heart is lost in thine,
Though thou forsakest a deceivéd thing;—
A dove forlorn and lost with sick unprunéd wing."

"My Madeline! sweet dreamer! lovely bride!
Say, may I be for aye thy vassal blest?
Thy beauty's shield, heart-shaped and vermeil-dyed?
Ah, silver shrine, here will I take my rest
After so many hours of toil and quest,
A famished pilgrim,—saved by miracle.
Though I have found, I will not rob thy nest,   340
Saving of thy sweet self; if thou think'st well
To trust, fair Madeline, to no rude infidel.

"Hark! 'tis an elfin storm from fairy land,
Of haggard seeming, but a boon indeed:
Arise—arise! the morning is at hand;—
The bloated wassailers will never heed;—
Let us away, my love, with happy speed;
There are no ears to hear, or eyes to see,—
Drowned all in Rhenish and the sleepy mead.
Awake! arise! my love, and fearless be,   350
For o'er the southern moors I have a home for thee."

She hurried at his words, beset with fears,
For there were sleeping dragons all around,
At glaring watch, perhaps, with ready spears—
Down the wide stairs a darkling way they found;
In all the house was heard no human sound.
A chain-drooped lamp was flickering by each door;

The arras, rich with horseman, hawk, and hound,
Fluttered in the besieging wind's uproar;
And the long carpets rose along the gusty floor.   360

They glide, like phantoms, into the wide hall;
Like phantoms to the iron porch they glide;
Where lay the Porter, in uneasy sprawl,
With a huge empty flagon by his side:
The wakeful bloodhound rose, and shook his hide,
But his sagacious eye an inmate owns:
By one, and one, the bolts full easy slide:—
The chains lie silent on the footworn stones;
The key turns, and the door upon its hinges groans.

And they are gone: ay, ages long ago   370
These lovers fled away into the storm.
That night the Baron dreamed of many a woe,
And all his warrior-guests, with shade and form
Of witch, and demon, and large coffin-worm,
Were long be-nightmared. Angela the old
Died palsy-twitched, with meager face deform;
The Beadsman, after thousand aves told,
For aye unsought-for slept among his ashes cold.

1820

ALFRED, LORD TENNYSON

The Lady of Shalott

PART I

On either side the river lie
Long fields of barley and of rye,
That clothe the wold and meet the sky;
And through the field the road runs by
    To many-towered Camelot;
And up and down the people go,
Gazing where the lilies blow
Round an island there below,
    The island of Shalott.

Willows whiten, aspens quiver,   10
Little breezes dusk and shiver
Through the wave that runs for ever
By the island in the river
   Flowing down to Camelot.
Four gray walls, and four gray towers,
Overlook a space of flowers,
And the silent isle imbowers
   The Lady of Shalott.

By the margin, willow-veiled,
Slide the heavy barges trailed   20
By slow horses; and unhailed
The shallop flitteth silken-sailed
   Skimming down to Camelot:
But who hath seen her wave her hand?
Or at the casement seen her stand?
Or is she known in all the land,
   The Lady of Shalott?

Only reapers, reaping early
In among the bearded barley,
Hear a song that echoes cheerly   30
From the river winding clearly,
   Down to towered Camelot;
And by the moon the reaper weary,
Piling sheaves in uplands airy,
Listening, whispers " 'Tis the fairy
   Lady of Shalott."

PART II

There she weaves by night and day
A magic web with colors gay.
She has heard a whisper say,
A curse is on her if she stay   40
   To look down to Camelot.
She knows not what the curse may be,
And so she weaveth steadily,

And little other care hath she,
   The Lady of Shalott.

And moving through a mirror clear
That hangs before her all the year,
Shadows of the world appear.
There she sees the highway near
   Winding down to Camelot;   50
There the river eddy whirls,
And there the surly village-churls,
And the red cloaks of market girls,
   Pass onward from Shalott.

Sometimes a troop of damsels glad,
An abbot on an ambling pad,
Sometimes a curly shepherd-lad,
Or long-haired page in crimson clad,
   Goes by to towered Camelot;
And sometimes through the mirror blue   60
The knights come riding two and two:
She hath no loyal knight and true,
   The Lady of Shalott.

But in her web she still delights
To weave the mirror's magic sights,
For often through the silent nights
A funeral, with plumes and lights
   And music, went to Camelot;
Or when the moon was overhead,
Came two young lovers lately wed: 70
"I am half sick of shadows," said
   The Lady of Shalott.

PART III

A bow-shot from her bower-eaves,
He rode between the barley-sheaves,
The sun came dazzling through the leaves,
And flamed upon the brazen greaves
   Of bold Sir Lancelot.

A red-cross knight for ever kneeled
To a lady in his shield,
That sparkled on the yellow field, 80
Beside remote Shalott.

The gemmy bridle glittered free,
Like to some branch of stars we see
Hung in the golden Galaxy.
The bridle bells rang merrily
    As he rode down to Camelot;
And from his blazoned baldric slung
A mighty silver bugle hung,
And as he rode his armor rung,
    Beside remote Shalott. 90

All in the blue unclouded weather
Thick-jeweled shone the saddle-leather,
The helmet and the helmet-feather
Burned like one burning flame together,
    As he rode down to Camelot;
As often through the purple night,
Below the starry clusters bright,
Some bearded meteor, trailing light,
    Moves over still Shalott.

His broad clear brow in sunlight glowed; 100
On burnished hooves his war-horse trode;
From underneath his helmet flowed
His coal-black curls as on he rode,
    As he rode down to Camelot.
From the bank and from the river
He flashed into the crystal mirror,
"Tirra lirra," by the river
    Sang Sir Lancelot.

She left the web, she left the loom,
She made three paces through the room, 110
She saw the water-lily bloom,
She saw the helmet and the plume,
    She looked down to Camelot.

Out flew the web and floated wide;
The mirror cracked from side to side;
"The curse is come upon me," cried
    The Lady of Shalott.

PART IV

In the stormy east-wind straining,
The pale yellow woods were waning,
The broad stream in his banks complaining,   120
Heavily the low sky raining
    Over towered Camelot;
Down she came and found a boat
Beneath a willow left afloat,
And round about the prow she wrote
    The Lady of Shalott.

And down the river's dim expanse
Like some bold seër in a trance,
Seeing all his own mischance—
With a glassy countenance   130
    Did she look to Camelot.
And at the closing of the day
She loosed the chain, and down she lay;
The broad stream bore her far away,
    The Lady of Shalott.

Lying, robed in snowy white
That loosely flew to left and right—
The leaves upon her falling light—
Through the noises of the night
    She floated down to Camelot;   140
And as the boat-head wound along
The willowy hills and fields among,
They heard her singing her last song,
    The Lady of Shalott.

Heard a carol, mournful, holy,
Chanted loudly, chanted lowly,
Till her blood was frozen slowly,

And her eyes were darkened wholly,
    Turned to towered Camelot.
For ere she reached upon the tide   150
The first house by the water-side,
Singing in her song she died,
    The Lady of Shalott.

Under tower and balcony,
By garden-wall and gallery,
A gleaming shape she floated by,
Dead-pale between the houses high,
    Silent into Camelot.
Out upon the wharfs they came,
Knight and burgher, lord and dame,   160
And round the prow they read her name,
    The Lady of Shalott.

Who is this? and what is here?
And in the lighted palace near
Died the sound of royal cheer;
And they crossed themselves for fear,
    All the knights at Camelot:
But Lancelot mused a little space;
He said, "She has a lovely face;
God in his mercy lend her grace,   170
    The Lady of Shalott."

                                        1842

ROBERT BROWNING

My Last Duchess

FERRARA

That's my last Duchess painted on the wall,
Looking as if she were alive. I call
That piece a wonder, now: Fra Pandolf's hands
Worked busily a day, and there she stands.
Will't please you sit and look at her? I said
"Fra Pandolf" by design, for never read

Strangers like you that pictured countenance,
The depth and passion of its earnest glance,
But to myself they turned (since none puts by
The curtain I have drawn for you, but I)   10
And seemed as they would ask me, if they durst,
How such a glance came there; so, not the first
Are you to turn and ask thus. Sir, 't was not
Her husband's presence only, called that spot
Of joy into the Duchess' cheek: perhaps
Fra Pandolf chanced to say, "Her mantle laps
Over my lady's wrist too much," or "Paint
Must never hope to reproduce the faint
Half-flush that dies along her throat": such stuff
Was courtesy, she thought, and cause enough   20
For calling up that spot of joy. She had
A heart—how shall I say?—too soon made glad,
Too easily impressed: she liked whate'er
She looked on, and her looks went everywhere.
Sir, 'twas all one! My favor at her breast,
The dropping of the daylight in the West,
The bough of cherries some officious fool
Broke in the orchard for her, the white mule
She rode with round the terrace—all and each
Would draw from her alike the approving speech,   30
Or blush, at least. She thanked men,—good! but thanked
Somehow—I know not how—as if she ranked
My gift of a nine-hundred-years-old name
With anybody's gift. Who'd stoop to blame
This sort of trifling? Even had you skill
In speech—(which I have not)—to make your will
Quite clear to such an one, and say, "Just this
Or that in you disgusts me; here you miss,
Or there exceed the mark"—and if she let
Herself be lessoned so, nor plainly set   40
Her wits to yours, forsooth, and made excuse,
—E'en then would be some stooping; and I choose
Never to stoop. Oh sir, she smiled, no doubt,
Whene'er I passed her; but who passed without
Much the same smile? This grew; I gave commands;

Then all smiles stopped together. There she stands
As if alive. Will 't please you rise? We'll meet
The company below, then. I repeat
The Count your master's known munificence
Is ample warrant that no just pretense   50
Of mine for dowry will be disallowed;
Though his fair daughter's self, as I avowed
At starting, is my object. Nay, we'll go
Together down, sir. Notice Neptune, though,
Taming a sea-horse, thought a rarity,
Which Claus of Innsbruck cast in bronze for me!

1842

Andrea Del Sarto [1]

(CALLED "THE FAULTLESS PAINTER")

But do not let us quarrel any more,
No, my Lucrezia; bear with me for once:
Sit down and all shall happen as you wish.
You turn your face, but does it bring your heart?
I'll work then for your friend's friend, never fear,
Treat his own subject after his own way,
Fix his own time, accept too his own price,
And shut the money into this small hand
When next it takes mine. Will it? tenderly?
Oh, I'll content him,—but to-morrow, Love!   10
I often am much wearier than you think,
This evening more than usual, and it seems
As if—forgive now—should you let me sit
Here by the window with your hand in mine
And look a half-hour forth on Fiesole,
Both of one mind, as married people use,
Quietly, quietly the evening through,
I might get up to-morrow to my work
Cheerful and fresh as ever. Let us try.
To-morrow, how you shall be glad for this!   20

[1] For an account of the life of Andrea del Sarto (1486-1531) see Vasari's *Lives of the Painters*.

Your soft hand is a woman of itself,
And mine the man's bared breast she curls inside.
Don't count the time lost, neither; you must serve
For each of the five pictures we require:
It saves a model. So! keep looking so—
My serpentining beauty, rounds on rounds!
—How could you ever prick those perfect ears,
Even to put the pearl there! oh, so sweet—
My face, my moon, my everybody's moon,
Which everybody looks on and calls his,   30
And, I suppose, is looked on by in turn,
While she looks—no one's: very dear, no less.
You smile? why, there's my picture ready made,
There's what we painters call our harmony!
A common greyness silvers everything,—
All in a twilight, you and I alike
—You, at the point of your first pride in me
(That's gone you know),—but I, at every point;
My youth, my hope, my art, being all toned down
To yonder sober pleasant Fiesole.   40
There's the bell clinking from the chapel-top;
That length of convent-wall across the way
Holds the trees safer, huddled more inside;
The last monk leaves the garden; days decrease,
And autumn grows, autumn in everything.
Eh? the whole seems to fall into a shape
As if I saw alike my work and self
And all that I was born to be and do,
A twilight-piece. Love, we are in God's hand.
How strange now, looks the life he makes us lead;   50
So free we seem, so fettered fast we are!
I feel he laid the fetter: let it lie!
This chamber for example—turn your head—
All that's behind us! You don't understand
Nor care to understand about my art,
But you can hear at least when people speak:
And that cartoon, the second from the door
—It is the thing, Love! so such things should be—
Behold Madonna!—I am bold to say.

I can do with my pencil what I know,   60
What I see, what at bottom of my heart
I wish for, if I ever wish so deep—
Do easily, too—when I say, perfectly,
I do not boast, perhaps: yourself are judge,
Who listened to the Legate's talk last week,
And just as much they used to say in France.
At any rate 'tis easy, all of it!
No sketches first, no studies, that's long past:
I do what many dream of, all their lives,
—Dream? strive to do, and agonise to do,   70
And fail in doing. I could count twenty such
On twice your fingers, and not leave this town,
Who strive—you don't know how the others strive
To paint a little thing like that you smeared
Carelessly passing with your robes afloat,—
Yet do much less, so much less, Someone says,
(I know his name, no matter)—so much less!
Well, less is more, Lucrezia: I am judged.
There burns a truer light of God in them,
In their vexed beating stuffed and stopped-up brain,   80
Heart, or whate'er else, than goes on to prompt
This low-pulsed forthright craftsman's hand of mine.
Their works drop groundward, but themselves, I know,
Reach many a time a heaven that's shut to me,
Enter and take their place there sure enough,
Though they come back and cannot tell the world.
My works are nearer heaven, but I sit here.
The sudden blood of these men! at a word—
Praise them, it boils, or blame them, it boils too.
I, painting from myself and to myself,   90
Know what I do, am unmoved by men's blame
Or their praise either. Somebody remarks
Morello's outline there is wrongly traced,
His hue mistaken; what of that? or else,
Rightly traced and well ordered; what of that?
Speak as they please, what does the mountain care?
Ah, but a man's reach should exceed his grasp,
Or what's a heaven for? All is silver-grey

Placid and perfect with my art: the worse!
I know both what I want and what might gain,   100
And yet how profitless to know, to sigh
'Had I been two, another and myself,
Our head would have o'erlooked the world!' No doubt.
Yonder 's a work now, of that famous youth
The Urbinate who died five years ago.
('T is copied, George Vasari sent it me.)
Well, I can fancy how he did it all,
Pouring his soul, with kings and popes to see,
Reaching, that heaven might so replenish him,
Above and through his art—for it gives way;   110
That arm is wrongly put—and there again—
A fault to pardon in the drawing's lines,
Its body, so to speak: its soul is right,
He means right—that, a child may understand.
Still, what an arm! and I could alter it:
But all the play, the insight and the stretch—
Out of me, out of me! And wherefore out?
Had you enjoined them on me, given me soul,
We might have risen to Rafael, I and you!
Nay, Love, you did give all I asked, I think—   120
More than I merit, yes, by many times.
But had you—oh, with the same perfect brow,
And perfect eyes, and more than perfect mouth,
And the low voice my soul hears, as a bird
The fowler's pipe, and follows to the snare—
Had you, with these the same, but brought a mind!
Some women do so. Had the mouth there urged
'God and the glory! never care for gain.
The present by the future, what is that?
Live for fame, side by side with Agnolo!   130
Rafael is waiting: up to God, all three!'
I might have done it for you. So it seems:
Perhaps not. All is as God over-rules.
Beside, incentives come from the soul's self;
The rest avail not. Why do I need you?

105. Raphael was born at Urbino in 1483; he died in 1520.
130. Michael Angelo (1475–1564).

What wife had Rafael, or has Agnolo?
In this world, who can do a thing, will not;
And who would do it, cannot, I perceive:
Yet the will 's somewhat—somewhat, too, the power—
And thus we half-men struggle. At the end,   140
God, I conclude, compensates, punishes.
'Tis safer for me, if the award be strict,
That I am something underrated here,
Poor this long while, despised, to speak the truth.
I dared not, do you know, leave home all day,
For fear of chancing on the Paris lords.
The best is when they pass and look aside;
But they speak sometimes; I must bear it all.
Well may they speak! That Francis, that first time,
And that long festal year at Fontainebleau!   150
I surely then could sometimes leave the ground,
Put on the glory, Rafael's daily wear,
In that humane great monarch's golden look,—
One finger in his beard or twisted curl
Over his mouth's good mark that made the smile,
One arm about my shoulder, round my neck,
The jingle of his gold chain in my ear,
I painting proudly with his breath on me,
All his court round him, seeing with his eyes,
Such frank French eyes, and such a fire of souls   160
Profuse, my hand kept plying by those hearts,—
And, best of all, this, this, this face beyond,
This in the background, waiting on my work,
To crown the issue with a last reward!
A good time, was it not, my kingly days?
And had you not grown restless . . . but I know—
'T is done and past; 't was right, my instinct said;
Too live the life grew, golden and not gray,
And I'm the weak-eyed bat no sun should tempt
Out of the grange whose four walls make his world.   170
How could it end in any other way?
You called me, and I came home to your heart.
The triumph was—to reach and stay there; since

149. King Francis I of France.

I reached it ere the triumph, what is lost?
Let my hands frame your face in your hair's gold,
You beautiful Lucrezia that are mine!
'Rafael did this, Andrea painted that;
The Roman's is the better when you pray,
But still the other's Virgin was his wife—'
Men will excuse me. I am glad to judge
Both pictures in your presence; clearer grows
My better fortune, I resolve to think.
For, do you know, Lucrezia, as God lives,
Said one day Agnolo, his very self,
To Rafael . . . I have known it all these years . . .
(When the young man was flaming out his thoughts
Upon a palace-wall for Rome to see,
Too lifted up in heart because of it)
'Friend, there 's a certain sorry little scrub
Goes up and down our Florence, none cares how,
Who, were he set to plan and execute
As you are, pricked on by your popes and kings,
Would bring the sweat into that brow of yours!'
To Rafael's!—And indeed the arm is wrong.
I hardly dare . . . yet, only you to see,
Give the chalk here—quick, thus the line should go!
Ay, but the soul! he 's Rafael! rub it out!
Still, all I care for, if he spoke the truth,
(What he? why, who but Michael Agnolo?
Do you forget already words like those?)
If really there was such a chance, so lost,—
Is, whether you're—not grateful—but more pleased.
Well, let me think so. And you smile indeed!
This hour has been an hour! Another smile?
If you would sit thus by me every night
I should work better, do you comprehend?
I mean that I should earn more, give you more.
See, it is settled dusk now; there 's a star;
Morello 's gone, the watch-lights show the wall,
The cue-owls speak the name we call them by.
Come from the window, love,—come in, at last,
Inside the melancholy little house

We built to be so gay with. God is just.
King Francis may forgive me: oft at nights
When I look up from painting, eyes tired out,
The walls become illumined, brick from brick
Distinct, instead of mortar, fierce bright gold,
That gold of his I did cement them with!
Let us but love each other. Must you go?
That Cousin here again? he waits outside?   220
Must see you—you, and not with me? Those loans?
More gaming debts to pay? you smiled for that?
Well, let smiles buy me! have you more to spend?
While hand and eye and something of a heart
Are left me, work 's my ware, and what 's it worth?
I'll pay my fancy. Only let me sit
The gray remainder of the evening out,
Idle, you call it, and muse perfectly
How I could paint, were I but back in France,
One picture, just one more—the Virgin's face,   230
Not your's this time! I want you at my side
To hear them—that is, Michael Agnolo—
Judge all I do and tell you of its worth.
Will you? To-morrow, satisfy your friend.
I take the subjects for his corridor,
Finish the portrait out of hand—there, there,
And throw him in another thing or two
If he demurs; the whole should prove enough
To pay for this same Cousin's freak. Beside,
What 's better and what 's all I care about,   240
Get you the thirteen scudi for the ruff!
Love, does that please you? Ah, but what does he,
The Cousin! what does he to please you more?

I am grown peaceful as old age to-night.
I regret little, I would change still less.
Since there my past life lies, why alter it?
The very wrong to Francis!—it is true
I took his coin, was tempted and complied,
And built this house and sinned, and all is said.
My father and my mother died of want.   250

Well, had I riches of my own? you see
How one gets rich! Let each one bear his lot.
They were born poor, lived poor, and poor they died:
And I have laboured somewhat in my time
And not been paid profusely. Some good son
Paint my two hundred pictures—let him try!
No doubt, there 's something strikes a balance. Yes,
You loved me quite enough, it seems tonight.
This must suffice me here. What would one have?
In heaven, perhaps, new chances, one more chance—   260
Four great walls in the New Jerusalem,
Meted on each side by the angel's reed,
For Leonard, Rafael, Agnolo and me
To cover—the three first without a wife,
While I have mine! So—still they overcome
Because there 's still Lucrezia,—as I choose.

Again the Cousin's whistle! Go, my Love.

1855

MATTHEW ARNOLD

Sohrab and Rustum

AN EPISODE

And the first gray of morning filled the east,
And the fog rose out of the Oxus stream.
But all the Tartar camp along the stream
Was hushed, and still the men were plunged in sleep;
Sohrab alone, he slept not: all night long
He had lain wakeful, tossing on his bed;
But when the gray dawn stole into his tent,
He rose, and clad himself, and girt his sword,
And took his horseman's cloak, and left his tent,
And went abroad into the cold wet fog,   10
Through the dim camp to Peran-Wisa's tent.
Through the black Tartar tents he passed, which stood

263. Leonardo da Vinci (1452–1519).

Clustering like bee-hives on the low flat strand
Of Oxus, where the summer-floods o'erflow
When the sun melts the snows in high Pamere:
Through the black tents he passed, o'er that low strand,
And to a hillock came, a little back
From the stream's brink—the spot where first a boat,
Crossing the stream in summer, scrapes the land.
The men of former times had crowned the top   20
With a clay fort; but that was fallen, and now
The Tartars built there Peran-Wisa's tent,
A dome of laths, and o'er it felts were spread.
And Sohrab came there, and went in, and stood
Upon the thick piled carpets in the tent,
And found the old man sleeping on his bed
Of rugs and felts, and near him lay his arms.
And Peran-Wisa heard him, though the step
Was dulled; for he slept light, an old man's sleep;
And he rose quickly on one arm, and said: 30
    "Who art thou? for it is not yet clear dawn.
Speak! is there news, or any night alarm?"
    But Sohrab came to the bedside, and said:—
"Thou knowest me, Peran-Wisa: it is I.
The sun is not yet risen, and the foe
Sleep; but I sleep not; all night long I lie
Tossing and wakeful, and I come to thee,
For so did King Afrasiab bid me seek
Thy counsel, and to heed thee as thy son,
In Samarcand, before the army marched;   40
And I will tell thee what my heart desires.
Thou knowest if, since from Ader-baijan first
I came among the Tartars and bore arms,
I have still served Afrasiab well, and shown,
At my boy's years, the courage of a man.
This too thou know'st, that, while I still bear on
The conquering Tartar ensigns through the world,
And beat the Persians back on every field,
I seek one man, one man, and one alone—
Rustum, my father; who I hoped should greet,   50
Should one day greet, upon some well-fought field

His not unworthy, not inglorious son.
So I long hoped, but him I never find.
Come then, hear now, and grant me what I ask.
Let the two armies rest to-day: but I
Will challenge forth the bravest Persian lords
To meet me, man to man: if I prevail,
Rustum will surely hear it; if I fall—
Old man, the dead need no one, claim no kin.
Dim is the rumor of a common fight,   60
Where host meets host, and many names are sunk;
But of a single combat fame speaks clear."
    He spoke; and Peran-Wisa took the hand
Of the young man in his, and sighed, and said:—
    "O Sohrab, an unquiet heart is thine!
Canst thou not rest among the Tartar chiefs,
And share the battle's common chance with us
Who love thee, but must press forever first,
In single fight incurring single risk,
To find a father thou hast never seen?   70
That were far best, my son, to stay with us
Unmurmuring; in our tents, while it is war,
And when 'tis truce, then in Afrasiab's towns.
But, if this one desire indeed rules all,
To seek out Rustum—seek him not through fight:
Seek him in peace, and carry to his arms,
O Sohrab, carry an unwounded son!
But far hence seek him, for he is not here.
For now it is not as when I was young,
When Rustum was in front of every fray;   80
But now he keeps apart, and sits at home,
In Seistan, with Zal, his father old.
Whether that his own mighty strength at last
Feels the abhorred approaches of old age;
Or in some quarrel with the Persian King.
    There go!—Thou wilt not? Yet my heart forebodes
Danger or death awaits thee on this field.
Fain would I know thee safe and well, though lost
To us; fain therefore send thee hence, in peace
To seek thy father, not seek single fights   90

In vain:—but who can keep the lion's cub
From ravening, and who govern Rustum's son?
Go, I will grant thee what thy heart desires."
   So said he, and dropped Sohrab's hand, and left
His bed, and the warm rugs whereon he lay;
And o'er his chilly limbs his woollen coat
He passed, and tied his sandals on his feet,
And threw a white cloak round him, and he took
In his right hand a ruler's staff, no sword;
And on his head he set his sheep-skin cap,   100
Black, glossy, curled, the fleece of Kara-Kul;
And raised the curtain of his tent, and called
His herald to his side, and went abroad.
   The sun by this had risen, and cleared the fog
From the broad Oxus and the glittering sands.
And from their tents the Tartar horsemen filed
Into the open plain; so Haman bade—
Haman, who next to Peran-Wisa ruled
The host, and still was in his lusty prime.
From their black tents, long files of horse, they streamed:
As when, some gray November morn, the files,   111
In marching order spread, of long-necked cranes,
Stream over Casbin, and the southern slopes
Of Elburz, from the Aralian estuaries,
Or some frore Caspian reed-bed, southward bound
For the warm Persian sea-board—so they streamed.
The Tartars of the Oxus, the King's guard,
First, with black sheep-skin caps and with long spears;
Large men, large steeds; who from Bokhara come
And Khiva, and ferment the milk of mares.   120
Next, the more temperate Toorkmuns of south,
The Tukas, and the lances of Salore,
And those from Attruck and the Caspian sands;
Light men, and on light steeds, who only drink
The acrid milk of camels, and their wells.
And then a swarm of wandering horse, who came
From far, and a more doubtful service owned;
The Tartars of Ferghana, from the banks
Of the Jaxartes, men with scanty beards

And close-set skull-caps; and those wilder hordes   130
Who roam o'er Kipchak and the northern waste,
Kalmuks and unkempt Kuzzaks, tribes who stray
Nearest the Pole, and wandering Kirghizzes,
Who come on shaggy ponies from Pamere;
These all filed out from camp into the plain.
    And on the other side the Persians formed:
First a light cloud of horse, Tartars they seemed,
The Ilyats of Khorassan: and behind,
The royal troops of Persia, horse and foot,
Marshalled battalions bright in burnished steel.   140
    But Peran-Wisa with his herald came,
Threading the Tartar squadrons to the front,
And with his staff kept back the foremost ranks.
And when Ferood, who led the Persians, saw
That Peran-Wisa kept the Tartars back,
He took his spear, and to the front he came,
And checked his ranks, and fixed them where they stood.
And the old Tartar came upon the sand
Betwixt the silent hosts, and spake, and said:—
    "Ferood, and ye, Persians and Tartars, hear!   150
Let there be truce between the hosts to-day.
But choose a champion from the Persian lords
To fight our champion Sohrab, man to man."
    As, in the country, on a morn in June,
When the dew glistens on the pearlèd ears
A shiver runs through the deep corn for joy—
So, when they heard what Peran-Wisa said,
A thrill through all the Tartar squadrons ran
Of pride and hope for Sohrab, whom they loved.
    But as a troop of pedlars, from Cabool,   160
Cross underneath the Indian Caucasus,
That vast sky-neighboring mountain of milk snow;
Crossing so high, that, as they mount, they pass
Long flocks of travelling birds dead on the snow,
Choked by the air, and scarce can they themselves
Slake their parched throats with sugared mulberries—
In single file they move, and stop their breath,
For fear they should dislodge the o'er-hanging snows—

So the pale Persians held their breath with fear.
And to Ferood his brother chiefs came up   170
To counsel: Gudurz and Zoarrah came,
And Feraburz, who ruled the Persian host
Second, and was the uncle of the King;
These came and counselled, and then Gudurz said:—
    "Ferood, shame bids us take their challenge up.
Yet champion have we none to match this youth.
He has the wild stag's foot, the lion's heart.
But Rustum came last night; aloof he sits
And sullen, and has pitched his tents apart.
Him will I seek, and carry to his ear   180
The Tartar challenge, and this young man's name.
Haply he will forget his wrath, and fight.
Stand forth the while, and take their challenge up."
    So spake he; and Ferood stood forth and cried:—
"Old man, be it agreed as thou hast said!
Let Sohrab arm, and we will find a man."
    He spake; and Peran-Wisa turned, and strode
Back through the opening squadrons to his tent.
But through the anxious Persians Gudurz ran,
And crossed the camp which lay behind, and reached,   190
Out on the sands beyond it, Rustum's tents.
Of scarlet cloth they were, and glittering gay,
Just pitched: the high pavilion in the midst
Was Rustum's, and his men lay camped around.
And Gudurz entered Rustum's tent, and found
Rustum; his morning meal was done, but still
The table stood before him, charged with food;
A side of roasted sheep, and cakes of bread,
And dark green melons; and there Rustum sate
Listless, and held a falcon on his wrist,   200
And played with it; but Gudurz came and stood
Before him; and he looked, and saw him stand,
And with a cry sprang up, and dropped the bird,
And greeted Gudurz with both hands, and said:—
    "Welcome! these eyes could see no better sight.
What news? but sit down first, and eat and drink."
    But Gudurz stood in the tent-door, and said:—

"Not now; a time will come to eat and drink,
But not to-day; to-day has other needs.
The armies are drawn out, and stand at gaze;   210
For from the Tartars is a challenge brought
To pick a champion from the Persian lords
To fight their champion—and thou knowest his name—
Sohrab men call him, but his birth is hid.
O Rustum, like thy might is this young man's!
He has the wild stag's foot, the lion's heart;
And he is young, and Iran's chiefs are old,
Or else too weak; and all eyes turn to thee.
Come down and help us, Rustum, or we lose!"
   He spoke: but Rustum answered with a smile:—   220
"Go to! if Iran's chiefs are old, then I
Am older: if the young are weak, the King
Errs strangely; for the King, for Kai-Khosroo,
Himself is young, and honors younger men,
And lets the agèd moulder to their graves.
Rustum he loves no more, but loves the young—
The young may rise at Sohrab's vaunts, not I.
For what care I, though all speak Sohrab's fame?
For would that I myself had such a son,
And not that one slight helpless girl I have—   230
A son so famed, so brave, to send to war,
And I to tarry with the snow-haired Zal,
My father, whom the robber Afghans vex,
And clip his borders short, and drive his herds,
And he has none to guard his weak old age.
There would I go, and hang my armor up,
And with my great name fence that weak old man,
And spend the goodly treasures I have got,
And rest my age, and hear of Sohrab's fame,
And leave to death the hosts of thankless kings,   240
And with these slaughterous hands draw sword no more."
   He spoke, and smiled; and Gudurz made reply:—
"What then, O Rustum, will men say to this,
When Sohrab dares our bravest forth, and seeks
Thee most of all, and thou, whom most he seeks,
Hidest thy face? Take heed, lest men should say:

'Like some old miser, Rustum hoards his fame,
And shuns to peril it with younger men.' "
And, greatly moved, then Rustum made reply:—
"O Gudurz, wherefore dost thou say such words?   250
Thou knowest better words than this to say.
What is one more, one less, obscure or famed,
Valiant or craven, young or old, to me?
Are not they mortal, am not I myself?
But who for men of nought would do great deeds?
Come, thou shall see how Rustum hoards his fame!
But I will fight unknown, and in plain arms;
Let not men say of Rustum, he was matched
In single fight with any mortal man."
    He spoke, and frowned; and Gudurz turned,.and ran   260
Back quickly through the camp in fear and joy—
Fear at his wrath, but joy that Rustum came.
But Rustum strode to his tent door, and called
His followers in, and bade them bring his arms,
And clad himself in steel: the arms he chose
Were plain, and on his shield was no device,
Only his helm was rich, inlaid with gold,
And from the fluted spine atop, a plume
Of horsehair waved, a scarlet horsehair plume.
So armed, he issued forth; and Ruksh, his horse,   270
Followed him like a faithful hound at heel—
Ruksh, whose renown was noised through all the earth,
The horse whom Rustum on a foray once
Did in Bokhara by the river find,
A colt beneath its dam, and drove him home,
And reared him; a bright bay, with lofty crest;
Dight with a saddle-cloth of broidered green
Crusted with gold, and on the ground were worked
All beasts of chase, all beasts which hunters know.
So followed, Rustum left his tents, and crossed   280
The camp, and to the Persian host appeared.
And all the Persians knew him, and with shouts
Hailed; but the Tartars knew not who he was.
And dear as the wet diver to the eyes
Of his pale wife who waits and weeps on shore,

By sandy Bahrein, in the Persian Gulf,
Plunging all day into the blue waves, at night,
Having made up his tale of precious pearls,
Rejoins her in their hut upon the sands—
So dear to the pale Persians Rustum came.   290
    And Rustum to the Persian front advanced,
And Sohrab armed in Haman's tent, and came.
And as afield the reapers cut a swath
Down through the middle of a rich man's corn,
And on each side are squares of standing corn,
And in the midst a stubble, short and bare—
So on each side were squares of men, with spears
Bristling, and in the midst, the open sand.
And Rustum came upon the sand, and cast
His eyes towards the Tartar tents, and saw   300
Sohrab come forth, and eyed him as he came.
    As some rich woman, on a winter's morn,
Eyes through her silken curtains the poor drudge
Who with numb blackened fingers makes her fire—
At cock-crow on a starlit winter's morn,
When the frost flowers the whitened windowpanes—
And wonders how she lives, and what the thoughts
Of that poor drudge may be; so Rustum eyed
The unknown adventurous youth, who from afar
Came seeking Rustum, and defying forth   310
All the most valiant chiefs: long he perused
His spirited air, and wondered who he was.
For very young he seemed, tenderly reared;
Like some young cypress, tall, and dark, and straight,
Which in a queen's secluded garden throws
Its slight dark shadow on the moonlit turf,
By midnight, to a bubbling fountain's sound—
So slender Sohrab seemed, so softly reared.
And a deep pity entered Rustum's soul
As he beheld him coming; and he stood,   320
And beckoned to him with his hand, and said:—
    "O thou young man, the air of Heaven is soft,
And warm, and pleasant; but the grave is cold!
Heaven's air is better than the cold dead grave.

Behold me! I am vast, and clad in iron,
And tried; and I have stood on many a field
Of blood, and I have fought with many a foe—
Never was that field lost, or that foe saved.
O Sohrab, wherefore wilt thou rush on death?   •
Be governed! quit the Tartar host, and come   330
To Iran, and be as my son to me,
And fight beneath my banner till I die.
There are no youths in Iran brave as thou."
     So he spake, mildly: Sohrab heard his voice,
The mighty voice of Rustum, and he saw
His giant figure planted on the sand,
Sole, like some single tower, which a chief
Has builded on the waste in former years
Against the robbers; and he saw that head,
Streaked with its first gray hairs;—hope filled his soul,   340
And he ran forward and embraced his knees,
And clasped his hand within his own, and said:—
     "O, by thy father's head! by thine own soul!
Art thou not Rustum? speak! art thou not he?"
     But Rustum eyed askance the kneeling youth,
And turned away, and spake to his own soul:—
     "Ah me, I muse what this young fox may mean!
False, wily, boastful, are these Tartar boys.
For if I now confess this thing he asks,
And hide it not, but say: *Rustum is here!*   350
He will not yield indeed, nor quit our foes,
But he will find some pretext not to fight,
And praise my fame, and proffer courteous gifts,
A belt or sword perhaps, and go his way.
And on a feast day, in Afrasiab's hall,
In Samarcand, he will arise and cry:
'I challenged once, when the two armies camped
Beside the Oxus, all the Persian lords
To cope with me in single fight; but they
Shrank, only Rustum dared; then he and I   360
Changed gifts, and went on equal terms away.'
So will he speak, perhaps, while men applaud;
Then were the chiefs of Iran shamed through me."

And then he turned, and sternly spake aloud:—
"Rise! wherefore dost thou vainly question thus
Of Rustum? I am here, whom thou hast called
By challenge forth: make good thy vaunt, or yield!
· Is it with Rustum only thou wouldst fight?
Rash boy, men look on Rustum's face and flee.
For well I know, that did great Rustum stand   370
Before thy face this day, and were revealed,
There would be then no talk of fighting more.
But being what I am, I tell thee this—
Do thou record it in thine inmost soul:
Either thou shalt renounce thy vaunt and yield;
Or else thy bones shall strew this sand, till winds
Bleach them, or Oxus with his summer-floods,
Oxus in summer wash them all away "
     He spoke: and Sohrab answered, on his feet:—
"Art thou so fierce? Thou wilt not fright me so!   380
I am no girl, to be made pale by words.
Yet this thou hast said well, did Rustum stand
Here on this field, there were no fighting then.
But Rustum is far hence, and we stand here.
Begin! thou art more vast, more dread than I,
And thou art proved, I know, and I am young—
But yet success sways with the breath of Heaven.
And though thou thinkest that thou knowest sure
Thy victory, yet thou canst not surely know.
For we are all, like swimmers in the sea,   390
Poised on the top of a huge wave of fate,
Which hangs uncertain to which side to fall.
And whether it will heave us up to land,
Or whether it will roll us out to sea,
Back out to sea, to the deep waves of death,
We know not, and no search will make us know;
Only the event will teach us in its hour."
     He spoke, and Rustum answered not, but hurled
His spear; down from the shoulder, down it came
As on some partridge in the corn a hawk   400
That long has towered in the airy clouds
Drops like a plummet; Sohrab saw it come,

And sprang aside, quick as a flash: the spear
Hissed, and went quivering down into the sand,
Which it sent flying wide;—then Sohrab threw
In turn, and full struck Rustum's shield; sharp rang,
The iron plates rang sharp, but turned the spear.
And Rustum seized his club, which none but he
Could wield: an unlopped trunk it was, and huge,
Still rough—like those which men in treeless plains   410
To build them boats fish from the flooded rivers,
Hyphasis or Hydaspes, when, high up
By their dark springs, the wind in wintertime
Has made in Himalayan forests wrack,
And strewn the channels with torn boughs—so huge
The club which Rustum lifted now, and struck
One stroke; but again Sohrab sprang aside,
Lithe as the glancing snake, and the club came
Thundering to earth, and leaped from Rustum's hand.
And Rustum followed his own blow, and fell   420
To his knees, and with his fingers clutched the sand.
And now might Sohrab have unsheathed his sword,
And pierced the mighty Rustum while he lay
Dizzy, and on his knees, and choked with sand;
But he looked on, and smiled, nor bared his sword,
But courteously drew back, and spoke, and said:—
    "Thou strikest too hard! that club of thine will float
Upon the summer-floods, and not my bones.
But rise, and be not wroth! not wroth am I;
No, when I see thee, wrath forsakes my soul.   430
Thou sayst thou art not Rustum: be it so.
Who art thou then, that canst so touch my soul?
Boy as I am, I have seen battles too—
Have waded foremost in their bloody waves,
And heard their hollow roar of dying men;
But never was my heart thus touched before.
Are they from Heaven, these softenings of the heart?
O thou old warrior, let us yield to Heaven!
Come, plant we here in earth our angry spears,
And make a truce, and sit upon this sand,   440
And pledge each other in red wine, like friends,

And thou shalt talk to me of Rustum's deeds.
There are enough foes in the Persian host,
Whom I may meet, and strike, and feel no pang;
Champions enough Afrasiab has, whom thou
Mayst fight; fight *them*, when they confront thy spear!
But oh, let there be peace 'twixt thee and me!"
He ceased: but while he spake, Rustum had risen,
And stood erect, trembling with rage: his club
He left to lie, but had regained his spear,   450
Whose fiery point now in his mailed right-hand
Blazed bright and baleful, like that autumn-star, .
The baleful sign of fevers: dust had soiled
His stately crest, and dimmed his glittering arms.
His breast heaved, his lips foamed, and twice his voice
Was choked with rage: at last these words broke way:—
"Girl! nimble with thy feet, not with thy hands!
Curled minion, dancer, coiner of sweet words!
Fight, let me hear thy hateful voice no more!
Thou art not in Afrasiab's gardens now   460
With Tartar girls, with whom thou art wont to dance;
But on the Oxus-sands, and in the dance
Of battle, and with me, who make no play
Of war; I fight it out, and hand to hand.
Speak not to me of truce, and pledge, and wine!
Remember all thy valor: try thy feints
And cunning! all the pity I had is gone;
Because thou hast shamed me before both the hosts
With thy light skipping tricks, and thy girl's wiles."
He spoke, and Sohrab kindled at his taunts,   470
And he too drew his sword: at once they rushed
Together, as two eagles on one prey
Come rushing down together from the clouds,
One from the east, one from the west; their shields
Dashed with a clang together, and a din
Rose, such as that the sinewy woodcutters
Make often in the forest's heart at morn,
Of hewing axes, crashing trees—such blows
Rustum and Sohrab on each other hailed.
And you would say that sun and stars took part   480

In that unnatural conflict; for a cloud
Grew suddenly in Heaven, and darked the sun
Over the fighters' heads; and a wind rose
Under their feet, and moaning swept the plain,
And in a sandy whirlwind wrapped the pair.
In gloom they twain were wrapped, and they alone;
For both the on-looking hosts on either hand
Stood in broad daylight, and the sky was pure,
And the sun sparkled on the Oxus stream.
But in the gloom they fought, with bloodshot eyes   490
And laboring breath; first Rustum struck the shield
Which Sohrab held stiff out; the steel-spiked spear
Rent the tough plates, but failed to reach the skin,
And Rustum plucked it back with angry groan.
Then Sohrab with his sword smote Rustum's helm,
Nor clove its steel quite through; but all the crest
He shore away, and that proud horse-hair plume,
Never till now defiled, sank to the dust;
And Rustum bowed his head; but then the gloom
Grew blacker, thunder rumbled in the air,   500
And lightnings rent the cloud; and Ruksh, the horse,
Who stood at hand, uttered a dreadful cry;—
No horse's cry was that, most like the roar
Of some pained desert lion, who all day
Hath trailed the hunter's javelin in his side,
And comes at night to die upon the sand.
The two hosts heard that cry, and quaked for fear,
And Oxus curdled as it crossed his stream.
But Sohrab heard, and quailed not, but rushed on,
And struck again; and again Rustum bowed   510
His head; but this time all the blade, like glass,
Sprang in a thousand shivers on the helm,
And in his hand the hilt remained alone.
Then Rustum raised his head; his dreadful eyes
Glared, and he shook on high his menacing spear,
And shouted, *Rustum!*—Sohrab heard that shout,
And shrank amazed: back he recoiled one step,
And scanned with blinking eyes the advancing form;
And then he stood bewildered; and he dropped

His covering shield, and the spear pierced his side.   520
He reeled, and staggering back, sank to the ground;
And then the gloom dispersed, and the wind fell,
And the bright sun broke forth, and melted all
The cloud; and the two armies saw the pair—
Saw Rustum standing, safe upon his feet,
And Sohrab, wounded, on the bloody sand.
　　Then with a bitter smile, Rustum began:—
"Sohrab, thou thoughtest in thy mind to kill
A Persian lord this day, and strip his corpse,
And bear thy trophies to Afrasiab's tent.   530
Or else that the great Rustum would come down
Himself to fight, and that thy wiles would move
His heart to take a gift, and let thee go.
And then that all the Tartar host would praise
Thy courage or thy craft, and spread thy fame,
To glad thy father in his weak old age.
Fool, thou art slain, and by an unknown man!
Dearer to the red jackals shalt thou be
Than to thy friends, and to thy father old."
　　And, with a fearless mien, Sohrab replied:—   540
"Unknown thou art; yet thy fierce vaunt is vain.
Thou dost not slay me, proud and boastful man!
No! Rustum slays me, and this filial heart.
For were I matched with ten such men as thee,
And I were that which till to-day I was,
They should be lying here, I standing there.
But that belovèd name unnerved my arm—
That name, and something, I confess, in thee,
Which troubles all my heart, and made my shield
Fall; and thy spear transfixed an unarmed foe.   550
And now thou boastest, and insultest my fate.
But hear thou this, fierce man, tremble to hear!
The mighty Rustum shall avenge my death!
My father, whom I seek through all the world,
He shall avenge my death, and punish thee!"
　　As when some hunter in the spring hath found
A breeding eagle sitting on her nest,
Upon the craggy isle of a hill-lake,

And pierced her with an arrow as she rose,
And followed her to find her where she fell 560
Far off;—anon her mate comes winging back
From hunting, and a great way off descries
His huddling young left sole; at that, he checks
His pinion, and with short uneasy sweeps
Circles above his eyry, with loud screams
Chiding his mate back to her nest; but she
Lies dying, with the arrow in her side,
In some far stony gorge out of his ken,
A heap of fluttering feathers—never more
Shall the lake glass her, flying over it; 570
Never the black and dripping precipices
Echo her stormy scream as she sails by:—
As that poor bird flies home, nor knows his loss,
So Rustum knew not his own loss, but stood
Over his dying son, and knew him not.
    But, with a cold incredulous voice, he said:—
"What prate is this of fathers and revenge?
The mighty Rustum never had a son."
    And, with a failing voice, Sohrab replied:—
"Ah! yes, he had! and that lost son am I. 580
Surely the news will one day reach his ear,
Reach Rustum, where he sits, and tarries long,
Somewhere, I know not where, but far from here,
And pierce him like a stab, and make him leap
To arms, and cry for vengeance upon thee.
Fierce man, bethink thee, for an only son!
What will that grief, what will that vengeance be?
Oh, could I live, till I that grief had seen!
Yet him I pity not so much, but her,
My mother, who in Ader-baijan dwells 590
With that old king, her father, who grows gray
With age, and rules over the valiant Koords.
Her most I pity, who no more will see
Sohrab returning from the Tartar camp,
With spoils and honor, when the war is done.
But a dark rumor will be bruited up,
From tribe to tribe, until it reach her ear;

And then will that defenceless woman learn
That Sohrab will rejoice her sight no more;
But that in battle with a nameless foe,   600
By the far-distant Oxus, he is slain."
   He spoke; and as he ceased, he wept aloud,
Thinking of her he left, and his own death.
He spoke; but Rustum listened, plunged in thought.
Nor did he yet believe it was his son
Who spoke, although he called back names he knew;
For he had had sure tidings that the babe,
Which was in Ader-baijan born to him,
Had been a puny girl, no boy at all—
So that sad mother sent him word, for fear   610
Rustum should take the boy, to train in arms;
And so he deemed that either Sohrab took,
By a false boast, the style of Rustum's son;
Or that men gave it him, to swell his fame.
So deemed he; yet he listened, plunged in thought,
And his soul set to grief, as the vast tide
Of the bright rocking Ocean sets to shore
At the full moon: tears gathered in his eyes;
For he remembered his own early youth,
And all its bounding rapture; as, at dawn,   620
The shepherd from his mountain-lodge descries
A far, bright city, smitten by the sun,
Through many rolling clouds—so Rustum saw
His youth; saw Sohrab's mother, in her bloom;
And that old king, her father, who loved well
His wandering guest, and gave him his fair child
With joy; and all the pleasant life they led,
They three, in that long-distant summertime—
The castle, and the dewy woods, and hunt
And hound, and morn on those delightful hills   630
In Ader-baijan. And he saw that youth,
Of age and looks to be his own dear son,
Piteous and lovely, lying on the sand,
Like some rich hyacinth which by the scythe
Of an unskilful gardener has been cut,
Mowing the garden grass-plots near its bed,

And lies, a fragrant tower of purple bloom,
On the mown, dying grass—so Sohrab lay,
Lovely in death, upon the common sand.
And Rustum gazed on him with grief, and said:—   640
    "O Sohrab, thou indeed art such a son
Whom Rustum, wert thou his, might well have loved.
Yet here thou errest, Sohrab, or else men
Have told thee false—thou art not Rustum's son.
For Rustum had no son: one child he had—
But one—a girl; who with her mother now
Plies some light female task, nor dreams of us—
Of us she dreams not, nor of wounds, nor war."
    But Sohrab answered him in wrath; for now
The anguish of the deep-fixed spear grew fierce,   650
And he desired to draw forth the steel,
And let the blood flow free, and so to die—
But first he would convince his stubborn foe;
And, rising sternly on one arm, he said:—
    "Man, who art thou who dost deny my words?
Truth sits upon the lips of dying men,
And falsehood, while I lived, was far from mine.
I tell thee, pricked upon this arm I bear
That seal which Rustum to my mother gave,
That she might prick it on the babe she bore." ·   660
    He spoke; and all the blood left Rustum's cheeks,
And his knees tottered, and he smote his hand
Against his breast, his heavy mailèd hand,
That the hard iron corslet clanked aloud;
And to his heart he pressed the other hand,
And in a hollow voice he spake, and said:—
    "Sohrab, that were a proof which could not lie!
If thou show this, then art thou Rustum's son."
    Then, with weak hasty fingers, Sohrab loosed
His belt, and near the shoulder bared his arm,   670
And showed a sign in faint vermilion points
Pricked; as a cunning workman, in Pekin,
Pricks with vermilion some clear porcelain vase,
An emperor's gift—at early morn he paints,
And all day long, and, when night comes, the lamp

Lights up his studious forehead and thin hands—
So delicately pricked the sign appeared
On Sohrab's arm, the sign of Rustum's seal.
It was that griffin, which of old reared Zal,
Rustum's great father, whom they left to die,   680
A helpless babe, among the mountain rocks;
Him that kind creature found, and reared, and loved—
Then Rustum took it for his glorious sign.
And Sohrab bared that image on his arm,
And himself scanned it long with mournful eyes,
And then he touched it with his hand and said:—
    "How say'st thou? Is that sign the proper sign
Of Rustum's son, or of some other man's?"
    He spoke: but Rustum gazed, and gazed, and stood
Speechless; and then he uttered one sharp cry: 690
    "O boy—thy father!"—and his voice choked there.
And then a dark cloud passed before his eyes,
And his head swam, and he sank down to earth.
But Sohrab crawled to where he lay, and cast
His arms about his neck, and kissed his lips,
And with fond faltering fingers stroked his cheeks,
Trying to call him back to life; and life
Came back to Rustum, and he oped his eyes,
And they stood wide with horror; and he seized
In both his hands the dust which lay around,   700
And threw it on his head, and smirched his hair,—
His hair, and face, and beard, and glittering arms;
And strong convulsive groanings shook his breast,
And his sobs choked him; and he clutched his sword,
To draw it, and forever let life out.
But Sohrab saw his thought, and held his hands,
And with a soothing voice he spake, and said:—
    "Father, forbear! for I but meet to-day
The doom that at my birth was written down
In Heaven, and thou art Heaven's unconscious hand.   710
Surely my heart cried out that it was thou,
When first I saw thee; and thy heart spoke too,
I know it! but fate trod those promptings down
Under its iron heel; fate, fate engaged

The strife, and hurled me on my father's spear.
But let us speak no more of this! I find
My father; let me feel that I have found!
Come, sit beside me on this sand, and take
My head betwixt thy hands, and kiss my cheeks,
And wash them with thy tears, and say:
      '*My son!*'   720
Quick! quick! for numbered are my sands of life,
And swift; for like the lightning to this field
I came, and like the wind I go away—
Sudden, and swift, and like a passing wind.
But it was writ in Heaven that this should be."
   So said he: and his voice released the heart
Of Rustum, and his tears broke forth; he cast
His arms round his son's neck, and wept aloud,
And kissed him. And awe fell on both the hosts
When they saw Rustum's grief: and Ruksh, the horse, 730
With his head bowing to the ground and mane
Sweeping the dust, came near, and in mute woe
First to the one, then to the other moved
His head, as if inquiring what their grief
Might mean; and from his dark, compassionate eyes,
The big warm tears rolled down, and caked the sand.
But Rustum chid him with stern voice, and said:—
   "Ruksh, now thou grievest; but, O Ruksh, thy feet
Should first have rotted on their nimble joints,
Or ere they bore thy master to this field!"   730
   But Sohrab looked upon the horse and said:—
"Is this, then, Ruksh? How often, in past days,
My mother told me of thee, thou brave steed,
My terrible father's terrible horse! and said,
That I should one day find thy lord and thee.
Come, let me lay my hand upon thy mane!
O Ruksh, thou art more fortunate than I;
For thou hast gone where I shall never go,
And snuffed the breezes of my father's home.
And thou hast trod the sands of Seïstan,   750
And seen the river of Helmund, and the Lake
Of Zirrah; and the aged Zal himself

Has often stroked thy neck, and given thee food,
Corn in a golden platter soaked with wine,
And said 'O Ruksh! bear Rustum well!' but I
Have never known my grandsire's furrowed face,
Nor seen his lofty house in Seïstan,
Nor slaked my thirst at the clear Helmund stream;
But lodged among my father's foes, and seen
Afrasiab's cities only, Samarcand,   760
Bokhara, and lone Khiva in the waste,
And the black Toorkmun tents; and only drunk
The desert rivers, Moorghab and Tejend,
Kohik, and where the Kalmuks feed their sheep,
The northern Sir; and this great Oxus stream—
The yellow Oxus, by whose brink I die."
     And, with a heavy groan, Rustum bewailed:—
"Oh, that its waves were flowing over me!
Oh, that I saw its grains of yellow silt
Roll tumbling in the current o'er my head!"   770
     But, with a grave mild voice, Sohrab replied:—
"Desire not that, my father! thou must live.
For some are born to do great deeds, and live,
As some are born to be obscured, and die.
Do thou the deeds I die too young to do,
And reap a second glory in thine age;
Thou art my father, and thy gain is mine.
But come! thou seest this great host of men
Which follow me; I pray thee, slay not these!
Let me entreat for them; what have they done?   780
They followed me, my hope, my fame, my star.
Let them all cross the Oxus back in peace.
But me thou must bear hence, not send with them,
But carry me with thee to Seïstan,
And place me on a bed, and mourn for me,
Thou, and the snow-haired Zal, and all thy friends.
And thou must lay me in that lovely earth,
And heap a stately mound above my bones,
And plant a far-seen pillar over all:
That so the passing horseman on the waste   790
May see my tomb a great way off, and cry:

'*Sohrab, the mighty Rustum's son, lies there,*
Whom his great father did in ignorance kill'—
And I be not forgotten in my grave."
    And, with a mournful voice, Rustum replied:—
"Fear not! as thou hast said, Sohrab, my son,
So shall it be; for I will burn my tents,
And quit the host, and bear thee hence with me,
And carry thee away to Seïstan,
And place thee on a bed, and mourn for thee,   800
With the snow-headed Zal, and all my friends.
And I will lay thee in that lovely earth,
And heap a stately mound above thy bones,
And plant a far-seen pillar over all,
And men shall not forget thee in thy grave.
And I will spare thy host; yea, let them go!
Let them all cross the Oxus back in peace!
What should I do with slaying any more?
For would that all whom I have ever slain
Might be once more alive; my bitterest foes,   810
And they who were called champions in their time.
And through whose death I won that fame I have—
And I were nothing but a common man,
A poor, mean soldier, and without renown,
So thou mightest live too, my son, my son!
Or rather would that I, even I myself,
Might now be lying on this bloody sand,
Near death, and by an ignorant stroke of thine,
Not thou of mine! and I might die, not thou;
And I, not thou, be borne to Seïstan;   820
And Zal might weep above my grave, not thine;
And say '*O son, I weep thee not too sore,*
For willingly, I know, thou met'st thine end.'
But now in blood and battles was my youth,
And full of blood and battles is my age,
And I shall never end this life of blood."
    Then, at the point of death, Sohrab replied:—
"A life of blood indeed, thou dreadful man!
But thou shalt yet have peace; only not now,
Not yet! but thou shalt have it on that day,   830

When thou shalt sail in a high-masted ship,
Thou and the other peers of Kai-Khosroo,
Returning home over the salt blue sea,
From laying thy dear master in his grave."
    And Rustum gazed on Sohrab's face, and said:—
"Soon be that day, my son, and deep that sea!
Till then, if fate so wills, let me endure."
    He spoke; and Sohrab smiled on him, and took
The spear, and drew it from his side, and eased
His wound's imperious anguish; but the blood   840
Came welling from the open gash, and life
Flowed with the stream;—all down his cold white side
The crimson torrent ran, dim now and soiled
Like the soiled tissue of white violets
Left, freshly gathered, on their native bank,
By romping children, whom their nurses call
Indoors from the sun's eye; his head drooped low,
His limbs grew slack; motionless, white, he lay—
White, with eyes closed; only when heavy gasps,
Deep heavy gasps quivering through all his frame,   850
Convulsed him back to life, he opened them,
And fixed them feebly on his father's face;
Till now all strength was ebbed, and from his limbs
Unwillingly the spirit fled away,
Regretting the warm mansion which it left,
And youth, and bloom, and this delightful world.
    So, on the bloody sand, Sohrab lay dead;
And the great Rustum drew his horseman's cloak
Down o'er his face, and sate by his dead son.
As those black granite pillars, once high-reared   860
By Jemshid in Persepolis, to bear
His house, now 'mid their broken flights of steps
Lie prone, enormous, down the mountain side—
So in the sand lay Rustum by his son.
    And night came down over the solemn waste,
And the two gazing hosts, and that sole pair,
And darkened all; and a cold fog, with night,
Crept from the Oxus. Soon a hum arose,
As of a great assembly loosed, and fires

Began to twinkle through the fog: for now   870
Both armies moved to camp, and took their meal;
The Persians took it on the open sands
Southward, the Tartars by the river marge;
And Rustum and his son were left alone.
   But the majestic river floated on,
Out of the mist and hum of that low land,
Into the frosty starlight, and there moved,
Rejoicing, through the hushed Chorasmian waste,
Under the solitary moon;—he flowed
Right for the polar star, past Orgunjè,   880
Brimming, and bright, and large; then sands begin
To hem his watery march, and dam his streams,
And split his currents; that for many a league
The shorn and parcelled Oxus strains along
Through beds of sand and matted rushy isles—
Oxus, forgetting the bright speed he had
In his high mountain cradle in Pamere,
A foiled circuitous wanderer—till at last
The longed-for dash of waves is heard, and wide
His luminous home of waters opens, bright   890
And tranquil, from whose floor the new-bathed stars
Emerge, and shine upon the Aral Sea.

1853

DANTE GABRIEL ROSSETTI

Sister Helen

"Why did you melt your waxen man,
                    Sister Helen?
Today is the third since you began."
"The time was long, yet the time ran,
                    Little brother."
                    (*O Mother, Mary Mother,*
Three days today, between Hell and Heaven!)

"But if you have done your work aright,
                    Sister Helen,
You'll let me play, for you said I might."   10

"Be very still in your play tonight,
        Little brother."
    (*O Mother, Mary Mother,*
Third night, tonight, between Hell and Heaven!)

"You said it must melt ere vesper-bell,
        Sister Helen;
If now it be molten, all is well."
"Even so—nay, peace! you cannot tell,
        Little brother."
    (*O Mother, Mary Mother,*   20
Oh, what is this, between Hell and Heaven?)

"Oh, the waxen knave was plump today,
        Sister Helen;
How like dead folk he has dropped away!"
"Nay now, of the dead what can you say,
        Little brother?"
    (*O Mother, Mary Mother,*
What of the dead, between Hell and Heaven?)

"See, see, the sunken pile of wood,
        Sister Helen,   30
Shines through the thinned wax red as blood!"
"Nay now, when looked you yet on blood,
        Little brother?"
    (*O Mother, Mary Mother,*
How pale she is, between Hell and Heaven!)

"Now close your eyes, for they're sick and sore,
        Sister Helen,
And I'll play without the gallery door."
"Aye, let me rest—I'll lie on the floor,
        Little brother."   40
    (*O Mother, Mary Mother,*
What rest tonight, between Hell and Heaven?)

"Here high up in the balcony,
        Sister Helen,
The moon flies face to face with me."

"Aye, look and say whatever you see,
                    Little brother."
              (*O Mother, Mary Mother,*
What sight tonight, between Hell and Heaven?)

"Outside it's merry in the wind's wake,   50
                    Sister Helen;
In the shaken trees the chill stars shake."
"Hush, heard you a horse-tread as you spake,
                    Little brother?"
              (*O Mother, Mary Mother,*
What sound tonight, between Hell and Heaven?)

"I hear a horse-tread, and I see,
                    Sister Helen,
Three horsemen that ride terribly."
"Little brother, whence come the three,   60
                    Little brother?"
              (*O Mother, Mary Mother,*
Whence should they come, between Hell and Heaven?)

"They come by the hill-verge from Boyne Bar,
                    Sister Helen,
And one draws nigh, but two are afar."
"Look, look, do you know them who they are,
                    Little brother?"
              (*O Mother, Mary Mother,*
Who should they be, between Hell and Heaven?)   70

"Oh, it's Keith of Eastholm rides so fast,
                    Sister Helen,
For I know the white mane on the blast."
"The hour has come, has come at last,
                    Little brother!"
              (*O Mother, Mary Mother,*
Her hour at last, between Hell and Heaven!)

"He has made a sign and called Halloo!
                    Sister Helen,
And he says that he would speak with you."   80

"Oh, tell him I fear the frozen dew,
      Little brother."
    (*O Mother, Mary Mother,*
Why laughs she thus, between Hell and Heaven?)

"The wind is loud, but I hear him cry,
      Sister Helen,
That Keith of Ewern's like to die."
"And he and thou, and thou and I,
      Little brother."
    (*O Mother, Mary Mother,*   90
And they and we, between Hell and Heaven!)

"Three days ago, on his marriage-morn,
      Sister Helen,
He sickened, and lies since then forlorn."
"For bridegroom's side is the bride a thorn,
      Little brother?"
    (*O Mother, Mary Mother,*
Cold bridal cheer, between Hell and Heaven!)

"Three days and nights now he has lain abed,
      Sister Helen,   100
And he prays in torment to be dead."
"The thing may chance, if he have prayed,
      Little brother!"
    (*O Mother, Mary Mother,*
If he have prayed, between Hell and Heaven!)

"But he has not ceased to cry today,
      Sister Helen,
That you should take your curse away."
"*My* prayer was heard—he need but pray,
      Little brother!"   110
    (*O Mother, Mary Mother,*
Shall God not hear, between Hell and Heaven?)

"But he says, till you take back your ban,
      Sister Helen,
His soul would pass, yet never can."

"Nay then, shall I slay a living man,
   Little brother?"
   (O Mother, Mary Mother,
A living soul, between Hell and Heaven!)

"But he calls forever on your name,   120
   Sister Helen,
And says that he melts before a flame."
"My heart for his pleasure fared the same,
   Little brother."
   (O Mother, Mary Mother,
Fire at the heart, between Hell and Heaven!)

"Here's Keith of Westholm riding fast,
   Sister Helen,
For I know the white plume on the blast."
"The hour, the sweet hour I forecast,   130
   Little brother!"
   (O Mother, Mary Mother,
Is the hour sweet, between Hell and Heaven!)

"He stops to speak, and he stills his horse,
   Sister Helen;
But his words are drowned in the wind's course."
"Nay hear, nay hear, you must hear perforce,
   Little brother!"
   (O Mother, Mary Mother,
What word now heard, between Hell and Heaven!) 140

"Oh, he says that Keith of Ewern's cry,
   Sister Helen,
Is ever to see you ere he die."
"In all that his soul sees, there am I,
   Little brother!"
   (O Mother, Mary Mother,
The soul's one sight, between Hell and Heaven!)

"He sends a ring and a broken coin,
   Sister Helen,
And bids you mind the banks of Boyne."   150

"What else he broke will he ever join,
                    Little brother?"
              (*O Mother, Mary Mother,*
No, never joined, between Hell and Heaven!)

"He yields you these and craves full fain,
                    Sister Helen,
You pardon him in his mortal pain."
"What else he took will he give again,
                    Little brother?"
              (*O Mother, Mary Mother,*   160
Not twice to give, between Hell and Heaven!)

"He calls your name in an agony,
                    Sister Helen,
That even dead Love must weep to see."
"Hate, born of Love, is blind as he,
                    Little brother!"
              (*O Mother, Mary Mother,*
Love turned to hate, between Hell and Heaven!)

"Oh, it's Keith of Keith now that rides fast,
                    Sister Helen,   170
For I know the white hair on the blast."
"The short, short hour will soon be past,
                    Little brother!"
              (*O Mother, Mary Mother,*
Will soon be past, between Hell and Heaven!)

"He looks at me and he tries to speak,
                    Sister Helen,
But oh! his voice is sad and weak!"
"What here should the mighty Baron seek,
                    Little brother?"   180
              (*O Mother, Mary Mother,*
Is this the end, between Hell and Heaven?)

"Oh, his son still cries, if you forgive,
                    Sister Helen,
The body dies, but the soul shall live."

"Fire shall forgive me as I forgive,
   Little brother!"
   (*O Mother, Mary Mother,*
As she forgives, between Hell and Heaven!)

"Oh, he prays you, as his heart would rive,   190
   Sister Helen,
To save his dear son's soul alive." •
"Fire cannot slay it; it shall thrive,
   Little brother!"
   (*O Mother, Mary Mother,*
Alas, alas, between Hell and Heaven!)

"He cries to you, kneeling in the road,
   Sister Helen,
To go with him for the love of God!"
"The way is long to his son's abode,   200
   Little brother."
   (*O Mother, Mary Mother,*
The way is long, between Hell and Heaven!)

"A lady's here, by a dark steed brought,
   Sister Helen,
So darkly clad, I saw her not."
"See her now or never see aught,
   Little brother!"
   (*O Mother, Mary Mother,*
What more to see, between Hell and Heaven!) 210

"Her hood falls back, and the moon shines fair,
   Sister Helen,
On the Lady of Ewern's golden hair."
"Blest hour of my power and her despair,
   Little brother!"
   (*O Mother, Mary Mother,*
Hour blest and banned, between Hell and Heaven!)

"Pale, pale her cheeks, that in pride did glow,
   Sister Helen,
'Neath the bridal-wreath three days ago." 220

"One morn for pride and three days for woe,
    Little brother!"
    (*O Mother, Mary Mother,*
Three days, three nights, between Hell and Heaven!)

"Her clasped hands stretch from her bending head,
    Sister Helen;
With the loud wind's wail her sobs are wed."
"What wedding-strains hath her bridal-bed,
    Little brother?"
    (*O Mother, Mary Mother,*   230
What strain but death's, between Hell and Heaven!)

"She may not speak, she sinks in a swoon,
    Sister Helen—
She lifts her lips and gasps on the moon."
"Oh! might I but hear her soul's blithe tune,
    Little brother!"
    (*O Mother, Mary Mother,*
Her woe's dumb cry, between Hell and Heaven!)

"They've caught her to Westholm's saddlebow,
    Sister Helen,   240
And her moonlit hair gleams white in its flow."
"Let it turn whiter than winter snow,
    Little brother!"
    (*O Mother, Mary Mother,*
Woe-withered gold, between Hell and Heaven!)

"O Sister Helen, you heard the bell,
    Sister Helen!
More loud than the vesper-chime it fell."
"No vesper-chime, but a dying knell,
    Little brother!"   250
    (*O Mother, Mary Mother,*
His dying knell, between Hell and Heaven!)

"Alas! but I fear the heavy sound,
    Sister Helen;
Is it in the sky or in the ground?"

"Say, have they turned their horses round,
Little brother?"
(*O Mother, Mary Mother,
What would she more, between Hell and Heaven?*)

"They have raised the old man from his knee,   260
Sister Helen,
And they ride in silence hastily."
"More fast the naked soul doth flee,
Little brother!"
(*O Mother, Mary Mother,
The naked soul, between Hell and Heaven!*)

"Flank to flank are the three steeds gone,
Sister Helen,
But the lady's dark steed goes alone."
"And lonely her bridegroom's soul hath flown,   270
Little brother."
(*O Mother, Mary Mother,
The lonely ghost, between Hell and Heaven!*)

"Oh, the wind is sad in the iron chill,
Sister Helen,
And weary sad they look by the hill."
"But Keith of Ewern's sadder still,
Little brother!"
(*O Mother, Mary Mother,
Most sad of all, between Hell and Heaven!*)   280

"See, see, the wax has dropped from its place,
Sister Helen,
And the flames are winning up apace!"
"Yet here they burn but for a space,
Little brother!"
(*O Mother, Mary Mother,
Here for a space, between Hell and Heaven!*)

"Ah! what white thing at the door has crossed,
Sister Helen?
Ah! what is this that sighs in the frost?"   290

"A soul that's lost as mine is lost,
    Little brother!"
   (*O Mother, Mary Mother,*
Lost, lost, all lost, between Hell and Heaven!)
               1854

LYRIC POETRY

THE LYRIC was born when men first had the impulse to sing a song. Before this they had danced to music as a release to their emotions. Then they found words to accompany their instruments. Finally, in comparatively recent times, they composed songs for unaccompanied recitation. But still the idea of a tune prevailed, and to this day, whether or not lyrics are put to music, we think of them as songs, and we think of the poets as singers.

Lyrical poetry is an outlet to the emotions, which seem to be most commonly aroused by thoughts on love and religion. It is not surprising, therefore, that amorous and religious themes are those most frequently found in the lyric. But the subject matter of lyrical poetry extends to almost all aspects of life. Next to love and religion possibly the contemplation of nature has been the subject of most lyrics, though lyrics on death, even when divorced from religious expression, are almost as numerous. As we all know, songs often accompany work; they are also a usual means of exhorting men before battle and of cheering soldiers on the march, for they are often admirable expressions of triumphant patriotism. Reflective moods, too, perhaps Wordsworth's "emotion recollected in tranquillity," induce true poets to sing. And one should not neglect to mention, when enumerating some of the sources of lyrical inspiration, the high spirits and happiness that often lead to humorous verse, which sometimes takes its place among the great poetry of the race. Good company, especially in the presence of the flowing bowl, has led men to sing from time immemorial. Every period of English lyric poetry from the Middle Ages to the present has produced lyrics on all the more important of these themes.

Lyric Poetry of the Middle Ages

The earliest extant English lyrics were written in the first half of the thirteenth century. Already they were the products of literary poets and singers and were not popular songs of the folk. These older songs, sung by the people about their work and play, have unfortunately perished. That they once existed, however, we cannot doubt, for many records of complaints against them by the Church have survived. Probably because of the attitude of the clergy, the lyrics which have come down to us from the thirteenth, fourteenth, and fifteenth centuries were made by learned poets, of a moral turn of mind. They may be divided into the religious and moral lyrics, which form the larger part, and the secular lyrics, which constitute the smaller, but no less significant, part.

Life was hard to endure in the northern climate of England, and this fact may explain the congeniality of the story of the sufferings of Christ with the English temperament. Among the religious poems, one of the earliest, *Sunset on Calvary*, depicts the crucifixion:

> Nou goth sonne vnder wod,—
> me reweth, marie, thi faire Rode.
> Nou goth sonne vnder tre,—
> me reweth, marie, thi sone and the.

Without mentioning the dead Christ, the poet has made us see the body hanging from the cross with Mary weeping beneath it. The whole tragic tale of suffering and death is suggested.

The typically English mood of despair, usually expressed by the medieval word, *Weilawei!*, runs through a great deal of the medieval lyric poetry. We find it in a lullaby of Mary to her Child:

> Lollai, lollai, litil child, whi wepistou so sore?
> nedis mostou wepe, hit was igarkid the yore
> euer to lib in sorow, and sich and mourne euere,

as thin eldren did er this, whil he aliues were.
Lollai, lollai, litil child, child lolai, lullow,
In-to vncuth world icommen so ertow!

Here is the note of the vanity, the sorrow, the transitoriness of all things in this life which is one mark of the medieval English spirit.

Not only do the religious lyrics reflect the mood of the people; they also reveal aspects of the thought of the times. Two examples will illustrate the point.

In the poem beginning, "Adam lay ibounden," we find a logical argument which is derived from the scholastic training of the medieval schools. The poet assures us that Adam did us a good service by eating the apple, for, although he lay in bonds four thousand winters to pay for his transgression,

Ne hadde the appil take ben,
The appil taken ben,
Ne hadde never our lady
A ben hevene quene.

The clerk-author concludes by blessing the time when the apple was eaten:

Blessed be the time
That appil take was.
Therefore we moun singen
"Deo gracias."

The paradox may well have come from a students' debate in the colleges of Oxford or Cambridge. Its appearance in this humorous religious poem is an indication of the prevalence of scholastic thought.

The second illustration which we shall give of a common medieval thought pattern in the lyrics concerns the conventions of courtly love. When we find references in the lyrics of the Middle Ages to Mary as a lady to be served by her vassal, or to Mary as a rose, we are reminded of the days of chivalry. The first stanza of *A Song of Love to the Blessed Virgin* reflects this medieval way of thinking:

Off alle floures feirest fall on,
And that is Marie, Moder fre,
That bar the child of flesch and bon,
Ihesu, Godes sone in Maieste.
A loue-likyng is come to me
To serue that ladi, qwen of blis,
Ay better and better in my degre,
The lengor that I liue, I-wis.

As we find many aspects of medieval thought imbeded in
the religious poetry, so in the secular poetry these same traits,
and some others, appear. The tradition of courtly love runs
all through such a lyric as *Alysoun*, that very personal cry of
an anonymous fourteenth century lover. The lyrics which
Geoffrey Chaucer wrote for the sophisticated ladies of the
court are full of it. This worship of women is not the only
note, however, which we hear in the medieval poetry, for
some of the poets were neither so happy in their loves nor so
gallant. The satirist gibes:

In sorow and care he lede his life,
That have a schrow ontill his wife.

Chaucer in jest writes to his friend Bukton of "the wo that is
in mariage." And an unmarried man sings:

The bachelor most joyfully
In pleasant plight doth pass his days;
Good fellowship and company
He doth maintain and keep always.

Such a young man in his hours of good fellowship might have
sung:

Ale make many a man to stik at a brere;
Ale make many a man to ly in the miere;
And ale make many a man to slepe by the fiere.
With doll!

From these and dozens of other lyrics one can draw for oneself
a picture of the life and modes of thought of England in the

Middle Ages. Religious feeling predominates here, but love
and satire and jollity have their places.

Lyric Poetry of the Sixteenth and Seventeenth Centuries

With the coming of the sixteenth century many new in-.
fluences began to appear in the English lyric. England was
united and peaceful; from Flodden Field to the Civil War
no battle was fought on English soil. English ships were voyag-
ing to all parts of the world and returning laden with exotic
luxuries. The country was growing in wealth, and the people
were cultivating the arts of painting, music, sculpture, architecture, and poetry. In science a few men were already con-
ducting experiments in private laboratories and in the one or
two anatomical theaters which existed. English travellers were
bringing back exciting tales from their tours on the Continent,
and were including in their luggage books of French and
Italian poetry and texts of the Greek and Latin classics, which
were constantly coming from the foreign presses. The English production of books rose enormously in this century and
the next. This wide circulation of all sorts of literature,
coupled with the stimulation to the intellectual life of the nation caused by the beginnings of scientific investigation and
the voyages of discovery, inspired the greatest lyrical flowering that England has ever known.

King Henry the Eighth, himself a poet, encouraged this
growth, which blossomed before the end of his reign in hundreds of new lyrics in the manner of the French and Italian
poets. The most distinguished of these early writers were Sir
Thomas Wyatt and the Earl of Surrey, both of whom naturalized the sonnet of Petrarch in England. Wyatt was the older
and more powerful lyrist, though many of his sonnets are
translations from or adaptations of the sonnets of Petrarch
and other Italians. In this dawn of the Renascence his step was
still uneasy and at times heavy. But in such verses as *My Galley
Charged with Forgetfulness*, in spite of the trite Petrarchan

figure, he achieved force and dignity of language. He is
at times still medieval, as in the lyric *Forget not yet,* the
second stanza of which is a good example of the crudity of
Wyatt's versifying. But all English lyrists for the next century
looked to him as the father of the sonnet in English. Henry
Howard, Earl of Surrey, wrote more smoothly than Wyatt,
though less memorably. His sonnets often seem medieval in
tone, as, for instance, the *Description of Spring,* the first few
lines of which, so far as their thought goes, might as well
have sprung from the fourteenth century:

> The soote season that bud and bloom forth brings
> With green hath clad the hill and eke the vale,
> The nightingale with feathers new she sings,
> The turtle to her make hath told her tale.

The poems of both these men remained in manuscript until
1557 when Richard Tottel, the publisher, collected them,
together with the work of a good many other poets of the first
half of the century, and issued a miscellany under the title
Songs and Sonnets. This, the earliest anthology of poems of
the new writers, may be regarded as the first harvest of the
lyric fruit of the English Renascence.

The next important event after the publication of Tottel's
miscellany was the appearance in 1579 of *The Shepherds'
Calendar.* In the following songlike dialogue one feels the
vernal quality of this spring of English poetry:

> PERIGOT. It fell upon a holy eve,
> WILLYE.   Hey, ho, holidaye!
> PER. When holly fathers wont to shrieve;
> WIL.   Now gynneth this roundelay.
> PER. Sitting upon a hill so high,
> WIL.   Hey, ho, the high hyll!
> PER. The while my flocke did feede thereby;
> WIL.   The while the shepheard selfe did spill;
> PER. I saw the bouncing Bellibone,

WIL.   Hey, ho, bonibel!
PER.   Tripping over the dale alone,
WIL.   She can trippe it very well!

Delicately making use of the ballad stanza, the song of Perigot
and Willie achieves a clarity new to the English language.

Within the next generation it seemed that all England had
turned to composing verses. Poetry was the fashion at Court.
Every gentleman knew how to compose at least one sonnet to
his lady's eyebrow. Long sonnet sequences were written by
Spenser, Sidney, Daniel, Drayton, and Shakespeare. Spenser
moulded his verses into many forms, and in the *Epithalamion*,
the rapturous song for his own marriage, reached perhaps his
grandest notes. The chorus was swelled by such men as Sidney
and Watson, Lodge and Marlowe, Breton and Campion, to
name only a few out of many dozens of young men who were
now singing in England. And it is especially proper to call
their poems songs, for during these same years English musi-
cians were taking the lead in Europe, and to their tunes scores
of Elizabethan lyrics were sung. Of all the lyrists of this time,
Shakespeare holds the first place with his unforgettable songs.
The very breath of spring runs through

> On a day—alack the day!—
> Love, whose month is ever May,
> Spied a blossom, passing fair,
> Playing in the wanton air:
> Through the velvet leaves the wind,
> All unseen, gan passage find;
> That the lover, sick to death,
> Wished himself the heaven's breath.

Dozens of such joyous nothings are scattered through the
plays of the next twenty years. Nor was Shakespeare alone.
Greene, Nashe, Kyd, Munday, Dekker, Marston, all filled the
stages with some of the loveliest songs ever written.

With the passing of the sixteenth century the character of
the lyric began to change, and three tendencies, now divergent

now coincident, may be marked. One group of conservative poets, following in the footsteps of Spenser, wrote in the pastoral vein. Giles and Phineas Fletcher and William Browne are perhaps the best known representatives of this school. Their type of imitation of Spenser flourished for only a few years and then became merged in the other movements of the time, though the influence of Spenser himself continued straight down to the nineteenth century, if indeed, it may be said to have ceased yet. The other two tendencies sprang from the work of Ben Jonson and John Donne, who first became known in the last two or three years of the sixteenth century, and exercised dominant influences on the poetry of the entire seventeenth.

The carefree, and seemingly careless, ecstasies which had marked the lyrics of Shakespeare and many other poets of the day became in Ben Jonson less rhapsodic, somewhat more precise and intellectual. In the stanzaic form, with its formal final line repeated in all three stanzas, Jonson's *Hymn to Diana* illustrates this subtle change:

> Queen and huntress, chaste and fair,
>   Now the sun is laid to sleep,
> Seated in thy silver chair,
>   State in wonted manner keep:
>   Hesperus entreats thy light,
>   Goddess excellently bright.

The poet has not simply lifted up his voice and sung; rather he has chiseled out of his imagination each word with which he expresses his thought. In the manner of the ancients whom he so greatly admired, he has striven for balance of word and phrase and for clarity of image. His poem is no less pleasing than those more free songs of the older poets, but it is more formal.

The "Sons of Ben" sought in their poems the same restraint and directness of phrase as had marked the work of their master. Thomas Carew in *Spring* presents a picture which is probably inspired by Jonson and the poets of antiquity. Robert Herrick, though more personal than Jonson, preserves simplicity of phrase and clarity of image. Waller, Lovelace, Suckling, and at the end of the century, Rochester and Dryden, all carried on the tradition, which proved ideal for the poets of the "Age of Reason." The very directness of statement which they admired had come to them with the authority of the name of Ben Jonson. Under their treatment, however, the lyrical devices of Jonson and his "Sons" lost their ecstasy.

The third tendency in the lyric poetry of the seventeenth century emanated from the work of John Donne. Although himself an Elizabethan, Donne belonged to the younger, realistic school which sprang up at the very end of the sixteenth century. His poetry is characterized by a new use of figures of speech which are unusual and which heighten the emotional effect by their intellectual appeal. In his effort to express his thought with precision, Donne was attempting to break down the conventional categories of comparison in order to focus the reader's attention more accurately on some one aspect of his subject. To accomplish this, he pointed out similarities in seemingly unlike things and almost startled his readers into fresh intellectual and emotional experience. For example, in Donne's best known lyric, *A Valediction Forbidding Mourning*, he counsels his wife not to weep because he has to leave her for an extended trip to France. He continues:

> Our two souls, therefore, which are one,
>   Though I must go, endure not yet
> A breach, but an expansion,
>   Like gold to airy thinness beat.

The thought of the two souls of Donne and his wife being like goldleaf beaten to "airy thinness" requires intellectual effort because it is startlingly unusual. This type of figure of speech is called "conceit." It runs all through Donne's early love poems, and one finds it giving power to his later religious lyrics, such, for instance, as, *The Funeral, The Relic,* and the *Hymn to God, my God, in my Sickness.*

After Donne had shown the way, many of the most brilliant poets of the seventeenth century wrote "metaphysical" poetry, as Dr. Johnson termed it. In such a poem as *The Collar,* George Herbert carries the conceit through from the very title to the last line. In *Life* the figure of the fading flowers is a particularly touching reminder of the death that comes to all. Richard Crashaw employed the metaphysical conceit, which seems especially suitable to his devoutly Catholic, emotional experience. By its use in *The World,* Henry Vaughan makes one actually see Eternity:

> I saw Eternity the other night
> Like a great *Ring* of pure and endless light,
>   All calm as it was bright.

The conceit is here sublime. Other metaphysical poets whom one must not forget to mention include Thomas Traherne, Aurelian Townsend, Abraham Cowley, and Andrew Marvell. The last named, in particular, brings together in the *Bermudas, The Garden, To His Coy Mistress,* and elsewhere, both the method of Donne and that of Jonson. Thus, writing almost at the Restoration, he seems to complete a circle which began to be drawn by two divergent tendencies at the end of the sixteenth century and only closed its arc two generations later.

One more lyrist of the seventeenth century, in whom nearly all literary forms and tendencies combine, remains to be considered. John Milton has been called the last of the Elizabethans. He is also the epitome of all seventeenth century lyric poetry. The spirit of a *Song on a May Morning* is that of an earlier generation. Through it and through *L'Allegro* and *Il Penseroso* we catch echos of Shakespeare warbling "his native wood-notes wild." The sonnets, too, though in Italian form, are in the tradition of the late Elizabethans. Milton's poetry likewise contains evidences of all three tendencies of seventeenth century poetry which we have just discussed. The influence of Spenser runs through the pastoral elegy *Lycidas*. In *Comus* the Jonsonian masque has been adapted. Finally, the conceit of the metaphysical poets appears in *On the Morning of Christ's Nativity*. Beyond all of these influences and tendencies Milton added something for which no better word has yet been found than "Miltonic."

Lyric Poetry of the Eighteenth and Nineteenth Centuries

Though Milton's three long poems, through which are sprinkled many lyric passages, were not completed until some years after the Restoration, all of his strictly lyrical poetry was finished before 1660. The work of most of the other lyrists of the seventeenth century also ended about this time or within a few years thereafter. Then followed an age, lasting nearly a century, when England was virtually without lyric poetry. It is true that hundreds of verses were composed, but in only a handful, notably the lyrics of William Collins and several passages in Gray's poems, do we discern the true lyric note. The reason for this curious lack in the literature of the latter seventeenth century and the first three quarters of the eighteenth century must be sought in the temperament of the time. In our essay on narrative poetry, we said that it was the "Age of Reason"; in our essay on moral poetry, we shall have a good deal more to say concerning this period as one in which prose and the formal heroic couplet were the prevailing literary mediums. In commenting here on the lyric, we shall only remark that the social life of England in the late seventeenth century was dominated by an idea of formality and decorum. Even the songs had to be "reasonable." Men seldom let themselves go in the freedom of a lyric, the whole point of which might be merely the joy of singing a song. The song had to have a rational thought and be expressed with more dignity than seemed to the people of this era to reside in an

Elizabethan "Heigh, ho!" And so a hundred years passed, and great poetry was written, but few men sang.

In the late eighteenth century, however, many changes came about. In political theory the "Age of Reason" was reaching its height. In France, Rousseau was explaining the nature of the state in terms of *The Social Contract;* in America, Tom Paine was preaching democratic doctrine in *The Age of Reason;* and in England, William Godwin was expounding his social theories in *Political Justice.* All of these men were unorthodox in their Christianity and for the most part called themselves deists. But their anti-Christianity was not pessimistic as to the future of man; rather it was extremely optimistic and hopeful, for they believed wholeheartedly in the power of men to improve their situation. When the French Revolution broke out in 1789, they rejoiced. "How much it is the greatest event that ever happened; and how much it is the best," exclaimed the politician Charles James Fox on hearing the news. He was expressing the thought of thousands of his countrymen. William Blake greeted the event. After some delay, Wordsworth accepted the cause. The popular feeling was that at last men might achieve freedom. But as time went on and England herself became embroiled in a war with France, the retreat set in and patriotism was revived. Finally, the victory at Waterloo in 1815 which ensured the freedom of England from foreign invasion, was the knell of the freedom of individuals to express their feelings. This left only freedom of the imagination for the poets.

The belief in the power of *reason,* which had been one of the characteristics of the thought of the early eighteenth century, was by the end of that period greatly weakened. Men were beginning to distrust what their *minds* could tell them. They demanded, on the contrary, the right to consult their *feelings* for an interpretation of the world about them. Nature, whose counsels come to us through our senses, they considered the surest guide to knowledge. Wordsworth exclaims to his sister Dorothy:

> One moment now may give us more
> Than fifty years of reason;
> Our minds shall drink at every pore
> The spirit of the season.

This attitude of mind which permeated the literature of the time was called "Romanticism", and of course it was far more complex than one can say in few words. In their attempts to express the knowledge derived from their feelings, the Romantic poets paid a new and much greater attention to the influence of natural objects on our lives; they were inspired in part by the new study of and interest in the Middle Ages; they wrote with a special consciousness of the supernatural; and very frequently they displayed a particular sympathy for childhood and the intuitive understanding of children.

One of the first poets to respond to the new spirit was Robert Burns, who found among the simple folk from whom he sprang material from which he created new songs. The lyric note is again heard as we read:

> Green grow the rashes, O;
> Green grow the rashes, O;
> The sweetest hours that e'er I spend,
> Are spent amang the lasses, O.

Writing during exactly the same years, William Blake was even more truly the herald of the new poetic movement. His *Poetical Sketches* are the work of the mystic who is also the great artist. Indeed, these two powers come together perfectly in such a poem as *To the Evening Star*. The *Songs of Innocence and Experience* which reveal Blake as the true modernist, appeared in 1789. Here, in *The Lamb, The Little Black Boy, The Chimney Sweeper*, for instance, the poets of the present day have found inspiration and technical suggestion. But Blake was disregarded by his own generation and given his proper place in the history of English poetry only within comparatively recent years. Meantime, another poet was given credit for beginning the movement toward Romanticism.

William Wordsworth and Samuel Taylor Coleridge published in 1798 a little volume of poems entitled *Lyrical Ballads*. In this collection Wordsworth tried to get away from the old eighteenth century theory of poetry which differentiated the language of poets from that of prose writers. On the contrary, he attempted to write poetry in the words and phrases which men used in their daily intercourse. The subject matter of his poems, also, was the every day life he saw around him. *Lines Written in Early Spring* illustrates the point. It is a simple meditation in the language of everyday people, but the thought is profound and the poetry moving. Of the poems which Coleridge contributed to the volume, *The Rime of the Ancient Mariner* is his greatest and his most characteristic. In it one finds the medievalism and the supernaturalism so characteristic of the Romantics, and one also feels the magical music which is the author's own. *Lyrical Ballads* pointed the way for poets of the Romantic movement and gave a promise of the future works of its own two authors.

Of the other great poets of this period, Lord Byron cannot be regarded as essentially a lyric poet. This sharp, satirical man saw things too much in terms of stories, of personal dislikes, and of lessons to be driven home. We include *So We'll Go No More A-Roving* and two or three other song-like poems among the lyrics of this volume, but Byron did not have the spirit of a lyrist. Shelley and Keats, on the other hand, were predominantly poets of song. As we read almost any of the songs from Shelley's *Prometheus Unbound* we feel this. In *Love's Philosophy* he achieved the lyric ecstasy and a perfection of form. It ends with this stanza:

> See the mountains kiss high Heaven
>   And the waves clasp one another;
> No sister-flower would be forgiven
>   If it disdained its brother,
> And the sunlight clasps the earth
>   And the moonbeams kiss the sea:
> What is all this sweet work worth
>   If thou kiss not me?

One feels this ecstasy sustained to extraordinary lengths in the *Ode to the West Wind, The Cloud, To a Skylark.* If one must point to a lyrical defect in this poet, it is that he so frequently felt the need to espouse a cause in his lyrics. His *Song to the Men of England,* for instance, has not the freedom, the joy, which belongs to the true lyric. He was at his best when dealing with great ideas, such as the Platonism which runs through *Adonais,* the *Hymn to Intellectual Beauty,* and many another of his poems.

With Keats we encounter the most finished artist of the poets of the early nineteenth century. His was a power to envision a pure image. As we read the *Ode on a Grecian Urn,* we see without cloud the urn and the "flowery tale" pictured on it. We sense the "unheard" melodies; we partake of the "happy love" of the youth and maiden; we see as through a glass, the folk gathering for the sacrifice of the heifer. Finally, we are left with the clear image of the storied urn and the knowledge that

> "Beauty is truth, truth beauty,"—that is all
> Ye know on earth, and all ye need to know.

The poem is finished in every detail, and the image is complete. Although such perfection is not found in Keats' earliest work, one might analyze any one of the other odes, or almost any other of the later poems, and find the same clarity of thought and image.

The Romantic poets had written out of the confidence of their religious, political, and artistic philosophies. Their successors the Victorians were less certain of any philosophical verities. Tennyson seems to affirm his faith the more vehemently because he is unsure. Matthew Arnold could only conclude:

> . . . we are here as on a darkling plain
> Swept with confused alarms of struggle and flight,
> Where ignorant armies clash by night.

And Browning cries:

> God's in his heaven—
> All's right with the world!

as if to brace himself against the fact that the world is obviously not all right.

In the midst of their doubts, however, all three of these men were able to sing. Tennyson's lyrics have an enchantment which endears them even to a generation which rejects much of his poetry. One is caught by the ring of

> Blow, bugle, blow: set the wild echoes flying;
> Answer, bugle; answer, echoes,—dying, dying, dying.

The short lyrics from *Maud* and the long *Ode on the Death of the Duke of Wellington* alike have a musical power. With Arnold the music is of a different sort, more quiet and more subtle. But one catches it clearly in *The Forsaken Merman* and elsewhere. The third of this group, Robert Browning, possessed a particularly acute ear for the subtleties of sound, and occasionally he came out with a fine downright marching song as in *Cavalier Tunes:*

> Marching along, fifty-score strong,
> Great-hearted gentlemen, singing this song.

Many others of the Victorians wrote lovely lyrics. Christina Rossetti's *When I am dead*, Thomas Lovell Beddoes' *To Sea, To Sea!*, a number of Dante Gabriel Rossetti's sonnets from *The House of Life*, and Elizabeth Barrett Browning's *Sonnets from the Portuguese*, all possess the spirit of song.

The lyrics of this generation are marked, moreover, by philosophical tone. Browning's Pippa sings

> All service ranks the same with God,

and in *The Garden of Proserpine*, Swinburne meditates on change and the passage of time. This philosophical bent took the particular form in Tom Hood, and other poets of the workers, of propaganda lyrics for better labor conditions.

The Victorians were serious, and their seriousness comes out constantly in their fine lyrics. Their love of verbal smoothness, which even a slight acquaintance with their prose will reveal, is no where more evident than in their lyric poetry.

As the nineteenth century drew to a close and the twentieth opened, the spirit of the great Victorians seemed only slightly altered. Robert Bridges followed Tennyson and others of his generation in their feeling for the music of verse and in their philosophical musings. But his poems are also individual. *When my Love was away* and *So Sweet Love Seemed That April Morn* illustrate the delicacy of thought and the polish of form which characterize his work. At the very end of his life Bridges published *The Testament of Beauty*, a long poem in which occur many lyrical passages. Here we find an experimentalism in poetry which brings his work down to the thought of our own times. Also writing in the nineties was A. E. Housman, the most precise of modern poets. The lyrics from *A Shropshire Lad* are formed with the exactness of the classical poems, short, to the point, verbally perfect.

> With rue my heart is laden
>   For golden friends I had,
> For many a rose-lipped maiden
>   And many a lightfoot lad.
>
> By brooks too broad for leaping
>   The lightfoot boys are laid;
> The rose-lipped girls are sleeping
>   In fields where roses fade.

In this pellucid poem not a word is idly used. It is typical of the best in Housman—and most of his poetry is the best. With William Butler Yeats we come to the most distinguished of the Irish national poets of the nineties. His lyrics are marked by the author's use of the stories of Irish legend. *The Stolen Child*, based on one of the old tales, has the refrain:

Come away, O human child!
To the waters and the wild
With a faery, hand in hand,
For the world's more full of weeping than
you can understand.

The Celtic vein of Yeats' poetry is manifest in *The White Birds* and *The Rose of the World*, where he employs symbols to express a mystical thought. Throughout his poetry runs a feeling for the elves and fairies who inhabit his Ireland. Finally, we end with the lyrics of John Masefield, the present Poet Laureate. He stole away from home as a boy of fourteen and went to sea, and *Sea-Fever, Cargoes, St. Mary's Bells*, all in their ways reflect this experience. *The West Wind* illustrates the ballad-like lilt of many of his poems, and in it, too, we find the love of the out-of-doors and the spring.

Three different periods from the thirteenth century to the twentieth have witnessed the flourishing of English lyrical poetry. The first came in the Middle Ages, and to it belongs some of the most moving Christian poetry written in England. With the sixteenth century a second period begins, and from Tottel's miscellany in 1557 to the time of the Restoration nearly every kind of lyric poem was written. During this time, moreover, it seemed that poetry was in the air, for lyrics were produced by courtiers and statesmen, by parsons and rakes, by everyone who could carry a tune. Finally, towards the close of the eighteenth century, a third period of the lyric commenced, which has already extended from the time of Wordsworth down to that of the present Poet Laureate. The poets of this last period have imitated all the devices used by their predecessors and have developed others of their own.

FURTHER READING

John Drinkwater, *The Lyric*, 1915.
John Erskine, *The Elizabethan Lyric*, 1905.
Ernest Rhys, *Lyric Poetry*, 1913.
Felix E. Schelling, *The English Lyric*, 1913.

ANONYMOUS

I Syng of a Mayden

I syng of a mayden
  That is makeles;
Kyng of alle kynges
  To here sone che ches.

He cam also stylle
  Ther his moder was,
As dew in aprylle
  That fallyt on the gras.

He cam also stylle
  To his moderes bowr   10
As dew in aprille
  That fallyt on the flour.

He cam also stylle
  Ther his moder lay,
As dew in aprille
  That fallyt on the spray.

Moder and maydyn
  Was never non but che;
Wel may swych a lady
  Godes moder be.   20
About 1300

Sumer Is Icumen In

Sumer is icumen in,
  Lhude sing cuccu;
Groweth sed and bloweth med
  And springth the wude nu.
    Sing cuccu;

2. *makeles*, without a mate.   4. *Che ches*, she chose.   2. *Lhude*, loud.

Awe bleteth after lomb,
Lhouth after calve cu;
Bulluc sterteth, bucke verteth;
Murie sing cuccu.
    Cuccu, cuccu,   10
Wel singes thu, cuccu,
Ne swik thu naver nu.
About 1240

Lenten Ys Come with Love to Toune

Lenten ys come with love to toune,
With blosmen ant with briddes roune,
    That al this blisse bryngeth;
Dayes-eyes in this dales,
Notes suete of nyhtegales,
    Vch foul song singeth;
The threstlecoc him threteth oo,
Away is huere wynter wo,
    When woderove springeth;
This foules singeth ferly fele,   10
Ant wlyteth on huere winter wele,
    That al the wode ryngeth.

The rose rayleth hire rode,
The leves on the lyhte wode
    Waxen al with wille;
The mone mandeth hire bleo,
The lilie is lossom to seo,
    The fenyl ant the fille;
Wowes this wilde drakes,

6. *awe*, ewe.   7. *Lhouth*, loweth.   7. *cu*, cow.   8. *sterteth*, jumps.
8. *verteth*, leaps.   9. *murie*, merry.   11. *thu*, thou.
12. *swik*, rest.   12. *naver*, never.
1. *to toune*, in turn.   6. *Vch*, each.   7. *threteth oo*, chides them.
8. *huere*, their.   9. *woderove*, woodruff.
10. *ferly fele*, wonderfully many.   11. *wlyteth*, look.   13. *rayleth*, clothes.
13. *rode*, red.   16. *mandeth hire bleo*, sends her light.
17. *lossom*, lovesome.   18. *fille*, thyme.   19. *wowes*, woo.

Miles murgeth huere makes;   20
    Ase strem that striketh stille,
Mody meneth; so doth mo
(Ichot ycham on of tho)
    For love that likes ille.

The mone mandeth hire lyht,
So doth the semly sonne bryht,
    When briddes singeth breme;
Deawes donketh the dounes,
Deores with huere derne rounes
    Domes forte deme;   30
Wormes woweth under cloude,
Wymmen waxeth wounder proude
    So wel hit wol hem seme,
Yef me shal wonte wille of on,
This wunne weole y wole forgon
    Ant wyht in wode be fleme.
About 1300

Alysoun

Bytuene Mersh ant Averil
    When spray biginneth to springe,
The lutel foul hath hire wyl
    On hyre lud to synge.
Ic libbe in love-longinge
    For semlokest of alle thinge;
He may me blisse bringe;
    Icham in hire baundoun.

20. *miles*, males.   20. *murgeth*, please.   20. *makes*, mates.
21. *striketh*, flows.   22. *mody meneth*, the moody man laments.
22. *mo*, many.   23. *Ichot*, I think.   23. *ycham*, I am.
27. *breme*, gaily.   28. *deawes*, dews.   28. *donketh*, make wet.
29. *deores*, lovers.   29. *derne*, secret.   29. *rounes*, tales.
30. *domes*, decisions.   30. *deme*, to judge.   31. *cloude*, clod.
34. *Yef*, if.   34. *wonte*, win.   35. *wunne weole*, wealth of joy.
36. *wyht*, wight.   36. *fleme*, banished.
4. *On hyre lud*, in her language.   5. *Ic libbe*, I live.
6. *semlokest*, seemliest.   7. *He*, She.
8. *Icham*, I am. *baundoun*, bondage.

An hendy hap ichabbe yhent;
Ichot from hevene it is me sent;   10
From alle wymmen mi love is lent
Ant lyht on Alysoun.

On heu hire her is fayr ynuh,
   Hire browe broune, hire eye blake;
With lossum chere he on me loh,
   With middel smal ant wel ymake.
   Bote he me wolle to hire take,
   Forte buen hire owen make,
   Longe to lyven ichulle forsake,
Ant feye fallen adoun.   20

Nihtes when I wende ant wake,
   Forthi myn wonges waxeth won.
Levedi, al for thine sake
   Longinge is ylent me on.
   In world nis non so wytermon,
   That al hire bounte telle con.
   Hire swyre is whittore then the swon,
Any feyrest may in toune.

Icham for wowing al forswake,
   Wery so water in wore.   30
Lest eny reve me my make,
   Icbhabe y-yerned yore.
   Beter is tholien whyle sore,
   Then mournen evermore.
   Geynest under gore,

9. *hendy*, pleasant. *ichabbe*, I have. *yhent*, seized.   10. *Ichot*, I think.
13. *On heu*, In hew. *hire*, her. *her*, hair. *ynuh*, enough.
15. *lossum*, devoted. *loh*, smiled.   17. *he*, she.
18. *forte buen*, for to be. *make*, mate.   19. *ichulle*, I shall.
20. *feye*, like to die.   21. *wende*, turn.
22. *Forthi*, because. *wonges waxeth won*, cheeks become wan.
23. *Levedi*, Lady.   24. *ylent*, come.   25. *wytermon*, wise a man.
27. *swyre*, neck.   28. *may*, maid.
29. *wowing*, wooing. *forswake*, worn out.   30. *wore*, weir.
31. *reve*, rob.   33. *tholien*, endure.
35. *geynest*, prettiest. *gore*, woman's dress.

Herkne to my roun.
  An hendy hap ichabbe yhent;
  Ichot from hevene it is me sent;
  From alle wymmen mi love is lent
Ant lyht on Alysoun.   40
About 1300

GEOFFREY CHAUCER

Now Welcom Somer

Now welcom somer, with thy sonne softe
That hast this wintres weders over-shake,
And driven awey the longe nightes blake!
Seynt Valentyn, that art ful hy on-lofte;—
Thus singen smale foules for thy sake—
  Now welcom somer, with thy sonne softe
  That hast this wintres weders over-shake.
Wel han they cause for to gladen ofte,
Sith ech of hem recovered hath his make
Ful blisful may they singen whan they wake;   10

  Now welcom somer, with thy sonne softe,
  That hast this wintres weders over-shake,
  And driven awey the longe nightes blake.
The Parliament of Fowls, about 1382

SIR THOMAS WYATT

Forget Not Yet the Tried Intent

Forget not yet the tried intent
Of such a truth as I have meant,
My great travail, so gladly spent,
    Forget not yet.

Forget not yet when first began
The weary life ye know, since whan

9. *make*, mate.

The suit, the service none tell can,
   Forget not yet.

Forget not yet the great assays,
The cruel wrong, the scornful ways;   10
The painful patience in denays,
   Forget not yet.

Forget not yet, forget not this,
How long ago hath been, and is,
The mind that never meant amiss,
   Forget not yet.

Forget not, then, thine own approved,
The which so long hath thee so loved,
Whose steadfast faith yet never moved;
   Forget not this.   20
Before 1533

The Lover Complaineth the Unkindness of His Love

My lute, awake! perform the last
Labour that thou and I shall waste,
And end that I have now begun;
And when this song is sung and past,
My lute, be still, for I have done.

   As to be heard where ear is none,
As lead to grave in marble stone,
My song may pierce her heart as soon.
Should we then sigh, or sing, or moan?
No, no, my lute, for I have done.   10

   The rocks do not so cruelly
Repulse the waves continually,
As she my suit and affection;
So that I am past remedy,
Whereby my lute and I have done.

   Proud of the spoil that thou hast got
Of simple hearts, through love's shot;

By whom unkind thou hast them won,
Think not he hath his bow forgot,
Although my lute and I have done.   20

Vengeance shall fall on thy disdain,
That makest but game on earnest pain;
Think not alone under the sun
Unquit to cause thy lover's plain,
Although my lute and I have done.

May chance thee lie withered and old,
In winter nights that are so cold,
Plaining in vain unto the moon;
Thy wishes then dare not be told.
Care then who list, for I have done.   30

And then may chance thee to repent
The time that thou hast lost and spent
To cause thy lover's sigh and swoon;
Then shalt thou know beauty but lent,
And wish and want as I have done.

Now cease, my lute, this is the last
Labour that thou and I shall waste,
And ended is that we begun.
Now is this song both sung and past,
My lute, be still, for I have done.   40
Before 1533

HENRY HOWARD, EARL OF SURREY

Description of Spring Wherein Each Thing Renews, Save Only the Lover

The soote season that bud and bloom forth brings,
With green hath clad the hill and eke the vale;
The nightingale with feathers new she sings;   ·
The turtle to her make hath told her tale:
Summer is come, for every spray now springs;
The hart hath hung his old head on the pale;

1. *soote*, sweet.   4. *make*, mate.

The buck in brake his winter coat he flings;
The fishes float with new repairéd scale;
The adder all her slough away she slings;
The swift swallow pursueth the flies smale;   10
The busy bee her honey now she mings.
Winter is worn, that was the flowers' bale:
And thus I see among these pleasant things
Each care decays, and yet my sorrow springs!
Before 1547

Complaint of a Lover Rebuked

Love that liveth and reigneth in my thought,
That built his seat within my captive brest,
Clad in the arms wherein with me he fought,
Oft in my face he doth his banner rest.
She, that me taught to love, and suffer pain,
My doubtful hope and eke my hot desire
With shamefast cloak to shadow and refrain,
Her smiling grace converteth straight to ire.
And coward Love then to the heart apace
Taketh his flight, whereas he lurks and plains   10
His purpose lost, and dare not show his face.
For my lord's guilt thus faultless bide I pains.
Yet from my lord shall not my foot remove;
Sweet is his death that takes his end by love.
Before 1547

EDMUND SPENSER

Prothalamion [1]

Calme was the day, and through the trembling ayre
Sweete breathing Zephyrus did softly play,
A gentle spirit, that lightly did delay
Hot Titans beames, which then did glyster fayre:
When I, whom sullein care,

[1] Spenser wrote *Prothalamion* to honor the approaching marriage of the Ladies Elizabeth and Katherine Somerset in 1596.

Through discontent of my long fruitlesse stay
In princes court, and expectation vayne
Of idle hopes, which still doe fly away,
Like empty shaddowes, did aflict my brayne,
Walkt forth to ease my payne   10
Along the shoare of silver streaming Themmes;
Whose rutty bancke, the which his river hemmes,
Was paynted all with variable flowers,
And all the meades adornd with daintie gemmes,
Fit to decke maydens bowres,
And crowne their paramours,
Against the brydale day, which is not long:
    Sweete Themmes, runne softly, till I end my song.

There, in a meadow, by the rivers side,
A flocke of nymphes I chaunced to espy,   20
All lovely daughters of the flood thereby,
With goodly greenish locks all loose untyde,
As each had bene a bryde:
And each one had a little wicker basket,
Made of fine twigs entrayled curiously,
In which they gathered flowers to fill their flasket;
And with fine fingers cropt full feateously
The tender stalkes on hye.
Of every sort, which in that meadow grew,
They gathered some; the violet pallid blew,   30
The little dazie, that at evening closes,
The virgin lillie, and the primrose trew,
With store of vermeil roses,
To decke their bridegromes posies
Against the brydale day, which was not long:
    Sweete Themmes, runne softly, till I end my song.

With that I saw two swannes of goodly hewe
Come softly swimming downe along the lee;
Two fairer birds I yet did never see:
The snow which doth the top of Pindus strew   40
Did never whiter shew,
Nor Jove himselfe, when he a swan would be
For love of Leda, whiter did appear:

Yet Leda was, they say, as white as he,
Yet not so white as these, nor nothing neare:
So purely white they were,
That even the gentle streame, the which them bare,
Seem'd foule to them, and bad his billows spare
To wet their silken feathers, least they might
Soyle their fayre plumes with water not so fayre,   50
And marre their beauties bright,
That shone as heavens light,
Against their brydale day, which was not long:
　　Sweete Themmes, runne softly, till I end my song.

Eftsoones the nymphes, which now had flowers their fill,
Ran all in haste to see that silver brood,
As they came floating on the christal flood;
Whom when they sawe, they stood amazed still,
Their wondring eyes to fill.
They seem'd they never saw a sight so fayre,   60
Of fowles so lovely, that they sure did deeme
Them heavenly borne, or to be that same payre
Which through the skie draw Venus silver teeme;
For sure they did not seeme
To be begot of any earthly seede,
But rather angels or of angels breede:
Yet were they bred of Somers-heat, they say,
In sweetest season, when each flower and weede
The earth did fresh aray;
So fresh they seem'd as day,   70
Even as their brydale day, which was not long:
　　Sweete Themmes, runne softly, till I end my song.

Then forth they all out of their baskets drew
Great store of flowers, the honour of the field,
That to the sense did fragrant odours yeild,
All which upon those goodly birds they threw,
And all the waves did strew,
That like old Peneus waters they did seeme,
When downe along by pleasant Tempes shore,
Scattred with flowres, through Thessaly they streeme,   80
That they appeare, through lillies plenteous store,

Like a brydes chamber flore.
Two of those nymphes, meane while, two garlands bound
Of freshest flowres which in that mead they found,
The which presenting all in trim array,
Their snowie foreheads therewithall they crownd,
Whil'st one did sing this lay,
Prepar'd against that day,
Against their brydale day, which was not long:
   Sweete Themmes, runne softly, till I end my song.   90

"Ye gentle birdes, the worlds faire ornament,
And heavens glorie, whom this happie hower
Doth leade unto your lovers blissfull bower,
Joy may you have and gentle hearts content
Of your loves couplement:
And let faire Venus, that is Queene of Love,
With her heart-quelling sonne upon you smile,
Whose smile, they say, hath vertue to remove
All loves dislike, and friendships faultie guile
For ever to assoile.   100
Let endlesse peace your steadfast hearts accord,
And blessed plentie wait upon your bord;
And let your bed with pleasures chast abound,
That fruitfull issue may to you afford,
Which may your foes confound,
And make your joyes redound,
Upon your brydale day, which is not long:
   Sweete Themmes, runne softlie, till I end my song."

So ended she; and all the rest around
To her redoubled that her undersong,   110
Which said, their bridale daye should not be long.
And gentle Eccho from the neighbour ground
Their accents did resound.
So forth those joyous birdes did passe along,
Adowne the lee, that to them murmurde low,
As he would speake, but that he lackt a tong,
Yeat did by signes his glad affection show,
Making his streame run slow.
And all the foule which in his flood did dwell

Gan flock about these twaine, that did excell   120
The rest so far as Cynthia doth shend
The lesser starres. So they, enranged well,
Did on those two attend,
And their best service lend,
Against their wedding day, which was not long:
    Sweete Themmes, runne softly, till I end my song.

At length they all to mery London came,
To mery London, my most kyndly nurse,
That to me gave this lifes first native sourse:
Though from another place I take my name,   130
An house of auncient fame.
There when they came, whereas those bricky towres,
The which on Themmes brode aged backe doe ryde,
Where now the studious lawyers have their bowers,
There whylome wont the Templer Knights to byde,
Till they decayd through pride:
Next whereunto there standes a stately place,
Where oft I gayned giftes and goodly grace
Of that great lord which therein wont to dwell,
Whose want too well now feeles my freendles case: 140
But ah! here fits not well
Olde woes, but joyes to tell,
Against the bridale daye, which is not long:
    Sweete Themmes, runne softly, till I end my song.

Yet therein now doth lodge a noble peer,
Great Englands glory and the worlds wide wonder,
Whose dreadfull name late through all Spaine did thunder,
And Hercules two pillors standing neere
Did make to quake and feare.
Faire branch of honor, flower of chevalrie,   150
That fillest England with thy triumphes fame,
Joy have thou of thy noble victorie,
And endlesse happinesse of thine owne name
That promiseth the same:
That through thy prowesse and victorious armes
Thy country may be freed from forraine harmes;
And great Elisaes glorious name may ring

Through al the world, fil'd with thy wide alarmes,
Which some grave Muse may sing
To ages following,   160
Upon the brydale day, which is not long:
  Sweete Themmes, runne softly, till I end my song.

From those high towers this noble lord issuing,
Like radiant Hesper when his golden hayre
In th'ocean billows he hath bathed fayre,
Descended to the rivers open vewing,
With a great traine ensuing.
Above the rest were goodly to bee seene
Two gentle knights of lovely face and feature,
Beseeming well the bower of anie queene,   170
With gifts of wit and ornaments of nature,
Fit for so goodly stature:
That like the twins of Jove they seem'd in sight,
Which decke the bauldricke of the heavens bright.
They two, forth pacing to the rivers side,
Received those two faire brides, their loves delight,
Which, at th'appointed tyde,
Each one did make his bryde,
Against their brydale day, which is not long:
  Sweete Themmes, runne softly, till I end my song.   180

                                              1596

Epithalamion [1]

Ye learned sisters which have oftentimes
Beene to me ayding, others to adorne:
Whom ye thought worthy of your gracefull rymes,
That even the greatest did not greatly scorne
To heare theyr names sung in your simple layes,
But joyed in theyr prayse.
And when ye list your owne mishaps to mourne,
Which death, or love, or fortunes wreck did rayse,
Your string could soone to sadder tenor turne,

[1] Spenser wrote this poem in honor of his marriage, 1596.

And teach the woods and waters to lament   10
Your dolefull dreriment.
Now lay those sorrowfull complaints aside,
And having all your heads with girland crownd,
Helpe me mine owne loves prayses to resound,
Ne let the same of any be envide:
So Orpheus did for his owne bride,
So I unto my selfe alone will sing,
The woods shall to me answer and my Eccho ring.

Early before the worlds light giving lampe,
His golden beame upon the hils doth spred,   20
Having disperst the nights unchearefull dampe,
Doc ye awake, and with fresh lusty-hed,
Go to the bowre of my beloved love,
My truest turtle dove,
Bid her awake; for Hymen is awake,
And long since ready forth his maske to move,
With his bright Tead that flames with many a flake,
And many a bachelor to waite on him,
In theyr fresh garments trim.
Bid her awake therefore and soone her dight,   30
For lo the wished day is come at last,
That shall for al the paynes and sorrowes past,
Pay to her usury of long delight:
And whylest she doth her dight,
Doe ye to her of joy and solace sing,
That all the woods may answer and your eccho ring.

Bring with you all the Nymphes that you can heare
Both of the rivers and the forrests greene:
And of the sea that neighbours to her neare,
Al with gay girlands goodly wel beseene.   40
And let them also with them bring in hand,
Another gay girland
For my fayre love of lillyes and of roses,
Bound truelove wize with a blew silke riband.
And let them make great store of bridale poses,

27. *Tead*, torch.

And let them eeke bring store of other flowers
To deck the bridale bowers.
And let the ground whereas her foot shall tread,
For feare the stones her tender foot should wrong
Be strewed with fragrant flowers all along,   50
And diapred lyke the discolored mead.
Which done, doe at her chamber dore awayt,
For she will waken strayt,
The whiles doe ye this song unto her sing,
The woods shall to you answer and your Eccho ring.

Ye Nymphes of Mulla which with carefull heed,
The silver scaly trouts doe tend full well,
And greedy pikes which use therein to feed,
(Those trouts and pikes all others doo excell)
And ye likewise which keepe the rushy lake,   60
Where none doo fishes take,
Bynd up the locks the which hang scatterd light,
And in his waters which your mirror make,
Behold your faces as the christall bright,
That when you come whereas my love doth lie,
No blemish she may spie.
And eke ye lightfoot mayds which keepe the deere,
That on the hoary mountayne use to towre,
And the wylde wolves which seeke them to devoure,
With your steele darts doo chace from comming neer   70
Be also present heere,
To helpe to decke her and to help to sing,
That all the woods may answer and your eccho ring.

Wake, now my love, awake; for it is time,
The Rosy Morne long since left Tithones bed,
All ready to her silver coche to clyme,
And Phoebus gins to shew his glorious hed.
Hark how the cheerefull birds do chaunt theyr laies
And carroll of loves praise.
The merry Larke hir mattins sings aloft,   80
The thrush replyes, the Mavis descant playes,
The Ouzell shrills, the Ruddock warbles soft,

82. *Mavis*, thrush. *Ouzell*, blackbird. *Ruddock*, Redbreast.

So goodly all agree with sweet consent,
To this dayes merriment.
Ah, my deere love, why doe ye sleepe thus long,
When meeter were that ye should now awake,
T'awayt the comming of your joyous make,
And hearken to the birds love-learned song,
The deawy leaves among.
For they of joy and pleasance to you sing,   90
That all the woods them answer and theyr eccho ring.

My love is now awake out of her dreame,
And her fayre eyes like stars that dimmed were
With darksome cloud, now shew theyr goodly beams
More bright then Hesperus his head doth rere.
Come now ye damzels, daughters of delight,
Helpe quickly her to dight,
But first come ye fayre houres which were begot
In Jove's sweet paradice, of Day and Night,
Which doe the seasons of the yeare allot,   100
And al that ever in this world is fayre
Doe make and still repayre.
And ye three handmayds of the Cyprian Queene,
The which doe still adorne her beauties pride,
Helpe to addorne my beautifullest bride:
And as ye her array, still throw betweene
Some graces to be seene,
And as ye use to Venus, to her sing,
The whiles the woods shal answer and your eccho ring.

Now is my love all ready forth to come,   110
Let all the virgins therefore well awayt,
And ye fresh boyes that tend upon her groome
Prepare your selves; for he is comming strayt.
Set all your things in seemely good aray
Fit for so joyfull day,
The joyfulst day that ever sunne did see.
Faire Sun, shew forth thy favourable ray,
And let thy lifull heat not fervent be
For feare of burning her sunshyny face,
Her beauty to disgrace.   120

O fayrest Phoebus, father of the Muse,
If ever did honour thee aright,
Or sing the thing that mote thy mind delight,
Doe not thy servants simple boone refuse,
But let this day, let this one day, be myne;
Let all the rest be thine.
Then I thy soverayne prayses loud wil sing,
That all the woods shal answer and theyr eccho ring.

Harke how the Minstrels gin to shrill aloud
Their merry Musick that resounds from far,   130
The pipe, the tabor, and the trembling Croud,
That well agree withouten breach or jar.
But most of all the Damzels doe delite,
When they their tymbrels smyte,
And thereunto doe daunce and carrol sweet,
That all the sences they doe ravish quite,
The whyles the boyes run up and downe the street,
Crying aloud with strong confused noyce,
As if it were one voyce.
Hymen, iô Hymen, Hymen they do shout,   140
That even to the heavens theyr shouting shrill
Doth reach, and all the firmament doth fill,
To which the people standing all about,
As in approvance doe thereto applaud
And loud advaunce her laud,
And evermore they Hymen, Hymen sing,
That al the woods them answer and theyr eccho ring.

Loe where she comes along with portly pace
Lyke Phoebe from her chamber of the East,
Arysing forth to run her mighty race,   150
Clad all in white, that seemes a virgin best.
So well it her beseemes that ye would weene
Some angell she had beene.
Her long loose yellow locks lyke golden wyre,
Sprinckled with perle, and perling flowres a tweene,
Doe lyke a golden mantle her attyre,

131. *Croud*, violin.

And being crowned with a girland greene,
Seeme lyke some mayden Queene.
Her modest eyes abashed to behold
So many gazers, as on her do stare,   160
Upon the lowly ground affixed are.
Ne dare lift up her countenance too bold,
But blush to heare her prayses sung so loud,
So farre from being proud.
Nathlesse doe ye still loud her prayses sing.
That all the woods may answer and your eccho ring.

Tell me ye merchants daughters did ye see
So fayre a creature in your towne before,
So sweet, so lovely, and so mild as she,
Adornd with beautyes grace and vertues store,   170
Her goodly eyes lyke Saphyres shining bright,
Her forehead yvory white,
Her cheekes lyke apples which the sun hath rudded,
Her lips lyke cherryes charming men to byte,
Her brest like to a bowle of creame uncrudded,
Her paps lyke lyllies budded,
Her snowie necke lyke to a marble towre,
And all her body like a pallace fayre,
Ascending uppe with many a stately stayre,
To honours seat and chastities sweet bowre.   180
Why stand ye still ye virgins in amaze,
Upon her so to gaze,
Whiles ye forget your former lay to sing,
To which the woods did answer and your eccho ring.

But if ye saw that which no eyes can see,
The inward beauty of her lively spright,
Garnisht with heavenly guifts of high degree,
Much more then would ye wonder at that sight,
And stand astonisht lyke to those which red
Medusaes mazeful hed.   190
There dwels sweet love and constant chastity,
Unspotted fayth and comely womanhood,
Regard of honour and mild modesty,
There vertue raynes as Queene in royal throne,

And giveth lawes alone.
The which the base affections doe obay,
And yeeld theyr services unto her will,
Ne thought of thing uncomely ever may
Thereto approch to tempt her mind to ill.
Had ye once seene these her celestial threasures,   200
And unrevealed pleasures,
Then would ye wonder and her prayses sing,
That al the woods should answer and your eccho ring.

Open the temple gates unto my love,
Open them wide that she may enter in,
And all the postes adorne as doth behove,
And all the pillours deck with girlands trim,
For to recyve this Saynt with honour dew,
That commeth in to you.
With trembling steps and humble reverence,   210
She commeth in, before th'almighties vew,
Of her ye virgins learne obedience,
When so ye come into those holy places,
To humble your proud faces:
Bring her up to th'high altar, that she may
The sacred ceremonies there partake,
The which do endlesse matrimony make,
And let the roring Organs loudly play
The praises of the Lord in lively notes,
The whiles with hollow throates   220
The Choristers the joyous Antheme sing,
That al the woods may answere and their eccho ring.

Behold whiles she before the altar stands
Hearing the holy priest that to her speakes
And blesseth her with his two happy hands,
How the red roses flush up in her cheekes,
And the pure snow with goodly vermill stayne,
Like crimsin dyde in grayne,
That even th'Angels which continually,
About the sacred Altare doe remaine,   230
Forget their service and about her fly,
Ofte peeping in her face that seemes more fayre,

The more they on it stare.
But her sad eyes still fastened on the ground,
Are governed with goodly modesty,
That suffers not one looke to glaunce awry,
Which may let in a little thought unsownd.
Why blush ye love to give to me your hand,
The pledge of all our band?
Sing, ye sweet Angels, Alleluya sing,   240
That all the woods may answere and your eccho ring.

Now al is done; bring home the bride againe,
Bring home the triumph of our victory,
Bring home with you the glory of her gaine,
With joyance bring her and with jollity.
Never had man more joyfull day then this,
Whom heaven would heape with blis.
Make feast therefore now all this live long day,
This day for ever to me holy is,
Poure out the wine without restraint or stay,   250
Poure not by cups, but by the belly full,
Poure out to all that wull,
And sprinkle all the postes and wals with wine,
That they may sweat, and drunken be withall.
Crowne ye God Bacchus with a coronall,
And Hymen also crowne with wreathes of vine,
And let the Graces daunce unto the rest;
For they can doo it best:
The whiles the maydens doe theyr carroll sing,
To which the woods shal answer and theyr eccho ring.   260

Ring ye the bels, ye yong men of the towne,
And leave your wonted labors for this day:
This day is holy; doe ye write it downe,
That ye for ever it remember may.
This day the sunne is in his chiefest hight,
With Barnaby the bright,
From whence declining daily by degrees,
He somewhat loseth of his heat and light,
When once the Crab behind his back he sees.
But for this time it ill ordained was,   270

To chose the longest day in all the yeare,
And shortest night, when longest fitter weare:
Yet never day so long, but late would passe.
Ring ye the bels, to make it weare away,
And bonefiers make all day,
And daunce about them, and about them sing:
That all the woods may answer, and your eccho ring.

Ah when will this long weary day have end,
And lende me leave to come unto my love?
How slowly do the houres theyr numbers spend?   280
How slowly does sad Time his feathers move
Hast thee, O fayrest Planet, to thy home
Within the Westerne fome:
Thy tyred steedes long since have need of rest.
Long though it be, at last I see it gloome,
And the bright evening star with golden creast
Appeare out of the East.
Fayre childe of beauty, glorious lampe of love
That all the host of heaven in rankes doost lead,
And guydest lovers through the nightes dread,   290
How chearefully thou lookest from above,
And seemst to laugh atweene thy twinkling light
As joying in the sight
Of these glad many which for joy doe sing,
That all the woods them answer and their eccho ring.

Now ceasse, ye damsels, your delights forepast;
Enough is it, that all the day was youres:
Now day is doen, and night is nighing fast:
Now bring the Bryde into the brydall boures.
Now night is come, now soone her disaray,   300
And in her bed her lay;
Lay her in lillies and in violets,
And silken courteins over her display,
And odourd sheetes, and Arras coverlets.
Behold how goodly my faire love does ly
In proud humility;
Like unto Maia, when as Jove her tooke,
In Tempe, lying on the flowry gras,

Twixt sleepe and wake, after she weary was,
With bathing in the Acidalian brooke.   310
Now it is night, ye damsels may be gon,
And leave my love alone,
And leave likewise your former lay to sing:
The woods no more shal answere, nor your eccho ring.

Now welcome night, thou night so long expected,
That long daies labour doest at last defray,
And all my cares, which cruell love collected,
Hast sumd in one, and cancelled for aye:
Spread thy broad wing over my love and me,
That no man may us see,   320
And in thy sable mantle us enwrap,
From feare of perrill and foule horror free.
Let no false treason seeke us to entrap,
Nor any dread disquiet once annoy
The safety of our joy:
But let the night be calme and quietsome,
Without tempestuous storms or sad afray:
Lyke as when Jove with fayre Alcmena lay,
When he begot the great Tirynthian groome:
Or lyke as when he with thy selfe did lie,   330
And begot Majesty.
And let the mayds and yongmen cease to sing:
Ne let the woods them answer, nor theyr eccho ring.

Let no lamenting cryes, nor dolefull teares,
Be heard all night within nor yet without:
Ne let false whispers, breeding hidden feares,
Breake gentle sleepe with misconceived dout.
Let no deluding dreames, nor dreadful sights
Make sudden sad affrights;
Ne let housefyres, nor lightnings helpelesse harmes,   340
Ne let the Pouke, nor other evill sprights,
Ne let mischivous witches with theyr charmes,
Ne let hob Goblins, names whose sence we see not,
Fray us with things that be not.
Let not the shriech Oule, nor the Storke be heard:
Nor the night Raven that still deadly yels,

Nor damned ghosts cald up with mighty spels,
Nor griesly vultures make us once affeard:
Ne let th'unpleasant Quyre of Frogs still croking
Make us to wish theyr choking.   350
Let none of these theyr drery accents sing;
Ne let the woods them answer, nor theyr eccho ring.

But let stil Silence trew night watches keepe,
That sacred peace may in assurance rayne,
And tymely sleep, when it is tyme to sleepe,
May poure his limbs forth on your pleasant playne,
The whiles an hundred little winged loves,
Like divers fethered doves,
Shall fly and flutter round about your bed,
And in the secret darke, that none reproves,   360
Their prety stealthes shal worke, and snares shal spread
To filch away sweet snatches of delight,
Conceald through covert night.
Ye sonnes of Venus, play your sports at will,
For greedy pleasure, carelesse of your toyes,
Thinks more upon her paradise of joyes,
Then what ye do, albe it good or ill.
All night therefore attend your merry play,
For it will soone be day:
Now none doth hinder you, that say or sing,   370
Ne will the woods now answer, nor your Eccho ring.

Who is the same, which at my window peepes?
Or whose is that faire face, that shines so bright,
Is it not Cinthia, she that never sleepes,
But walkes about high heaven al the night?
A fayrest goddesse, do thou not envy
My love with me to spy:
For thou likewise didst love, though now unthought,
And for a fleece of woll, which privily,
The Latmian shepherd once unto thee brought,   380
His pleasures with thee wrought.
Therefore to us be favorable now;
And sith of wemens labours thou hast charge,
And generation goodly dost enlarge,

Encline thy will t'effect our wishfull vow,
And the chast wombe informe with timely seed,
That may our comfort breed:
Till which we cease our hopefull hap to sing,
Ne let the woods us answere, nor our Eccho ring.

And thou great Juno, which with awful might   390
The lawes of wedlock still dost patronize,
And the religion of the faith first plight
With sacred rites hast taught to solemnize:
And eeke for comfort often called art
Of women in their smart,
Eternally bind thou this lovely band,
And all thy blessings unto us impart.
And thou glad Genius, in whose gentle hand,
The bridale bowre and geniall bed remaine,
Without blemish or staine,   400
And the sweet pleasures of theyr loves delight
With secret ayde dost succour and supply,
Till they bring forth the fruitfull progeny,
Send us the timely fruit of this same night.
And thou fayre Hebe, and thou Hymen free,
Grant that it may so be.
Til which we cease your further prayse to sing,
Ne any woods shal answer, nor your Eccho ring.

And ye high heavens, the temple of the gods,
In which a thousand torches flaming bright   410
Doe burne, that to us wretched earthly clods,
In dreadful darknesse lend desired light;
And all ye powers which in the same remayne,
More then we men can fayne,
Poure out your blessings on us plentiously,
And happy influence upon us raine,
That we may raise a large posterity,
Which from the earth, which they may long possesse,
With lasting happinesse,
Up to your haughty pallaces may mount,   420
And for the guerdon of theyr glorious merit
May heavenly tabernacles there inherit,

Of blessed Saints for to increase the count.
So let us rest, sweet love, in hope of this,
And cease till then our tymely joyes to sing,
The woods no more us answer, nor our eccho ring.

Song made in lieu of many ornaments,
With which my love should duly have bene dect,
Which cutting off through hasty accidents,
Ye would not stay your dew time to expect,   430
But promist both to recompens,
Be unto her a goodly ornament,
And for short time an endlesse moniment.

1595

MICHAEL DRAYTON

Since There's No Help

Since there's no help, come, let us kiss and part!
Nay, I have done; you get no more of me!
And I am glad, yea, glad, with all my heart,
That thus so cleanly I myself can free.
Shake hands for ever! Cancel all our vows!
And when we meet at any time again,
Be it not seen in either of our brows,
That we one jot of former love retain!
Now at the last gasp of Love's latest breath,
When, his pulse failing, Passion speechless lies;   10
When Faith is kneeling by his bed of death,
And Innocence is closing up his eyes—
    Now, if thou wouldst, when all have given him over,
    From death to life thou might'st him yet recover!

1619

WILLIAM SHAKESPEARE

Sonnets [1]

15

When I consider everything that grows
Holds in perfection but a little moment,
That this huge stage presenteth nought but shows
Whereon the stars in secret influence comment;
When I perceive that men as plants increase,
Cheeréd and checked even by the self-same sky,
Vaunt in their youthful sap, at height decrease,
And wear their brave state out of memory—
Then the conceit of this inconstant stay
Sets you most rich in youth before my sight,   10
Where wasteful Time debateth with Decay,
To change your day of youth to sullied night;
   And all in war with Time for love of you,
   As he takes from you, I engraft you new.

18

Shall I compare thee to a summer's day?
Thou art more lovely and more temperate:
Rough winds do shake the darling buds of May,
And summer's lease hath all too short a date;
Sometime too hot the eye of heaven shines,
And often is his gold complexion dimméd;
And every fair from fair sometime declines,
By chance or nature's changing course untrimmed:
But thy eternal summer shall not fade
Nor lose possession of that fair thou ow'st;   10
Nor shall Death brag thou wand'rest in his shade,
When in eternal lines to time thou grow'st;
   So long as men can breathe or eyes can see,
   So long lives this and this gives life to thee.

[1] The *Sonnets* were written before 1599.

29

When in disgrace with fortune and men's eyes,
I all alone beweep my outcast state,
And trouble deaf heaven with my bootless cries,
And look upon myself, and curse my fate,
Wishing me like to one more rich in hope,
Featured like him, like him with friends possessed,
Desiring this man's art and that man's scope,
With what I most enjoy contented least;
Yet in these thoughts myself almost despising,
Haply I think on thee—and then my state,   10
Like to the lark at break of day arising
From sullen earth, sings hymns at heaven's gate;
    For thy sweet love remembered such wealth brings
    That then I scorn to change my state with kings.   ·

30

When to the sessions of sweet silent thought
I summon up remembrance of things past,
I sigh the lack of many a thing I sought,
And with old woes new wail my dear time's waste.
Then can I drown an eye, unused to flow,
For precious friends hid in death's dateless night,
And weep afresh love's long since canceled woe,
And moan the expense of many a vanished sight.
Then can I grieve at grievances foregone,
And heavily from woe to woe tell o'er   10
The sad account of fore-bemoanéd moan,
Which I new pay as if not paid before.
    But if the while I think on thee, dear friend,
    All losses are restored and sorrows end.

33

Full many a glorious morning have I seen
Flatter the mountain-tops with sovereign eye,
Kissing with golden face the meadows green,
Gilding pale streams with heavenly alchemy;
Anon permit the basest clouds to ride

With ugly rack on his celestial face,
And from the forlorn world his visage hide,
Stealing unseen to west with this disgrace.
Even so my sun one early morn did shine
With all-triumphant splendor on my brow;
But, out, alack! he was but one hour mine,
The region cloud hath masked him from me now.
    Yet him for this my love no whit disdaineth;
     Suns of the world may stain when heaven's sun
     staineth.

55

Not marble, nor the gilded monuments
Of princes, shall outlive this powerful rime;
But you shall shine more bright in these contents
Than unswept stone besmeared with sluttish time.
When wasteful war shall statues overturn,
And broils root out the work of masonry,
Nor Mars his sword nor war's quick fire shall burn
The living record of your memory.
'Gainst death and all-oblivious enmity
Shall you pace forth; your praise shall still find room 10
Even in the eyes of all posterity
That wear this world out to the ending doom.
    So, till the judgment that yourself arise,
     You live in this, and dwell in lovers' eyes.

73

That time of year thou mayst in me behold
When yellow leaves, or none, or few, do hang
Upon those boughs which shake against the cold,
Bare ruined choirs, where late the sweet birds sang.
In me thou see'st the twilight of such day
As after sunset fadeth in the west,
Which by and by black night doth take away,
Death's second self, that seals up all in rest.
In me thou see'st the glowing of such fire
That on the ashes of his youth doth lie,   10
As the death-bed whereon it must expire,

Consumed with that which it was nourished by.
　This thou perceivest, which makes thy love more
　　strong,
　To love that well which thou must leave ere long.

106

When in the chronicle of wasted time
I see descriptions of the fairest wights,
And beauty making beautiful old rime
In praise of ladies dead and lovely knights,
Then, in the blazon of sweet beauty's best,
Of hand, of foot, of lip, of eye, of brow,
I see their antique pen would have expressed
Even such a beauty as you master now.
So all their praises are but prophecies
Of this our time, all you prefiguring;　　　　　　　10
And, for they looked but with divining eyes,
They had not skill enough your worth to sing.
　For we, which now behold these present days,
　Have eyes to wonder, but lack tongues to praise.

116

Let me not to the marriage of true minds
Admit impediments. Love is not love
Which alters when it alteration finds,
Or bends with the remover to remove.
Oh, no! it is an ever-fixéd mark
That looks on tempests and is never shaken;
It is the star to every wandering bark,
Whose worth's unknown, although his height be taken.
Love's not Time's fool, though rosy lips and cheeks
Within his bending sickle's compass come;　　　　　10
Love alters not with his brief hours and weeks,
But bears it out even to the edge of doom.
　If this be error and upon me proved,
　I never writ, nor no man ever loved.

130

My mistress' eyes are nothing like the sun;
Coral is far more red than her lips' red;

If snow be white, why then her breasts are dun;
If hairs be wires, black wires grow on her head.
I have seen roses damasked, red and white,
But no such roses see I in her cheeks;
And in some perfumes is there more delight
Than in the breath that from my mistress reeks.
I love to hear her speak, yet well I know
That music hath a far more pleasing sound;   10
I grant I never saw a goddess go;
My mistress, when she walks, treads on the ground:
  And yet, by heaven, I think my love as rare
  As any she belied with false compare.

SONGS FROM THE PLAYS

When Daisies Pied

When daisies pied and violets blue,
  And lady-smocks all silver-white,
And cuckoo-buds of yellow hue
  Do paint the meadows with delight,
The cuckoo then, on every tree,
Mocks married men; for thus sings he,
          Cuckoo!
Cuckoo, cuckoo!—O word of fear,
Unpleasing to a married ear!

When shepherds pipe on oaten straws,   10
  And merry larks are plowmen's clocks,
When turtles tread, and rooks, and daws,
  And maidens bleach their summer smocks
The cuckoo then, on every tree,
Mocks married men; for thus sings he,
          Cuckoo!
Cuckoo, cuckoo!—O word of fear,
Unpleasing to a married ear!

About 1591   *Love's Labor's Lost, 1598*

When Icicles Hang by the Wall

When icicles hang by the wall,
　　And Dick the shepherd blows his nail,
And Tom bears logs into the hall,
　　And milk comes frozen home in pail,
When blood is nipped and ways be foul,
Then nightly sings the staring owl,
"Tu-whit, tu-who!" a merry note,
While greasy Joan doth keel the pot.

When all aloud the wind doth blow,
　　And coughing drowns the parson's saw,　　　　10
And birds sit brooding in the snow,
　　And Marian's nose looks red and raw,
When roasted crabs hiss in the bowl,
Then nightly sings the staring owl,
"Tu-whit, tu-who!" a merry note,
While greasy Joan doth keel the pot.
About 1591　　　　*Love's Labor's Lost, 1598.*

Who Is Sylvia?

Who is Sylvia? what is she,
　　That all our swains commend her?
Holy, fair, and wise is she;
　　The heaven such grace did lend her,
That she might admiréd be.

Is she kind as she is fair?
　　For beauty lives with kindness.
Love doth to her eyes repair
　　To help him of his blindness,
And, being helped, inhabits there.　　　　10
About 1591　　*The Two Gentlemen of Verona, 1623*

8. *keel*, skim.

Where the Bee Sucks

Where the bee sucks, there suck I;
In a cowslip's bell I lie;
There I couch when owls do cry.
On the bat's back I do fly
After summer merrily.
Merrily, merrily, shall I live now
Under the blossom that hangs on the bough.
About 1611   *The Tempest, 1623*

Tell Me, Where Is Fancy Bred

Tell me, where is fancy bred,
Or in the heart, or in the head?
How begot, how nourishéd?
        Reply, reply.
It is engendered in the eyes,
With gazing fed; and fancy dies
In the cradle where it lies:
Let us all ring fancy's knell;
I'll begin it,—Ding-dong, bell.
        Ding, dong, bell.   10
About 1595   *The Merchant of Venice, 1600*

Under the Greenwood Tree

Under the greenwood tree
Who loves to lie with me,
And turn his merry note
Unto the sweet bird's throat,
Come hither! come hither! come hither!
Here shall he see
No enemy
But winter and rough weather.

Who doth ambition shun
And loves to live i' the sun,   10
Seeking the food he eats

And pleased with what he gets,
Come hither! come hither! come hither!
Here shall he see
No enemy
But winter and rough weather.
About 1599   *As You Like It, 1623*

Blow, Blow, Thou Winter Wind

Blow, blow, thou winter wind!
Thou art not so unkind
    As man's ingratitude;
Thy tooth is not so keen,
Because thou art not seen,
    Although thy breath be rude.

Heigh ho! sing, heigh ho! unto the green holly:
Most friendship is feigning, most loving mere folly:
    Then, heigh ho, the holly!
    This life is most jolly.   10

Freeze, freeze, thou bitter sky!
That dost not bite so nigh
    As benefits forgot;
Though thou the waters warp,
Thy sting is not so sharp
    As friend remembered not.

Heigh ho! sing, heigh ho! *etc.*
About 1599   *As You Like It, 1599*

Sigh No More

Sigh no more, ladies, sigh no more!
    Men were deceivers ever,
One foot in sea and one on shore,
    To one thing constant never:
Then sigh not so, but let them go,
    And be you blithe and bonny,

Converting all your sounds of woe
Into Hey nonny, nonny!

Sing no more ditties, sing no moe
Of dumps so dull and heavy!   10
The fraud of men was ever so,
Since summer first was leafy:
Then sigh not so, but let them go,
And be you blithe and bonny,
Converting all your sounds of woe
Into Hey nonny, nonny!
                    Much Ado about Nothing, 1600

O Mistress Mine

O Mistress mine, where are you roaming?
O, stay and hear; your true love's coming,
That can sing both high and low:
Trip no further, pretty sweeting,
Journeys end in lovers meeting,
Every wise man's son doth know.

What is love? 't is not hereafter;
Present mirth hath present laughter;
What's to come is still unsure:
In delay there lies no plenty;   10
Then come kiss me, sweet and twenty,
Youth's a stuff will not endure.
About 1601   *Twelfth Night, 1623*

Hark, Hark! The Lark

Hark, hark! The lark at heaven's gate sings,
And Phoebus gins arise,
His steeds to water at those springs
On chaliced flowers that lies;
And winking Mary-buds begin
To ope their golden eyes.

With every thing that pretty is,
    My lady sweet, arise!
        Arise, arise!
    About 1610   *Cymbeline, 1623*

Fear No More the Heat o' the Sun

Fear no more the heat o' the sun,
    Nor the furious winter's rages;
Thou thy worldly task hast done,
    Home art gone, and ta'en thy wages.
Golden lads and girls all must,
As chimney-sweepers, come to dust.

Fear no more the frown o' the great;
    Thou art past the tyrant's stroke;
Care no more to clothe and eat;
    To thee the reed is as the oak.   10
The scepter, learning, physic, must
All follow this, and come to dust.

Fear no more the lightning-flash,
    Nor the all-dreaded thunder-stone;
Fear not slander, censure rash;
    Thou hast finished joy and moan.
All lovers young, all lovers must
Consign to thee, and come to dust.

No exorciser harm thee!
    Nor no witchcraft charm thee!
Ghost unlaid forbear thee!
    Nothing ill come near thee!
Quiet consummation have;
    And renownéd be thy grave!
    About 1610   *Cymbeline, 1623*

Full Fathom Five Thy Father Lies

Full fathom five thy father lies:
    Of his bones are coral made;
Those are pearls that were his eyes;

Nothing of him that doth fade
But doth suffer a sea-change
Into something rich and strange.
Sea-nymphs hourly ring his knell:
                    Ding-dong!
Hark! now I hear them—Ding-dong, bell!
About 1611   *The Tempest, 1623*

THOMAS CAMPION

Follow Your Saint

Follow your saint, follow with accents sweet!
Haste you, sad notes, fall at her flying feet!
There, wrapped in cloud of sorrow, pity move,
And tell the ravisher of my soul I perish for her love:
But if she scorns my never-ceasing pain,
Then burst with sighing in her sight and ne'er return again!

All that I sung still to her praise did tend;
Still she was first, still she my songs did end;
Yet she my love and music both doth fly,
The music that her echo is and beauty's sympathy: 10
Then let my notes pursue her scornful flight!
It shall suffice that they were breathed and died for her de-
    light.

                                        1601

I Care Not for These Ladies

I care not for these ladies,
That must be wooed and prayed,
Give me kind Amarillis
The wanton country maid;
Nature art disdaineth,
Her beauty is her own;
    Her when we court and kiss,
    She cries, forsooth, let go.
    But when we come where comfort is,
    She never will say no.   10

If I love Amarillis,
She gives me fruit and flowers,
But if we love these ladies,
We must give golden showers,
Give them gold that sell love,
Give me the nutbrown lass,
    Who when we court and kiss,
    She cries, forsooth, let go.
    But when we come where comfort is,
    She never will say no.   20

These ladies must have pillows,
And beds by strangers wrought,
Give me a bower of willows,
Of moss and leaves unbought,
And fresh Amarillis,
With milk and honey fed,
    Who, when we court and kiss,
    She cries, forsooth, let go.
    But when we come where comfort is,
    She never will say no.   30

1601

Rose-Cheeked Laura

Rose-cheeked Laura, come
Sing thou smoothly with thy beauty's
Silent music, either other
        Sweetly gracing.

Lovely forms do flow
From consent divinely framéd;
Heaven is music, and thy beauty's
        Birth is heavenly.

These dull notes we sing
Discords need for helps to grace them.   10
Only beauty purely loving
        Knows no discord,

But still moves delight,
Like clear springs renewed by flowing,
Ever perfect, ever in them-
        selves eternal.

                                            1602

Beauty Is but a Painted Hell

Beauty is but a painted hell:
    Aye me, aye me,
She wounds them that admire it,
She kills them that desire it;
    Give her pride but fuel,
    No fire is more cruel.

Pity from ev'ry heart is fled:
    Aye me, aye me,
Since false desire could borrow
Tears of dissembled sorrow,   10
    Constant vows turn truthless,
    Love cruel, Beauty ruthless.

Sorrow can laugh, and Fury sing:
    Aye me, aye me,
My raving griefs discover
I lived too true a lover;
    The first step to madness
    Is the excess of sadness.

                                            1617

BEN JONSON

Slow, Slow, Fresh Fount

Slow, slow, fresh fount, keep time with my salt teares;
    Yet slower, yet, O faintly, gentle springs;
List to the heavy part the musick beares,
    Woe weeps out her division, when shee sings.
        Droup hearbs and flowres;
        Fall griefe in showres;

Our beauties are not ours:
        O, I could still
(Like melting snow upon some craggy hill,)
                        drop, drop, drop, drop,   10
Since natures pride is now a wither'd daffodil.
                        Cynthia's Revels, 1616

To Celia

Come, my Celia, let us prove,
While wee can, the sports of love,
Time will not be ours, for ever:
He, at length, our good will sever.
Spend not then his gifts in vaine.
Sunnes that set may rise againe;
But, if once wee lose this light,
'Tis, with us, perpetuall night.
Why should we deferre our joyes?
Fame and rumor are but toies.   10
Cannot wee delude the eyes
Of a few poore houshold spyes?
Or his easier eares beguile,
So removéd by our wile?
'Tis no sinne loves fruit to steele;
But the sweet thefts to reveale:
To bee taken, to be seene,
These have crimes accounted beene.
                        Volpone, 1607

Hymn to Diana

Queen and Huntress, chaste and fair,
    Now the sun is laid to sleep,
Seated in thy silver chair
    State in wonted manner keep:
        Hesperus entreats thy light,
        Goddess excellently bright.

Earth, let not thy envious shade
Dare itself to interpose;
Cynthia's shining orb was made
Heaven to clear when day did close: 10
Bless us then with wishèd sight,
Goddess excellently bright.

Lay thy bow of pearl apart
And thy crystal-shining quiver;
Give unto the flying hart
Space to breathe, how short soever:
Thou that mak'st a day of night,
Goddess excellently bright.

Cynthia's Revels, 1616

Song to Celia

Drink to me only with thine eyes,
And I will pledge with mine;
Or leave a kiss but in the cup,
And I'll not look for wine.
The thirst that from the soul doth rise
Doth ask a drink divine;
But might I of Jove's nectar sup,
I would not change for thine.

I sent thee late a rosy wreath,
Not so much honoring thee 10
As giving it a hope, that there
It could not withered be.
But thou thereon didst only breathe,
And sent'st it back to me;
Since when it grows, and smells, I swear,
Not of itself, but thee.

1616

Her Triumph

See the chariot at hand here of Love,
Wherein my Lady rideth!
Each that draws is a swan or a dove,
And well the car Love guideth.

As she goes, all hearts do duty
    Unto her beauty;
And enamored, do wish, so they might
    But enjoy such a sight,
That they still were to run by her side,
Through swords, through seas, whither she would
    ride.   10

Do but look on her eyes, they do light
    All that Love's world compriseth!
Do but look on her hair, it is bright
    As Love's star when it riseth!
Do but mark, her forehead's smoother
    Than words that soothe her;
And from her arched brows, such a grace
    Sheds itself through the face
As alone there triumphs to the life
All the gain, all the good, of the elements' strife.   20

Have you seen but a bright lily grow
    Before rude hands have touched it?
Have you marked but the fall of the snow
    Before the soil hath smutched it?
Have you felt the wool of the beaver?
    Or swan's down ever?
Or have smelt o' the bud of the briar?
    Or the nard in the fire?
Or have tasted the bag of the bee!
O so white! O so soft! O so sweet is she!   30
1616   *1631*

JOHN DONNE

A Valediction: Forbidding Mourning

As virtuous men passe mildly away,
    And whisper to their soules, to goe,
Whilst some of their sad friends doe say,
    The breath goes now, and some say, no:

So let us melt, and make no noise,
　No teare-floods, nor sigh-tempests move,
T'were prophanation of our joyes
　To tell the layetie our love.

Moving of th'earth brings harmes and feares;
　Men reckon what it did and meant,   10
But trepidation of the spheares,
　Though greater farre, is innocent.

Dull sublunary lovers love
　(Whose soule is sense) cannot admit
Absence, because it doth remove
　Those things which clemented it.

But we by a love so much refin'd,
　That our selves know not what it is,
Inter-assuréd of the mind,
　Care lesse, eyes, lips, and hands to misse,   20

Our two soules therefore, which are one,
　Though I must goe, endure not yet
A breach, but an expansion,
　Like gold to ayery thinnesse beate.

If they be two, they are two so
　As stiffe twin compasses are two;
Thy soule the fixt foot, makes no show
　To move, but doth, if the other doe.

And though it in the center sit,
　Yet when the other far doth rome,   30
It leanes, and hearkens after it,
　And growes erect, as that comes home.

Such wilt thou be to mee, who must
　Like th'other foot, obliquely runne;
Thy firmnes makes my circle just,
　And makes me end, where I begunne.

1633

The Relique

When my grave is broke up againe
Some second ghest to entertaine,
(For graves have learn'd that womanhead
To be to more then one a bed)
    And he that digs it, spies
A bracelet of bright haire about the bone,
    Will he not let us alone,
And thinke that there a loving couple lies,
Who thought that this device might be some way
To make their soules, at the last busie day,   10
Meet at this grave, and make a little stay?

If this fall in a time, or land,
Where mis-devotion doth command,
Then, he that digges us up, will bring
Us to the bishop, and the king,
    To make us reliques; then
Thou shalt be a Mary Magdalen, and I
    A something else thereby;
All women shall adore us, and some men;
And since at such time, miracles are sought,   20
I would have that age by this paper taught
What miracles wee harmlesse lovers wrought.

First, we lov'd well and faithfully,
Yet knew not what wee lov'd, nor why;
Difference of sex no more wee knew,
Then our guardian angells doe;
    Comming and going, wee
Perchance might kisse, but not between those meales;
    Our hands ne'r toucht the seales,
Which nature, injur'd by late law, sets free.   30
These miracles wee did; but now alas,
All measure, and all language, I should passe,
Should I tell what a miracle shee was.

1633

Go and Catch a Falling Star

Go and catch a falling star,
　Get with child a mandrake root,
Tell me where all past years are,
　Or who cleft the devil's foot;
Teach me to hear mermaids singing,
Or to keep off envy's stinging,
　　　And find
　　　What wind
Serves to advance an honest mind.

If thou be'st born to strange sights,   10
　Things invisible go see,
Ride ten thousand days and nights
　Till Age snow white hairs on thee;
Thou, when thou return'st, wilt tell me
All strange wonders that befell thee,
　　　And swear
　　　No where
Lives a woman true and fair.

If thou find'st one, let me know;
　Such a pilgrimage were sweet.   20
Yet do not; I would not go,
　Though at next door we might meet.
Though she were true when you met her,
And last till you write your letter,
　　　Yet she
　　　Will be
False, ere I come, to two or three.

1633

The Ecstasy

Where, like a pillow on a bed,
　A pregnant bank swelled up, to rest
The violet's reclining head,
　Sat we two, one another's best.

Our hands were firmly cemented
    With a fast balm, which thence did spring,
Our eye-beams twisted, and did thread
    Our eyes, upon one double string;
So t' intergraft our hands, as yet
    Was all the means to make us one,   10
And pictures in our eyes to get
    Was all our propagation.
As 'twixt two equal armies, fate
    Suspends uncertain victory,
Our souls (which to advance their state,
    Were gone out) hung 'twixt her, and me.
And whil'st our souls negotiate there,
    We like sepulchral statues lay;
All day, the same our postures were,
    And we said nothing, all the day.   20
If any, so by love refined
    That he soul's language understood,
And by good love were grown all mind,
    Within convenient distance stood,
He (though he knew not which soul spake,
    Because both meant, both spake the same)
Might thence a new concoction take,
    And part far purer than he came.
This Ecstasy doth unperplex
    (We said) and tell us what we love;   30
We see by this, it was not sex,
    We see, we saw not what did move:
But as all several souls contain
    Mixture of things, they know not what,
Love, these mixed souls, doth mix again,
    And makes both one, each this and that.
A single violet transplant,
    The strength, the color, and the size,
(All which before was poor, and scant)
    Redoubles still, and multiplies.   40
When love, with one another so
    Interinanimates two souls,

That abler soul, which thence doth flow,
    Defects of loneliness controls.
We then, who are this new soul, know
    Of what we are composed, and made,
For, th' atomies of which we grow,
    Are souls, whom no change can invade.
But O alas, so long, so far
    Our bodies why do we forbear?   50
They are ours, though they are not we; we are
    The intelligences, they the sphere.
We owe them thanks, because they thus,
    Did us, to us, at first convey,
Yielded their forces, sense, to us,
    Nor are dross to us, but allay.
On man heaven's influence works not so,
    But that it first imprints the air,
So soul into the soul may flow,
    Though it to body first repair.   60
As our blood labors to beget
    Spirits, as like souls as it can,
Because such fingers need to knit
    That subtle knot, which makes us man:
So must pure lovers' souls descend
    T' affections, and to faculties,
Which sense may reach and apprehend,
    Else a great prince in prison lies.
T' our bodies turn we then, that so
    Weak men on love revealed may look;   70
Love's mysteries in souls do grow,
    But yet the body is his book.
And if some lover, such as we,
    Have heard this dialogue of one,
Let him still mark us, he shall see
    Small change, when we're to bodies gone.

1633

Holy Sonnet

Death, be not proud, though some have calléd thee
Mighty and dreadful, for thou art not so;
For those whom thou think'st thou dost overthrow
Die not, poor Death; nor yet canst thou kill me.
From rest and sleep, which but thy picture be,
Much pleasure; then from thee much more must flow;
And soonest our best men with thee do go—
Rest of their bones and souls' delivery!
Thou'rt slave to fate, chance, kings, and desperate men,
And dost with poison, war, and sickness dwell;   10
And poppy or charms can make us sleep as well
And better than thy stroke. Why swell'st thou then?
One short sleep past, we wake eternally,
And Death shall be no more: Death, thou shalt die!

1633

A Hymn to God the Father

Wilt thou forgive that sin where I begun,
    Which was my sin, though it were done before?
Wilt thou forgive that sin through which I run,
    And do run still, though still I do deplore?
When thou hast done, thou hast not done;
        For I have more.

Wilt thou forgive that sin which I have won
    Others to sin, and made my sins their door?
Wilt thou forgive that sin which I did shun
    A year or two, but wallowed in a score?   10
When thou hast done, thou hast not done;
        For I have more.

I have a sin of fear, that when I've spun
    My last thread, I shall perish on the shore;
But swear by thyself that at my death thy Son
    Shall shine as he shines now and heretofore;
And having done that, thou hast done;
        I fear no more.

1633

ROBERT HERRICK

The Argument of His Book

I sing of brooks, of blossoms, birds and bowers,
Of April, May, of June and July-flowers;
I sing of May-poles, hock-carts, wassails, wakes,
Of bridegrooms, brides, and of their bridal cakes;
I write of youth, of love, and have access
By these to sing of cleanly wantonness;
I sing of dews, of rains, and, piece by piece,
Of balm, of oil, of spice and ambergris;
I sing of times trans-shifting, and I write
How roses first came red and lilies white;   10
I write of groves, of twilights, and I sing
The court of Mab, and of the Fairy King
I write of hell; I sing (and ever shall)
Of heaven, and hope to have it after all.

1648

Corinna's Going A-Maying

Get up, get up for shame, the blooming morn
Upon her wings presents the god unshorn.
    See how Aurora throws her fair
    Fresh-quilted colors through the air;
    Get up, sweet slug-a-bed, and see
    The dew bespangling herb and tree.
Each flower has wept and bowed toward the east
Above an hour since: yet you not dressed;
    Nay! not so much as out of bed?
    When all the birds have matins said   10
    And sung their thankful hymns, 'tis sin,
    Nay, profanation, to keep in,
Whenas a thousand virgins on this day
Spring, sooner than the lark, to fetch in May.

Rise and put on your foliage, and be seen
To come forth, like the spring-time, fresh and green,

And sweet as Flora. Take no care
For jewels for your gown or hair:
Fear not; the leaves will strew
Gems in abundance upon you: 20
Besides, the childhood of the day has kept,
Against you come, some orient pearls upwept;
   Come and receive them while the light
   Hangs on the dew-locks of the night:
   And Titan on the eastern hill
   Retires himself, or else stands still
Till you come forth.   Wash, dress, be brief in praying:
Few beads are best when once we go a-Maying.

Come, my Corinna, come; and, coming, mark
How each field turns a street, each street a park
   Made green and trimmed with trees; see how
   Devotion gives each house a bough
   Or branch: each porch, each door ere this
   An ark, a tabernacle is,
Made up of white-thorn, neatly interwove;
As if here were those cooler shades of love.
   Can such delights be in the street
   And open fields and we not see't?
   Come, we'll abroad; and let's obey
   The proclamation made for May: 40
And sin no more, as we have done, by staying;
But, my Corinna, come, let's go a-Maying.

There's not a budding boy or girl this day
But is got up, and gone to bring in May.
   A deal of youth, ere this, is come
   Back, and with white-thorn laden home.
   Some have despatched their cakes and cream
   Before that we have left to dream:
And some have wept, and wooed, and plighted troth,
And chose their priest, ere we can cast off sloth: 50
   Many a green-gown has been given;
   Many a kiss, both odd and even:
   Many a glance too has been sent
   From out the eye, love's firmament;

Many a jest told of the keys betraying
This night, and locks picked, yet we're not a-Maying.

Come, let us go while we are in our prime;
And take the harmless folly of the time.
   We shall grow old apace, and die
   Before we know our liberty.   60
   Our life is short, and our days run
   As fast away as does the sun;
And, as a vapor or a drop of rain,
Once lost, can ne'er be found again,
   So when or you or I are made
   A fable, song, or fleeting shade,
   All love, all liking, all delight
   Lies drowned with us in endless night.
Then while time serves, and we are but decaying,
Come, my Corinna, come, let's go a-Maying.   70
                                        1648

Upon Prue His Maid

   In this little urne is laid
   Prewdence Baldwin (once my maid)
   From whose happy spark here let
   Spring the purple violet.
                    1648

Upon Julia's Clothes

   Whenas in silks my Julia goes,
   Then, then (me thinks) how sweetly flowes
   That liquefaction of her clothes.

   Next, when I cast mine eyes and see
   That brave vibration each way free;
   O how that glittering taketh me!
                    1648

To Music, to Becalm His Fever

Charm me asleep, and melt me so
  With thy delicious numbers,
That being ravished, hence I go
  Away in easy slumbers.
Ease my sick head,
And make my bed,
  Thou power that canst sever
From me this ill;
And quickly still,
Though thou not kill   10
  My fever.

Thou sweetly canst convert the same
  From a consuming fire,
Into a gentle-licking flame,
  And make it thus expire.
Then make me weep
My pains asleep,
  And give me such reposes,
That I, poor I,
May think, thereby,   20
I live and die
  'Mongst roses.

Fall on me like a silent dew,
  Or like those maiden showers,
Which, by the peep of day, do strew
  A baptism o'er the flowers.
Melt, melt my pains
With thy soft strains;
  That having ease me given,
With full delight,   30
I leave this light,
And take my flight
  For heaven.

1648

To Anthea, Who May Command Him Anything

Bid me to live, and I will live
  Thy protestant to be:
Or bid me love, and I will give
  A loving heart to thee.

A heart as soft, a heart as kind,
  A heart as sound and free
As in the whole world thou canst find,
  That heart I'll give to thee.

Bid that heart stay, and it will stay,
  To honor thy decree: 10
Or bid it languish quite away,
  And 't shall do so for thee.

Bid me to weep, and I will weep,
  While I have eyes to see:
And having none, yet I will keep
  A heart to weep for thee.

Bid me despair, and I'll despair,
  'Under that cypress tree:
Or bid me die, and I will dare
  E'en death, to die for thee.   20

Thou art my life, my love, my heart,
  The very eyes of me,
And hast command of every part,
  To live and die for thee.
                    1648

To Daffodils

Fair Daffodils, we weep to see
  You haste away so soon;
As yet the early rising sun
  Has not attained his noon.

Stay, stay,
Until the hasting day
Has run
But to the even-song;
And, having prayed together, we
Will go with you along.   10

We have short time to stay, as you,
We have as short a spring;
As quick a growth to meet decay,
As you, or anything.
We die
As your hours do, and dry
Away,
Like to the summer's rain;
Or as the pearls of morning's dew,
Ne'er to be found again.   20

1648

A Meditation for His Mistress

You are a tulip seen to-day,
But, dearest, of so short a stay
That where you grew scarce man can say.

You are a lovely July-flower,
Yet one rude wind or ruffling shower
Will force you hence, and in an hour.

You are a sparkling rose i' th' bud,
Yet lost ere that chaste flesh and blood
Can show where you or grew or stood.

You are a full-spread, fair-set vine,   10
And can with tendrils love entwine,
Yet dried ere you distil your wine.

You are like balm enclosed well
In amber or some crystal shell,
Yet lost ere you transfuse your smell.

You are a dainty violet,
Yet wither'd ere you can be set
Within the virgin's coronet.

You are the queen all flowers among;
But die you must, fair maid, ere long,   20
As he, the maker of this song.

1648

How Roses Came Red

Roses at first were white,
    Till they could not agree,
Whether my Sapho's breast
    Or they more white should be.

But being vanquished quite,
    A blush their cheeks bespread;
Since which, believe the rest,
    The roses first came red.

1648

Night-Piece, to Julia

Her eyes the glow-worm lend thee,
The shooting stars attend thee;
    And the elves also,
    Whose little eyes glow
Like the sparks of fire, befriend thee.

No will-o'-th'-Wisp mis-light thee,
Nor snake nor slow-worm bite thee;
    But on, on thy way,
    Not making a stay,
Since ghost there's none to affright thee.   10

Let not the dark thee cumber;
What though the moon does slumber?
    The stars of the night
    Will lend thee their light,
Like tapers clear without number.

Then, Julia, let me woo thee,
Thus, thus, to come unto me;
    And when I shall meet
    Thy silvery feet
My soul I'll pour into thee.   20

1648

GEORGE HERBERT

The Collar

I struck the board, and cried, "No more; I will abroad!
What! shall I ever sigh and pine?
My lines and life are free; free as the road,
    Loose as the wind, as large as store.
        Shall I be still in suit?
    Have I no harvest but a thorn
    To let me blood, and not restore
What I have lost with cordial fruit?
        Sure there was wine
    Before my sighs did dry it; there was corn   10
        Before my tears did drown it;
    Is the year only lost to me?
        Have I no bays to crown it,
No flowers, no garlands gay? all blasted,
        All wasted?
    Not so, my heart, but there is fruit,
        And thou hast hands.
    Recover all thy sigh-blown age
On double pleasures; leave thy cold dispute
Of what is fit and not; forsake thy cage,   20
        Thy rope of sands
Which petty thoughts have made, and made to thee
    Good cable, to enforce and draw,
        And be thy law,
While thou didst wink and wouldst not see.
        Away! take heed;
        I will abroad.

Call in thy death's head there, tie up thy fears;
    He that forbears
To suit and serve his need   30
    Deserves his load."
But as I raved, and grew more fierce and wild
    At every word,
Methought I heard one calling, "Child";
    And I replied, "My Lord."
                    1633

Virtue

Sweet day, so cool, so calm, so bright,
    The bridal of the earth and sky,
The dew shall weep thy fall to-night;
    For thou must die.

Sweet rose, whose hue, angry and brave,
    Bids the rash gazer wipe his eye,
Thy root is ever in its grave,
    And thou must die.

Sweet spring, full of sweet days and roses,
    A box where sweets compacted lie,   10
My music shows ye have your closes,
    And all must die.

Only a sweet and virtuous soul,
    Like seasoned timber, never gives;
But though the whole world turn to coal,
    Then chiefly lives.
                1633

THOMAS CAREW

The Spring

Now that the winter's gone, the earth hath lost
Her snow-white robes, and now no more the frost
Candies the grass, or casts an icy cream
Upon the silver lake or crystal stream;

But the warm sun thaws the benumbed earth,
And makes it tender; gives a sacred birth
To the dead swallow; wakes in hollow tree
The drowsy cuckoo and the humble-bee.
Now a choir of chirping minstrels bring
In triumph to the world the youthful spring. 10
The valleys, hills, and woods in rich array
Welcome the coming of the longed-for May.
Now all things smile, only my love doth lour;
Nor hath the scalding noonday sun the power
To melt that marble ice, which still doth hold
Her heart congealed, and makes her pity cold.
The ox, which lately did for shelter fly
Into the stall, doth now securely lie
In open fields; and love no more is made
By the fireside, but in the cooler shade 20
Amyntas now doth with his Chloris sleep
Under a sycamore, and all things keep
Time with the season; only she doth carry
June in her eyes, in her heart January.

1640

Ask Me No More Where Jove Bestows

Ask me no more where Jove bestows,
When June is past, the fading rose;
For in your beauties orient deep,
These flow'rs as in their causes sleep.

Ask me no more whither doe stray
The golden atomes of the day;
For in pure love heaven did prepare
Those powders to inrich your hair.

Ask me no more whither doth haste
The nightingale, when May is past; 10
For in your sweet dividing throat
She winters, and keeps warm her note.

Ask me no more where those stars light
That downwards fall in dead of night;
For in your eyes they sit, and there
Fixéd become as in their sphere.

Ask me no more if east or west,
The phenix builds her spicy nest;
For unto you at last she flies,
And in your fragrant bosom dies.   20

1640

Disdain Returned

He that loves a rosy cheek,
    Or a coral lip admires,
Or from starlike eyes doth seek
    Fuel to maintain his fires,
As old Time makes these decay,
So his flames must waste away.

But a smooth and steadfast mind,
    Gentle thoughts and calm desires,
Hearts with equal love combined,
    Kindle never-dying fires.   10
Where these are not, I despise
Lovely cheeks or lips or eyes.

No tears, Celia, now shall win
    My resolved heart to return;
I have searched thy soul within,
    And find naught but pride and scorn;
I have learned thy arts, and now
    Can disdain as much as thou.
Some power, in my revenge, convey
    That love to her I cast away.   20

1640

JOHN MILTON

On Shakespeare

What needs my Shakespeare for his honour'd bones,
The labour of an age in piléd stones,
Or that his hallow'd reliques should be hid
Under a star-ypointing pyramid?
Dear son of memory, great heir of fame,
What need'st thou such weak witness of thy name?
Thou in our wonder and astonishment
Hast built thy self a live-long monument.
For whilst to th'shame of slow-endeavouring art,
Thy easie numbers flow, and that each heart   10
Hath from the leaves of thy unvalu'd book,
Those Delphick lines with deep impression took,
Then thou our fancy of it self bereaving,
Dost make us marble with too much conceaving;
And so sepulcher'd in such pomp dost lie,
That kings for such a tomb would wish to die.

1632

Lycidas [1]

Yet once more, O ye laurels, and once more,
Ye myrtles brown, with ivy never sere,
I come to pluck your berries harsh and crude,
And with forced fingers rude
Shatter your leaves before the mellowing year.
Bitter constraint and sad occasion dear
Compels me to disturb your season due;
For Lycidas is dead, dead ere his prime,
Young Lycidas, and hath not left his peer.
Who would not sing for Lycidas? he knew   10
Himself to sing, and build the lofty rime.
He must not float upon his watery bier
Unwept, and welter to the parching wind,
Without the meed of some melodious tear.

[1] This poem was written to Milton's friend, Edward King.

Begin, then, Sisters of the sacred well
That from beneath the seat of Jove doth spring;
Begin, and somewhat loudly sweep the string.
Hence with denial vain and coy excuse:
So may some gentle Muse
With lucky words favor *my* destined urn,   20
And as he passes turn,
And bid fair peace be to my sable shroud!
    For we were nursed upon the self-same hill,
Fed the same flock, by fountain, shade, and rill;
Together both, ere the high lawns appeared
Under the opening eyelids of the Morn,
We drove a-field, and both together heard
What time the gray-fly winds her sultry horn
Battening our flocks with the fresh dews of night,
Oft till the star that rose at evening bright   30
Toward heaven's descent had sloped his westering wheel.
Meanwhile the rural ditties were not mute;
Tempered to the oaten flute,
Rough Satyrs danced, and Fauns with cloven heel
From the glad sound would not be absent long;
And old Damœtas loved to hear our song.
    But, oh! the heavy change, now thou art gone,
Now thou art gone and never must return!
Thee, Shepherd, thee the woods and desert caves,
With wild thyme and the gadding vine o'ergrown,   40
And all their echoes, mourn.
The willows, and the hazel copses green,
Shall now no more be seen
Fanning their joyous leaves to thy soft lays.
As killing as the canker to the rose,
Or taint-worm to the weanling herds that graze,
Or frost to flowers, that their gay wardrobe wear,
When first the white-thorn blows;
Such, Lycidas, thy loss to shepherd's ear.
    Where were ye, Nymphs, when the remorseless deep   50
Closed o'er the head of your loved Lycidas?
For neither were ye playing on the steep
Where your old bards, the famous Druids, lie,

Nor on the shaggy top of Mona high,
Nor yet where Deva spreads her wizard stream.
Ay me! I fondly dream
"Had ye been there," . . . for what could that have done?
What could the Muse herself that Orpheus bore,
The Muse herself, for her enchanting son,
Whom universal nature did lament,   60
When, by the rout that made the hideous roar,
His gory visage down the stream was sent,
Down the swift Hebrus to the Lesbian shore?
    Alas! what boots it with uncessant care
To tend the homely, slighted, shepherd's trade,
And strictly meditate the thankless Muse?
Were it not better done, as others use,
To sport with Amaryllis in the shade,
Or with the tangles of Neæra's hair?
Fame is the spur that the clear spirit doth raise   70
(That last infirmity of noble mind)
To scorn delights and live laborious days;
But the fair guerdon when we hope to find,
And think to burst out into sudden blaze,
Comes the blind Fury with the abhorréd shears,
And slits the thin-spun life. "But not the praise,"
Phœbus replied, and touched my trembling ears:
"Fame is no plant that grows on mortal soil,
Nor in the glistening foil
Set off to the world, nor in broad rumor lies,   80
But lives and spreads aloft by those pure eyes
And perfect witness of all-judging Jove;
As he pronounces lastly on each deed,
Of so much fame in heaven expect thy meed."
    O fountain Arethuse, and thou honored flood,
Smooth-sliding Mincius, crowned with vocal reeds,
That strain I heard was of a higher mood.
But now my oat proceeds,
And listens to the Herald of the Sea,
That came in Neptune's plea.   90
He asked the waves, and asked the felon winds,
What hard mishap hath doomed this gentle swain?

And questioned every gust of rugged wings
That blows from off each beakéd promontory.
They knew not of his story;
And sage Hippotades their answer brings,
That not a blast was from his dungeon strayed:
The air was calm, and on the level brine
Sleek Panope with all her sisters played.
It was that fatal and perfidious bark,   100
Built in the eclipse, and rigged with curses dark,
That sunk so low that sacred head of thine.
   Next, Camus, reverend sire, went footing slow,
His mantle hairy, and his bonnet sedge,
Inwrought with figures dim, and on the edge
Like to that sanguine flower inscribed with woe.
"Ah! who hath reft," quoth he, "my dearest pledge?"
Last came, and last did go,
The Pilot of the Galilean Lake;
Two massy keys he bore of metals twain   110
(The golden opes, the iron shuts amain).
He shook his mitered locks, and stern bespake:—
"How well could I have spared for thee, young swain,
Enow of such as, for their bellies' sake,
Creep, and intrude, and climb into the fold!
Of other care they little reckoning make
Than how to scramble at the shearers' feast,
And shove away the worthy bidden guest.
Blind mouths! that scarce themselves know how to hold
A sheep-hook, or have learned ought else the least   120
That to the faithful herdman's art belongs!
What recks it them? What need they? They are sped;
And, when they list, their lean and flashy songs
Grate on their scrannel pipes of wretched straw;
The hungry sheep look up, and are not fed,
But, swoln with wind and the rank mist they draw,
Rot inwardly, and foul contagion spread;
Besides what the grim wolf with privy paw
Daily devours apace, and nothing said.
But that two-handed engine at the door   130
Stands ready to smite once, and smite no more."

Return, Alpheus; the dread voice is past
That shrunk thy streams; return, Sicilian Muse,
And call the vales, and bid them hither cast
Their bells and flowerets of a thousand hues.
Ye valleys low, where the mild whispers use
Of shades, and wanton winds, and gushing brooks,
On whose fresh lap the swart star sparely looks,
Throw hither all your quaint enameled eyes
That on the green turf suck the honeyed showers,   140
And purple all the ground with vernal flowers.
Bring the rathe primrose that forsaken dies,
The tufted crow-toe, and pale jessamine,
The white pink, and the pansy freaked with jet,
The growing violet,
The musk rose, and the well-attired woodbine,
With cowslips wan that hang the pensive head,
And every flower that sad embroidery wears;
Bid amaranthus all his beauty shed,
And daffadillies fill their cups with tears,   150
To strew the laureate hearse where Lycid lies.
For so, to interpose a little ease,
Let our frail thoughts dally with false surmise,
Ay me! whilst thee the shores and sounding seas
Wash far away, where'er thy bones are hurled;
Whether beyond the stormy Hebrides,
Where thou perhaps under the whelming tide
Visit'st the bottom of the monstrous world;
Or whether thou, to our moist vows denied,
Sleep'st by the fable of Bellerus old,   160
Where the great Vision of the guarded mount
Looks toward Namancos and Bayona's hold.
Look homeward, Angel, now, and melt with ruth:
And, O ye dolphins, waft the hapless youth.
    Weep no more, woeful shepherds, weep no more,
For Lycidas, your sorrow, is not dead,
Sunk though he be beneath the watery floor.
So sinks the day-star in the ocean bed,
And yet anon repairs his drooping head,
And tricks his beams, and with new-spangled ore   170

Flames in the forehead of the morning sky:
So Lycidas sunk low, but mounted high,
Through the dear might of him that walked the waves,
Where, other groves and other streams along,
With nectar pure his oozy locks he laves,
And hears the unexpressive nuptial song,
In the blest kingdoms meek of joy and love.
There entertain him all the Saints above,
In solemn troops, and sweet societies,
That sing, and singing in their glory move,   180
And wipe the tears for ever from his eyes.
Now, Lycidas, the shepherds weep no more;
Henceforth thou art the Genius of the shore,
In thy large recompense, and shalt be good
To all that wander in that perilous flood.
    Thus sang the uncouth swain to the oaks and rills,
While the still morn went out with sandals gray:
He touched the tender stops of various quills,
With eager thought warbling his Doric lay:
And now the sun had stretched out all the hills,   190
And now was dropped into the western bay.
At last he rose, and twitched his mantle blue:
To-morrow to fresh woods, and pastures new.

1638

Song on a May Morning

Now the bright morning Star, Day's harbinger,
Comes dancing from the East, and leads with her
The flowery May, who from her green lap throws
The yellow cowslip, and the pale primrose.
    Hail bounteous May that dost inspire
    Mirth and youth, and warm desire,
    Woods and groves, are of thy dressing,
    Hill and dale doth boast they blessing.
Thus we salute thee with our early song,
And welcome thee and wish thee long.   10

1645

On Time

Fly, envious Time, till thou run out thy race:
Call on the lazy leaden-stepping Hours,
Whose speed is but the heavy plummet's pace;
And glut thyself with what thy womb devours,
Which is no more than what is false and vain,
And merely mortal dross;
So little is our loss,
So little is thy gain!
For, when as each thing bad thou hast entombed,
And, last of all, thy greedy self consumed,   10
Then long Eternity shall greet our bliss
With an individual kiss,
And Joy shall overtake us as a flood;
When everything that is sincerely good,
And perfectly divine,
With Truth, and Peace, and Love, shall ever shine
About the supreme throne
Of him, to whose happy-making sight alone
When once our heavenly-guided soul shall climb,
Then, all this earthly grossness quit,   20
Attired with stars we shall for ever sit,
    Triumphing over Death, and Chance, and thee, O Time!
                                                  1645

How Soon Hath Time

How soon hath Time, the suttle theef of youth,
    Stoln on his wing my three and twentieth yeer!
    My hasting dayes flie on with full career,
    But my late spring no bud or blossom shew'th.
Perhaps my semblance might deceive the truth,
    That I to manhood am arriv'd so near,
    And inward ripenes doth much less appear,
    That som more timely-happy spirits indu'th.
Yet be it less or more, or soon or slow,
    It shall be still in strictest measure eev'n,   10

To that same lot, however mean, or high,
Toward which Time leads me, and the will of Heav'n;
All is, if I have grace to use it so,
As ever in my great task Masters eye.

1645

When I Consider How My Light Is Spent

When I consider how my light is spent
  Ere half my days in this dark world and wide,
  And that one talent which is death to hide
  Lodged with me useless, though my soul more bent
To serve therewith my Maker, and present
  My true account, lest He returning chide,
  "Doth God exact day-labor, light denied?"
  I fondly ask. But Patience, to prevent
That murmur, soon replies, "God doth not need
  Either man's work or his own gifts. Who best   10
  Bear his mild yoke, they serve him best. His state
Is kingly: thousands at his bidding speed,
  And post o'er land and ocean without rest;
  They also serve who only stand and wait."

1655   *1673*

On His Deceased Wife

Methought I saw my late espoused saint
Brought to me like Alcestis from the grave,
Whom Jove's great son to her glad husband gave,
Rescued from death by force though pale and faint.
Mine as whom washed from spot of child-bed taint,
Purification in the old law did save,
And such, as yet once more I trust to have
Full sight of her in Heaven without restraint,
Came vested in all white, pure as her mind.
Her face was veiled, yet to my fancied sight,   10
Love, sweetness, goodness, in her person shined,

So clear, as in no face with more delight.
But O, as to embrace me she inclined,
I waked, she fled, and day brought back my night.

1673

Sweet Is the Breath of Morn

Sweet is the breath of morn, her rising sweet,
With charm of earliest birds; pleasant the sun
When first on this delightful land he spreads
His orient beams, on herb, tree, fruit, and flower,
Glistring with dew; fragrant the fertile earth
After soft showers; and sweet the coming on
Of grateful evening mild, then silent night
With this her solemn bird and this fair moon,
And these the gems of Heaven, her starry train:
But neither breath of morn when she ascends   10
With charm of earliest birds, nor rising sun
On this delightful land, nor herb, fruit, flower,
Glistring with dew, nor fragrance after showers,
Nor grateful evening mild, nor silent night
With this her solemn bird, nor walk by moon,
Or glittering star-light without thee is sweet.

Paradise Lost, 1667

RICHARD LOVELACE

To Althea, from Prison

When Love with unconfinèd wings
    Hovers within my gates,
And my divine Althea brings
    To whisper at the grates;
When I lie tangled in her hair
    And fettered to her eye,
The gods that wanton in the air
    Know no such liberty.

When flowing cups run swiftly round
  With no allaying Thames,   10
Our careless heads with roses bound,
  Our hearts with loyal flames;
When thirsty grief in wine we steep,
  When healths and draughts go free,
Fishes that tipple in the deep
  Know no such liberty.

When, like committed linnets, I
  With shriller throat shall sing
The sweetness, mercy, majesty,
  And glories of my king;   20
When I shall voice aloud how good
  He is, how great should be,
Enlargèd winds, that curl the flood,
  Know no such liberty.

Stone walls do not a prison make,
  Nor iron bars a cage;
Minds innocent and quiet take
  That for an hermitage;
If I have freedom in my love,
  And in my soul am free,   30
Angels alone, that soar above,
  Enjoy such liberty.

              1649

ANDREW MARVELL

To His Coy Mistress

Had we but world enough, and time,
This coyness, lady, were no crime.
We would sit down, and think which way
To walk, and pass our long love's day.
Thou by the Indian Ganges' side
Shouldst rubies find: I by the tide
Of Humber would complain. I would
Love you ten years before the flood,

And you should, if you please, refuse
Till the conversion of the Jews;   10
My vegetable love should grow
Vaster than empires and more slow;
An hundred years should go to praise
Thine eyes, and on thy forehead gaze;
Two hundred to adore each breast,
But thirty thousand to the rest;
An age at least to every part,
And the last age should show your heart.
For, lady, you deserve this state;
Nor would I love at lower rate.   20

But at my back I always hear
Time's wingéd chariot hurrying near;
And yonder all before us lie
Deserts of vast eternity.
Thy beauty shall no more be found,
Nor in thy marble vault shall sound
My echoing song; then worms shall try
That long preserved virginity;
And your quaint honor turn to dust,
And into ashes all my lust: 30
The grave's a fine and private place,
But none, I think, do there embrace.

Now therefore, while the youthful hue
Sits on thy skin like morning dew,
And while thy willing soul transpires
At every pore with instant fires,
Now let us sport us while we may,
And now, like amorous birds of prey,
Rather at once our time devour
Than languish in his slow-chapped power,   40
Let us roll all our strength and all
Our sweetness up into one ball,
And tear our pleasures with rough strife
Thorough the iron gates of life:
Thus, though we cannot make our sun
Stand still, yet we will make him run.
1681

The Garden

How vainly men themselves amaze,
To win the palm, the oak, or bays,
And their uncessant labors see
Crowned from some single herb or tree
Whose short and narrow-vergéd shade
Does prudently their toils upbraid,
While all flowers and trees do close
To weave the garlands of repose!

Fair Quiet, have I found thee here,
And Innocence, thy sister dear?   10
Mistaken long, I sought you then
In busy companies of men.
Your sacred plants, if here below,
Only among the plants will grow;
Society is all but rude
To this delicious solitude.

No white nor red was ever seen
So amorous as this lovely green.
Fond lovers, cruel as their flame,
Cut in these trees their mistress' name.   20
Little, alas! they know or heed,
How far these beauties hers exceed!
Fair trees! wheres'e'er your barks I wound,
No name shall but your own be found.

When we have run our passion's heat,
Love hither makes his best retreat.
The gods that mortal beauty chase,
Still in a tree did end their race:
Apollo hunted Daphne so,
Only that she might laurel grow;   30
And Pan did after Syrinx speed,
Not as a nymph, but for a reed.

What wond'rous life is this I lead!
Ripe apples drop about my head;

The luscious clusters of the vine
Upon my mouth do crush their wine;
The nectarine and curious peach
Into my hands themselves do reach;
Stumbling on melons as I pass,
Ensnared with flowers, I fall on grass.   40

Meanwhile the mind from pleasure less
Withdraws into its happiness;
The mind, that ocean where each kind
Does straight its own resemblance find,
Yet it creates, transcending these,
Far other worlds and other seas,
Annihilating all that's made
To a green thought in a green shade.

Here at the fountain's sliding foot,
Or at some fruit tree's mossy root,   50
Casting the body's vest aside,
My soul into the boughs does glide;
There like a bird it sits and sings,
Then whets, then combs its silver wings;
And till prepared for longer flight,
Waves in its plumes the various light.

Such was that happy garden-state,
While man there walked without a mate;
After a place so pure and sweet,
What other help could yet be meet!   60
But 'twas beyond a mortal's share
To wander solitary there;
Two paradises 'twere, in one,
To live in paradise alone.

How well the skillful gard'ner drew
Of flowers and herbs this dial new,
Where, from above, the milder sun
Does through a fragrant zodiac run;
And as it works, th' industrious bee
Computes its time as well as we.   70

How could such sweet and wholesome hours
Be reckoned but with herbs and flowers?

1681

Bermudas

Where the remote Bermudas ride
In the ocean's bosom unespied,
From a small boat that rowed along
The listening winds received this song:

"What should we do but sing His praise
That led us through the watery maze
Unto an isle so long unknown,
And yet far kinder than our own?
Where He the huge sea-monsters wracks
That lift the deep upon their backs,   10
He lands us on a grassy stage,
Safe from the storms' and prelates' rage.
He gave us this eternal spring
Which here enamels everything,
And sends the fowls to us in care
On daily visits through the air.
He hangs in shades the orange bright
Like golden lamps in a green night,
And does in the pomegranates close
Jewels more rich than Ormus shows.   20
He makes the figs our mouths to meet
And throws the melons at our feet;
But apples plants of such a price,
No tree could ever bear them twice.
With cedars chosen by His hand
From Lebanon He stores the land;
And makes the hollow seas that roar
Proclaim the ambergris on shore.
He cast (of which we rather boast)
The Gospel's pearl upon our coast;   30
And in these rocks for us did frame
A temple where to sound His name.

Oh, let our voice His praise exalt
Till it arrive at heaven's vault,
Which thence, perhaps, rebounding may
Echo beyond the Mexique bay!"

Thus sung they in the English boat
A holy and a cheerful note;
And all the way, to guide their chime,
With falling oars they kept the time.   40

1681

HENRY VAUGHAN

The Retreat

Happy those early days, when I
Shined in my angel-infancy!
Before I understood this place
Appointed for my second race,
Or taught my soul to fancy aught
But a white, celestial thought;
When yet I had not walked above
A mile or two from my first love,
And looking back at that short space,
Could see a glimpse of his bright face;   10
When on some gilded cloud or flower
My gazing soul would dwell an hour,
And in those weaker glories spy
Some shadows of eternity;
Before I taught by tongue to wound
My conscience with a sinful sound,
Or had the black art to dispense,
A several sin to every sense,
But felt through all this fleshly dress
Bright shoots of everlastingness.   20
    O, how I long to travel back,
And tread again that ancient track,
That I might once more reach that plain,
Where first I felt my glorious train;

From whence the enlightened spirit sees
That shady city of palm trees.
But ah! my soul with too much stay
Is drunk, and staggers in the way!
Some men a forward motion love,
But I by backward steps would move;   30
And when this dust falls to the urn,
In that state I came, return.

1655

The World

I saw Eternity the other night,
Like a great ring of pure and endless light,
  All calm, as it was bright;
And round beneath it, Time, in hours, days, years,
  Driven by the spheres
Like a vast shadow moved; in which the world
  And all her train were hurled.
The doting lover in his quaintest strain
  Did there complain;
Near him, his lute, his fancy, and his flights,   10
  Wit's sour delights,
With gloves, and knots, the silly snares of pleasure,
  Yet his dear treasure,
All scattered lay, while he his eyes did pour
  Upon a flower.

The darksome statesman, hung with weights and woe,
Like a thick midnight-fog moved there so slow,
  He did not stay, nor go;
Condemning thoughts, like sad eclipses, scowl
  Upon his soul,   20
And clouds of crying witnesses without
  Pursued him with one shout.
Yet digged the mole, and lest his ways be found,
  Worked under ground,
Where he did clutch his prey; but one did see
  That policy;

Churches and altars fed him; perjuries
  Were gnats and flies;
It rained about him blood and tears, but he
  Drank them as free.   30

The fearful miser on a heap of rust
Sat pining all his life there, did scarce trust
  His own hands with the dust,
Yet would not place one piece above, but lives
  In fear of thieves.
Thousands there were as frantic as himself,
  And hugged each one his pelf;
The downright epicure placed heaven in sense,
  And scorned pretense;
While others, slipped into a wide excess,   40
  Said little less;
The weaker sort, slight, trivial wares enslave,
  Who think them brave;
And poor, despiséd Truth sat counting by
  Their victory.

Yet some, who all this while did weep and sing,
And sing and weep, soared up into the ring;
  But most would use no wing.
O fools, said I, thus to prefer dark night
  Before true light!   50
To live in grots and caves, and hate the day
  Because it shows the way,
The way, which from this dead and dark abode
  Leads up to God;
A way there you might tread the sun, and be
  More bright than he!
But, as I did their madness so discuss,
  One whispered thus
"This ring the Bridegroom did for none provide,
  But for his bride."   60

1655

JOHN DRYDEN
Alexander's Feast

OR, THE POWER OF MUSIC; AN ODE
IN HONOR OF ST. CECILIA'S DAY: 1697

I

'T was at the royal feast, for Persia won
   By Philip's warlike son.
   Aloft in awful state
   The godlike hero sate
   On his imperial throne:
   His valiant peers were placed around;
Their brows with roses and with myrtles bound.
   (So should desert in arms be crowned).
The lovely Thais, by his side,
Sate like a blooming Eastern bride
In flow'r of youth and beauty's pride.
   Happy, happy, happy pair!
   None but the brave,
   None but the brave,
   None but the brave deserves the fair.

CHORUS

   Happy, happy, happy pair!
   None but the brave,
   None but the brave,
   None but the brave deserves the fair.

II

Timotheus, placed on high   20
   Amid the tuneful choir,
   With flying fingers touched the lyre:
The trembling notes ascend the sky,
   And heav'nly joys inspire.
The song began from Jove,
Who left his blissful seats above
(Such is the power of mighty love).

A dragon's fiery form belied the god:
Sublime on radiant spires he rode,
    When he to fair Olympia pressed;   30
    And while he sought her snowy breast:
Then, round her slender waist he curled,
And stamped an image of himself, a sov'reign of the world.
The list'ning crowd admire the lofty sound;
"A present deity," they shout around;
"A present deity," the vaulted roofs rebound:
      With ravished ears
      The monarch hears,
      Assumes the god,
      Affects to nod,   40
   And seems to shake the spheres.

CHORUS

      With ravished ears
      The monarch hears,
      Assumes the god,
      Affects to nod,
   And seems to shake the spheres.

III

The praise of Bacchus then the sweet musician sung,
  Of Bacchus ever fair and ever young:
    The jolly god in triumph comes;
    Sound the trumpets; beat the drums;   50
      Flushed with a purple grace
      He shows his honest face:
Now give the hautboys breath; he comes, he comes.
    Bacchus, ever fair and young,
      Drinking joys did first ordain:
    Bacchus' blessings are a treasure.
    Drinking is the soldier's pleasure:
      Rich the treasure,
      Sweet the pleasure,
      Sweet is pleasure after pain.   60

CHORUS

Bacchus' blessings are a treasure,
Drinking is the soldier's pleasure:
   Rich the treasure,
    Sweet the pleasure,
   Sweet is pleasure after pain.

IV

Soothed with the sound, the king grew vain;
   Fought all his battles o'er again;
And thrice he routed all his foes; and thrice he slew the slain.
The master saw the madness rise;
His glowing cheeks, his ardent eyes;   70
And, while he heav'n and earth defied,
Changed his hand, and checked his pride.
    He chose a mournful Muse,
    Soft pity to infuse:
He sung Darius great and good,
    By too severe a fate,
Fallen, fallen, fallen, fallen,
    Fallen from his high estate,
      And welt'ring in his blood;
Deserted, at his utmost need,   80
By those his former bounty fed;
On the bare earth exposed he lies,
With not a friend to close his eyes.
With downcast looks the joyless victor sate,
   Revolving in his altered soul
    The various turns of chance below;
  And, now and then, a sigh he stole;
    And tears began to flow.

CHORUS

Revolving in his altered soul
   The various turns of chance below;   90
And, now and then, a sigh he stole;
   And tears began to flow.

V

The mighty master smiled, to see
That love was in the next degree:
'Twas but a kindred sound to move,
For pity melts the mind to love.
   Softly sweet, in Lydian measures,
   Soon he soothed his soul to pleasures.
"War," he sung, "is toil and trouble;
Honor, but an empty bubble;   100
    Never ending, still beginning,
    Fighting still, and still destroying;
    If the world be worth thy winning,
    Think, O think it worth enjoying;
     Lovely Thais sits beside thee,
     Take the good the gods provide thee."
The many rend the skies with loud applause;
So Love was crowned, but Music won the cause.
   The prince, unable to conceal his pain,
    Gazed on the fair   110
    Who caused his care,
  And sighed and looked, sighed and looked,
  Sighed and looked, and sighed again:
At length, with love and wine at once oppressed,
The vanquished victor sunk upon her breast.

    CHORUS

   The prince, unable to conceal his pain,
    Gazed on the fair
    Who caused his care,
  And sighed and looked, sighed and looked,
  Sighed and looked, and sighed again: 120
At length, with love and wine at once oppressed,
The vanquished victor sunk upon her breast.

VI

Now strike the golden lyre again:
A louder yet, and yet a louder strain.
Break his bands of sleep asunder,

And rouse him, like a rattling peal of thunder.
    Hark, hark, the horrid sound
      Has raised up his head:
      As awaked from the dead,
    And amazed, he stares around.   130
"Revenge, revenge!" Timotheus cries,
    "See the Furies arise!
    See the snakes that they rear,
    How they hiss in their hair,
And the sparkles that flash from their eyes!
    Behold a ghastly band,
    Each a torch in his hand!
Those are Grecian ghosts, that in battle were slain,
    And unburied remain
    Inglorious on the plain: 140
    Give the vengeance due
    To the valiant crew.
Behold how they toss their torches on high,
    How they point to the Persian abodes,
And glitt'ring temples of their hostile gods!"
The princes applaud, with a furious joy;
And the king seized a flambeau with zeal to destroy;
    Thais led the way,
    To light him to his prey,
And, like another Helen, fired another Troy.   150

CHORUS

And the king seized a flambeau with zeal to destroy;
    Thais led the way,
    To light him to his prey,
And, like another Helen, fired another Troy.

VII

    Thus, long ago,
Ere heaving bellows learned to blow,
    While organs yet were mute;
    Timotheus, to his breathing flute,
    And sounding lyre,
Could swell the soul to rage, or kindle soft desire.   160

At last, divine Cecilia came,
Inventress of the vocal frame;
The sweet enthusiast, from her sacred store,
Enlarged the former narrow bounds,
And added length to solemn sounds,
With nature's mother wit, and arts unknown before.
    Let old Timotheus yield the prize,
      Or both divide the crown;
    He raised a mortal to the skies;
    She drew an angel down.   170

GRAND CHORUS

At last, divine Cecilia came,
Inventress of the vocal frame;
The sweet enthusiast, from her sacred store,
Enlarged the former narrow bounds,
And added length to solemn sounds,
With nature's mother wit, and arts unknown before.
    Let old Timotheus yield the prize,
      Or both divide the crown;
    He raised a mortal to the skies;
    She drew an angel down.   180

1700

WILLIAM COLLINS

A Song from Shakespeare's Cymbeline

I

To fair Fidele's grassy tomb
  Soft maids and village hinds shall bring
Each op'ning sweet, of earliest bloom,
  And rifle all the breathing Spring.

II

No wailing ghost shall dare appear
  To vex with shrieks this quiet grove:
But shepherd lads assemble here,
  And melting virgins own their love.

III

No wither'd witch shall here be seen,
  No goblins lead their nightly crew: 10
The female fays shall haunt the green,
  And dress thy grave with pearly dew!

IV

The redbreast oft at ev'ning hours
  Shall kindly lend his little aid:
With hoary moss, and gather'd flow'rs,
  To deck the ground where thou art laid.

V

When howling winds, and beating rain,
  In tempests shake the sylvan cell:
Or midst the chace on ev'ry plain,
  The tender thought on thee shall dwell.   20

VI

Each lonely scene shall thee restore,
  For thee the tear be duly shed:
Belov'd, till life could charm no more;
  And mourn'd, till Pity's self be dead.

1744

Ode to Evening

If aught of oaten stop, or pastoral song,
May hope, chaste Eve, to soothe thy modest ear,
  Like thy own solemn springs,
  Thy springs and dying gales,

O nymph reserved, while now the bright-haired sun
Sits in yon western tent, whose cloudy skirts,
  With brede ethereal wove,
  O'erhang his wavy bed:

Now air is hushed, save where the weak-eyed bat,
With short shrill shriek, flits by on leathern wing,   10
    Or where the beetle winds
    His small but sullen horn,

As oft he rises 'midst the twilight path,
Against the pilgrim borne in heedless hum:
    Now teach me, maid composed,
    To breathe some softened strain,

Whose numbers, stealing through thy dark'ning vale,
May not unseemly with its stillness suit,
    As, musing slow, I hail
    Thy genial loved return!   20

For when thy folding-star arising shows
His paly circlet, at his warning lamp
    The fragrant Hours, and elves
    Who slept in flowers the day,

And many a nymph who wreaths her brows with sedge,
And sheds the fresh'ning dew, and, lovelier still,
    The pensive Pleasures sweet,
    Prepare thy shadowy car.

Then lead, calm vot'ress, where some sheety lake
Cheers the lone heath, or some time-hallowed pile   30
    Or upland fallows gray
    Reflect its last cool gleam.

But when chill blust'ring winds, or driving rain,
Forbid my willing feet, be mine the hut
    That from the mountain's side
    Views wilds, and swelling floods,

And hamlets brown, and dim-discovered spires,
And hears their simple bell, and marks. o'er all
    Thy dewy fingers draw
    The gradual dusky veil.   40

While Spring shall pour his show'rs, as oft he wont,
And bathe thy breathing tresses, meekest Eve;
  While Summer loves to sport
  Beneath thy ling'ring light;

While sallow Autumn fills thy lap with leaves;
Or Winter, yelling through the troublous air,
  Affrights thy shrinking train,
  And rudely rends thy robes;

So long, sure-found beneath the sylvan shed,
Shall Fancy, Friendship, Science, rose-lipped Health,   50
  Thy gentlest influence own,
  And hymn thy fav'rite name!

1747

Ode [1]

WRITTEN IN THE BEGINNING OF THE YEAR 1746

1

How sleep the brave, who sink to rest,
By all their country's wishes blest!
When Spring, with dewy fingers cold,
Returns to deck their hallow'd mold,
She there shall dress a sweeter sod,
Than Fancy's feet have ever trod.

2

By fairy hands their knell is rung,
By forms unseen their dirge is sung;
There Honour comes, a pilgrim grey,
To bless the turf that wraps their clay,   10
And Freedom shall awhile repair,
To dwell a weeping hermit there!

1746

[1] In 1745 and 1746 England suffered the loss of many men killed in battle both at home and abroad.

WILLIAM BLAKE

How Sweet I Roam'd

How sweet I roam'd from field to field
And tasted all the summer's pride,
Till I the Prince of Love beheld
Who in the sunny beams did glide!

He show'd me lilies for my hair,
And blushing roses for my brow;
He led me through his gardens fair
Where all his golden pleasures grow.

With sweet May dews my wings were wet,
And Phoebus fir'd my vocal rage;   10
He caught me in his silken net,
And shut me in his golden cage.

He loves to sit and hear me sing,
Then, laughing, sports and plays with me;
Then stretches out my golden wing,
And mocks my loss of liberty.

1783

My Silks and Fine Array

My silks and fine array,
My smiles and languish'd air,
By love are driv'n away;
And mournful lean Despair
Brings me yew to deck my grave;
Such end true lovers have.

His face is fair as heav'n
When springing buds unfold;
O why to him was't giv'n
Whose heart is wintry cold?   10
His breast is love's all-worshipp'd tomb,
Where all love's pilgrims come.

Bring me an axe and spade,
Bring me a winding-sheet;
When I my grave have made
Let winds and tempests beat:
Then down I'll lie as cold as clay.
True love doth pass away!

1783

To the Muses

Whether on Ida's shady brow,
Or in the chambers of the East,
The chambers of the sun, that now
From ancient melody have ceas'd;

Whether in Heaven ye wander fair,
Or the green corners of the earth,
Or the blue regions of the air
Where the melodious winds have birth;

Whether on crystal rocks ye rove,
Beneath the bosom of the sea   10
Wand'ring in many a coral grove,
Fair Nine, forsaking Poetry!

How have you left the ancient love
That bards of old enjoy'd in you!
The languid strings do scarcely move!
The sound is forc'd, the notes are few!

1783

Piping Down the Valleys Wild

Piping down the valleys wild,
Piping songs of pleasant glee,
On a cloud I saw a child,
And he laughing said to me:

"Pipe a song about a Lamb!"
So I piped with merry cheer.

"Piper, pipe that song again;"
So I piped: he wept to hear.

"Drop thy pipe, thy happy pipe;
Sing thy songs of happy cheer:"   10
So I sang the same again,
While he wept with joy to hear.

"Piper, sit thee down and write
In a book, that all may read."
So he vanished from my sight,
And I plucked a hollow reed,

And I made a rural pen,
And I stained the water clear,
And I wrote my happy songs
Every child may joy to hear.   20

1789

London

I wander through each chartered street,
Near where the chartered Thames does flow,
And mark in every face I meet
Marks of weakness, marks of woe.

In every cry of every man,
In every infant's cry of fear,
In every voice, in every ban,
The mind-forged manacles I hear:

How the chimney-sweeper's cry
Every blackening church appalls,   10
And the hapless soldier's sigh
Runs in blood down palace walls.

But most, through midnight streets I hear
How the youthful harlot's curse
Blasts the new-born infant's tear,
And blights with plagues the marriage hearse.

1794

The Tiger

Tiger! Tiger! burning bright
In the forests of the night,
What immortal hand or eye
Could frame thy fearful symmetry?

In what distant deeps or skies
Burnt the fire of thine eyes?
On what wings dare he aspire?
What the hand dare seize the fire?

And what shoulder, and what art,
Could twist the sinews of thy heart?   10
And when thy heart began to beat,
What dread hand? and what dread feet?

What the hammer? what the chain?
In what furnace was thy brain?
What the anvil? what dread grasp
Dare its deadly terrors clasp?

When the stars threw down their spears,
And watered heaven with their tears,
Did he smile his work to see?
Did he who made the Lamb make thee?   20

Tiger! Tiger! burning bright
In the forests of the night,
What immortal hand or eye
Dare frame thy fearful symmetry?

1794

And Did Those Feet in Ancient Time

And did those feet in ancient time
Walk upon England's mountains green?
And was the holy Lamb of God
On England's pleasant pastures seen?

And did the Countenance Divine
   Shine forth upon our clouded hills?
And was Jerusalem builded here
   Among these dark Satanic Mills?

Bring me my bow of burning gold!
   Bring me my arrows of desire!   10
Bring me my spear! O clouds, unfold!
   Bring me my chariot of fire!

I will not cease from mental fight,
   Nor shall my sword sleep in my hand,
Till we have built Jerusalem
   In England's green and pleasant land.
                 Milton, about 1808

To Winter

"O winter! bar thine adamantine doors:
The north is thine; there hast thou built thy dark
Deep-founded habitation. Shake not thy roofs,
Nor bend thy pillars with thine iron car."

He hears me not, but o'er the yawning deep
Rides heavy; his storms are unchained, sheathéd
In ribbéd steel; I dare not lift mine eyes,
For he hath reared his scepter o'er the world.

Lo! now the direful monster, whose skin clings
To his strong bones, strides o'er the groaning rocks: 10
He withers all in silence, and in his hand
Unclothes the earth, and freezes up frail life.

He takes his seat upon the cliffs,—the mariner
Cries in vain. Poor little wretch, that deal'st
With storms!—till heaven smiles, and the monster
Is driv'n yelling to his caves beneath mount Hecla.
                 1783

A Poison Tree

I was angry with my friend:
I told my wrath, my wrath did end.
I was angry with my foe:
I told it not, my wrath did grow.

And I water'd it in fears,
Night and morning with my tears;
And I sunnéd it with smiles,
And with soft deceitful wiles.

And it grew both day and night,
Till it bore an apple bright;   10
And my foe beheld it shine,
And he knew that it was mine,

And into my garden stole
When the night had veil'd the pole:
In the morning glad I see
My foe outstretch'd beneath the tree.

1794

The Garden of Love

I went to the Garden of Love,
And saw what I never had seen:
A chapel was built in the midst,
Where I used to play on the green.

And the gates of this chapel were shut,
And "Thou shalt not" writ over the door;
So I turned to the Garden of Love,
That so many sweet flowers bore:

And I saw it was filléd with graves,
And tombstones where flowers should be;   10
And priests in black gowns were walking their rounds,
And binding with briars my joys and desires.

1794

ROBERT BURNS

To a Mouse

ON TURNING HER UP IN HER NEST WITH THE PLOW

Wee, sleekit, cow'rin', tim'rous beastie,
O what a panic's in thy breastie!
Thou need na start awa sae hasty,
    Wi' bickering brattle!
I wad be laith to rin an' chase thee
    Wi' murd'ring pattle!

I'm truly sorry man's dominion
Has broken nature's social union,
An' justifies that ill opinion
    Which makes thee startle   10
At me, thy poor earth-borne companion,
    An' fellow-mortal!

I doubt na, whyles, but thou may thieve;
What then? poor beastie, thou maun live!
A daimen-icker in a thrave
    'S a sma' request:
I'll get a blessin' wi' the lave,
    And never miss't!

Thy wee bit housie, too, in ruin!
Its silly wa's the win's are strewin'!   20
An' naething, now, to big a new ane,
    O' foggage green!
An' bleak December's winds ensuin',
    Baith snell an' keen!

Thou saw the fields laid bare and waste,
An' weary winter comin' fast,

1. *sleekit*, slinking.   4. *brattle*, scampering.
6. *pattle*, instrument for cleaning the plow.
15. *daimen*, odd. *icker*, ear of corn. *thrave*, twenty-four sheaves.
17. *lave*, leavings.   21. *to big*, to build.   22. *foggage*, forrage.
24. *snell*, biting.

An' cozie here, beneath the blast,
    Thou thought to dwell,
Till crash! the cruel coulter past
    Out-thro' thy cell.   30

That wee bit heap o' leaves an' stibble
Has cost thee mony a weary nibble!
Now thou's turned out, for a' thy trouble,
    But house or hald,
To thole the winter's sleety dribble,
    An' cranreuch cauld!

But, Mousie, thou art no thy lane,
In proving foresight may be vain:
The best laid schemes o' mice an' men
    Gang aft a-gley,   '   40
An' lea'e us nought but grief an' pain
    For promis'd joy.

Still thou art blest compar'd wi' me!
The present only toucheth thee:
But oh! I backward cast my e'e
    On prospects drear!
An' forward tho' I canna see,
    I guess an' fear!
                     1786

Of A' the Airts

Of a' the airts the wind can blaw,
    I dearly like the west,
For there the bonnie lassie lives,
    The lassie I lo'e best:
There's wild woods grow, and rivers row,
    And mony a hill between;
But day and night my fancy's flight
    Is ever wi' my Jean.

29. *coulter's,* cutter on a plow.   35. *To thole,* endure.
36. *cranreuch,* hoar frost.   37. *no thy lane,* not alone.
  1. *airts,* points of the compass.   5. *row,* roll.

I see her in the dewy flowers,
   I see her sweet and fair: 10
I hear her in the tunefu' birds,
   I hear her charm the air:
There's not a bonnie flower that springs
   By fountain, shaw, or green;
There's not a bonnie bird that sings,
   But minds me o' my Jean.

1790

Highland Mary

Ye banks, and braes, and streams around
   The castle o' Montgomery,
Green be your woods and fair your flowers,
   Your waters never drumlie!
There simmer first unfald her robes,
   And there the langest tarry;
For there I took the last fareweel,
   O' my sweet Highland Mary.

How sweetly bloomed the gay green birk,
   How rich the hawthorn's blossom,   10
As underneath their fragrant shade
   I clasped her to my bosom!
The golden hours on angel wings
   Flew o'er me and my dearie;
For dear to me as light and life,
   Was my sweet Highland Mary.

Wi' monie a vow and locked embrace
   Our parting was fu' tender;
And, pledging aft to meet again,
   We tore oursels asunder;   20
But O! fell death's untimely frost,
   That nipt my flower sae early!
Now green's the sod, and cauld's the clay,
   That wraps my Highland Mary!

14. *shaw*, a copse.   4. *drumlie*, miry.

O pale, pale now, those rosy lips,
　　I aft hae kissed sae fondly!
And closed for ay the sparkling glance,
　　That dwalt on me sae kindly!
And mouldering now in silent dust,
　　That heart that lo'ed me dearly!　　　　　30
But still within my bosom's core
　　Shall live my Highland Mary.

1799

Ae Fond Kiss

Ae fond kiss, and then we sever!
Ae fareweel, alas, for ever!
Deep in heart-wrung tears I'll pledge thee,
Warring sighs and groans I'll wage thee.
Who shall say that fortune grieves him
While the star of hope she leaves him?
Me, nae cheerfu' twinkle lights me,
Dark despair around benights me.

I'll ne'er blame my partial fancy,
Naething could resist my Nancy;　　　　　10
But to see her was to love her,
Love but her, and love for ever.
Had we never loved sae kindly,
Had we never loved sae blindly,
Never met—or never parted—
We had ne'er been broken-hearted.

Fare thee weel, thou first and fairest!
Fare thee weel, thou best and dearest!
Thine be ilka joy and treasure,
Peace, enjoyment, love, and pleasure.　　　　20
Ae fond kiss, and then we sever;
Ae fareweel, alas, for ever!
Deep in heart-wrung tears I'll pledge thee,
Warring sighs and groans I'll wage thee.

1792

Sweet Afton

Flow gently, sweet Afton, among thy green braes,
Flow gently, I'll sing thee a song in thy praise;
My Mary's asleep by thy murmuring stream,
Flow gently, sweet Afton, disturb not her dream.

Thou stock-dove whose echo resounds through the glen,
Ye wild whistling blackbirds in yon thorny den,
Thou green-crested lapwing, thy screaming forbear,
I charge you disturb not my slumbering fair.

How lofty, sweet Afton, thy neighboring hills,
Far marked with the courses of clear winding rills;   10
There daily I wander as noon rises high,
My flocks and my Mary's sweet cot in my eye.

How pleasant thy banks and green valleys below,
Where wild in the woodlands the primroses blow;
There oft as mild ev'ning weeps over the lea,
The sweet-scented birk shades my Mary and me.

Thy crystal stream, Afton, how lovely it glides,
And winds by the cot where my Mary resides;
How wanton thy waters her snowy feet lave,
As gathering sweet flow'rets she stems thy clear wave.   20

Flow gently, sweet Afton, among thy green braes,
Flow gently, sweet river, the theme of my lays;
My Mary's asleep by thy murmuring stream,
Flow gently, sweet Afton, disturb not her dream.

1792

Scots Wha Hae

Scots, wha hae wi' Wallace bled,
Scots, wham Bruce has aften led,
Welcome to your gory bed,
    Or to victorie.

Now's the day, and now's the hour;
See the front o' battle lour!
See approach proud Edward's power—
   Chains and slaverie!

Wha will be a traitor knave?
Wha can fill a coward's grave?   10
Wha sae base as be a slave?
   Let him turn and flee!

Wha for Scotland's King and law
Freedom's sword will strongly draw,
Freeman stand, or freeman fa'?
   Let him follow me!

By oppression's woes and pains!
By your sons in servile chains!
We will drain our dearest veins,
   But they shall be free!   20

Lay the proud usurpers low!
Tyrants fall in every foe!
Liberty's in every blow!
   Let us do or die!

1794

My Love Is Like a Red Red Rose

My love is like a red red rose
   That's newly sprung in June:
My love is like the melodie
   That's sweetly play'd in tune.

So fair art thou, my bonnie lass,
   So deep in love am I:
And I will love thee still, my dear,
   Till a' the seas gang dry.

Till a' the seas gang dry, my dear,
   And the rocks melt wi' the sun: 10
And I will love thee still, my dear,
   While the sands o' life shall run.

And fare thee weel, my only love,
    And fare thee weel awhile!
And I will come again, my love,
    Tho' it were ten thousand mile.

1794

O, Wert Thou in the Cauld Blast

O, wert thou in the cauld blast
    On yonder lea, on yonder lea,
My plaidie to the angry airt,
    I'd shelter thee, I'd shelter thee.
Or did misfortune's bitter storms
    Around thee blaw, around thee blaw,
Thy bield should be my bosom,
    To share it a', to share it a'.

Or were I in the wildest waste,
    Sae black and bare, sae black and bare,   10
The desert were a paradise,
    If thou wert there, if thou wert there.
Or were I monarch o' the globe,
    Wi' thee to reign, wi' thee to reign,
The brightest jewel in my crown
    Wad be my queen, wad be my queen.

1800

Mary Morison

O Mary, at thy window be,
    It is the wished, the trysted hour!
Those smiles and glances let me see,
    That make the miser's treasure poor:
How blithely wad I bide the stoure,
    A weary slave frae sun to sun,
Could I the rich reward secure,
    The lovely Mary Morison.

3. *airt*, quarter of the wind.   7. *bield*, shelter.   5. *stoure*, turmoil.

Yestreen, when to the trembling string
   The dance gaed thro' the lighted ha',   10
To thee my fancy took its wing,
   I sat, but neither heard nor saw:
Tho' this was fair, and that was braw,
   And yon the toast of a' the town,
I sighed, and said amang them a',
   "Ye are na Mary Morison."

O Mary, canst thou wreck his peace,
   Wha for thy sake wad gladly die?
Or canst thou break that heart of his,
   Whase only faut is loving thee?   20
If love for love thou wilt na gie,
   At least be pity to me shown!
A thought ungentle canna be
   The thought o' Mary Morison.

1800

Ye Flowery Banks o' Bonnie Doon

Ye flowery banks o' bonnie Doon,
   How can ye blume sae fair?
How can ye chant, ye little birds,
   And I sae fu' o' care?

Thou'll break my heart, thou bonnie bird,
   That sings upon the bough;
Thou minds me o' the happy days,
   When my fause luve was true.

Thou'll break my heart, thou bonnie bird,
   That sings beside thy mate;   10
For sae I sat, and sae I sang,
   And wist na o' my fate.

Aft hae I roved by bonnie Doon,
   To see the woodbine twine,
And ilka bird sang o' its love,
   And sae did I o' mine.

10. *gaed,* went.   20. *Whase,* whose.

Wi' lightsome heart I pu'd a rose
　Frae off its thorny tree:
And my fause luver staw my rose,
　But left the thorn wi' me.　　　　　　20

1808

WILLIAM WORDSWORTH

Lines Written in Early Spring

I heard a thousand blended notes,
While in a grove I sate reclined,
In that sweet mood when pleasant thoughts
Bring sad thoughts to the mind.

To her fair works did Nature link
The human soul that through me ran;
And much it grieved my heart to think
What man has made of man.

Through primrose tufts, in that green bower,
The periwinkle trailed its wreaths;　　　　10
And 'tis my faith that every flower
Enjoys the air it breathes.

The birds around me hopped and played,
Their thoughts I cannot measure—
But the least motion which they made,
It seemed a thrill of pleasure.

The budding twigs spread out their fan,
To catch the breezy air;
And I must think, do all I can,
That there was pleasure there.　　　　　　20

If this belief from heaven be sent,
If such be Nature's holy plan,
Have I not reason to lament
What man has made of man?

1798

A Slumber Did My Spirit Seal

A slumber did my spirit seal;
    I had no human fears:
She seemed a thing that could not feel
    The touch of earthly years.

No motion has she now, no force;
    She neither hears nor sees;
Rolled round in earth's diurnal course,
    With rocks, and stones, and trees.

                                        1800

Three Years She Grew in Sun and Shower

Three years she grew in sun and shower,
Then Nature said, 'A lovelier flower
On earth was never sown;
This Child I to myself will take;
She shall be mine, and I will make
A Lady of my own.

'Myself will to my darling be
Both law and impulse: and with me
The Girl, in rock and plain,
In earth and heaven, in glade and bower,   10
Shall feel an overseeing power
To kindle or restrain.

'She shall be sportive as the fawn
That wild with glee across the lawn
Or up the mountain springs;
And hers shall be the breathing balm,
And hers the silence and the calm
Of mute insensate things.

'The floating clouds their state shall lend
To her; for her the willow bend;   20
Nor shall she fail to see
Even in the motions of the Storm

Grace that shall mould the Maiden's form
By silent sympathy.

'The stars of midnight shall be dear
To her; and she shall lean her ear
In many a secret place
Where rivulets dance their wayward round,
And beauty born of murmuring sound
Shall pass into her face.   30

'And vital feelings of delight
Shall rear her form to stately height,
Her virgin bosom swell;
Such thoughts to Lucy I will give
While she and I together live
Here in this happy dell.'

Thus Nature spake—The work was done—
How soon my Lucy's race was run!
She died, and left to me
This heath, this calm, and quiet scene;   40
The memory of what has been,
And never more will be.

1800

She Dwelt among the Untrodden Ways

She dwelt among the untrodden ways
   Beside the springs of Dove,
A Maid whom there were none to praise
   And very few to love:

A violet by a mossy stone
   Half hidden from the eye!
—Fair as a star, when only one
   Is shining in the sky.

She lived unknown, and few could know
   When Lucy ceased to be;   10
But she is in her grave, and, oh,
   The difference to me!

1800

The Solitary Reaper

Behold her, single in the field,
Yon solitary Highland Lass!
Reaping and singing by herself;
Stop here, or gently pass!
Alone she cuts and binds the grain,
And sings a melancholy strain;
O listen! for the Vale profound
Is overflowing with the sound.

No Nightingale did ever chaunt
More welcome notes to weary bands   10
Of travelers in some shady haunt,
Among Arabian sands:
A voice so thrilling ne'er was heard
In spring-time from the Cuckoo-bird,
Breaking the silence of the seas
Among the farthest Hebrides.

Will no one tell me what she sings?—
Perhaps the plaintive numbers flow
For old, unhappy, far-off things,
And battles long ago: 20
Or is it some more humble lay,
Familiar matter of to-day?
Some natural sorrow, loss, or pain,
That has been, and may be again?

Whate'er the theme, the Maiden sang
As if her song could have no ending;
I saw her singing at her work,
And o'er the sickle bending;—
I listened, motionless and still;
And, as I mounted up the hill   30
The music in my heart I bore,
Long after it was heard no more.

1807

I Wandered Lonely as a Cloud

I wandered lonely as a cloud
That floats on high o'er vales and hills,
When all at once I saw a crowd,
A host, of golden daffodils;
Beside the lake, beneath the trees,
Fluttering and dancing in the breeze.

Continuous as the stars that shine
And twinkle on the milky way,
They stretched in never-ending line
Along the margin of a bay: 10
Ten thousand saw I at a glance,
Tossing their heads in sprightly dance.

The waves beside them danced; but they
Out-did the sparkling waves in glee:
A poet could not but be gay,
In such a jocund company:
I gazed—and gazed—but little thought
What wealth the show to me had brought:

For oft, when on my couch I lie
In vacant or in pensive mood,   20
They flash upon that inward eye
Which is the bliss of solitude;
And then my heart with pleasure fills,
And dances with the daffodils.
                                    1807

Ode

INTIMATIONS OF IMMORTALITY FROM RECOLLECTIONS
OF EARLY CHILDHOOD

The Child is father of the Man;
And I could wish my days to be
Bound each to each by natural piety.

I

There was a time when meadow, grove, and stream,
The earth, and every common sight,
    To me did seem
    Appareled in celestial light,
The glory and the freshness of a dream.
It is not now as it hath been of yore;—
    Turn wheresoe'er I may,
        By night or day,
The things which I have seen I now can see no more.

II

    The Rainbow comes and goes,   10
    And lovely is the Rose,
    The Moon doth with delight
Look round her when the heavens are bare,
    Waters on a starry night
    Are beautiful and fair;
    The sunshine is a glorious birth;
    But yet I know, where'er I go,
That there hath passed away a glory from the earth.

III

Now, while the birds thus sing a joyous song,
    And while the young lambs bound   20
        As to' the tabor's sound,
To me alone there came a thought of grief:
A timely utterance gave that thought relief,
    And I again am strong:
The cataracts blow their trumpets from the steep;
Nor more shall grief of mine the season wrong;
I hear the Echoes through the mountains throng,
The Winds come to me from the fields of sleep,
    And all the earth is gay;
        Land and sea   30
    Give themselves up to jollity,
        And with the heart of May

Doth every Beast keep holiday;—
Thou Child of Joy,
Shout round me, let me hear thy shouts, thou happy
Shepherd-boy!

IV

Ye blessèd Creatures, I have heard the call
Ye to each other make; I see
The heavens laugh with you in your jubilee;
My heart is at your festival,
My head hath its coronal,   40
The fullness of your bliss, I feel—I feel it all.
Oh evil day! if I were sullen
While Earth herself is adorning,
This sweet May-morning,
And the Children are culling
On every side,
In a thousand valleys far and wide,
Fresh flowers; while the sun shines warm,
And the Babe leaps up on his Mother's arm:—
I hear, I hear, with joy I hear!   50
—But there's a Tree, of many, one,
A single Field which I have looked upon,
Both of them speak of something that is gone:
The Pansy at my feet
Doth the same tale repeat:
Whither is fled the visionary gleam?
Where is it now, the glory and the dream?

V

Our birth is but a sleep and a forgetting:
The Soul that rises with us, our life's Star,
Hath had elsewhere its setting,   60
And cometh from afar:
Not in entire forgetfulness,
And not in utter nakedness,
But trailing clouds of glory do we come
From God, who is our home:
Heaven lies about us in our infancy!

Shades of the prison-house begin to close
  Upon the growing Boy,
But He beholds the light, and whence it flows,
  He sees it in his joy;   70
The Youth, who daily farther from the east
  Must travel, still is Nature's Priest,
  And by the vision splendid
  Is on his way attended;
At length the Man perceives it die away,
And fade into the light of common day.

VI

Earth fills her lap with pleasures of her own;
Yearnings she hath in her own natural kind,
And, even with something of a Mother's mind,
  And no unworthy aim,   80
  The homely Nurse doth all she can
To make her Foster-child, her Inmate man,
  Forget the glories he hath known,
And that imperial palace whence he came.

VII

Behold the Child among his new-born blisses,
A six years' Darling of a pigmy size!
See, where 'mid work of his own hand he lies,
Fretted by sallies of his mother's kisses,
With light upon him from his father's eyes!
See, at his feet, some little plan or chart,   90
Some fragment from his dream of human life,
Shaped by himself with newly-learnéd art;
  A wedding or a festival,
  A mourning or a funeral;
    And this hath now his heart,
  And unto this he frames his song:
    Then will he fit his tongue
To dialogues of business, love, or strife;
  But it will not be long
  Ere this be thrown aside,   100
  And with new joy and pride

The little Actor cons another part;
Filling from time to time his "humorous stage"
With all the Persons, down to palsied Age,
That Life brings with her in her equipage;
   As if his whole vocation
   Were endless imitation.

VIII

Thou, whose exterior semblance doth belie
   Thy Soul's immensity;
Thou best Philosopher, who yet dost keep   110
Thy heritage, thou Eye among the blind,
That, deaf and silent, read'st the eternal deep,
Haunted for ever by the eternal mind,—
   Mighty Prophet! Seer bless'd!
   On whom those truths do rest,
Which we are toiling all our lives to find,
In darkness lost, the darkness of the grave;
Thou, over whom thy Immortality
Broods like the Day, a Master o'er a Slave,
A Presence which is not to be put by;   120
Thou little Child, yet glorious in the might
Of heaven-born freedom on thy being's height,
Why with such earnest pains dost thou provoke
The years to bring the inevitable yoke,
Thus blindly with thy blessedness at strife?
Full soon thy Soul shall have her earthly freight,
And custom lie upon thee with a weight,
Heavy as frost, and deep almost as life!

IX

   O joy! that in our embers
   Is something that doth live,   130
   That nature yet remembers
   What was so fugitive!
The thought of our past years in me doth breed
Perpetual benediction: not indeed
For that which is most worthy to be bless'd—
Delight and liberty, the simple creed

Of Childhood, whether busy or at rest,
With new-fledged hope still fluttering in his breast:—
    Not for these I raise
    The song of thanks and praise; 140
  But for those obstinate questionings
  Of sense and outward things,
  Fallings from us, vanishings;
  Blank misgivings of a Creature
Moving about in worlds not realized,
High instincts before which our mortal Nature
Did tremble like a guilty Thing surprised:
    But for those first affections,
    Those shadowy recollections,
  Which, be they what they may, 150
Are yet the fountain light of all our day,
Are yet a master light of all our seeing;
  Uphold us, cherish, and have power to make
Our noisy years seem moments in the being
Of the eternal Silence: truths that wake,
    To perish never;
Which neither listlessness, nor mad endeavor,
    Nor Man nor Boy,
Nor all that is at enmity with joy,
Can utterly abolish or destroy! 160
    Hence in a season of calm weather
    Though inland far we be,
Our Souls have sight of that immortal sea
    Which brought us hither,
    Can in a moment travel thither,
And see the Children sport upon the shore,
And hear the mighty waters rolling evermore.

          X

Then sing, ye Birds, sing, sing a joyous song!
  And let the young Lambs bound
  As to the tabor's sound! 170
We in thought will join your throng,
  Ye that pipe and ye that play,
  Ye that through your hearts to-day

Feel the gladness of the May!
What though the radiance which was once so bright
Be now for ever taken from my sight,
　　Though nothing can bring back the hour
　　Of splendor in the grass, of glory in the flower;
　　We will grieve not, rather find
　　Strength in what remains behind;　　　　　　180
　　In the primal sympathy
　　　　Which having been must ever be;
　　In the soothing thoughts that spring
　　Out of human suffering;
　　In the faith that looks through death,
In years that bring philosophic mind.

XI

And O, ye Fountains, Meadows, Hills, and Groves,
Forebode not any severing of our loves!
Yet in my heart of hearts I feel your might;
I only have relinquished one delight　　　　　　190
To live beneath your more habitual sway.
I love the Brooks which down their channels fret,
Even more than when I tripped lightly as they;
The innocent brightness of a new-born Day
　　　　Is lovely yet;
The Clouds that gather round the setting sun
Do take a sober coloring from an eye
That hath kept watch o'er man's mortality;
Another race hath been, and other palms are won.
Thanks to the human heart by which we live,　　200
Thanks to its tenderness, its joys, and fears,
To me the meanest flower that blows can give
Thoughts that do often lie too deep for tears.

1807

Composed upon Westminster Bridge

Earth has not anything to show more fair:
Dull would he be of soul who could pass by
A sight so touching in its majesty:

This City now doth like a garment wear
The beauty of the morning; silent, bare,
Ships, towers, domes, theaters, and temples lie
Open unto the fields, and to the sky;
All bright and glittering in the smokeless air.
Never did sun more beautifully steep
In his first splendor valley, rock, or hill;   10
Ne'er saw I, never felt, a calm so deep!
The river glideth at his own sweet will:
Dear God! the very houses seem asleep;
And all that mighty heart is lying still!

1807

London, 1802

Milton! thou shouldst be living at this hour:
England hath need of thee: she is a fen
Of stagnant waters: altar, sword, and pen,
Fireside, the heroic wealth of hall and bower,
Have forfeited their ancient English dower
Of inward happiness. We are selfish men:
Oh! raise us up, return to us again;
And give us manners, virtue, freedom, power.
Thy soul was like a Star, and dwelt apart:
Thou hadst a voice whose sound was like the sea,   10
Pure as the naked heavens, majestic, free;
So didst thou travel on life's common way
In cheerful godliness; and yet thy heart
The lowliest duties on herself did lay.

1807

My Heart Leaps Up When I Behold

My heart leaps up when I behold
    A rainbow in the sky:
So was it when my life began;
So is it now I am a man:

So be it when I shall grow old,
    Or let me die!
The Child is father of the Man;
And I could wish my days to be
Bound each to each by natural piety.

1807

SAMUEL TAYLOR COLERIDGE

Frost at Midnight

The Frost performs its secret ministry,
Unhelped by any wind. The owlet's cry
Came loud—and hark, again! loud as before.
The inmates of my cottage, all at rest,
Have left me to that solitude, which suits
Abstruser musings: save that at my side
My cradled infant slumbers peacefully.
'Tis calm indeed! so calm, that it disturbs
And vexes meditation with its strange
And extreme silentness. Sea, hill, and wood,   10
This populous village! Sea, and hill, and wood,
With all the numberless goings-on of life,
Inaudible as dreams! the thin blue flame
Lies on my low-burnt fire, and quivers not;
Only that film, which fluttered on the grate,
Still flutters there, the sole unquiet thing.
Methinks, its motion in this hush of nature
Gives it dim sympathies with me who live,
Making it a companionable form,
Whose puny flaps and freaks the idling Spirit   20
By its own moods interprets, every where
Echo or mirror seeking of itself,
And makes a toy of Thought.

                              But O! how oft,
How oft, at school, with most believing mind,
Presageful, have I gazed upon the bars,
To watch that fluttering *stranger!* and as oft

With unclosed lids, already had I dreamt
Of my sweet birth-place, and the old church-tower,
Whose bells, the poor man's only music, rang
From morn to evening, all the hot Fairday,   30
So sweetly, that they stirred and haunted me
With a wild pleasure, falling on mine ear
Most like articulate sounds of things to come!
So gazed I, till the soothing things, I dreamt,
Lulled me to sleep, and sleep prolonged my dreams!
And so I brooded all the following morn,
Awed by the stern preceptor's face, mine eye
Fixed with mock study on my swimming book:
Save if the door half opened, and I snatched
A hasty glance, and still my heart leaped up,   40
For still I hoped to see the *stranger's* face,
Townsman, or aunt, or sister more beloved,
My play-mate when we both were clothed alike!

    Dear Babe, that sleepest cradled by my side,
Whose gentle breathings, heard in this deep calm,
Fill up the intersperséd vacancies
And momentary pauses of the thought!
My babe so beautiful! it thrills my heart
With tender gladness, thus to look at thee,
And think that thou shalt learn far other lore,   50
And in far other scenes! For I was reared
In the great city, pent 'mid cloisters dim,
And saw nought lovely but the sky and stars.
But *thou*, my babe! shalt wander like a breeze
By lakes and sandy shores, beneath the crags
Of ancient mountain, and beneath the clouds,
Which image in their bulk both lakes and shores
And mountain crags: so shalt thou see and hear
The lovely shapes and sounds intelligible
Of that eternal language, which thy God   60
Utters, who from eternity doth teach
Himself in all, and all things in himself.
Great universal Teacher! he shall mould
Thy spirit, and by giving make it ask.

Therefore all seasons shall be sweet to thee,
Whether the summer clothe the general earth
With greenness, or the redbreast sit and sing
Betwixt the tufts of snow on the bare branch
Of mossy apple-tree, while the nigh thatch
Smokes in the sun-thaw; whether the eavedrops fall
Heard only in the trances of the blast,   71
Or if the secret ministry of frost
Shall hang them up in silent icicles,
Quietly shining to the quiet Moon.

1798

Kubla Khan

In Xanadu did Kubla Khan
  A stately pleasure-dome decree:
Where Alph, the sacred river, ran
Through caverns measureless to man
  Down to a sunless sea.
So twice five miles of fertile ground
With walls and towers were girdled round:
And here were gardens bright with sinuous rills
Where blossomed many an incense-bearing tree,
And here were forests ancient as the hills,   10
Enfolding sunny spots of greenery.

But oh! that deep romantic chasm which slanted
Down the green hill athwart a cedarn cover!
A savage place! as holy and enchanted
As e'er beneath a waning moon was haunted
By woman wailing for her demon-lover!
And from this chasm, with ceaseless turmoil seething,
As if this earth in fast thick pants were breathing,
A mighty fountain momently was forced,
Amid whose swift half-intermitted burst   20
Huge fragments vaulted like rebounding hail,
Or chaffy grain beneath the thresher's flail:
And 'mid these dancing rocks at once and ever
It flung up momently the sacred river.

Five miles meandering with a mazy motion
Through wood and dale the sacred river ran,
Then reached the caverns measureless to man,
And sank in tumult to a lifeless ocean:
And 'mid this tumult Kubla heard from far
Ancestral voices prophesying war!   30

  The shadow of the dome of pleasure
  Floated midway on the waves;
  Where was heard the mingled measure
  From the fountain and the caves.
It was a miracle of rare device,
A sunny pleasure-dome with caves of ice!

  A damsel with a dulcimer
  In a vision once I saw:
  It was an Abyssinian maid,
  And on her dulcimer she played,   40
  Singing on Mount Abora.
  Could I revive within me
  Her symphony and song,
  To such a deep delight 'twould win me,
That with music loud and long,
I would build that dome in air,
That sunny dome! those caves of ice!
And all who heard should see them there,
And all should cry, Beware! Beware!
His flashing eyes, his floating hair!   50
Weave a circle round him thrice,
And close your eyes with holy dread,
For he on honey-dew hath fed,
And drunk the milk of Paradise.
                              1816

SIR WALTER SCOTT

Hunting Song

Waken, lords and ladies gay,
On the mountain dawns the day,
All the jolly chase is here,
With hawk, and horse, and hunting-spear!
Hounds are in their couples yelling,
Hawks are whistling, horns are knelling;
Merrily, merrily, mingle they,
"Waken, lords and ladies gay."

Waken, lords and ladies gay,
The mist has left the mountain gray,   10
Springlets in the dawn are steaming,
Diamonds on the brake are gleaming:
And foresters have busy been,
To track the buck in thicket green;
Now we come to chant our lay,
"Waken, lords and ladies gay."

Waken, lords and ladies gay,
To the greenwood haste away;
We can show you where he lies,
Fleet of foot, and tall of size;   20
We can show the marks he made,
When 'gainst the oak his antlers frayed;
You shall see him brought to bay;
"Waken, lords and ladies gay."

Louder, louder chant the lay,
Waken, lords and ladies gay!
Tell them youth, and mirth, and glee,
Run a course as well as we;
Time, stern huntsman! who can balk,
Stanch as hound, and fleet as hawk: 30
Think of this, and rise with day,
Gentle lords and ladies gay.

1808

Proud Maisie

Proud Maisie is in the wood,
    Walking so early;
Sweet Robin sits on the bush,
    Singing so rarely.

'Tell me, thou bonny bird,
    When shall I marry me?'
'When six braw gentlemen
    Kirkward shall carry ye.'

'Who makes the bridal bed,
    Birdie, say truly?'   10
'The grey-headed sexton
    That delves the grave duly.

'The glow-worm o'er grave and stone
    Shall light thee steady.
The owl from the steeple sing,
    Welcome, proud lady.'
                    The Heart of Midlothian, 1818

WALTER SAVAGE LANDOR

Rose Aylmer

Ah, what avails the sceptred race,
    Ah, what the form divine!
What every virtue, every grace!
    Rose Aylmer, all were thine.
Rose Aylmer, whom these wakeful eyes
    May weep, but never see,
A night of memories and of sighs
    I consecrate to thee.
                    1806

Past Ruin'd Ilion Helen Lives

Past ruin'd Ilion Helen lives,
   Alcestis rises from the shades;
Verse calls them forth; 'tis verse that gives
   Immortal youth to mortal maids.

Soon shall Oblivion's deepening veil
   Hide all the peopled hills you see,
The gay, the proud, while lovers hail
   These many summers you and me.

The tear for fading beauty check,
   For passing glory cease to sigh;
One form shall rise above the wreck,
   One name, Ianthe, shall not die.

1831

Ianthe

From you, Ianthe, little troubles pass
   Like little ripples down a sunny river;
Your pleasures spring like daisies in the grass,
   Cut down, and up again as blithe as ever.

1846

On His Seventy-Fifth Birthday

I strove with none; for none was worth my strife,
   Nature I loved, and next to Nature, Art;
I warmed both hands before the fire of life,
   It sinks, and I am ready to depart.

1853

LEIGH HUNT

Jenny Kissed Me

Jenny kissed me when we met,
   Jumping from the chair she sat in;
Time, you thief, who love to get
   Sweets into your list, put that in;

Say I'm weary, say I'm sad,
   Say that health and wealth have missed me,
Say I'm growing old, but add,
   Jenny kissed me.

1838

GEORGE GORDON, LORD BYRON

She Walks in Beauty

I

She walks in beauty, like the night
   Of cloudless climes and starry skies;
And all that's best of dark and bright
   Meet in her aspect and her eyes:
Thus mellowed to that tender light
   Which heaven to gaudy day denies.

II

One shade the more, one ray the less,
   Had half impaired the nameless grace
Which waves in every raven tress,
   Or softly lightens o'er her face;   10
Where thoughts serenely sweet express
   How pure, how dear their dwelling-place.

III

And on that cheek, and o'er that brow,
   So soft, so calm, yet eloquent,
The smiles that win, the tints that glow,
   But tell of days in goodness spent,
A mind at peace with all below,
   A heart whose love is innocent!

1815

When We Two Parted

When we two parted
   In silence and tears,
Half broken-hearted
   To sever for years,

Pale grew thy cheek and cold,
Colder thy kiss;
Truly that hour foretold
Sorrow to this.

The dew of the morning
Sunk chill on my brow—   10
It felt like the warning
Of what I feel now.
Thy vows are all broken,
And light is thy fame:
I hear thy name spoken,
And share in its shame.

They name thee before me,
A knell to mine ear;
A shudder comes o'er me—
Why wert thou so dear?   20
They know not I knew thee,
Who knew thee too well:—
Long, long shall I rue thee,
Too deeply to tell.

In secret we met—
In silence I grieve,
That thy heart could forget,
Thy spirit deceive.
If I should meet thee
After long years,   30
How should I greet thee?—
With silence and tears.

                              1816

Stanzas for Music

There be none of Beauty's daughters
With a magic like thee;
And like music on the waters
Is thy sweet voice to me:
When, as if its sound were causing

The charmed ocean's pausing,
The waves lie still and gleaming,
And the lull'd winds seem dreaming:

And the midnight moon is weaving
    Her bright chain o'er the deep;   10
Whose breast is gently heaving,
    As an infant's asleep:
So the spirit bows before thee,
To listen and adore thee;
With a full but soft emotion,
Like the swell of Summer's ocean.

                                        1816

So We'll Go No More A-Roving

So we'll go no more a-roving
    So late into the night,
Though the heart be still as loving,
    And the moon be still as bright.

For the sword outwears its sheath,
    And the soul wears out the breast,
And the heart must pause to breathe,
    And Love itself have rest.

Though the night was made for loving,
    And the day returns too soon,   10
Yet we'll go no more a-roving
    By the light of the moon.

                                        1830

PERCY BYSSHE SHELLEY

Love's Philosophy

I

The fountains mingle with the river
    And the rivers with the Ocean,
The winds of Heaven mix for ever
    With a sweet emotion;

Nothing in the world is single;
    All things by a law divine
In one spirit meet and mingle.
    Why not I with thine?—

II

See the mountains kiss high Heaven
    And the waves clasp one another;
No sister-flower would be forgiven
    If it disdained its brother,
And the sunlight clasps the earth
    And the moonbeams kiss the sea:
What is all this sweet work worth
    If thou kiss not me?

1819

Ode to the West Wind

I

O Wild West Wind, thou breath of Autumn's being,
Thou, from whose unseen presence the leaves dead
Are driven, like ghosts from an enchanter fleeing,

Yellow, and black, and pale, and hectic red,
Pestilence-stricken multitudes: O thou,
Who chariotest to their dark wintry bed

The wingéd seeds, where they lie cold and low,
Each like a corpse within its grave, until
Thine azure sister of the Spring shall blow

Her clarion o'er the dreaming earth, and fill
(Driving sweet buds like flocks to feed in air)
With living hues and odors plain and hill:

Wild Spirit, which are moving everywhere;
Destroyer and preserver; hear, oh, hear!

II

Thou on whose stream, 'mid the steep sky's commotion,
Loose clouds like earth's decaying leaves are shed,
Shook from the tangled boughs of Heaven and Ocean,

Angels of rain and lightning: there are spread
On the blue surface of thine aëry surge,
Like the bright hair uplifted from the head   20

Of some fierce Mænad, even from the dim verge
Of the horizon to the zenith's height,
The locks of the approaching storm. Thou dirge

Of the dying year, to which this closing night
Will be the dome of a vast sepulcher,
Vaulted with all thy congregated might

Of vapors, from whose solid atmosphere
Black rain, and fire, and hail will burst: oh, hear!

III

Thou who didst waken from his summer dreams
The blue Mediterranean, where he lay,   30
Lulled by the coil of his crystálline streams,

Beside a pumice isle in Baiæ's bay,
And saw in sleep old palaces and towers
Quivering within the wave's intenser day,

All overgrown with azure moss and flowers
So sweet, the sense faints picturing them! Thou
For whose path the Atlantic's level powers

Cleave themselves into chasms, while far below
The sea-blooms and the oozy woods which wear
The sapless foliage of the ocean, know   40

Thy voice, and suddenly grow gray with fear,
And tremble and despoil themselves: oh, hear!

IV

If I were a dead leaf thou mightest bear;
If I were a swift cloud to fly with thee;
A wave to pant beneath thy power, and share

The impulse of thy strength, only less free
Than thou, O uncontrollable! If even
I were as in my boyhood, and could be

The comrade of thy wanderings over Heaven,
As then, when to outstrip thy skyey speed   50
Scarce seemed a vision; I would ne'er have striven

As thus with thee in prayer in my sore need.
Oh, lift me as a wave, a leaf, a cloud!
I fall upon the thorns of life! I bleed!

A heavy weight of hours has chained and bowed
One too like thee: tameless, and swift, and proud.

V

Make me thy lyre, even as the forest is:
What if my leaves are falling like its own!
The tumult of thy mighty harmonies

Will take from both a deep, autumnal tone,   60
Sweet though in sadness. Be thou, Spirit fierce,
My spirit! Be thou me, impetuous one!

Drive my dead thoughts over the universe
Like withered leaves to quicken a new birth!
And, by the incantation of this verse,

Scatter, as from an unextinguished hearth
Ashes and sparks, my words among mankind!
Be through my lips to unawakened earth

The trumpet of a prophecy! O, Wind,
If Winter comes, can Spring be far behind?   70

1820

The Cloud

I bring fresh showers for the thirsting flowers,
    From the seas and the streams;
I bear light shade for the leaves when laid
    In their noonday dreams.
From my wings are shaken the dews that waken
    The sweet buds every one,
When rocked to rest on their mother's breast,
    As she dances about the sun.
I wield the flail of the lashing hail,
    And whiten the green plains under,   10
And then again I dissolve it in rain,
    And laugh as I pass in thunder.

I sift the snow on the mountains below,
    And their great pines groan aghast;
And all the night 'tis my pillow white,
    While I sleep in the arms of the blast.
Sublime on the towers of my skyey bowers,
    Lightning my pilot sits;
In a cavern under is fettered the thunder,
    It struggles and howls at fits;   20
Over earth and ocean, with gentle motion,
    This pilot is guiding me,
Lured by the love of the genii that move
    In the depths of the purple sea;
Over the rills, and the crags, and the hills,
    Over the lakes and the plains,
Wherever he dream, under mountain or stream,
    The Spirit he loves remains;
And I all the while bask in Heaven's blue smile,
    Whilst he is dissolving in rains.   30

The sanguine Sunrise, with his meteor eyes,
    And his burning plumes outspread,
Leaps on the back of my sailing rack,
    When the morning star shines dead;
As on the jag of a mountain crag,
    Which an earthquake rocks and swings,

An eagle alit one moment may sit
  In the light of its golden wings.
And when Sunset may breathe, from the lit sea beneath,
  Its ardors of rest and of love,   40
And the crimson pall of eve may fall
  From the depth of Heaven above,
With wings folded I rest, on mine aëry nest,
  As still as a brooding dove.

That orbéd maiden with white fire laden,
  Whom mortals call the Moon,
Glides glimmering o'er my fleece-like floor,
  By the midnight breezes strewn;
And wherever the beat of her unseen feet,
  Which only the angels hear,   50
May have broken the woof of my tent's thin roof,
  The stars peep behind her and peer;
And I laugh to see them whirl and flee,
  Like a swarm of golden bees,
When I widen the rent in my wind-built tent,
  Till the calm rivers, lakes, and seas,
Like strips of the sky fallen through me on high,
  Are each paved with the moon and these.

I bind the Sun's throne with a burning zone,
  And the Moon's with a girdle of pearl;   60
The volcanoes are dim, and the stars reel and swim,
  When the whirlwinds my banner unfurl.
From cape to cape, with a bridge-like shape,
  Over a torrent sea,
Sunbeam-proof, I hang like a roof,—
  The mountains its columns be.
The triumphal arch through which I march
  With hurricane, fire, and snow,
When the Powers of the air are chained to my chair,
  Is the million-colored bow;   70
The sphere-fire above its soft colors wove,
  While the moist Earth was laughing below.

I am the daughter of Earth and Water,
    And the nursling of the Sky;
I pass through the pores of the ocean and shores;
    I change, but I cannot die.
For after the rain when with never a stain
    The pavilion of Heaven is bare,
And the winds and sunbeams with their convex gleams
    Build up the blue dome of air,   80
I silently laugh at my own cenotaph,
    And out of the caverns of rain,
Like a child from the womb, like a ghost from the tomb,
    I arise and unbuild it again.

                1820

To a Skylark

    Hail to thee, blithe spirit!
      Bird thou never wert,
    That from heaven, or near it,
      Pourest thy full heart
In profuse strains of unpremeditated art.

    Higher still and higher
      From the earth thou springest
    Like a cloud of fire;
      The blue deep thou wingest,
And singing still dost soar, and soaring ever singest.   10

    In the golden lightning
      Of the sunken sun,
    O'er which clouds are bright'ning,
      Thou dost float and run;
Like an unbodied joy whose race is just begun.

    The pale purple even
      Melts around thy flight;
    Like a star of heaven
      In the broad day-light
Thou art unseen, but yet I hear thy shrill delight,   20

Keen as are the arrows
Of that silver sphere,
Whose intense lamp narrows
In the white dawn clear,
Until we hardly see, we feel that it is there.

All the earth and air
With thy voice is loud,
As, when night is bare,
From one lonely cloud
The moon rains out her beams, and heaven is overflowed.

What thou art we know not;   31
What is most like thee?
From rainbow clouds there flow not
Drops so bright to see
As from thy presence showers a rain of melody.

Like a poet hidden
In the light of thought,
Singing hymns unbidden,
Till the world is wrought
To sympathy with hopes and fears it heeded not: 40

Like a high-born maiden
In a palace tower,
Soothing her love-laden
Soul in secret hour
With music sweet as love, which overflows her bower:

Like a glow-worm golden
In a dell of dew,
Scattering unbeholden
Its aërial hue
Among the flowers and grass which screen it from the
    view: 50

Like a rose embowered
In its own green leaves,
By warm winds deflowered,

Till the scent it gives
Makes faint with too much sweet these heavy-wingèd
thieves.

Sound of vernal showers
On the twinkling grass,
Rain-awakened flowers,
All that ever was
Joyous, and clear, and fresh, thy music doth surpass.   60

Teach us, sprite or bird,
What sweet thoughts are thine;
I have never heard
Praise of love or wine
That panted forth a flood of rapture so divine:

Chorus Hymenaeal,
Or triumphal chant,
Matched with thine would be all
But an empty vaunt,
A thing wherein we feel there is some hidden want.   70

What objects are the fountains
Of thy happy strain?
What fields, or waves, or mountains?
What shapes of sky or plain?
What love of thine own kind? what ignorance of pain?

With thy clear keen joyance
Languor cannot be:
Shadow of annoyance
Never came near thee:
Thou lovest, but ne'er knew love's sad satiety.   80

Waking or asleep,
Thou of death must deem
Things more true and deep
Than we mortals dream,
Or how could thy notes flow in such a crystal stream?

We look before and after,
And pine for what is not:

Our sincerest laughter
With some pain is fraught;
Our sweetest songs are those that tell of saddest thought.

Yet if we could scorn   91
    Hate, and pride, and fear;
If we were things born
    Not to shed a tear,
I know not how thy joy we ever should come near.

Better than all measures
    Of delightful sound,
Better than all treasures
    That in books are found,
Thy skill to poet were, thou scorner of the ground!   100

Teach me half the gladness
    That thy brain must know,
Such harmonious madness
    From my lips would flow,
The world should listen then, as I am listening now.

                                             1820

The Indian Serenade

I arise from dreams of Thee
    In the first sweet sleep of night,
When the winds are breathing low
    And the stars are shining bright:
I arise from dreams of thee,
    And a spirit in my feet
Hath led me—who knows how?
    To thy chamber-window, Sweet!

The wandering airs, they faint
    On the dark, the silent stream—   10
The champak odors fail
    Like sweet thoughts in a dream;
The nightingale's complaint,
    It dies upon her heart,

As I must die on thine,
    O beloved as thou art!

Oh, lift me from the grass!
    I die, I faint, I fail!
Let thy love in kisses rain
    On my lips and eyelids pale.   20
My cheek is cold and white, alas!
    My heart beats loud and fast;
Oh! press it close to thine again,
    Where it will break at last.

1822

Lines: 'When the Lamp Is Shattered'

I

When the lamp is shattered
The light in the dust lies dead—
    When the cloud is scattered
The rainbow's glory is shed.
    When the lute is broken,
Sweet tones are remembered not;
    When the lips have spoken,
Loved accents are soon forgot.

II

As music and splendour
Survive not the lamp and the lute,
    The heart's echoes render   10
No song when the spirit is mute:—
    No song but sad dirges,
Like the wind through a ruined cell,
    Or the mournful surges
That ring the dead seaman's knell.

III

When hearts have once mingled
Love first leaves the well-built nest;
    The weak one is singled

To endure what it once possessed.   20
O Love! who bewailest
The frailty of all things here,
Why choose you the frailest
For your cradle, your home, and your bier?

IV

Its passions will rock thee
As the storms rock the ravens on high;
Bright reason will mock thee,
Like the sun from a wintry sky.
From thy nest every rafter
Will rot, and thine eagle home   30
Leave thee naked to laughter,
When leaves fall and cold winds come.

1824

Music, When Soft Voices Die

Music, when soft voices die,
Vibrates in the memory—
Odors, when sweet violets sicken,
Live within the sense they quicken.
Rose-leaves, when the rose is dead,
Are heaped for the beloved's bed;
And so thy thoughts, when thou art gone,
Love itself shall slumber on.

1824

One Word Is Too Often Profaned

I

One word is too often profaned
For me to profane it,
One feeling too falsely disdained
For thee to disdain it;
One hope is too like despair
For prudence to smother,

And pity from thee more dear
Than that from another.

II

I can give not what men call love,
    But wilt thou accept not   10
The worship the heart lifts above
    And the Heavens reject not,—
The desire of the moth for the star,
    Of the night for the morrow,
The devotion to something afar
    From the sphere of our sorrow?

1824

To Night

Swiftly walk o'er the western wave,
        Spirit of Night!
Out of the misty eastern cave,
Where all the long and lone daylight
Thou wovest dreams of joy and fear,
Which make thee terrible and dear,—
        Swift be thy flight!

Wrap thy form in a mantle gray,
        Star in-wrought!
Blind with thine hair the eyes of Day: 10
Kiss her until she be wearied out;
Then wander o'er city, and sea, and land,
Touching all with thine opiate wand—
        Come, long sought!

When I arose and saw the dawn,
        I sighed for thee;
When light rode high, and the dew was gone,
And noon lay heavy on flower and tree,
And the weary Day turned to his rest,
Lingering like an unloved guest,   20
        I sighed for thee.

Thy brother Death came, and cried,
       Wouldst thou me?
Thy sweet child Sleep, the filmy-eyed,
Murmured like a noon-tide bee,
Shall I nestle near thy side?
Wouldst thou me?—And I replied,
       No, not thee!

Death will come when thou art dead,
       Soon, too soon—   30
Sleep will come when thou art fled;
Of neither would I ask the boon
I ask of thee, belovèd Night—
Swift be thine approaching flight,
       Come soon, soon!

1824

JOHN KEATS

On First Looking into Chapman's Homer

Much have I traveled in the realms of gold,
  And many goodly states and kingdoms seen;
  Round many western islands have I been
Which bards in fealty to Apollo hold.
Oft of one wide expanse had I been told,
  That deep-browed Homer ruled as his demesne:
  Yet did I never breathe its pure serene
Till I heard Chapman speak out loud and bold:
Then felt I like some watcher of the skies
  When a new planet swims into his ken;   10
Or like stout Cortez when with eagle eyes
  He stared at the Pacific—and all his men
Looked at each other with a wild surmise—
  Silent, upon a peak in Darien.

1817

To One Who Has Been Long in City Pent

To one who has been long in city pent,
  'Tis very sweet to look into the fair
  And open face of heaven,—to breathe a prayer
Full in the smile of the blue firmament.
Who is more happy, when, with heart's content,
  Fatigued he sinks into some pleasant lair
  Of wavy grass, and reads a debonair
And gentle tale of love and languishment?
Returning home at evening, with an ear
  Catching the notes of Philomel,—an eye   10
Watching the sailing cloudlet's bright career,
  He mourns that day so soon has glided by:
E'en like the passage of an angel's tear
  That falls through the clear ether silently.

1817

Induction to Endymion

A thing of beauty is a joy for ever:
Its loveliness increases; it will never
Pass into nothingness; but still will keep
A bower quiet for us, and a sleep
Full of sweet dreams, and health, and quiet breathing.
Therefore, on every morrow, are we wreathing
A flowery band to bind us to the earth,
Spite of despondence, of the inhuman dearth
Of noble natures, of the gloomy days,
Of all the unhealthy and o'er-darkened ways   10
Made for our searching: yes, in spite of all,
Some shape of beauty moves away the pall
From our dark spirits. Such the sun, the moon,
Trees old and young, sprouting a shady boon
For simple sheep: and such are daffodils
With the green world they live in; and clear rills
That for themselves a cooling covert make
'Gainst the hot season; the mid-forest brake,
Rich with a sprinkling of fair musk-rose blooms:

And such too is the grandeur of the dooms 20
We have imagined for the mighty dead;
All lovely tales that we have heard or read:
An endless fountain of immortal drink,
Pouring unto us from the heaven's brink.
　Nor do we merely feel these essences
For one short hour; no, even as the trees
That whisper round a temple become soon
Dear as the temple's self, so does the moon,
The passion poesy, glories infinite,
Haunt us till they become a cheering light 30
Unto our souls, and bound to us so fast,
That, whether there be shine, or gloom o'ercast,
They always must be with us, or we die.
　Therefore, 'tis with full happiness that I
Will trace the story of Endymion.
The very music of the name has gone
Into my being, and each pleasant scene
Is growing fresh before me as the green
Of our own valleys: so I will begin
Now while I cannot hear the city's din; 40
Now while the early budders are just new,
And run in mazes of the youngest hue
About old forests; while the willow trails
Its delicate amber; and the dairy pails
Bring home increase of milk. And, as the year
Grows lush in juicy stalks, I'll smoothly steer
My little boat, for many quiet hours.
With streams that deepen freshly into bowers
Many and many a verse I hope to write,
Before the daisies, vermeil rimmed and white, 50
Hide in deep herbage; and ere yet the bees
Hum about globes of clover and sweet peas,
I must be near the middle of my story.
O may no wintry season, bare and hoary,
See it half finished: but let Autumn bold,
With universal tinge of sober gold,
Be all about me when I make an end.
And now at once, adventuresome, I send

My herald thought into a wilderness:
There let its trumpet blow, and quickly dress   60
My uncertain path with green, that I may speed
Easily onward, thorough flowers and weed.

1818

Ode on Melancholy

No, no! go not to Lethe, neither twist
    Wolf's-bane, tight-rooted, for its poisonous wine;
Nor suffer thy pale forehead to be kissed
    By nightshade, ruby grape of Proserpine;
Make not your rosary of yew-berries,
    Nor let the beetle, nor the death-moth be
        Your mournful Psyche, nor the downy owl
A partner in your sorrow's mysteries;
    For shade to shade will come too drowsily,
    And drown the wakeful anguish of the soul.   10

But when the melancholy fit shall fall
    Sudden from heaven like a weeping cloud,
That fosters the droop-headed flowers all,
    And hides the green hill in an April shroud;
Then glut thy sorrow on a morning rose,
    Or on the rainbow of the salt sand-wave,
        Or on the wealth of globèd peonies;
Or if thy mistress some rich anger shows,
    Emprison her soft hand, and let her rave,
    And feed deep, deep upon her peerless eyes.   20

She dwells with Beauty—Beauty that must die;
    And Joy, whose hand is ever at his lips
Bidding adieu; and aching Pleasure nigh,
    Turning to poison while the bee-mouth sips:
Ay, in the very temple of Delight
    Veiled Melancholy has her sovran shrine,
        Though seen of none save him whose strenuous
            tongue
Can burst Joy's grape against his palate fine;

His soul shall taste the sadness of her might,
And be among her cloudy trophies hung.   30

1820

Ode to a Nightingale

My heart aches, and a drowsy numbness pains
  My sense, as though of hemlock I had drunk,
Or emptied some dull opiate to the drains
  One minute past, and Lethe-wards had sunk:
'Tis not through envy of thy happy lot,
  But being too happy in thine happiness—
    That thou, light-wingéd Dryad of the trees,
        In some melodious plot
  Of beechen green, and shadows numberless,
    Singest of summer in full-throated ease.   10

O, for a draught of vintage! that hath been
  Cooled a long age in the deep-delvéd earth,
Tasting of Flora and the country green,
  Dance, and Provençal song, and sunburnt mirth!
O for a beaker full of the warm South,
  Full of the true, the blushful Hippocrene,
    With beaded bubbles winking at the brim,
        And purple-stainéd mouth;
  That I might drink, and leave the world unseen,
    And with thee fade away into the forest dim: 20

Fade far away, dissolve, and quite forget
  What thou among the leaves hast never known,
The weariness, the fever, and the fret
  Here, where men sit and hear each other groan;
Where palsy shakes a few, sad, last gray hairs,
  Where youth grows pale, and specter-thin,
        and dies;
  Where but to think is to be full of sorrow
        And leaden-eyed despairs,
  Where Beauty cannot keep her lustrous eyes,
    Or new Love pine at them beyond tomorrow.   30

Away! away! for I will fly to thee,
  Not charioted by Bacchus and his pards,
But on the viewless wings of Poesy,
  Though the dull brain perplexes and retards:
Already with thee! tender is the night,
  And haply the Queen-Moon is on her throne,
    Clustered around by all her starry Fays;
      But here there is no light,
Save what from heaven is with the breezes
      blown
    Through verdurous glooms and winding
      mossy ways.   40

I cannot see what flowers are at my feet,
  Nor what soft incense hangs upon the boughs,
But, in embalméd darkness, guess each sweet
  Wherewith the seasonable month endows
The grass, the thicket, and the fruit-tree wild;
  White hawthorn, and the pastoral eglantine;
    Fast fading violets covered up in leaves;
      And mid-May's eldest child,
The coming musk-rose, full of dewy wine,
  The murmurous haunt of flies on summer
      eves.   50

Darkling I listen; and, for many a time,
  I have been half in love with easeful Death,
Called him soft names in many a muséd rime,
  To take into the air my quiet breath;
Now more than ever seems it rich to die,
  To cease upon the midnight with no pain,
    While thou art pouring forth thy soul
      abroad
      In such an ecstasy!
Still wouldst thou sing, and I have ears in vain—
  To thy high requiem become a sod.   60

Thou wast not born for death, immortal Bird!
  No hungry generations tread thee down;

The voice I hear this passing night was heard
    In ancient days by emperor and clown:
Perhaps the self-same song that found a path
    Through the sad heart of Ruth, when, sick
        for home,
        She stood in tears amid the alien corn;
            The same that oft-times hath
Charmed magic casements, opening on the
        foam
        Of perilous seas, in faery lands forlorn.   70

Forlorn! the very word is like a bell
    To toll me back from thee to my sole self!
Adieu! the fancy cannot cheat so well
    As she is famed to do, deceiving elf.
Adieu! adieu! thy plaintive anthem fades
    Past the near meadows, over the still stream,
        Up the hillside; and now 'tis buried deep
            In the next valley glades:
    Was it a vision, or a waking dream?
        Fled is that music—Do I wake or sleep?   80

                                        1819

Ode on a Grecian Urn

Thou still unravished bride of quietness,
    Thou foster-child of silence and slow time,
Sylvan historian, who canst thus express
    A flowery tale more sweetly than our rhyme:
What leaf-fringed legend haunts about thy shape
    Of deities or mortals, or of both,
        In Tempe or the dales of Arcady?
What men or gods are these? What maidens loth?
    What mad pursuit? What struggle to escape?
        What pipes and timbrels? What wild ecstasy?   10

Heard melodies are sweet, but those unheard
    Are sweeter; therefore, ye soft pipes, play on;
Not to the sensual ear, but, more endeared,
    Pipe to the spirit ditties of no tone:

Fair youth, beneath the trees, thou canst not leave
　　Thy song, nor ever can those trees be bare;
　　　Bold Lover, never, never canst thou kiss,
Though winning near the goal—yet, do not grieve;
　　She cannot fade, though thou hast not thy bliss,
　　　Forever wilt thou love, and she be fair!   20

Ah, happy, happy boughs! that cannot shed
　　Your leaves, nor ever bid the Spring adieu:
And, happy melodist, unwearièd,
　　Forever piping songs forever new;
More happy love! more happy, happy love!
　　Forever warm and still to be enjoyed,
　　　Forever panting, and forever young;
All breathing human passion far above,
　　That leaves a heart high-sorrowful and cloyed,
　　　A burning forehead, and a parching tongue.   30

Who are these coming to the sacrifice?
　　To what green altar, O mysterious priest,
Lead'st thou that heifer lowing at the skies,
　　And all her silken flanks with garlands dressed?
What little town by river or sea shore,
　　Or mountain-built with peaceful citadel,
　　　Is emptied of its folk, this pious morn?
And, little town, thy streets for evermore
　　Will silent be; and not a soul to tell
　　　Why thou art desolate, can e'er return.   40

O Attic shape! Fair attitude! with brede
　　Of marble men and maidens overwrought,
With forest branches and the trodden weed;
　　Thou, silent form, dost tease us out of thought
As doth eternity: Cold Pastoral!
　　When old age shall this generation waste,
　　　Thou shalt remain, in midst of other woe
Than ours, a friend to man, to whom thou say'st,
　　"Beauty is truth, truth beauty,"—that is all
　　　Ye know on earth, and all ye need to know.   50

1820

To Autumn

Season of mists and mellow fruitfulness,
  Close bosom-friend of the maturing sun;
Conspiring with him how to load and bless
  With fruit the vines that round the thatch-eaves
      run;
To bend with apples the mossed cottage-trees,
  And fill all fruit with ripeness to the core;
    To swell the gourd, and plump the hazel shells
With a sweet kernel; to set budding more,
  And still more, later flowers for the bees,
  Until they think warm days will never cease,   10
    For Summer has o'er-brimmed their clammy
      cells.

Who hath not seen thee oft amid thy store?
  Sometimes whoever seeks abroad may find
Thee sitting careless on a granary floor,
  Thy hair soft-lifted by the winnowing wind;
Or on a half-reaped furrow sound asleep,
  Drowsed with the fume of poppies, while thy
      hook
    Spares the next swath and all its twinèd
      flowers:
And sometimes like a gleaner thou dost keep
  Steady thy laden head across a brook;   20
  Or by a cider-press, with patient look,
    Thou watchest the last oozings hours by hours.

Where are the songs of Spring? Ay, where are
    they?
  Think not of them, thou hast thy music too.—
While barrèd clouds bloom the soft-dying day,
  And touch the stubble-plains with rosy hue;
Then in a wailful choir the small gnats mourn
  Among the river sallows, borne aloft
    Or sinking as the light wind lives or dies;

And full-grown lambs loud bleat from hilly bourn;   30
Hedge-crickets sing; and now with treble soft
The red-breast whistles from a garden-croft;
And gathering swallows twitter in the skies.

1820

Ode to Psyche

O Goddess! hear these tuneless numbers, wrung
    By sweet enforcement and remembrance dear,
And pardon that thy secrets should be sung
    Even into thine own soft-conchèd ear:
Surely I dreamt to-day, or did I see
    The wingèd Psyche with awaken'd eyes?
I wander'd in a forest thoughtlessly,
    And, on the sudden, fainting with surprise,
Saw two fair creatures, couchèd side by side
In deepest grass, beneath the whisp'ring roof   10
Of leaves and trembled blossoms, where there ran
    A brooklet, scarce espied:

'Mid hush'd, cool-rooted flowers, fragrant-eyed,
    Blue, silver-white, and budded Tyrian,
They lay calm-breathing on the bedded grass;
    Their arms embracèd, and their pinions too;
    Their lips touch'd not, but had not bade adieu,
As if disjoined by soft-handed slumber,
And ready still past kisses to outnumber
    At tender eye-dawn of aurorean love: 20
        The wingèd boy I knew;
    But who wast thou, O happy, happy dove?
        His Psyche true!

O latest born and loveliest vision far
    Of all Olympus' faded hierarchy!
Fairer than Phœbe's sapphire-region'd star,
    Or Vesper, amorous glow-worm of the sky;
Fairer than these, though temple thou hast none,
        Nor altar heap'd with flowers;

JOHN KEATS

Nor virgin-choir to make delicious moan   30
    Upon the midnight hours;
No voice, no lute, no pipe, no incense sweet
    From chain-swung censer teeming;
No shrine, no grove, no oracle, no heat
    Of pale-mouth'd prophet dreaming.

O brightest! though too late for antique vows,
    Too, too late for the fond believing lyre,
When holy were the haunted forest boughs,
    Holy the air, the water, and the fire;
Yet even in these days so far retir'd   40
    From happy pieties, thy lucent fans,
    Fluttering among the faint Olympians,
I see, and sing, by my own eyes inspir'd.
So let me be thy choir, and make a moan
    Upon the midnight hours;
Thy voice, thy lute, thy pipe, thy incense sweet
    From swinged censer teeming;
Thy shrine, thy grove, thy oracle, thy heat
    Of pale-mouth'd prophet dreaming.

Yes, I will be thy priest, and build a fane   50
    In some untrodden region of my mind,
Where branched thoughts, new grown with pleasant
    pain,
    Instead of pines shall murmur in the wind:
Far, far around shall those dark-cluster'd trees
    Fledge the wild-ridged mountains steep by steep;
And there by zephyrs, streams, and birds, and bees,
The moss-lain Dryads shall be lull'd to sleep;
And in the midst of this wide quietness
A rosy sanctuary will I dress
With the wreath'd trellis of a working brain,   60
    With buds, and bells, and stars without a name,
With all the gardener Fancy e'er could feign,
    Who breeding flowers, will never breed the same:
And there shall be for thee all soft delight
    That shadowy thought can win,

A bright torch, and a casement ope at night,
To let the warm Love in!

1820

Bright Star! Would I Were Steadfast As Thou Art

Bright star! would I were steadfast as thou art—
    Not in lone splendor hung aloft the night,
And watching, with eternal lids apart,
    Like Nature's patient sleepless Eremite,
The moving waters at their priestlike task
    Of pure ablution round earth's human shores,
Or gazing on the new soft fallen mask
    Of snow upon the mountains and the moors—
No—yet still steadfast, still unchangeable,
    Pillowed upon my fair love's ripening breast,   10
To feel forever its soft fall and swell,
    Awake forever in a sweet unrest,
Still, still to hear her tender-taken breath,
And so live ever—or else swoon to death.

1819   *1848*

When I Have Fears That I May Cease to Be

When I have fears that I may cease to be
    Before my pen has gleaned my teeming brain,
Before high-pilèd books, in charact'ry,
    Hold like rich garners the full-ripened grain;
When I behold, upon the night's starred face,
    Huge cloudy symbols of a high romance,
And think that I may never live to trace
    Their shadows, with the magic hand of chance;
And when I feel, fair creature of an hour,
    That I shall never look upon thee more,   10
Never have relish in the faery power
    Of unreflecting love;—then on the shore
Of the wide world I stand alone, and think,
Till Love and Fame to nothingness do sink.

1818   *1848*

JOHN HENRY NEWMAN

The Pillar of the Cloud

Lead, Kindly Light, amid the encircling gloom,
  Lead Thou me on!
The night is dark, and I am far from home—
  Lead Thou me on!
Keep Thou my feet; I do not ask to see
The distant scene—one step enough for me.

I was not ever thus, nor prayed that Thou
  Shouldst lead me on.
I loved to choose and see my path; but now
  Lead Thou me on!   10
I loved the garish day, and, spite of fears,
Pride ruled my will; remember not past years.

So long Thy power hath blessed me, sure it still
  Will lead me on,
O'er moor and fen, o'er crag and torrent, till
  The night is gone;
And with the morn those angel faces smile
Which I have loved long since and lost awhile.

1836

ALFRED, LORD TENNYSON

Break, Break, Break

Break, break, break,
  On thy cold gray stones, O Sea!
And I would that my tongue could utter
  The thoughts that arise in me.

O well for the fisherman's boy,
  That he shouts with his sister at play!
O well for the sailor lad,
  That he sings in his boat on the bay!

And the stately ships go on
  To their haven under the hill;   10
But O for the touch of a vanished hand,
  And the sound of a voice that is still!

Break, break, break,
  At the foot of thy crags, O Sea!
But the tender grace of a day that is dead
  Will never come back to me.
            1842

The Splendour Falls on Castle Walls

  The splendour falls on castle walls
    And snowy summits old in story:
  The long light shakes across the lakes,
    And the wild cataract leaps in glory.
Blow, bugle, blow, set the wild echoes flying,
Blow, bugle; answer, echoes, dying, dying, dying.

  O hark, O hear! how thin and clear,
    And thinner, clearer, farther going!
  O sweet and far from cliff and scar
    The horns of Elfland faintly blowing!   10
Blow, let us hear the purple glens replying:
Blow, bugle; answer, echoes, dying, dying, dying.

  O love, they die in yon rich sky,
    They faint on hill or field or river:
  Our echoes roll from soul to soul,
    And grow for ever and for ever.
Blow, bugle, blow, set the wild echoes flying,
And answer, echoes, answer, dying, dying, dying.
            The Princess, 1850

Tears, Idle Tears

  Tears, idle tears, I know not what they mean,
  Tears from the depth of some divine despair   20
  Rise in the heart, and gather to the eyes,

In looking on the happy Autumn-fields,
And thinking of the days that are no more.

    Fresh as the first beam glittering on a sail,
That brings our friends up from the underworld,
Sad as the last which reddens over one
That sinks with all we love below the verge;
So sad, so fresh, the days that are no more.

                                        The Princess, 1850

Come Into the Garden, Maud

Come into the garden, Maud,
    For the black bat, night, has flown,
Come into the garden, Maud,
    I am here at the gate alone;
And the woodbine spices are wafted abroad,
    And the musk of the rose is blown.

For a breeze of morning moves,
    And the planet of Love is on high,
Beginning to faint in the light that she loves
    On a bed of daffodil sky,   10
To faint in the light of the sun she loves,
    To faint in his light, and to die.

All night have the roses heard
    The flute, violin, bassoon;
All night has the casement jessamine stirred
    To the dancers dancing in tune;
Till a silence fell with the waking bird,
    And a hush with the setting moon.

I said to the lily, "There is but one,
    With whom she has heart to be gay.   20
When will the dancers leave her alone?
    She is weary of dance and play."
Now half to the setting moon are gone,
    And half to the rising day;

Low on the sand and loud on the stone
   The last wheel echoes away.

I said to the rose, "The brief night goes
   In babble and revel and wine.
O young lord-lover, what sighs are those,
   For one that will never be thine?   30
But mine, but mine," so I sware to the rose,
   "Forever and ever, mine."

And the soul of the rose went into my blood,
   As the music clashed in the hall;
And long by the garden lake I stood,
   For I heard your rivulet fall
From the lake to the meadow and on to the wood,
   Our wood, that is dearer than all;

From the meadow your walks have left so sweet
   That whenever a March wind sighs   40
He sets the jewel-print of your feet
   In violets blue as your eyes,
To the woody hollows in which we meet
   And the valleys of Paradise.

The slender acacia would not shake
   One long milk-bloom on the tree;
The white lake-blossom fell into the lake
   As the pimpernel dozed on the lea;
But the rose was awake all night for your sake,
   Knowing your promise to me;   50
The lilies and roses were all awake,
   They sighed for the dawn and thee.

Queen rose of the rosebud garden of girls,
   Come hither, the dances are done,
In gloss of satin and glimmer of pearls,
   Queen lily and rose in one;
Shine out, little head, sunning over with curls,
   To the flowers, and be their sun.

There has fallen a splendid tear
   From the passion-flower at the gate. 60
She is coming, my dove, my dear;
   She is coming, my life, my fate.
The red rose cries, "She is near, she is near";
   And the white rose weeps, "She is late";
The larkspur listens, "I hear, I hear";
   And the lily whispers, "I wait."

She is coming, my own, my sweet;
   Were it ever so airy a tread,
My heart would hear her and beat,
   Were it earth in an earthy bed; 70
My dust would hear her and beat,
   Had I lain for a century dead,
Would start and tremble under her feet,
   And blossom in purple and red.

1855

Crossing the Bar

Sunset and evening star,
   And one clear call for me!
And may there be no moaning of the bar,
   When I put out to sea,

But such a tide as moving seems asleep,
   Too full for sound and foam,
When that which drew from out the boundless
    deep
   Turns again home.

Twilight and evening bell,
   And after that the dark! 10
And may there be no sadness of farewell,
   When I embark;

For tho' from out our bourne of Time and Place
   The flood may bear me far,
I hope to see my Pilot face to face
   When I have crost the bar.

1889

ELIZABETH BARRETT BROWNING

Sonnets from the Portuguese

XIV

If thou must love me, let it be for nought
  Except for love's sake only. Do not say,
  "I love her for her smile—her look—her way
Of speaking gently,—for a trick of thought
That falls in well with mine, and certes brought
  A sense of pleasant ease on such a day;"—
  For these things in themselves, Beloved, may
Be changed, or change for thee,—and love, so
    wrought,
May be unwrought so. Neither love me for
  Thine own dear pity's wiping my cheeks dry: 10
A creature might forget to weep, who bore
  Thy comfort long, and lose thy love thereby.
But love me for love's sake, that evermore
  Thou may'st love on through love's eternity.

XLIII

How do I love thee? Let me count the ways.
  I love thee to the depth and breadth and height
  My soul can reach, when feeling out of sight
For the ends of Being and ideal Grace.
I love thee to the level of everyday's
  Most quiet need, by sun and candle-light.   20
  I love thee freely, as men strive for Right;
I love thee purely, as they turn from Praise.
I love thee with the passion put to use
  In my old griefs, and with my childhood's faith.
I love thee with a love I seemed to lose
  With my lost saints,—I love thee with the breath,
Smiles, tears, of all my life!—and, if God choose,
  I shall but love thee better after death.

1850

A Musical Instrument

I

What was he doing, the great god Pan,
   Down in the reeds by the river?
Spreading ruin and scattering ban,
Splashing and paddling with hoofs of a goat,
And breaking the golden lilies afloat
   With the dragon-fly on the river.

II

He tore out a reed, the great god Pan,
   From the deep cool bed of the river;
The limpid water turbidly ran,
And the broken lilies a-dying lay,   10
And the dragon-fly had fled away,
   Ere he brought it out of the river.

III

High on the shore sat the great god Pan,
   While turbidly flowed the river;
And hacked and hewed as a great god can,
With his hard bleak steel at the patient reed,
Till there was not a sign of the leaf indeed
   To prove it fresh from the river.

IV

He cut it short, did the great god Pan
   (How tall it stood in the river!),   20
Then drew the pith, like the heart of a man,
Steadily from the outside ring,
And notched the poor dry empty thing
   In holes, as he sat by the river.

V

'This is the way,' laughed the great god Pan
   (Laughed while he sat by the river),
'The only way, since gods began

To make sweet music, they could succeed.'
Then, dropping his mouth to a hole in the reed,
He blew in power by the river.　　　　30

VI

Sweet, sweet, sweet, O Pan!
　Piercing sweet by the river!
Blinding sweet, O great god Pan!
The sun on the hill forgot to die,
And the lilies revived, and the dragon-fly
　Came back to dream on the river.

VII

Yet half a beast is the great god Pan,
　To laugh as he sits by the river,
Making a poet out of a man:
The true gods sigh for the cost and pain,—　　　　40
For the reed which grows nevermore again
　As a reed with the reeds in the river.

1860

ROBERT BROWNING

Home-Thoughts, from Abroad

I

Oh, to be in England
Now that April's there,
And whoever wakes in England
Sees, some morning, unaware,
That the lowest boughs and the brushwood sheaf
Round the elm-tree bole are in tiny leaf,
While the chaffinch sings on the orchard bough
In England—now!

II

And after April, when May follows,
And the whitethroat builds, and all the swallows!　10
Hark, where my blossomed pear-tree in the hedge

Leans to the field and scatters on the clover
Blossoms and dewdrops—at the bent spray's edge—
That's the wise thrush; he sings each song twice over,
Lest you should think he never could recapture
The first fine careless rapture!
And though the fields look rough with hoary dew,
All will be gay when noontide wakes anew
The buttercups, the little children's dower
—Far brighter than this gaudy melonflower!   20

1845

Meeting at Night

I

The grey sea and the long black land;
And the yellow half-moon large and low;
And the startled little waves that leap
In fiery ringlets from their sleep,
As I gain the cove with pushing prow,
And quench its speed in the slushy sand.

II

Then a mile of warm sea-scented beach;
Three fields to cross till a farm appears;
A tap at the pane, the quick sharp scratch
And blue spurt of a lighted match,   10
And a voice less loud, thro' its joys and fears,
Than the two hearts beating each to each!

1845

The Last Ride Together

I said—Then, dearest, since 'tis so,
Since now at length my fate I know,
Since nothing all my love avails,
Since all, my life seemed meant for, fails,
    Since this was written and needs must be—
My whole heart rises up to bless

Your name in pride and thankfulness!
Take back the hope you gave,—I claim
Only a memory of the same,
—And this beside, if you will not blame,   10
    Your leave for one more last ride with me.

My mistress bent that brow of hers;
Those deep dark eyes where pride demurs
When pity would be softening through,
Fixed me a breathing-while or two
    With life or death in the balance: right!
The blood replenished me again;
My last thought was at least not vain:
I and my mistress, side by side
Shall be together, breathe and ride,   20
So, one day more am I deified.
    Who knows but the world may end tonight?

Hush! if you saw some western cloud
All billowy-bosomed, over-bowed
By many benedictions—sun's
And moon's and evening-star's at once—
    And so, you, looking and loving best,
Conscious grew, your passion drew
Cloud, sunset, moonrise, star-shine too,
Down on you, near and yet more near,   30
Till flesh must fade for heaven was here!—
Thus leant she and lingered—joy and fear!
    Thus lay she a moment on my breast.

Then we began to ride. My soul
Smoothed itself out, a long-cramped scroll
Freshening and fluttering in the wind.
Past hopes already lay behind.
    What need to strive with a life awry?
Had I said that, had I done this,
So might I gain, so might I miss.   40
Might she have loved me? just as well
She might have hated, who can tell!
Where had I been now if the worst befell?
    And here we are riding, she and I.

Fail I alone, in words and deeds?
Why, all men strive, and who succeeds?
We rode; it seemed my spirit flew,
Saw other regions, cities new,
   As the world rushed by on either side.
I thought,—All labor, yet no less   50
Bear up beneath their unsuccess.
Look at the end of work, contrast
The petty done, the undone vast,
This present of theirs with the hopeful past!
   I hoped she would love me; here we ride.

What hand and brain went ever paired?
What heart alike conceived and dared?
What act proved all its thought had been?
What will but felt the fleshly screen?
   We ride and I see her bosom heave.   60
There's many a crown for who can reach.
Ten lines, a statesman's life in each!
The flag stuck on a heap of bones,
A soldier's doing! what atones?
They scratch his name on the Abbey-stones.
   My riding is better, by their leave.

What does it all mean, poet? Well,
Your brains beat into rhythm, you tell
What we felt only; you expressed
You hold things beautiful the best,   70
   And place them in rime so, side by side.
'Tis something, nay 'tis much: but then,
Have you yourself what's best for men?
Are you—poor, sick, old ere your time—
Nearer one whit your own sublime
Than we who never have turned a rime?
   Sing, riding's a joy! For me, I ride.

And you, great sculptor—so, you gave
A score of years to Art, her slave,
And that's your Venus, whence we turn   80
To yonder girl that fords the burn!
   You acquiesce, and shall I repine?

What, man of music, you grown gray
With notes and nothing else to say,
Is this your sole praise from a friend,
"Greatly his opera's strains intend,
But in music we know how fashions end!"
　　I gave my youth; but we ride, in fine.

Who knows what's fit for us? Had fate
Proposed bliss here should sublimate　　　　　　　90
My being—had I signed the bond—
Still one must lead some life beyond,
　　Have a bliss to die with, dim-descried.
This foot once planted on the goal,
This glory-garland round my soul,
Could I descry such? Try and test!
I sink back shuddering from the quest.
Earth being so good, would heaven seem best?
　　Now, heaven and she are beyond this ride.

And yet—she has not spoke so long!　　　　　　100
What if heaven be that, fair and strong
At life's best, with our eyes upturned
Whither life's flower is first discerned,
　　We, fixed so, ever should so abide?
What if we still ride on, we two,
With life for ever old yet new,
Changed not in kind but in degree,
The instant made eternity,—
And heaven just prove that I and she
　　Ride, ride together, for ever ride?　　　　　　110

　　　　　　　　　　　　　　　　　1855

Two in the Campagna

I

I wonder do you feel to-day
　　As I have felt since, hand in hand,
We sat down on the grass, to stray
　　In spirit better through the land,
This morn of Rome and May?

II

For me, I touched a thought, I know,
　Has tantalized me many times,
(Like turns of thread the spiders throw
　Mocking across our path) for rhymes
To catch at and let go.　　　　　　　10

III

Help me to hold it! First it left
　The yellowing fennel, run to seed
There, branching from the brickwork's cleft,
　Some old tomb's ruin: yonder weed
Took up the floating weft,

IV

Where one small orange cup amassed
　Five beetles,—blind and green they grope
Among the honey-meal: and last,
　Everywhere on the grassy slope
I traced it. Hold it fast!　　　　　　　20

V

The champaign with its endless fleece
　Of feathery grasses everywhere!
Silence and passion, joy and peace,
　An everlasting wash of air—
Rome's ghost since her decease.

VI

Such life there, through such lengths of hours,
　Such miracles performed in play,
Such primal naked forms of flowers,
　Such letting nature have her way
While heaven looks from its towers!　　　　　　30

VII

How say you? Let us, O my dove,
　Let us be unashamed of soul,

As earth lies bare to heaven above!
    How is it under our control
To love or not to love?

VIII

I would that you were all to me,
    You that are just so much, no more.
Nor yours nor mine, nor slave nor free!
    Where does the fault lie? What the core
Of the wound, since wound must be?   40

IX

I would I could adopt your will,
    See with your eyes, and set my heart
Beating by yours, and drink my fill
    At your soul's springs,—your part my part
In life, for good and ill.

X

No. I yearn upward, touch you close,
    Then stand away. I kiss your cheek,
Catch your soul's warmth,—I pluck the rose
    And love it more than tongue can speak—
Then the good minute goes.   50

XI

Already how am I so far
    Out of that minute? Must I go
Still like the thistle-ball, no bar,
    Onward, whenever light winds blow,
Fixed by no friendly star?

XII

Just when I seemed about to learn!
    Where is the thread now? Off again!
The old trick! Only I discern—
    Infinite passion, and the pain
Of finite hearts that yearn.   60

1855

MATTHEW ARNOLD

Shakespeare

Others abide our question. Thou art free.
We ask and ask—Thou smilest and art still,
Out-topping knowledge. For the loftiest hill,
Who to the stars uncrowns his majesty,
Planting his steadfast footsteps in the sea,
Making the heaven of heavens his dwelling-place,
Spares but the cloudy border of his base
To the foiled searching of mortality;
And thou, who didst the stars and sunbeams know,
Self-schooled, self-scanned, self-honored, self-secure, 10
Didst walk on earth unguessed at.—Better so!
All pains the immortal spirit must endure,
   All weakness which impairs, all griefs which bow,
   Find their sole speech in that victorious brow.

1849

Requiescat

   Strew on her roses, roses,
      And never a spray of yew!
   In quiet she reposes;
      Ah, would that I did too!

   Her mirth the world required;
      She bathed it in smiles of glee.
   But her heart was tired, tired,
      And now they let her be.

   Her life was turning, turning,
      In mazes of heat and sound.   10
   But for peace her soul was yearning,
      And now peace laps her round.

   Her cabin'd, ample spirit,
      It flutter'd and fail'd for breath.

To-night it doth inherit
The vasty hall of death.

1853

Philomela

Hark! ah, the nightingale—
The tawny-throated!
Hark, from that moonlit cedar what a burst!
What triumph! hark!—what pain!

O wanderer from a Grecian shore,
Still, after many years, in distant lands,
Still nourishing in thy bewilder'd brain
That wild, unquench'd, deep-sunken, old-world pain—
Say, will it never heal?
And can this fragrant lawn   10
With its cool trees, and night,
And the sweet, tranquil Thames,
And moonshine, and the dew,
To thy rack'd heart and brain
Afford no balm?

Dost thou to-night behold,
Here, through the moonlight on this English grass,
The unfriendly palace in the Thracian wild?
Dost thou again peruse
With hot cheeks and sear'd eyes   20
The too clear web, and thy dumb sister's shame?
Dost thou once more assay
Thy flight, and feel come over thee,
Poor fugitive, the feathery change
Once more, and once more seem to make resound
With love and hate, triumph and agony,
Lone Daulis, and the high Cephissian vale?
Listen, Eugenia—
How thick the bursts come crowding through the leaves!
Again—thou hearest?   30

Eternal passion!
Eternal pain!

1853

Thyrsis

A MONODY, TO COMMEMORATE THE AUTHOR'S FRIEND,
ARTHUR HUGH CLOUGH, WHO DIED AT FLORENCE, 1861

How changed is here each spot man makes or fills!
  In the two Hinkseys nothing keeps the same;
    The village street its haunted mansion lacks,
  And from the sign is gone Sibylla's name
    And from the roofs the twisted chimney-stacks—
      Are ye too changed, ye hills?
  See, 'tis no foot of unfamiliar men
    Tonight from Oxford up your pathway strays!
  Here came I often, often, in old days—
Thyrsis and I; we still had Thyrsis then.   10

Runs it not here, the track by Childsworth Farm,
  Past the high wood, to where the elm-tree crowns
    The hill behind whose ridge the sunset flames?
  The signal-elm, that looks on Ilsley Downs,
    The Vale, the three lone weirs, the youthful
      Thames?—
      This winter's eve is warm,
  Humid the air! leafless, yet soft as spring,
    The tender purple spray on copse and briers!
  And that sweet city with her dreaming spires,
  She needs not June for beauty's heightening,   20

Lovely all times she lies, lovely tonight!—
  Only, methinks, some loss of habit's power
    Befalls me wandering through this upland dim;
  Once passed I blindfold here, at any hour;
    Now seldom come I, since I came with him.
      That single elm tree bright
  Against the west—I miss it! it is gone?
  We prized it dearly; while it stood, we said,

Our friend, the gypsy-scholar, was not dead;
While the tree lived, he in these fields lived on.　　　30

Too rare, too rare, grow now my visits here,
　　But once I knew each field, each flower, each stick;
　　　And with the country folk acquaintance made
　　By barn in threshing-time, by new-built rick.
　　　Here, too, our shepherd-pipes we first assayed.
　　　　Ah me! this many a year
　　My pipe is lost, my shepherd's holiday!
　　　Needs must I lose them, needs with heavy heart
　　　Into the world and wave of men depart;
　　But Thyrsis of his own will went away.　　　40

It irked him to be here; he could not rest.
　　He loved each simple joy the country yields,
　　　He loved his mates; but yet he could not keep,
　　For that a shadow lowered on the fields,
　　　Here with the shepherds and the silly sheep.
　　　　Some life of men unblest
　　He knew, which made him droop, and filled his head.
　　　He went; his piping took a troubled sound
　　　Of storms that rage outside our happy ground;
　　He could not wait their passing, he is dead.　　　50

So, some tempestuous morn in early June,
　　When the year's primal burst of bloom is o'er,
　　　Before the roses and the longest day—
　　When garden-walks and all the grassy floor
　　　With blossoms red and white of fallen May
　　　　And chestnut flowers are strewn—
　　So have I heard the cuckoo's parting cry,
　　　From the wet field, through the vexed garden-trees,
　　　Come with the volleying rain and tossing breeze:
　　The bloom is gone, and with the bloom go I!　　　60

Too quick despairer, wherefore wilt thou go?
　　Soon will the high midsummer pomps come on.
　　　Soon will the musk carnations break and swell,

Soon shall we have gold-dusted snapdragon,
　　Sweet-William with his homely cottage-smell,
　　　And stocks in fragrant blow;
Roses that down the alleys shine afar,
　　And open, jasmine-muffled lattices,
　　And groups under the dreaming garden-trees,
And the full moon, and the white evening-star. 　70

He hearkens not! light comer, he is flown!
　　What matters it? next year he will return,
　　　And we shall have him in the sweet spring days,
With whitening hedges, and uncrumpling fern,
　　And bluebells trembling by the forest-ways,
　　And scent of hay new-mown.
But Thyrsis never more we swains shall see;
　　See him come back, and cut a smoother reed,
　　And blow a strain the world at last shall heed—
For Time, not Corydon, hath conquered thee! 　80

Alack, for Corydon no rival now!—
　　But when Sicilian shepherds lost a mate,
　　　Some good survivor with his flute would go,
Piping a ditty sad for Bion's fate;
　　And cross the unpermitted ferry's flow,
　　And relax Pluto's brow,
And make leap up with joy the beauteous head
　　Of Proserpine, among whose crownéd hair
　　Are flowers first opened on Sicilian air,
And flute his friend, like Orpheus, from the dead. 　90

O easy access to the hearer's grace
　　When Dorian shepherds sang to Proserpine!
　　　For she herself had trod Sicilian fields,
She knew the Dorian water's gush divine,
　　She knew each lily white which Enna yields,
　　Each rose with blushing face;
She loved the Dorian pipe, the Dorian strain.
　　But, ah, of our poor Thames she never heard!
　　Her foot the Cumner cowslips never stirred;
And we should tease her with our plaint in vain! 　100

Well! wind-dispersed and vain the words will be,
Yet, Thyrsis, let me give my grief its hour
    In the old haunt, and find our tree-topped hill!
Who, if not I, for questing here hath power?
    I know the wood which hides the daffodil,
        I know the Fyfield tree,
    I know what white, what purple fritillaries
        The grassy harvest of the river-fields,
        Above by Ensham, down by Sandford, yields,
And what sedged brooks are Thames's tributaries;   110

I know these slopes; who knows them if not I?—
    But many a dingle on the loved hillside,
        With thorns once studded, old, white-blossomed trees,
    Where thick the cowslips grew, and far descried
        High towered the spikes of purple orchises,
            Hath since our day put by
    The coronals of that forgotten time;
        Down each green bank hath gone the plowboy's team,
        And only in the hidden brookside gleam
Primroses, orphans of the flowery prime.   120

Where is the girl, who by the boatman's door,
    Above the locks, above the boating throng,
        Unmoored our skiff when through the Wytham flats,
    Red loosestrife and blond meadow-sweet among
        And darting swallows and light water-gnats,
            We tracked the shy Thames shore?
    Where are the mowers, who, as the tiny swell
        Of our boat passing heaved the river-grass,
        Stood with suspended scythe to see us pass?—
They are all gone, and thou art gone as well!   130

Yes, thou art gone! and round me too the night
    In ever-nearing circle weaves her shade.
        I see her veil draw soft across the day,
    I feel her slowly chilling breath invade
        The cheek grown thin, the brown hair sprent with
            gray;
        I feel her finger light

Laid pausefully upon life's headlong train—
 The foot less prompt to meet the morning dew,
 The heart less bounding at emotion new,
And hope, once crushed, less quick to spring again.   140

And long the way appears, which seemed so short
 To the less practiced eye of sanguine youth;
 And high the mountain-tops, in cloudy air,
The mountain-tops, where is the throne of Truth,
 Tops in life's morning-sun so bright and bare!
  Unbreachable the fort
Of the long-battered world uplifts its wall;
 And strange and vain the earthly turmoil grows,
 And near and real the charm of thy repose,
And night as welcome as a friend would fall.   150

But hush! the upland hath a sudden loss
 Of quiet!—Look, adown the dusk hillside,
 A troop of Oxford hunters going home,
As in old days, jovial and talking, ride!
 From hunting with the Berkshire hounds they come.
  Quick! let me fly, and cross
Into yon farther field;—'Tis done; and see,
 Backed by the sunset, which doth glorify
 The orange and pale violet evening sky,
Bare on its lonely ridge, the Tree! the Tree!   160

I take the omen! Eve lets down her veil,
 The white fog creeps from bush to bush about,
 The west unflushes, the high stars grow bright,
And in the scattered farms the lights come out.
 I cannot reach the signal-tree tonight,
  Yet, happy omen, hail!
Hear it from thy broad lucent Arno-vale
 (For there thine earth-forgetting eyelids keep
 The morningless and unawakening sleep
Under the flowery oleanders, pale),   170

Hear it, O Thyrsis, still our tree is there!—
 Ah, vain! These English fields, this upland dim,
 These brambles pale with mist engarlanded,

That lone, sky-pointing tree, are not for him;
    To a boon southern country he is fled,
        And now in happier air,
Wandering with the great Mother's train divine
    (And purer or more subtle soul than thee,
        I trow, the mighty Mother doth not see)
Within a folding of the Apennine,   180

Thou hearest the immortal chants of old!—
    Putting his sickle to the perilous grain
        In the hot cornfield of the Phrygian king,
    For thee the Lityerses-song again
        Young Daphnis with his silver voice doth sing;
            Sings his Sicilian fold,
    His sheep, his hapless love, his blinded eyes—
        And how a call celestial round him rang,
        And heavenward from the fountain-brink he sprang,
    And all the marvel of the golden skies.   190

There thou art gone, and me thou leavest here
    Sole in these fields! yet will I not despair.
        Despair I will not, while I yet descry
    'Neath the mild canopy of English air
        That lonely tree against the western sky.
            Still, still these slopes, 'tis clear,
    Our gypsy-scholar haunts, outliving thee!
        Fields where soft sheep from cages pull the hay,
        Woods with anemones in flower till May,
    Know him a wanderer still; then why not me?   200

A fugitive and gracious light he seeks,
    Shy to illumine; and I seek it too.
        This does not come with houses or with gold,
    With place, with honor, and a flattering crew;
        'Tis not in the world's market bought and sold—
            But the smooth-slipping weeks
    Drop by, and leave its seeker still untired;
        Out of the heed of mortals he is gone,
        He wends unfollowed, he must house alone;
    Yet on he fares, by his own heart inspired.   210

Thou too, O Thyrsis, on like quest wast bound;
  Thou wanderedst with me for a little hour!
    Men gave thee nothing; but this happy quest,
  If men esteemed thee feeble, gave thee power,
    If men procured thee trouble, gave thee rest.
      And this rude Cumner ground,
  Its fir-topped Hurst, its farms, its quiet fields,
    Here cam'st thou in thy jocund youthful time,
    Here was thine height of strength, thy golden prime!
  And still the haunt beloved a virtue yields.   220

What though the music of thy rustic flute
  Kept not for long its happy, country tone;
    Lost it too soon, and learned a stormy note
Of men contention-tossed, of men who groan,
    Which tasked thy pipe too sore, and tired thy throat—
      It failed, and thou wast mute!
  Yet hadst thou alway visions of our light,
    And long with men of care thou couldst not stay,
    And soon thy foot resumed its wandering way,
  Left human haunt, and on alone till night.   230

Too rare, too rare, grow now my visits here!
  'Mid city-noise, not, as with thee of yore,
    Thyrsis! in reach of sheep-bells is my home.
  —Then through the great town's harsh, heart-wearying
      roar,
    Let in thy voice a whisper often come,
      To chase fatigue and fear:
Why faintest thou? I wondered till I died.
Roam on! The light we sought is shining still.
 Dost thou ask proof? Our tree yet crowns the hill,
Our scholar travels yet the loved hillside.   240
        1866

Dover Beach

  The sea is calm to-night.
  The tide is full, the moon lies fair
  Upon the straits;—on the French coast the light

Gleams and is gone; the cliffs of England stand,
Glimmering and vast, out in the tranquil bay.
Come to the window, sweet is the night-air!
Only, from the long line of spray
Where the sea meets the moon-blanched land,
Listen! you hear the grating roar
Of pebbles which the waves draw back, and fling,   10
At their return, up the high strand,
Begin, and cease, and then again begin,
With tremulous cadence slow, and bring
The eternal note of sadness in.

Sophocles long ago
Heard it on the Ægean, and it brought
Into his mind the turbid ebb and flow
Of human misery; we
Find also in the sound a thought,
Hearing it by this distant northern sea.   20
The Sea of Faith
Was once, too, at the full, and round earth's shore
Lay like the folds of a bright girdle furled.
But now I only hear
Its melancholy, long, withdrawing roar,
Retreating, to the breath
Of the night-wind, down the vast edges drear
And naked shingles of the world.

Ah, love, let us be true
To one another! for the world, which seems   30
To lie before us like a land of dreams,
So various, so beautiful, so new,
Hath really neither joy, nor love, nor light,
Nor certitude, nor peace, nor help for pain;
And we are here as on a darkling plain
Swept with confused alarms of struggle and flight,
Where ignorant armies clash by night.

1867

DANTE GABRIEL ROSSETTI

The Blessed Damozel

The blessèd damozel leaned out
    From the gold bar of Heaven;
Her eyes were deeper than the depth
    Of waters stilled at even;
She had three lilies in her hand,
    And the stars in her hair were seven.

Her robe, ungirt from clasp to hem,
    No wrought flowers did adorn,
But a white rose of Mary's gift,
    For service meetly worn;   10
Her hair that lay along her back
    Was yellow like ripe corn.

Herseemed she scarce had been a day
    One of God's choristers;
The wonder was not yet quite gone
    From that still look of hers;
Albeit, to them she left, her day
    Had counted as ten years.

(To one, it is ten years of years.
    . . . Yet now, and in this place,   20
Surely she leaned o'er me—her hair
    Fell all about my face. . . .
Nothing: the autumn-fall of leaves.
    The whole year sets apace.)

It was the rampart of God's house
    That she was standing on;
By God built over the sheer depth
    The which is Space begun;
So high, that looking downward thence
    She scarce could see the sun.   30

It lies in Heaven, across the flood,
    Of ether, as a bridge.

Beneath, the tides of day and night
　　With flame and darkness ridge
The void, as low as where this earth
　　Spins like a fretful midge.

Around her, lovers, newly met
　　'Mid deathless love's acclaims,
Spoke evermore among themselves
　　Their heart-remembered names;　　　　40
And the souls mounting up to God
　　Went by her like thin flames.

And still she bowed herself and stooped
　　Out of the circling charm;
Until her bosom must have made
　　The bar she leaned on warm,
And the lilies lay as if asleep
　　Along her bended arm.

From the fixed place of Heaven she saw
　　Time like a pulse shake fierce　　　　50
Through all the worlds. Her gaze still strove
　　Within the gulf to pierce
Its path; and now she spoke as when
　　The stars sang in their spheres.

The sun was gone now; the curled moon
　　Was like a little feather
Fluttering far down the gulf; and now
　　She spoke through the still weather.
Her voice was like the voice the stars
　　Had when they sang together.　　　　60

(Ah sweet! Even now, in that bird's song,
　　Strove not her accents there,
Fain to be hearkened? When those bells
Possessed the mid-day air,
Strove not her steps to reach my side
　　Down all the echoing stair?)

"I wish that he were come to me,
    For he will come," she said.
"Have I not prayed in Heaven?—on earth,
    Lord, Lord, has he not prayed?   70
Are not two prayers a perfect strength?
    And shall I feel afraid?

"When round his head the aureole clings,
    And he is clothed in white,
I'll take his hand and go with him
    To the deep wells of light;
As unto a stream we will step down,
    And bathe there in God's sight.

"We two will stand beside that shrine,
    Occult, withheld, untrod,   80
Whose lamps are stirred continually
    With prayer sent up to God;
And see our old prayers, granted, melt
    Each like a little cloud.

"We two will lie i' the shadow of
    That living mystic tree
Within whose secret growth the Dove
    Is sometimes felt to be,
While every leaf that His plumes touch
    Saith His Name audibly.   90

"And I myself will teach to him,
    I myself, lying so,
The songs I sing here; which his voice
    Shall pause in, hushed and slow,
And find some knowledge at each pause,
    Or some new thing to know."

(Alas! we two, we two, thou say'st!
    Yea, one wast thou with me
That once of old. But shall God lift
    To endless unity   100
The soul whose likeness with thy soul
    Was but its love for thee?)

"We two," she said, "will seek the groves
　　Where the lady Mary is,
With her five handmaidens, whose names
　　Are five sweet symphonies,
Cecily, Gertrude, Magdalen,
　　Margaret and Rosalys.

"Circlewise sit they, with bound locks
　　And foreheads garlanded;   110
Into the fine cloth white like flame
　　Weaving the golden thread,
To fashion the birth-robes for them
　　Who are just born, being dead.

"He shall fear, haply, and be dumb:
　　Then will I lay my cheek
To his, and tell about our love,
　　Not once abashed or weak:
And the dear Mother will approve
　　My pride, and let me speak.   120

"Herself shall bring us, hand in hand,
　　To Him round whom all souls
Kneel, the clear-ranged unnumbered heads
　　Bowed with their aureoles:
And angels meeting us shall sing
　　To their citherns and citoles.

"There will I ask of Christ the Lord
　　Thus much for him and me:—
Only to live as once on earth
　　With Love,—only to be,   130
As then awhile, for ever now
　　Together, I and he."

She gazed and listened and then said,
　　Less sad of speech than mild,—
"All this is when he comes." She ceased.
　　The light thrilled towards her, filled
With angels in strong level flight.
　　Her eyes prayed, and she smiled.

(I saw her smile.) But soon their path
   Was vague in distant spheres: 140
And then she cast her arms along
   The golden barriers,
And laid her face between her hands,
And wept. (I heard her tears.)

1850

SONNETS FROM THE HOUSE OF LIFE

4. *Lovesight*

When do I see thee most, beloved one?
   When in the light the spirits of mine eyes
   Before thy face, their altar, solemnize
The worship of that Love through thee made known?
Or when in the dusk hours, (we two alone,)
   Close-kissed and eloquent of still replies
   Thy twilight-hidden glimmering visage lies,
And my soul only sees thy soul its own?

O love, my love! if I no more should see
Thyself, nor on the earth the shadow of thee,   10
   Nor image of thine eyes in any spring,—
How then should sound upon Life's darkening slope
The ground-whirl of the perished leaves of Hope,
   The wind of Death's imperishable wing?

1870

19. *Silent Noon*

Your hands lie open in the long, fresh grass—
   The finger-points look through like rosy blooms;
   Your eyes smile peace. The pasture gleams and glooms
'Neath billowing skies that scatter and amass.
All round our nest, far as the eye can pass,
   Are golden kingcup-fields with silver edge
   Where the cow-parsley skirts the hawthorn hedge.
'Tis visible silence, still as the hour-glass.

Deep in the sun-searched growths the dragonfly
Hangs like a blue thread loosened from the sky—   10
    So this winged hour is dropped to us from above.
Oh! clasp we to our hearts, for deathless dower,
This close-companioned inarticulate hour
    When twofold silence was the song of love.

1881

26. Mid-Rapture

Thou lovely and beloved, thou my love;
    Whose kiss seems still the first; whose summoning
      eyes,
    Even now, as for our love-world's new sunrise,
Shed very dawn; whose voice, attuned above
All modulation of the deep-bowered dove,
    Is like a hand laid softly on the soul;
    Whose hand is like a sweet voice to control
Those worn tired brows it hath the keeping of:—

What word can answer to thy word,—what gaze
    To thine, which now absorbs within its sphere   10
    My worshiping face, till I am mirrored there
Light-circled in a heaven of deep-drawn rays?
    What clasp, what kiss mine inmost heart can prove,
    O lovely and belovéd, O my love?

1881

49. Willowwood

I sat with Love upon a woodside well,
    Leaning across the water, I and he;
    Nor ever did he speak nor looked at me,
But touched his lute wherein was audible
The certain secret thing he had to tell:
    Only our mirrored eyes met silently
    In the low wave; and that sound came to be
The passionate voice I knew; and my tears fell.

And at their fall, his eyes beneath grew hers;
And with his foot and with his wingfeathers   10
    He swept the spring that watered my heart's
    drouth.
Then the dark ripples spread to waving hair,
And as I stooped, her own lips rising there
    Bubbled with brimming kisses at my mouth.

                                            1869

CHRISTINA GEORGINA ROSSETTI

A Birthday

My heart is like a singing bird
    Whose nest is in a water'd shoot;
My heart is like an apple-tree
    Whose boughs are bent with thick-set fruit;
My heart is like a rainbow shell
    That paddles in a halcyon sea;
My heart is gladder than all these,
    Because my love is come to me.

Raise me a dais of silk and down;
    Hang it with vair and purple dyes;   10
Carve it in doves and pomegranates,
    And peacocks with a hundred eyes;
Work it in gold and silver grapes,
    In leaves and silver fleurs-de-lys;
Because the birthday of my life
    Is come, my love is come to me.

                                            1857

Uphill

Does the road wind uphill all the way?
    Yes, to the very end.
Will the day's journey take the whole long day?
    From morn to night, my friend.

But is there for the night a resting-place?
 A roof for when the slow dark hours begin.
May not the darkness hide it from my face?
 You cannot miss that inn.

Shall I meet other wayfarers at night?
 Those who have gone before.   10
Then must I knock, or call when just in sight?
 They will not keep you standing at that door.

Shall I find comfort, travel-sore and weak?
 Of labor you shall find the sum.
Will there be beds for me and all who seek?
 Yea, beds for all who come.

         1861

When I Am Dead

When I am dead, my dearest,
 Sing no sad songs for me;
Plant thou no roses at my head,
 Nor shady cypress tree.
Be the green grass above me
 With showers and dewdrops wet;
And if thou wilt, remember,
 And if thou wilt, forget.

I shall not see the shadows,
 I shall not feel the rain;   10
I shall not hear the nightingale
 Sing on as if in pain.
And dreaming through the twilight
 That doth not rise nor set,
Haply I may remember,
 And haply may forget.

         1862

Twice

I took my heart in my hand
 (O my love, O my love),

I said: Let me fall or stand,
    Let me live or die,
But this once hear me speak
    (O my love, O my love)—
Yet a woman's words are weak;
    You should speak, not I.

You took my heart in your hand
    With a friendly smile,   10
With a critical eye you scann'd,
    Then set it down,
And said, "It is still unripe,
    Better wait awhile;
Wait while the skylarks pipe,
    Till the corn grows brown."

As you set it down it broke—
    Broke, but I did not wince;
I smiled at the speech you spoke,
    At your judgement I heard: 20
But I have not often smiled
    Since then, nor question'd since,
Nor cared for cornflowers wild,
    Nor sung with the singing bird.

I take my heart in my hand,
    O my God, O my God,
My broken heart in my hand:
    Thou hast seen, judge Thou.
My hope was written on sand,
    O my God, O my God: 30
Now let thy judgement stand—
    Yea, judge me now.

This contemn'd of a man,
    This marr'd one heedless day,
This heart take thou to scan
    Both within and without:
Refine with fire its gold,
    Purge Thou its dross away—

Yea, hold it in Thy hold,
Whence none can pluck it out.   40

I take my heart in my hand—
I shall not die, but live—
Before Thy face I stand;
I, for Thou callest such:
All that I have I bring,
All that I am I give,
Smile Thou and I shall sing,
But shall not question much.

1864

Aloof

The irresponsive silence of the land,
    The irresponsive sounding of the sea,
    Speak both one message of one sense to me:—
Aloof, aloof, we stand aloof, so stand
Thou too aloof, bound with the flawless band
    Of inner solitude; we bind not thee;
    But who from thy self-chain shall set thee free?
What heart shall touch thy heart? What hand thy hand?
And I am sometimes proud and sometimes meek,
    And sometimes I remember days of old   10
When fellowship seem'd not so far to seek,
    And all the world and I seem'd much less cold,
    And at the rainbow's foot lay surely gold,
And hope felt strong, and life itself not weak.

Before 1882

GEORGE MEREDITH

Love in the Valley

Under yonder beech-tree single on the greensward,
    Couched with her arms behind her golden head,
Knees and tresses folded to slip and ripple idly,
    Lies my young love sleeping in the shade.

Had I the heart to slide an arm beneath her,
  Press her parting lips as her waist I gather slow,
Waking in amazement she could not but embrace me:
  Then would she hold me and never let me go?

  .   .   .   .   .

Shy as the squirrel and wayward as the swallow,
  Swift as the swallow along the river's light   10
Circleting the surface to meet his mirrored winglets,
  Fleeter she seems in her stay than in her flight.
Shy as the squirrel that leaps among the pinetops,
  Wayward as the swallow overhead at set of sun,
She whom I love is hard to catch and conquer,
  Hard, but O the glory of the winning were she won!

  .   .   .   .   .

When her mother tends her before the laughing mirror,
  Tying up her laces, looping up her hair,
Often she thinks, were this wild thing wedded,
  More love should I have, and much less care.   20
When her mother tends her before the lighted mirror,
  Loosening her laces, combing down her curls,
Often she thinks, were this wild thing wedded,
  I should miss but one for many boys and girls.

  .   .   .   .   .

Heartless she is as the shadow in the meadows
  Flying to the hills on a blue and breezy noon.
No, she is athirst and drinking up her wonder:
  Earth to her is young as the slip of the new moon.
Deals she an unkindness, 'tis but her rapid measure,
  Even as in a dance; and her smile can heal no less: 30
Like the swinging May-cloud that pelts the flowers
    with hailstones
Off a sunny border, she was made to bruise and bless.

  .   .   .   .   .

Lovely are the curves of the white owl sweeping
  Wavy in the dusk lit by one large star.

Lone on the fir-branch, his rattle-note unvaried,
   Brooding o'er the gloom, spins the brown eve-jar.
Darker grows the valley, more and more forgetting:
   So were it with me if forgetting could be willed.
Tell the grassy hollow that holds the bubbling well-
      spring,
   Tell it to forget the source that keeps it filled.   40

.   .   .   .   .

Stepping down the hill with her fair companions,
   Arm in arm, all against the raying West,
Boldly she sings, to the merry tune she marches,
   Brave in her shape, and sweeter unpossessed.
Sweeter, for she is what my heart first awaking
   Whispered the world was; morning light is she.
Love that so desires would fain keep her changeless;
   Fain would fling the net, and fain have her free.

.   .   .   .   .

Happy happy time, when the white star hovers
   Low over dim fields fresh with bloomy dew,   50
Near the face of dawn, that draws athwart the dark-
      ness,
   Threading it with color, like yewberries the yew.
Thicker crowd the shades as the grave East deepens
   Glowing, and with crimson a long cloud swells.
Maiden still the morn is; and strange she is, and secret;
   Strange her eyes; her cheeks are cold as cold sea-
      shells.

.   .   .   .   .

Sunrays, leaning on our southern hills and lighting
   Wild cloud-mountains that drag the hills along,
Oft ends the day of your shifting brilliant laughter
   Chill as a dull face frowning on a song.   60
Ay, but shows the South-West a ripple-feathered
      bosom
   Blown to silver while the clouds are shaken and
      ascend

Scaling the mid-heavens as they stream, there comes
   a sunset
Rich, deep like love in beauty without end.

. . . . .

When at dawn she sighs, and like an infant to the
   window
   Turns grave eyes craving light, released from dreams,
Beautiful she looks, like a white water-lily
   Bursting out of bud in havens of the streams.
When from bed she rises clothed from neck to ankle
   In her long nightgown sweet as boughs of May,   70
Beautiful she looks, like a tall garden lily
   Pure from the night, and splendid for the day.

. . . . .

Mother of the dews, dark eye-lashed twilight,
   Low-lidded twilight, o'er the valley's brim,
Rounding on thy breast sings the dew-delighted
   skylark,
   Clear as though the dewdrops had their voice in him.
Hidden where the rose-flush drinks the rayless planet,
   Fountain-full he pours the spraying fountain-showers.
Let me hear her laughter, I would have her ever
   Cool as dew in twilight, the lark above the flowers. 80

. . . . .

All the girls are out with their baskets for the primrose;
   Up lanes, woods through, they troop in joyful bands.
My sweet leads: she knows not why, but now she
   loiters,
   Eyes the bent anemones, and hangs her hands.
Such a look will tell that the violets are peeping,
   Coming the rose: and unaware a cry
Springs in her bosom for odors and for color,
   Covert and the nightingale; she knows not why.

. . . . .

Kerchiefed head and chin she darts between her tulips,
   Streaming like a willow gray in arrowy rain: 90

Some bend beaten cheek to gravel, and their angel
    She will be; she lifts them, and on she speeds again.
Black the driving raincloud breasts the iron gateway:
    She is forth to cheer a neighbor lacking mirth.
So when sky and grass met rolling dumb for thunder
    Saw I once a white dove, sole light of earth.

· · · · ·

Prim little scholars are the flowers of her garden,
    Trained to stand in rows, and asking if they please.
I might love them well but for loving more the wild
    ones:
    O my wild ones! they tell me more than these.   100
You, my wild one, you tell of honeyed fieldrose,
    Violet, blushing eglantine in life; and even as they,
They by the wayside are earnest of your goodness,
    You are of life's, on the banks that line the way.

· · · · ·

Peering at her chamber the white crowns the red rose,
    Jasmine winds the porch with stars two and three.
Parted is the window; she sleeps; the starry jasmine
    Breathes a falling breath that carries thoughts of me.
Sweeter unpossessed, have I said of her my sweetest?
    Not while she sleeps: while she sleeps the jasmine
    breathes,   110
Luring her to love; she sleeps; the starry jasmine
    Bears me to her pillow under white rose-wreaths.

· · · · ·

Yellow with birdfoot-trefoil are the grass-glades;
    Yellow with cinquefoil of the dew-gray leaf;
Yellow with stonecrop; the moss-mounds are yellow;
    Blue-necked the wheat sways, yellowing to the
    sheaf.
Green-yellow bursts from the copse the laughing
    yaffle;
    Sharp as a sickle is the edge of shade and shine:
Earth in her heart laughs looking at the heavens,
    Thinking of the harvest: I look and think of mine.   120

This I may know: her dressing and undressing
  Such a change of light shows as when the skies in
    sport
Shift from cloud to moonlight; or edging over thunder
  Slips a ray of sun; or sweeping into port
White sails furl; or on the ocean borders
  White sails lean along the waves leaping green.
Visions of her shower before me, but from eyesight
  Guarded she would be like the sun were she seen.

    .   .   .   .

Front door and back of the mossed old farmhouse
  Open with the morn, and in a breezy link   130
Freshly sparkles garden to stripe-shadowed orchard,
  Green across a rill where on sand the minnows wink.
Busy in the grass the early sun of summer
  Swarms, and the blackbird's mellow fluting notes
Call my darling up with round and roguish challenge:
  Quaintest, richest carol of all the singing throats!

    .   .   .   . .

Cool was the woodside; cool as her white dairy
  Keeping sweet the cream-pan; and there the boys
    from school,
Cricketing below, rushed brown and red with sunshine;
  O the dark translucence of the deep-eyed cool!   140
Spying from the farm, herself she fetched a pitcher
  Full of milk, and tilted for each in turn the beak.
Then a little fellow, mouth up and on tiptoe,
  Said, "I will kiss you": she laughed and leaned her
    cheek.

    .   .   .   .   .

Doves of the fir-wood walling high our red roof
  Through the long noon coo, crooning through
    the coo.
Loose droop the leaves, and down the sleepy roadway
  Sometimes pipes a chaffinch; loose droops the blue.
Cows flap a slow tail knee-deep in the river,

Breathless, given up to sun and gnat and fly.   150
Nowhere is she seen; and if I see her nowhere,
Lightning may come, straight rains and tiger sky.

.   .   .   .   .

O the golden sheaf, the rustling treasure-armful!
O the nutbrown tresses nodding interlaced!
O the treasure-tresses one another over
Nodding! O the girdle slack about the waist!
Slain are the poppies that shot their random scarlet
Quick amid the wheatears: wound about the waist,
Gathered, see these brides of Earth one blush of
ripeness!
O the nutbrown tresses nodding interlaced!   160

.   .   .   .   .

Large and smoky red the sun's cold disk drops,
Clipped by naked hills, on violet shaded snow:
Eastward large and still lights up a bower of moonrise,
Whence at her leisure steps the moon aglow.
Nightlong on black print-branches our beech-tree
Gazes in this whiteness: nightlong could I.
Here may life on death or death on life be painted.
Let me clasp her soul to know she cannot die!

.   .   .   .   .

Gossips count her faults; they scour a narrow chamber
Where there is no window, read not heaven or her.   170
"When she was a tiny," one aged woman quavers,
Plucks at my heart and leads me by the ear.
Faults she had once as she learned to run and tumbled:
Faults of feature some see, beauty not complete.
Yet, good gossips, beauty that makes holy
Earth and air, may have faults from head to feet.

.   .   .   .   .

Hither she comes; she comes to me; she lingers,
Deepens her brown eyebrows, while in new surprise
High rise the lashes in wonder of a stranger;
Yet am I the light and living of her eyes.   180

Something friends have told her fills her heart to
   brimming,
Nets her in her blushes, and wounds her, and
   tames.—
Sure of her haven, O like a dove alighting,
   Arms up, she dropped: our souls were in our names.

.   .   .   .   .

Soon will she lie like a white-frost sunrise.
   Yellow oats and brown wheat, barley pale as rye,
Long since your sheaves have yielded to the thresher,
   Felt the girdle loosened, seen the tresses fly.
Soon will she lie like a blood-red sunset.
   Swift with the to-morrow, green-winged Spring!   190
Sing from the South-West, bring her back the truants,
   Nightingale and swallow, song and dipping wing.

.   .   .   .   .

Soft new beech-leaves, up to beamy April
   Spreading bough on bough a primrose mountain,
      you,
Lucid in the moon, raise lilies to the skyfields,
   Youngest green transfused in silver shining through:
Fairer than the lily, than the wild white cherry:
   Fair as in image my seraph love appears
Borne to me by dreams when dawn is at my eyelids:
   Fair as in the flesh she swims to me on tears.   200

.   .   .   .   .

Could I find a place to be alone with heaven,
   I would speak my heart out: heaven is my need.
Every woodland tree is flushing like the dogwood,
   Flashing like the whitebeam, swaying like the reed.
Flushing like the dogwood crimson in October;
   Streaming like the flag-reed South-West blown;
Flashing as in gusts the sudden-lighted whitebeam:
   All seem to know what is for heaven alone.

1878

Sonnets from Modern Love

I

By this he knew she wept with waking eyes:
That, at his hand's light quiver by her head,
The strange low sobs that shook their common bed
Were called into her with a sharp surprise,
And strangled mute, like little gaping snakes,
Dreadfully venomous to him. She lay
Stone-still, and the long darkness flowed away
With muffled pulses. Then, as midnight makes
Her giant heart of Memory and Tears
Drink the pale drug of silence, and so beat   10
Sleep's heavy measure, they from head to feet
Were moveless, looking through their dead black
    years,
By vain regret scrawled over the blank wall.
Like sculptured effigies they might be seen
Upon their marriage-tomb, the sword between;
Each wishing for the sword that severs all.

47

We saw the swallows gathering in the sky,
And in the osier-isle we heard them noise.
We had not to look back on summer joys,
Or forward to a summer of bright dye;
But in the largeness of the evening earth
Our spirits grew as we went side by side.
The hour became her husband and my bride.
Love, that had robbed us so, thus blessed our dearth!
The pilgrims of the year waxed very loud
In multitudinous chatterings, as the flood   10
Full brown came from the West, and like pale blood
Expanded to the upper crimson cloud.
Love, that had robbed us of immortal things,
This little moment mercifully gave,
Where I have seen across the twilight wave
The swan sail with her young beneath her wings.

1862

ALGERNON CHARLES SWINBURNE

When the Hounds of Spring

When the hounds of spring are on winter's traces,
   The mother of months in meadow or plain
Fills the shadows and windy places
   With lisp of leaves and ripple of rain;
And the brown bright nightingale amorous
Is half assuaged for Itylus,
For the Thracian ships and the foreign faces,
   The tongueless vigil, and all the pain.

Come with bows bent and with emptying of quivers,
   Maiden most perfect, lady of light,   10
With a noise of winds and many rivers,
   With a clamor of waters, and with might;
Bind on thy sandals, O thou most fleet,
Over the splendor and speed of thy feet;
For the faint east quickens, the wan west shivers,
   Round the feet of the day and the feet of the night.

Where shall we find her, how shall we sing to her,
   Fold our hands round her knees, and cling?
O that man's heart were as fire and could spring to her,
   Fire, or the strength of the streams that spring!   20
For the stars and the winds are unto her
As raiment, as songs of the harp-player;
For the risen stars and the fallen cling to her,
   And the southwest-wind and the west-wind sing.

For winter's rains and ruins are over,
   And all the season of snows and sins;
The days dividing lover and lover,
   The light that loses, the night that wins;
And time remembered is grief forgotten,
And frosts are slain and flowers begotten,   30
And in green underwood and cover
   Blossom by blossom the spring begins.

The full streams feed on flower of rushes,
   Ripe grasses trammel a traveling foot,
The faint fresh flame of the young year flushes
   From leaf to flower and flower to fruit;
And fruit and leaf are as gold and fire,
And the oat is heard above the lyre,
And the hoofèd heel of a satyr crushes
   The chestnut-husk at the chestnut-root.   40

And Pan by noon and Bacchus by night,
   Fleeter of foot than the fleet-foot kid,
Follows with dancing and fills with delight
   The Mænad and the Bassarid;
And soft as lips that laugh and hide
The laughing leaves of the trees divide,
And screen from seeing and leave in sight
   The god pursuing, the maiden hid.

The ivy falls with the Bacchanal's hair
   Over her eyebrows hiding her eyes;   50
The wild vine slipping down leaves bare
   Her bright breast shortening into sighs;
The wild vine slips with the weight of its leaves,
But the berried ivy catches and cleaves
To the limbs that glitter, the feet that scare
   The wolf that follows, the fawn that flies.
                      Atalanta in Calydon, 1865

Before the Beginning of Years

Before the beginning of years
   There came to the making of man
Time, with a gift of tears;
   Grief, with a glass that ran;
Pleasure, with pain for leaven;
   Summer, with flowers that fell;
Remembrance fallen from heaven,
   And madness risen from hell;

Strength without hands to smite;
   Love that endures for a breath: 10
Night, the shadow of light,
   And life, the shadow of death.
And the high gods took in hand
   Fire, and the falling of tears,
And a measure of sliding sand
   From under the feet of the years;
And froth and drift of the sea;
   And dust of the laboring earth;
And bodies of things to be
   In the houses of death and of birth;   20
And wrought with weeping and laughter,
   And fashioned with loathing and love,
With life before and after
   And death beneath and above,
For a day and a night and a morrow,
   That his strength might endure for a span
With travail and heavy sorrow,
   The holy spirit of man.

From the winds of the north and the south
   They gathered as unto strife;   30
They breathed upon his mouth,
   They filled his body with life;
Eyesight and speech they wrought
   For the veils of the soul therein,
A time for labor and thought,
   A time to serve and to sin;
They gave him light in his ways,
   And love, and a space for delight,
And beauty and length of days,
   And night, and sleep in the night.   40
His speech is a burning fire;
   With his lips he travaileth;
In his heart is a blind desire,
   In his eyes foreknowledge of death;
He weaves, and is clothed with derision;
   Sows, and he shall not reap;

His life is a watch or a vision
Between a sleep and a sleep.

Atalanta in Calydon, 1865

FRANCIS THOMPSON

The Hound of Heaven

I fled Him, down the nights and down the days;
  I fled Him, down the arches of the years;
  I fled Him, down the labyrinthine ways
    Of my own mind; and in the mist of tears
I hid from Him, and under running laughter.
    Up vistaed hopes, I sped;
    And shot, precipitated,
    Adown Titanic glooms of chasmèd fears,
From those strong Feet that followed, followed
    after.
    But with unhurrying chase,   10
    And unperturbèd pace,
Deliberate speed, majestic instancy,
    They beat—and a Voice beat
    More instant than the Feet:
"All things betray thee, who betrayest Me."

    I pleaded, outlaw-wise,
By many a hearted casement, curtained red,
  Trellised with intertwining charities;
(For, though I knew His love Who followèd,
    Yet was I sore adread   20
Lest, having Him, I must have naught beside).
But, if one little casement parted wide,
  The gust of His approach would clash it to.
  Fear wist not to evade, as Love wist to pursue.
Across the margent of the world I fled,
  And troubled the gold gateways of the stars,
  Smiting for shelter on their clangèd bars;
    Fretted to dulcet jars
And silvern chatter the pale ports o' the moon.
I said to Dawn, Be sudden—to Eve, Be soon: 30

With thy young skyey blossoms heap me over
    From this tremendous Lover—
Float thy vague veil about me, lest He see!
    I tempted all His servitors, but to find
My own betrayal in their constancy,
In faith to Him their fickleness to me,
    Their traitorous trueness, and their loyal deceit.
To all swift things for swiftness did I sue;
    Clung to the whistling mane of every wind.
            But whether they swept, smoothly fleet,   40
    The long savannahs of the blue;
        Or whether, thunder-driven,
    They clanged His chariot 'thwart a heaven
Plashy with flying lightnings round the spurn o'
        their feet:
    Fear wist not to evade as Love wist to pursue.
        Still with unhurrying chase,
        And unperturbèd pace,
Deliberate speed, majestic instancy,
        Came on the following Feet,
        And a Voice above their beat: 50
"Naught shelters thee, who wilt not shelter Me."

I sought no more that after which I strayed
        In face of man or maid;
But still within the little children's eyes
        Seems something, something that replies,
They at least are for me, surely for me!
I turned me to them very wistfully;
But just as their young eyes grew sudden fair
        With dawning answers there,
Their angel plucked them from me by the hair.   60
"Come then, ye other children, Nature's,—share
With me" (said I) "your delicate fellowship;
        Let me greet you lip to lip,
        Let me twine with you caresses,
            Wantoning
        With our Lady-Mother's vagrant tresses;
            Banqueting

With her in her wind-walled palace,
Underneath her azured daïs;
Quaffing, as your taintless way is,   70
    From a chalice
Lucent-weeping out of the dayspring."
    So it was done:
I in their delicate fellowship was one—
Drew the bolt of Nature's secrecies.
    I knew all the swift importings
    On the willful face of skies;
    I knew how the clouds arise
    Spumèd of the wild sea-snortings—
      All that's born or dies,   80
    Rose and drooped with; made them shapers
Of mine own moods, or wailful or divine;
    With them joyed and was bereaven.
    I was heavy with the even,
  When she lit her glimmering tapers
    Round the day's dead sanctities;
    I laughed in the morning's eyes.
I triumphed and I saddened with all weather:
    Heaven and I wept together,
And its sweet tears were salt with mortal mine;   90
Against the red throb of its sunset-heart
    I laid my own to beat,
    And share commingling heat.
But not by that, by that, was eased my human
    smart;
In vain my tears were wet on Heaven's gray
    cheek.
For ah! we know not what each other says,
    These things and I: in sound *I* speak—
Their sound is but their stir, they speak by silences.
Nature, poor stepdame, cannot slake my drouth;
    Let her, if she would owe me,   100
Drop yon blue bosom-veil of sky, and show me
    The breasts o' her tenderness:
Never did any milk of hers once bless
    My thirsting mouth.

Nigh and nigh draws the chase,
With unperturbèd pace,
Deliberate speed, majestic instancy,
    And past those noisèd Feet
    A Voice comes yet more fleet—
"Lo! naught contents thee, who content'st not
    Me."   110

Naked I wait Thy love's uplifted stroke!
My harness piece by piece Thou hast hewn
        from me,
    And smitten me to my knee:
    I am defenseless utterly.
    I slept, methinks, and woke,
And, slowly gazing, find me stripped in sleep.
In the rash lustihead of my young powers,
    I shook the pillaring hours
And pulled my life upon me; grimed with smears,
I stand amid the dust o' the mounded years—   120
My mangled youth lies dead beneath the heap.
My days have crackled and gone up in smoke,
Have puffed and burst as sun-starts on a stream.
    Yea, faileth now even dream
The dreamer, and the lute the lutanist;
Even the linked fantasies, in whose blossomy twist
I swung the earth a trinket at my wrist,
Are yielding—cords of all too weak account
For earth, with heavy griefs so overplussed.
    Ah! is Thy love indeed   130
A weed, albeit an amaranthine weed,
Suffering no flowers except its own to mount?
    Ah! must—
    Designer infinite!—
'Ah! must Thou char the wood ere Thou canst
        limn with it?
My freshness spent its wavering shower i' the dust;
And now my heart is as a broken fount,
Wherein tear-drippings stagnate, spilt down ever
    From the dank thoughts that shiver

Upon the sighful branches of my mind.   140
  Such is: what is to be?
The pulp so bitter, how shall taste the rind?
I dimly guess what Time in mist confounds;
Yet ever and anon a trumpet sounds
From the hid battlements of Eternity:
Those shaken mists a space unsettle, then
Round the half-glimpsèd turrets slowly wash
  again.
  But not ere him who summoneth
  I first have seen, enwound
With glooming robes purpureal, cypress-
  crowned: 150
His name I know, and what his trumpet saith.
Whether man's heart or life it be which yields
  Thee harvest, must Thy harvest fields
  Be dunged with rotten death?

  Now of that long pursuit
  Comes on at hand the bruit;
That Voice is round me like a bursting sea:
  "And is thy earth so marred,
  Shattered in shard on shard?
Lo, all things fly thee, for thou fliest Me!   160
  Strange, piteous, futile thing!
Wherefore should any set thee love apart?
Seeing none but I makes much of naught"
  (He said),
"And human love needs human meriting:
  How hast thou merited—
Of all man's clotted clay the dingiest clot?
  Alack, thou knowest not
How little worthy of any love thou art!
Whom wilt thou find to love ignoble thee,
  Save Me, save only Me?   170
All which I took from thee I did but take,
  Not for thy harms,
But just that thou might'st seek it in My arms.
  All which thy child's mistake

Fancies as lost, I have stored for thee at home:
Rise, clasp My hand, and come!"

Halts by me that footfall:
Is my gloom, after all,
Shade of His hand, outstretched caressingly?—
"Ah, fondest, blindest, weakest,   180
I am He Whom thou seekest!
Thou dravest love from thee, who dravest Me."

                                                           1893

ALFRED EDWARD HOUSMAN

POEMS FROM A SHROPSHIRE LAD

Reveille

Wake! The silver dusk returning
  Up the beach of darkness brims,
And the ship of sunrise burning
  Strands upon the eastern rims.

Wake! The vaulted shadow shatters,
  Trampled to the floor it spanned,
And the tent of night in tatters
  Straws the sky-pavilioned land.

Up, lad, up! 'Tis late for lying.
  Hear the drums of morning play;   10
Hark, the empty highways crying,
  "Who'll beyond the hills away?"

Towns and countries woo together,
  Forelands beacon, belfries call;
Never lad that trod on leather
  Lived to feast his heart with all.

Up, lad; thews that lie and cumber
  Sunlit pallets never thrive;
Morns abed and daylight slumber
  Were not meant for man alive.   20

Clay lies still, but blood's a rover;
    Breath's a ware that will not keep.
Up, lad; when the journey's over
    There'll be time enough to sleep.

1896

When Smoke Stood Up from Ludlow

When smoke stood up from Ludlow,
    And mist blew off from Teme,
And blithe afield to plowing
    Against the morning beam
    I strode beside my team,

The blackbird in the coppice
    Looked out to see me stride,
And hearkened as I whistled
    The trampling team beside,
    And fluted and replied: 10

"Lie down, lie down, young yeoman;
    What use to rise and rise?
Rise man a thousand mornings
    Yet down at last he lies,
    And then the man is wise."

I heard the tune he sang me,
    And spied his yellow bill;
I picked a stone and aimed it
    And threw it with a will.
    Then the bird was still.   20

Then my soul within me
    Took up the blackbird's strain,
And still beside the horses
    Along the dewy lane
    It sang the song again:

"Lie down, lie down, young yeoman;
    The sun moves always west;
The road one treads to labor

Will lead one home to rest,
And that will be the best."   30

1896

Bredon Hill

In summertime on Bredon
   The bells they sound so clear;
Round both the shires they ring them
   In steeples far and near,
   A happy noise to hear.

Here of a Sunday morning
   My love and I would lie,
And see the coloured counties,
   And hear the larks so high
   About us in the sky.   10

The bells would ring to call her
   In valleys miles away:
"Come all to church, good people;
   Good people, come and pray."
   But here my love would stay.

And I would turn and answer
   Among the springtime thyme,
"Oh, peal upon our wedding,
   And we will hear the chime,
   And come to church in time."   20

But when the snows at Christmas
   On Bredon top were strown,
My love rose up so early
   And stole out unbeknown
   And went to church alone.

They tolled the one bell only,
   Groom there was none to see,
The mourners followed after,
   And to church went she,
   And would not wait for me.   30

The bells they sound on Bredon,
  And still the steeples hum.
"Come all to church, good people,"—
  Oh, noisy bells, be dumb;
  I hear you, I will come.

1896

In My Own Shire

  In my own shire, if I was sad,
Homely comforters I had:
The earth, because my heart was sore,
Sorrowed for the son she bore;
And standing hills, long to remain,
Shared their short-lived comrade's pain.
And bound for the same bourn as I,
On every road I wandered by,
Trod beside me, close and dear,
The beautiful and death-struck year: 10
Whether in the woodland brown
I heard the beechnut rustle down,
And saw the purple crocus pale
Flower about the autumn dale;
Or littering far the fields of May
Lady-smocks a-bleaching lay,
And like a skylit water stood
The bluebells in the azured wood.

  Yonder, lightening other loads,
The season's range the country roads,   20
But here in London streets I ken
No such helpmates, only men;
And these are not in plight to bear,
If they would, another's care.
They have enough as 'tis: I see
In many an eye that measures me
The mortal sickness of a mind
Too unhappy to be kind.
Undone with misery, all they can

Is to hate their fellow man;   30
And till they drop they needs must still
Look at you and wish you ill.

1896

ROBERT BRIDGES

I Will Not Let Thee Go

I will not let thee go.
Ends all our month-long love in this?
   Can it be summed up so,
   Quit in a single kiss?
I will not let thee go.

I will not let thee go.
If thy words' breath could scare thy deeds,
   As the soft south can blow
   And toss the feathered seeds,
Then might I let thee go.   10

I will not let thee go.
Had not the great sun seen, I might;
   Or were he reckoned slow
   To bring the false to light,
Then might I let thee go.

I will not let thee go.
The stars that crowd the summer skies
   Have watched us so below
   With all their million eyes,
I dare not let thee go.   20

I will not let thee go.
Have we not chid the changeful moon,
   Now rising late, and now
   Because she set too soon,
And shall I let thee go?

I will not let thee go.
Have not the young flowers been content,
Plucked ere their buds could blow,
To seal our sacrament?
I cannot let thee go.   30

I will not let thee go.
I hold thee by too many bands:
Thou sayest farewell, and lo!
I have thee by the hands,
And will not let thee go.

1890

A Passer-By

Whither, O splendid ship, thy white sails crowding,
  Leaning across the bosom of the urgent West,
That fearest nor sea rising, nor sky clouding,
  Whither away, fair rover, and what thy quest?
  Ah! soon, when Winter has all our vales oppressed,
When skies are cold and misty, and hail is hurling,
  Wilt thou glide on the blue Pacific, or rest
In a summer haven asleep, thy white sails furling.

I there before thee, in the country that well thou
    knowest,
  Already arrived am inhaling the odorous air: 10
I watch thee enter unerringly where thou goest,
  And anchor queen of the strange shipping there,
  Thy sails for awnings spread, thy masts bare;
Nor is aught from the foaming reef to the snow-
    capped, grandest
  Peak, that is over the feathery palms more fair
Than thou, so upright, so stately, and still thou standest.

And yet, O splendid ship, unhailed and nameless,
  I know not if, aiming a fancy, I rightly divine
That thou hast a purpose joyful, a courage blameless,
  Thy port assured in a happier land than mine.   20
  But for all I have given thee, beauty enough is thine,

As thou, aslant with trim tackle and shrouding,
  From the proud nostril curve of a prow's line
In the offing scatterest foam, thy white sails crowding.

1890

So Sweet Love Seemed That April Morn

So sweet love seemed that April morn,
When first we kissed beside the thorn,
So strangely sweet, it was not strange
We thought that love could never change.

But I can tell—let truth be told—
That love will change in growing old;
Though day by day is nought to see,
So delicate his motions be.

And in the end 'twill come to pass
Quite to forget what once he was,   10
Nor even in fancy to recall
The pleasure that was all in all.

His little spring, that sweet we found,
So deep in summer floods is drowned,
I wonder, bathed in joy complete,
How love so young could be so sweet.

1894

My Delight and Thy Delight

My delight and thy delight
Walking, like two angels white,
In the gardens of the night:

  My desire and thy desire
Twining to a tongue of fire,
Leaping live, and laughing higher;
Through the everlasting strife
In the mystery of life.

Love, from whom the world begun,
Hath the secret of the sun.   10
Love can tell, and love alone,
Whence the million stars were strewn,
Why each atom knows its own,
How, in spite of woe and death,
Gay is life, and sweet is breath:

This he taught us, this we knew,
Happy in his science true,
Hand in hand as we stood
Neath the shadows of the wood,
Heart to heart as we lay   20
In the dawning of the day.

1899

WILLIAM BUTLER YEATS

When You Are Old

When you are old and gray and full of sleep,
And nodding by the fire, take down this book,
And slowly read, and dream of the soft look
Your eyes had once, and of their shadows deep;

How many loved your moments of glad grace,
And loved your beauty with love false or true;
But one man loved the pilgrim soul in you,
And loved the sorrows of your changing face.

And bending down beside the glowing bars
Murmur, a little sadly, how love fled   10
And paced upon the mountains overhead
And hid his face amid a crowd of stars.

1893

The Song of Wandering Aengus

I went out to the hazel wood,
Because a fire was in my head,
And cut and peeled a hazel wand,

And hooked a berry to a thread;
And when white moths were on the wing,
And moth-like stars were flickering out,
I dropped the berry in a stream
And caught a little silver trout.

When I had laid it on the floor,
I went to blow the fire a-flame,   10
But something rustled on the floor,
And some one called me by my name:
It had become a glimmering girl
With apple blossom in her hair
Who called me by my name and ran
And faded through the brightening air.

Though I am old with wandering
Through hollow lands and hilly lands,
I will find out where she has gone,
And kiss her lips and take her hands;   20
And walk among long dappled grass,
And pluck till time and times are done
The silver apples of the moon,
The golden apples of the sun.

1899

He Remembers Forgotten Beauty

When my arms wrap you round I press
My heart upon the loveliness
That has long faded from the world;
The jewelled crowns that kings have hurled
In shadowy pools, when armies fled;
The love-tales wrought with silken thread
By dreaming ladies upon cloth
That has made fat the murderous moth;
The roses that of old time were
Woven by ladies in their hair,   10
The dew-cold lilies ladies bore
Through many a sacred corridor

Where such grey clouds of incense rose
That only God's eyes did not close:
For that pale breast and lingering hand
Come from a more dream-heavy land,
A more dream-heavy hour than this;
And when you sigh from kiss to kiss
I hear white Beauty sighing, too,
For hours when all must fade like dew,   20
But flame on flame, and deep on deep,
Throne over throne where in half sleep,
Their swords upon their iron knees,
Brood her high lonely mysteries.

                                    1899

The Wild Swans At Coole

The trees are in their autumn beauty,
The woodland paths are dry,
Under the October twilight the water
Mirrors a still sky;
Upon the brimming water among the stones
Are nine-and-fifty swans.

The nineteenth autumn has come upon me
Since I first made my count;
I saw, before I had well finished,
All suddenly mount   10
And scatter wheeling in great broken rings
Upon their clamorous wings.

I have looked upon those brilliant creatures,
And now my heart is sore.
All's changed since I, hearing at twilight,
The first time on this shore,
The bell-beat of their wings above my head,
Trod with a lighter tread.

Unwearied still, lover by lover,
They paddle in the cold   20

Companionable streams or climb the air;
Their hearts have not grown old;
Passion or conquest, wander where they will,
Attend upon them still.

But now they drift on the still water
Mysterious, beautiful;
Among what rushes will they build,
By what lake's edge or pool
Delight men's eyes when I awake some day
To find they have flown away? 30

1919

DIDACTIC POETRY

FROM THE EARLIEST TIMES English poets have wished to teach their readers as well as to delight them. Poetry in which men set out to teach a lesson, or give a definition, or express some point of view is called didactic. The lessons which they try to teach may be intensely practical, as in the case of the jingles used in the old days to teach children the alphabet:

> A is for Adam, who was the first man,
> He broke God's command, and thus sin began.

Or, the poet may simply define the "merry heart:"

> Jog on, jog on, the footpath way,
> And merrily hent the stile-a:
> A merry heart goes all the day,
> Your sad tires in a mile-a.

Or again, he may give vent in verse to literary criticism or to philosophical speculation. We shall not attempt to consider all phases of didactic poetical thought, but we shall point out the main tendencies in poetry of this kind through the centuries we are studying.

Didactic Poetry of the Middle Ages

Since the fourteenth-century Englishman was deeply religious, his didactic poetry reflected his anxiety about the life after death, in which he firmly believed. When he looked around him and saw the evils which were done on every hand, he was filled with concern for the souls of his fellowmen. He thought of their indubitable plight after death. They lived idly and wickedly; they spent both goods and time thoughtlessly; surely they would die in sin. Their future state could

be deduced from the certain knowledge of the fate of those
who had gone before:

> Were beth they biforen us weren,
> Houndes ladden and hauekes beren,
> And hadden feld and wode,
> The riche levedies in hoere bour,
> That wereden gold in hoere tressour,
> With hoere brighte rode?

Of course the answer to the question is that these gay ones had
gone to Hell. The moralist of the fourteenth century was
extremely anxious that men should behave themselves so as
to avoid this unhappy end. The moral poets of the period tried
almost every literary device to make men consider in time
the manner in which they were leading their lives.

Of all medieval methods of teaching lessons the favorite was
the allegory, wherein abstract ideas, such as Law, Truth, Love,
Charity, were conceived of as sensible objects or as persons:

> *Lex* is leyd adowne,
> And *veritas* is but small;
> *Amor* is owt of towne,
> And *caritas* is gon with all.

In *Piers the Plowman* we learn of William who falls asleep on
Malvern Hills. He dreams of a Field Full of Folk among whom
exist all the evils prevalent in England. The friars tell lies, the
lawyers cheat their clients, the courtiers deceive the king by
flattery. The seven deadly sins, Pride, Envy, Gluttony, and the
rest, all appear as actual persons who by their lives illustrate
the sins whose names they bear.

Living at the same time as William Langland, Geoffrey
Chaucer not only made use of allegory in his poems, but he
employed nearly all the other literary devices which were
characteristic of medieval English didactic writers. Indeed we
shall not need to go beyond his work for the remainder of our
discussion of this type of medieval poetry. The fable, for
instance, was a particularly delightful means by which to

portray the effects of sin. Chaucer's Pardoner relates the dire consequences of greed and blasphemy in his tale of the three young rioters who set out in the midst of a plague to seek and kill the malefactor Death. When they are directed by an old man to a spot where they find eight bushels of gold, their greed leads each to plot the death of the others, and so all in very truth find Death. The story carries the moral, which needs little pointing.

Chaucer is also one of the most able, albeit genial, satirists in English. By his shrewd observations on the Canterbury Pilgrims he reveals more clearly than all the ranting preachers of his time the corruptions current in his day. We know all the shady reeves of England when we learn how cleverly Chaucer's Reve could cheat his young lord:

> Ful riche he was astored prively,
> His lord wel coude he plesen subtilly,
> To yeve and lene him of his owne good,
> And have a thank, and yet a cote and hood.

All the corruptions of the clergy, which within the next century and a half were to add to the discontent which culminated in the Reformation and the establishment of the Church of England, are pointed out in Chaucer's humorous descriptions of the Friar, the Monk, the Prioress, and the other ecclesiastics.

If Chaucer was not precisely a didactic poet in that he was not avowedly attempting to reform men and manners, he is indirectly didactic in his satire and humor. In certain of his ballades, moreover, especially in the *Balade de Bon Conseyl*, the *Lak of Stedfastnesse*, and *Gentilesse*, he is openly didactic. But Chaucer's didacticism is seldom that of the typical medieval allegorist, for he describes men and women as individuals. He does not write of "Lex" or "Ceritas," but rather he tells of the learned lawyer and the parson whom he knew well on the streets of London and in the remote shire towns of England.

Didactic Poetry of the Sixteenth and Seventeenth Centuries

When we pass from the Middle Ages to the Renascence, the proportion of didactic to lyrical and dramatic poetry diminishes, though, as we shall see, a few remarkable didactic poems were written during just this period. Among the lyrics and plays, moreover, such as those of Ben Jonson, a clear didactic note is manifest. Just why the lyrical and dramatic poetry predominates is not easy to say, but reasons may be suggested. Since poetry is occupied with the emotions and since the poet is not able both to explain ideas and, at the same time, to suggest their emotional associations, he is forced to treat those concepts which are the easy assumptions of his public. The Renascence produced no philosopher of its own until the seventeenth century. Men continued to exercise their minds with the philosophy of the medieval church and to delve into the works of the Greek and Latin writers for their philosophical concepts. Plato, more than any other writer, became the philosopher of the Renascence, but Aristotle and the Stoics also greatly influenced the men of this period. Since, therefore, the sixteenth and seventeenth centuries were listening to many philosophical voices, the poets could not easily assume any one system of concepts to be familiar to all their readers. The times, moreover, were exciting ones in which to live, full of new discoveries and inventions and of stirring military and political exploits. All of these conditions made the poets tend towards lyrical and dramatic productions rather than towards didacticism, which was at that moment of English thought more the province of controversial prose writers. But in spite of these facts, a few didactic poems did come from the poets of the Renascence, and these few include the greatest narrative poems of the age, *The Faerie Queene* and *Paradise Lost*. Though we have already discussed these poems in our introduction to narrative poetry, we shall have to consider them again, from the point of view of their moral purpose.

In expounding to Sir Walter Raleigh "his whole intention" in *The Faerie Queene*, Spenser made abundantly clear the didactic aim of the poem:

The generall end therefore of all the booke is to fashion a gentleman or noble person in vertuous and gentle discipline.

The methods which he employed to do this are those already familiar to the medieval poets, the allegory, the moral fable, and the satire. The allegory is here used to the best advantage. The plan of the poem called for twelve books, six of which were actually written, representing each of the twelve Aristotelian virtues, which together make up the perfect man. The Faerie Queene herself represents both Queen Elizabeth and glory in general. Each book is really a moral fable, relating the deeds of a hero who goes in quest of a particular virtue. The first book tells of the adventures of the Red Cross Knight in his search for Holiness, the second those of Sir Guyon who seeks Temperance, and so on. Within the fabric of the poem thus broadly conceived, the poet introduces many descriptive, lyrical, and even satirical passages. The ideas of Plato, Boethius, and others of the ancient and medieval philosophers run through the whole, which may well be regarded as an Elizabethan book of conduct, based on the moral precepts which were accepted by Spenser's own generation.

Born several years after the death of Spenser, and acknowledging the elder poet as one of his own moral teachers, John Milton wrote the greatest didactic poem of the seventeenth century. In *Paradise Lost*, Milton set out "to justify the ways of God to man," to show to Englishmen of his day that man had once possessed every advantage with which to attain the best imaginable life but had fallen because he violated God's command. The power and righteousness of God are demonstrated; the weakness and folly of Adam and Eve are made clear; finally, the hope is held out that man may redeem his lost position. The whole lesson is taught by means of an epic narrative. Throughout the poem Milton has woven the philosophical and moral concepts of Plato, of Paul, of Augustine, and of his own countryman, Spenser. It is, in fact, a poem based on the ideas of the ancient and the medieval thinkers rather than on the philosophical speculations of the seventeenth century.

Didactic Poetry of the Late Seventeenth and Eighteenth Centuries

By the end of the seventeenth century and the early part of the eighteenth, philosophical ideas had spread from the work of such men as Sir Francis Bacon in England and René Descartes in France. From them men learned to think in scientific terms, to use the reason in order to establish hitherto unknown facts. By the method of science they discovered many ways in which nature works, the laws of gravity and Boyle's laws of gases, for instance, and came to understand as never before the order which underlies the qualities and motions of the natural bodies and substances. It was but a step from this new knowledge to the desire on the part of all men to introduce more exactitude and order into their own daily affairs. They tried to find rules by which they could correct their religion, their conduct, their architecture, their grammar. And so new religious sects arose, such as Methodism, which attempted to find an improved method in religion and conduct; new architectural designs were adopted, which aimed at greater symmetry and rationality in buildings; and new grammatical and rhetorical rules were laid down for the prose writers and poets. Support for this effort to find better methods in the arts was found in the classical writers themselves to whom scholars had been looking from the beginnings of the Renascence straight down to the eighteenth century. In the "Age of Reason," therefore, many of the rules of the Ancients were adapted to contemporary needs. To such an extent, in fact, was this done in literature that the early eighteenth century came to be known as the "Classical" or "Augustan Age" of English poetry.

In keeping with the thought of the time, the poets of the late seventeenth and early eighteenth centuries sought by the aid of their classical studies and by the use of their own reason to attain a more sustained orderliness and clarity of expression in their poetry. For this purpose they found the rimed couplet an exceedingly satisfactory verse form, and though many metrical forms were employed, the couplet was the most popular manner of writing poetry in this period. Since it lent itself well to aphorism and epigram and was particularly suitable for less emotional and more intellectual poetry, the "heroic couplet," as it was called, was commonly used by didactic writers. It was, indeed, a good medium for the new philosophical ideas of the period, and we find it constantly employed from 1660 to the end of the eighteenth century in philosophical and reflective poems, in meditative descriptions, and in moral essays, satire, and literary criticism.

Turning now to the actual work of the Restoration and eighteenth century poets, we come first to John Dryden, whose *Absalon and Achitophel* is a satire on the political intrigues of the Earl of Shaftesbury. The fable of the older didactic poets has been retained in a tale which only faintly conceals under biblical names the living figures of contemporary England. Dryden was perhaps at his best when writing political satire, but he was also a literary critic in verse. In *MacFlecknoe*, he satirizes his former friend, the poet Thomas Shadwell, who, he tells us, was the "last great prophet of tautology." He then becomes even more biting as he writes, "Shadwell never deviates into sense." Such judgments, however, are not the sort of general literary criticism which we shall find in the work of Pope. They are, rather, personal satire taken over from politics. Dryden's greatest literary criticism was in prose; in poetry he was the partisan politician.

Alexander Pope was a moralist and critic and humorist all at once. His humor never comes out better than in the mock-epic, *The Rape of the Lock*, which we have already discussed in our study of narrative poetry. We like to remember the sheer-nonsense of such lines as:

> Now lap-dogs give themselves the rousing shake,
> And sleepless lovers, just at twelve awake.

The poem was written for the avowed purpose of preventing a duel over a young lady, and part of its success lay in its light humor, untouched by malice.

In literary criticism Pope may be regarded as the spokesman of his age. He counselled young writers "first to follow nature," and he believed in the "Rules" derived from former times:

> Those Rules of old discover'd, not devis'd,
> Are Nature still, but Nature methodiz'd.

One must study the works of the Ancients and learn their precepts, but

> Some beauties yet no Precepts can declare,
> For there's a happiness as well as care.

In other words, Genius is necessary in producing art as well as a thorough knowledge of the Rules derived from Nature and Antiquity. Thus Pope explains a whole system of literary criticism, which is the outgrowth of the philosophical tendencies that we have already discussed.

Finally, in *An Essay on Man*, we find Pope the moral poet at his best. In the first few lines he announces his didactic purpose:

> Laugh where we must, be candid where we can;
> But vindicate the ways of God to Man.

All the scientific discoveries of his day and all the philosophical speculations are suggested in the following:

> Say first, of God above, or Man below,
> What can we reason, but from what we know?
> Of Man, what see we but his station here,

From which to reason, or to which refer?
Thro' worlds unnumber'd tho' the God be known,
'Tis ours to trace him only in our own.
He, who thro' vast immensity can pierce,
See worlds on worlds compose one universe,
Observe how system into system runs,
What other Planets circle other suns,
What vary'd Being peoples ev'ry star,
May tell why Heav'n has made us as we are.
But of this frame the bearings, and the ties,
The strong connections, nice dependencies,
Gradations just, has thy pervading soul
Look'd thro'? or can a part contain the whole?

Here, as in his literary criticism and, for that matter, as in his humorous gibes, Pope was trying to find the rational thought, the Rule drawn from Nature. In this search he was typical of his age; the *Essay* is probably the best mirror that exists of the moral thought of the early eighteenth century.

From the time of Pope to the end of the century, didactic poetry flourished, and the same thoughts on Reason and Rule, Nature and the Ancients, continued to be repeated by poet after poet. Isaac Watts, a contemporary of Pope, was one of the most charming and moving of didactic poets. His hymns are still sung in churches, and his *Divine Songs*, "How doth the little busy Bee," " 'Tis the Voice of the Sluggard," and others, have been memorized by little children for two hundred years. Writing at just the same time, James Thomson produced in blank verse, *The Seasons*, one of the most popular poems of the entire eighteenth century. Its long descriptions, now of the falling snow, now of the flowers of the English gardens, have a moral beauty which has endeared the poem to all readers of English poetry. Thomson's didacticism appears again in *The Castle of Indolence*, this time supported by the allegorical machinery of Spenser, whose stanza and style Thomson imitated. Here the allegory is a little too heavy, however, and the poem lacks the charm of *The Seasons*.

With the middle and end of the century we come to the work of Dr. Johnson, Oliver Goldsmith, George Crabbe, and William Cowper. In *The Vanity of Human Wishes* Johnson portrays the folly of "hope and fear, desire and hate," of all the devils, in fact, which drive men on to achieve whatever of good or bad fame they gain from life. His poem is, indeed, a verse sermon on vanity. The most famous lines in the poem give a gloomy picture of what a scholar may hope to get from his successes:

> Deign on the passing world to turn thine eyes,
> And pause awhile from letters, to be wise;
> There mark what ills the scholar's life assail,
> Toil, envy, want, the patron, and the jail.

Himself a scholar, Dr. Johnson knew some of these sorrows. Since he was a very religious man, he could only conclude his poem by counselling reliance on the power of Heaven. In *The Deserted Village* Goldsmith writes of the effects on the little village of Auburn of the "Industrial Revolution," a term which he, of course, did not know. But he knew the conditions of the countryside. He saw people being drawn off from the pretty and healthful towns of England and Ireland to work in the great cities under degenerating conditions, and he grieved. The enclosing of the fields meant the loss of free-holding farmers, with ruinous effects on the economic and social life of the country. From these facts he drew the moral:

> Ill fares the land, to hastening ills a prey,
> Where wealth accumulates, and men decay:
> Princes and lords may flourish, or may fade;
> A breath can make them, as a breath has made;
> But a bold peasantry, their country's pride,
> When once destroyed, can never be supplied.

Coming but a few years after Goldsmith's description of Auburn, George Crabbe's poem *The Village* presents a less sentimental picture of the small village community. Crabbe's work is marked by a realism which seems to link it closely with the Romantic poets who were within a few years to appear in public, but he still retains many of the characteristics of the poetry of the early century. One is all too familiar with the references to Virgil's "Mantuan song," and with the habit of capitalizing "Truth," "Nature," and "Fancy."

> On Mincio's banks, in Caesar's bounteous reign,
> If Tityrus found the Golden Age again,
> Must sleepy bards the flattering dream prolong,
> Mechanic echoes of the Mantuan song?
> From Truth and Nature shall we widely stray,
> Where Virgil, not where Fancy, leads the way?

This is far from Crabbe's best poetry and must only be read as an example of what the eighteenth century writers persisted in doing until they were laughed out of court by the newer poets. In *The Task* of Cowper we find many of the same poetical vices, but in his realism and in his love of nature, this poet, more definitely than Crabbe, belongs to the late eighteenth century and looks forward to the Romantics.

Didactic Poetry of the Nineteenth Century

The shift to Romanticism from the thought which had preceded in the eighteenth century may be traced to a philosophical change on the part of the poets of the time, and it is thus of particular importance from the standpoint of didactic poetry. We have noted the desire on the part of Pope and the men of his generation to live by Reason and Rules. By the fourth quarter of the century a reaction was taking place. As Cowper says:

> In vain by reason and by rule,
> We try to bend the will.

If one compares Addison's hymn, *The Spacious Firmament on high*, in which the universe is viewed as a great impersonal orderly system, with almost any one of Cowper's hymns, for instance, *Oh! for a closer walk with God*, where the whole thought is the personal, intuitive understanding of God, one feels better than words can state the difference between the spirit of the earlier century and that of the later.

The philosophy which underlay the new spirit came in large measure from German writers, who conceived the world in terms of idealism and individualism. They saw the world of matter as an appearance or garment of the reality which is spirit. Matter, space, time, sensation, and reason lie outside of the spirit, which is viewed as absolute. Since each individual is a part of that spirit, each shares in the eternal reality. Such is the transcendentalism which forms the basis of the romantic theory of literature, which thus becomes a revelation to man of this divine reality. The emotions and the imagination are the approaches to the Absolute. Literature is the expression of intuitions and sympathies and is a means of union between the soul of man and the ideal. The poet has more of the divine than ordinary men; he is something of a priest and a mystic; and so, to the Romantics and their successors in the next generation, literature was, in truth, a religion. This fact was proclaimed in prose by Carlyle and Emerson and in poetry by Tennyson and Browning.

Transcendental thought permeates all of Wordsworth's poetry, and his didacticism is largely concerned with giving expression to it. One finds it in *Lines Composed a Few Miles above Tintern Abbey:*

> And I have felt
> A presence that disturbs me with the joy
> Of elevated thoughts; a sense sublime
> Of something far more deeply interfused,
> Whose dwelling is the light of setting suns,
> And the round ocean and the living air,
> And the blue sky, and in the mind of man:
> A motion and a spirit, that impels
> All thinking things, all objects of all thought,
> And rolls through all things.

In the sonnet *On Westminster Bridge* and in *The Prelude* in many lyrical passages, one catches this thought of the spirit as detached from the body and the world of things about us. It appears in the work of Coleridge also, in *Frost at Midnight*, for example, and it runs through much of Shelley's poetry.

The didacticism of the nineteenth-century poets comes out, moreover, in poems of literary criticism. Wordsworth's *Scorn Not the Sonnet*, the sonnets addressed to Milton, and the critical sections of *The Prelude* are examples of his interest in teaching the poetic art through poetry. In character this criticism differs greatly from the work of previous literary critics in verse. The technical precepts, as illustrated in the criticism of Pope, are here supplanted by criticism of an emotional character. Wordsworth writes of the contentment of nuns within their convent, of hermits in their cells, of students in seclusion, to prepare the reader for his conclusion that the sonnet has within its small compass sufficient room for the solace of the greatest spirits.

Of course these poets did not confine themselves to one type of literary comment. In Byron we have a recrudescence of satirical verse. Satire had never been dead, but in the hands of this fierce man its former spirit revived, and men heard the whip's crack and felt the malice of the early eighteenth century poets. Byron's satirical power is at its best in *English Bards and Scotch Reviewers*, and no portions of this poem are more scathing than the sections on Scott, Southey, Wordsworth, and Coleridge. *Don Juan*, too, for those who can wade through it, contains a great deal of good and bad satire. Byron's power as a satirist, however, is probably something of a measure of his failure as a lyrist. Wordsworth as a critic is more typical of the romantic poets than Byron, for he believed in giving sway to the emotions, and in literary criticism as in lyrical poetry, we find him true to the convictions of this group.

As we move towards the Victorian Age, the same tendencies that we have seen in the earlier century are visible. With the coming of the Industrial Revolution men had become more concerned with social problems, many of which arose for the first time as a result of the enclosing of the common lands in the rural districts and of the crowding of workers into cities. The advances of science, too, especially as science tended to give men religious doubts, produced new sorts of philosophical speculations in the mid-nineteenth century. The didactic poetry of the Victorians, then, was a continuation of that of the Romantics with new ideas, speculations, and doubts added.

As we have seen in our introduction to the lyrics, the social turmoil of the nineteenth century often comes out in the lyrical utterance of such men as Thomas Hood, whose *Song of the Shirt* was written to call attention to the miserable condition of garment workers. This poem is in every sense as didactic as are *Battle Song* and *Preston Mills* of Ebenezer Elliott. Writing to the same purpose but in a far more poetic strain, Elizabeth Barrett Browning still moves us with *The Cry of the Children*. Some years later William Morris preached social betterment in *The Day is Coming*, where he satirically promised a future time when

All folk that are in England shall be better lodged than swine.

Tennyson and many other poets of the period were aroused by social speculations, which have continued to interest poets down to our own day.

The philosophical and religious problems raised by the discoveries and inventions of science are reflected in the work of nearly every poet of the nineteenth century. To many men the old religious beliefs were incredible, but they could find no satisfactory substitute for them. They felt themselves to be, in Arnold's words,

Wandering between two worlds, one dead,
The other powerless to be born.

With the loss of religious conviction men seemed to have little to live for or to die for. Arnold regarded himself and others who were similarly disturbed as

> Light half-believers of our casual creeds,
> Who never deeply felt, nor clearly willed.

Through *Empedocles on Etna*, the Obermann poems, and almost all the rest, run Arnold's cries of doubt. Tennyson, gazing at a *Flower in the Crannied Wall*, thought that by knowing it fully one ought to be able to discover the whole secret of existence—if one only could. Throughout *In Memoriam*, as he struggles with the problem of belief, he tries to persuade himself to believe in God and immortality, but one is never satisfied that he is really convinced. At the end of his long life, he is still arguing with himself over the question of his faith:

> Let blow the trumpet strongly while I pray,
> Till this embattled wall of unbelief,—
> My prison, not my fortress,—fall away!

With Robert Browning this religious questioning took the form of preoccupation with moral affairs. The Grammarian of *The Grammarian's Funeral* had spent his life trying to learn all the knowledge of the world, but the poet's concern was not so much with the science of the old student as with the personal effort he had made to gain his knowledge.

> He ventured neck or nothing,—heaven's success
> Found, or earth's failure:
> "Wilt thou trust death or not?" He answered, "Yes!
> Hence with life's pale lure!"
> That low man seeks a little thing to do,
> Sees it and does it:
> This high man, with a great thing to pursue,
> Dies ere he knows it.

This poet bases his moral judgments on character; he makes little effort to pose ethical questions raised by science. In the closing years of the century, however, Thomas Hardy reaches the limits of unbelief when in *God-Forgotten* he accepts at their face value the findings of science and considers what these involve in terms of immediate supervision of man's life by God.

> I towered far, and lo! I stood within
> The presence of the Lord Most High,
> Sent thither by the sons of Earth, to win
>   Some answer to their cry.

> —"The Earth, sayest thou? The Human race?
> By Me created? Sad its lot?
> Nay: I have no remembrance of such place:
>   Such world I fashioned not."—

All of these nineteenth century poets were baffled in the presence of the new scientific thought, and they found their religious faith severely tested.

A study of didactic poetry, in and for itself, brings one to the basic moral nature of the English people. Throughout their long poetic history, their writers have been deeply concerned with the problems of religion, of social conduct, above all of character. Piers the Plowman whipped his age as he contemplated the evils of his contemporaries, Spenser sought "to fashion a gentleman or noble person in vertuous and gentle discipline," Pope taught the young poet to follow the classical rules, the nineteenth century poets stressed philosophical speculations in their verse. Didacticism runs through all English poetry and through all its forms, and is, indeed, the Englishman's principal reason for being a poet at all.

FURTHER READING

W. J. Courthope, *A History of English Poetry*, 1911. VOL. V, CHAP. 10.
Dwight L. Durling, *The Georgic Tradition in English Poetry*, 1935.
Hugh Walker, *English Satire and Satirists*, 1925.

GEOFFREY CHAUCER

Truth

BALADE DE BON CONSEYL

Flee fro the prees, and dwelle with sothfastnesse,
Suffyce unto thy good, though hit be smal;
For hord hath hate, and climbing tikelnesse,
Prees hath envye, and wele blent overal;
Savour no more than thee bihove shal;
Werk wel thy-self, that other folk canst rede;
And trouthe shal delivere, hit is no drede.

Tempest thee noght al croked to redresse,
In trust of hir that turneth as a bal:
Gret reste stant in litel besinesse;   10
And eek be war to sporne ageyn an al;
Stryve noght, as doth the crokke with the wal.
Daunte thy-self, that dauntest otheres dede;
And trouthe shal delivere, hit is no drede.

That thee is sent, receyve in buxumnesse,
The wrastling for this worlde axeth a fal.
Her nis non hoom, her nis but wildernesse:
Forth, pilgrim, forth! Forth, beste, out of thy stal!
Know thy contree, look up, thank God of al;
Hold the hye wey, and lat thy gost thee lede: 20
And trouthe shal delivere, hit is no drede.

1. *fro,* from; *prees,* crowd; *sothfastnesse,* steadfastness.
2. *Suffyce unto thy good,* be content with thy income.
3. *tikelnesse,* slipperyness.
4. *wele blent overal,* happiness blinds everything.   5. *Savour,* taste.
6. *rede,* counsel.   8. *croked,* evil, crookedness.
11. *sporne,* spurn; *al,* awl.   12. *crokke,* crock.   13. *Daunte,* subdue.
15. *buxumnesse,* submission.   16. *axeth,* asks, begs.

ENVOY

Therfore, thou vache, leve thyn old wrecchednesse
Unto the worlde; leve now to be thral;
Crye him mercy, that of his hy goodnesse
Made thee of noght, and in especial
Draw unto him, and pray in general
For thee, and eek for other, hevenlich mede;
And trouthe shal delivere, hit is no drede.
About 1390

The Compleint of Chaucer to His Empty Purse

To you, my purse, and to non other wight
Compleyne I, for ye be my lady dere!
I am so sory, now that ye be light;
For certes, but ye make me hevy chere,
Me were as leef be leyd up-on my bere;
For whiche un-to your mercy thus I crye:
Beth hevy ageyn, or elles mot I dye!

Now voucheth sauf this day, or hit be night,
That I of you the blisful soun may here,
Or see your colour lyk the sonne bright,   10
That of yelownesse hadde never pere.
Ye be my lyf, ye be myn hertes stere,
Quene of comfort and of good companye:
Beth hevy ageyn, or elles mot I dye!

Now, purs, that be to me my lyves light,
And saveour, as doun in this worlde here,
Out of this toune help me through your might,
Sin that ye wole nat been my tresorere;
For I am shave as nye as any frere.
But yit I pray un-to your curtesye: 20
Beth hevy ageyn, or elles mot I dye!

22. *vache*, a pun here intended, for the word "vache" means cow, and
the poem was addressed to Sir Philip la Vache, whom Chaucer was exhorting to bestir himself.
9. *soun*, sound.   12. *stere*, pilot.

LENVOY DE CHAUCER

O conquerour of Brutes Albioun!
Which that by lyne and free eleccioun
Ben verray king, this song to you I sende;
And ye, that mowen al our harm amende,
Have minde up-on my supplicacioun!
About 1399

SIR EDWARD DYER

My Mind to Me a Kingdom Is

My mind to me a kingdom is;
　　Such perfect joy therein I find
That it excels all other bliss
　　That world affords or grows by kind.
Though much I want which most would have,
Yet still my mind forbids to crave.

No princely pomp, no wealthy store,
　　No force to win the victory,
No wily wit to salve a sore,
　　No shape to feed a loving eye;　　　　　　10
To none of these I yield as thrall:
For why? My mind doth serve for all.

I see how plenty suffers oft,
　　And hasty climbers soon do fall;
I see that those which are aloft
　　Mishap doth threaten most of all;
They get with toil, they keep with fear:
Such cares my mind could never bear.

Content to live, this is my stay;
　　I seek no more than may suffice;　　　　　20
I press to bear no haughty sway;
　　Look, what I lack my mind supplies:

22. *conquerour of Brutes Albioun*, King Henry IV, who actually granted
this request of Chaucer for money.
25. *mowen*, may.

Lo, thus I triumph like a king,
Content with that my mind doth bring.

Some have too much, yet still do crave;
    I little have, and seek no more.
They are but poor, though much they have,
    And I am rich with little store:
They poor, I rich; they beg, I give;
They lack, I leave; they pine, I live.   30

I laugh not at another's loss;
    I grudge not at another's gain;
No worldly waves my mind can toss;
    My state at one doth still remain:
I fear no foe, I fawn no friend;
I loathe not life, nor dread my end.

Some weigh their pleasure by their lust,
    Their wisdom by their rage of will;
Their treasure is their only trust;
    A cloakéd craft their store of skill: 40
But all the pleasure that I find
Is to maintain a quiet mind.

My wealth is health and perfect ease;
    My conscience clear my chief defense;
I neither seek by bribes to please,
    Nor by deceit to breed offense:
Thus do I live; thus will I die;
Would all did so as well as I!

                                    1588

SIR WALTER RALEIGH

His Pilgrimage

Give me my scallop-shell of quiet,
    My staff of faith to walk upon,
My scrip of joy, immortal diet,
    My bottle of salvation,

My gown of glory, hope's true gage;
And thus I'll take my pilgrimage.

Blood must be my body's balmer;
  No other balm will there be given;
Whilst my soul, like a white palmer,
  Travels to the land of heaven,   10
Over the silver mountains,
Where spring the nectar fountains.
    There I'll kiss
    The bowl of bliss;
And drink my eternal fill
Upon every milken hill.
My soul will be a-dry before;
But, after, it will thirst no more.

And by the happy blissful day
  More peaceful pilgrims I shall see,   20
That have shook off their gowns of clay,
  And go apparelled fresh like me.
    I'll bring them first,
    To slake their thirst
And then to taste those nectar suckets
    At the clear wells
    Where sweetness dwells,
Drawn up by saints in crystal buckets.

  And when our bottles and all we
Are filled with immortality,   30
Then the holy paths we'll travel,
Strowed with rubies thick as gravel;
Ceilings of diamonds, sapphire floors,
High walls of coral, and pearl bowers.
  From thence to Heaven's bribeless hall,
Where no corrupted voices brawl;
No conscience molten into gold;
Nor forged accusers bought and sold;
No cause deferred; nor vain-spent journey;
For there Christ is the King's Attorney,   40
Who pleads for all without degrees,

And he hath angels, but no fees.
When the grand twelve million jury
Of our sins and sinful fury,
'Gainst our souls black verdicts give,
Christ pleads his death, and then we live.
Be thou my speaker, taintless Pleader,
Unblotted Lawyer, true Proceeder!
Thou movest salvation even for alms,
Not with a bribed lawyer's palms.   50
And this is my eternal plea
To him that made heaven, earth, and sea,
Seeing my flesh must die so soon,
And want a head to dine next noon,—
Just at the stroke, when my veins start and spread,
Set on my soul an everlasting head:
Then am I ready, like a palmer fit,
To tread those blest paths which before I writ.

1604

ROBERT GREENE

Sweet Are the Thoughts That Savor of Content

Sweet are the thoughts that savor of content;
     The quiet mind is richer than a crown;
Sweet are the nights in careless slumber spent;
     The poor estate scorns fortune's angry frown:
Such sweet content, such minds, such sleep, such bliss,
Beggars enjoy, when princes oft do miss.

The homely house that harbors quiet rest;
     The cottage that affords no pride nor care;
The mean that 'grees with country music best;
     The sweet consort of mirth and modest fare;   10
Obscuréd life sets down a type of bliss:
A mind content both crown and kingdom is.

1591

THOMAS CAMPION

The Man of Life Upright

The man of life upright,
   Whose guiltless heart is free
From all dishonest deeds,
   And thought of vanity,

The man whose silent days
   In harmless joys are spent,
Whom hopes cannot delude,
   Nor sorrow discontent;

That man needs neither towers
   Nor armour for defence,   10
Nor secret vaults to fly
   From thunder's violence.

He only can behold
   With unaffrighted eyes
The horrors of the deep
   And terrors of the skies.

Thus, scorning all the cares
   That fate, or fortune brings,
He makes the heaven his book,
   His wisdom heav'nly things,   20

Good thoughts his only friends,
   His wealth a well-spent age,
The earth his sober inn
   And quiet pilgrimage.

                                        1601

Never Love

Never love, unless you can
Bear with all the faults of man:
Men sometimes will jealous be,

Though but little cause they see,
And hang the head, as discontent,
And speak what straight they will repent.

Men that but one Saint adore,
Make a show of love to more:
Beauty must be scorned in none,
Though but truly served in one: 10
    For what is courtship, but disguise?
    True hearts may have dissembling eyes.

Men when their affairs require,
Must awhile themselves retire;
Sometimes hunt, and sometimes hawk,
And not ever sit and talk.
    If these, and such like you can bear,
    Then like, and love, and never fear.
                              About 1617

BEN JONSON

Still to Be Neat

Still to be neat, still to be drest,
As you were going to a feast;
Still to be powdered, still perfumed;—
Lady, it is to be presumed,
Though art's hid causes are not found,
All is not sweet, all is not sound.

Give me a look, give me a face,
That makes simplicity a grace;
Robes loosely flowing, hair as free:
Such sweet neglect more taketh me   10
Than all th' adulteries of art;
They strike mine eyes, but not my heart.
                              1616

ROBERT HERRICK

His Litany, to the Holy Spirit

In the hour of my distress,
When temptations me oppress,
And when I my sins confess,
  Sweet Spirit, comfort me!

When I lie within my bed,
Sick in heart, and sick in head,
And with doubts discomforted,
  Sweet Spirit, comfort me!

When the house doth sigh and weep,
And the world is drowned in sleep,   10
Yet mine eyes the watch do keep,
  Sweet Spirit, comfort me!

When the artless doctor sees
No one hope, but of his fees,
And his skill runs on the lees,
  Sweet Spirit, comfort me!

When his potion and his pill,
Has or none or little skill,
Meet for nothing but to kill,
  Sweet Spirit, comfort me!   20

When the passing-bell doth toll,
And the furies in a shoal
Come to fright a parting soul,
  Sweet Spirit, comfort me!

When the tapers now burn blue,
And the comforters are few,
And that number more than true,
  Sweet Spirit, comfort me!

When the priest his last hath prayed,
And I nod to what is said,   30
'Cause my speech is now decayed,
  Sweet Spirit, comfort me!

When, God knows, I'm tossed about,
Either with despair or doubt,
Yet before the glass be out,
    Sweet Spirit, comfort me!

When the Tempter me pursu'th
With the sins of all my youth,
And half damns me with untruth,
    Sweet Spirit, comfort me!   40

When the flames and hellish cries
Fright mine ears and fright mine eyes,
And all terrors me surprise,
    Sweet Spirit, comfort me!

When the judgment is revealed,
And that opened which was sealed,
When to thee I have appealed,
    Sweet Spirit, comfort me!
          1647

A Grace for a Child

Here, a little child, I stand,
Heaving up my either hand:
Cold as paddocks though they be,
Here I lift them up to thee,
For a benison to fall
On our meat, and on us all. Amen.
          1647

To the Virgins to Make Much of Time

Gather ye rosebuds while ye may,
  Old Time is still a-flying;
And this same flower that smiles today,
  Tomorrow will be dying.

The glorious lamp of heaven, the sun,
  The higher he's a-getting,
The sooner will his race be run,
  And nearer he's to setting.

That age is best which is the first,
  When youth and blood are warmer;   10
But being spent, the worse and worst
  Times still succeed the former.

Then be not coy, but use your time,
  And while ye may, go marry;
For, having lost but once your prime,
  You may forever tarry.

                                        1648

Delight in Disorder

  A sweet disorder in the dress
  Kindles in clothes a wantonness:
  A lawn about the shoulders thrown
  Into a fine distraction:
  An erring lace, which here and there
  Enthralls the crimson stomacher:
  A cuff neglectful, and thereby
  Ribbons to flow confusedly:
  A winning wave (deserving note)
  In the tempestuous petticoat: 10
  A careless shoe-string, in whose tye
  I see a wild civility:
  Do more bewitch me, then when art
  Is too precise in every part.

                                        1648

ANONYMOUS

The Guest

Yet if his majesty, our sovereign lord,
Should of his own accord
Friendly himself invite,
And say, "I'll be your guest to-morrow night,"
How should we stir ourselves, call and command
All hands to work! "Let no man idle stand.

Set me fine Spanish tables in the hall,
See they be fitted all;
Let there be room to eat,
And order taken that there want no meat.   10
See every sconce and candlestick made bright,
That without tapers they may give a light.
Look to the presence: are the carpets spread,
The dazie o'er the head,
The cushions in the chairs,
And all the candles lighted on the stairs?
Perfume the chambers, and in any case
Let each man give attendance in his place."
Thus if the king were coming would we do;
And 'twere good reason too: 20
For 'tis a duteous thing
To show all honor to an earthly king;
And, after all our travail and our cost,
So he be pleased, to think no labor lost.
But at the coming of the King of Heaven
All's set at six and seven:
We wallow in our sin;
Christ cannot find a chamber in the inn.
We entertain him always like a stranger,
And, as at first, still lodge him in the manger.   30
Before 1648

GEORGE HERBERT

Discipline

Throw away thy rod,
Throw away thy wrath:
    O my God,
Take the gentle path.

For my heart's desire
Unto thine is bent:
    I aspire
To a full consent.

Not a word or look
I affect to own,
    But by book,
And thy book alone.   10

Though I fail, I weep:
Though I halt in pace,
    Yet I creep
To the throne of grace.

Then let wrath remove;
Love will do the deed:
    For with love
Stony hearts will bleed.   20

Love is swift of foot;
Love's a man of war,
    And can shoot,
And can hit from far.

Who can scape his bow?
That which wrought on thee,
    Brought thee low,
Needs must work on me.

Throw away thy rod;
Though man frailties hath,   30
    Thou art God:
Throw away thy wrath.

        1633

The Pulley

When God at first made man,
Having a glass of blessing standing by;
  "Let us," said he, "pour on him all we can:
Let the world's riches, which dispersèd lie,
  Contract into a span."

  So Strength first made a way;
Then Beauty flowed; then Wisdom, Honor, Pleasure.
  When almost all was out, God made a stay,

Perceiving that alone, of all his treasure,
　　Rest in the bottom lay.　　　　　　　　　　10

"For if I should," said he,
"Bestow this jewel also on my creature,
　　He would adore my gifts instead of me,
And rest in Nature, not the God of Nature;
　　So both should losers be.

"Yet let him keep the rest,
But keep them with repining restlessness;
　　Let him be rich and weary, that at least,
If goodness lead him not, yet weariness
　　May toss him to my breast."　　　　　　　20
　　　　　　　　　　1633

Love

Love bade me welcome; yet my soul drew back,
　　Guilty of dust and sin.
But quick-eyed Love, observing me grow slack
　　From my first entrance in,
Drew nearer to me, sweetly questioning,
　　If I lacked anything.

"A guest," I answered, "worthy to be here:"
　　Love said, "You shall be he."
"I, the unkind, ungrateful? Ah, my dear,
　　I cannot look on thee!"　　　　　　　　10
Love took my hand and smiling did reply,
　　"Who made the eyes but I?"

"Truth, Lord; but I have marred them: let my shame
　　Go where it doth deserve."
"And know you not," says Love, "who bore the blame?"
　　"My dear, then I will serve."
"You must sit down," says Love, "and taste my meat."
　　So I did sit and eat.
　　　　　　　　　　1633

EDMUND WALLER

Go, Lovely Rose!

Go, lovely rose!
Tell her that wastes her time and me,
That now she knows,
When I resemble her to thee,
How sweet and fair she seems to be.

Tell her that's young,
And shuns to have her graces spied,
That hadst thou sprung
In deserts, where no men abide,
Thou must have uncommended died.   10

Small is the worth
Of beauty from the light retired;
Bid her come forth,
Suffer herself to be desired,
And not blush so to be admired.

Then die! that she
The common fate of all things rare
May read in thee;
How small a part of time they share
That are so wondrous sweet and fair!   20

1664

SIR JOHN SUCKLING

Why So Pale and Wan, Fond Lover?

Why so pale and wan, fond lover?
    Prithee, why so pale?
Will, when looking well can't move her,
    Looking ill prevail?
    Prithee, why so pale?

Why so dull and mute, young sinner?
    Prithee, why so mute?

Will, when speaking well can't win her,
    Saying nothing do't?
    Prithee, why so mute?   10

Quit, quit for shame! This will not move,
    This cannot take her.
If of herself she will not love,
    Nothing can make her:
    The devil take her!

1646

A Doubt of Martyrdom

O for some honest lover's ghost,
    Some kind unbodied post
        Sent from the shades below!
        I strangely long to know
Whether the noble chaplets wear,
Those that their mistress' scorn did bear,
        Or those that were used kindly.

For whatsoe'er they tell us here
    To make those sufferings dear,
        'Twill there, I fear, be found   10
        That to the being crowned
T'have loved alone will not suffice,
Unless we also have been wise
        And have our loves enjoyed.

What posture can we think him in
    That, here unloved, again
        Departs, and's thither gone
        Where each sits by his own?
Or how can that Elysium be
Where I my mistress still must see   20
        Circled in others' arms?

For there the judges all are just,
    And Sophonisba must
        Be his whom she held dear,
        Not his who loved her here:

The sweet Philoclea, since she died,
Lies by her Pirocles his side,
   Not by Amphialus.

Some bays, perchance, or myrtle bough,
  For difference crowns the brow   30
    Of those kind souls that were
    The noble martyrs here;
And if that be the only odds
(As who can tell?) ye kinder gods,
    Give me the woman here.
                1646

Constancy

Out upon it! I have loved
  Three whole days together;
And am like to love three more,
  If it prove fair weather.

Time shall moult away his wings
  Ere he shall discover
In the whole wide world again
  Such a constant lover.

But the spite on't is, no praise
  Is due at all to me: 10
Love with me had made no stays,
  Had it any been but she.

Had it any been but she,
  And that very face,
There had been at least ere this
  A dozen dozen in her place.
             1659

HENRY VAUGHAN

They Are All Gone

They are all gone into the world of light!
 And I alone sit ling'ring here;
Their very memory is fair and bright,
 And my sad thoughts doth clear.

It glows and glitters in my cloudy breast
 Like stars upon some gloomy grove,
Or those faint beams in which this hill is drest,
 After the sun's remove.

I see them walking in an air of glory,
 Whose light doth trample on my days: 10
My days, which are at best but dull and hoary,
 Mere glimmering and decays.

O holy hope! and high humility,
 High as the heavens above!
These are your walks, and you have showed them me
 To kindle my cold love.

Dear, beauteous death! the jewel of the just,
 Shining nowhere, but in the dark;
What mysteries do lie beyond thy dust;
 Could man outlook that mark!   20

He that hath found some fledged bird's nest may know
 At first sight, if the bird be flown;
But what fair well or grove he sings in now,
 That is to him unknown.

And yet, as angels in some brighter dreams
 Call to the soul, when man doth sleep:
So some strange thoughts transcend our wonted themes,
 And into glory peep.

If a star were confined into a tomb
 Her captive flames must needs burn there;   30

But when the hand that locked her up gives room,
  She'll shine through all the sphere.

O Father of eternal life, and all
  Created glories under thee!
Resume thy spirit from this world of thrall
  Into true liberty.

Either disperse these mists, which blot and fill
  My perspective (still) as they pass,
Or else remove me hence unto that hill,
  Where I shall need no glass.   40

                    1655

JOHN DRYDEN

Absalom and Achitophel[1]

In pious times, ere priestcraft did begin,
Before polygamy was made a sin;
When man on many multiplied his kind,
Ere one to one was cursedly confined;
When nature prompted, and no law denied
Promiscuous use of concubine and bride;
Then Israel's monarch after Heaven's own heart,
His vigorous warmth did variously impart
To wives and slaves; and, wide as his command,
Scattered his Maker's image through the land.   10
Michal of royal blood, the crown did wear;
A soil ungrateful to the tiller's care:
Not so the rest; for several mothers bore
To godlike David several sons before.
But since like slaves his bed they did ascend,

---

[1] Dryden uses the story of the revolt of Absalom (2 Samuel, xiii–xviii) as a cover for his satire on Anthony Ashley Cooper, Earl of Shaftesbury, who wished to make Charles II's illegitimate son, James, Duke of Monmouth, the heir to the throne, in place of Charles' Catholic brother, James, Duke of York.

7. *Israel's monarch,* David; Charles II.
11. *Michal,* Catharine of Portugal, Queen to Charles.

No true succession could their seed attend.
Of all this numerous progeny was none
So beautiful, so brave, as Absalon:
Whether, inspired by some diviner lust,
His father got him with a greater gust;   20
Or that his conscious destiny made way,
By manly beauty, to imperial sway.
Early in foreign fields he won renown
With kings and states allied to Israel's crown;
In peace the thoughts of war he could remove,
And seemed as he were only born for love.
Whate'er he did, was done with so much ease,
In him alone 't was natural to please:
His motions all accompanied with grace;
And paradise was opened in his face.   30
With secret joy indulgent David viewed
His youthful image in his son renewed:
To all his wishes nothing he denied;
And made the charming Annabel his bride.
What faults he had (for who from faults is free?)
His father could not or he would not see.
Some warm excesses which the law forbore,
Were construed youth that purged by boiling o'er,
And Amnon's murder, by a specious name,
Was called a just revenge for injured fame.   40
Thus praised and loved the noble youth remained,
While David, undisturbed, in Sion reigned.
But life can never be sincerely blest;
Heav'n punishes the bad, and proves the best.
The Jews, a headstrong, moody, murm'ring race,
As ever tried th' extent and stretch of grace;
God's pampered people, whom, debauched with ease,
No king could govern, nor no God could please
(Gods they had tried of every shape and size,
That god-smiths could produce, or priests devise);   50
These Adam-wits, too fortunately free,

18. *Absalon*, James, Duke of Monmouth.
34. *Annabel*, Anne Scott, Countess of Buccleuch.
42. *Sion*, London.   45. *The Jews*, the English.

Began to dream they wanted liberty;
And when no rule, no precedent was found,
Of men by laws less circumscribed and bound;
They led their wild desires to woods and caves,
And thought that all but savages were slaves.
They who, when Saul was dead, without a blow,
Made foolish Ishbosheth the crown forgo;
Who banished David did from Hebron bring,
And with a general shout proclaimed him king: 60
Those very Jews, who, at their very best,
Their humor more than loyalty expressed,
Now wondered why so long they had obeyed
An idol monarch, which their hands had made;
Thought they might ruin him they could create,
Or melt him to that golden calf, a State.
But these were random bolts; no formed design,
Nor interest made the factious crowd to join:
The sober part of Israel, free from stain,
Well knew the value of a peaceful reign;   70
And, looking backward with a wise affright,
Saw seams of wounds, dishonest to the sight:
In contemplation of whose ugly scars
They cursed the memory of civil wars.
The moderate sort of men, thus qualified,
Inclined the balance to the better side;
And David's mildness managed it so well,
The bad found no occasion to rebel.
But when to sin our biased nature leans,
The careful Devil is still at hand with means;   80
And providently pimps for ill desires:
The Good Old Cause, revived, a plot requires.
Plots, true or false, are necessary things,
To raise up commonwealths and ruin kings.
　　Th' inhabitants of old Jerusalem
Were Jebusites; the town so called from them;
And theirs the native right.

57. *Saul*, Oliver Cromwell.   58. *Ishbosheth*, Richard Cromwell.
59. *Hebron*, Scotland.   82. *Good Old Cause*, the Commonwealth.
85. *Jerusalem*, London.   86. *Jebusites*, Catholics.

But when the chosen people grew more strong,
The rightful cause at length became the wrong;
And every loss the men of Jebus bore,   90
They still were thought God's enemies the more.
Thus worn and weakened, well or ill content,
Submit they must to David's government:
Impoverished and deprived of all command,
Their taxes doubled as they lost their land;
And, what was harder yet to flesh and blood,
Their gods disgraced, and burned like common wood.
This set the heathen priesthood in a flame;
For priests of all religions are the same:
Of whatsoe'er descent their godhead be,   100
Stock, stone, or other homely pedigree,
In his defense his servants are as bold,
As if he had been born of beaten gold.
The Jewish rabbins, though their enemies,
In this conclude them honest men and wise:
For 'twas their duty, all the learnéd think,
T' espouse his cause, by whom they eat and drink.
From hence began that Plot, the nation's curse,
Bad in itself, but represented worse,
Raised in extremes, and in extremes decried,   110
With oaths affirmed, with dying vows denied,
Not weighed or winnowed by the multitude;
But swallowed in the mass, unchewed and crude.
Some truth there was, but dashed and brewed with lies,
To please the fools, and puzzle all the wise:
Succeeding times did equal folly call,
Believing nothing, or believing all.
Th' Egyptian rites the Jebusites embraced;
Where gods were recommended by their taste.
Such sav'ry deities must needs be good,   120
As served at once for worship and for food.
By force they could not introduce these gods,
For ten to one in former days was odds;

88. *chosen people*, Protestants.
104. *Jewish rabbins*, clergy of the Anglican Church.
108. *Plot*, Popish Plot.   118. *Egyptian*, French.

So fraud was used (the sacrificer's trade):
Fools are more hard to conquer than persuade.
Their busy teachers mingled with the Jews,
And raked for converts e'en the court and stews:
Which Hebrew priests the more unkindly took,
Because the fleece accompanies the flock.
Some thought they God's anointed meant to slay   130
By guns, invented since full many a day:
Our author swears it not; but who can know
How far the Devil and Jebusites may go?
This Plot, which failed for want of common sense,
Had yet a deep and dangerous consequence
For, as when raging fevers boil the blood,
The standing lake soon floats into a flood,
And every hostile humor, which before
Slept quiet in its channels, bubbles o'er;
So several factions from this first ferment   140
Work up to foam, and threat the government.
Some by their friends, more by themselves thought wise,
Opposed the power to which they could not rise.
Some had in courts been great, and thrown from thence,
Like fiends were hardened in impenitence.
Some, by their monarch's fatal mercy, grown
From pardoned rebels kinsmen to the throne,
Were raised in power and public office high;
Strong bands, if bands ungrateful men could tie.
    Of these the false Achitophel was first;   150
A name to all succeeding ages curst:
For close designs and crooked counsels fit;
Sagacious, bold, and turbulent of wit;
Restless, unfixed in principles and place;
In power unpleased, impatient of disgrace:
A fiery soul, which, working out its way,   ⎫
Fretted the pigmy body to decay,   ⎬
And o'er-informed the tenement of clay.   ⎭
A daring pilot in extremity;
Pleased with the danger, when the waves went high, 160
He sought the storms; but, for a calm unfit,

150. *Achitophel*, Anthony Ashley Cooper, Earl of Shaftesbury.

Would steer too nigh the sands, to boast his wit.
Great wits are sure to madness near allied,
And thin partitions do their bounds divide;
Else why should he, with wealth and honor blest,
Refuse his age the needful hours of rest?
Punish a body which he could not please;
Bankrupt of life, yet prodigal of ease?
And all to leave what with his toil he won,
To that unfeathered two-legg'd thing, a son   170
Got, while his soul did huddled notions try
And born a shapeless lump, like anarchy.
In friendship false, implacable in hate;
Resolved to ruin or to rule the State.
To compass this the triple bond he broke, ⎫
The pillars of the public safety shook;   ⎬
And fitted Israel for a foreign yoke;   ⎭
Then seized with fear, yet still affecting fame,
Usurped a patriot's all-atoning name.
So easy still it proves in factious times,   180
With public zeal to cancel private crimes.
How safe is treason, and how sacred ill,
Where none can sin against the people's will!
Where crowds can wink, and no offense be known,
Since in another's guilt they find their own!
Yet fame deserved no enemy can grudge;
The statesman we abhor, but praise the judge.
In Israel's courts ne'er sat an Abbethdin
With more discerning eyes, or hands more clean;
Unbribed, unsought, the wretched to redress;   190
Swift of dispatch, and easy of access.
Oh, had he been content to serve the crown,
With virtues only proper to the gown;
Or had the rankness of the soil been freed
From cockle, that oppressed the noble seed;
David for him his tuneful harp had strung,
And Heav'n had wanted one immortal song.
But wild *Ambition* loves to slide, not stand,
And *Fortune's* ice prefers to *Virtue's* land.
Achitophel, grown weary to possess   200

A lawful fame, and lazy happiness,
Disdained the golden fruit to gather free,
And lent the crowd his arm to shake the tree.
Now, manifest of crimes contrived long since,
He stood at bold defiance with his prince;
Held up the buckler of the people's cause
Against the crown, and skulked behind the laws.
The wished occasion of the Plot he takes;
Some circumstances finds, but more he makes.
By buzzing emissaries fills the ears   210
Of list'ning crowds with jealousies and fears
Of arbitrary counsels brought to light,
And proves the king himself a Jebusite.
Weak arguments! which yet he knew full well
Were strong with people easy to rebel.
For, governed by the moon, the giddy Jews
Tread the same track when she the prime renews;
And once in twenty years, their scribes record,
By natural instinct they change their lord. . . .

1681

JOSEPH ADDISON

Hymn

The spacious firmament on high,
With all the blue ethereal sky,
And spangled heavens, a shinging frame,
Their great Original proclaim.
Th' unwearied Sun from day to day
Does his Creator's power display;
And publishes to every land
The work of an Almighty hand.

Soon as the evening shades prevail,
The Moon takes up the wondrous tale;   10
And nightly to the listening Earth
Repeats the story of her birth:

Whilst all the stars that round her burn,
And all the planets in their turn,
Confirm the tidings as they roll,
And spread the truth from pole to pole.

What though in solemn silence all
Move round the dark terrestrial ball;
What though nor real voice nor sound
Amidst their radiant orbs be found?   20
In Reason's ear they all rejoice,
And utter forth a glorious voice;
For ever singing as they shine,
'The Hand that made us is divine.'

1712

ALEXANDER POPE

An Essay on Criticism

PART I

'Tis hard to say, if greater want of skill
Appear in writing or in judging ill;
But, of the two, less dang'rous is th' offense
To tire our patience, than mislead our sense.
Some few in that, but numbers err in this,
Ten censure wrong for one who writes amiss;
A fool might once himself alone expose,
Now one in verse makes many more in prose.
    'Tis with our judgments as our watches, none
Go just alike, yet each believes his own.   10
In Poets as true Genius is but rare,
True Taste as seldom is the Critic's share;
Both must alike from Heav'n derive their light,
These born to judge, as well as those to write.
Let such teach others who themselves excel,
And censure freely who have written well.
Authors are partial to their wit, 'tis true,
But are not Critics to their judgment too?
    Yet if we look more closely, we shall find

Most have the seeds of judgment in their mind: 20
Nature affords at least a glimm'ring light;
The lines, though touched but faintly, are drawn right.
But as the slightest sketch, if justly traced, ⎫
Is by ill-coloring but the more disgraced, ⎬
So by false learning is good sense defaced: ⎭
Some are bewildered in the maze of schools,
And some made coxcombs Nature meant but fools.
In search of wit these lose their common sense,
And then turn Critics in their own defense:
Each burns alike, who can, or cannot write,   30
Or with a Rival's, or an Eunuch's spite.
All fools have still an itching to deride,
And fain would be upon the laughing side.
If Mævius scribble in Apollo's spite,
There are who judge still worse than he can write.
   Some have at first for Wits, then Poets passed,
Turned Critics next, and proved plain fools at last.
Some neither can for Wits nor Critics pass,
As heavy mules are neither horse nor ass.
Those half-learn'd witlings, num'rous in our isle,   40
As half-formed insects on the banks of Nile;
Unfinished things, one knows not what to call,
Their generation's so equivocal:
To tell 'em, would a hundred tongues require,
Or one vain wit's, that might a hundred tire.
   But you who seek to give and merit fame,
And justly bear a Critic's noble name,
Be sure yourself and your own reach to know,
How far your genius, taste, and learning go;
Launch not beyond your depth, but be discreet,   50
And mark that point where sense and dullness meet.
   Nature to all things fixed the limits fit,
And wisely curbed proud man's pretending wit.
As on the land while here the ocean gains,
In other parts it leaves wide sandy plains;
Thus in the soul while memory prevails,
The solid pow'r of understanding fails;
Where beams of warm imagination play,

The memory's soft figures melt away.
One science only will one genius fit;   60
So vast is art, so narrow human wit:
Not only bounded to peculiar arts,
But oft in those confined to single parts.
Like kings we lose the conquests gained before,
By vain ambition still to make them more;
Each might his sev'ral province well command,
Would all but stoop to what they understand.
     First follow Nature, and your judgment frame
By her just standard, which is still the same:
Unerring Nature, still divinely bright,   70
One clear, unchanged, and universal light,
Life, force, and beauty, must to all impart,
At once the source, and end, and test of Art.
Art from that fund each just supply provides
Works without show, and without pomp presides:
In some fair body thus th' informing soul
With spirits feeds, with vigor fills the whole,
Each motion guides, and ev'ry nerve sustains
Itself unseen, but in th' effects, remains.
Some, to whom Heav'n in wit has been profuse,   80
Want as much more, to turn it to its use;
For wit and judgment often are at strife,
Though meant each other's aid, like man and wife.
'Tis more to guide, than spur the Muse's steed;
Restrain his fury, than provoke his speed;
The wingéd courser, like a gen'rous horse,
Shows most true mettle when you check his course.
     Those Rules of old discovered, not devised,
Are Nature still, but Nature methodized;
Nature, like liberty, is but restrained   90
By the same laws which first herself ordained.
     Hear how learn'd Greece her useful rules indites,
When to repress, and when indulge our flights:
High on Parnassus' top her sons she showed,
And pointed out those arduous paths they trod;
Held from afar, aloft, th' immortal prize,
And urged the rest by equal steps to rise.

Just precepts thus from great examples giv'n,
She drew from them what they derived from Heav'n.
The gen'rous Critic fanned the Poet's fire,   100
And taught the world with reason to admire.
Then Criticism the Muse's handmaid proved,
To dress her charms, and make her more belov'd:
But following wits from that intention strayed,
Who could not win the mistress, wooed the maid;
Against the Poets their own arms they turned
Sure to hate most the men from whom they learned.
So modern 'Pothecaries, taught the art
By Doctors' bills to play the Doctor's part,
Bold in the practice of mistaken rules,   110
Prescribe, apply, and call their masters fools
Some on the leaves of ancient authors prey
Nor time nor moths e'er spoiled so much as they.
Some dryly plain, without invention's aid,
Write dull receipts how poems may be made
These leave the sense, their learning to display
And those explain the meaning quite away.
    You then whose judgment the right course would steer,
Know well each Ancient's proper character;
His fable, subject, scope in ev'ry page;   120
Religion, Country, genius of his Age:
Without all these at once before your eyes,
Cavil you may, but never criticize.
Be Homer's works your study and delight,
Read them by day, and meditate by night;
Thence form your judgment, thence your maxims bring,
And trace the Muses upward to their spring.
Still with itself compared, his text peruse;
And let your comment be the Mantuan Muse.
    When first young Maro in his boundless mind   130
A work t' outlast immortal Rome designed,
Perhaps he seemed above the critic's law,
And but from Nature's fountains scorned to draw:
But when t' examine every part he came,
Nature and Homer were, he found, the same.

Convinced, amazed, he checks the bold design; ⎫
And rules as strict his labored work confine,   ⎬
As if the Stagirite o'erlooked each line.   ⎭
Learn hence for ancient rules a just esteem;
To copy Nature is to copy them.   140
    Some beauties yet no Precepts can declare,
For there's a happiness as well as care.
Music resembles Poetry, in each   ⎫
Are nameless graces which no methods teach,   ⎬
And which a master-hand alone can reach.   ⎭
If, where the rules not far enough extend
(Since rules were made but to promote their end),
Some lucky License answer to the full
Th' intent proposed, that License is a rule.
Thus Pegasus, a nearer way to take,   150
May boldly deviate from the common track;
From vulgar bounds with brave disorder part,
And snatch a grace beyond the reach of art,
Which without passing through the judgment, gains
The heart, and all its end at once attains.
In prospects thus, some objects please our eyes, ⎫
Which out of nature's common order rise,   ⎬
The shapeless rock, or hanging precipice.   ⎭
Great wits sometimes may gloriously offend,
And rise to faults true Critics dare not mend. 160
But though the Ancients thus their rules invade
(As Kings dispense with laws themselves have made),
Moderns, beware! or if you must offend
Against the precept, ne'er transgress its End;
Let it be seldom, and compelled by need;
And have, at least, their precedent to plead.
The Critic else proceeds without remorse,
Seizes your fame, and puts his laws in force.
    I know there are, to whose presumptuous thoughts
Those freer beauties, e'en in them, seem faults. 170
Some figures monstrous and mis-shaped appear,
Considered singly, or beheld too near,
Which, but proportioned to their light, or place,
Due distance reconciles to form and grace.

A prudent chief not always must display
His powers in equal ranks, and fair array.
But with th' occasion and the place comply,
Conceal his force, nay seem sometimes to fly.
Those oft are stratagems which error seem,
Nor is it Homer nods, but we that dream.   180
    Still green with bays each ancient Altar stands,
Above the reach of sacrilegious hands;
Secure from Flames, from Envy's fiercer rage,
Destructive War, and all-involving Age.
See, from each clime the learn'd their incense bring!
Hear, in all tongues consenting Pæans ring!
In praise so just let ev'ry voice be joined,
And fill the gen'ral chorus of mankind.
Hail, Bards triumphant! born in happier days;
Immortal heirs of universal praise!   190
Whose honors with increase of ages grow,
As streams roll down, enlarging as they flow;
Nations unborn your mighty names shall sound,
And worlds applaud that must not yet be found!
Oh may some spark of your celestial fire,
The last, the meanest of your sons inspire
(That on weak wings, from far, pursues your flights;
Glows while he reads, but trembles as he writes),
To teach vain Wits a science little known,
T' admire superior sense, and doubt their own!   200

1711

Epistle to Dr. Arbuthnot [1]

P. Shut, shut the door, good John! fatigued, I said,
Tie up the knocker, say I'm sick, I'm dead.
The Dog-star rages! nay 'tis past a doubt,
All Bedlam, or Parnassus, is let out:
Fire in each eye, and papers in each hand,

[1] This *Epistle* was written in reply to abusive attacks on Pope. Dr. Arbuthnot was Pope's physician and friend. Of the numerous persons of the time referred to by Pope only those who appear under pseudonyms are identified in the notes. In the opening line Pope speaks to his servant, John.
    1. *John*, John Searl, Pope's servant.

They rave, recite, and madden round the land.
      What walls can guard me, or what shade can hide?
They pierce my thickets, through my Grot they glide;
By land, by water, they renew the charge;
They stop the chariot, and they board the barge.   10
No place is sacred, not the Church is free;
E'en Sunday shines no Sabbath-day to me;
Then from the Mint walks forth the Man of rime,
Happy to catch me just at Dinner-time.
      Is there a Parson, much bemused in beer,
A maudlin Poetess, a riming Peer,
A Clerk, foredoomed his father's soul to cross,
Who pens a Stanza, when he should *engross?*
Is there, who, locked from ink and paper, scrawls
With desp'rate charcoal round his darkened walls?   20
All fly to Twit'nam, and in humble strain
Apply to me, to keep them mad or vain.
Arthur, whose giddy son neglects the Laws,
Imputes to me and my damned works the cause:
Poor Cornus sees his frantic wife elope,
And curses Wit, and Poetry, and Pope.
      Friend to my Life (which did not you prolong,
The world had wanted many an idle song)
What Drop or Nostrum can this plague remove?
Or which must end me, a Fool's wrath or love?   30
A dire dilemma! either way I'm sped,
If foes, they write, if friends, they read me dead.
Seized and tied down to judge, how wretched I!
Who can't be silent, and who will not lie.
To laugh, were want of goodness and of grace,
And to be grave, exceeds all Pow'r of face.
I sit with sad civility, I read
With honest anguish, and an aching head;
And drop at last, but in unwilling ears,
This saving counsel, "Keep your piece nine years."   40

    8. *Grot,* Pope had a grotto, which still exists, on his estate at Twickenham.
    13. *Mint,* a part of London used as a refuge by insolvent debtors, who
could only leave it on Sunday, when they were safe from arrest.
    23. *Arthur,* Arthur Moore.   25. *Cornus,* possibly Sir Robert Walpole.

"Nine years!" cries he, who high in Drury-Lane,
Lulled by soft Zephyrs through the broken pane,
Rimes ere he wakes, and prints before Term ends,
Obliged by hunger, and request of friends:
"The piece, you think, is incorrect? why, take it,
I'm all submission, what you'd have it, make it."
   Three things another's modest wishes bound,
My Friendship, and a Prologue, and ten pound.
   Pitholeon sends to me: "You know his Grace,
I want a Patron; ask him for a Place."   50
Pitholeon libeled me—"but here's a letter
Informs you, Sir, 'twas when he knew no better.
Dare you refuse him? Curll invites to dine,
He'll write a *Journal*, or he'll turn Divine."
   Bless me! a packet.—" 'Tis a stranger sues,
A Virgin Tragedy, an Orphan Muse."
If I dislike it, "Furies, death and rage!"
If I approve, "Commend it to the Stage."
There (thank my stars) my whole Commission ends,
The Play'rs and I are, luckily, no friends.   60
Fired that the house reject him, " 'Sdeath I'll print it,
And shame the fools——Your Int'rest, Sir, with Lintot!"
Lintot, dull rogue! will think your price too much:
"Not, Sir, if you revise it, and retouch."
All my demurs but double his Attacks;
At last he whispers, "Do; and we go snacks."
Glad of a quarrel, straight I clap the door,
Sir, let me see your works and you no more.
   'Tis sung, when Midas' Ears began to spring
(Midas, a sacred person and a king),   70
His very Minister who spied them first,
(Some say his Queen) was forced to speak, or burst.
And is not mine, my friend, a sorer case,
When ev'ry coxcomb perks them in my face?
A. Good friend, forbear! you deal in dang'rous things.

49. *Pitholeon*, Pope states that this was the name taken by a foolish poet of Rhodes.
53. *Curll*, Edmund Curll, a dishonest bookseller.
62. *Lintot*, Bernard Lintot, Pope's publisher.

I'd never name Queens, Ministers, or Kings;
Keep close to Ears, and those let asses prick;
'Tis nothing— P. Nothing? if they bite and kick?
Out with it, *Dunciad!* let the secret pass,
That secret to each fool, that he's an Ass: 80
The truth once told (and wherefore should we lie?)
The Queen of Midas slept, and so may I.
    You think this cruel? take it for a rule,
No creature smarts so little as a fool.
Let peals of laughter, Codrus! round thee break,
Thou unconcerned canst hear the mighty crack:
Pit, Box, and gall'ry in convulsions hurled,
Thou stand'st unshook amidst a bursting world.
Who shames a Scribbler? break one cobweb through,
He spins the slight, self-pleasing thread anew: 90
Destroy his fib or sophistry, in vain,
The creature's at his dirty work again,
Throned in the center of his thin designs,
Proud of a vast extent of flimsy lines!
Whom have I hurt? has Poet yet, or Peer,
Lost the arched eye-brow, or Parnassian sneer?
And has not Colley still his Lord and Whore?
His butchers Henley? his freemasons Moore?
Does not one table Bavius still admit?
Still to one Bishop Philips seem a wit?   100
Still Sappho— A. Hold! for God's sake—you'll offend,
No Names!—be calm!—learn prudence of a friend!
I too could write, and I am twice as tall;
But foes like these— P. One Flatt'rer's worse than all.
Of all mad creatures, if the learn'd are right,
It is the slaver kills, and not the bite.
A fool quite angry is quite innocent:
Alas! 'tis ten times worse when they *repent.*

97. *Colley,* Colley Cibber, made poet laureate in 1730.
    98. *Henley,* John Henley, a preacher known as "the Orator"; *Moore,*
James Moore-Smyth, son of Arthur Moore, mentioned above.
    99. *Bavius,* a Roman poetaster.
    100. *Philips,* Ambrose Philips, whose patron was Bishop Boulter.
    101. *Sappho,* Lady Mary Wortley Montagu.

One dedicates in high heroic prose,
And ridicules beyond a hundred foes: 110
One from all Grubstreet will my fame defend,
And, more abusive, calls himself my friend.
This prints my *Letters*, that expects a bribe,
And others roar aloud, "Subscribe, subscribe."
    There are, who to my person pay their court:
I cough like Horace, and, though lean, am short,
Ammon's great son one shoulder had too high,
Such Ovid's nose, and "Sir! you have an Eye"—
Go on, obliging creatures, make me see
All that disgraced my Betters, met in me.   120
Say for my comfort, languishing in bed,
"Just so immortal Maro held his head:"
And when I die, be sure you let me know
Great Homer died three thousand years ago.
    Why did I write? what sin to me unknown
Dipped me in ink, my parents', or my own?
As yet a child, nor yet a fool to fame,
I lisped in numbers, for the numbers came.
I left no calling for this idle trade,
No duty broke, no father disobeyed.   130
The Muse but served to ease some friend, not Wife,
To help me through this long disease, my Life,
To second, Arbuthnot! thy Art and Care,
And teach the Being you preserved, to bear.
    But why then publish? Granville the polite,
And knowing Walsh, would tell me I could write;
Well-natured Garth inflamed with early praise;
And Congreve loved, and Swift endured my lays;
The courtly Talbot, Somers, Sheffield, read;
E'en mitered Rochester would nod the head,   140

117. *Ammon's great son*, Alexander the Great.
122. *Maro*, Virgil.   135. *Granville*, George Granville, Lansdown.
136. *Walsh*, William Walsh, a literary friend of Pope.
137. *Garth*, Dr. Samuel Garth.
139. *Talbot*, Charles, Duke of Shrewsbury; *Somers*, John, Lord Somers; *Sheffield*, John, Earl of Mulgrave, Duke of Buckinghamshire. All three of these men encouraged Pope in his early work.
140. *Rochester*, Francis Atterbury, Bishop of Rochester.

And St. John's self (great Dryden's friends before)
With open arms received one Poet more.
Happy my studies, when by these approved!
Happier their author, when by these belov'd,
From these the world will judge of men and books,
Not from the Burnets, Oldmixons, and Cookes.
    Soft were my numbers; who could take offense,
While pure Description held the place of Sense?
Like gentle Fanny's was my flow'ry theme,
A painted mistress, or a purling stream.   150
Yet then did Gildon draw his venal quill;—
I wished the man a dinner, and sat still.
Yet then did Dennis rave in furious fret;
I never answered,—I was not in debt.
If want provoked, or madness made them print,
I waged no war with Bedlam or the Mint.
    Did some more sober Critic come abroad;
If wrong, I smiled; if right, I kissed the rod.
Pains, reading, study, are their just pretense,
And all they want is spirit, taste, and sense.   160
Commas and points they set exactly right,
And 'twere a sin to rob them of their mite.
Yet ne'er one sprig of laurel graced these ribalds,
From slashing Bentley down to pidling Tibalds:
Each wight, who reads not, and but scans and spells,
Each Word-catcher, that lives on syllables,
E'en such small Critics some regard may claim,
Preserved in Milton's or in Shakespeare's name.
Pretty! in amber to observe the forms
Of hairs, or straws, or dirt, or grubs, or worms!   170
The things, we know, are neither rich nor rare,

141. *St. John*, Bolingbroke, to whom Pope dedicated the *Essay on Man*.
146. *Burnets, Oldmixons, and Cookes*, Pope calls these men "Authors of secret and scandalous history."
149. *Fanny*, Lord Hervey, described in lines 305ff. as *Sporus*.
151. *Gildon*, Charles Gildon, a contemporary critic.
153. *Dennis*, John Dennis, a critic who was a life-long foe of Pope.
164. *Bentley*, Richard Bentley the famous classical scholar; *Tibalds*, Lewis Theobald, whom Pope made the hero of the *Dunciad* because he produced a better edition of Shakespeare than did Pope.

But wonder how the devil they got there.
   Were others angry: I excused them too;
Well might they rage, I gave them but their due.
A man's true merit 'tis not hard to find;
But each man's secret standard in his mind,
That Casting-weight pride adds to emptiness,
This, who can gratify? for who can guess?
The Bard whom pilfered Pastorals renown,
Who turns a Persian tale for half a Crown,   180
Just writes to make his barrenness appear,
And strains, from hard-bound brains, eight lines a year;
He, who still wanting, though he lives on theft,
Steals much, spends little, yet has nothing left:
And He, who now to sense, now nonsense leaning,
Means not, but blunders round about a meaning:
And He, whose fustian's so sublimely bad,
It is not Poetry, but prose run mad:
All these, my modest Satire bade translate,
And owned that nine such Poets made a Tate.   190
How did they fume, and stamp, and roar, and chafe!
And swear, not Addison himself was safe.
   Peace to all such! but were there One whose fires
True Genius kindles, and fair Fame inspires;
Bless'd with each talent and each art to please,
And born to write, converse, and live with ease:
Should such a man, too fond to rule alone,
Bear, like the Turk, no brother near the throne,
View him with scornful, yet with jealous eyes,
And hate for arts that caused himself to rise;   200
Damn with faint praise, assent with civil leer,
And without sneering, teach the rest to sneer;
Willing to wound, and yet afraid to strike,
Just hint a fault, and hesitate dislike;
Alike reserved to blame, or to commend,
A tim'rous foe, and a suspicious friend;
Dreading e'en fools, by Flatterers besieged,

179. *The Bard*, Ambrose Philips, author of pastoral poetry.
190. *Tate*, Nahum Tate, a poet laureate of the early eighteenth century.
192. *Addison*, Joseph Addison.

And so obliging, that he ne'er obliged;
Like Cato, give his little Senate laws,
And sit attentive to his own applause;   210
While Wits and Templars ev'ry sentence raise,
And wonder with a foolish face of praise:—
Who but must laugh, if such a man there be?
Who would not weep, if Atticus were he?
   What though my Name stood rubric on the walls
Or plastered posts, with claps, in capitals?
Or smoking forth, a hundred hawkers' load,
On wings of winds came flying all abroad?
I sought no homage from the Race that write;
I kept, like Asian Monarchs, from their sight: 220
Poems I heeded (now be-rimed so long)
No more than thou, great George! a birthday song.
I ne'er with wits or witlings passed my days,
To spread about the itch of verse and praise;
Nor like a puppy, daggled through the town,
To fetch and carry sing-song up and down;
Nor at Rehearsals sweat, and mouthed, and cried,
With handkerchief and orange at my side;
But sick of fops, and poetry, and prate,
To Bufo, left the whole Castalian state.   230
   Proud as Apollo on his forkéd hill,
Sat full-blown Bufo, puffed by ev'ry quill;
Fed with soft Dedication all day long,
Horace and he went hand in hand in song.
His Library (where busts of Poets dead
And a true Pindar stood without a head),
Received of wits an undistinguished race,
Who first his judgment asked, and then a place:
Much they extolled his pictures, much his seat,
And flattered ev'ry day, and some days eat: 240
Till grown more frugal in his riper days,
He paid some bards with port, and some with praise:
To some a dry rehearsal saw assigned,
And others (harder still) he paid in kind.

209. *Cato,* an allusion to Addison's play by that name.
214. *Atticus,* Addison.   230. *Bufo,* Charles Montagu, Earl of Halifax.

Dryden alone (what wonder?) came not nigh,
Dryden alone escaped this judging eye:
But still the Great have kindness in reserve,
He helped to bury whom he helped to starve.
    May some choice patron bless each gray goose quill!
May ev'ry Bavius have his Bufo still!   250
So, when a Statesman wants a day's defense,
Or Envy holds a whole week's war with Sense,
Or simple pride for flatt'ry makes demands,
May dunce by dunce be whistled off my hands!
Bless'd be the Great! for those they take away,
And those they left me; for they left me Gay;
Left me to see neglected Genius bloom,
Neglected die, and tell it on his tomb:
Of all thy blameless life the sole return
My Verse, and Queensb'ry weeping o'er thy urn.   260
    Oh, let me live my own, and die so too!
(To live and die is all I have to do)
Maintain a Poet's dignity and ease,
And see what friends, and read what books I please;
Above a Patron, though I condescend
Sometimes to call a minister my friend.
I was not born for Courts or great affairs;
I pay my debts, believe, and say my pray'rs;
Can sleep without a Poem in my head;
Nor know, if Dennis be alive or dead.   270
    Why am I asked what next shall see the light?
Heav'ns! was I born for nothing but to write?
Has Life no joys for me? or (to be grave)
Have I no friend to serve, no soul to save?
"I found him close with Swift"—"Indeed? no doubt"
(Cries prating Balbus), "something will come out."
'Tis all in vain, deny it as I will.
"No, such a Genius never can lie still;"
And then for mine obligingly mistakes

256. *Gay*, John Gay, who wrote the *Beggar's Opera*.
260. *Queensb'ry*, the Duchess of Queensbury, the friend of Gay.
276. *Balbus*, Lord Kinnoul.

The first Lampoon Sir Will or Bubo makes.　　　　　280
Poor guiltless I! and can I choose but smile,
When ev'ry Coxcomb knows me by my Style?
　　Cursed be the verse, how well soe'er it flow,
That tends to make one worthy man my foe,
Give Virtue scandal, Innocence a fear,
Or from the soft-eyed Virgin steal a tear!
But he who hurts a harmless neighbor's peace
Insults fall'n worth, or Beauty in distress,
Who loves a Lie, lame slander helps about,
Who writes a Libel, or who copies out:　　　　　290
That Fop, whose pride affects a patron's name,
Yet absent, wounds an author's honest fame.
Who can your merit selfishly approve,
And show the sense of it without the love;
Who has the vanity to call you friend,
Yet wants the honor, injured, to defend;
Who tells whate'er you think, whate'er you say,
And, if he lie not, must at least betray:
Who to the Dean, and silver bell can swear,
And sees at Canons what was never there;　　　　　300
Who reads, but with a lust to misapply,
Make Satire a Lampoon, and Fiction, Lie.
A lash like mine no honest man shall dread,
But all such babbling blockheads in his stead.
　　Let Sporus tremble— A. What? that thing of silk,
Sporus, that mere white curd of Ass's milk!
Satire or sense, alas! can Sporus feel?
Who breaks a butterfly upon a wheel?
P. Yet let me flap this bug with gilded wings,
This painted child of dirt, that stinks and stings;　　　310
Whose buzz the witty and the fair annoys,
Yet wit ne'er tastes, and beauty ne'er enjoys:
So well-bred spaniels civilly delight
In mumbling of the game they dare not bite.
Eternal smiles his emptiness betray,

280. *Sir Will*, Sir William Yonge; *Bubo*, Bubb Doddington, a courtier and
patron of men of letters.
305. *Sporus*, Lord Hervey, who had ridiculed Pope's physical deformities.

As shallow streams run dimpling all the way.
Whether in florid impotence he speaks,
And, as the prompter breathes, the puppet squeaks;
Or at the ear of Eve, familiar Toad,
Half froth, half venom, spits himself abroad,   320
In puns, or politics, or tales, or lies,
Or spite, or smut, or rimes, or blasphemies.
His wit all see-saw, between that and this,
Now high, now low, now master up, now miss,
And he himself one vile Antithesis.
Amphibious thing! that acting either part,
The trifling head or the corrupted heart,
Fop at the toilet, flatt'rer at the board,
Now trips a Lady, and now struts a Lord.
Eve's tempter thus the Rabbins have expressed,   330
A Cherub's face, a reptile all the rest;
Beauty that shocks you, parts that none will trust;
Wit that can creep, and pride that licks the dust.
    Not Fortune's worshiper, nor fashion's fool,
Not Lucre's madman, nor Ambition's tool,
Not proud, nor servile;—be one Poet's praise,
That, if he pleased, he pleased by manly ways:
That Flatt'ry, e'en to Kings, he held a shame,
And thought a Lie in verse or prose the same.
That not in Fancy's maze he wandered long,   340
But stooped to Truth, and moralized his song:
That not for Fame, but Virtue's better end,
He stood the furious foe, the timid friend,
The damning critic, half approving wit,
The coxcomb hit, or fearing to be hit;
Laughed at the loss of friends he never had,
The dull, the proud, the wicked, and the mad;
The distant threats of vengeance on his head,
The blow unfelt, the tear he never shed;
The tale revived, the lie so oft o'erthrown,   350
Th' imputed trash, and dullness not his own;
The morals blackened when the writings 'scape,
The libeled person, and the pictured shape;

319. *Eve,* Queen Caroline.

Abuse, on all he loved, or loved him, spread,
A friend in exile, or a father dead;
The whisper, that to greatness still too near,
Perhaps, yet vibrates on his Sov'reign's ear:—
Welcome for thee, fair Virtue! all the past;
For thee, fair Virtue! welcome e'en the last!

    A. But why insult the poor, affront the great?   360
P. A knave's a knave, to me, in ev'ry state:
Alike my scorn, if he succeed or fail.
Sporus at court, or Japhet in a jail,
A hireling scribbler, or a hireling peer,
Knight of the post corrupt, or of the shire;
If on a Pillory, or near a Throne,
He gain his Prince's ear, or lose his own.

    Yet soft by nature, more a dupe than wit,
Sappho can tell you how this man was bit;
This dreaded Sat'rist Dennis will confess   370
Foe to his pride, but friend to his distress:
So humble, he has knocked at Tibbald's door,
Has drunk with Cibber, nay has rimed for Moore.
Full ten years slandered, did he once reply?
Three thousand suns went down on Welsted's lie.
To please a Mistress one aspersed his life;
He lashed him not, but let her be his wife.
Let Budgell charge low Grubstreet on his quill,
And write whate'er he pleased, except his Will;
Let the two Curlls of Town and Court, abuse   380
His father, mother, body, soul, and muse.
Yet why? that Father held it for a rule,
It was a sin to call our neighbor fool;
That harmless Mother thought no wife a whore:
Hear this, and spare his family, James Moore!
Unspotted names, and memorable long!
If there be force in Virtue, or in Song.

    Of gentle blood (part shed in Honor's cause,

363. *Japhet*, Japhet Crook, a forger of the time.
375. *Welsted's lie*, Leonard Welsted falsely accused Pope of lampooning
the Duke of Chandos. This incident is also alluded to in lines 299–300.
378. *Budgell*, Eustace Budgell, a contributor to the *Spectator*.

While yet in Britain Honor had applause)
Each parent sprung— A. What fortune, pray?— P. Their
    own,   390
And better got, than Bestia's from the throne.
Born to no Pride, inheriting no Strife,
Nor marrying Discord in a noble wife,
Stranger to civil and religious rage,
The good man walked innoxious through his age.
Nor Courts he saw, no suits would ever try,
Nor dared an Oath, nor hazarded a Lie.
Unlearn'd, he knew no schoolman's subtle art,
No language, but the language of the heart.
By Nature honest, by Experience wise,   400
Healthy by temp'rance, and by exercise:
His life, though long, to sickness past unknown,
His death was instant, and without a groan.
O grant me, thus to live, and thus to die!
Who sprung from Kings shall know less joy than I.
   O Friend! may each domestic bliss be thine!
Be no unpleasing Melancholy mine:
Me, let the tender office long engage,
To rock the cradle of reposing Age,
With lenient arts extend a Mother's breath,   410
Make Languor smile, and smooth the bed of Death,
Explore the thought, explain the asking eye,
And keep a while one parent from the sky!
On cares like these if length of days attend,
May Heav'n, to bless those days, preserve my friend,
Preserve him social, cheerful, and serene,
And just as rich as when he served a Queen.
A. Whether that blessing be denied or giv'n,
Thus far was right, the rest belongs to Heav'n.

1735

391. *Bestia*, possibly the Duke of Marlborough.

JAMES THOMSON

Winter [1]

See, Winter comes to rule the varied year,
Sullen and sad, with all his rising train—
Vapors, and clouds, and storms. Be these my theme;
These, that exalt the soul to solemn thought
And heavenly musing. Welcome, kindred glooms!
Cogenial horrors, hail! With frequent foot,
Pleased have I, in my cheerful morn of life,
When nursed by careless solitude I lived
And sung of Nature with unceasing joy,
Pleased have I wandered through your rough domain;   10
Trod the pure virgin-snows, myself as pure;
Heard the winds roar, and the big torrent burst;
Or seen the deep-fermenting tempest brewed
In the grim evening-sky. Thus passed the time,
Till through the lucid chambers of the south
Looked out the joyous Spring—looked out and smiled. . . .
    Nature! great parent! whose unceasing hand
Rolls round the Seasons of the changeful year,
How mighty, how majestic are thy works!
With what a pleasing dread they swell the soul,   20
That sees astonished, and astonished sings!
Ye too, ye winds! that now begin to blow
With boisterous sweep, I raise my voice to you.
Where are your stores, ye powerful beings! say,
Where your aerial magazines reserved
To swell the brooding terrors of the storm?
In what far-distant region of the sky,
Hushed in deep silence, sleep you when 'tis calm?
    When from the pallid sky the Sun descends,
With many a spot, that o'er his glaring orb   30
Uncertain wanders, stained; red fiery streaks
Begin to flush around. The reeling clouds
Stagger with dizzy poise, as doubting yet

---

[1] "Winter" is one fourth of *The Seasons,* a long poem in which Thomson wrote of the four seasons of the year.

Which master to obey; while, rising slow,
Blank in the leaden-colored east, the moon
Wears a wan circle round her blunted horns.
Seen through the turbid, fluctuating air,
The stars obtuse emit a shivering ray;
Or frequent seem to shoot athwart the gloom,
And long behind them trail the whitening blaze.   40
Snatched in short eddies, plays the withered leaf;
And on the flood the dancing feather floats.
With broadened nostrils to the sky upturned,
The conscious heifer snuffs the stormy gale.
E'en as the matron, at her nightly task,
With pensive labor draws the flaxen thread,
The wasted taper and the crackling flame
Foretell the blast. But chief the plumy race,
The tenants of the sky, its changes speak.
Retiring from the downs, where all day long   50
They picked their scanty fare, a blackening train
Of clamorous rooks thick-urge their weary flight,
And seek the closing shelter of the grove.
Assiduous, in his bower, the wailing owl
Plies his sad song. The cormorant on high
Wheels from the deep, and screams along the land.
Loud shrieks the soaring hern; and with wild wing
The circling sea-fowl cleave the flaky clouds.
Ocean, unequal pressed, with broken tide
And blind commotion heaves; while from the shore,   60
Eat into caverns by the restless wave,
And forest-rustling mountain comes a voice
That, solemn-sounding, bids the world prepare.
Then issues forth the storm with sudden burst,
And hurls the whole precipitated air
Down in a torrent. On the passive main
Descends the ethereal force, and with strong gust
Turns from its bottom the discolored deep.
Through the black night that sits immense around,
Lashed into foam, the fierce-conflicting brine   70
Seems o'er a thousand raging waves to burn.
Meantime the mountain-billows, to the clouds

In dreadful tumult swelled, surge above surge,
Burst into chaos with tremendous roar,
And anchored navies from their stations drive
Wild as the winds, across the howling waste
Of mighty waters: now the inflated wave
Straining they scale, and now impetuous shoot
Into the secret chambers of the deep,
The wintry Baltic thundering o'er their head.   80
Emerging thence again, before the breath
Of full-exerted heaven they wing their course,
And dart on distant coasts—if some sharp rock
Or shoal insidious break not their career,
And in loose fragments fling them floating round.
   Nor less at land the loosened tempest reigns.
The mountain thunders, and its sturdy sons
Stoop to the bottom of the rocks they shade.
Lone on the midnight steep, and all aghast,
The dark wayfaring stranger breathless toils,   90
And, often falling, climbs against the blast.
Low waves the rooted forest, vexed, and sheds
What of its tarnished honors yet remain—
Dashed down and scattered, by the tearing wind's
Assiduous fury, its gigantic limbs.
Thus struggling through the dissipated grove,
The whirling tempest raves along the plain;
And, on the cottage thatched or lordly roof
Keen-fastening, shakes them to the solid base.
Sleep frighted flies; and round the rocking dome,   100
For entrance eager, howls the savage blast.
Then too, they say, through all the burdened air
Long groans are heard, shrill sounds, and distant sighs,
That, uttered by the demon of the night,
Warn the devoted wretch of woe and death.
   Huge uproar lords it wide. The clouds, commixed
With stars swift-gliding, sweep along the sky.
All Nature reels: till Nature's King, who oft
Amid tempestuous darkness dwells alone,
And on the wings of the careering wind   110
Walks dreadfully serene, commands a calm;

Then straight air, sea, and earth are hushed at once.
    As yet 'tis midnight deep. The weary clouds,
Slow-meeting, mingle into solid gloom.
Now, while the drowsy world lies lost in sleep,
Let me associate with the serious Night,
And Contemplation, her sedate compeer;
Let me shake off the intrusive cares of day,
And lay the meddling senses all aside.
    Where now, ye lying vanities of life!   120
Ye ever-tempting, ever-cheating train!
Where are you now? and what is your amount?
Vexation, disappointment, and remorse.
Sad, sickening thought! and yet deluded man,
A scene of crude disjointed visions past,
And broken slumbers, rises still resolved,
With new-flushed hopes, to run the giddy round.
    Father of light and life! thou Good Supreme!
O teach me what is good! teach me Thyself!
Save me from folly, vanity, and vice,   130
From every low pursuit; and feed my soul
With knowledge, conscious peace, and virtue pure—
Sacred, substantial, never-fading bliss!
    The keener tempests come: and, fuming dun
From all the livid east or piercing north,
Thick clouds ascend, in whose capacious womb
A vapory deluge lies, to snow congealed.
Heavy they roll their fleecy world along,
And the sky saddens with the gathered storm.
Through the hushed air the whitening shower descends, 140
At first thin-wavering; till at last the flakes
Fall broad and wide and fast, dimming the day
With a continual flow. The cherished fields
Put on their winter-robe of purest white.
'Tis brightness all!; save where the new snow melts
Along the mazy current. Low the woods
Bow their hoar head; and, ere the languid sun
Faint from the west emits his evening ray,
Earth's universal face, deep-hid and chill,
Is one wild dazzling waste, that buries wide   150

The works of man. Drooping, the laborer-ox
Stands covered o'er with snow, and then demands
The fruit of all his toil. The fowls of heaven,
Tamed by the cruel season, crowd around
The winnowing store, and claim the little boon
Which Providence assigns them. One alone,
The redbreast, sacred to the household gods,
Wisely regardful of the embroiling sky,
In joyless fields and thorny thickets leaves
His shivering mates, and pays to trusted man   160
His annual visit. Half afraid, he first
Against the window beats; then brisk alights
On the warm hearth; then, hopping o'er the floor,
Eyes all the smiling family askance,
And pecks, and starts, and wonders where he is—
Till, more familiar grown, the table-crumbs
Attract his slender feet. The foodless wilds
Pour forth their brown inhabitants. The hare,
Though timorous of heart, and hard beset
By death in various forms, dark snares, and dogs,   170
And more unpitying men, the garden seeks,
Urged on by fearless want. The bleating kind
Eye the bleak heaven, and next the glistening earth,
With looks of dumb despair; then, sad-dispersed,
Dig for the withered herb through heaps of snow.
    Now, shepherds, to your helpless charge be kind:
Baffle the raging year, and fill their pens
With food at will; lodge them below the storm,
And watch them strict: for, from the bellowing east,
In this dire season, oft the whirlwind's wing   180
Sweeps up the burden of whole wintry plains
In one wide waft, and o'er the hapless flocks,
Hid in the hollow of two neighboring hills,
The billowy tempest whelms; till, upward urged,
The valley to a shining mountain swells,
Tipped with a wreath high-curling in the sky.
    As thus the snows arise, and, foul and fierce,
All Winter drives along the darkened air,
In his own loose-revolving fields the swain

Disastered stands; sees other hills ascend,   190
Of unknown joyless brow; and other scenes,
Of horrid prospect, shag the trackless plain;
Nor finds the river nor the forest, hid
Beneath the formless wild; but wanders on
From hill to dale, still more and more astray—
Impatient flouncing through the drifted heaps,
Stung with the thoughts of home: the thoughts of home
Rush on his nerves and call their vigor forth
In many a vain attempt. How sinks his soul!
What black despair, what horror fills his heart,   200
When, for the dusky spot which fancy feigned
His tufted cottage rising through the snow,
He meets the roughness of the middle waste,
Far from the track and blest abode of man;
While round him night resistless closes fast,
And every tempest, howling o'er his head,
Renders the savage wilderness more wild.
Then throng the busy shapes into his mind
Of covered pits, unfathomably deep,
A dire descent! beyond the power of frost;   210
Of faithless bogs; of precipices huge,
Smoothed up with snow; and (what is land unknown,
What water) of the still unfrozen spring,
In the loose marsh or solitary lake,
Where the fresh fountain from the bottom boils.
These check his fearful steps; and down he sinks
Beneath the shelter of the shapeless drift,
Thinking o'er all the bitterness of death,
Mixed with the tender anguish nature shoots
Through the wrung bosom of the dying man—   220
His wife, his children, and his friends unseen.
In vain for him the officious wife prepares
The fire fair-blazing and the vestment warm;
In vain his little children, peeping out
Into the mingling storm, demand their sire
With tears of artless innocence. Alas!
Nor wife nor children more shall he behold,
Nor friends, nor sacred home. On every nerve

The deadly Winter seizes, shuts up sense,
And, o'er his inmost vitals creeping cold,   230
Lays him along the snows a stiffened corse,
Stretched out, and bleaching in the northern blast.

1726

SAMUEL JOHNSON

One-and-Twenty

Long-expected One-and-twenty,
    Ling'ring year, at length is flown:
Pride and pleasure, pomp and plenty,
    Great * * *, are now your own.

Loosen'd from the minor's tether,
    Free to mortgage or to sell,
Wild as wind and light as feather,
    Bid the sons of thrift farewell.

Call the Betsies, Kates, and Jennies,
    All the names that banish care;   10
Lavish of your grandsire's guineas,
    Show the spirit of an heir.

All that prey on vice and folly
    Joy to see their quarry fly:
There the gamester, light and jolly,
    There the lender, grave and sly.

Wealth, my lad, was made to wander,
    Let it wander as it will;
Call the jockey, call the pander,
    Bid them come and take their fill.   20

When the bonny blade carouses,
    Pockets full, and spirits high—
What are acres? What are houses?
    Only dirt, or wet or dry.

Should the guardian friend or mother
    Tell the woes or wilful waste,

Scorn their counsel, scorn their pother;—
You can hang or drown at last!

1794

THOMAS GRAY

Ode on the Death of a Favorite Cat

DROWNED IN A TUB OF GOLD FISHES

'Twas on a lofty vase's side,
Where China's gayest art had dyed
   The azure flowers, that blow;
Demurest of the tabby kind,
The pensive Selima reclined,
   Gazed on the lake below.

Her conscious tail her joy declared;
The fair round face, the snowy beard,
   The velvet of her paws,
Her coat, that with the tortoise vies,   10
Her ears of jet, and emerald eyes,   ·
   She saw; and purred applause.

Still had she gazed; but 'midst the tide
Two angel forms were seen to glide,
   The genii of the stream;
Their scaly armor's Tyrian hue
Through richest purple to the view
   Betrayed a golden gleam.

The hapless nymph with wonder saw:
A whisker first and then a claw,   20
   With many an ardent wish,
She stretched in vain to reach the prize.
What female heart can gold despise?
   What cat's averse to fish?

Presumptuous maid! with looks intent
Again she stretched, again she bent,
   Nor knew the gulf between.

(Malignant Fate sat by, and smiled)
The slippery verge her feet beguiled,
   She tumbled headlong in.   30

Eight times emerging from the flood
She mewed to every watery god,
   Some speedy aid to send.
No dolphin came, no nereid stirred:
Nor cruel Tom, nor Susan heard.
   A favorite has no friend!

From hence, ye beauties, undeceived,
Know, one false step is ne'er retrieved,
   And be with caution bold.
Not all that tempts your wandering eyes   40
And heedless hearts, is lawful prize;
   Nor all, that glisters, gold.

           1748

Elegy

WRITTEN IN A COUNTRY CHURCH-YARD

The Curfew tolls the knell of parting day,
   The lowing herd wind slowly o'er the lea,
The plowman homeward plods his weary way,
   And leaves the world to darkness and to me.

Now fades the glimmering landscape on the sight,
   And all the air a solemn stillness holds,
Save where the beetle wheels his droning flight,
   And drowsy tinklings lull the distant folds;

Save that from yonder ivy-mantled tower
   The moping owl does to the moon complain   10
Of such, as wand'ring near her secret bower,
   Molest her ancient solitary reign.

Beneath those rugged elms, that yew-tree's shade,
   Where heaves the turf in many a mold'ring heap,
Each in his narrow cell for ever laid,
   The rude Forefathers of the hamlet sleep.

The breezy call of incense-breathing Morn,
    The swallow twitt'ring from the straw-built shed,
The cock's shrill clarion, or the echoing horn,
    No more shall rouse them from their lowly bed.   20

For them no more the blazing hearth shall burn,
    Or busy housewife ply her evening care:
No children run to lisp their sire's return,
    Or climb his knees the envied kiss to share.

Oft did the harvest to their sickle yield,
    Their furrow oft the stubborn glebe has broke;
How jocund did they drive their team afield!
    How bowed the woods beneath their sturdy stroke!

Let not Ambition mock their useful toil,
    Their homely joys, and destiny obscure;   30
Nor Grandeur hear with a disdainful smile,
    The short and simple annals of the poor.

The boast of heraldry, the pomp of pow'r,
    And all that beauty, all that wealth e'er gave,
Awaits alike th' inevitable hour.
    The paths of glory lead but to the grave.

Nor you, ye Proud, impute to These the fault,
    If Mem'ry o'er their Tomb no Trophies raise,
Where through the long-drawn isle and fretted vault
    The pealing anthem swells the note of praise.   40

Can storied urn or animated bust
    Back to its mansion call the fleeting breath?
Can Honor's voice provoke the silent dust,
    Or Flatt'ry soothe the dull cold ear of Death?

Perhaps in this neglected spot is laid
    Some heart once pregnant with celestial fire;
Hands, that the rod of empire might have swayed,
    Or waked to ecstasy the living lyre.

But Knowledge to their eyes her ample page
    Rich with the spoils of time did ne'er unroll;   50
Chill Penury repressed their noble rage,
    And froze the genial current of the soul.

Full many a gem of purest ray serene,
    The dark unfathomed caves of ocean bear:
Full many a flower is born to blush unseen,
    And waste its sweetness on the desert air.

Some village-Hampden, that with dauntless breast
    The little Tyrant of his fields withstood;
Some mute inglorious Milton here may rest,
    Some Cromwell guiltless of his country's blood.   60

Th' applause of list'ning senates to command,
    The threats of pain and ruin to despise,
To scatter plenty o'er a smiling land,
    And read their hist'ry in a nation's eyes,

Their lot forbade: nor circumscribed alone
    Their growing virtues, but their crimes confined;
Forbade to wade through slaughter to a throne,
    And shut the gates of mercy on mankind,

The struggling pangs of conscious truth to hide,
    To quench the blushes of ingenuous shame,   70
Or heap the shrine of Luxury and Pride
    With incense kindled at the Muse's flame.

Far from the madding crowd's ignoble strife,
    Their sober wishes never learned to stray;
Along the cool sequestered vale of life
    They kept the noiseless tenor of their way.

Yet e'en these bones from insult to protect
    Some frail memorial still erected nigh,
With uncouth rimes and shapeless sculpture decked,
    Implores the passing tribute of a sigh.   80

Their name, their years, spelt by th' unlettered muse,
    The place of fame and elegy supply:

And many a holy text around she strews,
That teach the rustic moralist to die.

For who to dumb Forgetfulness a prey,
This pleasing anxious being e'er resigned,
Left the warm precincts of the cheerful day,
Nor cast one longing ling'ring look behind?

On some fond breast the parting soul relies,
Some pious drops the closing eye requires;   90
E'en from the tomb the voice of Nature cries,
E'en in our Ashes live their wonted Fires.

For thee, who mindful of th' unhonored Dead
Dost in these lines their artless tale relate;
If chance, by lonely contemplation led,
Some kindred Spirit shall inquire thy fate,

Haply some hoary-headed Swain may say,
"Oft have we seen him at the peep of dawn
Brushing with hasty steps the dews away
To meet the sun upon the upland lawn.   100

"There at the foot of yonder nodding beech
That wreathes its old fantastic roots so high,
His listless length at noontide would he stretch,
And pore upon the brook that babbles by.

"Hard by yon wood, now smiling as in scorn,
Mutt'ring his wayward fancies he would rove,
Now drooping, woeful wan, like one forlorn,
Or crazed with care, or crossed in hopeless love.

"One morn I missed him on the customed hill,
Along the heath and near his fav'rite tree;   110
Another came; nor yet beside the rill,
Nor up the lawn, nor at the wood was he;

"The next with dirges due in sad array
Slow through the church-way path we saw him borne.
Approach and read (for thou can'st read) the lay,
Graved on the stone beneath yon agéd thorn."

THE EPITAPH

Here rests his head upon the lap of Earth
  A Youth to Fortune and to Fame unknown.
Fair Science frowned not on his humble birth,
  And Melancholy marked him for her own.   120

Large was his bounty, and his soul sincere,
  Heav'n did a recompense as largely send:
He gave to Mis'ry all he had, a tear,
  He gained from Heav'n ('twas all he wished) a friend.

No farther seek his merits to disclose,
  Or draw his frailties from their dread abode
(There they alike in trembling hope repose),
  The bosom of his Father and his God.

1751

OLIVER GOLDSMITH

Song

When lovely woman stoops to folly,
  And finds, too late, that men betray,
What charm can soothe her melancholy?
  What art can wash her guilt away?

The only art her guilt to cover,
  To hide her shame from every eye,
To give repentance to her lover,
  And wring his bosom, is—to die.
        The Vicar of Wakefield, 1766

Deserted Village

Sweet Auburn! loveliest village of the plain,
Where health and plenty cheered the laboring swain,
Where smiling spring its earliest visit paid,
And parting summer's lingering blooms delayed;

Dear lovely bowers of innocence and ease,
Seats of my youth, when every sport could please;
How often have I loitered o'er thy green,
Where humble happiness endeared each scene!
How often have I paused on every charm,
The sheltered cot, the cultivated farm,   10
The never-failing brook, the busy mill,
The decent church that topped the neighboring hill;
The hawthorn bush, with seats beneath the shade,
For talking age and whispering lovers made!
How often have I blessed the coming day,
When toil, remitting, lent its turn to play,
And all the village train, from labor free,
Led up their sports beneath the spreading tree!
While many a pastime circled in the shade,
The young contending as the old surveyed;   20
And many a gambol frolicked o'er the ground,
And sleights of art and feats of strength went round;
And still, as each repeated pleasure tired,
Succeeding sports the mirthful band inspired—
The dancing pair that simply sought renown,
By holding out to tire each other down;
The swain mistrustless of his smutted face,
While secret laughter tittered round the place;
The bashful virgin's side-long looks of love;
The matron's glance, that would those looks reprove.   30
These were thy charms, sweet village! sports like these,
With sweet succession, taught e'en toil to please;
These round thy bowers their cheerful influence shed;
These were thy charms—but all these charms are fled.

   Sweet smiling village, loveliest of the lawn,
Thy sports are fled, and all thy charms withdrawn;
Amidst thy bowers the tyrant's hand is seen,
And desolation saddens all thy green;
One only master grasps the whole domain,
And half a tillage stints thy smiling plain.   40
No more thy glassy brook reflects the day,
But, choked with sedges, works its weedy way;

Along thy glades, a solitary guest,
The hollow-sounding bittern guards its nest;
Amidst thy desert walks the lapwing flies,
And tires their echoes with unvaried cries;
Sunk are thy bowers in shapeless ruin all,
And the long grass o'ertops the moldering wall;
And, trembling, shrinking from the spoiler's hand,
Far, far away thy children leave the land.   50

Ill fares the land, to hastening ills a prey,
Where wealth accumulates, and men decay.
Princes and lords may flourish, or may fade;
A breath can make them, as a breath has made;
But a bold peasantry, their country's pride,
When once destroyed, can never be supplied.

A time there was, ere England's griefs began,
When every rood of ground maintained its man;
For him light labor spread her wholesome store,
Just gave what life required, but gave no more: 60
His best companions, innocence and health;
And his best riches, ignorance of wealth.

But times are altered; trade's unfeeling train
Usurp the land, and dispossess the swain;
Along the lawn, where scattered hamlets rose,
Unwieldy wealth and cumbrous pomp repose;
And every want to opulence allied,
And every pang that folly pays to pride.
Those gentle hours that plenty bade to bloom,
Those calm desires that asked but little room,   70
Those healthful sports that graced the peaceful scene,
Lived in each look, and brightened all the green—
These, far departing, seek a kinder shore,
And rural mirth and manners are no more.

Sweet Auburn! parent of the blissful hour,
Thy glades forlorn confess the tyrant's power.
Here, as I take my solitary rounds,
Amidst thy tangling walks and ruined grounds,

And, many a year elapsed, return to view
Where once the cottage stood, the hawthorn grew—   80
Remembrance wakes with all her busy train,
Swells at my breast, and turns the past to pain.

In all my wanderings round this world of care,
In all my griefs—and God has given my share—
I still had hopes, my latest hours to crown,
Amidst these humble bowers to lay me down;
To husband out life's taper at the close,
And keep the flame from wasting by repose;
I still had hopes, for pride attends us still,
Amidst the swains to show my book-learned skill,   90
Around my fire an evening group to draw,
And tell of all I felt, and all I saw;
And, as a hare, whom hounds and horns pursue,
Pants to the place from whence at first she flew,
I still had hopes, my long vexations past,
Here to return—and die at home at last.

O blest retirement, friend to life's decline,
Retreats from care, that never must be mine,
How happy he who crowns, in shades like these,
A youth of labor with an age of ease;   100
Who quits a world where strong temptations try,
And, since 'tis hard to combat, learns to fly!
For him no wretches, born to work and weep,
Explore the mine, or tempt the dangerous deep;
No surly porter stands, in guilty state,
To spurn imploring famine from the gate;
But on he moves to meet his latter end,
Angels around befriending virtue's friend;
Bends to the grave with unperceived decay,
While resignation gently slopes the way;   110
And, all his prospects brightening to the last,
His heaven commences ere the world be past!

Sweet was the sound, when oft, at evening's close,
Up yonder hill the village murmur rose.

There, as I passed with careless steps and slow,
The mingled notes came softened from below;
The swain responsive as the milkmaid sung,
The sober herd that lowed to meet their young;
The noisy geese that gabbled o'er the pool,
The playful children just let loose from school;   120
The watch-dog's voice that bayed the whispering wind,
And the loud laugh that spoke the vacant mind;—
These all in sweet confusion sought the shade,
And filled each pause the nightingale had made.
But now the sounds of population fail,
No cheerful murmurs fluctuate in the gale,
No busy steps the grass-grown footway tread,
For all the bloomy flush of life is fled—
All but yon widowed, solitary thing,
That feebly bends beside the plashy spring;   130
She, wretched matron—forced, in age for bread,
To strip the brook with mantling cresses spread,
To pick her wintry faggot from the thorn,
To seek her nightly shed, and weep till morn—
She only left of all the harmless train,
The sad historian of the pensive plain.

Near yonder copse, where once the garden smiled,
And still where many a garden-flower grows wild,
There, where a few torn shrubs the place disclose,
The village preacher's modest mansion rose.   140
A man he was to all the country dear,
And passing rich with forty pounds a year.
Remote from towns he ran his godly race,
Nor e'er had changed, nor wished to change, his place;
Unpracticed he to fawn, or seek for power
By doctrines fashioned to the varying hour;
Far other aims his heart had learned to prize,
More skilled to raise the wretched than to rise.
His house was known to all the vagrant train;
He chid their wanderings, but relieved their pain;   150
The long-remembered beggar was his guest,
Whose beard descending swept his aged breast;

The ruined spendthrift, now no longer proud,
Claimed kindred there, and had his claims allowed;
The broken soldier, kindly bade to stay,
Sat by his fire, and talked the night away;—
Wept o'er his wounds, or, tales of sorrow done,
Shouldered his crutch, and showed how fields were won.
Pleased with his guests, the good man learned to glow,
And quite forgot their vices in their woe;   160
Careless their merits or their faults to scan,
His pity gave ere charity began.

    Thus to relieve the wretched was his pride,
And e'en his failings leaned to virtue's side;
But in his duty prompt at every call,
He watched and wept, he prayed and felt for all;
And, as a bird each fond endearment tries
To tempt its new-fledged offspring to the skies,
He tried each art, reproved each dull delay,
Allured to brighter worlds, and led the way.   170

    Beside the bed where parting life was laid,
And sorrow, guilt, and pain, by turns dismayed,
The reverend champion stood. At his control,
Despair and anguish fled the struggling soul;
Comfort came down the trembling wretch to raise,
And his last faltering accents whispered praise.

    At church, with meek and unaffected grace,
His looks adorned the venerable place;
Truth from his lips prevailed with double sway,
And fools, who came to scoff, remained to pray.   180
The service past, around the pious man
With steady zeal, each honest rustic ran;
E'en children followed, with endearing wile,
And plucked his gown, to share the good man's smile;
His ready smile a parent's warmth expressed;
Their welfare pleased him, and their cares distressed:
To them his heart, his love, his griefs were given,
But all his serious thoughts had rest in heaven.

As some tall cliff that lifts its awful form,
Swells from the vale, and midway leaves the storm,   190
Though round its breast the rolling clouds are spread,
Eternal sunshine settles on its head.

Beside yon straggling fence that skirts the way,
With blossomed furze unprofitably gay,
There, in his noisy mansion, skilled to rule,
The village master taught his little school.
A man severe he was, and stern to view;
I knew him well, and every truant knew;
Well had the boding tremblers learned to trace
The day's disasters in his morning face;   200
Full well they laughed with counterfeited glee
At all his jokes, for many a joke had he;
Full well the busy whisper, circling round,
Conveyed the dismal tidings when he frowned.
Yet he was kind, or if severe in aught,
The love he bore to learning was in fault.
The village all declared how much he knew;
'Twas certain he could write, and cipher too;
Lands he could measure, terms and tides presage,
And e'en the story ran that he could gauge.   210
In arguing, too, the parson owned his skill,
For e'en though vanquished, he could argue still;
While words of learnéd length and thundering sound
Amazed the gazing rustics ranged around;
And still they gazed, and still the wonder grew,
That one small head could carry all he knew.
But past is all his fame;—the very spot,
Where many a time he triumphed, is forgot.

Near yonder thorn, that lifts its head on high,
Where once the sign-post caught the passing eye,   220
Low lies that house where nut-brown drafts inspired,
Where gray-beard mirth and smiling toil retired,
Where village statesmen talked with looks profound,
And news much older than their ale went round.
Imagination fondly stoops to trace
The parlor splendors of that festive place;

The whitewashed wall, the nicely-sanded floor,
The varnished clock that clicked behind the door,
The chest, contrived a double debt to pay,
A bed by night, a chest of drawers by day,   230
The pictures placed for ornament and use,
The twelve good rules, the royal game of goose,
The hearth, except when winter chilled the day,
With aspen boughs, and flowers, and fennel, gay;—
While broken teacups, wisely kept for show,
Ranged o'er the chimney, glistened in a row.

Vain transitory splendors! could not all
Reprieve the tottering mansion from its fall?
Obscure it sinks, nor shall it more impart
An hour's importance to the poor man's heart.   240
Thither no more the peasant shall repair,
To sweet oblivion of his daily care;
No more the farmer's news, the barber's tale,
No more the woodman's ballad shall prevail;
No more the smith his dusky brow shall clear,
Relax his ponderous strength, and lean to hear;
The host himself no longer shall be found
Careful to see the mantling bliss go round;
Nor the coy maid, half willing to be pressed,
Shall kiss the cup to pass it to the rest.   250

Yes! let the rich deride, the proud disdain,
These simple blessings of the lowly train;
To me more dear, congenial to my heart,
One native charm, than all the gloss of art.
Spontaneous joys, where nature has its play,
The soul adopts, and owns their first-born sway;
Lightly they frolic o'er the vacant mind,
Unenvied, unmolested, unconfined:
But the long pomp, the midnight masquerade,
With all the freaks of wanton wealth arrayed,   260
In these, ere triflers half their wish obtain,
The toiling pleasure sickens into pain;
And, e'en while fashion's brightest arts decoy,
The heart distrusting asks, if this be joy.

Ye friends to truth, ye statesmen, who survey
The rich man's joys increase, the poor's decay,
'Tis yours to judge how wide the limits stand
Between a splendid and a happy land.
Proud swells the tide with loads of freighted ore,
And shouting folly hails them from her shore;   270
Hoards, e'en beyond the miser's wish, abound,
And rich men flock from all the world around.
Yet count our gains. This wealth is but a name
That leaves our useful products still the same.
Not so the loss. The man of wealth and pride
Takes up a space that many poor supplied;
Space for his lake, his park's extended bounds,
Space for his horses, equipage, and hounds;
The robe that wraps his limbs in silken sloth,
Has robbed the neighboring fields of half their growth;   280
His seat, where solitary sports are seen,
Indignant spurns the cottage from the green;
Around the world each needful product flies,
For all the luxuries the world supplies;
While thus the land, adorned for pleasure all,
In barren splendor feebly waits the fall.

As some fair female, unadorned and plain,
Secure to please while youth confirms her reign,
Slights every borrowed charm that dress supplies,
Nor shares with art the triumph of her eyes;   290
But when those charms are past, for charms are frail,
When time advances, and when lovers fail,
She then shines forth, solicitous to bless,
In all the glaring impotence of dress;
Thus fares the land by luxury betrayed;
In nature's simplest charms at first arrayed;—
But verging to decline, its splendors rise,
Its vistas strike, its palaces surprise;
While, scourged by famine, from the smiling land
The mournful peasant leads his humble band;   300
And while he sinks, without one arm to save,
The country blooms—a garden and a grave!

Where, then, ah! where shall poverty reside,
To 'scape the pressure of contiguous pride?
If to some common's fenceless limits strayed,
He drives his flock to pick the scanty blade,
Those fenceless fields the sons of wealth divide,
And e'en the bare-worn common is denied.

If to the city sped—what waits him there?
To see profusion that he must not share;   310
To see ten thousand baneful arts combined
To pamper luxury and thin mankind;
To see those joys the sons of pleasure know
Extorted from his fellow-creature's woe;
Here while the courtier glitters in brocade,
There the pale artist plies the sickly trade;
Here while the proud their long-drawn pomps display,
There the black gibbet glooms beside the way;
The dome where pleasure holds her midnight reign,
Here, richly decked, admits the gorgeous train;   320
Tumultuous grandeur crowds the blazing square,
The rattling chariots clash, the torches glare.
Sure scenes like these no troubles e'er annoy!
Sure these denote one universal joy!—
Are these thy serious thoughts?—ah, turn thine eyes
Where the poor houseless shivering female lies;
She once, perhaps, in village plenty blessed,
Has wept at tales of innocence distressed;
Her modest looks the cottage might adorn,
Sweet as the primrose peeps beneath the thorn;   330
Now lost to all, her friends, her virtue, fled,
Near her betrayer's door she lays her head,
And, pinched with cold, and shrinking from the
      shower,
With heavy heart deplores that luckless hour,
When idly first, ambitious of the town,
She left her wheel, and robes of country brown.

Do thine, sweet Auburn, thine, the loveliest train,
Do thy fair tribes participate her pain?

E'en now, perhaps, by cold and hunger led,
At proud men's doors they ask a little bread!   340

Ah, no. To distant climes, a dreary scene,
Where half the convex world intrudes between,
Through torrid tracts with fainting steps they go,
Where wild Altama murmurs to their woe.
Far different there from all that charmed before,
The various terrors of that horrid shore;
Those blazing suns that dart a downward ray,
And fiercely shed intolerable day;
Those matted woods where birds forget to sing,
But silent bats in drowsy clusters cling;   350
Those poisonous fields, with rank luxuriance crowned,
Where the dark scorpion gathers death around;
Where at each step the stranger fears to wake
The rattling terrors of the vengeful snake;
Where crouching tigers wait their hapless prey,
And savage men more murderous still than they;
While oft in whirls the mad tornado flies,
Mingling the ravaged landscape with the skies.
Far different these from every former scene,
The cooling brook, the grassy-vested green,   360
The breezy covert of the warbling grove,
That only sheltered thefts of harmless love.

Good Heaven! what sorrows gloomed that parting
    day,
That called them from their native walks away;
When the poor exiles, every pleasure past,
Hung round their bowers, and fondly looked their
    last,
And took a long farewell, and wished in vain,
For seats like these beyond the western main;
And shuddering still to face the distant deep,
Returned and wept, and still returned to weep!   370
The good old sire the first prepared to go
To new-found worlds, and wept for others' woe;
But for himself, in conscious virtue brave,
He only wished for worlds beyond the grave.

His lovely daughter, lovelier in her tears,
The fond companion of his helpless years,
Silent went next, neglectful of her charms,
And left a lover's for a father's arms.
With louder plaints the mother spoke her woes,
And blessed the cot where every pleasure rose, 380
And kissed her thoughtless babes with many a tear,
And clasped them close, in sorrow doubly dear;
Whilst her fond husband strove to lend relief
In all the silent manliness of grief.

O luxury, thou cursed by Heaven's decree,
How ill exchanged are things like these for thee!
How do thy potions, with insidious joy,
Diffuse their pleasures only to destroy!
Kingdoms by thee to sickly greatness grown,
Boast of a florid vigor not their own; 390
At every draft more large and large they grow,
A bloated mass of rank unwieldy woe;
Till sapped their strength, and every part unsound,
Down, down they sink, and spread a ruin round.

E'en now the devastation is begun,
And half the business of destruction done;
E'en now, methinks, as pondering here I stand,
I see the rural virtues leave the land.
Down where yon anchoring vessel spreads the sail,
That idly waiting flaps with every gale, 400
Downward they move, a melancholy band,
Pass from the shore, and darken all the strand;
Contented toil, and hospitable care,
And kind connubial tenderness are there;
And piety with wishes placed above,
And steady loyalty, and faithful love.

And thou, sweet Poetry, thou loveliest maid,
Still first to fly where sensual joys invade!
Unfit, in these degenerate times of shame,
To catch the heart, or strike for honest fame; 410

Dear charming nymph, neglected and decried,
My shame in crowds, my solitary pride;
Thou source of all my bliss and all my woe,
That found'st me poor at first, and keep'st me so;
Thou guide by which the nobler arts excel,
Thou nurse of every virtue, fare thee well!
Farewell! and oh! where'er thy voice be tried,
On Torno's cliffs, or Pambamarca's side,
Whether where equinoctial fervors glow,
Or winter wraps the polar world in snow,   420
Still let thy voice, prevailing over time,
Redress the rigors of th' inclement clime;
Aid slighted truth with thy persuasive strain;
Teach erring man to spurn the rage of gain;
Teach him that states, of native strength possessed,
Though very poor, may still be very blest;
That trade's proud empire hastes to swift decay,
As ocean sweeps the labored mole away;
While self-dependent power can time defy,
As rocks resist the billows and the sky.   430

1770

WILLIAM COWPER

The Task

Oh Winter, ruler of th' inverted year,
Thy scatter'd hair with sleet like ashes fill'd,
Thy breath congeal'd upon thy lips, thy cheeks
Fring'd with a beard made white with other
        snows
Than those of age, thy forehead wrapt in clouds,
A leafless branch thy sceptre, and thy throne
A sliding car, indebted to no wheels,
But urg'd by storms along its slipp'ry way,
I love thee, all unlovely as thou seem'st,
And dreaded as thou art! Thou hold'st the sun   10
A pris'ner in the yet undawning east,
Short'ning his journey between morn and noon,

And hurrying him, impatient of his stay,
Down to the rosy west; but kindly still
Compensating his loss with added hours
Of social converse and instructive ease,
And gath'ring, at short notice, in one group
The family dispers'd, and fixing thought,
Not less dispers'd by day-light and its cares.
I crown thee king of intimate delights,   20
Fire-side enjoyments, home-born happiness,
And all the comforts that the lowly roof
Of undisturb'd retirement, and the hours
Of long uninterrupted ev'ning, know.
No rattling wheels stop short before these gates;
No powder'd pert, proficient in the art
Of sounding an alarm, assaults these doors
Till the street rings; no stationary steeds
Cough their own knell, while, heedless of the
      sound,
The silent circle fan themselves, and quake: 30
But here the needle plies its busy task,
The pattern grows, the well-depicted flow'r,
Wrought patiently into the snowy lawn,
Unfolds its bosom; buds, and leaves, and sprigs,
And curling tendrils, gracefully dispos'd,
Follow the nimble finger of the fair;
A wreath that cannot fade, of flow'rs that blow
With most success when all besides decay.
The poet's or historian's page, by one
Made vocal for th' amusement of the rest;   40
The sprightly lyre, whose treasure of sweet
      sounds
The touch from many a trembling chord
      shakes out;
And the clear voice symphonious, yet distinct,
And in the charming strife triumphant still;
Beguile the night, and set a keener edge
On female industry: the threaded steel
Flies swiftly, and, unfelt, the task proceeds. . . .

Come, Ev'ning, once again, season of peace;
Return, sweet Ev'ning, and continue long!
Methinks I see thee in the streaky west,   50
With matron-step slow-moving, while the night
Treads on thy sweeping train; one hand
        employ'd
In letting fall the curtain of repose
On bird and beast, the other charg'd for man
With sweet oblivion of the cares of day:
Not sumptuously adorn'd, nor needing aid,
Like homely featur'd night, of clust'ring gems;
A star or two, just twinkling on thy brow,
Suffices thee; save that the moon is thine
No less than her's, not worn indeed on high   60
With ostentatious pageantry, but set
With modest grandeur in thy purple zone,
Resplendent less, but of an ampler round.
Come then, and thou shalt find thy vot'ry calm,
Or make me so. Composure is thy gift:
And, whether I devote thy gentle hours
To books, to music, or the poet's toil;
To weaving nets for bird-alluring fruit;
Or twining silken threads round iv'ry reels,
When they command whom man was born to
        please;   70
I slight thee not, but make thee welcome still.
    Just when our drawing-rooms begin to blaze
With lights, by clear reflection multiplied
From many a mirror, in which he of Gath,
Goliath, might have seen his giant bulk
Whole, without stooping, tow'ring crest and all,
My pleasures, too, begin. But me, perhaps,
The glowing hearth may satisfy awhile
With faint illumination, that uplifts
The shadow to the ceiling, there by fits   80
Dancing uncouthly to the quiv'ring flame.
Not undelightful is an hour to me
So spent in parlour twilight: such a gloom
Suits well the thoughtful or unthinking mind,

The mind contemplative, with some new theme
Pregnant, or indispos'd alike to all.
Laugh ye, who boast your more mercurial
    pow'rs,
That never feel a stupor, know no pause,
Nor need one; I am conscious, and confess,
Fearless, a soul that does not always think.   90
Me oft has fancy, ludicrous and wild,
Sooth'd with a waking dream of houses, tow'rs,
Trees, churches, and strange visages, express'd
In the red cinders, while with poring eye
I gaz'd, myself creating what I saw.
Nor less amus'd have I quiescent watch'd
The sooty films that play upon the bars,
Pendulous, and foreboding, in the view
Of superstition, prophesying still,
Though still deceiv'd, some stranger's near
    approach.   100
'Tis thus the understanding takes repose
In indolent vacuity of thought,
And sleeps and is refresh'd. Meanwhile the face
Conceals the mood lethargic with a mask
Of deep deliberation, as the man
Were task'd to his full strength, absorb'd and
    lost.
Thus oft, reclin'd at ease, I lose an hour
At ev'ning, till at length the freezing blast,
That sweeps the bolted shutter, summons home
The recollected pow'rs; and, snapping short   110
The glassy threads, with which the fancy
    weaves
Her brittle toys, restores me to myself.
How calm is my recess; and how the frost,
Raging abroad, and the rough wind, endear
The silence and the warmth enjoy'd within!

From Book IV, 1785

WILLIAM BLAKE

Auguries of Innocence

To see a World in a grain of sand,
And a Heaven in a wild flower,
Hold Infinity in the palm of your hand,
And Eternity in an hour.

A robin redbreast in a cage
Puts all Heaven in a rage.
A dove-house fill'd with doves and pigeons
Shudders Hell thro' all its regions.
A dog starv'd at his master's gate
Predicts the ruin of the State.   10
A horse misus'd upon the road
Calls to Heaven for human blood.
Each outcry of the hunted hare
A fibre from the brain does tear.
A skylark wounded in the wing,
A cherubim does cease to sing.
The game-cock clipt and arm'd for fight
Does the rising sun affright.
Every wolf's and lion's howl
Raises from Hell a Human soul.   20
The wild deer, wandering here and there,
Keeps the Human soul from care.
The lamb misus'd breeds public strife,
And yet forgives the butcher's knife.
The bat that flits at close of eve
Has left the brain that won't believe.
The owl that calls upon the night
Speaks the unbeliever's fright.
He who shall hurt the little wren
Shall never be belov'd by men.   30
He who the ox to wrath has mov'd
Shall never be by woman lov'd.
The wanton boy that kills the fly
Shall feel the spider's enmity.

He who torments the chafer's sprite
Weaves a bower in endless night.
The caterpillar on the leaf
Repeats to thee thy mother's grief.
Kill not the moth nor butterfly,
For the Last Judgement draweth nigh.   40
He who shall train the horse to war
Shall never pass the polar bar.
The beggar's dog and widow's cat,
Feed them, and thou wilt grow fat.
The gnat that sings his summer's song
Poison gets from Slander's tongue.
The poison of the snake and newt
Is the sweat of Envy's foot.
The poison of the honey-bee
Is the artist's jealousy.   50
The prince's robes and beggar's rags
Are toadstools on the miser's bags.
A truth that's told with bad intent
Beats all the lies you can invent.
It is right it should be so;
Man was made for joy and woe;
And when this we rightly know,
Thro' the world we safely go.
Joy and woe are woven fine,
A clothing for the soul divine;   60
Under every grief and pine
Runs a joy with silken twine.
The babe is more than swaddling-bands;
Throughout all these human lands
Tools were made, and born were hands,
Every farmer understands.
Every tear from every eye
Becomes a babe in Eternity;
This is caught by Females bright,
And return'd to its own delight.   70
The bleat, the bark, bellow, and roar
Are waves that beat on Heaven's shore.
The babe that weeps the rod beneath

Writes revenge in realms of death.
The beggar's rags, fluttering in air,
Does to rags the heavens tear.
The soldier, arm'd with sword and gun,
Palsied strikes the summer's sun.
The poor man's farthing is worth more
Than all the gold on Afric's shore.   80
One mite wrung from the labourer's hands
Shall buy and sell the miser's lands
Or, if protected from on high,
Does that whole nation sell and buy.
He who mocks the infant's faith
Shall be mock'd in Age and Death.
He who shall teach the child to doubt
The rotting grave shall ne'er get out.
He who respects the infant's faith
Triumphs over Hell and Death.   90
The child's toys and the old man's reasons
Are the fruits of the two seasons.
The questioner, who sits so sly,
Shall never know how to reply.
He who replies to words of Doubt
Doth put the light of knowledge out.
The strongest poison ever known
Came from Caesar's laurel crown.
Nought can deform the human race
Like to the armour's iron brace.   100
When gold and gems adorn the plough
To peaceful arts shall Envy bow.
A riddle, or the cricket's cry,
Is to Doubt a fit reply.
The emmet's inch and eagle's mile
Make lame Philosophy to smile.
He who doubts from what he sees
Will ne'er believe, do what you please.
If the Sun and Moon should doubt,
They'd immediately go out.   110
To be in a passion you good may do,
But no good if a passion is in you.

The whore and gambler, by the state
Licensed, build that nation's fate.
The harlot's cry from street to street
Shall weave Old England's winding-sheet.
The winner's shout, the loser's curse,
Dance before dead England's hearse.
Every night and every morn
Some to misery are born.   120
Every morn and every night
Some are born to sweet delight.
Some are born to sweet delight,
Some are born to endless night.
We are led to believe a lie
When we see not thro' the eye,
Which was born in a night, to perish in a night,
When the Soul slept in beams of light.
God appears, and God is Light,
To those poor souls who dwell in Night;   130
But does a Human Form display
To those who dwell in realms of Day.
About 1803

ROBERT BURNS

Address to the Deil

O Prince, O Chief of many thronéd Powers
That led the embattled Seraphim to war!
                                        —MILTON.

O thou! whatever title suit thee—
Auld Hornie, Satan, Nick, or Clootie—
Wha in yon cavern grim an' sootie,
            Clos'd under hatches,
Spairges about the brunstane cootie,
            To scaud poor wretches!

Hear me, Auld Hangie, for a wee,
An' let poor damnéd bodies be;

5. *spairges,* splashes. *cootie,* tub.

I'm sure sma' pleasure it can gie,
    Ev'n to a deil,   10
To skelp an' scaud poor dogs like me
    An' hear us squeel!

Great is thy pow'r, an' great thy fame;
Far kend an' noted is thy name;
An' tho' yon lowin heugh's thy hame,
    Thou travels far;
An' faith! thou's neither lag, nor lame,
    Nor blate, nor scaur.

Whyles, ranging like a roarin lion,
For prey, a' holes an' corners trying;   20
Whyles, on the strong-wing'd tempest flyin,
    Tirlin the kirks;
Whyles, in the human bosom pryin,
    Unseen thou lurks.

I've heard my rev'rend grannie say,
In lanely glens ye like to stray;
Or, where auld ruin'd castles gray
    Nod to the moon,
Ye fright the nightly wand'rer's way
    Wi' eldritch croon.   30

When twilight did my grannie summon,
To say her pray'rs, douce, honest woman!
Aft yont the dyke she's heard you bummin,
    Wi' eerie drone;
Or, rustlin, thro' the boortrees comin,
    Wi' heavy groan.

Ae dreary, windy, winter night,
The star shot down wi' sklentin' light,

11. *skelp*, slap.   15. *lowin*, glowing; *heugh*, cave.
18. *blate*, shy; *scaur*, timid.
22. *Tirlin' the kirks*, tearing the roofs off churches.
30. *eldritch*, unearthly.   32. *douce*, gentle.   35. *boortrees*, elder bushes.

Wi' you mysel, I gat a fright:
    Ayont the lough,   40
Ye, like a rash-buss, stood in sight,
    Wi' waving sough.

The cudgel in my nieve did shake,
Each bristl'd hair stood like a stake;
When wi' an eldritch, stoor "quaick, quaick,"
    Amang the springs,
Awa ye squattered like a drake,
    On whistling wings.

Let warlocks grim, an' wither'd hags,
Tell how wi' you, on ragweed nags,   50
They skim the muirs an' dizzy crags,
    Wi' wicked speed;
And in kirk-yards renew their leagues,
    Owre howkit dead.

Thence, countra wives, wi' toil an' pain,
May plunge an' plunge the kirn in vain;
For O! the yellow treasure's taen
    By witchin' skill;
An' dawtit, twal-pint Hawkie's gane
    As yell's the bill.   60

Thence, mystic knots mak great abuse
On young guidmen, fond, keen an' croose;
When the best wark-lume i' the house,
    By cantraip wit,
Is instant made no worth a louse,
    Just at the bit.

40. *lough*, lake.   42. *sough*, sigh.   43. *nieve*, hand.
45. *stoor*, stern.   49. *warlocks*, witches.   54. *Owre*, over; *howkit*, dugup.
56. *kirn*, churn.
59. *dawtit*, pampered; *twal-pint*, twelve-pint; *Hawkie*, chalk face.
60. *yell*, dry; *bill*, bull.
62. *young guidmen*, newly married men; *croose*, bold.
63. *wark-lume*, tool.

When thowes dissolve the snawy hoord,
An' float the jinglin icy-boord,
Then, water-kelpies haunt the foord,
     By your direction,   70
An' 'nighted trav'llers are allur'd
     To their destruction.

An' aft your moss-traversing spunkies
Decoy the wight that late an' drunk is:
The bleezin, curst, mischievous monkies
     Delude his eyes,
Till in some miry slough he sunk is,
     Ne'er mair to rise.

When Masons' mystic word an' grip
In storms an' tempests raise you up,   80
Some cock or cat your rage maun stop,
     Or, strange to tell!
The youngest brither ye wad whip
     Aff straught to hell.

Lang syne in Eden's bonie yard,
When youthfu' lovers first were pair'd,
An' all the soul of love they shar'd,
     The raptur'd hour,
Sweet on the fragrant flow'ry swaird,
     In shady bow'r: 90

Then you, ye auld, snick-drawing dog!
Ye cam to Paradise incog,
An' play'd on man a cursed brogue
     (Black be your fa'!),
An' gied the infant warld a shog,
     'Maist ruin'd a'.

D' ye mind that day when in a bizz
Wi' reekit duds, an' reestit gizz,

---

67. *thowes*, thaws.   73. *spunkies*, will-o-the-wisp.
91. *snick-drawing*, latch-lifting.   95. *shog*, shock.
98. *reekit*, smoky; *reestit gizz*, singed wig.

Ye did present your smoutie phiz
    'Mang better folk;   100
An' sklented on the man of Uzz
    Your spitefu' joke?

An' how ye gat him i' your thrall,
An' brak him out o' house an' hal',
While scabs an' botches did him gall,
    Wi' bitter claw;
An' lowsed his ill-tongu'd wicked scaul—
    Was warst ava?

But a' your doings to rehearse,
Your wily snares an' fechtin fierce,   110
Sin' that day Michael did you pierce
    Down to this time,
Wad ding a Lallan tongue, or Erse,
    In prose or rhyme.

An' now, Auld Cloots, I ken ye're thinkin,
A certain Bardie's rantin, drinkin,
Some luckless hour will send him linkin,
    To your black Pit;
But, faith! he'll turn a corner jinkin,
    An' cheat you yet.   120

But fare-you-weel, Auld Nickie-Ben!
O, wad ye tak a thought an' men'!
Ye aiblins might—I dinna ken—
    Still hae a stake:
I'm wae to think upo' yon den,
    Ev'n for your sake!

        1786

---

101. *sklented*, directed.   107. *lowsed*, let loose.
113. *ding*, outdo; *Lallan*, Lowland; *Erse*, Gaelic.   117. *linkin*, skipping.
119. *jinkin*, dodging.   123. *aiblins*, perhaps.   125. *wae*, woe.

Holy Willie's Prayer [1]

O Thou, wha in the Heavens dost dwell,
Wha, as it pleases best Thysel',
Sends ane to heaven an' ten to hell
    A' for Thy glory,
And no for onie guid or ill
    They've done afore Thee!

I bless and praise Thy matchless might,
Whan thousands Thou hast left in night,
That I am here before Thy sight,
    For gifts an' grace,   10
A burning an' a shining light,
    To a' this place.

What was I, or my generation,
That I should get sic exaltation?
I, wha deserv'd sic just damnation
    For broken laws,
Five thousand years 'fore my creation,
    Thro' Adam's cause!

When frae my mither's womb I fell,
Thou might hae plung'd me deep in hell,   20
To gnash my gums, to weep and wail,
    In burnin' lake,
Where damnéd devils roar and yell,
    Chain'd to a stake.

Yet I am here, a chosen sample,
To show Thy grace is great and ample;
I'm here a pillar in Thy temple,
    Strong as a rock,
A guide, a buckler, an example
    To a' Thy flock.   30

[1] "Holy Willie" was William Fisher, an elder of doubtful reputation in a small Scotch church. The following "prayer" was voiced by Willie after he was reproved before an ecclesiastical court, at the instigation of Mr. Gavin Hamilton, who is referred to in the poem.

O Lord, Thou kens what zeal I bear,
When drinkers drink, and swearers swear,
And singin' there and dancin' here,
    Wi' great an' sma':
For I am keepit by Thy fear,
    Free frae them a'.

But yet, O Lord! confess I must:
At times I'm fash'd wi' fleshly lust;
An' sometimes, too, wi' warldly trust,
    Vile self gets in;   40
But Thou remembers we are dust,
    Defil'd in sin.

O Lord! yestreen, Thou kens, wi' Meg—
Thy pardon I sincerely beg,
O! may it ne'er be a livin' plague
    To my dishonor!
An' I'll ne'er lift a lawless leg
    Again upon her.

Besides, I farther maun allow,
Wi' Lizzie's lass, three times, I trow;   50
But, Lord, that Friday I was fou,
    When I came near her,
Or else, Thou kens, Thy servant true
    Wad ne'er hae steered her.

May be Thou lets this fleshly thorn
Beset Thy servant e'en and morn,
Lest he owre high and proud should turn,
    'Cause he's sae gifted;
If sae, Thy hand maun e'en be borne,
    Until Thou lift it.   60

Lord, bless Thy chosen in this place,
For here Thou hast a chosen race;
But God confound their stubborn face,
    And blast their name,
Wha bring Thy elders to disgrace,
    An' public shame!

38. *fash'd,* tempted.

Lord, mind Gau'n Hamilton's deserts:
He drinks, an' swears, an' plays at cartes,
Yet has sae monie takin arts
    Wi' grit and sma',   70
Frae God's ain Priest the people's hearts
    He steals awa'.

An' whan we chasten'd him therefore,
Thou kens how he bred sic a splore,
As set the warld in a roar
    O' laughin at us;
Curse Thou his basket and his store,
    Kail and potatoes!

Lord, hear my earnest cry an' pray'r
Against that Presbyt'ry o' Ayr!   80
Thy strong right hand, Lord, make it bare
    Upo' their heads;
Lord, weigh it down, an' dinna spare,
    For their misdeeds!

O Lord my God! that glib-tongu'd Aiken,
My very heart and flesh are quakin,
To think how we stood sweatin, shakin,
    An' piss'd wi' dread,
While he, wi' hingin lip an' snakin,
    Held up his head.   90

Lord, in the day of vengeance try him;
Lord, visit him wha did employ him,
And pass not in Thy mercy by 'em,
    Nor hear their pray'r:
But, for Thy people's sake, destroy 'em,
    An' dinna spare.

But, Lord, remember me and mine
Wi' mercies temp'ral and divine,

---

68. *cartes*, cards.   70. *grit*, great.   74. *splore*, fuss.
89. *snakin*, sneering.

That I for gear and grace may shine,
   Excelled by nane;   100
And a' the glory shall be Thine,
   Amen, Amen.

1799

WILLIAM WORDSWORTH

Lines

COMPOSED A FEW MILES ABOVE TINTERN ABBEY, ON REVISITING
THE BANKS OF THE WYE DURING A TOUR. JULY 13, 1798

Five years have passed; five summers, with the
   length
Of five long winters! and again I hear
These waters, rolling from their mountain-springs
With a soft inland murmur.—Once again
Do I behold these steep and lofty cliffs,
That on a wild secluded scene impress
Thoughts of more deep seclusion; and connect
The landscape with the quiet of the sky.
The day is come when I again repose
Here, under this dark sycamore, and view   10
These plots of cottage-ground, these orchard-tufts,
Which at this season, with their unripe fruits,
Are clad in one green hue, and lose themselves
'Mid groves and copses. Once again I see
These hedge-rows, hardly hedge-rows, little lines
Of sportive wood run wild: these pastoral farms,
Green to the very door; and wreaths of smoke
Sent up, in silence, from among the trees!
With some uncertain notice, as might seem
Of vagrant dwellers in the houseless woods   20
Or of some Hermit's cave, where by his fire
The hermit sits alone.
                   These beauteous forms,
Through a long absence, have not been to me
As is a landscape to a blind man's eye:

99. *gear,* wealth.

But oft, in lonely rooms, and 'mid the din
Of towns and cities, I have owed to them
In hours of weariness, sensations sweet,
Felt in the blood, and felt along the heart;
And passing even into my purer mind,
With tranquil restoration:—feelings too   30
Of unremembered pleasure: such, perhaps,
As have no slight or trivial influence
On that best portion of a good man's life,
His little, nameless, unremembered, acts
Of kindness and of love. Nor less, I trust,
To them I may have owed another gift,
Of aspect more sublime; that blessed mood,
In which the burthen of the mystery,
In which the heavy and the weary weight
Of all this unintelligible world,   40
Is lightened:—that serene and blessed mood,
In which the affections gently lead us on,—
Until, the breath of this corporeal frame
And even the motion of our human blood
Almost suspended, we are laid asleep
In body, and become a living soul:
While with an eye made quiet by the power
Of harmony, and the deep power of joy,
We see into the life of things.
                                        If this
Be but a vain belief, yet, oh! how oft—   50
In darkness and amid the many shapes
Of joyless daylight; when the fretful stir
Unprofitable, and the fever of the world,
Have hung upon the beatings of my heart—
How oft, in spirit, have I turned to thee,
O sylvan Wye! thou wanderer through the woods,
How often has my spirit turned to thee!
    And now, with gleams of half-extinguished thought,
With many recognitions dim and faint,
And somewhat of a sad perplexity,   60
The picture of the mind revives again:
While here I stand, not only with the sense

Of present pleasure, but with pleasing thoughts
That in this moment there is life and food
For future years. And so I dare to hope,
Though changed, no doubt, from what I was when first
I came among these hills; when like a roe
I bounded o'er the mountains, by the sides
Of the deep rivers, and the lonely streams,
Wherever nature led: more like a man   70
Flying from something that he dreads, than one
Who sought the thing he loved. For nature then
(The coarser pleasures of my boyish days,
And their glad animal movements all gone by)
To me was all in all.—I cannot paint
What then I was. The sounding cataract
Haunted me like a passion; the tall rock,
The mountain, and the deep and gloomy wood,
Their colors and their forms, were then to me
An appetite; a feeling and a love,   80
That had no need of a remoter charm,
By thought supplied, nor any interest
Unborrowed from the eye.—That time is past,
And all its aching joys are now no more,
And all its dizzy raptures. Not for this
Faint I, nor mourn nor murmur; other gifts
Have followed; for such loss, I would believe,
Abundant recompense. For I have learned
To look on nature, not as in the hour
Of thoughtless youth; but hearing oftentimes   90
The still, sad music of humanity,
Nor harsh nor grating, though of ample power
To chasten and subdue. And I have felt
A presence that disturbs me with the joy
Of elevated thoughts; a sense sublime
Of something far more deeply interfused,
Whose dwelling is the light of setting suns,
And the round ocean and the living air,
And the blue sky, and in the mind of man;
A motion and a spirit, that impels   100
All thinking things, all objects of all thought,

And rolls through all things. Therefore am I still
A lover of the meadows and the woods,
And mountains; and of all that we behold
From this green earth; of all the mighty world
Of eye, and ear,—both what they half create,
And what perceive; well pleased to recognize
In nature and the language of the sense,
The anchor of my purest thoughts, the nurse,
The guide, the guardian of my heart, and soul   110
Of all my moral being.
                   Nor perchance,
If I were not thus taught, should I the more
Suffer my genial spirits to decay:
For thou art with me here upon the banks
Of this fair river; thou my dearest Friend,
My dear, dear Friend, and in thy voice I catch
The language of my former heart, and read
My former pleasures in the shooting lights
Of thy wild eyes. Oh! yet a little while
May I behold in thee what I was once,   120
My dear, dear Sister! and this prayer I make,
Knowing that Nature never did betray
The heart that loved her; 'tis her privilege,
Through all the years of this our life, to lead
From joy to joy: for she can so inform
The mind that is within us, so impress
With quietness and beauty, and so feed
With lofty thoughts, that neither evil tongues,
Rash judgments, nor the sneers of selfish men,
Nor greetings where no kindness is, nor all   130
The dreary intercourse of daily life,
Shall e'er prevail against us, or disturb
Our cheerful faith, that all which we behold
Is full of blessings. Therefore let the moon
Shine on thee in thy solitary walk;
And let the misty mountain-winds be free
To blow against thee: and, in after years,

115. Dorothy Wordsworth, the poet's sister.

When these wild ecstasies shall be matured
Into a sober pleasure; when thy mind
Shall be a mansion for all lovely forms,   140
Thy memory be as a dwelling-place
For all sweet sounds and harmonies; oh! then,
If solitude, or fear, or pain, or grief,
Should be thy portion, with what healing thoughts
Of tender joy wilt thou remember me,
And these my exhortations! Nor, perchance—
If I should be where I no more can hear
Thy voice, nor catch from thy wild eyes these gleams
Of past existence—wilt thou then forget
That on the banks of this delightful stream   150
We stood together; and that I, so long
A worshiper of Nature, hither came
Unwearied in that service: rather say
With warmer love—oh! with far deeper zeal
Of holier love. Nor wilt thou then forget,
That after many wanderings, many years
Of absence, these steep woods and lofty cliffs,
And this green pastoral landscape, were to me
More dear, both for themselves and for thy sake!

1798

When I Have Borne in Memory

When I have borne in memory what has tamed
Great Nations, how ennobling thoughts depart
When men change swords for ledgers, and desert
The student's bower for gold, some fears unnamed
I had, my Country—am I to be blamed?
Now, when I think of thee, and what thou art,
Verily, in the bottom of my heart,
Of those unfilial fears I am ashamed.
For dearly must we prize thee; we who find
In thee a bulwark for the cause of men;
And I by my affection was beguiled:
What wonder if a Poet now and then,

Among the many movements of his mind,
Felt for thee as a lover or a child!

1807

Nuns Fret Not at Their Convent's Narrow Room

Nuns fret not at their convent's narrow room;
And hermits are contented with their cells;
And students with their pensive citadels;
Maids at the wheel, the weaver at his loom,
Sit blithe and happy; bees that soar for bloom,
High as the highest Peak of Furness-fells,
Will murmur by the hour in foxglove bells:
In truth the prison, into which we doom
Ourselves, no prison is: and hence for me,
In sundry moods, 'twas pastime to be bound   10
Within the Sonnet's scanty plot of ground;
Pleased if some Souls (for such there needs must be)
Who have felt the weight of too much liberty,
Should find brief solace there, as I have found.

1807

It Is a Beauteous Evening, Calm and Free

It is a beauteous evening, calm and free,
The holy time is quiet as a Nun
Breathless with adoration; the broad sun
Is sinking down in its tranquillity;
The gentleness of heaven broods o'er the Sea:
Listen! the mighty Being is awake,
And doth with his eternal motion make
A sound like thunder—everlastingly.
Dear Child! dear Girl! that walkest with me here,
If thou appear untouched by solemn thought,   10
Thy nature is not therefore less divine:
Thou liest in Abraham's bosom all the year;
And worshipp'st at the Temple's inner shrine,
God being with thee when we know it not.

1807

Ode to Duty

Stern Daughter of the Voice of God!
O Duty! if that name thou love
Who art a light to guide, a rod
To check the erring, and reprove;
Thou, who art victory and law
When empty terrors overawe;
From vain temptations dost set free;
And calm'st the weary strife of frail humanity!

There are who ask not if thine eye
Be on them; who, in love and truth,   10
Where no misgiving is, rely
Upon the genial sense of youth:
Glad Hearts! without reproach or blot;
Who do thy work, and know it not:
Oh! if through confidence misplaced
They fail, thy saving arms, dread Power! around
   them cast.

Serene will be our days and bright,
And happy will our nature be,
When love is an unerring light,
And joy its own security.   20
And they a blissful course may hold
Even now, who, not unwisely bold,
Live in the spirit of this creed;
Yet seek thy firm support, according to their need.

I, loving freedom, and untried;
No sport of every random gust,
Yet being to myself a guide,
Too blindly have reposed my trust:
And oft, when in my heart was heard
Thy timely mandate, I deferred   30
The task, in smoother walks to stray;
But thee I now would serve more strictly, if I may.

Through no disturbance of my soul,
Or strong compunction in me wrought,

I supplicate for thy control;
But in the quietness of thought:
Me this unchartered freedom tires;
I feel the weight of chance-desires:
My hopes no more must change their name,
I long for a repose that ever is the same.   40

Stern Lawgiver! yet thou dost wear
The Godhead's most benignant grace;
Nor know we anything so fair
As is the smile upon thy face:
Flowers laugh before thee on their beds
And fragrance in thy footing treads;
Thou dost preserve the stars from wrong;
And the most ancient heavens, through Thee, are
    fresh and strong.

To humbler functions, awful Power!   50
I call thee: I myself commend
Unto thy guidance from this hour;
Oh, let my weakness have an end!
Give unto me, made lowly wise,
The spirit of self-sacrifice;
The confidence of reason give;
And in the light of truth thy Bondman let me live!
    1807

The World Is Too Much with Us

The world is too much with us: late and soon,
Getting and spending, we lay waste our powers:
Little we see in Nature that is ours;
We have given our hearts away, a sordid boon!
This Sea that bares her bosom to the moon;
The winds that will be howling at all hours,
And are up-gathered now like sleeping flowers;
For this, for everything, we are out of tune;
It moves us not.—Great God! I'd rather be
A Pagan suckled in a creed outworn;   10

So might I, standing on this pleasant lea,
Have glimpses that would make me less forlorn;
Have sight of Proteus rising from the sea;
Or hear old Triton blow his wreathèd horn.

1807

Scorn Not the Sonnet

Scorn not the Sonnet; Critic, you have frowned,
Mindless of its just honors; with this key
Shakespeare unlocked his heart; the melody
Of this small lute gave ease to Petrarch's wound;
A thousand times this pipe did Tasso sound;
With it Camoëns soothed an exile's grief;
The Sonnet glittered a gay myrtle leaf
Amid the cypress with which Dante crowned
His visionary brow; a glowworm lamp,
It cheered mild Spenser, called from Faeryland   10
To struggle through dark ways; and when a damp
Fell round the path of Milton, in his hand
The Thing became a trumpet; whence he blew
Soul-animating strains—alas, too few!

1827

The Prelude

CHILDHOOD AND SCHOOL-TIME

Fair seed-time had my soul, and I grew up
Fostered alike by beauty and by fear:
Much favoured in my birthplace, and no less
In that belovéd Vale to which erelong
We were transplanted—there were we let loose
For sports of wider range. Ere I had told
Ten birth-days, when among the mountain-slopes
Frost, and the breath of frosty wind, had snapped
The last autumnal crocus, 'twas my joy
With store of springes o'er my shoulder hung   10

To range the open heights where woodcocks run
Among the smooth green turf. Through half the night,
Scudding away from snare to snare, I plied
That anxious visitation;—moon and stars
Were shining o'er my head. I was alone,
And seemed to be a trouble to the peace
That dwelt among them. Sometimes it befell
In these night wanderings, that a strong desire
O'erpowered my better reason, and the bird
Which was the captive of another's toil   20
Became my prey; and when the deed was done
I heard among the solitary hills
Low breathings coming after me, and sounds
Of undistinguishable motion, steps
Almost as silent as the turf they trod.

   Nor less when spring had warmed the cultured Vale,
Moved we as plunderers where the mother-bird
Had in high places built her lodge; though mean
Our object and inglorious, yet the end
Was not ignoble. Oh! when I have hung   30
Above the raven's nest, by knots of grass   .
And half-inch fissures in the slippery rock
But ill sustained, and almost (so it seemed)
Suspended by the blast that blew amain,
Shouldering the naked crag, oh, at that time
While on the perilous ridge I hung alone,
With what strange utterance did the loud dry wind
Blow through my ear! the sky seemed not a sky
Of earth—and with what motion moved the clouds!

   Dust as we are, the immortal spirit grows   40
Like harmony in music; there is a dark
Inscrutable workmanship that reconciles
Discordant elements, makes them cling together
In one society. How strange that all
The terrors, pains, and early miseries,
Regrets, vexations, lassitudes interfused
Within my mind, should e'er have borne a part,
And that a needful part, in making up

The calm existence that is mine when I
Am worthy of myself! Praise to the end! 50
Thanks to the means which Nature deigned to employ;
Whether her fearless visitings, or those
That came with soft alarm, like hurtless light
Opening the peaceful clouds; or she may use
Severer interventions, ministry
More palpable, as best might suit her aim.

One summer evening (led by her) I found
A little boat tied to a willow tree
Within a rocky cave, its usual home.
Straight I unloosed her chain, and stepping in 60
Pushed from the shore. It was an act of stealth
And troubled pleasure, nor without the voice
Of mountain-echoes did my boat move on;
Leaving behind her still, on either side,
Small circles glittering idly in the moon,
Until they melted all into one track
Of sparkling light. But now, like one who rows,
Proud of his skill, to reach a chosen point
With an unswerving line, I fixed my view
Upon the summit of a craggy ridge, 70
The horizon's utmost boundary; far above
Was nothing but the stars and the grey sky.
She was an elfin pinnace; lustily
I dipped my oars into the silent lake,
And, as I rose upon the stroke, my boat
Went heaving through the water like a swan;
When, from behind that craggy steep till then
The horizon's bound, a huge peak, black and huge,
As if with voluntary power instinct
Upreared its head. I struck and struck again, 80
And growing still in stature the grim shape
Towered up between me and the stars, and still,
For so it seemed, with purpose of its own
And measured motion like a living thing,
Strode after me. With trembling oars I turned,
And through the silent water stole my way

Back to the covert of the willow tree;
There in her mooring-place I left my bark,—
And through the meadows homeward went, in grave
And serious mood; but after I had seen   90
That spectacle, for many days, my brain
Worked with a dim and undetermined sense
Of unknown modes of being; o'er my thoughts
There hung a darkness, call it solitude
Or blank desertion. No familiar shapes
Remained, no pleasant images of trees,
Of sea or sky, no colours of green fields;
But huge and mighty forms, that do not live
Like living men, moved slowly through the mind
By day, and were a trouble to my dreams.   100

Wisdom and Spirit of the universe!
Thou Soul that art the eternity of thought,
Thou givest to forms and images a breath
And everlasting motion, not in vain
By day or star-light thus from my first dawn
Of childhood didst thou intertwine for me
The passions that build up our human soul;
Not with the mean and vulgar works of man,
But with high objects, with enduring things—
With life and nature—purifying thus   110
The elements of feeling and of thought,
And sanctifying, by such discipline,
Both pain and fear, until we recognise
A grandeur in the beatings of the heart.
Nor was this fellowship vouchsafed to me
With stinted kindness. In November days,
When vapours rolling down the valley made
A lonely scene more lonesome, among woods,
At noon and 'mid the calm of summer nights,
When, by the margin of the trembling lake,   120
Beneath the gloomy hills homeward I went
In solitude, such intercourse was mine;
Mine was it in the fields both day and night,
And by the waters, all the summer long.

And in the frosty season, when the sun
Was set, and visible for many a mile
The cottage windows blazed through twilight gloom,
I heeded not their summons: happy time
It was indeed for all of us—for me
It was a time of rapture! Clear and loud   130
The village clock tolled six,—I wheeled about,
Proud and exulting like an untired horse
That cares not for his home. All shod with steel,
We hissed along the polished ice in games
Confederate, imitative of the chase
And woodland pleasures,—the resounding horn,
The pack loud chiming, and the hunted hare.
So through the darkness and the cold we flew,
And not a voice was idle; with the din
Smitten, the precipices rang aloud;   140
The leafless trees and every icy crag
Tinkled like iron; while far distant hills
Into the tumult sent an alien sound
Of melancholy not unnoticed, while the stars
Eastward were sparkling clear, and in the west
The orange sky of evening died away.
Not seldom from the uproar I retired
Into a silent bay, or sportively
Glanced sideway, leaving the tumultuous throng,
To cut across the reflex of a star   150
That fled, and, flying still before me, gleamed
Upon the glassy plain; and oftentimes,
When we had given our bodies to the wind,
And all the shadowy banks on either side
Came sweeping through the darkness, spinning still
The rapid line of motion, then at once
Have I, reclining back upon my heels,
Stopped short; yet still the solitary cliffs
Wheeled by me—even as if the earth had rolled
With visible motion her diurnal round!   160
Behind me did they stretch in solemn train,
Feebler and feebler, and I stood and watched
Till all was tranquil as a dreamless sleep.

                              From *Book I, 1850*

WALTER SAVAGE LANDOR

Resignation

Why, why repine, my pensive friend,
　　At pleasures slipp'd away?
Some the stern Fates will never lend,
　　And all refuse to stay.

I see the rainbow in the sky,
　　The dew upon the grass;
I see them, and I ask not why
　　They glimmer or they pass.

With folded arms I linger not
　　To call them back; 'twere vain:　　　　10
In this, or in some other spot,
　　I know they'll shine again.

1846

PERCY BYSSHE SHELLEY

Hymn To Intellectual Beauty

I

The awful shadow of some unseen Power
　　Floats though unseen among us,—visiting
　　This various world with as inconstant wing
As summer winds that creep from flower to flower,—
Like moonbeams that behind some piny mountain
　　　　shower,
　　It visits with inconstant glance
　　Each human heart and countenance;
Like hues and harmonies of evening,—
　　Like clouds in starlight widely spread,—
　　Like memory of music fled,—　　　　10
　　Like aught that for its grace may be
Dear, and yet dearer for its mystery.

II

Spirit of BEAUTY, that dost consecrate
  With thine own hues all thou dost shine upon
  Of human thought or form,—where art thou gone?
Why dost thou pass away and leave our state,
This dim vast vale of tears, vacant and desolate?
    Ask why the sunlight not for ever
    Weaves rainbows o'er yon mountain-river,
Why aught should fail and fade that once is shown,   20
    Why fear and dream and death and birth
    Cast on the daylight of this earth
    Such gloom,—why man has such a scope
For love and hate, despondency and hope?

III

No voice from some sublimer world hath ever
  To sage or poet these responses given—
  Therefore the names of Demon, Ghost, and Heaven,
Remain the records of their vain endeavor,
Frail spells—whose uttered charm might not avail to
    sever,
    From all we hear and all we see,   30
    Doubt, chance, and mutability.
Thy light alone—like mist o'er mountains driven,
    Or music by the night-wind sent
    Through strings of some still instrument,
    Or moonlight on a midnight stream,
Gives grace and truth to life's unquiet dream.

IV

Love, Hope, and Self-esteem, like clouds depart
  And come, for some uncertain moments lent.
  Man were immortal, and omnipotent,
Didst thou, unknown and awful as thou art,   40
Keep with thy glorious train firm state within his heart.
    Thou messenger of sympathies,
    That wax and wane in lovers' eyes—

Thou—that to human thought art nourishment,
    Like darkness to a dying flame!
    Depart not as thy shadow came,
    Depart not—lest the grave should be,
Like life and fear, a dark reality.

V

While yet a boy I sought for ghosts, and sped
    Through many a listening chamber, cave and ruin,   50
    And starlight wood, with fearful steps pursuing
Hopes of high talk with the departed dead.
I called on poisonous names with which our youth is fed;
    I was not heard—I saw them not—
    When musing deeply on the lot
Of life, at that sweet time when winds are wooing
    All vital things that wake to bring
    News of birds and blossoming,—
    Sudden, thy shadow fell on me;
I shrieked, and clasped my hands in ecstasy!   60

VI

I vowed that I would dedicate my powers
    To thee and thine—have I not kept the vow?
    With beating heart and streaming eyes, even now
I call the phantoms of a thousand hours
Each from his voiceless grave: they have in visioned
    bowers
    Of studious zeal or love's delight
    Outwatched with me the envious night—
They know that never joy illumed my brow
    Unlinked with hope that thou wouldst free
    This world from its dark slavery,   70
    That thou—O awful LOVELINESS,
Wouldst give whate'er these words cannot express.

VII

The day becomes more solemn and serene
    When noon is past—there is a harmony
    In autumn, and a luster in its sky,

Which through the summer is not heard or seen,
As if it could not be, as if it had not been!
　　Thus let thy power, which like the truth
　　Of nature on my passive youth
Descended, to my onward life supply　　　　　　　　80
　　Its calm—to one who worships thee,
　　And every form containing thee,
　　Whom, SPIRIT fair, thy spells did bind
To fear himself, and love all human kind.

1817

Ozymandias

I met a traveler from an antique land
Who said: Two vast and trunkless legs of stone
Stand in the desert. Near them, on the sand,
Half sunk, a shattered visage lies, whose frown,
And wrinkled lip, and sneer of cold command,
Tell that its sculptor well those passions read
Which yet survive, stamped on these lifeless things,
The hand that mocked them, and the heart that fed:
And on the pedestal these words appear:
"My name is Ozymandias, King of Kings:　　　　　　　10
Look on my works, ye Mighty, and despair!"
Nothing beside remains. Round the decay
Of that colossal wreck, boundless and bare
The lone and level sands stretch far away.

1818

ALFRED, LORD TENNYSON

Ulysses

It little profits that an idle king,
By this still hearth, among these barren crags,
Match'd with an aged wife, I mete and dole
Unequal laws unto a savage race,
That hoard, and sleep, and feed, and know not me.
I cannot rest from travel: I will drink

Life to the lees: all times I have enjoy'd
Greatly, have suffer'd greatly, both with those
That loved me, and alone; on shore, and when
Thro' scudding drifts the rainy Hyades   10
Vext the dim sea: I am become a name;
For always roaming with a hungry heart
Much have I seen and known; cities of men
And manners, climates, councils, governments,
Myself not least, but honour'd of them all;
And drunk delight of battle with my peers,
Far on the ringing plains of windy Troy.
I am a part of all that I have met;
Yet all experience is an arch wherethro'
Gleams that untravell'd world, whose margin fades   20
For ever and for ever when I move.
How dull it is to pause, to make an end,
To rust unburnish'd, not to shine in use!
As tho' to breathe were life. Life piled on life
Were all too little, and of one to me
Little remains: but every hour is saved
From that eternal silence, something more,
A bringer of new things; and vile it were
For some three suns to store and hoard myself,
And this gray spirit yearning in desire   30
To follow knowledge like a sinking star,
Beyond the utmost bound of human thought.
     This is my son, mine own Telemachus,
To whom I leave the sceptre and the isle—
Well-loved of me, discerning to fulfil
This labour, by slow prudence to make mild
A rugged people, and thro' soft degrees
Subdue them to the useful and the good.
Most blameless is he, centered in the sphere
Of common duties, decent not to fail   40
In offices of tenderness, and pay
Meet adoration to my household gods,
When I am gone. He works his work, I mine.
     There lies the port; the vessel puffs her sail:
There gloom the dark broad seas. My mariners,

Souls that have toil'd, and wrought, and thought with
    me— .
That ever with a frolic welcome took
The thunder and the sunshine, and opposed
Free hearts, free foreheads—you and I are old;
Old age hath yet his honour and his toil;   50
Death closes all: but something ere the end,
Some work of noble note, may yet be done,
Not unbecoming men that strove with Gods.
The lights begin to twinkle from the rocks:
The long day wanes: the slow moon climbs: the deep
Moans round with many voices. Come, my friends,
'Tis not too late to seek a newer world.
Push off, and sitting well in order smite
The sounding furrows; for my purpose holds
To sail beyond the sunset, and the baths   60
Of all the western stars, until I die.
It may be that the gulfs will wash us down:
It may be we shall touch the Happy Isles,
And see the great Achilles, whom we knew.
Tho' much is taken, much abides; and tho'
We are not now that strength which in old days
Moved earth and heaven; that which we are, we are;
One equal temper of heroic hearts,
Made weak by time and fate, but strong in will
To strive, to seek, to find, and not to yield.   70

                              1842

In Memoriam A. H. H.[1]

OBIIT MDCCCXXXIII

Strong Son of God, immortal Love,
    Whom we, that have not seen thy face,
    By faith, and faith alone, embrace,
Believing where we cannot prove;

[1] *In Memoriam* is a threnody to Tennyson's friend Arthur Henry Hallam
who died in 1833.

Thine are these orbs of light and shade;
　　Thou madest Life in man and brute;
　　Thou madest Death; and lo, thy foot
Is on the skull which thou hast made.

Thou wilt not leave us in the dust:
　　Thou madest man, he knows not why,   10
　　He thinks he was not made to die;
And thou hast made him: thou art just.

Thou seemest human and divine,
　　The highest, holiest manhood, thou:
　　Our wills are ours, we know not how;
Our wills are ours, to make them thine.

Our little systems have their day;
　　They have their day and cease to be:
　　They are but broken lights of thee,
And thou, O Lord, art more than they.   20

We have but faith: we cannot know;
　　For knowledge is of things we see;
　　And yet we trust it comes from thee,
A beam in darkness: let it grow.

Let knowledge grow from more to more,
　　But more of reverence in us dwell;
　　That mind and soul, according well,
May make one music as before,

But vaster. We are fools and slight;
　　We mock thee when we do not fear: 30
　　But help thy foolish ones to bear;
Help thy vain worlds to bear thy light.

II

Old Yew, which graspest at the stones
　　That name the under-lying dead,
　　Thy fibres net the dreamless head,
Thy roots are wrapt about the bones.

The seasons bring the flower again,
    And bring the firstling to the flock;
    And in the dusk of thee, the clock
Beats out the little lives of men.   40

O not for thee the glow, the bloom,
    Who changest not in any gale,
    Nor branding summer suns avail
To touch thy thousand years of gloom:

And gazing on thee, sullen tree,
    Sick for thy stubborn hardihood,
    I seem to fail from out my blood
And grow incorporate into thee.

XXVII

I envy not in any moods
    The captive void of noble rage,   50
    The linnet born within the cage,
That never knew the summer woods:

I envy not the beast that takes
    His license in the field of time,
    Unfetter'd by the sense of crime,
To whom a conscience never wakes;

Nor, what may count itself as blest,
    The heart that never plighted troth
    But stagnates in the weeds of sloth;
Nor any want-begotten rest.   60

I hold it true, whate'er befall;
    I feel it, when I sorrow most;
    'Tis better to have loved and lost
Than never to have loved at all.

LIV

Oh yet we trust that somehow good
    Will be the final goal of ill,
    To pangs of nature, sins of will,
Defects of doubt, and taints of blood;

That nothing walks with aimless feet;
   That not one life shall be destroy'd,   70
   Or cast as rubbish to the void,
When God hath made the pile complete;

That not a worm is cloven in vain;
   That not a moth with vain desire
   Is shrivell'd in a fruitless fire,
Or but subserves another's gain.

Behold, we know not anything;
   I can but trust that good shall fall
   At last—far off—at last, to all,
And every winter change to spring.   80

So runs my dream: but what am I?
   An infant crying in the night:
   An infant crying for the light:
And with no language but a cry.

CVI

Ring out, wild bells, to the wild sky,
   The flying cloud, the frosty light:
   The year is dying in the night;
Ring out, wild bells, and let him die.

Ring out the old, ring in the new,
   Ring, happy bells, across the snow: 90
   The year is going, let him go;
Ring out the false, ring in the true.

Ring out the grief that saps the mind,
   For those that here we see no more;
   Ring out the feud of rich and poor,
Ring in redress to all mankind.

Ring out a slowly dying cause,
   And ancient forms of party strife;
   Ring in the nobler modes of life,
With sweeter manners, purer laws.   100

Ring out the want, the care, the sin,
　The faithless coldness of the times
　Ring out, ring out my mournful rhymes,
But ring the fuller minstrel in.

Ring out false pride in place and blood,
　The civic slander and the spite;
　Ring in the love of truth and right,
Ring in the common love of good.

Ring out old shapes of foul disease;
　Ring out the narrowing lust of gold;
　Ring out the thousand wars of old,
Ring in the thousand years of peace.

Ring in the valiant man and free,
　The larger heart, the kindlier hand;
　Ring out the darkness of the land,
Ring in the Christ that is to be.

CXXX

Thy voice is on the rolling air;
　I hear thee where the waters run;
　Thou standest in the rising sun,
And in the setting thou art fair.

What art thou then? I cannot guess;
　But tho' I seem in star and flower
　To feel thee some diffusive power,
I do not therefore love thee less:

My love involves the love before;
　My love is vaster passion now;   110
　Tho' mix'd with God and Nature thou,
I seem to love thee more and more.

Far off thou art, but ever nigh;
　I have thee still, and I rejoice;
　I prosper, circled with thy voice;
I shall not lose thee tho' I die.

1850

Ode on the Death of the Duke of Wellington

I

Bury the Great Duke
  With an empire's lamentation,
Let us bury the Great Duke
  To the noise of the mourning of a mighty nation,
Mourning when their leaders fall,
Warriors carry the warrior's pall,
And sorrow darkens hamlet and hall.

II

Where shall we lay the man whom we deplore?
Here, in streaming London's central roar.
Let the sound of those he wrought for,   10
And the feet of those he fought for,
Echo round his bones for evermore.

III

Lead out the pageant: sad and slow,
As fits an universal woe,
Let the long, long procession go,
And let the sorrowing crowd about it grow,
And let the mournful martial music blow;
The last great Englishman is low.

IV

Mourn, for to us he seems the last,
Remembering all his greatness in the Past   20
No more in soldier fashion will he greet
With lifted hand the gazer in the street.
O friends, our chief state-oracle is mute!
Mourn for the man of long-enduring blood,
The statesman-warrior, moderate, resolute,
Whole in himself, a common good.
Mourn for the man of amplest influence,
Yet clearest of ambitious crime,

Our greatest yet with least pretense,
Great in council and great in war, 30
Foremost captain of his time,
Rich in saving common-sense,
And, as the greatest only are,
In his simplicity sublime.
O good gray head which all men knew,
O voice from which their omens all men drew,
O iron nerve to true occasion true,
O fall'n at length that tower of strength
Which stood four-square to all the winds that blew!
Such was he whom we deplore. 40
The long self-sacrifice of life is o'er.
The great World-victor's victor will be seen no more.

V

All is over and done:
Render thanks to the Giver,
England, for thy son.
Let the bell be tolled.
Render thanks to the Giver,
And render him to the mold.
Under the cross of gold
That shines over city and river, 50
There he shall rest for ever
Among the wise and the bold.
Let the bell be tolled:
And a reverent people behold
The towering car, the sable steeds:
Bright let it be with its blazoned deeds,
Dark in its funeral fold.
Let the bell be tolled:
And a deeper knell in the heart be knolled;
And the sound of the sorrowing anthem rolled 60
Through the dome of the golden cross;
And the volleying cannon thunder his loss;
He knew their voices of old.
For many a time in many a clime
His captain's-ear has heard them boom

Bellowing victory, bellowing doom:
When he with those deep voices wrought,
Guarding realms and kings from shame;
With those deep voices our dead captain taught
The tyrant, and asserts his claim   70
In that dread sound to the great name,
Which he has worn so pure of blame,
In praise and in dispraise the same,
A man of well-attempered frame.
O civic muse, to such a name,
To such a name for ages long,
To such a name,
Preserve a broad approach of fame,
And ever-echoing avenues of song!

VI

Who is he that cometh, like an honored guest,   80
With banner and with music, with soldier and with
        priest,
With a nation weeping, and breaking on my rest?
Mighty Seaman, this is he
Was great by land as thou by sea.
Thine island loves thee well, thou famous man,
The greatest sailor since our world began.
Now, to the roll of muffled drums,
To thee the greatest soldier comes;
For this is he
Was great by land as thou by sea;   90
His foes were thine; he kept us free;
O give him welcome, this is he
Worthy of our gorgeous rites,
And worthy to be laid by thee;
For this is England's greatest son,
He that gained a hundred fights,
Nor ever lost an English gun;
This is he that far away
Against the myriads of Assaye
Clashed with his fiery few and won;   100
And underneath another sun,

Warring on a later day,
Round affrighted Lisbon drew
The treble works, the vast designs
Of his labored rampart-lines,
Where he greatly stood at bay,
Whence he issued forth anew,
And ever great and greater grew,
Beating from the wasted vines
Back to France her banded swarms, 110
Back to France with countless blows,
Till o'er the hills her eagles flew
Beyond the Pyrenean pines,
Followed up in valley and glen
With blare of bugle, clamor of men,
Roll of cannon and clash of arms,
And England pouring on her foes.
Such a war had such a close.
Again their ravening eagle rose
In anger, wheeled on Europe-shadowing wings, 120
And barking for the thrones of kings;
Till one that sought but Duty's iron crown
On that loud sabbath shook the spoiler down;
A day of onsets of despair!
Dashed on every rocky square,
Their surging charges foamed themselves away;
Last, the Prussian trumpet blew;
Through the long-tormented air
Heaven flashed a sudden jubilant ray,
And down we swept and charged and overthrew. 130
So great a soldier taught us there
What long-enduring hearts could do
On that world-earthquake, Waterloo!
Mighty Seaman, tender and true,
And pure as he from taint of craven guile,
O savior of the silver-coasted isle,
O shaker of the Baltic and the Nile,
If aught of things that here befall
Touch a spirit among things divine,
If love of country move thee there at all, 140

Be glad, because his bones are laid by thine!
And through the centuries let a people's voice
In full acclaim,
A people's voice,
The proof and echo of all human fame,
A people's voice, when they rejoice
At civic revel and pomp and game,
Attest their great commander's claim
With honor, honor, honor, honor to him,
Eternal honor to his name.   150

VII

A people's voice! we are a people yet.
Though all men else their nobler dreams forget,
Confused by brainless mobs and lawless Powers,
Thank Him who isled us here, and roughly set
His Briton in blown seas and storming showers,
We have a voice, with which to pay the debt
Of boundless love and reverence and regret
To those great men who fought, and kept it ours.
And keep it ours, O God, from brute control;
O Statesmen, guard us, guard the eye, the soul   160
Of Europe, keep our noble England whole,
And save the one true seed of freedom sown
Betwixt a people and their ancient throne,
That sober freedom out of which there springs
Our loyal passion for our temperate kings;
For, saving that, ye help to save mankind
Till public wrong be crumbled into dust,
And drill the raw world for the march of mind,
Till crowds at length be sane and crowns be just.
But wink no more in slothful overtrust.   170
Remember him who led your hosts;
He bade you guard the sacred coasts.
Your cannons molder on the seaward wall;
His voice is silent in your council-hall
For ever; and whatever tempests lour
For ever silent; even if they broke
In thunder, silent; yet remember all

He spoke among you, and the Man who spoke;
Who never sold the truth to serve the hour,
Nor paltered with Eternal God for power;   180
Who let the turbid streams of rumor flow
Through either babbling world of high and low;
Whose life was work, whose language rife
With rugged maxims hewn from life;
Who never spoke against a foe;
Whose eighty winters freeze with one rebuke
All great self-seekers trampling on the right:
Truth-teller was our England's Alfred named;
Truth-lover was our English Duke;
Whatever record leap to light   190
He never shall be shamed.

VIII

Lo, the leader in these glorious wars
Now to glorious burial slowly borne,
Followed by the brave of other lands,
He, on whom from both her open hands
Lavish Honor showered all her stars,
And affluent Fortune emptied all her horn.
Yea, let all good things await
Him who cares not to be great,
But as he saves or serves the state.   200
Not once or twice in our rough island-story,
The path of duty was the way to glory:
He that walks it, only thirsting
For the right, and learns to deaden
Love of self, before his journey closes,
He shall find the stubborn thistle bursting
Into glossy purples, which outredden
All voluptuous garden-roses.
Not once or twice in our fair island-story,
The path of duty was the way to glory: 210
He, that ever following her commands,
On with toil of heart and knees and hands,
Through the long gorge to the far light has won
His path upward, and prevailed,

Shall find the toppling crags of Duty scaled
Are close upon the shining table-lands
To which our God Himself is moon and sun.
Such was he: his work is done.
But while the races of mankind endure,
Let his great example stand   220
Colossal, seen of every land,
And keep the soldier firm, the statesman pure:
Till in all lands and through all human story
The path of duty be the way to glory:
And let the land whose hearths he saved from shame
For many and many an age proclaim
At civic revel and pomp and game,
And when the long-illumined cities flame,
Their ever-loyal iron leader's fame,
With honor, honor, honor, honor to him,   230
Eternal honor to his name.

IX

Peace, his triumph will be sung
By some yet unmoulded tongue
Far on in summers that we shall not see:
Peace, it is a day of pain
For one about whose patriarchal knee
Late the little children clung:
O peace, it is a day of pain
For one, upon whose hand and heart and brain
Once the weight and fate of Europe hung.   240
Ours the pain, be his the gain!
More than is of man's degree
Must be with us, watching here
At this, our great solemnity.
Whom we see not we revere;
We revere, and we refrain
From talk of battles loud and vain
And brawling memories all too free
For such a wise humility
As befits a solemn fane: 250
We revere, and while we hear

The tides of Music's golden sea
Setting toward eternity,
Uplifted high in heart and hope are we,
Until we doubt not that for one so true
There must be other nobler work to do
Than when he fought at Waterloo,
And Victor he must ever be.
For though the Giant Ages heave the hill
And break the shore, and evermore   260
Make and break, and work their will;
Though world on world in myriad myriads roll
Round us, each with different powers,
And other forms of life than ours,
What know we greater than the soul?
On God and Godlike men we build our trust.
Hush, the Dead March wails in the people's ears:
The dark crowd moves, and there are sobs and tears:
The black earth yawns: the mortal disappears;
Ashes to ashes, dust to dust;   270
He is gone who seemed so great.—
Gone; but nothing can bereave him
Of the force he made his own
Being here, and we believe him
Something far advanced in State,
And that he wears a truer crown
Than any wreath that man can weave him.
Speak no more of his renown,
Lay your earthly fancies down,
And in the vast cathedral leave him.   280
God accept him, Christ receive him!

1852

ROBERT BROWNING

A Grammarian's Funeral

Let us begin and carry up this corpse,
    Singing together.
Leave we the common crofts, the vulgar thorpes
    Each in its tether

Sleeping safe on the bosom of the plain,
    Cared-for till cock-crow:
Look out if yonder be not day again
    Rimming the rock-row!
That's the appropriate country; there, men's thought,
    Rarer, intenser,   10
Self-gathered for an outbreak, as it ought,
    Chafes in the censer.
Leave we the unlettered plain its herd and crop;
    Seek we sepulture
On a tall mountain, cited to the top,
    Crowded with culture!
All the peaks soar, but one the rest excels;
    Clouds overcome it;
No! yonder sparkle is the citadel's
    Circling its summit.   20
Thither our path lies; wind we up the heights;
    Wait ye the warning?
Our low life was the level's and the night's;
    He's for the morning.
Step to a tune, square chests, erect each head,
    'Ware the beholders!
This is our master, famous, calm and dead
    Borne on our shoulders.
Sleep, crop and herd! sleep, darkling thorpe and croft,
    Safe from the weather!   30
He whom we convoy to his grave aloft,
    Singing together,
He was a man born with thy face and throat,
    Lyric Apollo!
Long he lived nameless: how should Spring take note
    Winter would follow?
Till lo, the little touch, and youth was gone!
    Cramped and diminished.
Moaned he, "New measures, other feet anon!
    My dance is finished"?   40
No, that's the world's way: (keep the mountain-side,
    Make for the city!)

He knew the signal, and stepped on with pride
    Over men's pity;
Left play for work, and grappled with the world
    Bent on escaping:
"What's in the scroll," quoth he, "thou keepest furled?
    Show me their shaping,
Theirs who most studied man, the bard and sage,—
    Give!"—So, he gowned him,   50
Straight got by heart that book to its last page:
    Learned, we found him.
Yea, but we found him bald too, eyes like lead,
    Accents uncertain:
"Time to taste life," another would have said,
    "Up with the curtain!"
This man said rather, "Actual life comes next?
    Patience a moment!
Grant I have mastered learning's crabbed text,
    Still there's the comment.   60
Let me know all! Prate not of most or least,
    Painful or easy!
Even to the crumbs I'd fain eat up the feast,
    Ay, nor feel queasy."
Oh, such a life as he resolved to live,
    When he had learned it,
When he had gathered all books had to give!
    Sooner, he spurned it.
Image the whole, then execute the parts—
    Fancy the fabric   70
Quite, ere you build, ere steel strike fire from quartz,
    Ere mortar dab brick!

(Here's the town-gate reached: there's the market-place
    Gaping before us.)
Yea, this in him was the peculiar grace
    (Hearten our chorus!)
That before living he'd learn how to live—
    No end to learning:
Earn the means first—God surely will contrive
    Use for our earning.   80

Others mistrust and say, "But time escapes:
　　Live now or never!"
He said, "What's time? Leave Now for dogs and apes!
　　Man has Forever."
Back to his book then: deeper drooped his head:
　　Calculus racked him:
Leaden before, his eyes grew dross of lead:
　　Tussis attacked him.
"Now, master, take a little rest!"—not he!
　　(Caution redoubled,　　　　　　　　　　　　　　90
Step two abreast, the way winds narrowly!)
　　Not a whit troubled,
Back to his studies, fresher than at first,
　　Fierce as a dragon
He (soul-hydroptic with a sacred thirst)
　　Sucked at the flagon.
Oh, if we draw a circle premature,
　　Heedless of far gain,
Greedy for quick returns of profit, sure
　　Bad is our bargain!　　　　　　　　　　　　　100
Was it not great? did not he throw on God,
　　(He loves the burthen)—
God's task to make the heavenly period
　　Perfect the earthen?
Did not he magnify the mind, show clear
　　Just what it all meant?
He would not discount life, as fools do here,
　　Paid by instalment.
He ventured neck or nothing—heaven's success
　　Found, or earth's failure:　　　　　　　　　　110
"Wilt thou trust death or not?" He answered "Yes!
　　Hence with life's pale lure!"
That low man seeks a little thing to do,
　　Sees it and does it:
This high man, with a great thing to pursue,
　　Dies ere he knows it.
That low man goes on adding one to one,
　　His hundred's soon hit:

This high man, aiming at a million,
　　Misses an unit. 120
That, has the world here—should he need the next,
　　Let the world mind him!
This, throws himself on God, and unperplexed
　　Seeking shall find him.
So, with the throttling hands of death at strife,
　　Ground he at grammar;
Still, through the rattle, parts of speech were rife:
　　While he could stammer
He settled *Hoti's* business—let it be!—
　　Properly based *Oun*— 130
Gave us the doctrine of the enclitic *De*,
　　Dead from the waist down.
Well, here's the platform, here's the proper place:
　　Hail to your purlieus,
All ye highfliers of the feathered race,
　　Swallows and curlews!
Here's the top-peak; the multitude below
　　Live, for they can, there:
This man decided not to Live but Know—
　　Bury this man there? 140
Here—here's his place, where meteors shoot, clouds form,
　　Lightnings are loosened,
Stars come and go! Let joy break with the storm,
　　Peace let the dew send!
Lofty designs must close in like effects:
　　Loftily lying,
Leave him—still loftier than the world suspects,
　　Living and dying.

1855

Prospice

Fear death?—to feel the fog in my throat,
　　The mist in my face,
When the snows begin, and the blasts denote
　　I am nearing the place,

The power of the night, the press of the storm,
   The post of the foe;
Where he stands, the Arch Fear in a visible form,
   Yet the strong man must go:
For the journey is done and the summit attained,
   And the barriers fall,   10
Though a battle's to fight ere the guerdon be gained,
   The reward of it all.
I was ever a fighter, so—one fight more,
   The best and the last!
I would hate that death bandaged my eyes, and forebore,
   And bade me creep past.
No! let me taste the whole of it, fare like my peers
   The heroes of old,
Bear the brunt, in a minute pay glad life's arrears
   Of pain, darkness and cold.   20
For sudden the worst turns the best to the brave,
   The black minute's at end,
And the elements' rage, the fiend-voices that rave,
   Shall dwindle, shall blend,
Shall change, shall become first a peace out of pain,
   Then a light, then thy breast,
O thou soul of my soul! I shall clasp thee again,
   And with God be the rest!

                    1864

Rabbi Ben Ezra

Grow old along with me!
The best is yet to be,
The last of life, for which the first was made:
Our times are in His hand
Who saith, "A whole I planned,
Youth shows but half; trust God: see all, nor
   be afraid!"

Not that, amassing flowers,
Youth sighed, "Which rose make ours,
Which lily leave and then as best recall?"
Not that, admiring stars,   10

It yearned, "Nor Jove, nor Mars;
Mine be some figured flame which blends,
    transcends them all!"

Not for such hopes and fears
Annulling youth's brief years,
Do I remonstrate: folly wide the mark!
Rather I prize the doubt
Low kinds exist without,
Finished and finite clods, untroubled by a spark.

Poor vaunt of life indeed,
Were man but formed to feed   20
On joy, to solely seek and find and feast:
Such feasting ended, then
As sure an end to men;
Irks care the crop full bird? Frets doubt the
    maw-crammed breast?

Rejoice we are allied
To That which doth provide
And not partake, effect, and not receive!
A spark disturbs our clod;
Nearer we hold of God
Who gives, than of His tribes that take, I must
    believe.   30

Then, welcome each rebuff
That turns earth's smoothness rough,
Each sting that bids nor sit nor stand but go!
Be our joys three-parts pain!
Strive, and hold cheap the strain;
Learn, nor account the pang; dare, never grudge
    the throe!

For thence,—a paradox
Which comforts while it mocks,—
Shall life succeed in that it seems to fail:
What I aspired to be,   40

And was not, comforts me:
A brute I might have been, but would not sink
   i' the scale.

What is he but a brute
Whose flesh has soul to suit,
Whose spirit works lest arms and legs want play?
To man, propose this test—
Thy body at its best,
How far can that project thy soul on its lone way?

Yet gifts should prove their use:
I own the Past profuse   50
Of power each side, perfection every turn:
Eyes, ears took in their dole,
Brain treasured up the whole;
Should not the heart beat once "How good to live
   and learn"?

Not once beat "Praise be thine!
I see the whole design,
I, who saw power, see now Love perfect too:
Perfect I call Thy plan:
Thanks that I was a man!
Maker, remake, complete,—I trust what Thou
   shalt do!"   60

For pleasant is this flesh;
Our soul, in its rose-mesh
Pulled ever to the earth, still yearns for rest:
Would we some prize might hold
To match those manifold
Possessions of the brute,—gain most, as we did
   best!

Let us not always say,
"Spite of this flesh to-day
I strove, made head, gained ground upon the
   whole!"
As the bird wings and sings,   70

Let us cry, "All good things
Are ours, nor soul helps flesh more, now, than
    flesh helps soul!"

Therefore I summon age
To grant youth's heritage,
Life's struggle having so far reached its term:
Thence shall I pass, approved
A man, for aye removed
From the developed brute; a God though in the
    germ.

And I shall thereupon
Take rest, ere I be gone   80
Once more on my adventure brave and new:
Fearless and unperplexed,
When I wage battle next,
What weapons to select, what armor to indue.

Youth ended, I shall try
My gain or loss thereby;
Leave the fire ashes, what survives is gold:
And I shall weigh the same,
Give life its praise or blame:
Young, all lay in dispute; I shall know, being old.   90

For note, when evening shuts,
A certain moment cuts
The deed off, calls the glory from the gray:
A whisper from the west
Shoots—"Add this to the rest,
Take it and try its worth: here dies another day."

So, still within this life,
Though lifted o'er its strife,
Let me discern, compare, pronounce at last,
"This rage was right i' the main,   100
That acquiescence vain:
The Future I may face now I have proved the
    Past."

For more is not reserved
To man, with soul just nerved
To act to-morrow what he learns to-day:
Here, work enough to watch
The Master work, and catch
Hints of the proper craft, tricks of the tool's true
    play.

As it was better, youth
Should strive, through acts uncouth,   110
Toward making, than repose on aught found made:
So, better, age, exempt
From strife, should know, than tempt
Further. Thou waitedst age: wait death nor be
    afraid!

Enough now, if the Right
And Good and Infinite
Be named here, as thou callest thy hand thine
    own,
With knowledge absolute,
Subject to no dispute
From fools that crowded youth, nor let thee
    feel alone.   120

Be there, for once and all,
Severed great minds from small,
Announced to each his station in the Past!
Was I, the world arraigned,
Were they, my soul disdained,
Right? Let age speak the truth and give us
    peace at last!

Now, who shall arbitrate?
Ten men love what I hate,
Shun what I follow, slight what I receive;
Ten, who in ears and eyes   130
Match me: we all surmise,
They this thing, and I that: whom shall my soul
    believe?

Not on the vulgar mass
Called "work," must sentence pass,
Things done, that took the eye and had the
   price;
O'er which, from level stand,
The low world laid its hand,
Found straightway to its mind, could value in a
   trice:

But all, the world's coarse thumb
And finger failed to plumb,   140
So passed in making up the main account;
All instincts immature,
All purposes unsure,
That weighed not as his work, yet swelled the
   man's amount:

Thoughts hardly to be packed
Into a narrow act,
Fancies that broke through language and escaped;
All I could never be,
All, men ignored in me,
This, I was worth to God, whose wheel the
   pitcher shaped.   150

Ay, note that Potter's wheel,
That metaphor! and feel
Why time spins fast, why passive lies our clay,—
Thou, to whom fools propound,
When the wine makes its round,
"Since life fleets, all is change; the Past gone,
   seize to-day!"

Fool! All that is, at all,
Lasts ever, past recall;
Earth changes, but thy soul and God stand sure:
What entered into thee,   160
That was, is, and shall be:
Time's wheel runs back or stops: Potter and
   clay endure.

He fixed thee 'mid this dance
Of plastic circumstance,
This Present, thou, forsooth, wouldst fain arrest:
Machinery just meant
To give thy soul its bent,
Try thee and turn thee forth, sufficiently
    impressed.

What though the earlier grooves,
Which ran the laughing loves   170
Around thy base, no longer pause and press;
What though, about thy rim,
Skull-things in order grim
Grow out, in graver mood, obey the sterner
    stress?

Look not thou down but up!
To uses of a cup,
The festal board, lamp's flash and trumpet's
    peal,
The new wine's foaming flow,
The Master's lips aglow!
Thou, heaven's consummate cup, what needst
    thou with earth's wheel?   180

But I need, now as then,
Thee, God, who moldest men;
And since, not even while the whirl was worst,
Did I—to the wheel of life
With shapes and colors rife,
Bound dizzily—mistake my end, to slake Thy
    thirst:

So, take and use Thy work:
Amend what flaws may lurk,
What strain o' the stuff, what warpings past the
    aim!
My times be in Thy hand!   190

Perfect the cup as planned!
Let age approve of youth, and death complete
the same!
        1864

MATTHEW ARNOLD

A Summer Night

In the deserted, moon-blanch'd street,
How lonely rings the echo of my feet!
Those windows, which I gaze at, frown,
Silent and white, unopening down,
Repellent as the world;—but see,
A break between the housetops shows
The moon! and, lost behind her, fading dim
Into the dewy dark obscurity
Down at the far horizon's rim,
Doth a whole tract of heaven disclose!   10

And to my mind the thought
Is on a sudden brought
Of a past night, and a far different scene.
Headlands stood out into the moonlit deep
As clearly as at noon;
The spring-tide's brimming flow
Heaved dazzlingly between;
Houses, with long white sweep,
Girdled the glistening bay;
Behind, through the soft air,   20
The blue haze-cradled mountains spread away,
That night was far more fair—
But the same restless pacings to and fro,
And the same vainly throbbing heart was there,
And the same bright, calm moon.

And the calm moonlight seems to say:
Hast thou then still the old unquiet breast,
Which neither deadens into rest,
Nor ever feels the fiery glow

That whirls the spirit from itself away,   30
But fluctuates to and fro,
Never by passion quite possess'd
And never quite benumb'd by the world's sway?—
And I, I know not if to pray
Still to be what I am, or yield and be
Like all the other men I see.

For most men in a brazen prison live,
Where, in the sun's hot eye,
With heads bent o'er their toil, they languidly
Their lives to some unmeaning taskwork give,   40
Dreaming of nought beyond their prison-wall.
And as, year after year,
Fresh products of their barren labour fall
From their tired hands, and rest
Never yet comes more near,
Gloom settles slowly down over their breast;
And while they try to stem
The waves of mournful thought by which they are
    prest,
Death in their prison reaches them,
Unfreed, having seen nothing, still unblest.   50

And the rest, a few,
Escape their prison and depart
On the wide ocean of life anew.
There the freed prisoner, where'er his heart
Listeth, will sail;
Nor doth he know how there prevail,
Despotic on that sea,
Trade-winds which cross it from eternity.
Awhile he holds some false way, underbarr'd
By thwarting signs, and braves   60
The freshening wind and blackening waves.
And then the tempest strikes him; and between
The lightning-bursts is seen
Only a driving wreck,
And the pale master on his spar-strewn deck
With anguish'd face and flying hair

Grasping the rudder hard,
Still bent to make some port he knows not where,
Still standing for some false, impossible shore.
And sterner comes the roar   70
Of sea and wind, and through the deepening gloom
Fainter and fainter wreck and helmsman loom,
And he too disappears, and comes no more.

Is there no life, but these alone?
Madman or slave, must man be one?

Plainness and clearness without shadow of stain!
Clearness divine!
Ye heavens, whose pure dark regions have no sign
Of languor, though so calm, and, though so great,
Are yet untroubled and unpassionate;   80
Who, though so noble, share in the world's toil,
And, though so task'd, keep free from dust and soil!
I will not say that your mild deeps retain
A tinge, it may be, of their silent pain
Who have long'd deeply once, and long'd in vain—
But I will rather say that you remain
A world above man's head, to let him see
How boundless might his soul's horizons be,
How vast, yet of what clear transparency!
How it were good to abide there, and breathe free;   90
How fair a lot to fill
Is left to each man still!

1852

The Scholar-Gypsy

Go, for they call you, shepherd, from the hill;
  Go, shepherd, and untie the wattled cotes!
    No longer leave thy wistful flock unfed,
  Nor let thy bawling fellows rack their throats,
    Nor the cropped herbage shoot another head.
      But when the fields are still,
    And the tired men and dogs all gone to rest,
      And only the white sheep are sometimes seen

Cross and recross the strips of moon-blanched green,
Come, shepherd, and again begin the quest!   10

Here, where the reaper was at work of late—
    In this high field's dark corner, where he leaves
        His coat, his basket, and his earthen cruse,
        And in the sun all morning binds the sheaves,
            Then here, at noon, comes back his stores to use—
            Here will I sit and wait,
        While to my ear from uplands far away
            The bleating of the folded flocks is borne,
            With distant cries of reapers in the corn—
    All the live murmur of a summer's day.   20

Screened is this nook o'er the high, half-reaped field,
    And here till sun-down, shepherd! will I be.
        Through the thick corn the scarlet poppies peep,
        And round green roots and yellowing stalks I see
            Pale pink convolvulus in tendrils creep;
            And air-swept lindens yield
        Their scent, and rustle down their perfumed showers
            Of bloom on the bent grass where I am laid,
            And bower me from the August sun with shade;
    And the eye travels down to Oxford's towers.   30

And near me on the grass lies Glanvil's book—
    Come, let me read the oft-read tale again!
        The story of the Oxford scholar poor,
        Of pregnant parts and quick inventive brain,
            Who, tired of knocking at preferment's door,
            One summer morn forsook
        His friends, and went to learn the gypsy-lore,
            And roamed the world with that wild brotherhood,
            And came, as most men deemed, to little good,
    But came to Oxford and his friends no more.   40

But once, years after, in the country lanes,
    Two scholars, whom at college erst he knew,
        Met him, and of his way of life inquired;

Whereat he answered, that the gypsy-crew,
  His mates, had arts to rule as they desired
    The workings of men's brains,
And they can bind them to what thoughts they will.
  "And I," he said, "the secret of their art,
    When fully learned, will to the world impart;
But it needs heaven-sent moments for this skill."   50

This said, he left them, and returned no more.—
  But rumors hung about the country-side,
    That the lost Scholar long was seen to stray,
Seen by rare glimpses, pensive and tongue-tied,
  In hat of antique shape, and cloak of gray,
    The same the gypsies wore.
Shepherds had met him on the Hurst in spring;
  At some lone alehouse in the Berkshire moors,
  On the warm ingle-bench, the smock-frocked boors
Had found him seated at their entering,   60

But, 'mid their drink and clatter, he would fly.
  And I myself seem half to know thy looks,
    And put the shepherds, wanderer! on thy trace;
And boys who in lone wheatfields scare the rooks
  I ask if thou hast passed their quiet place;
    Or in my boat I lie
Moored to the cool bank in the summer heats,
  'Mid wide grass meadows which the sunshine fills,
  And watch the warm, green-muffled Cumner hills,
And wonder if thou haunt'st their shy retreats.   70

For most, I know, thou lov'st retired ground!
  Thee at the ferry Oxford riders blithe,
    Returning home on summer nights, have met
Crossing the stripling Thames at Bab-lock-hithe,
  Trailing in the cool stream thy fingers wet,
    As the punt's rope chops round;
And leaning backward in a pensive dream,
  And fostering in thy lap a heap of flowers
  Plucked in shy fields and distant Wychwood bowers,
And thine eyes resting on the moonlit stream.   80

And then they land, and thou art seen no more!—
  Maidens, who from the distant hamlets come
    To dance around the Fyfield elm in May,
  Oft through the darkening fields have seen thee roam,
    Or cross a stile into the public way.
      Oft thou hast given them store
  Of flowers—the frail-leafed, white anemone,
    Dark bluebells drenched with dews of summer eves,
    And purple orchises with spotted leaves—
  But none hath words she can report to thee.   90

And, above Godstow Bridge, when hay-time's here
  In June, and many a scythe in sunshine flames,
    Men who through those wide fields of breezy grass
  Where black-winged swallows haunt the glittering Thames,
    To bathe in the abandoned lasher pass,
      Have often passed thee near
  Sitting upon the river bank o'ergrown;
    Marked thine outlandish garb, thy figure spare,
    Thy dark vague eyes, and soft abstracted air—
  But, when they came from bathing, thou wast gone!   100

At some lone homestead in the Cumner hills,
  Where at her open door the housewife darns,
    Thou hast been seen, or hanging on a gate
  To watch the threshers in the mossy barns.
    Children, who early range these slopes and late
      For cresses from the rills,
  Have known thee eying, all an April-day,
    The springing pastures and the feeding kine;
    And marked thee, when the stars come out and shine,
  Through the long dewy grass move slow away.   110

In autumn, on the skirts of Bagley wood—
  Where most the gypsies by the turf-edged way
    Pitch their smoked tents, and every bush you see
  With scarlet patches tagged and shreds of gray,
    Above the forest ground called Thessaly—
      The blackbird, picking food,

Sees thee, nor stops his meal, nor fears at all;
So often has he known thee past him stray,
Rapt, twirling in thy hand a withered spray,
And waiting for the spark from heaven to fall.   120

And once, in winter, on the causeway chill
Where home through flooded fields foot-travelers go,
   Have I not passed thee on the wooden bridge,
Wrapped in thy cloak and battling with the snow,
   Thy face tow'rd Hinksey and its wintry ridge?
      And thou hast climbed the hill
And gained the white brow of the Cumner range;
   Turned once to watch, while thick the snowflakes fall,
   The line of festal light in Christ-Church hall—
Then sought thy straw in some sequestered grange.   130

But what—I dream! Two hundred years are flown
Since first thy story ran through Oxford halls,
   And the grave Glanvil did the tale inscribe
That thou wert wandered from the studious walls
   To learn strange arts, and join a gypsy-tribe;
      And thou from earth art gone
Long since, and in some quiet churchyard laid—
   Some country-nook, where o'er thy unknown grave
   Tall grasses and white flowering nettles wave,
Under a dark, red-fruited yew-tree's shade.   140

—No, no, thou hast not felt the lapse of hours!
For what wears out the life of mortal men?
   'Tis that from change to change their being rolls;
'Tis that repeated shocks, again, again,
   Exhaust the energy of strongest souls
      And numb the elastic powers.
Till having used our nerves with bliss and teen,
   And tired upon a thousand schemes our wit,
   To the just-pausing Genius we remit
Our worn-out life, and are—what we have been.   150

Thou hast not lived, why should'st thou perish, so?
   Thou hadst *one* aim, *one* business, *one* desire;
      Else wert thou long since numbered with the dead!

Else hadst thou spent, like other men, thy fire!
   The generations of thy peers are fled,
      And we ourselves shall go;
   But thou possessest an immortal lot,
      And we imagine thee exempt from age
      And living as thou liv'st on Glanvil's page,
Because thou hadst—what we, alas! have not.   160

For early didst thou leave the world, with powers
   Fresh, undiverted to the world without,
      Firm to their mark, not spent on other things;
   Free from the sick fatigue, the languid doubt,
      Which much to have tried, in much been baffled, brings.
        O life unlike to ours!
Who fluctuate idly without term or scope,
   Of whom each strives, nor knows for what he strives,
   And each half lives a hundred different lives;
Who wait like thee, but not, like thee, in hope.   170

Thou waitest for the spark from heaven! and we,
   Light half-believers of our casual creeds,
      Who never deeply felt, nor clearly willed,
   Whose insight never has borne fruit in deeds,
      Whose vague resolves never have been fulfilled;
        For whom each year we see
Breeds new beginnings, disappointments new;
   Who hesitate and falter life away,
   And lose to-morrow the ground won to-day—
Ah! do not we, wanderer! await it too?   180

Yes, we await it!—but it still delays,
   And then we suffer! and amongst us one,
      Who most has suffered, takes dejectedly
   His seat upon the intellectual throne;
      And all his store of sad experience he
        Lays bare of wretched days;
Tells us his misery's birth and growth and signs,
   And how the dying spark of hope was fed,
   And how the breast was soothed, and how the head,
And all his hourly varied anodynes.   190

This for our wisest! and we others pine,
   And wish the long unhappy dream would end,
     And waive all claim to bliss, and try to bear;
   With close-lipped patience for our only friend,
     Sad patience, too near neighbor to despair—
       But none has hope like thine!
   Thou through the fields and through the woods dost stray,
     Roaming the country-side, a truant boy,
     Nursing thy project in unclouded joy,
   And every doubt long blown by time away.   200

O born in days when wits were fresh and clear,
   And life ran gayly as the sparkling Thames;
     Before this strange disease of modern life,
   With its sick hurry, its divided aims,
     Its heads o'ertaxed, its palsied hearts, was rife—
       Fly hence, our contact fear!
   Still fly, plunge deeper in the bowering wood!
     Averse, as Dido did with gesture stern
     From her false friend's approach in Hades turn,
   Wave us away, and keep thy solitude!   210

Still nursing the unconquerable hope,
   Still clutching the inviolable shade,
     With a free, onward impulse brushing through,
   By night, the silvered branches of the glade—
     Far on the forest skirts, where none pursue,
       On some mild pastoral slope
   Emerge, and resting on the moonlit pales
     Freshen thy flowers as in former years
     With dew, or listen with enchanted ears,
   From the dark dingles, to the nightingales!   220

But fly our paths, our feverish contact fly!
   For strong the infection of our mental strife,
     Which, though it gives no bliss, yet spoils for rest;
   And we should win thee from thy own fair life,
     Like us distracted, and like us unblest.
       Soon, soon thy cheer would die,

Thy hopes grow timorous, and unfixed thy powers,
   And thy clear aims be cross and shifting made;
   And then thy glad perennial youth would fade,
Fade, and grow old at last, and die like ours.   230

Then fly our greetings, fly our speech and smiles!
   —As some grave Tyrian trader, from the sea,
   Descried at sunrise an emerging prow
Lifting the cool-haired creepers stealthily,
   The fringes of a southward-facing brow
      Among the Ægean isles;
And saw the merry Grecian coaster come,
   Freighted with amber grapes, and Chian wine,
   Green, bursting figs, and tunnies steeped in brine—
And knew the intruders on his ancient home,   240

The young light-hearted masters of the waves—
   And snatched his rudder, and shook out more sail;
   And day and night held on indignantly
O'er the blue Midland waters with the gale,
   Betwixt the Syrtes and soft Sicily,
      To where the Atlantic raves
Outside the western straits; and unbent sails
   There, where down cloudy cliffs, through sheets of foam,
   Shy traffickers, the dark Iberians come;
And on the beach undid his corded bales.   250

1853

Stanzas from the Grande Chartreuse

Through Alpine meadows soft-suffused
With rain, where thick the crocus blows,
Past the dark forges long disused,
The mule-track from Saint Laurent goes.
The bridge is crossed, and slow we ride,
Through forest, up the mountain-side.

The autumnal evening darkens round,
The wind is up, and drives the rain;

The cells!—the suffering Son of Man
Upon the wall—the knee-worn floor—
And where they sleep, that wooden bed,
Which shall their coffin be, when dead!

The library, where tract and tome
Not to feed priestly pride are there,   50
To hymn the conquering march of Rome,
Nor yet to amuse, as ours are!
They paint of souls the inner strife,
Their drops of blood, their death in life.

The garden, overgrown—yet mild,
See, fragrant herbs are flowering there!
Strong children of the Alpine wild
Whose culture is the brethren's care;
Of human tasks their only one,
And cheerful works beneath the sun.   60

Those halls, too, destined to contain
Each its own pilgrim-host of old,
From England, Germany, or Spain—
All are before me! I behold
The House, the Brotherhood austere!
—And what am I, that I am here?

For rigorous teachers seized my youth,
And purged its faith, and trimmed its fire,
Showed me the high, white star of Truth,
There bade me gaze, and there aspire.   70
Even now their whispers pierce the gloom:
What dost thou in this living tomb?

Forgive me, masters of the mind!
At whose behest I long ago
So much unlearned, so much resigned—
I come not here to be your foe!
I seek these anchorites, not in ruth,
To curse and to deny your truth;

Not as their friend, or child, I speak!
But as, on some far northern strand,   80

While, hark! far down, with strangled sound
Doth the Dead Guier's stream complain
Where that wet smoke, among the woods,
Over his boiling caldron broods.

Swift rush the spectral vapors white
Past limestone scars with ragged pines,
Showing—then blotting from our sight!—
Halt—through the cloud-drift something shines!
High in the valley, wet and drear,
The huts of Courrerie appear.

Strike leftward! cries our guide; and higher
Mounts up the stony forest-way.   20
At last the encircling trees retire;
Look! through the showery twilight gray
What pointed roofs are these advance?—
A palace of the Kings of France?

Approach, for what we seek is here!
Alight, and sparely sup, and wait
For rest in this outbuilding near;
Then cross the sward and reach that gate.
Knock; pass the wicket! Thou art come
To the Carthusians' world-famed home.   30

The silent courts, where night and day
Into their stone-carved basins cold
The splashing icy fountains play—
The humid corridors behold!
Where, ghostlike in the deepening night,
Cowled forms brush by in gleaming white.

The chapel, where no organ's peal
Invests the stern and naked prayer—
With penitential cries they kneel
And wrestle; rising then, with bare   40
And white uplifted faces stand,
Passing the Host from hand to hand;

Each takes, and then his visage wan
Is buried in his cowl once more.

Thinking of his own Gods, a Greek
In pity and mournful awe might stand
Before some fallen Runic stone—
For both were faiths, and both are gone.

Wandering between two worlds, one dead,
The other powerless to be born,
With nowhere yet to rest my head,
Like these, on earth I wait forlorn.
Their faith, my tears, the world deride—
I come to shed them at their side.   90

Oh, hide me in your gloom profound,
Ye solemn seats of holy pain!
Take me, cowled forms, and fence me round,
Till I possess my soul again;
Till free my thoughts before me roll,
Not chafed by hourly false control!

For the world cries your faith is now
But a dead time's exploded dream;
My melancholy, sciolists say,
Is a passed mode, an outworn theme—   100
As if the world had ever had
A faith, or sciolists been sad!

Ah, if it *be* passed, take away,
At least, the restlessness, the pain;
Be man henceforth no more a prey
To these out-dated stings again!
The nobleness of grief is gone—
Ah, leave us not the fret alone!

But—if you cannot give us ease—
Last of the race of them who grieve   110
Here leave us to die out with these
Last of the people who believe!
Silent, while years engrave the brow;
Silent—the best are silent now.

Achilles ponders in his tent,
The kings of modern thought are dumb;

Silent they are, though not content,
And wait to see the future come.
They have the grief men had of yore,
But they contend and cry no more.   120

Our fathers watered with their tears
This sea of time whereon we sail,
Their voices were in all men's ears
Who passed within their puissant hail.
Still the same ocean round us raves,
But we stand mute, and watch the waves.

For what availed it, all the noise
And outcry of the former men?—
Say, have their sons achieved more joys,
Say, is life lighter now than then?   130
The sufferers died, they left their pain—
The pangs which tortured them remain.

What helps it now, that Byron bore,
With haughty scorn which mocked the smart,
Through Europe to the Ætolian shore
The pageant of his bleeding heart?
That thousands counted every groan,
And Europe made his woe her own?

What boots it, Shelley! that the breeze
Carried thy lovely wail away,   140
Musical through Italian trees
Which fringe thy soft blue Spezzian bay?
Inheritors of thy distress
Have restless hearts one throb the less?

Or are we easier, to have read,
O Obermann! the sad, stern page,
Which tells us how thou hidd'st thy head
From the fierce tempest of thine age
In the lone brakes of Fontainebleau,
Or chalets near the Alpine snow?   150

Ye slumber in your silent grave!—
The world, which for an idle day

Grace to your mood of sadness gave,
Long since hath flung her weeds away.
The eternal trifler breaks your spell;
But we—we learned your lore too well!

Years hence, perhaps, may dawn an age,
More fortunate, alas! than we,
Which without hardness will be sage,
And gay without frivolity.   160
Sons of the world, oh, speed those years;
But, while we wait, allow our tears!

Allow them! We admire with awe
The exulting thunder of your race;
You give the universe your law,
You triumph over time and space!
Your pride of life, your tireless powers,
We laud them, but they are not ours.

We are like children reared in shade
Beneath some old-world abbey wall,   170
Forgotten in a forest-glade,
And secret from the eyes of all.
Deep, deep the greenwood round them waves,
Their abbey, and its close of graves!

But, where the road runs near the stream,
Oft through the trees they catch a glance
Of passing troops in the sun's beam—
Pennon, and plume, and flashing lance!
Forth to the world those soldiers fare,
To life, to cities, and to war!   180

And through the wood, another way,
Faint bugle-notes from far are borne,
Where hunters gather, staghounds bay,
Round some fair forest-lodge at morn.
Gay dames are there, in sylvan green;
Laughter and cries—those notes between!

The banners flashing through the trees
Make their blood dance and chain their eyes,

That bugle-music on the breeze
Arrests them with a charmed surprise.   190
Banner by turns and bugle woo:
Ye shy recluses, follow too!

O children, what do ye reply?—
"Action and pleasure, will ye roam
Through these secluded dells to cry
And call us?—but too late ye come!
Too late for us your call ye blow,
Whose bent was taken long ago.

"Long since we pace this shadowed nave;
We watch those yellow tapers shine,   200
Emblems of hope over the grave,
In the high altar's depth divine;
The organ carries to our ear
Its accents of another sphere.

"Fenced early in this cloistral round
Of reverie, of shade, of prayer,
How should we grow in other ground?
How can we flower in foreign air?
—Pass, banners, pass, and bugles, cease;
And leave our desert to its peace!"   210

1855

Rugby Chapel

NOVEMBER, 1857

Coldly, sadly descends
The autumn evening. The field
Strewn with its dank yellow drifts
Of withered leaves, and the elms,
Fade into dimness apace,
Silent—hardly a shout
From a few boys late at their play!
The lights come out in the street,
In the schoolroom windows;—but cold,

Solemn, unlighted, austere, 10
Through the gathering darkness, arise
The chapel walls, in whose bound
Thou, my father! art laid.

There thou dost lie, in the gloom
Of the autumn evening. But ah!
That word, *gloom*, to my mind
Brings thee back, in the light
Of thy radiant vigor, again;
In the gloom of November we passed
Days not dark at thy side; 20
Seasons impaired not the ray
Of thy buoyant cheerfulness clear.
Such thou wast! and I stand
In the autumn evening, and think
Of by-gone autumns with thee.

Fifteen years have gone round
Since thou arosest to tread,
In the summer morning, the road
Of death, at a call unforeseen,
Sudden. For fifteen years, 30
We who till then in thy shade
Rested as under the boughs
Of a mighty oak, have endured
Sunshine and rain as we might,
Bare, unshaded, alone,
Lacking the shelter of thee.

O strong soul, by what shore
Tarriest thou now? For that force,
Surely, has not been left vain!
Somewhere, surely, afar, 40
In the sounding labor-house vast
Of being, is practiced that strength,
Zealous, beneficent, firm!

Yes, in some far-shining sphere,
Conscious or not of the past,

Still thou performest the word
Of the Spirit in whom thou dost live—
Prompt, unwearied, as here!
Still thou upraisest with zeal
The humble good from the ground,   50
Sternly repressest the bad!
Still, like a trumpet, dost rouse
Those who with half-open eyes
Tread the border-land dim
'Twixt vice and virtue; revivest,
Succorest!—this was thy work,
This was thy life upon earth.

What is the course of the life
Of mortal men on the earth?—
Most men eddy about   60
Here and there—eat and drink,
Chatter and love and hate,
Gather and squander, are raised
Aloft, are hurled in the dust,
Striving blindly, achieving
Nothing; and then they die—
Perish;—and no one asks
Who or what they have been,
More than he asks what waves,
In the moonlit solitudes mild   70
Of the midmost Ocean, have swelled,
Foamed for a moment, and gone.

And there are some, whom a thirst
Ardent, unquenchable, fires,
Not with the crowd to be spent,
Not without aim to go round
In an eddy of purposeless dust,
Effort unmeaning and vain.
Ah, yes! some of us strive
Not without action to die   80
Fruitless, but something to snatch
From dull oblivion, nor all
Glut the devouring grave!

We, we have chosen our path—
Path to a clear-purposed goal,
Path of advance!—but it leads
A long, steep journey, through sunk
Gorges, o'er mountains in snow.
Cheerful, with friends, we set forth—
Then, on the height, comes the storm. 90
Thunder crashes from rock
To rock, the cataracts reply,
Lightnings dazzle our eyes.
Roaring torrents have breached
The track, the stream-bed descends
In the place where the wayfarer once
Planted his footstep—the spray
Boils o'er its borders! aloft
The unseen snow-beds dislodge
Their hanging ruin; alas, 100
Havoc is made in our train!
Friends, who set forth at our side,
Falter, are lost in the storm.
We, we only are left!
With frowning foreheads, with lips
Sternly compressed, we strain on,
On—and at nightfall at last
Come to the end of our way,
To the lonely inn 'mid the rocks;
Where the gaunt and taciturn host 110
Stands on the threshold, the wind
Shaking his thin white hairs—
Holds his lantern to scan
Our storm-beat figures, and asks:
Whom in our party we bring?
Whom we have left in the snow?

Sadly we answer: We bring
Only ourselves! we lost
Sight of the rest in the storm.
Hardly ourselves we fought through, 120
Stripped, without friends, as we are.

Friends, companions, and train,
The avalanche swept from our side.

But thou would'st not *alone*
Be saved, my father! *alone*
Conquer and come to thy goal,
Leaving the rest in the wild.
We were weary, and we
Fearful, and we in our march
Fain to drop down and to die.   130
Still thou turnedst, and still
Beckonedst the trembler, and still
Gavest the weary thy hand.

If, in the paths of the world,
Stones might have wounded thy feet,
Toil or dejection have tried
Thy spirit, of that we saw
Nothing—to us thou wast still
Cheerful, and helpful, and firm!
Therefore to thee it was given   140
Many to save with thyself;
And, at the end of thy day,
O faithful shepherd! to come,
Bringing thy sheep in thy hand.
And through thee I believe
In the noble and great who are gone;
Pure souls honored and blessed
By former ages, who else—
Such, so soulless, so poor,
Is the race of men whom I see—   150
Seemed but a dream of the heart,
Seemed but a cry of desire.
Yes! I believe that there lived
Others like thee in the past,
Not like the men of the crowd
Who all round me today
Bluster or cringe, and make life
Hideous, and arid, and vile;
But souls tempered with fire,

Fervent, heroic, and good, 160
Helpers and friends of mankind.

Servants of God!—or sons
Shall I not call you? because
Not as servants ye knew
Your Father's innermost mind,
His, who unwillingly sees
One of his little ones lost—
Yours is the praise, if mankind
Hath not as yet in its march
Fainted, and fallen, and died! 170

See! In the rocks of the world
Marches the host of mankind,
A feeble, wavering line.
Where are they tending?—A God
Marshaled them, gave them their goal.
Ah, but the way is so long!
Years they have been in the wild!
Sore thirst plagues them, the rocks,
Rising all round, overawe;
Factions divide them, their host 180
Threatens to break, to dissolve.
—Ah, keep, keep them combined!
Else, of the myriads who fill
That army, not one shall arrive;
Sole they shall stray; in the rocks
Stagger forever in vain,
Die one by one in the waste.

Then, in such hour of need
Of your fainting, dispirited race,
Ye, like angels, appear, 190
Radiant with ardor divine!
Beacons of hope, ye appear!
Languor is not in your heart,
Weakness is not in your word,
Weariness not on your brow.
Ye alight in our van! at your voice,

Panic, despair, flee away.
Ye move through the ranks, recall
The stragglers, refresh the outworn,
Praise, re-inspire the brave!   200
Order, courage, return.
Eyes rekindling, and prayers,
Follow your steps as ye go.
Ye fill up the gaps in our files,
Strengthen the wavering line,
Stablish, continue our march,
On, to the bound of the waste,
On, to the City of God.

1867

GEORGE MEREDITH

The Discipline of Wisdom

Rich labor is the struggle to be wise,
While we make sure the struggle cannot cease.
Else better were it in some bower of peace
Slothful to swing, contending with the flies.
You point at Wisdom fixed on lofty skies,
As mid barbarian hordes a sculptured Greece:
She falls. To live and shine, she grows her fleece,
Is shorn, and rubs with follies and with lies.
So following her, your hewing may attain
The right to speak unto the mute, and shun   10
That sly temptation of the illumined brain,
Deliveries oracular, self-spun.
Who sweats not with the flock will seek in vain.
To shed the words which are ripe fruit of sun.

1883

Hard Weather

Bursts from a rending East in flaws
The young green leaflet's harrier, sworn
To strew the garden, strip the shaws,
And show our Spring with banner torn.

Was ever such virago morn?
The wind has teeth, the wind has claws.
All the wind's wolves through woods are loose,
The wild wind's falconry aloft.
Shrill underfoot the grassblade shrews,
At gallop, clumped, and down the croft   10
Bestrid by shadows, beaten, tossed;
It seems a scythe, it seems a rod.
The howl is up at the howl's accost;
The shivers greet and the shivers nod.

Is the land ship? we are rolled, we drive
Tritonly, cleaving hiss and hum;
Whirl with the dead, or mount or dive,
Or down in dregs, or on in scum.
And drums the distant, pipes the near,
And vale and hill are gray in gray,   20
As when the surge is crumbling sheer,
And sea-mews wing the haze of spray.
Clouds—are they bony witches?—swarms,
Darting swift on the robber's flight,
Hurry an infant sky in arms:
It peeps, it becks; 'tis day, 'tis night.
Black while over the loop of blue
The swathe is closed, like shroud on corse.
Lo, as if swift the Furies flew,
The Fates at heel at a cry to horse!   30

Interpret me the savage whirr:
And is it Nature scourged, or she,
Her offspring's executioner,
Reducing land to barren sea?
But is there meaning in a day
When this fierce angel of the air,
Intent to throw, and haply slay,
Can for what breath of life we bear
Exact the wrestle? Call to mind
The many meanings glistening up   40
When Nature, to her nurslings kind,
Hands them the fruitage and the cup!

And seek we rich significance
Not otherwhere than with those tides
Of pleasure on the sunned expanse,
Whose flow deludes, whose ebb derides?

Look in the face of men who fare
Lock-mouthed, a match in lungs and thews
For this fierce angel of the air,
To twist with him and take his bruise.   50
That is the face beloved of old
Of Earth, young mother of her brood:
Nor broken for us shows the mold
When muscle is in mind renewed:
Though farther from her nature rude,
Yet nearer to her spirit's hold:
And though of gentler mood serene,
Still forceful of her fountain-jet.
So shall her blows be shrewdly met,
Be luminously read the scene   60
Where Life is at her grindstone set,
That she may give us edging keen,
String us for battle, till as play
The common strokes of fortune shower.
Such meaning in a dagger-day
Our wits may clasp to wax in power.
Yea, feel us warmer at her breast,
By spin of blood in lusty drill,
Than when her honeyed hands caressed,
And Pleasure, sapping, seemed to fill.   70

Behold the life at ease; it drifts.
The sharpened life commands its course.
She winnows, winnows roughly; sifts,
To dip her chosen in her source:
Contention is the vital force,
Whence pluck they brain, her prize of gifts,
Sky of the senses! on which height,
Not disconnected, yet released,
They see how spirit comes to light,
Through conquest of the inner beast,   80

Which Measure tames to movement sane,
In harmony with what is fair.
Never is Earth misread by brain:
That is the welling of her, there
The mirror: with one step beyond,
For likewise is it voice; and more,
Benignest kinship bids respond,
When wail the weak, and them restore
Whom days as fell as this may rive,
While Earth sits ebon in her gloom,   90
Us atomies of life alive
Unheeding, bent on life to come.
Her children of the laboring brain,
These are the champions of the race,
True parents, and the sole humane,
With understanding for their base.
Earth yields the milk, but all her mind
Is vowed to thresh for stouter stock.
Her passion for old giantkind,
That scaled the mount, uphurled the rock,   100
Devolves on them who read aright
Her meaning and devoutly serve;
Nor in her starlessness of night
Peruse her with the craven nerve:
But even as she from grass to corn,
To eagle high from grubbing mole,
Prove in strong brain her noblest born,
The station for the flight of soul.

1888

THOMAS HARDY

Wives in the Sere

I

Never a careworn wife but shows,
   If a joy suffuse her,
Something beautiful to those
   Patient to peruse her,

Some one charm the world unknows
　　Precious to a muser,
Haply what, ere years were foes,
　　Moved her mate to choose her.

II

But, be it a hint of rose
　　That an instant hues her,
Or some early light or pose
　　Wherewith thought renews her—
Seen by him at full, ere woes
　　Practised to abuse her—
Sparely comes it, swiftly goes,
　　Time again subdues her.

1901

The Conformers

Yes; we'll wed, my little fay,
　　And you shall write you mine,
And in a villa chastely gray
　　We'll house, and sleep, and dine.
　　But those night-screened, divine,
　　Stolen trysts of heretofore,
We of choice ecstasies and fine
　　　　Shall know no more.

The formal faced cohue
　　Will then no more upbraid
With smiting smiles and whisperings two
　　Who have thrown less loves in shade.
　　We shall no more evade
　　The searching light of the sun,
Our game of passion will be played,
　　　　Our dreaming done.

We shall not go in stealth
　　To rendezvous unknown,

But friends will ask me of your health,
   And you about my own.   20
When we abide alone,
   No leapings each to each,
But syllables in frigid tone
      Of household speech.

When down to dust we glide
   Men will not say askance,
As now: "How all the country side
   Rings with their mad romance!"
But as they graveward glance
   Remark: "In them we lose   30
A worthy pair, who helped advance
      Sound parish views."

1909

Ah, Are You Digging on My Grave?

"Ah, are you digging on my grave
   My loved one?—planting rue?"
—"No: yesterday he went to wed
One of the brightest wealth has bred.
'It cannot hurt her now,' he said,
   'That I should not be true.'"

"Then who is digging on my grave?
   My nearest dearest kin?"
—"Ah, no: they sit and think, 'What use!
What good will planting flowers produce?   10
No tendance of her mound can loose
   Her spirit from Death's gin'"

"But some one digs upon my grave?
   My enemy?—prodding sly?"
—"Nay: when she heard you had passed the Gate
That shuts on all flesh soon or late,
She thought you no more worth her hate,
   And cares not where you lie."

"Then, who is digging on my grave?
    Say—since I have not guessed!"   20
—"O it is I, my mistress dear,
Your little dog, who still lives near,
And much I hope my movements here
    Have not disturbed your rest?"

"Ah, yes! *You* dig upon my grave . . .
    Why flashed it not on me
That one true heart was left behind!
What feeling do we ever find
To equal among human kind
    A dog's fidelity!"   30

"Mistress, I dug upon your grave
    To bury a bone, in case
I should be hungry near this spot
When passing on my daily trot.
I am sorry, but I quite forgot
    It was your resting-place."

1914

At Tea

The kettle descants in a cosy drone,
And the young wife looks in her husband's face,
And then at her guest's, and shows in her own
Her sense that she fills an envied place;
And the visiting lady is all abloom,
And says there was never so sweet a room.

And the happy young housewife does not know
That the woman beside her was first his choice,
Till the fates ordained it could not be so. . . .
Betraying nothing in look or voice   10
The guest sits smiling and sips her tea,
And he throws her a stray glance yearningly.

1911

DEFINITIONS

IN OUR INTRODUCTION to this anthology and in our arrangement of the poems, we have suggested that an understanding of form in poetry must take into consideration the intent of the poet to tell a story, sing a song or teach a lesson. We have suggested, further, that no poet writes strictly according to the rules, but is himself, in as much as he is a true poet, a "creator" of rules. In every discussion of the problems of form, however, certain technical terms are used, and it is convenient to understand the meaning of these terms.

Blank Verse is properly any unrimed verse, but the term is usually employed to denote unrimed, five-stress, iambic lines. See Milton's *Paradise Lost*, and Wordsworth's *Tintern Abbey*.

Couplets are written in either four- or five-stress riming lines. The five-stress line is known as the heroic couplet. See Burns' *Tam o'Shanter* and Pope's *Rape of the Lock*.

Tercets are stanzas arranged in groups of three riming lines. See Herrick's *Meditation for his Mistress* and the first stanza of Bridges' *My Delight and Thy Delight*.

Terza Rima is a series of three-line stanzas, interlocked by rime, arranged aba, bcb, cdc, ded, etc. See Shelley's *Ode to the West Wind*.

Quatrains are four-line stanzas, arranged according to a wide variety of rime schemes. The lines may be of any length and foot-pattern. See the early ballads and Coleridge's *Rime of the Ancient Mariner*.

Rime Royal is a stanza form consisting of five-stress, iambic, lines, arranged in the pattern, ababbcc. See Chaucer's *Compleint of Chaucer to his Empty Purse*.

Spenserian Stanza was invented by Spenser and used by him in *The Faerie Queene*. In this verse-form eight iambic, five-stress lines are followed by a final six-stress line (called an alexandrine). The rime is arranged according to a definite pattern, ababbcbcc. See Keats' *Eve of Saint Agnes*.

The Sonnet is a fourteen line stanza, written in five-stress, iambic lines. Many varieties of sonnets have been written, but the two principal ones are the Petrarchan (composed of two sets of lines, an octave and a sestet, riming abbaabbacddcee) and the Shakespearian (composed of three quatrains and a final couplet, riming ababcdcdefefgg). See Donne's *Holy Sonnet* and Arnold's *Shakespeare*, as examples of the former, and Drayton's *Since There's No Help* and Keats' *When I Have Fears That I May Cease to Be*, as examples of the latter.

The Ode was used first in English by Spenser in his *Prothalamion* and *Epithalamion*. See also Dryden's *Alexander's Feast* and Keats' five odes. A freer use of the ode, called by Cowley the "Pindaric Ode," is exemplified by Wordsworth's *Intimations of Immortality*, and by Tennyson's *The Death of the Duke of Wellington*.

INDEX TO AUTHORS, TITLES,
AND FIRST LINES

The names of authors are printed in capitals; titles are printed in roman; and first lines are printed in italics.